THE STATE
AND
FEDERAL
COURTS

THE STATE AND FEDERAL COURTS

A COMPLETE GUIDE TO HISTORY, POWERS, AND CONTROVERSY

Christopher P. Banks, Editor

An Imprint of ABC-CLIO, LLC

Santa Barbara, California • Denver, Colorado

Library of Congress Cataloging-in-Publication Data
Names: Banks, Christopher P., editor.
Title: The state and federal courts : a complete guide to history, powers, and controversy / Christopher P. Banks, editor.
Description: Santa Barbara, California : ABC-CLIO, [2017] | Includes bibliographical references and index.
Identifiers: LCCN 2016034520 (print) | LCCN 2016035178 (ebook) | ISBN 9781440841453 (hard copy : alk. paper) | ISBN 9781440841460 (ebook)
Subjects: LCSH: Courts—United States—History. | State courts—United States—History. | Judicial power—United States—History. | Judicial independence—United States. | Judicial process—United States. | Judges—Selection and appointment—United States. | Justice, Administration of—United States.
Classification: LCC KF8720 .S73 2017 (print) | LCC KF8720 (ebook) | DDC 347.73/12—dc23
LC record available at https://lccn.loc.gov/2016034520

ISBN: 978-1-4408-4145-3
EISBN: 978-1-4408-4146-0

21 20 19 18 17   1 2 3 4 5

This book is also available as an eBook.

ABC-CLIO
An Imprint of ABC-CLIO, LLC

ABC-CLIO, LLC
130 Cremona Drive, P.O. Box 1911
Santa Barbara, California 93116-1911
www.abc-clio.com

This book is printed on acid-free paper ∞

Manufactured in the United States of America

Contents

Introduction

The State and Federal Courts: A Complete Guide to History, Powers, and Controversy stands as a comprehensive, one-stop resource for understanding the inner workings of the judicial branch of government, as well as the tremendous political and cultural impact of courts and judges in this hyper-partisan political era.

Many political observers believe that we live today in an era of spiraling political gridlock between the executive and congressional branches of government. This gridlock, which has sometimes given rise to conditions of virtual paralysis, has been most visible at the federal level. However, similar struggles have played out at the state level in numerous regions of the country. As a result, the judicial branch has assumed new prominence in our political system, with the power to make sweeping changes to the legal and political systems of the United States. And in this age of judicial activism at both the state and federal levels, courts have shown a willingness to exert that power like never before.

This volume will explain the foundations of the U.S. judicial system, discuss the impact of the courts on American society from the colonial era to today, and explore the many ways in which political calculations and considerations shape the allegedly nonpartisan world of the judicial branch.

Chapter 1 of *The State and Federal Courts: A Complete Guide to History, Powers, and Controversy* provides a detailed history of the American judiciary system at both the state and federal levels. It explains not only how the courts came to have the powers they possess but also how those powers are exercised.

Chapter 2 examines and explains the specific roles, functions, and powers of the state and federal judiciary branches, from the smallest circuit and district courts to the U.S. Supreme Court. The contents of this chapter encompass everything from the authority, responsibilities, and hierarchy of various courts to the selection, compensation, terms of service, and responsibilities of different kinds of judges.

Chapter 3 provides an overview of the processes of the judicial branch. Coverage includes the constitutional foundations of courts, the roles played by judges and juries, differences between original and appellate jurisdictions, types of courts (appeals, superior, family, probate, criminal, civil, etc.), and explanations of civil and criminal proceedings.

Chapter 4 shines a spotlight on political issues and controversies of the judicial branch. Essays in this chapter explore specific areas in which politics have influenced the actions, character, and effectiveness of the judiciary. Readers will thus find authoritative and objective overviews of such topics as blue slips, filibusters of presidential nominations to the federal bench, partisan judicial elections, judicial review, judicial federalism, U.S. Supreme Court nominations and hearings, judicial activism, mandatory sentencing, impeachment/removal of federal judges, cameras in the courtroom, judicial specialization, public access to courts, and judicial independence. Other entries, meanwhile, will survey trends in federal and state rulings on such hot-button issues as abortion restrictions, gay marriage, gerrymandering, voting rights, the Affordable Care Act, property rights, privacy rights, defendants' rights, free speech, capital punishment, campaign finance, and gun ownership rights and restrictions.

The State and Federal Courts: A Complete Guide to History, Powers, and Controversy closes with three valuable supplemental features:

- A comprehensive glossary of legal and court terms
- An annotated bibliography of sources useful to readers interested in learning more about the history and workings of state and federal courts in the United States
- A detailed subject index

Together, these chapters and supplemental features constitute a unique and important resource for the study of the American judicial branch and the role it plays in shaping U.S. laws, politics, and society.

CHAPTER ONE

HISTORY OF THE JUDICIARY: FEDERAL AND STATE

Most of us know something about the basic structure of the federal and state governments in the United States. At the very least, we can name the three branches—executive, legislative, and judicial—and discuss the differences between them. At an early age, we are taught in school about the president of the United States and the different roles and responsibilities of the person who occupies the White House; we learn about Congress and the courts and their place in our government. In civics classes, we often get a skeletal picture of how the nation's government works; we are told that Congress writes the laws, the president executes them, and the Supreme Court acts as the interpreter of the U.S. Constitution. News reports, blogs, and editorials we read add to this knowledge. Many of us can go further and explain some of the basic interactions among the branches or how our local governments work. We know that the laws Congress passes are subject to the president's veto power and the Supreme Court's powers of judicial review; we understand that the president names the members of his cabinet and nominates justices to the Supreme Court and that the Senate has to confirm these nominations. We can discuss how the Supreme Court, as the "caretaker" of the Constitution, can declare laws unconstitutional, but that it is up to the legislative and executive branches to enforce these rulings—at both the state and federal levels. We discuss the relationships between the branches using such terms as *checks and balances* and *separation of powers*.

For most of us, though, this is about as far as our knowledge goes. According to media accounts that span decades, most Americans have trouble naming members of the Supreme Court, key figures in the congressional leadership, state legislators, or members of the president's cabinet. Still fewer of us can explain in detail how a bill becomes a law, the president's authority in foreign affairs, or how the Supreme Court decides a case. If we ask about the historical development of these institutions and officials or their powers, the numbers of those who understand how our federal and state governments work declines even further.

The ensuing chapters seek to explore and explain the workings and impact of the federal and state courts. The approach used here is both historical and topical. Both of these institutions have evolved over time, so only by placing the current powers and effects of the courts into this evolving history can we fully understand the true nature of the third branch of government. In the process, we will more fully understand the constitutional role of the federal and state courts and the proper application of the judicial function by the judges who operate them.

At the heart of our constitutional system is a vital principle—that the government has enough power to vindicate national interests while being limited enough to be subject to sufficient checks and balances. The operation of checks and balances helps to protect individual rights and preserve the legitimacy of competing institutions of government.

The principle of checks and balances takes several forms in the U.S. constitutional system. One is separation of powers. In some cases, some authority is assigned to a given institution. For example, courts have the authority to make formal decisions, or judgments (adjudications), about legitimate cases and controversies before them, without interference from the other branches of government. In other cases, such as with the exercise of war powers, the constitutional text presents what the political scientist Edward S. Corwin called an "invitation to struggle" between Congress and the president. In still other cases, the concept of federalism sorts out spheres of authority between the federal and state governments. In some realms, the federal government is supreme, and the states may not interfere; in others, the states are supreme, and the federal government has little or no power to interfere; in still others, the federal government and the states share concurrent powers over the same spheres of activity. The result is an ongoing tension and balance between the different levels of government as well as between institutions at the same level of government.

In the American court system, the concepts of limited government, separation of powers, checks and balances, and federalism are directly linked to the power of judicial review. Judicial review is the courts' power to review actions of other branches of government or other levels of government to determine whether they have complied with or violated the commands of the Constitution, and to set aside the actions challenged if they violate the Constitution.

Many people say that the courts, with their powers of judicial review, have the final say as to the meaning and proper reach of the Constitution. This is not entirely correct. It is always possible, for example, through a process sometimes called "jurisdiction stripping," for Congress to enact laws limiting the powers of federal courts to hear certain kinds of cases. In addition, per Article V of the U.S. Constitution, the original Constitution can be amended by the people. Congress rarely uses this power, however.

It is more likely, but still an exception, that Congress may propose a constitutional amendment, and the states may ratify it to overrule an unpopular Supreme Court decision. Further, because the modern court's decisions are the focus of rigorous study within the legal academic community and the legal profession, and because they are scrutinized in the news media, the resulting academic, professional, and public debate may shape the justices' views and even coerce them to change their minds.

Viewed over time, much of the doctrinal history of the federal courts can be largely seen as the center of an ongoing debate on the extent of these principles and their role in directing the governance of the United States in relation to state governments. In fact, for much of our nation's history, the federal courts have determined the evolving meanings of these principles—sometimes grabbing this power for themselves, sometimes distributing it to the other branches or the states. Without understanding this cluster of principles, we cannot understand the work and powers of the federal courts.

Americans have always lived under a complex and complicated court system, one with a difficult and ever-changing purpose. Hemmed in by rules and structures, and usually involved in a constant tug-of-war for power and impact with the other branches of government (at both state and federal levels), the courts nonetheless have had a clear and significant impact on American policymaking and social or political development. Political scientists Robert A. Carp and Ronald Stidham note the following in their book *The Federal Courts* (2010, 3):

> The decisions of federal judges and justices affect all our lives. Whether it is the upholding of laws already in place or broader policymaking decisions, the output of federal courts permeates the . . . body politic in the United States. No one can have a full and accurate understanding of the American political system without being cognizant of the work of the men and women who wear the black robe.

What follows is a detailed discussion of both the federal and state courts.

HISTORICAL DEVELOPMENT OF FEDERAL COURTS

From its small, contested, and somewhat inauspicious beginnings to today, the federal judiciary has grown steadily in size, resources, and prestige. It has also grown in the scope of its jurisdiction, the authority of its mandate, and the impact of its rulings. Originally hearing mostly private law matters and enforcing federal statutes, over the course of the 19th century, the federal courts developed into a major force in establishing and articulating national policy and values through cases posing vital issues of private and public law. From its early influence as a nationalizing force that helped shape a national economy, its identification with "big business" in the decades around the turn of the 20th century, its administrative responsibilities in the first half of the 20th century, and then to its growing focus on individual rights after the New Deal "constitutional revolution," the federal judiciary has experienced a constant increase in both the number and complexity of the cases it hears. Today, the federal courts hear fewer cases than the state courts, and while the numbers of filings rise and fall in response to changes within society and the law, it is unlikely that the federal courts' workloads will decline significantly in the future.

Today's federal court system traces its history back to the Constitutional Convention of 1787. Both the Virginia Plan and the New Jersey Plan, the two main proposals for forming a national government, provided for trial courts and appellate courts. The plan that was ultimately adopted by the convention delegates called for the establishment in the Constitution of a supreme court, leaving the creation of other courts to Congress. Specifically, Article III, Section 1 of the U.S. Constitution provides that "The judicial Power of the United States, shall be vested in one supreme Court, and in such inferior Courts as the Congress may from time to time ordain and establish."

The District and Circuit Courts

In the meeting of the First Congress in 1789, the outline of the nation's judicial system took shape. Members of Congress reflected upon their prior experiences in practical governance (with the Articles of Confederation and the state systems of courts created during and after the Revolution, but before the Convention) in framing the new federal judicial system. They thought about the nature of the British court system, the state court systems that operated under the Articles of Confederation, and the power that would be handed to the new government. At the same time that they were debating the need for a written Bill of Rights, they were also creating the courts that would decide disputes over those rights. The Judiciary Act of 1789, signed into law by President George Washington on September 24, 1789, outlined the organization and jurisdiction of the federal courts.

The Judiciary Act established 13 district courts to be located in the 11 states that had, to that date, ratified the Constitution, as well as in Maine and Kentucky (which were at that time territories of the states of Massachusetts and Virginia, respectively). Each district court had one district judge. The law provided for the number of sessions of court to be held each year and the location of the sessions. It also stipulated the salaries to be paid to the judges, which varied to reflect the expected differences in caseloads between the districts. The district judge was authorized to appoint a clerk to assist him. The act also allowed the president to appoint a prosecutor and a marshal in each district.

The caseload of the early district courts was limited because each one served as the trial court principally for admiralty and maritime cases and some minor civil and criminal matters, all of which had to arise within that district. In addition, the Act created a second type of trial court, the U.S. circuit court, which had limited appellate jurisdiction but also became the nation's principal trial court in the early years. Notably, district court judges spent more of their time on circuit court matters than district court cases.

Each of the state-located districts was also placed in a circuit. Three circuits were created: eastern, middle, and southern. The act outlined the circuit courts' meeting schedule and the location of the circuit courts' sessions, which were to be held in cities within each district. Supreme Court justices were to be assigned to each circuit, and the circuit court session would be heard by the two justices assigned to that circuit sitting with the district court judge of the district. (This requirement was soon reduced to a single justice sitting with a district judge.) The circuit courts served a dual role, as trial courts for some matters and as appeal courts for others. The Maine and Kentucky district courts performed the tasks of the circuit courts for their districts.

The circuit courts served as the trial courts for most federal matters, including cases brought by the United States, as well as diversity of citizenship cases. The circuit courts also exercised appellate jurisdiction over matters that were tried in district courts. The circuit courts met in each federal judicial district. The reality of "riding circuit" was very unpleasant for many Supreme Court justices who disliked the rigors of traveling across the nation and from state to state.

While the idea of riding circuit may seem odd, it made sense at the time. The caseload of the Supreme Court was small, and using the justices as trial judges saved the government funds that would have been otherwise required to hire separate circuit judges. Moreover, the practice was a well-known one for state courts and so was not seen as unusual at the time. Additionally, riding circuits exposed the justices to state laws and practices. It also made known to the people in the states the members of the least-visible branch of the national government.

The justices themselves, however, opposed circuit riding for various personal and professional reasons and eventually began doing it less and less. The first significant effort to do away with riding circuit was the Judiciary Act of 1801. This legislation created six circuits with separate circuit judgeships, relieving the Supreme Court justices of their circuit-riding duties. In 1802, however, a new Congress repealed the law and did away with the circuit judgeships (while keeping the circuits intact), so the Supreme Court justices rode circuit once again. The 1802 law allowed a district judge to sit by himself as a circuit judge, but it still required the presence of a Supreme Court justice in the circuit court to hear any appeals from district court proceedings. This remained the state of affairs until 1869, when Congress, mindful of steadily increasing caseloads, created separate circuit judgeships for each of the circuits. These judges were given the same authority that a Supreme Court justice had while sitting in the circuit. Now a circuit judge could sit with a district judge *or* with a justice and hear appeals.

From the time of the First Congress to the middle of the 19th century, the United States steadily grew in size and in the number of states and territories subject to U.S. law. By the beginning of the Civil War, there were more than 30 states. The implication of the Judiciary Act of 1789 seemed to be that each state should have district and circuit courts, but the existing circuit-riding burden was weighing heavily on the justices who had to travel the circuits. Congress responded to the growing need for courts and justices by creating new circuits and gradually expanding the size of the Supreme Court. In the 19th century, as well as in later years, Supreme Court appointments were affected by the politics of the time, so the process proceeded haltingly, and it was not until the Civil War that every circuit and district was served by a Supreme Court justice.

The Supreme Court's expansion in the first half of the 19th century was accomplished in a series of steps. After the Judiciary Act of 1802 and with new legislation, the Congress in 1807 created the Seventh Circuit, comprising Tennessee, Kentucky, and Ohio. A Supreme Court justice was added, and this seventh justice was assigned to the new circuit.

Over the next 30 years, nine new states were added to the United States, leading Congress to create two new circuits, the Eighth and Ninth, in 1837. Congress also added two new justices to the Supreme Court, one each for the new circuits. The nine circuits were reorganized in 1842, but no new circuit was added.

In 1855, a 10th circuit court, known as the California Circuit, was added to handle matters in the state of California's two districts. This particular circuit court was a milestone of sorts because Congress did not add a 10th justice to the Supreme Court to lead the new court. Instead, it created a separate circuit court judgeship for the first time.

In 1861, President Abraham Lincoln pressed Congress to address the effect of the nation's growth on the judicial system, especially the circuit court system. Noting that continually adding justices to the Supreme Court to handle circuit duties would make the Court unwieldy, Lincoln recommended setting a set number of justices for the Supreme Court, without regard to the number of circuits. He also wanted the circuits to be reorganized, perhaps to be served by newly created circuit judges, with or without the presence of a Supreme Court justice. In 1863, Congress created the 10th Circuit, replacing the California Circuit and adding to it the Oregon courts. And, in 1866, Congress reduced the number of circuits to nine, redistributing the states among the circuits.

Just as the nation had expanded, so too had the workload of the national court system. As the national economy grew and business corporations increased the amount of commercial activity, more cases came to the courts. As federal legislation increased, especially in the wake of the Civil War, so did the litigation caseload of the courts. Backlogs in the district and circuit courts mounted, and the caseload of the Supreme Court also grew at a staggering rate. In 1860, the Supreme Court docket had more than 300 cases. By 1890, that had increased

600 percent. Trial court workloads also increased dramatically in the 1870s and 1880s, and the increase in the number of district and circuit judges could not begin to keep pace with the cases pending.

As mentioned previously, in 1869, Congress responded to these increased caseloads by creating separate circuit judgeships for each of the circuits, which meant a circuit judge could sit with a district judge or with a Supreme Court justice and hear appeals. Nonetheless, these changes were not sufficient to keep pace with expanding caseloads. A jurisdictional change in 1875 shifted much of the circuit court burden to the district courts, increasing their already too-heavy load. Small changes were made, and many more substantial changes were proposed, but no real solution was crafted until 1891, when a solution was adopted that would endure into the 21st century.

The Circuit Court of Appeals Act of 1891 created a new court—the circuit court of appeals. This appellate court sat above the district and circuit trial courts. One circuit court of appeals was created for each of the nine circuits. Distributed among the circuit courts of appeals were the district courts of the 44 states of the United States. Each circuit court of appeals had two circuit judges and a district judge. Circuit riding for Supreme Court justices had not been abolished, but it was left up to the justice individually. (A vestige of the old arrangement remains in that Supreme Court members are still allotted circuits to hear emergency motions.) The law funneled many district court decisions to the court of appeals for final disposition and did away with the appellate jurisdiction of the old circuit courts. These circuit courts were abolished in 1911, leaving federal district courts as the sole federal trial courts. The 1891 act allowed some direct appeals to the highest court from the district court and allowed the intermediate appellate court to certify other appeals. The effect was a dramatic reduction in Supreme Court filings.

Since the Circuit Court of Appeals Act of 1891, the three-tiered structure of the federal court system has undergone only modest changes. Trial courts are at the bottom level, appeals courts are above them at the intermediate level, and the U.S. Supreme Court is at the highest appeals court level. The number of circuits has increased to 13, including a Circuit Court of Appeals for the District of Columbia. The number of district court and circuit court of appeals judgeships has increased roughly tenfold. New positions, bankruptcy courts, and federal magistrates have been added as units to the district courts.

U.S. Courts of Appeals

The circuit court of appeals was created in 1891 to hear appeals from the trial courts, which at that time were the district court and the circuit court. (This new title, "circuit court of appeals," led to confusion between the circuit court sitting as trial court and the newly created appeals court. This was corrected in

1948 by changing the title of the appeals courts to the court of appeals for the enumerated circuit. In the Judiciary Act of 1891, Congress created nine courts of appeals. The judges on these courts were the existing circuit judges and the newly appointed appellate judges. District court judges in the circuit were permitted to sit with the circuit justices to create three-judge appellate panels. Supreme Court justices were still assigned to particular circuits, but circuit riding was no longer required of them, and few did it.

The 1891 law gave the courts of appeals jurisdiction over a major portion of the appeals from district and circuit courts and restricted the types of cases that had previously been commonly appealed to the Supreme Court. In 1893, Congress established the Court of Appeals of the District of Columbia. In 1911, the U.S. circuit courts—the trial courts—were abolished in a judicial reorganization. In 1925, further legislation expanded the appellate jurisdiction of the courts of appeals. In 1916, the courts of appeals were given jurisdiction over certain railroad regulatory appeals, and, in the 1930s, as the number of federal administrative agencies exploded, the courts of appeals were given jurisdiction over appeals of decisions made by the new regulatory agencies. These actions reduced the review burden of the Supreme Court. In 1948, Congress changed the title of the federal appellate courts to the U.S. Court of Appeals (for the respective numbered circuits).

The number of and membership in the courts of appeals has increased. By the 1930s, it was no longer necessary for district judges to sit on court of appeals panels, as each court of appeals had at least three judges. New circuits were established by Congress. In 1929, the 10th Circuit was created, and, in 1980, the 11th Circuit was added. In 1982, Congress established the U.S. Court of Appeals for the Federal Circuit, combining the jurisdictions of two previously existing federal court systems (the U.S. Court of Customs and Patent Appeals and the U.S. Court of Claims).

The Supreme Court of the United States

The Constitution of the United States allocates the judicial power of the nation to "one supreme Court." The Constitution gives the Supreme Court original jurisdiction in matters where a state is a party or in cases involving diplomats but leaves it to Congress to determine the composition and responsibilities of our nation's highest court. The Judiciary Act of 1789 was the first act of Congress to make these determinations. The act established the Supreme Court with one chief justice and five associate justices. It defined the appellate jurisdiction of the Court in civil cases and in cases where state courts had entered decisions on the meaning or application of federal law. As mentioned previously, the law of 1789 required Supreme Court justices to ride circuit, presiding with federal judges on the circuit courts that sat in federal districts around the country. In part, this was done so that the justices would remain close to the state courts and the people of the nation, and they would be visibly involved with the legal processes around the country.

As noted earlier, circuit riding was time-consuming and strenuous, and justices immediately sought to have the task eliminated from their duties. After four years, Congress lightened the circuit load of the justices by reducing the number of justices from two to one that had to sit in a circuit court session. Congress tried to create separate judgeships for the circuit courts in 1801 to free the Supreme Court of circuit duty. To ease the circuit-riding burden, Congress allowed district judges to sit alone in circuit courts in some cases. In 1869, Congress created separate circuit court judge positions, further reducing the burden of circuit-riding. The Circuit Court of Appeals Act of 1891 created the circuit courts of appeals, which made circuit-riding optional for the justices. As stated previously, few continued the practice.

The Supreme Court of the United States first gathered on February 1, 1790. The justices met in New York City, the capital of the United States at that time. Some of the justices were unable to attend the meeting, so it was postponed until the next day. The Court met mainly to deal with matters of court administration and organization. The first cases to reach the Court came in 1791, and the first opinion was issued in 1792. The Court may have initially moved slower than desired, but in its first decade, the Supreme Court set a number of important precedents for the future of American law.

As the number of judicial circuits increased, so did the number of Supreme Court justices. In 1807, a seventh justice took the bench. In 1837, justices eight and nine were added to the Court. In 1863, with the creation of a 10th circuit, another justice joined the Court. Three years later, Congress reduced the membership of the Court to seven justices, ordering that no vacancies be filled until that number was reached. In 1869, when the number of justices on the bench stood at eight, Congress mandated that the Court have nine justices, one for each of the circuits then existing. This number has remained unchanged since then.

In the first hundred years of the nation, the justices asserted little control over their docket. They heard civil appeals and cases where Congress had provided for automatic appeals to the Supreme Court. The 1891 act, however, brought many changes in that regard. It created courts of appeals that heard many cases that would have previously gone to the Supreme Court and gave the high Court some discretion regarding which appeals of court of appeals rulings it would hear. The Judges Bill of 1925 expanded the Court's control over what cases it would hear, and, in 1988, Congress further restricted what cases the Court must hear on appeal. Nonetheless, the Supreme Court's docket has steadily increased since then. In 1945, there were fewer than 1,500 cases on the docket. In 1960, the number was just over 2,300. The number has continued to rise steadily, though, to more than 8,000 requests per year. The Court typically accepts about 80 cases per term for review. In 2014, for example, the Supreme Court issued decisions on 74 cases.

EVOLVING WORKLOADS OF THE FEDERAL COURTS

If we were to ask a federal court judge today what cases the federal courts predominantly handle, the judge would list cases dealing with major public law issues, such as criminal prosecutions or civil rights cases. That is because public law cases have had the greatest impact on the lower federal courts' caseload, in particular, and on society, in general. As Wolf Heydebrand and Carroll Seron noted in their study of the political economy of federal district courts, *Rationalizing Justice: The Political Economy of Federal District Courts* (1990), "The organizational history of the federal . . . courts is closely intertwined with the expanding role of the government in the twentieth century." Growing out of "a much larger change in the state's role to administer, regulate, and enforce policy, . . . public law litigation has increased dramatically" in direct response to federal-question suits brought as a result of the civil rights and regulatory reforms of the 1960s and 1970s and administrative law cases in which the United States was either plaintiff or defendant. By the 1980s, these cases "dominate[d] the civil docket of federal district courts" (159, 161–162). Add to this the sizable increase in criminal filings due to Congress's expansion of the number and severity of federal crimes during the 1990s, and public law's dominance in the workload, priorities, and functions of the federal district courts was the inevitable result. All told, from 2001 to 2014, federal circuit filings increased twentyfold.

If we had asked federal court judges a hundred years earlier what cases they handle, we would have received a quite different answer. Although criminal prosecutions would still figure in the judge's perceptions of his court's workload (though not necessarily in the judge's perceptions of the court's priorities), and administrative law cases would provide a small, but growing segment of the judge's caseload, civil rights cases would hardly have entered into the judge's consciousness. Nor would there be the sort of regulatory cases that have become a feature of federal civil litigation—"toxic tort" cases, Environmental Protection Agency (EPA) or Occupational Safety and Health Administration (OSHA) cases, or labor law cases. Rather, private lawsuits, most brought under the federal courts' diversity jurisdiction, along with land title and taxation cases, dominated the lower federal courts' dockets and priorities in the late 19th and early 20th centuries. Even the Supreme Court, which has the greatest opportunity and responsibility of any federal court to shape public policy, concerned itself with such private matters—at least as far as they interacted with the powers of the national and state governments to regulate and promote economic growth.

To be sure, although the numbers of lawsuits filed were minuscule, litigants did file civil rights cases in federal courts in the late 19th and early 20th centuries. And, the federal courts were able to hear and decide such cases, thanks to a series of constitutional and legal changes following the Civil War and the abolition of slavery. The framing and ratification of the Thirteenth, Fourteenth, and Fifteenth Amendments, accompanied by the enactment of a series of federal civil rights statutes, began a slow transformation of American law and the ways in which individuals could seek redress for denial of their rights. In particular, the enactment of the Jurisdiction and Removal Act of 1875 gave the lower federal courts the authority—for the first time—to hear cases posing "federal questions," that is, questions pertaining to the scope and meaning of federal statutes and of rights claimed under the Constitution or federal laws. With the enactment of this law, the district courts had near complete jurisdictional power to attend to civil rights matters, had they wished. Yet few judges of that era would have stressed or even mentioned handling civil rights cases as a major part of their court's functions.

During that same period, a category of cases that loom large in modern law and policymaking—government suits to enforce federal laws, in particular laws relating to taxation and admiralty—were few in number, no matter how important they were as matters of substance or procedure. Rather, the mix of state concerns with federal powers implicit in the creation and slow evolution of the federal court system assured that local concerns predominated in the early years of the federal bench. In fact, the federal courts had a relatively stable and traditional set of categories of cases that they heard and adjudicated: (1) admiralty cases; (2) criminal cases enforcing federal laws (of which there were only a few on the books until the 20th century); (3) disputes over land titles between states and, more commonly, within states newly added to the nation; (4) diversity cases (wherein the federal courts enforced state laws but applied federal procedures); and (5) federal tax code violations.

Take, for example, the workload of the federal district courts. In their first 60 years, disputes over land titles often made up as much as 50 percent of their workloads. Commercial credit suits involving issues of contractual rights and obligations often accounted for an equal and, in some states, an even greater number of private economic cases on district court dockets. In Alabama, for instance, cases involving commercial credit transactions made up the most common type of case during the antebellum period. Debt collection and other issues associated with economic insolvency added still more private economic cases to the list (e.g., in Kentucky, between 1789 and 1815, debt collection totaled 22 percent of all cases filed); tort suits added a small percentage to court caseloads. Finally, admiralty cases constituted a substantial share of the federal docket from 1790 through 1815; their primary impact was in fostering private economic growth in the economically important shipping industry and in

American trade overseas. This was especially the case in districts that bordered on major waterways, such as the District Court of Ohio, whose jurisdiction covered the Ohio River; the Northern District of California, which oversaw the busy port of San Francisco; and the Southern District of New York (Zelden 2007).

At the appellate level, after a slow start under Chief Justices John Jay, John Rutledge, and Oliver Ellsworth, the Supreme Court under Chief Justices John Marshall and Roger Taney stressed the twin themes of economic development and nationalization of the law. The justices understood the potential for the individual parts of the economy and law to pull away from each other in a diverse federal system. They also understood how a unified national economy not only could resist these tendencies, but also could promote American economic growth and prosperity. Their approach was twofold. First, they stressed the supremacy of the national government in matters of interstate commerce (often defining commerce widely in the process), admiralty, and the enforcement of contracts. In some cases, the judicial commitment to national supremacy in interstate commerce meant overturning state laws; in others, it meant demanding that the states honor their commitments. The result was a series of decisions creating, promoting, and defending a national marketplace.

Second, the justices provided those people employed in or taking part in this new marketplace a friendly forum to which they could bring their disputes and receive a uniform application of the law. A landmark Supreme Court decision, *Swift v. Tyson* (1842), recognized the right of federal judges to use their own judgment in interpreting the meaning of the common law, regardless of what state judicial precedent might require. In other words, a federal judge had the power to brush aside contrary principles of law that were derived from state cases. In practice, this meant that federal judges could adopt a similar approach to handling economic matters, no matter in what state the dispute arose. In the process, they were able to generate precedents and procedures that were favorable both to the interests of business (national and local) and to the promotion of economic development. *Swift* remained good law until 1938, when the Court overruled it in *Erie Railroad Company v. Tompkins*, a ruling that forced federal courts to apply state common law principles in the governing jurisdiction.

Post–Civil War Expansion of the Workload

Although the institutional structures that organized the courts were not changed significantly after the Civil War, Congress greatly expanded the courts' powers and jurisdiction in the latter half of the 19th century. Responding to the crisis of the Civil War and especially the Reconstruction Era that followed, Congress and the president joined forces to expand the federal courts' jurisdiction to include a mix of military and nonmilitary matters, including confiscation, emancipation, disloyalty, military government, reconstruction, and bankruptcy cases.

Congress also expanded the rights of litigants to transfer certain kinds of cases from state to federal courts—a procedure that lawyers call *removal*. The Judiciary Act of 1789 had authorized removals but limited them to only a few categories of cases. The Habeas Corpus Act of 1863 gave federal officers protection from civil and criminal actions that arose out of official acts by permitting removal of such lawsuits to federal court, thus arguably avoiding the prejudices of local jurors who would favor in-state litigants over out-of-state litigants. The Civil Rights Act of 1866 (and later the Enforcement Act of 1871) granted similar removal rights to private litigants for similar reasons. The Separable Controversies Act of 1866 expanded this access, allowing nonresident parties to split their case and bring their part of the case into federal court under diversity of citizenship. One year later, the Local Prejudice Act increased access even more, authorizing any party in a state case to remove suit if, as the law stated, "he had reason to . . . believe that, from prejudice or local influence, he will not be able to obtain justice in a state court." Finally, the Jurisdiction and Removal Act of 1875 gave the lower federal courts original and removal jurisdiction "as broad as the Constitution authorized" by permitting any party in a case to remove a case from state to federal court, authorizing removal of the whole suit if the actual controversy was between diverse parties, allowing for removal on the grounds of diversity even where one of the parties involved lived in the forum state (the state in which the suit originated), and permitting removal of all federal-question suits.

This expanded jurisdiction altered the balance of judicial federalism—a term describing how judicial power is divided and decentralized between federal and state courts—and swelled the demand on the federal courts. The national government, through its courts, now had the authority to respond to a wide range of public and private actions within the states. Although the government often hesitated to use this authority, over time, this access would result in an increase in the number of cases filed in the federal courts. While all this was happening, some jurisdictions opened the door for even greater use of the federal courts by private litigants, especially the new corporations that operated across the states. Exploiting a new and growing national marketplace that was full of opportunities—albeit also filled with significant uncertainties and hidden problems—these corporations saw the federal courts as friendly forums where they could seek judicial aid in solving a host of economic and political problems arising from the fact that every state had its own laws and precedents.

When we add to the mix the older types of litigation that persisted in the dockets of the federal judiciaries, we find that the growth in the workload of the federal courts was explosive. Between 1865 and 1900, federal dockets more than doubled. Not only were these cases more numerous than the number of cases that district judges had to handle in previous decades, but these cases were also generally larger and more complex than those filed a generation earlier.

On the private law side (as opposed to public law) of the docket, for example, district courts faced cases in which corporations had to defend against negligence actions that were brought by injured employees and by customers, and contract actions brought by policyholders against insurance company defendants. Many corporations facing insolvency or bankruptcy also turned to the federal courts for the protections of an equity receivership—a legal procedure by which an insolvent company is protected from its creditors while reorganizing its operations. And, of course, corporations that were increasingly subject to the complexity of aggressive regulatory efforts by state governments turned to federal courts, a move that allowed them to invoke removal jurisdiction in search of a friendly forum.

The growth in federal court caseloads was often staggering and socially significant. Consider the impact that tort filings (actions that claimed negligent conduct or defective products caused personal injury) had on the federal courts. As Edward A. Purcell Jr. notes in his *Litigation and Inequality* (1992, 19), a landmark study of business corporations' use of federal diversity jurisdiction, "The development of a national market and the dominance of corporate enterprise meant that more and more individuals came into contact with [interstate] corporations." In turn, this increase in interactions between corporations and individuals increased the chances for accidents. As Purcell points out:

> Railroads and streetcars, mass-produced consumer products, machines powered by steam and electricity, and the escalating dangers of industrial labor all combined to cause an enormous increase in the number and severity of accidental injuries to persons and property. (1992, 19–20)

The results were horrific: Between 1889 and 1906, accidents claimed the lives of 2,000 railroad workers per year and injured another 25,000 to 35,000; rail injuries among nonemployees tacked on an additional 15,000 to 35,000 accidents, and one-third of these were fatal. In Boston, streetcar injuries rose from 200 in 1889 to more than 1,700 in 1900. Nationwide, industrial accidents of all kinds were estimated to cause some 35,000 deaths and 2 million injuries each year after 1900.

High rates of injuries meant high rates of tort filings. In one California county, between 1880 and 1900, 340 personal injury suits were filed, 110 of which were heard in federal court; the ensuing decade saw the trend continue. Nationwide, between 1908 and 1911, the railroad lines of the New York Central faced almost 11,000 tort cases. Most of these actions were filed by the injured party in their local state courts. The defendant corporation then removed the cases, whenever possible, to federal court. The result was an ever-growing number of tort cases on federal court dockets. A U.S. House of Representatives committee report in 1876 found that the biggest and fastest-growing class of federal cases was diversity cases removed from state court by defendant corporations. Twenty years later, another House committee reported the same finding (Zeldon 2007, 22–23).

Twentieth-Century Changes

In the early 20th century, the number of such cases proliferated at an even greater pace. However, this story was not simply one of increasing numbers and cases. Over time, the content of the cases filed began to shift, transforming the federal courts' caseload that featured new issues and matters of concern in response to the era's social, economic, and technological changes. Even though the older, private law–dominated workload of the federal courts remained strong (as late as 1930, a National Commission on Law Observance and Enforcement study found that 52 percent of all diversity cases filed in the federal courts were private tort actions), public law cases came to dominate the time and effort of the federal courts.

The Progressive Era and World War I

The shift began during the Progressive Era in response to congressional enactment of social and economic reforms against illegal railroad combinations, interstate prostitution, and unsafe food products. (Yet another example was the ratification of the Sixteenth Amendment in 1913, creating the federal income tax and the need to enforce the federal income tax code by prosecuting those who refused to file or who sought to defraud the government in paying income taxes—a source of growth in federal courts' workloads that continues to this day.) Although the initial enforcement of these laws rested with federal executive agencies, litigation arising from the tax enforcement effort quickly poured into the federal courts as the litigants invoked the courts' jurisdiction to hear cases posing a "federal question." World War I strengthened the trend. For example, the federal courts had the job of enforcing the draft by hearing cases under the selective service laws. Draft compliance stood at 85 to 90 percent, but this still left some 2 to 3 million men who either refused to register, or failed to serve, when called up for service. Within six months of the war's start, the Justice Department ordered the arrest of more than 6,000 men nationwide. By mid-1918, about 10,000 men had been prosecuted in the federal courts for draft law violations. By December 1918, more than half of all known "draft dodgers" were indicted or had their cases settled in some manner. Smaller in numbers but greater in impact, cases under national security laws also came to the federal courts. In particular, the Espionage Act of 1917, the Sedition Act of 1918, and regulations that aimed to control enemy aliens generated some 600 federal cases in just two years.

Prohibition

The real shift began, however, with the ratification of the Eighteenth Amendment, which provided the constitutional warrant for Prohibition—the policy outlawing the production, transportation, and sale of alcohol across the United States. Enforced by federal authorities invoking the Volstead Act (1919), the statutory counterpart of the Eighteenth Amendment, Prohibition effectively took what had been a purely local problem—whether and how to impose limits on alcohol—and made it a national priority. The result was a massive increase in the federal courts' criminal workload. Criminal filings in the federal district courts increased by more than 300 percent nationwide—from 19,628 cases in 1917 to 87,305 cases in 1930. Most of this increase was directly attributable to Prohibition.

Prohibition also generated large numbers of civil lawsuits in which the government acted to seize the property of those violating Prohibition laws. Most common in this regard were equity suits—abatement suits aimed at declaring the property used in bootlegging a public nuisance. The federal courts had the power to close a property to all use for one year and a day if it was declared a public nuisance. Applied to Prohibition cases, the use of federal power meant shutting down the speakeasies and other stores dispensing liquor. Almost unheard of before 1920, federal nuisance abatement cases reached a high of 15,455 filings in 1932—Prohibition's last full year in effect.

The New Deal

Thirteen years of experience with Prohibition persuaded the American people and their state and federal legislators that the Eighteenth Amendment had been a mistake. In 1933, the Twenty-First Amendment repealed the Eighteenth Amendment, thus bringing Prohibition to an end. Though Prohibition's demise sharply cut back on the number of federal criminal filings, the general trend toward public law matters continued unchecked into the 1930s. The years of the Great Depression saw perhaps the greatest increase in federal power since the creation of the federal government itself. Under the leadership of President Franklin D. Roosevelt, the national government began to enact and enforce laws that affected the everyday lives of most Americans. From new banking and securities laws to Social Security, from price controls under the National Industrial Recovery Act (NIRA) to support of unions under the Wagner National Labor Relations Act (NLRA), FDR's New Deal greatly multiplied the reach and scope of federal law. The expansion of federal law was accompanied by a corresponding increase in federal-question suits in federal courts.

The impact was twofold. On the one hand, the federal courts had the job of hearing and deciding cases brought by the federal government to enforce these laws. Consequently, the district courts heard tens of thousands of price control and regulatory cases brought under NIRA. By the end of 1933 alone, the National Recovery Administration (NRA), created by NIRA, had brought some 10,000 cases to federal courts. The numbers continued at this pace through 1935. At the same time, the federal courts also heard constitutional challenges as well, often from defendants being prosecuted under them. In federal district courts across the nation, local businessmen and large farmers challenged NIRA and the Agricultural Adjustment Act (a statute analogous to NIRA but applied to the nation's farmers). Soon these cases were moving up the appellate ladder. However, in 1935, the Supreme Court ruled that both laws were unconstitutional. These defeats in the Supreme Court did not stop FDR's New Deal. In late 1935, the Roosevelt administration sought enactment of new regulatory laws aimed at combating the Great Depression. Collectively known as the Second New Deal, these laws generated even more federal-question work for the federal courts, as new filings percolated through the entire federal judiciary, from the district courts, then rising through the circuit courts, and finally reaching the Supreme Court. Better written and more internally coherent than the first round of New Deal legislation, the laws of the Second New Deal passed constitutional muster and were often upheld by the Supreme Court.

The Second New Deal marked a significant transition point for the federal courts. Whereas formerly the courts had often questioned and even attacked the legitimacy of governmental regulation, now they accepted Congress's declarations of need and legitimacy; thus, they upheld the continued growth of government regulation of economic matters and social issues. The effect of this shift was twofold. First, by supporting the federal regulation of administrative agencies, there was less need for the federal district courts to adjudicate prosecutions to enforce federal regulatory laws. Consequently, federal-question suits decreased, and the rate of filings stayed at this lower level until the 1970s. Even so, the decline in federal-question suits was overshadowed by a growing wave of diversity cases brought by corporations that were a significant part of business activity related to the economic boom caused by World War II.

Civil Rights and Civil Liberties

Of greater impact was the shift in the Supreme Court's focus toward developing American constitutional law. The shift began quietly when Justice Harlan Fiske Stone included Footnote 4 in his opinion for the Court in *U.S. v. Carolene Products* (1938). Presented to the Court as a challenge to Congress's Filled Milk Act (1923), which prohibited the addition of other fats to skim milk in order to make it seem more like whole milk or cream, *Carolene Products* seemed to be yet another case in which the Court routinely upheld a federal law regulating the economy. Yet, in the course of recognizing the legitimacy of congressional economic power, Justice Stone added a now-famous Footnote 4 which declared that, "There may be narrower scope for operation of the presumption of constitutionality when legislation appears on its face to be within a specific prohibition of the Constitution, such as those of the first ten Amendments, which are deemed equally specific when held to be embraced within the Fourteenth." He continued by noting how "prejudice against discrete and insular minorities" might present a "special condition . . . seriously . . . curtail[ing] the operation of those political processes ordinarily to be relied upon to protect minorities," and that this fact "may call for a correspondingly more searching judicial inquiry." The language in *Carolene Product*'s Footnote 4 signaled that the Supreme Court would be more proactive in defending civil rights and liberties in future cases.

In the years that followed, Justice Stone's warning that violations of the Bill of Rights (as incorporated into the Fourteenth Amendment's due process clause) were problems that would increasingly concern the Court became a call to arms that reshaped both the federal courts and the nation as a whole. From the mid-1940s on, the federal courts began to rule in favor of racial minorities as they sought protections for their long-neglected civil rights. The visible shift began in 1944, when the Supreme Court in *Smith v. Allwright* overturned state laws and party rules that limited the voting rights of qualified African American voters. Two years later, the Court ruled in *Morgan v. Virginia* that segregated public buses could not operate in interstate commerce. In 1948, *Shelley v. Kraemer* invalidated restrictive covenants—clauses written into real-estate deeds and contracts for sale of homes that barred the sale of those homes to African Americans. In 1950, the Court in *Sweatt v. Painter* ordered the state of Texas to desegregate its state university's law school. By 1954, when the Court issued its landmark ruling in *Brown v. Board of Education* that all separate public educational facilities for blacks were inherently unequal, the trend had already been set.

In the years that followed, under the leadership of Chief Justice Earl Warren, the Supreme Court reformed criminal law procedure, demanding that state courts follow the rule that illegally obtained evidence must be excluded from the trial (*Mapp v. Ohio*, 1961); that, in *Gideon v. Wainwright* (1963) and other cases, the accused have a right to an attorney and that this right is mandatory for all defendants at all major stages in an arrest and trial up through the first appeal of a conviction (Banks and O'Brien 2015, 159); and that police inform the accused of a suspect's constitutional rights before questioning (*Miranda v. Arizona*, 1966). Other changes included the judicial declaration that a constitutionally protected right to privacy in intimate matters of sex and procreation existed as a consequence of other specified constitutional rights (*Griswold v. Connecticut*, 1965); the interpretation of the Fourteenth Amendment's equal protection clause to require states to redistrict their legislative seats to meet a "one person, one vote" standard every 10 years (*Baker v. Carr*, 1962; *Gray v. Sanders*, 1963); and the beginnings of what would come to be called "affirmative action" (*Jones v. Alfred H. Mayer*, 1968).

Side by side with these constitutional reforms, the Court pursued doggedly its efforts to enforce *Brown*'s command that state and local governments desegregate public schools. In 1968, in *Green v. Board of Education*, the Court ruled that, given the 14 years that had passed since *Brown*, the time for delay had ended; thus, it ordered the immediate integration of southern public schools. One year later, in *Alexander v. Holmes County Board of Education*, the Court reiterated its demand that school boards take immediate steps to integrate their schools. Finally, in 1971, the Court upheld a mandatory busing plan to promote integration in *Swann v. Charlotte-Mecklenburg Board of Education*.

Changes at the Supreme Court level meant changes for the lower federal courts as well. Whereas the Supreme Court set the tone in matters of civil rights and liberties, the lower federal courts had the job of enforcing these changes. The result was the rise of a new category of cases on the district and circuit court dockets—civil rights cases. Though never as numerous as criminal prosecutions or private diversity cases, civil rights cases posed a unique burden for the lower federal courts. Unlike criminal or civil trials that end relatively quickly, civil rights suits stayed active for years, and even decades. Merely ordering a school to desegregate or a business to change its hiring practices was not enough. Without constant oversight, the average school or corporate board figured out ways to ignore or sidestep judicial orders and did nothing (or, if necessary, did the minimum that was required to stave off contempt-of-court charges). If the rights of minorities were to be vindicated, judges had to monitor the defendants' progress toward compliance with the law. Hence, not only did civil rights suits stay on the dockets for seemingly forever, they also took a significant amount of the judges' time to process and complete.

As the 1960s came to an end, there was a growing range of cases requiring the sort of day-to-day supervision represented by desegregation suits. In the 1970s, federal courts took on the frustrating tasks of reforming state prison systems as a result of lawsuits brought by prisoners that challenged the often horrific conditions of incarceration. The federal courts also had to oversee extensive affirmative action reforms in schools and private-sector employment. In addition, spurred on by the rise of the environmental movement and the discovery of massive cases of pollution that endangered the lives and health of millions of Americans, the courts had to supervise the cleanup of major environmental troubles. While all of these developments were unfolding, the growth in federal-question suits renewed its ever-constant upward climb.

Similar developments increasingly strained the federal courts' criminal dockets. The ongoing war on drugs drastically expanded the number and scope of federal crimes. With this growth came a parallel spike in federal criminal cases. By the late 1970s and early 1980s, things had gotten so bad that cries of "caseload crisis" were numerous. In repeated public statements and reports to Congress, Chief Justice Warren E. Burger (1969–1986) warned of the impending collapse of the federal court system unless something was done to lower the number of cases. Many legal scholars and jurists echoed Burger's warnings of disaster and pleas for action.

Relief from the Overload in Cases in the 21st Century

Dire as these warnings were, they ultimately proved overstated. During the middle years of the 20th century, Congress gradually increased the numbers of federal trial and appellate judges; reworked the structure of the circuit courts; and created specialized federal courts to siphon off cases in the areas of bankruptcy, immigration, and taxation from the general federal caseload. Rewriting the Federal Rules of Civil Procedure and the Federal Rules of Criminal Procedure, which are the systems of rules governing the vast majority of federal cases, also helped the federal judges cope with their increasing caseloads. The court system began to reform itself as well, adopting in the 1970s and 1980s more efficient case-processing methods and systems of judicial administration. Finally, the suggestions of legal scholars Samuel Estreicher and John Sexton (that the Supreme Court ought to see itself as the manager of the federal judicial system and thus ought to take cases based on that view of its judicial role) helped to ease the justices' workload and, in the process, to fend off the creation of another level of federal appellate review between the circuit courts and the Supreme Court. To be sure, the numbers of suits filed and cases heard did not go down, but nonetheless the result of all these reforms was a general lessening of pressure on the federal courts.

In the 2010s, federal judges have been required to give priority to criminal cases over civil ones. This has forced civil cases to be delayed, sometimes up to five or six years. In general, all cases have been delayed, as judges retire and have not been replaced in a timely manner. Because federal judges need to receive Senate confirmation, and the Republican-led Senate from 2010 to 2014 delayed or blocked many of President Obama's nominations, the federal courts have had a high percentage of judicial vacancies. In 2014, the Senate confirmed more nominations, but there is still about a 10 percent vacancy rate, especially in the lower federal courts.

HISTORICAL DEVELOPMENT OF STATE COURTS

To understand today's state courts, which are quite different from the federal courts, it is helpful to reflect on their origins. Originally, American national law and the judiciary grew out of British legal traditions and doctrines. Past British customs were not entirely welcome or appropriate for the remote and rustic conditions of the colonies, but at the time, prior practices were the only law familiar to them. Following the American Revolution, British legal and judicial traditions were rejected just as surely as the hereditary monarchy. Later, however, as the United States grew out of its infancy and revolutionary tempers cooled, American courts turned again to their British origins for advice.

The traditions, character, and structures of the state court systems are rooted both in national and local histories. The laws of individual states grew out of their colonial or territorial experiences, industrial and technological evolutions, and internal political struggles. The earliest colonial courts were quite different in many ways from modern state courts. Over time, as new political issues arose and new demands confronted the states, state courts had to adapt structural and doctrinal reforms. As the loosely connected states of a new nation became more economically and politically integrated, courts began adopting more uniform qualities and laws to help facilitate economic evolution. In American law, there is a constant tension between continuity and change—between the stability and wisdom that tradition promises and the opportunities and innovation hoped for through progress.

The Colonial Courts

During the colonial period, the structure of the courts differed vastly among the 13 colonies because they were established under differing charters. Some were created by edict of the Crown (Virginia), some were owned by corporations (Massachusetts Bay), and others initially were the private property of an individual (Pennsylvania). Thus, the justice systems in each colony evolved to serve the political needs of different masters. This helps explain some surviving disparities in court structures and doctrines across the states today.

Because the courts evolved from different grants of power, judges gained their power from various sources of judicial selection. In this way, they were responsive only to the one who chose them for judicial service. Perhaps most notably, the British monarch appointed many judges—either directly or authorized their very existence—in a colony's charter. This ensured that Crown-appointed judges displayed sympathy for the king.

For example, in Virginia, the general court included the governor and the council, or colonial senate. In his official capacity, the governor himself served as a judge in many colonies to resolve business disputes. Because the Virginian governor was the king's appointee, his economic decisions reflected the king's interests in trade disputes.

The Colonial Judge

During the colonial and early days of the new republic, lawyers and judges typically were not products of law schools. Rather, they had served as apprentices for established lawyers before going into practices of their own. Their studies often focused on political theory and philosophy, of which law was one part. Judging in the colonial era was a part-time job, and judges often were responsible for overlapping local chores. In addition to their judicial duties, justices of the peace administered local government, levied and collected taxes, and made local appointments in the way modern mayors and city councils would. On top of these duties, justices of the peace ran their own businesses and farms. In other words, fulfilling their judicial responsibilities was a part-time job that did not pay particularly well. They were usually prominent and upright members of their communities and tried to reflect the sensibilities of their communities as consistent with the demands of the colonial charter. They meted out punishment for cursing, failure to attend church, horse theft, treason, and murder.

While governors sat as judges, so too did legislators. In Virginia, members of the senate could hear criminal cases when it convened as the Court of Oyer & Terminer. Royal grants permitted some measure of local responsiveness in this way. Another way of accommodating the separation between London and the American colonies was a grant of authority to governors to appoint prominent, landowning, white, Protestant men of their own choosing to serve as justices of the peace. The selection of judges in the colonies more closely resembles the way in which federal judges are selected with legislative approval. Today, in many states, judges must face some type of election. As it had become the custom in England, judges were appointed in many of the colonies to serve during "good behavior."

The American Revolution and the Courts

As the American Revolution drew near, disputes between royally appointed governors and locally elected legislators escalated. So too did tensions related to establishing court systems, punishments, and crimes. In addition, the government in London frustrated colonial attempts to continue giving judges life tenure. Parliament also demanded that many types of cases be taken from colonial courts and transferred to London. The debate over the terms of judges and the demand that an increasing number of cases be heard in England became important points of contention leading up to the American Revolution. The Crown complained that its prerogatives were undermined by life terms for judges because it created fewer vacancies for the king to fill with like-minded judges. The colonial revolutionaries, meanwhile, said transporting trials across the Atlantic Ocean took justice out of the hands of those closest to the events and denied defendants, witnesses, and victims an opportunity to follow trials. The nature of administering justice was at the core of the American Revolution and its identity after independence was won.

Liberty and Justice for Some

Protestant free men were able to serve as justices of the peace. Usually, it was a justice of the peace who resolved disputes and meted out punishment for committing crimes during the colonial and founding eras. In many ways, the character of these courts was considerably different from modern courts. First, as noted previously, only Protestant, landowning, white men were eligible for decision-making positions. As parties to a case, white Protestant men could appeal their cases to the higher judicial authorities, including the governor, his council, or the state legislature. For white men convicted of a felony who had hoped to escape harsh capital punishment, there was the option of appealing to the "benefit of clergy." This meant they could turn their case over for a church trial and punishment. In some instances, the punishment was time spent in a convent or monastery, rather than the stockades, whipping, or hanging.

For women, slaves, and Native Americans, the story was different. They were not permitted to sit on a jury or to enjoy the prerogative of having cases heard beyond the local justices of the peace. The benefit of clergy for slaves and women was often contested, and this privilege turned on the mood of the colony (or state), whether the slave practiced Christianity, or whether the defendant could read the Bible. When a woman was in court, she was usually a witness and seldom the plaintiff. When free or enslaved Africans appeared in court, it almost always meant they were being tried for an offense. Blacks in most places through the mid-1800s enjoyed none of the protections enjoyed by British subjects or U.S. citizens. As witnesses, blacks could not testify against whites—only against other blacks.

State Courts in the New Republic

As the new republic emerged, the former colonies struggled to determine the role and function of courts. Many courts wanted to establish new traditions and legal reasoning that were more appropriate for a republic, as opposed to a monarchy. One of the most important changes to emerge occurred when the courts began to rely less frequently on British common law; instead, they began to develop law more suited to American needs. Change was often slow in coming. For example, the New York Constitution of 1777 explicitly kept the British-style court system intact during the Revolution, with the caveat that the legislature could make revisions as necessary. For the first 40 years of the new state's history, the New York high court remained untouched, save for the elimination of the king's name as authorizing its orders. Yet in other colonies, change was more rapid.

When Thomas Jefferson was serving as Secretary of State in President George Washington's administration, a mentor and friend of Jefferson's came to the

Virginia Chancery Court and gave the United States a remarkable new theory of justice. Now a bedrock concept of constitutional law, in 1782, Virginia Chancery Judge George Wythe first suggested the concept of *judicial review.* This is the legal theory that courts have the authority to interpret the meaning of a constitution and nullify any legislative or executive act that conflicts with it.

In *Commonwealth v. Caton* (1782), Judge Wythe wrote, "Pointing to the constitution, [I] will say, to them [state legislators], here is the limit of your authority; and, hither shall you go, but no further." Inspired from English common law, the idea of judicial review was expressed in state court decisions and later enshrined as federal constitutional law in the U.S. Supreme Court's 1803 decision *Marbury v. Madison*, from which the national high court today claims this power.

Almost as soon as its British roots left American legal tradition, so too did the charters that created local courts and authorized justices of the peace. Constitutions would take their place, and through the rest of U.S. history, they would be adopted, amended, and replaced in various ways. Another quality quickly abandoned was the French legal heritage in what is now much of the Midwest, as well as Spanish colonial law in the Southwest. With the Northwest Ordinance, the French common law was imposed between Pennsylvania and the Mississippi River.

Without law, though, early state courts realized elements of British tradition were better than chaos. The common law was reintroduced and modified to address citizens rather than subjects and an economy based on landowners rather than tenants. State legislatures also hastily passed statutes rescinding British legal principles that were repugnant to the revolutionary spirit, often later realizing some had utility.

Post-Revolutionary Law and Constitutions

Seeing the utility of decisions in British law, New York adopted colonial regulations in 1821 that did not otherwise contradict the state constitution. Courts also got into the act, claiming that the new republic had adopted the common law. There were, of course, loud outbursts of anxiety about turning to a foreign system—and to the British in particular—for legal advice. The Kentucky legislature, for example, noisily condemned British influences. At the same time that New York allowed British tradition to seep back into state law, Kentucky declared that "reports and books" containing British decisions, "shall not be read or considered as authority" in its courts (Friedman 2003, 68). For the laws and courts of the new republic, this would be a checkered part of their history. Thus, much of the tension among the industrial, rural, and frontier states remained until after the Civil War.

During this time period, no two state constitutions were exactly alike. On the contrary, state constitutions became more divergent during much of this era, generally reflecting tensions over suffrage, apportionment, and trade. What was common among these charters, though, was the deference paid to legislatures. Executive power generally was kept in check and held in some contempt. With *Marbury v. Madison* and the establishment of judicial review, judicial powers expanded, but they were used haltingly and with great caution. Suffice it to say, what these loosely united states held in common was a core faith in representative government, with voting rights available to a broader section of the public than elsewhere in the world.

Courts and Judges of the Jacksonian Era

Colonial judges were often beholden to executive authorities, and, in fact, they were executives themselves. However, during the 80 years between the founding era and the Civil War, the doctrine of separating powers between political institutions spread rapidly in the individual states as it was in the central national government. The idea of the part-time lay judge receded into memory as well.

Americans of this era placed emphasis on political control from below, not from above; that is, judges were selected by vote in many, but not all, counties in the new republic. In the wake of Andrew Jackson's presidency, however, the appointed judge became extinct. In 1777, Vermont began this march, requiring the popular election of judges. The rest of the states followed suit, with New Yorkers finally adopting popular election of their state Supreme Court judges in 1846. The theme of popular control of government remained powerful until the turn of the next century, when faith in the voter was shaken when waves of immigrants sided with scandalous political machines, and merit selection of judges gained fashion.

Also falling by the wayside between the founding and Civil War eras was legislative and executive interference in the business of state judiciaries. While governors in New Jersey and Connecticut retained high judicial authority in the founding era, this slowly faded into history as New York and Rhode Island constitutions in the 1840s took their governors off their courts of last resort.

Other American traditions emerged during the antebellum era, affecting the courts' personnel. The federal Constitution remained true to the executive appointment of judges. It also maintained lifetime tenure—another theme antithetical to Jacksonian democracy. Whereas federal judges could be forced out only by impeachment, usually for serious offenses, states such as Pennsylvania and South Carolina made it easy to remove judges for misdemeanor infractions.

Industrialization and Individualism in the Progressive Era

After the Civil War, between the 1880s and the 1920s, two intertwined events— the industrialization of the United States and massive immigration to U.S.

cities from impoverished parts of Europe and China—ushered in new ideas about law and courts.

The shift in attitudes toward injury and responsibility began in the mid-1800s, but it became more prominent by the early 20th century. By that time, industrialization, railroading, and immigration brought about the adoption of wage and work safety regulations. Among these laws were limits on the hours and conditions that pregnant women and children could toil in factories and other strenuous work environments. Industrial innovations also introduced heavy moving equipment into agriculture, railroading, and manufacturing processes. These machines and factories increased productivity, but they also sometimes jeopardized the health and even the lives of workers.

With economic innovation came the need to evaluate how law responded and understood the dangers and opportunities in the marketplace. Courts and legislatures adapted to the industrial revolution by putting forward political ideas in much the same way they had 100 years before—by purging and reintroducing common law traditions. Legal innovation came in fits and starts. Courts in California, Illinois, and Pennsylvania held tightly to rugged individualism as an organizing ideology despite legislative language attempting to address harsh labor conditions. Courts such as these argued against many types of legislative interference in employment regulation on two primary principles: first, regulation undermined a right to a contract, which was premised on the dignity of the rational individual who should decide for himself whether to accept dangerous employment conditions. Second, it treated all workers or certain types of laborers as a class, separate and unequal in the law only because of membership in that class.

Employers generally had little legal obligation for the safety of their workers, and consumers had high hurdles to surmount to sue for faulty manufacturing in courts such as these. Judges trained by mentors educated at the time of the Civil War placed high value on the individual's right to contract, and they denied legislatures' rights to interfere in the private relationship between employer and employee. In doing so, the courts did not let government deny a man the right to work 12-hour days, 6 days a week in a hot, dusty coal mine for a paltry wage. Using similar logic for the consumer, the legal motto "caveat emptor" (let the buyer beware) was in effect. The right to contract, or purchase, was not to be upset by unnecessary common law or regulation. The federal courts and Congress generally took a laissez-faire (let it be) attitude toward American enterprise.

During the Progressive era of the late 19th and early 20th centuries, however, reformers and journalists shed light on the economic power held by monopolies in the petroleum, rubber, steel, and mining industries, as well as the deplorable living and workplace conditions of urban laborers. A new generation of state judges revisited legal theories in light of new realities about economic forces, productivity, and human safety. Judges were also moved by the forces of political organization. Emerging labor unions pointed out the value of friendly judges on the bench with respect to forming unions and addressing labor conditions. The influence of urban political machines in New York City, Boston, Albany, and Kansas City thrived on the support of working-class voters as well. Democratic machines were able to keep courts staffed with judges favorable to worker-friendly legislation and patronage for lawyers, government attorneys, and would-be judges.

By the end of this era, courts had had a change of heart. New York Supreme Court Justice Benjamin Cardozo led the way in the 1920s by articulating modern ideas of product liability law. Under this new legal doctrine, state courts across the nation began to hold manufacturers responsible for injuries that occurred because of their products. This change has been slow and deliberate. Between the 1930s and 1990s, California, New Jersey, and other states' judges shifted the burdens of product liability from caveat emptor to *caveat venditor* (let the seller beware).

The changes in legal thought on issues of liability are some of the most profound transformations in legal philosophies since the nation's founding. These have redefined the position of different groups within society. In addition, the transformation demonstrates how broader changes in society affect the courts.

Other underdogs gained the attention of influential members of society as well. The plight of the poor, orphans, immigrants, and the mentally disabled, all of whom had virtually nothing in the way of legal protections, attracted the attention of women such as Jane Addams, who dedicated her life to helping poor people. These champions of the poor and powerless also urged legal reforms to protect those who were unable to defend themselves, such as widows and children. Laws were gradually enacted that empowered state agencies to represent the interests of wards of the state. Laws for the poor distinguished between worthy and unworthy. Vagrants and drunks continued to be afforded no quarter, but support grew for providing the disabled, veterans, widows, and orphans with some modest assistance. Along with these changing views, common law adjustments were made. For example, changing economic realities recognized in other parts of society brought awareness to judges of how courts should think about the legal relationship between a vulnerable worker or an illiterate consumer and that of a powerful, well-educated manufacturer.

Selection Method Reforms at the End of the Progressive Era
Since the early 1900s, many reformers have sought to have judges appointed, rather than elected. Because political machines controlled the tools of election campaigning, it was thought that partisan elections led to scandalous judging and patronage staffing of justice systems. Reformers, both in industry and in

the American Bar Association, worried that unqualified party loyalists were unable to decide fairly. The principles of popular control remained strong in the United States, however. Trusted progressives such as President Woodrow Wilson advocated a government run by technicians or well-qualified administrators. In this political environment, merit selection methods, most notably the Missouri Plan, reintroduced executive influence to the selection process while trying to keep some semblance of popular control. With some variation among the states, Missouri Plan states have a committee that sends to the governor a list of qualified candidates; the governor makes a nomination from this list, sometimes with some type of legislative or executive approval; at the next election, voters decide to keep or remove the judge; and often the judge faces no opponent in the election.

After the Great Depression

World War II put a pause on interest in state courts, as did growing national power to regulate commerce. After the 1937 Supreme Court case *NLRB v. Jones-Laughlin Steel Corporation*, which decided the types of activities that Congress could regulate under the commerce clause, doctrinal issues receded, and structural issues became the focus on reform in the state courts.

In particular, court reformers have wanted two things: (1) merit selection of judges and consolidation of the courts, and (2) to remove the idiosyncrasies and confusion that resulted from the fact that there were so many different types of limited-jurisdiction courts in each state. The reforms have sought to streamline and increase the efficiency of state courts so that they operated and looked more like the federal court structure, which allowed the public to understand better how state courts worked. The efforts to reform, however, have often been difficult to achieve because many local governments and court employees object to state intrusion into their territories. In the past, local political machines had used court staffing for patronage, and their opposition made reform efforts difficult. Local lawyers, who navigated these systems more effectively than outsiders, had an advantage over out-of-town lawyers and fought reform.

The Illinois court system is said to have been the first to adopt a *unified system*, which is modeled after the structure of the U.S. federal judicial system. Under the Illinois structure, there are no limited-jurisdiction courts; rather, there is a single local circuit court at the county level. In heavily populated areas, such as Cook County, the court may assign judges to hear specific case types, but it still remains a single court jurisdiction. Above the circuit court, Illinois has five district appellate courts, each with jurisdiction over some region of the state. Finally, there is a single supreme court with statewide jurisdiction.

During the late 1900s and early 2000s, most states made an effort to unify their court systems, though not all mirrored the reforms in Illinois. Some states retain limited jurisdiction courts, and others have separate appeals systems for criminal and civil litigation. For example, Wisconsin reduced its special-function courts to the municipal courts, which hear cases arising from the violation of city laws. In states such as Arkansas, Massachusetts, and Rhode Island, officials have opted to keep a broader array of special-function and appellate courts. New York's government has decided to stay with many limited jurisdiction courts and multiple appeals courts.

In addition to efforts to consolidate court structures, there has also been an effort to improve the appellate process. Although many states historically had a wide variety of low-level courts, they had few appellate courts. In 1960, only 14 states had middle-level appellate courts. Without this buffer, supreme courts were swamped with cases that had little or no broad social impact. The state's supreme courts were forced to play a supervisory role, overturning poor trial decisions, rather than assuming a policymaking role of interpreting laws and constitutions, as the U.S. Supreme Court does. Much of that has changed over the past few decades, as all but 10 states now have intermediate appellate courts. Even in some of the states that do not formally have intermediate courts, the trial courts can hear appeals from limited-jurisdiction courts. This provides a buffer between the trial court and the state supreme court. In Delaware's court system, for example, this alleviated caseload pressures on the final court of last resort (COLR). Although the appellate courts are considered higher in the structure of the court system, they have little control over who actually occupies judicial offices in trial courts. The higher courts are able to set aside legally incorrect decisions, but they cannot control incompetent judges by firing or suspending them for issuing rulings contrary to precedence unless there is judicial ethical misconduct. States have distinct disciplinary procedures for judges accused of serious misconduct; however, removing judges for disagreeable rulings is not common.

Modern Reform Efforts

Perhaps the four most visible efforts to reform state law and courts have been (1) movements to ease the burden of punitive damages on parties found liable in tort law; (2) imposing stringent sentences on criminal offenders; (3) continued emphasis on consolidating court systems; and, (4) de-politicizing the selection methods of judges. The selection method questions have been extended since the Progressive era. States that maintain partisan election methods do so because political parties exert greater influence than reform movements. States having more watered-down versions, in parts of the South and Midwest, have led to nonpartisan elections. The Missouri Plan remains the selection method of choice among most bar associations and reform movements, even though merit systems are increasingly under attack (Banks and O'Brien 2015).

The push to reduce legal liability began in the 1980s and has continued to generate debate. Claiming that high-priced punitive damages are detrimental to businesses and health care, an array of physician groups, insurance companies, hospitals, and manufacturers have sought to limit the dollar amount of awards in personal injury cases that judges and juries can assign. Between 1986 and 1997, 11 state legislatures enacted limits on awards for noneconomic damages. Also during that time span, 17 states placed limits on the amounts that plaintiffs can collect in punitive awards. New Hampshire prohibited awarding punitive damages altogether. Other states insisted on more stringent courtroom findings before punitive awards could be issued. Undoubtedly, many state governments found the issues surrounding tort law to be of critical concern. Central to these concerns are unresolved arguments about the questions of the economic effect and fairness of civil litigation, as well as the influence of various pressure groups.

Critics also say civil fines are so high they drive up the market price of goods and services, which harms consumers. However, there is reason to think that several of these initiatives will be reversed. By the end of the 1990s, 11 state supreme courts dismissed these limitations for failure to comply with the constitutions in these states. Some 87 decisions in these states have found that liability limitation statutes, at least in part, violate plaintiffs' state constitutional rights to recovery and interfere with the prerogatives of the judiciary.

Consumer advocates and trial lawyers say that in order for punitive awards to work, they should "hurt" the party that causes the damage (see, for example, Poukas 1992). The threat of civil penalty would make businesses cautious only if the fine is steep enough to take away the profit motive of bringing a defective product into the marketplace. They also say these penalties help the economy by giving consumers confidence in the products they buy. Some state court judges have charged that damage caps are counterproductive and have resisted legislative efforts to impose these rules (Glabberson 1999).

In 1996, the U.S. Supreme Court entered the debate over punitive damage awards by imposing strict guidelines on the prerogatives of state courts. In its decision *BMW of North America Inc. v. Gore*, the Court gave its first hint that it had grown concerned with punitive awards. Punitive awards hope to punish deliberately harmful behavior by causing the culpable party to pay the victim more than enough to compensate for lost wages, medical expenses, and repair of damaged property. In *State Farm Mutual Automobile Insurance Co. v. Campbell* (2003), the Supreme Court went further in restraining the state courts' ability to issue large penalties. The divided Court ruled that punitive damages that were 145 times greater than the actual damages were excessive (a violation of the Eighth Amendment's restriction against excessive penalties and the Fourteenth Amendment's due process clause) because civil process is less demanding than a criminal process. The Court, however, stopped short of giving clear guidelines about the size of punitive awards.

The Court has been reluctant to identify concrete constitutional limits on the ratio between harm, or potential harm, to the plaintiff and the punitive damages award; but, in practice, few awards exceeding a single-digit ratio between punitive and compensatory damages will satisfy due process (*State Farm Mutual Automobile Insurance Co. v. Campbell*, 2003).

The *Campbell* decision did not end the debate. Rather, President George W. Bush, delighted with the outcome, two years later mustered congressional support for legislation to impose stricter liability limits, especially for suits against drug manufacturers and physicians. His legal reform program also made it easier for tort defendants to move cases out of state courts and into less plaintiff-friendly federal courts (see Banks and O'Brien 2015).

Along with pressures on the courts to limit punitive damages, there has also been an effort to impose stricter sentences on criminal offenders. During the latter part of the 1980s and early 1990s, concerns about drug-related violence grew as the rates of assaults, robberies, homicides, and incarcerations rose dramatically. The rising crime rate led to demands for reform from both the political Right and Left. For those on the Right, the rising crime rate led to concerns that violent offenders were being treated lightly and allowed to repeat their offenses. For those on the Left, there were concerns over the uneven sentencing of defendants convicted of similar crimes. As a result of these concerns, many states adopted new guidelines as to how judges should sentence felons. Among these were three-strikes rules requiring long-term sentences for certain repeat offenders and minimum sentencing guidelines for a variety of offenses.

The get-tough-on-crime movement ran into turmoil in the early 2000s. For starters, then Governor George Ryan of Illinois suspended executions in the state. This came after a group of enterprising undergraduate college students and private investigators demonstrated that police brought faulty, if not fictional, evidence against 13 defendants who were convicted for murders they did not commit. Moreover, state and federal sentencing guidelines were found unconstitutional and unreasonable via the Sixth Amendment in the *Blakely v. Washington* (2004) decision (pertaining to state guidelines) and in the *U.S. v. Booker* (2005) decision (pertaining to federal guidelines). Here the U.S. Supreme Court held that (1) "aggravating" factors that might lead to harsh sentences must be proven at trial, not merely presented at sentencing (this might include the actual weight of some drugs being sold), and (2) legislatures could not give judges authority to "enhance" sentences based on unproven evidence. This ruling has left state and federal prosecutors trying to recraft legislation to impose sentences appropriate to the level of a crime.

Contemporary Judicial Authority

After having sharpened current national debates over economic issues such as punitive damages, as well as hot social topics such as assisted suicide, same-sex marriage, crime, and election law, state courts sit at the heart of current events and social controversies in the United States. On many issues, state courts have been early bellwethers of changing national perceptions and viewpoints. In the case of gay marriage, for example, a Massachusetts appeals court ruled in *Goodridge v. Department of Public Health* in 2003 that gay couples had a right to marry. Twelve years after this decision, the first in which a state's highest court endorsed the legality of same-sex marriage, the U.S. Supreme Court sided with this position in *Obergefell v. Hodges*.

It would be an exaggeration, however, to think they alone are determining the outcomes of these controversies. Rather, with 50 states, courts in each of these states continue to raise and revise cutting-edge legal theories. Therefore, it benefits the observer of news, politics, and policy to understand how these vital institutions function, how judges reason, and how their environments place pressures on them. Students of state courts have begun to examine the structure, function, and politics of state courts systematically as a group. Some 400 years after the first local courts were established in the American colonies and more than 200 years after Virginia's Judge Wythe helped to establish the power of a state court to exercise judicial review, our state courts have begun to receive something more than local attention.

Today's state judges are better organized, educated, and paid than any of their predecessors. Constant training opportunities and electronic communications allow judges across the country to be familiar with common legal topics and arguments. Similarly, the supporting casts for judges, clerks, and legal research staff enjoy similar organization and training. This allows state courts to function at a higher level of efficiency and competence. Moreover, judges are subject to the environments in which they serve. This environment includes elections, interest group activity in the courts, media attention, and pressures from other actors in government, who also enjoy improved information and research.

THE RELATIONSHIP BETWEEN FEDERAL AND STATE COURTS

As you can see, it is not accurate to say the United States has *a* judicial system; rather, it has many judicial systems. Each state has a judiciary, and no two states have systems that are exactly the same. Parallel to the state systems is the federal judicial system, beginning with a trial court (federal district courts), leading to an appellate court (usually the circuit court of appeals), and ending with the U.S. Supreme Court. Some state court systems can have even simpler structures, with only a trial and a supreme court, while other states may have more complex judicial systems with a variety of special-purpose courts, or two separate supreme courts—one to review civil cases and another for criminal cases.

The relationship between these two court systems—federal and state—is sometimes referred to as judicial federalism. Federalism is the distribution of power and responsibility between the national government and the individual states. State courts play an important role in American federalism because they are given considerable legal decision-making powers and responsibilities. In addition, state courts are significant because they serve to bring new legal issues and ideas into the nation's court system, and they act to apply U.S. Supreme Court rulings to the states. In the late 1900s and early 2000s, state supreme courts emerged as even more important players within judicial federalism as these courts discovered the use of state constitutions for deciding rights cases. Judicial federalism is both a cause and consequence of American law, national politics, and the structure of the federal system.

At the top of the U.S. federal court system is the U.S. Supreme Court. The Supreme Court's decisions, in particular, receive the most attention in popular news coverage, high school civics courses, and law school reading assignments. The great attention devoted to the Supreme Court reflects the Court's authority to decide the most profound legal issues confronting the nation. Before about one-third of the cases reach the Supreme Court, however, they first pass through state court systems. The opinions of state supreme courts help the U.S. Supreme Court think through emerging, thorny legal issues.

Despite the slim chance that any case will be brought to the U.S. Supreme Court, state noncompliance with federal Supreme Court decisions has historically been relatively uncommon. The compliance of state courts to U.S. Supreme Court decisions reinforces the high court's stature and indicates to all who enter a state courtroom where the final authority rests in American judicial federalism. Sometimes one decision may become the source of new legal questions. When that happens, states may pioneer novel legal theories or, more commonly, distinguish a case from an issue already decided by the U.S. Supreme Court. In this way, state courts play an important role in both defining and redefining issues for the U.S. Supreme Court. State supreme courts are at the intersection of U.S. law, filtering cases and ideas up to the U.S. Supreme Court and interpreting them for the trial courts closer to home.

One of the most important trends in judicial federalism has been the increased reliance by state supreme courts on state constitutions in making rights rulings. This type of judicial behavior has been labeled "the new judicial federalism" (see Banks and Blakeman 2012). While some observers think the U.S.

Supreme Court of the 1990s and early 2000s is more "conservative" than the Court of the 1960s and 1970s, and has become less supportive of civil rights and liberties suits, many state courts have expanded personal rights based on their own constitutions. Supreme Court Justice William Brennan (1977) was one of the first advocates for expanding individual rights through state constitutional interpretation. In the early 2000s, state courts used their authority to do exactly that. Even prior to Brennan's advocacy, Oregon Supreme Court Justice Hans Linde argued that the state constitutions, rather than the federal Bill of Rights, were "first in right and first in logic" (Linde 1980).

It is from Linde's theory that state courts have turned to their own state constitutional provisions to find rights unlikely to be found from the U.S. Supreme Court. These include a right to educational funding (see, for example, *Tennessee Small School Systems v. McWherter*, 1993), to low-income housing (see *Southern Burlington County NAACP v. Township of Mount Laurel*, 1975), and to firearm possession outside the home (*State of Wisconsin v. Hamdan*, 2003). The U.S. Supreme Court, as a rule, refrains from upsetting the state courts' interpretation of state law, even when both would come to contradictory conclusions about the meaning of very similar language.

The emergence of new judicial federalism is important because it means that the state high courts do not have to rely solely on the interpretations of the U.S. Supreme Court when they issue rulings (see Banks and Blakeman 2012). They may be responsive to local state political concerns and state history, thus remaining faithful to the text of state constitutions.

Even when federal issues are involved, the U.S. Supreme Court increasingly has turned in favor of states' rights. This places state courts in a more central decision-making position. For example, with the 1995 decision *United States v. Lopez*, the U.S. Supreme Court struck down a federal law that banned guns within "x" number of feet of schools, saying Congress exceeded its commerce power in making the law. Following the *United States v. Lopez* precedent, two other cases—*United States v. Morrison* in 1999 and *Solid Waste Agency of Northern Cook County v. United States Army Corps of Engineers* in 2001—also limited the reach of the federal government over states' rights.

One final aspect of judicial federalism is the relationship each state has with other states. Often states deal with many of the same issues, and they borrow ideas from one another. This sharing among state court opinions is referred to as "horizontal federalism." States such as California and New York are considered to have among the most innovative court systems in the nation, and their opinions are widely cited by the courts of other states (Caldiera 1985). State supreme court judges also frequently refer to judges with whom they share a point of view.

Charles L. Zelden, Sean O. Hogan, and Ginny Hollinger

Further Reading

Amar, Akhil Reed. 2015. *The Law of the Land: A Grand Tour of Our Constitutional Republic*. New York: Basic Books.

Aquinas, Thomas. 1988. *On Law, Morality and Politics*. Indianapolis, IN: Hackett.

Banks, Christopher P., and John C. Blakeman. 2012. *The U.S. Supreme Court and New Federalism: From the Rehnquist to the Roberts Court*. Lanham, MD: Rowman & Littlefield.

Banks, Christopher P., and David M. O'Brien. 2015. *The Judicial Process: Law, Courts, and Judicial Politics*. Thousand Oaks, CA: CQ Press.

Barrow, Deborah J., Gerard S. Gryski, and Gary Zuk. 1996. *The Federal Judiciary and Institutional Change*. Ann Arbor: University of Michigan Press.

Bermant, Gordon, and Russell R. Wheeler. 1995. "Federal Judges and the Judicial Branch: Their Independence and Accountability." *Mercer Law Review* 46: 835–861.

Bordewich, Fergus M. 2016. *The First Congress: How James Madison, George Washington, and a Group of Extraordinary Men Invented the Government*. New York: Simon & Schuster.

Brace, Paul, and Melinda Gann Hall. 1990. "Neo-Institutionalism and Dissent in the State Supreme Courts." *Journal of Politics* 52 (February): 54–70.

Brace, Paul, and Melinda Gann Hall. 1995. "Studying Courts Comparatively: The View from the American States." *Political Research Quarterly* 48 (March): 5–29.

Brennan, William J. 1977. "State Constitutions and the Protection of Individual Rights." *Harvard Law Review* 90 (January): 489–504.

Caldiera, Gregory A. 1983. "On the Reputation of State Supreme Courts." *Political Behavior* 5 (1): 83–108.

Carp, Robert A., and C. K. Rowland. 1983. *Policymaking and Politics in the Federal District Courts*. Knoxville: University of Tennessee Press.

Carp, Robert A., and Ronald Stidham. 2010. *The Federal Courts*. 5th ed. Washington, D.C.: CQ Press.

Carp, Robert A., and Ronald Stidham. 2013. *Judicial Process in America*. 9th ed. Washington, D.C.: CQ Press.

Church, Thomas W. 1995. "Plea Bargaining and Local Legal Culture." In *Contemplating Courts*, edited by Lee Epstein, 132–154. Washington, D.C.: CQ Press.

Clayton, Cornell W., and H. Gillman, eds. 1999. Judicial Choice. In *Supreme Court Decision-Making: New Institutionalist Approaches*. Chicago: University of Chicago Press.

Cotterrell, Bill. 2003. "Bush Given Power in Case." *Tallahassee Democrat*, October 22. http://www.Tallahassee.com.

Dailey, Debra. 1998. "Minnesota Sentencing Guidelines: A Structure for Change." *Law and Policy* 20 (July): 311–332.

Doernberg, Donald. 2016. *Federal Courts in a Nutshell*. St. Paul, MN: West Academic Publishing.

Farnsworth, E. Allan, and Steve Sheppard. 2010. *An Introduction to the Legal System of the United States*. 4th ed. New York: Oxford University Press.

Fino, Susan P. 1987. *The Role of State Supreme Courts in the New Judicial Federalism*. Westport, CT: Greenwood Press.

Fish, Peter Graham. 1973. *The Politics of Federal Judicial Administration*. Princeton, NJ: Princeton University Press.

Flango, Carol A., Victor E. Flango, and H. Ted Rubin. 1999. *How Are Courts Coordinating Family Cases?* (report 96–12C-B-222). Alexandria, VA: State Justice Institute.

Frankfurter, Felix, and James Landis. 1927. *The Business of the Supreme Court: A Study in the Federal Judicial System*. New York: Macmillan.

Friedman, Lawrence M. 2003. *A History of American Law*. 3rd ed. New York: Touchstone.

George, Robert P., and Christopher Wolfe, eds. 2000. *Natural Law and Public Reason*. Washington, D.C.: Georgetown University Press.

Gillman, Howard. 1993. *The Constitution Besieged: The Rise & Demise of Lochner Era Police Powers Jurisprudence*. Durham, NC: Duke University Press.

Glabberson, William. 1999. "State Laws Limiting Injury Suits Are Falling like Dominoes." *New York Times*, July 16.

Guide to the Federal Courts: An Introduction to the Federal Courts and Their Operation: Includes Explanation of How a Case Is Litigated. 1984. Washington, D.C.: Want Publishing.

Hall, Melinda Gann. 1987. "Constituent Influence in State Supreme Courts: Conceptual Notes and a Case Study." *Journal of Politics* 49 (November): 1117–1166.

Hall, Melinda Gann. 1994. "The Vicissitudes of Death by Decree: Forces Influencing Capital Punishment in State Supreme Courts." *Social Science Quarterly* 75 (March): 136–151.

Hall, Melinda Gann. 1999. "State Supreme Courts and Their Environments: Avenues to General Theories of Judicial Choice." In *Supreme Court Decision Making: New Institutionalist Approaches*, edited by Cornell W. Clayton and Howard Gillman, 281–300. Chicago: University of Chicago Press.

Hall, Melinda Gann, and Paul Brace. 1993. "Integrated Models of Judicial Dissent." *Journal of Politics* 55 (November): 419–435.

Handberg, Roger, and Harold F. Hill, Jr. 1980. "Court Curbing, Court Reversals, and Judicial Review: The Supreme Court versus Congress." *Law & Society Review* 14 (Winter): 309–322.

Heydebrand, Wolf, and Carroll Seron. 1990. *Rationalizing Justice: The Political Economy of Federal District Courts*. Albany: State University of New York Press.

Hoffer, Peter Charles, William James Hull Hoffer, and N. E. H. Hull. 2016. *The Federal Courts: An Essential History*. New York: Oxford University Press.

Hogan, Sean O. 2000. "Continuity and Change in the Common Law: The Illinois Supreme Court's Tort Doctrine 1970–1996." Unpublished PhD diss., University of Illinois-Chicago.

Klaversma, Laura G., and Daniel J. Hall. 2003. *Organizational and Administrative Review of the Fulton County, Georgia, Juvenile Court*. Denver, CO: Court Services Consulting.

Kramer, Larry D. 2001. "The Supreme Court 2000 Term: Foreword: We The Court." *Harvard Law Review* 115 (November): 4–168.

LaFountain, Robert C., Richard Y. Schauffler, Shauna M. Strickland, and Kathryn A. Holt. 2012. *Examining the Work of State Courts: An Analysis of 2010 State Court Caseloads*. Williamsburg, VA: National Center for State Courts.

Langan, Patrick A., and David P. Farrington. 1998. *Crime and Justice in the United States and in England and Wales, 1981–1996*. Washington, D.C.: U.S. Department of Justice.

Linde, Hans. 1995. "Are State Constitutions Common Law?" In *Intellect and Craft: The Contributions of Justice Hans Linde to American Constitutionalism*, edited by R. F. Nagel. Boulder, CO: Westview Press.

Marcus, Maeva, ed. 1992. *Origins of the Federal Judiciary: Essays on the Judiciary Act of 1789*. New York: Oxford University Press.

Mecham, Leonidas Ralph. 2002. *Judicial Business of the United States: 2002 Annual Report of the Director*. Washington, D.C.: Administrative Office of the U.S. Courts, Government Printing Office.

Mikeska, Jennifer L. 2000. "Court Consolidation: Reinventing Missouri State Courts." Institute for Court Management, Court Executive Development Program, Phase III Project. N.p.: McDonald County Circuit Court.

National Center for State Courts. 2002. "Civil Justice Reform Initiative: Advancing Civil Justice Reform." Williamsburg, VA: National Center for State Courts.

Nelson, Marilyn. 2001. "Customer Service and Court Consolidation: Are Consolidated Courts Better Able to Serve Their Customers?" Report to Institute for Court Management (May). Williamsburg, VA: National Center for State Courts.

Pinello, Daniel R. 1995. *The Impact of Judicial-Selection Method on State Supreme Court Policy Innovation, Reaction, and Atrophy*. Westport, CT: Greenwood Press.

Posner, Richard A. 1996. *The Federal Courts: Challenge and Reform*. Cambridge, MA: Harvard University Press.

Poukas, Erick P. 1992. "*Loitz v. Remington Arms Co.*: The Illinois Supreme Court Sets a Tougher Standard for Reviewing Punitive Damage Awards in Product Liability Cases." *John Marshall Law Review* 25 (Winter): 427.

Purcell, Edward A. 1992. *Litigation and Inequality: Federal Diversity Jurisdiction in Industrial America, 1870–1958*. New York: Oxford University Press.

Puzzanchera, Charles M. 2001. "Delinquency Cases Waived to Criminal Court, 1989–1998." *OJJDP Fact Sheet*, Office of Juvenile Justice and Delinquency Prevention, vol. 35. Washington, D.C.: U.S. Department of Justice.

Robertson, Pat. 2004. *Courting Disaster: How the Supreme Court Is Usurping the Power of Congress and the People*. Franklin, TN: Integrity Publishers.

Scalia, Antonin. 1997. *A Matter of Interpretation: Federal Courts and the Law*. Princeton, NJ: Princeton University Press.

Serrano, Richard A., and David G. Savage. 2004. "Scalia's Talk to Anti-Gay Group Spurs Ethics Debate." *Boston Globe*, March 8.

Steiger, John. 1998. "Taking the Law into Our Own Hands: Structured Sentencing, Fear of Violence and Citizen Initiatives in Washington State." *Law and Policy* 20 (July): 333–356.

Sunstein, Cass R. 2005. *Radicals in Robes: Why Extreme Right-Wing Courts Are Wrong for America*. New York: Basic Books.

Surrency, Erwin C. 2002. *History of the Federal Courts*. New York: Oceana Publications.

Tushnet, Mark V. 1999. *Taking the Constitution Away from the Courts*. Princeton, NJ: Princeton University Press.

Urofsky, Melvin I. 2015. *Dissent and the Supreme Court: Its Role in the Court's History and the Nation's Constitutional Dialogue*. New York: Pantheon.

U.S. Department of Justice. 2000. *Compendium of Federal Justice Statistics*. Washington, D.C.: U.S. Bureau of Justice Statistics, Department of Justice.

Weil, Jonathan, and Cassell Bryan-Low. 2003. "Audit Firms Overbilled Clients for Travel, Arkansas Suit Alleges." *Wall Street Journal*, September 17, A–1.

White, G. Edward. 2012. *Law in American History: Volume 1: From the Colonial Years Through the Civil War*. New York: Oxford University Press.

White, G. Edward. 2016. *Law in American History: Volume 2: From the Colonial Years Through the Civil War*. New York: Oxford University Press.

Yackle, Larry W. 1994. *Reclaiming the Federal Courts*. Cambridge, MA: Harvard University Press.

Yackle, Larry W. 2009. *Federal Courts*. 3rd ed. Durham, NC: Carolina Academic Press.

Zelden, Charles L. 2007. *The Judicial Branch of Federal Government: People, Process, and Politics*. Santa Barbara, CA: ABC-CLIO.

Cases

Erie Railroad Company v. Tompkins. 1938. 304 U.S. 64.
Gideon v. Wainwright. 1963. 372 U.S. 355.

On the Web
General Resources on Federal Courts
Administrative Office of the U.S. Courts, http://www.uscourts.gov

Biographical Directory of Federal Judges, 1789–present, http://www.fjc.gov/public/home.nsf/page/index.html

Federal Judicial Center, http://www.fjc.gov

History of the Federal Judiciary, http://www.fjc.gov/history/home.nsf/page/courts_district.html

Judicial Branch, http://www.4uth.gov.ua/usa/english/politics/judbranc.htm

The Supreme Court Database, http://scdb.wustl.edu

Supreme Court Historical Society, http://www.supremecourthistory.org

General Resources on State Courts
American Judges Association, http://aja.ncsc.dni.us

Center for State Constitutional Studies, Rutgers University-Camden, http://www-camlaw.rutgers.edu/statecon

Compendium of Federal Justice Statistics, Bureau of Justice Statistics, U.S. Department of Justice, http://www.ojp.usdoj.gov/bjs

Conference of State Court Administrators, http://cosca.ncsc.dni.us

National Center for State Courts, http://www.ncsc.org

State Supreme Court Data Project, http://www.ruf.rice.edu/~pbrace/statecourt/index.html

Criminal and Civil Court Activity
National Association of Drug Court Professionals, http://www.nadcp.org

RAND Corp. Institute for Civil Justice, http://www.rand.org/icj

U.S. Justice Department's National Criminal Justice Reference Service, http://www.ncjrs.gov

CHAPTER TWO

ROLES, FUNCTIONS, AND POWERS

When talking about the roles, functions, and powers of a court of law, there are three related questions of particular importance: What services does a court provide? Which level of court provides these services? What are the outcomes of the decisions and actions made by the court in question? The ensuing discussion answers these important questions.

ROLES, FUNCTIONS, AND POWERS OF FEDERAL COURTS

For the federal courts, the first question leads to the matter of their workloads—the types, locations, and quantities of cases that they hear and adjudicate. The second question requires examination of the different duties and roles of trial and appellate courts, as well as distinguishing between the roles of intermediate appellate courts (circuit courts of appeals) from those of the U.S. Supreme Court. The answers to those questions help us explore the impact these cases have had—and continue to have—on American law, governmental policy, and society.

One lesson that the history of the federal courts teaches is that each side in the political war of words to control the makeup of the federal bench is convinced with absolute certainty that it is right and the other side is wrong. Worse yet, each side is convinced that the other side's view of the courts is dangerous and that the very foundations of American culture, society, and law lie in the balance. The vehemence found in the rhetoric of both sides is a direct reflection of the central role the federal courts have come to exert in shaping the public debate and of the belief that this central role will continue unchecked in the years to come. That said, courts are also collegial institutions that work together to reach case outcomes, and, more often than not, the judges are in agreement about the cases. Courts divide ideologically less often.

How then to resolve the dispute? Who is right? Is it the judges or the politicians who have overstepped the bounds of constitutional governance? In addition, what are the proper bounds of constitutional governance?

Confusion and ignorance are at the heart of the bitter, polemical debate—confusion as to the constitutional role of the federal courts and ignorance as to the proper application of the judicial function by judges. Most of those who rage against the courts, on the Left and Right alike, have little grasp of the often technical and sometimes arcane workings of the judiciary and American law. At its core, the partisan warfare over the federal courts' proper place in American government is a debate over what issues the courts should hear and what sort of answers they should arrive at. To bring light to this debate, certain questions must be answered: Who are these federal judges? Where do they come from? What are their powers? What limits, if any, do these powers have? How do we organize the courts? What impact, if any, does this organization have on the courts' wider impact on American life? What role does politics play in shaping the work and opinions of the courts, is that role a good or a bad thing? Finally, how do the federal courts interact with the other branches of the federal government, with the state governments, and with the people?

Among the topics covered in achieving this task are the functions and roles of the judiciary. What does a court do? What jobs do the U.S. Constitution and the laws assign to courts and why? What mission must the judiciary complete and how? What responsibilities rest upon the shoulders of the men and women in the black robes, and how well do they meet these responsibilities? Why do we need courts in the first place? These questions lie at the heart of the federal judiciary's roles and functions in constitutional government. Answers, in turn, rest upon understanding the workloads, duties, and impact of federal courts.

DIFFERING ROLES AND FUNCTIONS OF FEDERAL COURTS

If *workloads* describe the sort of cases a court hears, descriptions of the courts' functions and roles illustrate the impact of their rulings. After all, people turn to courts for a reason: they want some specific result in a legal dispute or they would not turn to the courts in the first place. When we talk of the "functions of a court of law," what we are really talking about is matching the results with the impacts. What results does one get from the court? What needs are being met, and, more important, whose needs? In essence, who "wins" and who "loses"? The scope of a court's service can be individual (what you got out of the court), general (the overall impact of this service on the society as a whole), or both. It also can vary from court to court. Trial courts, for instance, have a different job than appellate courts, and, as such, the results and services they provide are different.

The U.S. Supreme Court

The most prominent of all the federal courts is the U.S. Supreme Court. The U.S. Constitution lays out the Supreme Court's powers. Article III of the Constitution declares: "The judicial Power of the United States, shall be vested in one supreme Court, and in such inferior Courts as the Congress may from time to time ordain and establish." It then provides:

> The judicial Power shall extend to all Cases, in Law and Equity, arising under this Constitution, the Laws of the United States, and Treaties made, or which shall be made, under their Authority [including] all Cases affecting Ambassadors, other public Ministers and Consuls, . . . all Cases of admiralty and maritime Jurisdiction, . . . Controversies to which the United States shall be a Party, . . . Controversies between two or more States, . . . between a State and Citizens of another State—between Citizens of different States—between Citizens of the same State claiming Lands under Grants of different States, and between a State, or the Citizens thereof, and foreign States, Citizens or Subjects.

Clause 2 of Article VI, in turn, makes clear that "This Constitution, and the Laws of the United States which shall be made in Pursuance thereof . . . shall be the supreme Law of the Land; and the Judges in every State shall be bound thereby. . . ."

Together, these constitutional requirements produce a court whose primary job is to say what the law is and what it is not. In a federal system of government, with multiple state court systems producing (often varying) rulings on similar topics, the need for a unifying center is imperative, which is one vital thing that the Supreme Court provides. In all matters of federal statutory law and for any issues arising under the Constitution, the Supreme Court is the final arbiter—the court that gets the last say in the ordinary course of business, and sometimes even in political disputes, like the contested 2000 presidential election between Al Gore and George W. Bush (see Banks et al., 2005). This function, in turn, is founded on the Court's power of judicial review.

Implicit in the Constitution, the Supreme Court's ability to determine if state and federal laws (and executive actions) are in compliance with the Constitution (judicial review) was made explicit in the case of *Marbury v. Madison* (1803). In his opinion, Chief Justice John Marshall declared for a unanimous Court that a federal law was unconstitutional, arguing that Congress had tried to vest in the Court powers beyond the maximum powers granted to the Court by the Constitution. If Congress, as an agent for the people, had exceeded and violated the commands of the Constitution, the act of "the People of the United States," then the Court's obligation was to heed the command of the people as specified in the Constitution and not the act of the people's agent who had overstepped its powers under the Constitution.

In so ruling, Marshall set up the Court as the final interpreter of the Constitution. He was arguing that the Court's position as the court of final resort in all cases under the Constitution or federal laws (i.e., the last court to hear a case on appeal) granted to it the unique right to determine the Constitution's final meaning—subject only to a constitutional amendment overriding a decision of the Supreme Court. In *Fletcher v. Peck* (1810), *Dartmouth College v. Woodward* (1819), and *McCulloch v. Maryland* (1819), Marshall extended this power of judicial review to the states as well. Here, Marshall was on stronger ground, for the supremacy clause of the Constitution (Article VI, Clause 2, already quoted) provides a firmer basis for this type of judicial review. To distinguish the two versions of judicial review, it might help to remember two sets of phrases. As the Supreme Court, Congress, and the presidency are co-equal institutions at the heads of the three coordinate branches of the federal government, *Marbury* judicial review is federal-federal review, or co-equal review. That is, a federal court is reviewing the constitutionality of actions of co-equal federal institutions. By contrast, *McCulloch* judicial review is federal-state review, or supervisory review. In such cases, a federal court is reviewing the constitutionality of actions of state institutions, supervising their compliance with the supremacy clause.

Although the Court rarely used its power of judicial review in the 50 years after *Marbury*, the precedent was set. The Supreme Court was the keeper of the Constitution. The Marshall Court laid the foundations that provide the institution of the Supreme Court its authority and importance in the federal government today.

The power to declare laws constitutional or not permits the Supreme Court to shape public policies established by Congress and the president. True, it is a negative power—the power to say no to congressional laws and presidential actions—but a significant power nonetheless. Political scientist Robert Birkly (1983) explained how this process works:

> Courts in any political system participate to some degree in the policy-making process because it is their job. Any judge faced with a choice between two or more interpretations and applications of a legislative act, executive order, or constitutional provision must choose among them because the controversy must be decided. And when the judge chooses, his or her interpretation becomes policy for the specific litigations. If the interpretation is accepted by the other judges, the judge has made policy for all jurisdictions in which that view prevails.

With the Supreme Court, this process is magnified. Unique among the federal courts, the Supreme Court gets to choose which cases it hears. Virtually all cases that the Court hears arrive via a process known as certiorari; that is, a party who has lost in a lower federal court or in a state court asks the Supreme Court justices to review the lower court's decision. If the justices decide to take the case, they issue a legal order known as a writ of certiorari to the lower court, asking that court to send the record of the case below to the justices for their review and consideration. The justices determine whether to grant this review. Their standard for acceptance, in turn, rests on the impact that their decision would have on the law. The justices are not interested in cases whose resolution are of importance only to those involved in the case (the justices describe these cases as "fact bound"). Only when a case raises a unique legal or constitutional question, or when the lower federal courts have offered conflicting answers to an important legal question, do the justices see a reason to act. Of the 8,000 to 9,000 cases the Court considers each year, the justices grant review in only 75 to 80 of those cases (Banks and O'Brien 2015, 79–80). The result is that the Supreme Court only rules on important and controversial questions in which the resolution may well reshape public policy.

Plessy v. Ferguson

In the realm of civil rights, for example, the Supreme Court has had an enormous impact on the legal landscape. In the late 1800s, southern states enacted laws requiring separate railroad facilities for blacks and whites. Even if an African American had bought a first-class ticket, he or she was required to ride in a black-only railcar. If no first-class, black-only railcar was available, the railroad forced the African American passenger to ride in a lower-class car where African Americans could sit. Such was the case in Louisiana, which in 1890 enacted a "separate but equal" railroad policy.

In 1892, Homer Plessy bought a first-class ticket, announced himself to be legally African American (he was one-eighth African American, but his appearance was indistinguishable from that of a white passenger), and was refused his first-class seat under the Louisiana law. He thereupon filed suit to challenge the Louisiana policy. The case had worked its way up to the Supreme Court by 1896. At issue in the case was the constitutionality of laws requiring separate facilities for persons of African descent. Plessy and his lawyers argued that the Fourteenth Amendment's equal protection clause prohibited such exclusions. The railroad disagreed, arguing that it had equal facilities available for African American riders and therefore satisfied the equal protection requirements of the Fourteenth Amendment.

The Court, by a 7–1 vote, sided with the Louisiana statute and the railroad sheltering itself under that law. Writing for the majority, Justice Henry B. Brown held:

> The object of the [Fourteenth] amendment was undoubtedly to enforce the absolute equality of the two races before the law, but in the nature of things it could not have been intended to abolish distinctions based upon color, or to enforce social, as distinguished from political, equality, or a

commingling of the two races upon terms unsatisfactory to either. Laws permitting, and even requiring, their separation in places where they are liable to be brought into contact do not necessarily imply the inferiority of either race to the other, and have been generally, if not universally, recognized as within the competency of the state legislatures in the exercise of their police power.

This being the case, Brown declared that:

. . . the case reduces itself to the question whether the statute of Louisiana is a reasonable regulation, and with respect to this there must necessarily be a large discretion on the part of the legislature. In determining the question of reasonableness, it is at liberty to act with reference to the established usages, customs, and traditions of the people, and with a view to the promotion of their comfort, and the preservation of the public peace and good order.

He concluded, therefore, that:

Gauged by this standard, we cannot say that a law which authorizes or even requires the separation of the two races in public conveyances is unreasonable, or more obnoxious to the Fourteenth Amendment than the Acts of Congress requiring separate schools for colored children in the District of Columbia, the constitutionality of which does not seem to have been questioned, or the corresponding acts of state legislatures.

And, lest his point be missed, Brown added:

Legislation is powerless to eradicate racial instincts or to abolish distinctions based upon physical differences, and the attempt to do so can only result in accentuating the difficulties of the present situation. If the civil and political rights of both races be equal one cannot be inferior to the other civilly or politically. If one race be inferior to the other socially, the Constitution of the United States cannot put them upon the same plane.

As long as the state of Louisiana required that separate facilities for the races be "equal"—and the Louisiana law explicitly required "that all railway companies carrying passengers in their coaches in this state, shall provide *equal* but separate accommodations for the white, and colored races" [emphasis added]—then separate accommodations were constitutional. So too, it turned out, were separate buses, train terminals, theaters, schools, restrooms, water fountains, and restaurants. Encouraged by the Supreme Court's ruling in *Plessy* that separate but equal facilities were constitutional, southern states began expanding on rules mandating the segregation of blacks and whites—an effort of misplaced legislative ingenuity that they pursued for half a century. By the end of the 1940s, the result was the almost total exclusion of African Americans from most aspects of public life in the South, combined with a sweeping separation of the races in all other aspects.

Brown v. Board of Education

So things largely stood until May 17, 1954, when the Supreme Court—composed of different justices living in a different era—ruled in *Brown v. Board of Education* that separate but equal facilities were inherently unequal and thus inherently unconstitutional, violating the Fourteenth Amendment's command of equal protection of the laws. The Court's ruling stated:

> We come then to the question presented: Does segregation of children in public schools solely on the basis of race, even though the physical facilities and other "tangible" factors may be equal, deprive the children of the minority group of equal educational opportunities? We believe that it does.

Chief Justice Earl Warren spoke for a unanimous Court (having worked long and hard to win over every one of his colleagues to back the decision and his opinion for the Court):

> To separate [children in grade and high schools] from others of similar age and qualifications solely because of their race generates a feeling of inferiority as to their status in the community that may affect their hearts and minds in a way unlikely ever to be undone. . . . Whatever may have been the extent of psychological knowledge at the time of *Plessy v. Ferguson,* this finding is amply supported by modern authority.

The justices consequently concluded that, "in the field of public education, the doctrine of 'separate but equal' has no place. Separate educational facilities are inherently unequal."

A complete and total reversal of the Court's 1896 reading of the Constitution (though without explicitly overruling the *Plessy* case), *Brown v. Board of Education* fundamentally changed our understanding of that document. It also transformed the social and political structure of life in the South (though, granted, after a generation-long fight to implement the reforms demanded by *Brown*). Integration of public schools in both the South and North became a reality, and the Court's ruling in *Brown* initiated a period of civil rights reform whose reverberations still shake our society today. Since that historic decision, however, the Supreme Court has adopted a less activist stance regarding school segregation. In cases such as *Milliken v. Bradley* (1974), *Board of Education of Oklahoma*

City v. Dowell (1991), and *Parents Involved in Community Schools v. Seattle School District No 1.* (2007), the Court has stipulated that school districts do not bear responsibility for changing social, cultural, and economic conditions that result in de facto education segregation, such as housing segregation. Indeed, the United States has experienced a slow but inexorable slide toward resegregation in the American education system—a slide driven by socioeconomic inequality rather than racist laws. According to a 2014 report by UCLA's Civil Rights Project (Orfield and Frankenberg 2014), in fact, students from minority groups in the United States are actually more likely to attend so-called "Minority Majority" schools than they were in the 1970s.

Circuit Courts of Appeals

The intermediate level of federal courts is occupied by courts organized by geographical region, such as the U.S. Court of Appeals for the First Circuit, and so on. There are 11 numbered circuits, plus 2 others in the District of Columbia: the D.C. Circuit, and the Federal Circuit. Like the Supreme Court, these are legal institutions that have considerable power to shape public policy. They also have the job of determining the meaning and proper reach of the law and, in this way, are able to shape the policy choices available to the other levels of government and the individual. The method by which they achieve this policy-making impact, however, is different from that of the Supreme Court. Whereas the Supreme Court shapes policy by controlling its own docket—and in doing so, choosing the important cases for ruling—the circuit courts generate impact by ruling on a wide range of varied cases brought to them on appeal from trial courts. Another vital distinction between circuit courts and the Supreme Court is that the former are obliged to follow the precedents set by the Supreme Court, whereas the justices of the Supreme Court may revisit or even set aside their previous decisions and opinions.

Circuit courts are the "enforcers" of the federal system. They hear appeals from the federal trial courts—the district courts—challenging the use or interpretation of the law (both statutes and judicial precedents) by the trial judge. Did the trial judge admit evidence that should have been excluded, or vice versa? Did the trial judge properly apply the law that he or she used to decide the legal issues in the case? Did the trial judge follow all appropriate precedents? Circuit judges must consider these sorts of questions each day. Their answers, in turn, either agree or disagree with the trial judge's reading of the law. If the circuit judges determine that the trial judge got the case right, the lower court's ruling is affirmed. If the circuit judges find otherwise, they either reverse the trial court ruling and substitute the opposite ruling, or they remand (return) the case to the trial court for rehearing and decision consistent with the circuit court's opinion. In either case, the circuit court is correcting a legal mistake. Consequently, we call this the "error correction" function of the appellate courts.

One reason the circuit courts of appeals can provide this error correction function is that, unlike the Supreme Court, circuit courts are required to hear all appeals filed in their courts. In any given year, this means ruling on literally tens of thousands of cases. Consequently, these courts hear a wide range of issues and are thus able to assure uniformity in the application of the law.

The circuit court's policymaking function builds on its error correction duties. Hearing thousands of cases a year, these courts control the flow of federal court precedents. Answering the various questions posed by an appeal from a federal district court's decision requires circuit judges to interpret the law themselves. Their rulings, in turn, are subsequently passed back to the trial judges who, under the rules of precedent, follow this new interpretation of the law in ruling future cases. Often, to be sure, circuit court judges base their rulings on the directives of the Supreme Court—when they exist. Given the vast number of cases the circuit courts hear and the limited number of cases the Supreme Court hears, there often are no Supreme Court directions to follow. In such cases, the circuit judges are forced to interpret the relevant precedents themselves. Sometimes, they find that the case before them is what lawyers call "one of first impression"— that is, the first time that a given legal or constitutional issue has appeared before a federal court. In any case, with interpretation comes the ability to affect policymaking choices and public policy.

The policymaking role of the circuit courts is even more apparent when we look at the types of cases the Supreme Court accepts for review from the circuit courts. With only a limited amount of time, the Supreme Court only takes the most important cases. In most instances, "most important" means "constitutional." As the historian and judicial biographer J. Woodford Howard Jr. noted in his *Courts of Appeals in the Federal Judicial System: A Study of the Second, Fifth, and District of Columbia Circuits*:

> First of all, the distribution of labor among the Supreme Court and the Courts of Appeals, . . . has matured into full differentiated functions for the federal appellate courts. Substantively, the Supreme Court has become more and more a constitutional tribunal. Courts of Appeals concentrate on statutory interpretation, administrative review, and error correction in masses of routine adjudications. (1981, 10)

In light of this relationship, appellate courts show deference to the Supreme Court in a variety of ways. For example, scholar Stephen L. Wasby wrote the following on SCOTUSblog in 2012:

> the courts of appeals' *anticipatory deference* to the Supreme Court—in particular, the lower courts' tendency to defer action when they believe that the Justices are likely to issue a ruling on follow-up questions that would affect cases pending in the courts of appeals. There is considerable

evidence that court of appeals judges wait for the Supreme Court to act and that they do so independent of competing judicial ideologies (or "agendas"). . . . Cases that the court of appeals hands down after a major Supreme Court ruling may well have been held pending that ruling to await developments once tendered to the Justices for possible review. The courts of appeals also exhibit deference to the Supreme Court by facilitating the movement of cases to the Court.

Yet because the Supreme Court nearly always takes only cases with clear constitutional implications, the answers the circuit courts reach on statutory matters largely go unreviewed. This, in effect, makes the circuit courts of appeals the courts of last resort for statutory interpretation. As with the Supreme Court, when a court is the court with the last say on a matter, its interpretation is the controlling view of the law—a view that all other branches of government have to accept and follow. (To be sure, if Congress is sufficiently provoked by a circuit court ruling interpreting a point of federal statutory or administrative law, it can pass a statute reversing the court's interpretation of the given point of federal law. This kind of reversal is the exception rather than the rule, however.)

District Courts

The federal district courts make up the base of the federal judicial pyramid. As noted, district courts are trial courts. In federal district courts, federal trials—whether civil or criminal—take place, where litigants are able to argue the merits of their case and seek justice. Lawyers get a chance to call witnesses and to present evidence and the unique facts of the case, the factual record, are established and set for all later proceedings. District courts, in other words, are primarily forums for resolving factual disputes through an application of the law. As a result, the focus in district courts is on the litigants themselves—their needs and demands. The law is a tool applied to seek a proper resolution of the dispute before the court. It shapes the judge's rulings, but it is not the primary reason the judge is holding court. It is for these reasons that one long-time district court judge argued that justice is found in the district courts, and litigants either get their justice there or they do not get it at all.

District courts also serve another important function. In the process of resolving disputes (both civil and criminal), they provide enforcement for legal rules and procedures. These rules, in turn, provide standards of acceptable and unacceptable behavior, of permitted and forbidden actions. Political scientists call this process *norm enforcement*. Norms are values and expectations, the informal and formal rules that shape our everyday behavior. They can be criminal in nature (do not murder) or civil (do not allow your car to crash into another vehicle). In either case, they assert the expectations of proper behavior that society demands of all its members. By applying these norms in settling private disputes or enforcing federal criminal laws, the district judge is reinforcing the necessity for adopting this behavior.

Finally, district courts also have a policymaking function. It is a much less obvious function than that found in the appellate branches of the federal courts. After all, most of the rules that district courts enforce—and the precedents shaping their application—are set by Congress and the higher courts. In addition, where the district judge does step out on his or her own to propose a new reading of the law, that decision is subject to review by the relevant circuit court of appeals. So even where the circuit court agrees with the district judge's reading of the law, it is the circuit judges' approval that creates the "official" precedent. Still, the initial reworking of the law was carried out at the district court level.

Policymaking: Civil Rights

A more effective policymaking role is available to the district courts through their oversight powers. The civil rights revolution of the second half of the 20th century profoundly changed the scope of cases filed with the district courts. Whereas criminal suits and traditional tort or contract matters remained largely disputes between small numbers of people, civil rights cases normally involved large populations and institutions of government. School desegregation, for example, drew in the entire population of a community, parents and children, and at least two levels of government (school boards and local government). More to the point, cases of this sort have been very complicated, taking extended periods of time to resolve. It has only been since 1990 or so, in fact, that many of the desegregation cases filed in the immediate aftermath of *Brown v. Board of Education* in the 1950s were finally closed. Responsibility to oversee the successful completion of those suits rested with the district courts. It was the district judges, therefore, who approved the plans and oversaw the process by which such civil rights reforms as desegregation were implemented. Given the complexity of the cases, this responsibility forced the district judges to make many decisions shaping the process of reform.

Policymaking: Prison Reform

One example should suffice to show how this process works. Beginning in the 1970s, district judges began to face a flood of complaints about conditions in southern state penitentiaries and jails. Although most judges attempted to ignore the problem, the scope of the complaints forced them to investigate. What they found horrified them. The Orleans Parish Jail, for instance, was built in 1929 and designed to house from 400 to 450 inmates. Yet in 1970, a federal district judge in the Southern District of Louisiana found between 800 and 900 inmates incarcerated there. These inmates faced "toilets . . . so badly corroded and rusted that cleanliness [was] impossible" and which, in some cells, they had to use as hand basins. Mattresses, where provided, "were rarely if ever sunned or cleaned, even though they may have been vomited or urinated upon." Ventilation was so lacking that the temperature often reached more than 100 degrees in summer, and conditions were extremely cold and damp in winter. Meanwhile, "the roof and sidewalls leak[ed] . . . [and were] infested with rats, mice, roaches and vermin," while the windows were "boarded up" to prevent inmates "from . . . pulling the bars out of the decaying windows and rotting plaster walls" (*Hamilton v. Schiro*, 1970). In Houston, federal District Judge Carl O. Bue discovered a Harris County Jail "represent[ing] some of the most dire and inhumane conditions in correction facilities across the United States." The average living space per inmate was only 20 square feet. Most cells were at double capacity, which forced more than 500 prisoners to sleep on the floor and others to sleep on so-called beds made out of tabletops or attached benches. Adding to the prisoners' woes, inadequate ventilation and heating "geometrically magnifi[ed] existing outside temperature conditions: in summer, the heat and humidity [were] stifling; in winter, the cold [was] all-pervasive." Worse yet, pervading everywhere was an "intolerable stench" (*Alberti v. Sheriff of Harris County, Texas*, 1980). Hard as it is to believe, the conditions were even worse at the state penitentiaries.

The problems facing a district judge attempting to come to grips with such overwhelming problems—and more important, seeking to shepherd these complex matters to a successful conclusion—were legion. The first problem arose in relation to the lack of credible challenges to prison conditions. Without documentary evidence and collaborating testimony, few cases were likely to survive appeal. Yet how could one correct for this problem when most prisoners were not represented by counsel? At the time, no law existed that provided payment for lawyers who took on prisoner cases; and, as most prisoners were already filing their petitions in forma pauperis (a pauper's petition), they clearly lacked the means to pay for an attorney. Yet without an attorney to organize the case, it was unlikely that the necessary facts could be sufficiently collated and properly presented to justify court action. Nor did the problems stop here. Even assuming one found a solution to the procedural problems posed by pro se filings (when the party to the case represents themselves without a lawyer), given the vast number of cases coming before the courts, providing remedies in each separate case posed a vast challenge. So too did the complex nature of the problems found in southern state institutions, most of which would require wrenching and expensive reforms to fix. Add in the usual opposition of the state to any court-ordered reform, along with the bias of state officials and the public against improving conditions for convicted criminals who, after all, were being punished by being incarcerated, and the difficulties posed in meeting the prisoners' legitimate demands for justice became acute.

Responding to these challenges, federal district judges across the South began ordering sweeping reforms. In 1972, in the Northern District of Mississippi, for instance, Chief Judge William Keady found Parchman Farm Prison in violation of the Eighth Amendment, which bars cruel and unusual punishments. Addressing a wide range of infractions, including mail censorship, deficient medical facilities, racial segregation and discrimination, irrational classification methods, a corrupt and violent trustee system, the inappropriate use of corporal punishment, and the inadequate protection of inmates (not to mention prison overcrowding and the deplorable condition of the physical plant), Keady issued a detailed injunction requiring immediate and long-term relief. In the short term (10 days), he demanded the end of censorship and corporal punishment. Soon after, he expected the end of racial segregation and the trustee system, as well as the implementation of procedures to protect inmates' safety and to upgrade the physical facilities. In the long term, Judge Keady demanded a complete renovation of the prison's physical plant, including the construction of new buildings, sewage facilities, and a hospital, as well as an end to forced labor. Retaining jurisdiction in the case, the court reserved the right to take further action if called for by events (*Gates v. Collier*, 1972).

Those events were quickly forthcoming. Faced with the state's unwillingness to pay for the required reforms, Judge Keady responded forcefully to its repeated failures or refusals to comply with his reform orders. Reiterating his position that the prison was "unfit for human habitation," in August 1975, Judge Keady ordered the closure of several decrepit cell blocks and mandated that each new prisoner receive at least 50 square feet of living space. He also appointed a monitor to report on the state's day-to-day compliance—or as the case usually turned out, noncompliance—with his order. This set the pattern: in the years that followed, the court issued more than 150 orders relating to the administration of corrections in Mississippi and forcing countless changes in the system's operating procedures (*Gates v. Collier*, 1975).

In Dallas, New Orleans, and Jacksonville, federal district courts' findings that the conditions in the city jails were unconstitutional resulted in judicial orders to forgo the use of inmates in employee tasks involving security risks and to hire additional staff to replace them. Other judicial orders required mandatory recreation programs; massive substantial repairs of existing facilities; and the expansion, construction, or subcontracting of new medical and jail facilities. All three jails were also compelled to classify inmates based on their status, and in the cases of Jacksonville and New Orleans, to house different classifications of prisoners separately.

The list of district judges ordering states to pay for expensive reforms—and the examples of the states' unwillingness to do so—can go on and on. What is important here is how the simple job of settling a dispute between prisoners demanding their civil rights and state officials refusing to pay for such reforms resulted in district judges mandating public policy in these matters—policies that affected most citizens of the South (if only in terms of taxes paid and government services provided).

JUDICIAL REASONING IN THE FEDERAL COURTS

As discussed previously, the actions of the federal courts historically have had a significant impact on the lives of the American people. The examples by which a federal court ruling—be it Supreme Court, circuit court, or district court—fashioned the policy choices of the nation are legion. For that reason, we now shift our focus to consider the wider context of this impact.

Before moving on, though, it is important to understand the forces that shape the federal courts' many roles and functions: not the jobs that they do—norm enforcer, policymaker, adjudicator—but the answers they arrive at while performing these roles. It is clear from the preceding discussion that judges do not have a free hand to rule as they wish. So what factors shape and limit their decision-making process?

The answer to this question is not as straightforward as we might think. The process of judicial reasoning is shaped by a number of interlocking forces and judicial duties—some formal and some informal. In addition, we cannot remove the human factor from the equation (Baum 2006). Judges are people, and as such, they have their own views and values, and it would be unrealistic to dismiss these views and values and their impact on what the judge does or does not do. In fact, observers across the political spectrum have expressed growing anxiety in recent years that judges at all levels of the judicial system are increasingly prone to deciding how they want to rule based on their political beliefs—and only then seeking out legal justifications for their positions. In fact, while their conclusions are open to debate in the scholarly community, some political scientists argue that judges ignore the law and solely decide cases on the basis of their personal preferences (Spaeth and Segal 1993; but see Symposium 1994). Lastly, we must keep in mind the institutional setting of the courts as a part of the federal government. Strategic interactions on the courts and with the other branches and levels of government, as well as historical and institutional factors, also affect the process by which judges shape their rulings (see, e.g., Murphy 1964; Clayton and Gillman 1999).

Limitations on the Judiciary

A first limitation on judicial power grows out of the specific demands made on the courts for action. Courts are by their very nature reactive institutions. Under the Constitution, they can only hear actual disputes involving actual harms that are brought by those directly involved in the matter under dispute. (The language that captures this concept, derived from Article III of the Constitution, is that courts can only hear *cases or controversies*.) Made-up, hypothetical, or test cases in which the goal of both sides is to get a particular reading of the law are not permitted. Federal courts also cannot issue advisory opinions based on hypothetical issues. In fact, when President George Washington and Secretary of State Thomas Jefferson asked the Supreme Court in 1793 for an advisory opinion that the president had the power to proclaim the United States neutral in the war between France and Great Britain, the Court unanimously answered that the matter called for an advisory opinion that the Court could not issue, even though individual members of the Court had provided informal advice to the Washington administration on many issues. These requirements limit the federal courts solely to matters brought before them by litigants in actual disputes. They depend, therefore, almost exclusively on the actions of others to initiate proceedings that fit within their agendas of decision making. While they can, and do, "invite" litigation by the way they handle their cases, they still are dependent on the choices of others to bring particular cases and controversies to their doorstep.

Jurisdictional Rules

Similarly, jurisdictional rules can limit the ability of a particular court to hear a case and thus to provide a remedy with policy implications. Jurisdiction means the authority of a court to hear and rule on a matter of fact or law. For one thing, federal trial courts are limited geographically as to their jurisdiction. Every state has at least one district court. Many have more than one. No district court's boundaries cross state lines. Because each individual district court is responsible only for cases arising within its own boundaries, each court is limited to those cases that arise locally. Consequently, the particular social, economic, and political makeup of that district will shape the sort of cases filed. For example, the District of Wyoming covers a mostly rural state. As such, it is more likely to hear cases involving agricultural issues than, say, the Southern District of New York, where many financial issues and securities-regulation issues arise due to the presence of Wall Street, NASDAQ, and the nerve centers of many of the nation's leading banks and investment firms.

Jurisdiction also limits the types of disputes that can be filed in a federal, as opposed to a state, court. The federal courts are empowered to hear civil actions and statutory actions (Banks and O'Brien 2015, Ch. 3). Also included under the title of federal questions are cases enforcing federal administrative rules and procedures and interpreting the reach of the Constitution, treaties, and executive orders.

The second category is criminal cases and refers only to those cases arising under the laws of the United States. In 1963, for example, there was no federal statute making it a crime to assassinate the president of the United States. Thus, had Lee Harvey Oswald not been murdered by Jack Ruby, he ultimately would have been tried in a Texas state court for the murder of President John F. Kennedy. Unless Congress sets out the necessity to act by appropriate legislation, as it did following the Kennedy assassination by making assassinations of federal officials a federal crime, the federal courts simply cannot act in these matters. Consequently, the only criminal laws enforced by the federal courts are federal laws.

Finally, there are diversity cases. These are private law cases brought under state law that the federal courts are empowered to hear because the plaintiff or plaintiffs and the defendant or defendants are from different states, and the amount in controversy is $75,000 or more. This type of jurisdiction was adopted in response to the unique political structure of the United States. With both state and national governments, we have a multijurisdictional political and legal system in this country. In fact, we really have 51 separate but interlocking constitutional, political, and legal systems—one for each state and one for the federal government. Each of these legal systems has its own different laws, procedures, court structures, and political traditions. Granted, the differences are not that great in most instances, but they do exist. Diversity jurisdiction has its roots in the recognition of this difference by the architects of the federal judicial system in 1789. Their fear was that a resident from one state would not be fairly treated in the courts of another state. For example, could a New York creditor expect a Rhode Island jury to rule in favor of his claim against a Rhode Island debtor, or vice versa? At the least, the differences in the two states' legal procedures would place the outsider at a disadvantage. To remedy this, the Judiciary Act of 1789 allowed the federal courts to hear cases under state law in which the litigants were from different states.

At first, all that was needed was that one person in the litigation be from a different state; thus, in a case pitting 5 plaintiffs against 7 defendants, if 11 of the 12 were from Rhode Island, but the 12th was from New York, that would be enough to trigger diversity jurisdiction and allow a federal court to hear the case. Gradually, the rule shifted from one of minimal diversity to one of complete diversity—that is, a case in which every plaintiff and every defendant was from a different state. If any plaintiff was from the same state as any defendant, that case could not be brought in federal court, no matter how much diversity existed among the other parties to the case. In addition, to limit the potential flood of diversity cases, statutes set a minimum amount at controversy for diversity cases to be eligible to be heard in federal court. Originally set at $500, this amount now stands at $75,000. If the plaintiff or plaintiffs in a diversity case cannot show that they have complete diversity of citizenship from the defendants, or they cannot show that what is at stake in the case is of a value at least equal to the minimum set by the federal statute, or both, then the case cannot be brought in a federal court.

Federal Procedural Rules and Values

Moving on to the judge's decision-making process, a factor shaping the impact of a federal ruling is the constellation of federal procedural rules and values that limit the range of decisions available to the judge. Anglo-American law is based on "reasoning by example" (Levi 2013). An outcome or legal doctrine is stated in case A. A similar (but not exact) set of facts occurs in case B. Under the law, the legal doctrine of A may be applied to determine B's decision. Lawyers call this process "following precedent," and its purpose is to provide the law with a necessary uniformity and consistency. What makes this legal reasoning system work is the fact that judges are *supposed* to adhere to past precedents. It is a requirement. The legal doctrine behind this rule is called stare decisis (literally, "stand by what has been decided"), and it is a key rule to the common law. Without it, the logic of the law collapses. As such, appellate courts require lower courts to follow the appropriate precedents. When judges refuse to do this, their rulings will be overturned on appeal. Assuring the proper application of precedent makes up the largest portion of the appellate courts' error correction function.

One exception to this rule of following precedent is that, for valid and sufficient reasons, the case in question may differ from the precedents so much that the precedents no longer seem relevant. Lawyers work hard to draw lines between precedents that cut against their position and the case they are arguing. This is known as "distinguishing a case." Judges, too, may be persuaded that a precedent that seems directly relevant to the case before them actually is too different from the facts of the case to be followed. One thing that appellate courts must do is to review how lower courts have handled any arguably relevant precedent and to decide whether the lower court rightly or wrongly distinguished a case that might otherwise have disposed of the case before them. One exception to this general pattern is that the Supreme Court is the only federal court that can revisit an issue of law already decided by one of its earlier cases and choose to follow it, to set it aside, or even to overrule it explicitly.

Even more explicit judicial self-restraint rules reinforce the limits implicit in the procedural rules of precedent. For example, the need for an actual "case or controversy" to exist for the court to hear the matter before it limits the range of cases available to the judge—and with it, the range of issues the judge can affect, shape, or modify. Similarly, the law requires that the case must involve the protection or enforcement of valuable legal rights or the punishment, prevention, or redress of wrongs directly related to the litigants in the case. All parties to a lawsuit must have proper standing (a direct, substantial personal interest in the outcome of the case). Outsiders to the case are not welcome and will be excluded from the proceedings. Moreover, as we have seen, judges may not issue advisory opinions. If Congress or the president wants to know if a particular action is constitutional or not, the only choice available is to enact the law and let those who are harmed by it bring the case before the courts. If no one is hurt by the law, or if nobody hurt by the law wants to bring the case, the matter will stand unresolved.

Other Limitations

A judge or court cannot hear a case unless all other legal remedies are exhausted. The courts only step in when no other forum is available to settle the dispute. This process of exhausting all legal remedies before seeking the intervention of a court ensures that litigants are properly before the court in resolving disputes, an effect that limits the powers of courts to hear disputes.

A judge cannot hear cases that pose political questions best left to the political branches of government for resolution. Examples here include the conduct of foreign relations and the internal political structures of the states. A famous example is the case of *Luther v. Borden* (1845), in which two factions in Rhode Island differed over the need to write a new state constitution to replace the state's revamped colonial charter, framed in the 1630s and revised in 1776. One faction actually held a constitutional convention, wrote a new constitution, and held elections under it, claiming that it was authorized to do so by the right of revolution set forth in the Declaration of Independence. Chief Justice Roger Taney and his colleagues agreed that this matter was a political question not suitable for resolution by a court of law.

Judges are also obliged to give the benefit of the doubt to statutes and to official actions whose constitutionality is questioned; they can only strike down a law or act of government on clear constitutional grounds—not just because they disagree with it on policy grounds.

CHOOSING FEDERAL JUDGES

Under Article II of the U.S. Constitution, the president and his executive branch are the key players in the judicial appointment process along with the U.S. Senate. The Senate must give "advice and consent," or approve, the president's choices for judicial service. However, each president is free to decide how personally involved he will be. Some have taken an active, even predominant, role. President Andrew Jackson, for example, chose to select most of his judicial candidates personally, with little administrative support. More commonly, presidents assign some if not most of the recruitment and even selection tasks to a cabinet officer or, in modern times, to another administrative entity in the executive branch, such as the Department of Justice or close advisors in the White House (Banks and O'Brien 2015, 105–113). Originally, the secretary of state was responsible for supervising the appointment of federal judges, but Franklin Pierce, the Democratic president elected in 1852, was overwhelmed with his patronage responsibilities. Because of the acquisition of new territories and the authorization of additional judgeships, Pierce had to nominate the largest number of judges of any antebellum president, including 53 to the lower federal courts, which included territorial judges. He decided that the job was too time-consuming for his secretary of state. Furthermore, his attorney general, Caleb Cushing, sought to enhance his role in the administration and in the cabinet by taking charge of at least one major component of patronage. Thus, in 1853, Pierce assigned Cushing the job of supervising judicial patronage. Ever since, that has been one of the leading responsibilities of the attorney general, especially in the recruitment of the lower federal bench.

As the attorney general's responsibilities have grown with the growing number of congressionally authorized judgeships, the recruitment process has become more bureaucratized. At least since the Eisenhower administration in the 1950s, the attorney general has assigned the primary duty of investigating potential candidates to a deputy attorney general. In some administrations, the White House staff has also played a prominent role. When Ronald Reagan came into office in 1981, he was so determined to appoint only those men and women who were committed to his judicial views of judicial restraint, law and order, and a strict interpretation of the Constitution that he brought control of judicial appointments into the White House more so than any previous president, creating a presidential committee on federal judicial selection composed of nine key staff members, including the attorney general, the White House chief of staff, the White House counsel, and leading political advisers. This committee conducted investigations of potential candidates independent of the Justice Department, the FBI, and the American Bar Association (ABA).

Since at least the start of the 20th century, the Department of Justice has maintained files on potential candidates for judicial positions, but the impetus for generating the list of potential nominees comes from a different source depending on the position. When a vacancy occurs or a new judgeship is authorized, the process of recruitment and selection begins.

For district court nominees, the initial impetus generally comes from the senator or senators of the state to which the appointment is to be made if they are from the president's party, or from a committee of state party leaders or members of the House of Representatives if neither senator is from the president's party—although a few senators have preferred not to become actively involved, leaving the choice to the Department of Justice and the president while maintaining their right to veto a distasteful choice. These senators or political committees will solicit recommendations, investigate the various candidates, and then submit either one or a number of names to the president for nomination. It is logical that local leaders play a key role, given the jurisdictional structure of the lower courts. From the beginning, Congress organized district courts along state lines and stipulated that district judges must reside in their districts. In addition, when the Constitution required the advice and consent of the Senate, it ensured that local interests would play an important role in the appointment process.

The prerogatives asserted by the senators, however, developed only gradually. Originally, state and local bar groups and local political leaders flooded the secretary of state with recommendations and comments on leading contenders. However, in the 1840s, during the administration of James K. Polk, congressional influence came to the fore, with Polk using it as a tool to garner support for himself and his policies. Under the Pierce administration during the 1850s, most of Pierce's district court openings were in states with at least one Democratic U.S. senator. Therefore, Pierce allowed those senators to make the selection, thus turning what had been a privilege into what senators would now claim as a prerogative. Some presidents have tried to minimize this senatorial prerogative, but without notable success. Reagan asked senators to submit from three to five names to the Justice Department, whose officials would then investigate and interview the candidates before making recommendations to the president; many senators, however, refused, maintaining that it was their prerogative to submit only one name.

Of course, even in the case of district court nominations, the executive branch—usually with the Department of Justice playing the leading role—still determines the final candidate. However, if the senator or committee of party leaders submits the name of a district court candidate whom the Justice Department and the ABA's Standing Committee on the Federal Judiciary find acceptable, the president nearly always nominates that person. Occasionally, investigations by either the Justice Department or the ABA raise concerns. In such cases, Justice Department officials might enter into negotiations with the senators or party leaders involved to find a candidate acceptable to all. When party leaders cannot agree on a candidate, they often enter into heated battles, usually with the White House or the Justice Department arbitrating. For example, in 1845, when Texas entered the Union, the two new U.S. senators, Sam Houston and Thomas Rusk, could not agree on who would become the District of Texas's first judge. Several other leading Texas politicians endorsed each of their candidates, and neither senator, political opponents for many years, would accept the other's choice. Finally, John C. Watrous, who had initiated efforts to be the nominee long before Texas entered the Union, emerged as a compromise candidate. A lawyer in the town of Houston and close friend of then-Congressman Polk, Watrous specialized in land title cases and served as attorney general when Texas was a republic. He and his supporters organized a petition drive to push his candidacy, and this—along with the deadlock and Watrous's friendship with the appointing president, Polk—led to his appointment to the bench. In the case of Lester Cecil's appointment to the District Court of the Southern District of Ohio by President Dwight Eisenhower in 1953, one leading political leader gave in to another. Cecil, then chief justice of the Montgomery County common pleas court, competed against Harry N. Routzohn, a former congressman from Dayton's Third Congressional District, for the nomination. Routzohn, who had the backing of a powerful Republican national committeewoman from the area, Katharine Kennedy Brown, was assumed to have the inside track, but he was 71 years old. Cecil had just been re-elected to the court of common pleas; if he were confirmed for the federal bench, Ohio's Democratic governor, Frank J. Lausche, would appoint Cecil's replacement to the county judgeship. After weeks of bickering, the Montgomery County Republican Committee endorsed Cecil, but the party remained fractured. The county committee chairman went to Washington to lobby Ohio's two Republican senators, Robert A. Taft and John W. Bricker, for Cecil, but Brown continued her battle for Routzohn. This infighting led many to speculate that because of the political deadlock in Dayton, the president might select someone from another area. It was such speculation that probably enabled Cecil supporters to convince Brown to endorse their candidate. After the infighting was over, Taft and Bricker endorsed the local party's choice, and Eisenhower nominated Cecil for the district court post.

Circuit Court and Supreme Court Appointments

For circuit court appointments, the balance of power shifts to the president. Because each circuit covers at least three states, no senator can claim that he or she is the key decision maker. Furthermore, there is no legal requirement that circuit court appointments be distributed among people from each state in the circuit. Generally, the leading players in the executive branch will pick and choose from among candidates urged upon them by the senators of the president's party from all the states in the circuit. However, often the president and his team will have their own candidates, sometimes urged upon them by other influential interest groups. For Supreme Court appointments, the president and his people generate their own list. The various entities already described also propose names for consideration. For both circuit and Supreme Court appointments, many presidents have their key people interview the candidates to determine their judicial philosophy.

After potential candidates are identified, they are investigated by a deputy attorney general, who contacts community leaders and prominent attorneys and jurists in the area to assess the candidates' qualifications, judicial temperament, jurisprudential views, and popularity. After the list is narrowed to leading contenders, the president considers reports by the FBI, the rankings of the ABA's Standing Committee on the Federal Judiciary, and the reaction of the senators from the circuit before making his final nomination decision.

The Senatorial Role

However, senatorial courtesy—which dictates that the president should not appoint a candidate that the home state senators oppose—can limit a president's choice. Although senatorial courtesy has never been absolute, the Senate has rarely supported the president over the objecting senator in a confirmation struggle. Senatorial courtesy even extends to senators not of the president's party. When any senator objects to an appointment to an office in his own state, other senators have historically been very reluctantly to criticize such actions.

After the president submits the name of his candidate to the Senate, a standard procedure, fully established by the beginning of the 20th century, is followed. The chairperson of the Senate Judiciary Committee, upon receiving a nomination from the president, sends out "blue slips" that officially notify senators from the nominee's home state that a nomination has been received. The form provides the senator with an opportunity to comment on the nomination, with the understanding that if no reply is received within a week, then the senator has no objections, and the nomination can proceed forward. If a senator replies that the nominee is "personally obnoxious" to that senator, that is generally enough to kill the approval if that senator is from the president's party. Especially before the 1980s, when the Senate operated more informally, senators who opposed a nominee but preferred not to return the blue slip and go on the record were able to block a nomination by quietly going to the chairperson of the Senate Judiciary Committee with objections. The chairperson would then bury the nomination, which would never come to a vote unless the president decided to make an issue of it by resubmitting the candidate's name.

Since the Constitution granted the Senate advice and consent powers, senators have passively or actively blocked a significant percentage of presidential nominees. Short of outright rejection, many nominations fail when the Senate refuses to vote on the president's candidates. Most often, this has occurred when a lame-duck president made the nomination or in times of intense political gridlock. But when a president's popularity declines, he might also find it difficult to get his judicial nominees confirmed. Thus, after 1986, when the Democrats gained a majority in the Senate, and the Reagan administration came under attack with the exposure of the Iran-Contra scandal, the Senate failed to take action on nine district court nominations in a two-year period. When Bill Clinton was threatened by impeachment in the fall of 1999, confirmation of his judicial nominations slowed to a trickle, with the Senate refusing to take action on 41 of his 62 nominations. Not until February 1999, when the impeachment threat disappeared, did the Senate begin confirming his judicial nominations again. Senators also have occasionally blocked votes on nominees in order to win concessions from the president. For example, in 1999, when Republican Orrin Hatch was chairperson of the Senate Judiciary Committee, he halted votes on all pending judicial nominations until Democratic president Clinton nominated

Hatch's candidate, Ted Stewart, for a federal judgeship in his home state of Utah. In 1959, Democratic then-senator Lyndon Johnson, the Senate majority leader, stalled the votes on all of Republican President Dwight D. Eisenhower's nominees until the president nominated Johnson's friend, Joe Fisher, for a federal district judgeship. On other occasions, presidents have withdrawn nominees in the face of opposition rather than wage a battle for the selected candidate. For example, in 1968, Justice Abe Fortas asked Lyndon Johnson to withdraw his nomination of Fortas as chief justice after charges were leveled against the latter for extrajudicial ethical improprieties. In 1987, Douglas H. Ginsburg, bowing to heavy pressure, asked Reagan to withdraw his name as a Supreme Court nominee after revealing that he had smoked marijuana. Similar political battles over judicial nominations have been a part of the political landscape in the G. W. Bush and Obama administrations as well.

However, the Senate has not been shy about exercising its "consent" function directly. For Supreme Court nominees alone, the Senate has formally rejected or postponed—thereby effectively killing—22 presidential nominations, representing over 20 percent of those nominated, all but 5 occurring in the 19th century. In fact, during the 19th century, the Senate rejected one out of every three nominees. Such action illustrates the difference in perception of the advice and consent function in the 19th compared to the 20th century. In the 19th century, the Senate had no qualms about rejecting candidates simply because the majority of the senators opposed the politics of the nominating president. John Tyler, who alienated the party that had placed him on the ballot, had the most Supreme Court nominees rejected—five. The Senate also rejected some nominees because of their involvement with a contentious public policy issue. For example, in 1795, the Senate rejected George Washington's nomination of John Rutledge to be chief justice of the Supreme Court because Rutledge opposed the Federalist-supported Jay Treaty. Senators also rejected candidates because of their jurisprudential approaches or other indications of policy or political unreliability. Ulysses S. Grant saw two of his nominations—those of Ebenezer R. Hoar in 1870 and Caleb Cushing in 1874—fail because the Senate was leery of their political and jurisprudential stands. Senatorial courtesy also blocked some nominations. For example, in the 1890s, because New York's Democratic senator, David B. Hill, opposed Grover Cleveland's choices of William B. Hornblower and Wheeler S. Peckham, the Senate rejected the nominees.

With few exceptions, but increasingly in modern times, since the start of the 20th century, the Senate has been more reluctant to reject presidential nominees outright. Often, but not exclusively, the nomination has been successfully blocked when powerful special interest groups have been able to convince senators that the candidate lacked the qualifications or judicial temperament to be a justice. This happened in three cases during the 20th century: John J. Parker, nominated by Herbert Hoover in 1930, and Clement Haynsworth and G. Harrold Carswell, nominated by Richard Nixon in 1969. The rejection of Robert Bork, nominated by Reagan in 1987, was largely due to Bork's controversial jurisprudential views and his role in the so-called Saturday Night Massacre and the Watergate scandal during the Nixon administration in the 1970s. However, one political scientist has claimed that since the Reagan administration's emphasis on transforming the courts by having, some said, ideological litmus tests for nominees, the Senate has reasserted its consent role, seeing itself as the guardian of the independence of the judicial branch. "No president after Reagan," Gary L. McDowell asserted, "whatever his political party or ideological predilections, is likely to enjoy as free a hand in judicial nominations—especially to the Supreme Court—as did his predecessors" (Abraham et al. 1990, xiii).

McDowell's prediction has certainly proven accurate in the early 21st century. During the two-term presidencies of both Republican George W. Bush and Democrat Barack Obama, the Senate's advice and consent role has been increasingly tainted by partisan obstructionism. Both Bush and Obama found that when the Senate was controlled by the opposition party, it became virtually a standard practice for their judicial nominations to be kept in limbo lest they tip the ideological makeup of the courts in ways that the opposing party disliked. Democrats and Republicans alike increasingly see court appointments as just another partisan battleground. This state of affairs reached a particular nadir in early 2016 when Supreme Court Justice Antonin Scalia passed away, leaving an empty seat on the Court. Leaders of the Republican-controlled U.S. Senate announced their refusal to consider any nominee put forward by Democratic President Barack Obama, despite their clear constitutional responsibility to do so. This stance, clearly taken in hopes that a Republican might win the White House in November 2016 and nominate a stalwart conservative to take the open seat, was widely criticized by legal experts—including many conservatives—for further damaging the nomination and confirmation process in federal judicial selection. According to a March 2016 editorial by the *Los Angeles Times* editorial board, the problem is that "if Senate Republicans can't be reasoned or shamed into abandoning their obstructionism, the damage won't be confined to this nomination. 'It will provoke an endless cycle of more tit-for-tat, and make it increasingly impossible for any president, Democrat or Republican, to carry out their constitutional function,' Obama said. 'The reputation of the Supreme Court will inevitably suffer. Faith in our justice system will inevitably suffer. Our democracy will ultimately suffer, as well.'"

Other Influences

In addition to the president, the president's advisers in the executive branch and the White House, and the senators, several others influence the recruitment and selection of federal judges. In 1952, Truman's Department of Justice asked the ABA to investigate, evaluate, and advise the department as to their candidates' suitability for judicial positions. Since then, the ABA routinely evaluates those the president is considering for appointment. However, President George W. Bush disregarded its evaluations because he considered it a liberal interest group. After the ABA's circuit member conducts a field investigation, contacting area lawyers and judges, he or she submits a report to the association's Standing Committee on the Federal Judiciary, which then issues its conclusions on whether the candidate is "exceptionally well qualified," "well qualified," "qualified," or "not qualified."

Those who nominate judicial positions also experience pressure from other interest groups. Local political leaders pressure senators and key members of the executive branch to appoint those who have rendered important service to the president, the senators in the state involved, or the party generally. Influential members of the local bar often organize petition drives or in other ways campaign for the candidates of their choice. Interest groups such as the League of Women Voters, labor unions, and others representing various political and economic positions have sometimes waged campaigns for or against candidates. Especially for Supreme Court appointments, interest groups with an ideological agenda gather information either extolling a candidate's virtues or exposing his or her flaws in hope of generating enough public pressure to influence the Senate's vote.

The candidates themselves comprise yet another pressure group. Federal judgeships have always been coveted positions. In the late 18th and early 19th centuries, candidates were attracted to the lifetime appointment and a steady salary despite the rigors of traveling circuit. By the 20th century, the prestige of the position made such posts the pinnacle of a legal career. Thus, by the time a position becomes vacant, potential candidates have generally made their interest known to the influential players in a variety of ways. Many actively campaign on their own behalf or solicit others to do so. They organize petition drives and flood the attorney general and key senators with testimonials about their qualifications and their loyalty to the party.

No matter how much they want a judgeship or how close they are to influential decision makers, successful candidates also need luck—that is, they need to be in the right place at the right time. No matter how talented or how politically active, lawyers will generally not even be considered if they are not a member of the appointing president's party, from the right region to give balance to the court, and of the right age—generally in his or her 40s or 50s. As one circuit court judge explained, no one wins nomination unless a highly placed politician takes an interest in his appointment.

No matter how presidents organize their staff for the recruitment and selection of federal judges, they will be sure the staff knows the explicit and implicit criteria for nomination. Although only presidents and their advisers know for sure why they selected one candidate over others, legal scholars have identified several factors that affect this decision. These factors, as we will see, affect all judicial nominations but vary somewhat depending on the judicial position.

FOUR KEY FACTORS IN CHOOSING A FEDERAL JUDGE

Although there are others, legal scholars have named at least four basic factors that have motivated presidents to select judicial candidates, especially for the Supreme Court.

Shared Philosophy and Policy Goals

The first factor is to appoint candidates that share the president's political and judicial philosophy. Sometimes this is referred to as "packing the court." The extent to which presidents do this varies with their governing style and political priorities. Some presidents have only vague policy objectives. President John F. Kennedy, for example, claimed he wanted only people of ability, respected for their professional skill, with an incorruptible character and firm judicial temperament, and a sense of justice tempered with mercy. Other presidents have insisted that their judicial nominees hold specific political and jurisprudential views. Andrew Jackson, for example, sought only candidates who would vigorously support the fugitive slave laws and oppose a national bank. Like Jackson, William Howard Taft, a former federal judge himself, took an active role in all his judicial appointments to ensure that he would select only those who believed in economic substantive due process and who would enforce personal property rights by critically examining progressive legislation attempting to regulate them.

In order to achieve the goal of appointing those who share their philosophy, some of America's early presidents turned to personal and political friends. These are people who, the president believed, deserved rewards for their consistent support of him and his political ambitions, who are trusted allies, and whose views he knows well. For Supreme Court appointees, perhaps the leading example was Jackson's appointment of Roger B. Taney in 1836 as chief justice to replace John Marshall. Taney was both Jackson's personal friend as well as a loyal political ally. After two secretaries of the treasury refused Jackson's demand to transfer $10 million in government funds from the Bank of the United States, which Jackson was determined to destroy, to state banks, Jackson appointed Taney—who had been serving as his attorney general—as a recess appointment as secretary of the treasury (this meant that the president could appoint a justice in between congressional sessions when Congress was not in session). Taney then willingly complied with Jackson's plan to transfer the funds. To punish Jackson, the Senate refused to approve Taney's nomination as treasury secretary. It then refused to vote on his appointment by Jackson as an associate justice to the Supreme Court. After a three-month battle, however, the Senate confirmed his appointment as chief justice of the Court by a narrow 14-vote margin. To illustrate further, Harry Truman's four appointments to the High Court—Harold H. Burton, Fred M. Vinson, Tom C. Clark, and Sherman Minton—were all close friends and political allies. The appointments of Horace H. Lurton by William Howard Taft, Louis D. Brandeis by Woodrow Wilson, Harlan Fiske Stone by Calvin Coolidge, William O. Douglas and Felix Frankfurter by Franklin Roosevelt, and Byron R. White by John F. Kennedy were also examples of this phenomenon. Occasionally, however, efforts to appoint personal friends or longtime associates to the Court have failed. In 1968, Republicans in the Senate successfully scuttled the nomination of associate justice Abe Fortas by Lyndon Johnson to serve as chief justice, allegedly on the basis of the nominee's ethical misdeeds. Thirty-seven years later, George W. Bush nominated White House counsel Harriet Miers for the Supreme Court. After three weeks of intense criticism from both Republicans and Democrats who charged that the nomination was an egregious example of political cronyism, Bush withdrew the nomination.

Kinship, or personal friendship, has also been a factor in the appointment of judges to the lower courts. In certain presidencies, those judges with close relationships with either the appointing president, the senators from his state, or other principal players in the appointment process have had a clear advantage over other candidates who might have been equally active in their party and equally qualified. For example, one-fourth of all of Polk's judicial nominees had family ties to their principal mediators. At least four appointees were the president's personal friends. Zachary Taylor, too, allowed kinship and instrumental friendship to dictate many of his judicial selections. Of his 10 nominees, 3 had kinship ties to those responsible for their selection and 3 others, all from Taylor's home state, were the president's instrumental friends. In the Pierce administration, 22 percent of the nominees had kinship connections to their primary supporters. Overall for the period from 1789 through 1899, 71.5 percent of the lower federal court Article III judges had kinship ties to or were instrumental friends with the principal mediators in the selection process.

Kinship and personal friendship, however, were far more important during the early national period and steadily declined as America's political parties became more formalized, institutionalized, and modern. During the Federalist era, fewer than 14 percent of district court appointees had no relationship by marriage, blood, or friendship with the principal mediators in the selection process; over 30 percent were related by blood; and another 22 percent by marriage to those selecting the candidates. The number without relatives or instrumental friendship connections to those choosing candidates climbed to 17.5 percent from the presidency of Jefferson through that of John Quincy Adams. Also, the number related by blood or marriage to those making decisions dropped dramatically; only 17.5 percent were related by blood and 15 percent by marriage to the chief decision makers. During the second party system (from Jackson through James Buchanan), the number with kinship or instrumental friendship ties again rose slightly—to 21.3 percent—and climbed somewhat more during the Civil War and Reconstruction Era to 29.3 percent. After 1877, however, kinship and friendship connections became significantly less important. Almost 44 percent of judges appointed between 1877 and 1899 had no ties by blood, marriage, or instrumental friendship with the principal mediators of the selection process; only 3.4 percent had blood relationships; and 1.2 percent had relationships through marriage to those selecting them. As kinship became less important, partisan considerations increased, with appointments going more often to those the principal mediators sought to reward for their party loyalty and political activities on behalf of the president or other influential party leaders.

Partisanship considerations are also connected to the president's desire to further policy goals. From the beginning, most appointees to all judgeships have shared the same political affiliation as their appointing president. After political parties became established in the early 1790s, all of George Washington's appointees were active members of his Federalist Party. Even prior to that, his appointees shared Washington's pro-federalist views. Similarly, from the 1830s to 1860, during the era of the second party system, all the nominees were members of the nominating presidents' parties with only one exception. Only during the Harrison-Tyler administration, when political affiliation was confused, were the numbers less than 100 percent, with 16.7 percent of the appointees being Jacksonian Democrats, 50 percent being Whig, and 33.3 percent being of unknown affiliation.

This same partisanship continued throughout the 20th century. Taft, the president from 1909 to 1913, was the least partisan of the presidents. Having been a federal appellate court judge before becoming president, Taft was more concerned about the qualifications of his nominees and their judicial philosophy than their party affiliation. From Franklin D. Roosevelt through Reagan in the latter part of the 20th century, 84 percent of appointees to the Supreme Court have been people from the president's party. All the justices appointed by Kennedy, Johnson, and Reagan were members of the appointing president's party. Furthermore, when a president selected a candidate from the opposition party, he did so only after he was convinced, based on either personal experience or faith in some influential adviser, that the candidate reflected his political and judicial philosophy. These considerations have heavily influenced the nominee selections of both the conservative Republican George W. Bush and the progressive Democrat Barack Obama.

But in the early years of the Republic, partisanship went beyond merely naming candidates who were affiliated with the appointing president's party. Presidents and the other key decision makers sought party activists. Clearly, judicial appointments were rewards for those who had faithfully served their party as well as for those who had supported the president's policies. In fact, presidents have often used judicial appointments to reward a faction of their party at the expense of those factions that had been loyal to their opponents within the party. President Andrew Jackson, for example, relied only on trusted political friends and longtime supporters to advise him on judicial nominees. Viewing judicial appointments as an opportunity to solidify the Democratic Party behind him and his supporters, he rewarded past personal loyalty over the desires of other local Democratic leaders. Martin Van Buren also rewarded past personal loyalty rather than using judicial appointments as a means of trying to garner support from those Democrats who had wavered in their support of him. These considerations have lessened in importance over time, but they are still a factor. Between 54 and 61 percent of all judicial nominees of Presidents Clinton, George H. W. Bush, Reagan, and Carter, for example, had records of political activity on either the president's or the senator's behalf as well as reputations for being competent or distinguished attorneys.

Political Needs of the Party and the President

Partisanship is also associated with a president's selection. During certain times, presidents have been influenced to select one candidate over another based on the perceived needs of his party or his political future. For example, the need to maintain political unity or to further the interests of important constituencies has played a prominent role in the selection of many Supreme Court justices. In 1862, Abraham Lincoln appointed Samuel F. Miller of Iowa to the Supreme Court largely in response to congressional demands, the need to woo western interests, the president's determination to hold intact the coalition supporting his efforts to fight vigorously the Civil War, and his desire to further the interests of the fledgling Republican Party. Miller had the support of virtually all the western governors and the entire western delegation in Congress. Lincoln also received a unique congressional petition bearing the names of 129 of the 140 members of the House of Representatives and almost every senator. Although Lincoln apparently succumbed to political pressure from Congress and other leading politicians, before the appointment, he had to be assured that Miller had the key values and qualifications Lincoln insisted on for his judicial appointees—loyalty to the Republican Party, a determination to preserve the Union, opposition to slavery, professional ability, judicial experience, and geographical suitability.

In 1864, with the war apparently won, Lincoln's concerns focused on unifying the Republican Party, which had suffered some losses in the congressional elections of 1864. Although without such pressures he would have probably nominated his longtime friend and political ally, Postmaster General Montgomery Blair, to replace Roger Taney as chief justice, Lincoln realized that Blair was too controversial to unite the party. Thus, the president selected instead his longtime political adversary, Salmon Chase, who had served as his secretary of the treasury and had campaigned vigorously for his re-election. Chase's appointment, Lincoln hoped, would solidify the support of the Radical Republicans and former Democrats, with Chase representing both these groups.

A century and a half later, political analysts believe that political considerations might have played a role, however minor, in President Barack Obama's 2009 selection of Sonia Sotomayor to fill a Supreme Court vacancy. Sotomayor's legal credentials were impressive, but qualifications aside, her nomination curried favor with America's growing Latino population. It also put the GOP in an awkward position, as opposition to Sotomayor might well worsen their already shaky standing with a rising voter demographic with which they were already struggling.

Generally, other important decision makers, especially senators and other political leaders, also rely chiefly on personal or professional friendships and party loyalty as their two chief criteria when they submit names to the president. Like presidents, senators tend to name personal friends, former law partners or business associates, active campaign workers, financial contributors, and others personally associated with them. When such close friends are not available, senators tend to choose those who have supported the state party organization or that faction aligned behind the senator. The experience of Griffin Bell, Carter's attorney general, is indicative of what it takes to get nominated for a federal judgeship. Bell claimed that it was not very difficult for him to get Kennedy to name him to the Fifth Circuit Court of Appeals: "I managed John F. Kennedy's presidential campaign in Georgia. Two of my oldest and closest friends were the two senators from Georgia. And I was campaign manager and special, unpaid counsel for the governor. . . . It [didn't] hurt to be a good lawyer, either" (Howard 1981, 93).

Balanced Representation

The third set of factors that influence the selection of federal judges is the need to balance representation, be it geographically or ethnically. Geographical representation has always been an important consideration for Supreme Court appointments. For lower court nominees, roots in the locality are of vital importance. Nearly all district court nominees have been selected to serve in the regions of their birth. In the antebellum period, for example, all New England judges, 85.7 percent of mid-Atlantic appointees, and 92.6 percent of Upper South jurists were born in their region of service. Even in newly created states filled with migrants from other areas, judges tended to have settled in the region and become active there before their appointments. Every antebellum district court judge resided in the state in which he was appointed to serve. In the 20th century, this pattern persisted. In 1963, for example, at least 58 percent of district court judges were born in the district to which they were appointed and almost 67 percent were born in the state. Furthermore, over 60 percent received their law school education in the state in which their court was located. Appellate court judges also have deep roots in their region. Of those sitting in 1963, over 77 percent were born in a state of their circuit, and more than 86 percent attended law school in the same state as their circuit. Ethnic and gender considerations became important only in the latter half of the 20th century, when the nation became increasingly supportive of a Supreme Court membership that reflected the diversity of the American people. That change in attitude helped pave the way for the acceptance of African Americans Thurgood Marshall and Clarence Thomas, women justices Sandra Day O'Connor, Ruth Bader Ginsburg, and Elena Kagan, and the Court's first justice of Hispanic descent in Sonia Sotomayor.

Merit

Objective merit has almost always been an important criterion; presidents seek well-qualified candidates. Yet objective merit has not generally been the major motivating factor in determining a final selection. Occasionally, however, there have been candidates who have been such prominent jurists that they became the obvious choice, despite their political affiliation, place of residence, ethnic background, or other traditional factors. The classic example was the appointment of Democrat Benjamin Cardozo by President Herbert Hoover, who was a Republican, to the Supreme Court in 1932. Cardozo had no friendship or kinship ties with either the president or any of his leading advisers. Further, he shared no ideological ties with Hoover. Moreover, there were already "too many" New Yorkers on the bench, and there was already a Jewish justice on the Court. Hoover wanted to appoint someone from the West, preferably a politically noncontroversial person who could be confirmed by the liberal Republican Senate. But Senator George Norris chaired the Senate Judiciary Committee at the time, and he made it clear that he and his fellow committeemen wanted Cardozo. In addition, law professors and deans of law schools inundated Hoover with petitions for the nomination of Cardozo, labeling him one of the most brilliant jurists in American history. Labor and business leaders, liberals and conservatives, and politicians in many areas of government as well as other influential Republican senators all urged Cardozo's appointment due to Cardozo's obvious merit.

THE MAKEUP OF THE FEDERAL JUDICIARY

No matter what motivated the decision makers to select them and despite pressures of politics and patronage, those who have served on the federal bench have generally represented America's elite. In no decade, on either the Supreme Court or the lower federal courts, have the judges been representative of the American population, whether based on class, education, ethnic background, or other demographic factors. What are the general characteristics of the typical federal judge? How have their backgrounds, educations, and prior experiences changed from 1789 through 2017? What variations does one see in their backgrounds based on the judicial position to which they are appointed? The answers to these questions will demonstrate that while there have been some notable changes over time, the picture of a "typical" federal justice has remained surprisingly consistent. What changes there have been reflect the increased complexity and sophistication of American society and well as its changing values, especially in regard to gender and ethnic considerations.

As of 2016, 40 presidents had appointed 114 people to serve as Supreme Court justices. Only four presidents, through President Barack Obama, made no Supreme Court appointments: William Henry Harrison, Zachary Taylor, Andrew Johnson, and Jimmy Carter. Of those appointed, 108 were men and 2 were women. All were white with the exception of 2 African Americans, and this deviation from the white male model did not occur until Lyndon Johnson's appointment of Thurgood Marshall in 1967 and Reagan's appointment of Sandra Day O'Connor in 1981. All but 6 have been native born, and all but 15 have been Anglo-Saxon. Nearly 90 percent were Protestant, with the vast majority of these belonging to the so-called high-status Protestant sects, that is, Episcopalian, Unitarian, and the like. However, 12 have been Catholics, and 8 have been Jewish.

Geographically, most have hailed from large, politically influential states in the South and East. Supreme Court justices have tended to come from upper-middle to upper-class social backgrounds, generally reared in nonrural although not necessarily urban environments. Further, they were reared in politically active and influential families. There were some variations over time, however. In the early national period (1789–1828), 95 percent of the future justices came from high status or socially prominent families, and their fathers were plantation owners, colonial lawyers, manufacturers, physicians, and land speculators, actively engaged in the political events of their era. This picture did not change significantly during the antebellum years, when politics was supposedly becoming more democratic, opening up opportunities for more Americans. There were differences, but they were slight: 3 of the 14 justices appointed from 1829 to 1861 were reared in families engaged in low-status occupations. One of these had an influential half-brother who paid his sibling's way through Yale College, another married the daughter of an influential political leader, and the third was the only self-made man without relatives with important political influence.

From the latter part of the 19th century through the early 20th century, from 1862 to 1933, the picture changes somewhat. While the number of justices whose fathers had high-status careers remained high, the number of those who were politically active declined. During this era, over 90 percent of the judges still came from wealthy backgrounds, but only about 60 percent of their families were politically active. One also sees a shift in the occupations of the justices' fathers. During the earlier years, most of their fathers were wealthy farmers or manufacturers and commercial men who also actively pursued political careers. After the Civil War, this began to change. Increasingly, the fathers of the justices were professionals, working in law, medicine, religion, or occasionally, higher education. Furthermore, many now came from families without a tradition of political involvement, although the families were still prominent, either economically or socially. No significant democratization in the appointment of Supreme Court jurists occurred until the 1930s. From the 1930s through 2015, about one-fourth of the justices have come from humble origins. Thurgood Marshall, for example, was the great-grandson of slaves and the son of a Pullman car steward, while Chief Justice Warren E. Burger's father earned his living as a traveling salesman and railroad car inspector. In the 21st century, the turn toward selecting nominees from non-"elite" socioeconomic backgrounds has become even more evident. In fact, the three justices appointed to the Court from 2006 to 2015—Samuel Alito, Elena Kagan, and Sonia Sotomayor—all hailed from middle-class or working-class backgrounds.

Although neither the Constitution nor any federal statute places any educational requirements on Article III judges, all Supreme Court appointees have been attorneys with the requisite legal training for their era, and all had practiced law at some point before their appointment. And, the vast majority have been well educated. Close to 85 percent either read law, which was the typical legal education in the 19th century, with prominent lawyers and judges, or attended the best undergraduate or law schools. By the late 20th century, however, probably reflecting the increasingly strong academic reputations of state-supported law schools, the number of judges attending Ivy League or private law schools, as opposed to state-supported schools, had declined. No significant pattern based on political affiliation is apparent in this trend. Roughly one-third of those appointed by Eisenhower and Kennedy graduated from state-supported law schools. That number steadily increased with subsequent presidents, reaching 48 percent with the Carter administration. Further, the number attending Ivy League schools fell from a high of almost 25 percent during the Nixon administration to a low of approximately 14 percent during the Reagan presidency.

Professionally, most Supreme Court nominees had been members of the lower federal judiciary or state judiciaries or had held various positions in the federal executive or administrative branches of government before their appointments to the bench. During the late 18th and early 19th centuries, over 85 percent of the justices had held primarily political positions before their appointments to the bench. This percentage dropped significantly in the post–Civil War period. Of the 16 justices appointed between 1862 and 1888, only 9, or a little over half, had held primarily political positions before their appointments; the rest were engaged as corporate lawyers. The numbers are even more dramatic from the period 1889–1919, when only 33 percent of the appointees had held primarily political positions before appointment: 61 percent were corporate lawyers and 5.6 percent were law professors.

By the late 20th century, turning to those with judicial experience had become the trend. Of the 18 appointees from Eisenhower through Reagan, for example, two-thirds had judicial experience. At the time of their appointments, 61 percent were members of the judiciary; specifically, 5 were government officials, and only 2 were in private practice, both with large law firms. This new trend of elevating judges from state or lower federal courts probably reflects not only the move toward greater professionalization of the judicial corps but also perhaps the determination of several late-20th-century presidents to appoint only those who reflect their own judicial philosophy. Those with judicial experience already have clear track records that the presidents and their staffs can examine for the nominees' ideological and jurisprudential views, their judicial temperament, and other factors that presidents deem essential for their appointees.

In the Court's more than 200-year history, however, only about a quarter of the 112 justices who have served or are serving have had 10 or more years of experience on any tribunal, federal or state; 42 had no judicial experience. Although, for example, all of the late-20th-century appointees were elevated from the circuit courts, some had served for only a very short time. Clarence Thomas, for example, had held a variety of government posts, including state prosecuting attorney, legal consultant to a senator, and chair of the U.S. Equal Employment Opportunity Commission; however, he had served for only a little more than one year on the U.S. Court of Appeals for the District of Columbia Circuit before President George H. W. Bush appointed him an associate Supreme Court justice. But lack of judicial experience has not been a bar to judicial greatness. Many of the most highly rated justices had no previous judicial experience, including John Marshall, Joseph Story, Roger Taney, Salmon Chase, Felix Frankfurter, Louis D. Brandeis, and Earl Warren.

Although a majority of the justices lacked a long history of prior judicial experience, most had been politically active citizens, serving in a variety of public capacities and allowing them to acquire key political connections before their appointments to the bench. Similar backgrounds are found among lower federal court appointments. Based on a study of their backgrounds from 1789 to the end of the 19th century, Kermit Hall concluded that while there were differences during different eras and among different appointing presidents, as a rule, judicial appointees tended to be "upwardly mobile sons of a prosperous middle class, who were committed to the party of the President in power when they were appointed and benefitted from personal ties with mediators of the selection process" (1980, 449).

District court judges appointed before the Civil War were young men, with their average age being 46.2 years, and 30 percent were 40 or younger. Typically, they viewed their appointment as the culmination of their career and as a chance to get away from the world of elective office to the security of a lifetime appointment with a steady income. As federal judgeships became more prestigious, the average age steadily increased. Only 10 percent of the Article III lower federal court judges named between 1877 and 1899 were 40 years old or under at the time of their appointment, while more than 53 percent were over 50 years old.

Ethnically, they were a homogeneous group. All were white males, mostly of Anglo-Saxon origins. Seventy percent came from English or Welsh origins, while 17.5 percent had Scotch-Irish backgrounds, and another 7.2 percent came from Irish origins. This largely Anglo-Saxon group also had long ties with the United States. Almost two-thirds were third generation or longer, while only one appointee, Henry Boyce of Louisiana, an Irishman, was not native born.

The federal judiciary was also dominated by the economic elite, that is, men who generally came from wealthy families whose members had been politically active in their communities. Thus, although the national average wealth for adult white males in the 1850s was approximately $2,580, the mean wealth of those judges' fathers for whom data is available was five times that average.

For analytical purposes, Hall (1987a, 1987b) divided the period of time that he studied into five subdivisions: 1789–1800 (the Federalist era); 1801–1828 (the Jeffersonian era and the Era of Good Feelings); 1829–1860 (the era of the second party system, when partisan politics developed more fully and the two major parties competed vigorously for domination); 1861–1876 (the era of Republican domination during the Civil War and Reconstruction); and 1877–1899 (the Gilded Age, with its rise of big business and the reemergence of a competitive two-party system). Many historians claim that the 19th century was a time of increased democratization as more people participated in the political process, property requirements for voting disappeared, and parties appealed to the masses. However, federal judges continued to come from society's elite, although the greatest variation in the social origins of federal judges occurred during the Civil War and Reconstruction.

In analyzing the social origins of these jurists, Hall (1976) examined the occupations of their fathers as well as other information about their wealth and family connections to determine what proportions were from the elite families (i.e., the landed gentry, merchants, and professionals such as doctors and lawyers who held positions of prominence—whether they were elected, judicial, or appointed—in the national or the upper echelons of state government), from

the prominent or well-to-do class (i.e., those whose fathers were artisans, pro-
prietors, teachers, sea captains, shopkeepers, tavern keepers, ministers, and successful farmers who were involved in state and local government and might
have held minor federal positions), or from humble origins (i.e., those whose
fathers were small farmers, mechanics, and laborers uninvolved, at least based
on extant sources, in the political world in which they lived). Hall concluded
that roughly one-third of the future judges came from the elite, and nearly one-
half (46.3%) came from well-to-do families. Thus, they began their lives in
secure environments, tending to grow up in urban areas. Only 20.7 percent of
the antebellum lower federal court judges came from humble backgrounds, generally from a class of small farmers.

Looking at the individual eras, one sees some fluctuations. During the Federalist era, almost 29 percent of Article III judges were from elite social backgrounds while only 9.6 percent came from humble origins. That changed little
until the Civil War. During the Jeffersonian era and the Era of Good Feelings,
the same percentage came from elite backgrounds, while 10.3 percent had been
reared in humble homes. Although not dramatic, there is some democratization
during the supposedly more democratic Jacksonian era and the era of the second party system. From Jackson through Buchanan, 20.7 percent came from
elite social origins, and 24 percent from humble-to-modest backgrounds. However, during the Civil War and Reconstruction era, those from the elite increased
to almost 31 percent. On the other hand, those from humble-to-modest backgrounds also increased slightly, to a little over 26 percent. The remaining judges
(43 percent) were from prominent backgrounds compared to about 62 percent
for the previous three eras. During the Gilded Age, the pattern changed dramatically with only 13 percent of these judges from elite backgrounds. Of these,
73 percent hailed from prominent families, and only 14 percent from humble
origins.

In contrast to 20th- and 21st century patterns, the social origins of the jurists
did not reflect the supposed difference between the major parties. During the
antebellum period, Democrats allegedly appealed to the common man, the non-
Anglo-Saxons, and the nonevangelical and non-Protestant religious groups,
whereas Whigs supposedly represented the "gentleman" classes of merchants,
planters, and evangelical Protestants. However, such differences are not found
among the judicial appointees. For example, 47.1 percent of Jackson's appointees, all Democrats, had elite backgrounds, while another 23.5 percent came
from well-to-do families. During the Taylor-Fillmore administration, where all
the appointees were Whigs, only 25 percent had elite backgrounds, and another
37.5 percent came from well-to-do families. Twenty-five percent came from
humble origins compared with 23.5 percent of Jackson appointees.

Despite the differences in socioeconomic backgrounds, the professions of the
judges' fathers were about the same for all eras. Between 33 percent and
39 percent had fathers who were engaged in the professions, between 16 percent

and 23 percent were engaged in commerce, and between 7 percent and 13 percent were engaged in manufacturing. The only real fluctuation was for those engaged in agriculture. Only 26 percent of the judges appointed by Federalist presidents had fathers who had engaged in agriculture. This might reflect the Federalists' procommercial policies. During the Jeffersonian and Era of Good Feelings periods, almost 41 percent of the fathers of judicial appointees had been engaged in agriculture, perhaps reflecting the biases of the Jeffersonians. After that, the percentage engaged in agriculture remained at about 34 percent. Thus, from the late 18th to the end of the 19th century, most judges had a background that at least indirectly exposed them to the commercial and manufacturing life of the nation, a background very different from that of the typical American of these times. Most judges (almost 59 percent) had been raised in towns and cities rather than on farms and in rural areas. Thus, overall, at a time when approximately 80 percent of the male labor force was engaged in farming, at most only about 40 percent of the judges had fathers who were farmers or planters.

The background of the federal jurists of the 19th century also differed from the general population by the fact that they came from families with traditions of political activism. Some 60 percent of the jurists' fathers had held either elective or appointed governmental positions, thus exposing their sons to the world of politics and service as well as facilitating the formation of important friendships that could lead to judicial appointments. Furthermore, of the district court judges appointed between 1789 and 1899, almost 80 percent had either a blood relative or someone related through marriage who held public office. During the first 40 years under the Constitution, the numbers were the highest: over 90 percent of appointees had kin in public office during that time. The most dramatic numbers were for the Federalist era, when the political elite clearly dominated: 56.5 percent had more than one relative in office, and only 6.5 percent had none. During the Jeffersonian era and the Era of Good Feelings, the numbers dropped only slightly, to 47 percent having more than one relative in office but only 6.1 percent having none. During the Age of Jackson, the numbers dropped as individual connections rather than kinship became more important. During those years, 17.9 percent of the district court judges had no relatives holding public office. The numbers steadily climbed from the Civil War, with almost 26 percent having no relatives in office during the Civil War and Reconstruction era, and almost 33 percent having none during the Gilded Age (Hall 1976; 1987a; 1987b).

Socioeconomic Status, Education, and Government Experience of 19th-Century Judges

Although a small percentage of judges were reared by parents with only modest means, by the time of their appointments, most were prominent socially, having acquired enough wealth that they could be placed comfortably in at least the middle class. At the time of their appointments, less than 2 percent were deemed to be of humble background in any era before the 20th century. During the Federalist era, almost 80 percent were elite while 20 percent were prominent. This declines steadily to the Civil War with 66 percent elite during the Jeffersonian era and the Era Good Feelings and only 40 percent during the era of the second party system. Then, during and after the Civil War, there was a slow rise in the number of elite judges appointed, with 47 percent having elite status at the time of their appointment by Civil War and Reconstruction era presidents, and 50 percent having that status at the time of appointment by late-19th-century presidents.

Judges serving before the 20th century were less formally educated than those appointed in the 20th and 21st centuries; this is a reflection both of changes in education as well as the social origins of the appointees. Still, those appointed before 1900 comprised an educated elite. Despite the fact that the Constitution fails to stipulate any educational requirements for Article III judges, all but one appointee have been attorneys. During the antebellum period, 85 percent of federal jurists read law to prepare for their legal careers, while the remainder graduated from or attended a law school. The only appointee without legal training was William Rossell of New Jersey, who had extensive judicial experience before his appointment to the federal bench, serving as a justice of the peace, a judge of the state common pleas court, and a state supreme court judge. Despite their general lack of law school training, most federal judges had education that went far beyond the minimum expected during these years. At a time when fewer than 4 percent of the American population attended college and when most attorneys had no college education, almost 61 percent of Article III lower federal court judges appointed between 1789 and 1899 had graduated from college, and another 8.5 percent had attended college. Further, 43.4 percent of these had attended or graduated from elite Ivy League institutions. Those appointed by Federalist presidents were the most highly educated, with 69.8 percent having graduated from college, and another 4.6 percent having attended. During the antebellum and Civil War and Reconstruction years, the numbers drop most dramatically—ranging from 50 percent to 53.5 percent having graduated from college with another 5 percent to 8.4 percent having attended. During the Gilded Age, the numbers again climb dramatically, to 66 percent college graduates and another 12.1 percent attendees. These percentages vary not only by era but also based on the social origins of the jurists. Of those appointed before the Civil War, only one-fourth of those from humble origins graduated college, while over 50 percent of those from well-to-do and elite backgrounds did.

Not only were 19th-century judges generally well educated, but they also had extensive experience in government before taking up their posts on the federal bench. Almost 80 percent of the pre-20th-century appointees had held elective office before becoming federal judges. During the Federalist period, the number was the highest, with over 85 percent having some previous elective political experience; about 41 percent had held state office, and almost 43 percent had been elected to a federal post. Some 75 percent of lower court federal judges appointed during the antebellum period had held an elective office before their appointments to the federal bench, most serving in the legislative branch. Over half had been a legislator, and almost 29 percent had served in the federal Congress. Only 19 percent had held executive positions, served in the cabinet, or had been members of the diplomatic corps. Those who had not held elective office had been politically active as presidential electors, party organizers, or appointees to executive or legal-judicial posts. During the post–Civil War period, the numbers of those having held elective positions before being appointed a federal judge were about the same, but more had held local offices (24 percent) than federal offices (17 percent).

More than 44 percent of 19th-century federal judges had judicial experience, with almost 87 percent having served as local and state judges, and the rest as federal territorial judges. However, the numbers fluctuated during different eras. Those appointed by Federalist presidents had the highest percentage of prior judicial service—53 percent. A little more than 40 percent of those appointed during the rest of the antebellum period had previous judicial experience, but this percentage varied dramatically, depending upon the appointing president. Jackson, Van Buren, and Fillmore, for example, were more concerned with balancing partisan and sectional interests and responding to pressures from key supporters than selecting candidates with extensive judicial experience. Thus, only 11.8 percent of Fillmore's, 23.5 percent of Van Buren's, and 28.1 percent of Jackson's appointees had prior judicial experience. Of those appointed by the other antebellum presidents, at least 42 percent had judicial experience. During the Civil War and Reconstruction Era, the number with previous judicial experience dropped to 35 percent, but the number went up again during the Gilded Age to 38.6 percent. Furthermore, in a period lacking mass communication, a surprising number of these men had achieved national prominence before their appointments to the lower federal judiciary. Almost 10 percent of Article III judges had gained such prominence while another 40 percent had statewide reputations (see Hall 1975; 1976; 1980).

Characteristics of Judges of the Modern Era

Since the beginning of the 20th century, the portrait of the typical lower court judge has changed in many ways. The vast majority of these judges are still members of the same political party as their appointing president. Similarly, the age of judicial appointees at the time of their appointments has not changed significantly over time, hovering around 50 years of age. Judicial appointees to courts of appeals tended to be slightly older than district court nominees, indicating that those selecting them sought people with more experience practicing law and statewide if not national reputations.

Ethnicity and Gender

The most dramatic change in the backgrounds of judicial appointees has been in their ethnic and gender composition. The lower federal court did not become diversified ethnically and by gender until the middle of the 20th century. Until Franklin Roosevelt appointed Florence Allen to the Sixth Circuit Court of Appeals in 1934, all had been men. Not until three decades later, in the Lyndon Johnson administration, was another woman appointed to an appellate court bench. Harry Truman appointed Burnita Shelton Matthews as the first woman district court judge, while Ronald Reagan broke the gender barrier on the Supreme Court with his appointment of Sandra Day O'Connor in 1981. But until Jimmy Carter's presidency, fewer than 2 percent of the lower judiciary were female. While Carter made the appointment of women and minorities an important objective, only 14.4 percent of his appointees were women. Although the percentage dropped during the Reagan administration to 8.3 percent, the number of federal judgeships filled by women increased during the Clinton presidency to 28.2 percent. The percentage of women federal judicial nominees dropped again during the administration of Republican president George W. Bush, to 22 percent. During the first seven years of the Obama administration, by contrast, 41 percent of openings for federal judgeships were filled by women.

It took even longer for racial minorities to have any representation on the federal bench. Harry Truman was the first president to appoint an African American when, in 1945, he named Chicago attorney Irvin C. Mollison to the U.S. Customs Court sitting in New York. Then, after his re-election in 1948, Harry Truman—acknowledging that the support of the African American community helped him win that tight election and that it expected a judicial appointment in return—nominated William Hastie to the Third Circuit Court of Appeals. Kennedy was the first to name an African American, James B. Parson, to the federal district court bench when appointing him to the U.S. District Court for the Northern District of Illinois, which includes Chicago. Kennedy also appointed Wade H. McCree Jr. to the Eastern District of Michigan, which includes Detroit, and A. Leon Higginbotham Jr. to the district court that includes Philadelphia. Lyndon Johnson's appointment of Thurgood Marshall to the Supreme Court broke the color barrier on the highest court. John F. Kennedy and Johnson were also the first to appoint judges from other previously unrepresented minority groups; combined, they appointed almost 4 percent blacks, 1.8 percent Hispanics, and 0.4 percent Asians. An example of the changing climate was Kennedy's appointment of Reynaldo G. Garza to the U.S. District Court for the Southern District of Texas in 1961. After a vacancy on that court developed in 1960, Dwight Eisenhower selected a prominent, well-connected white male as his nominee. But Lyndon Johnson, the senior senator from Texas and Kennedy's running mate in the 1960 election, quietly withheld his support until the 1960 election results were in. The Senate then delayed voting until Kennedy took office. The Eisenhower nominee's name was withdrawn, and Garza's was proposed in its place. The choice of a Hispanic lawyer from Brownsville over a white corporate attorney from Houston symbolized the types of changes taking place in the nation.

It was not until Carter, however, that the appointment of minorities was made an important priority. Almost 14 percent of Carter's judicial appointees were African American. Of the 37 African Americans he appointed, he placed 28 on district court benches and 9 on the courts of appeals. In addition, 6.9 percent of his nominees were Hispanic, and 0.5 percent were Asian. Reagan reversed this trend, however, with 92.4 percent of his appointees being white. In fact, Reagan appointed the smallest proportion of African Americans to the federal bench since the Eisenhower administration, which had selected no African Americans. Bush Sr.'s appointees were nearly 90 percent white. It was not until Clinton's presidency that the appointment of women and minorities approached their percentage of the population, with almost 50 percent of appointees being women and minorities: 19 percent were African American, 5.2 percent Hispanic, and 1.6 percent Asian. Bill Clinton was also the first president to appoint a Native American as an Article III judge. During the eight-year presidency of George W. Bush (2001–2009), 18 percent of judicial appointments were filled by minorities. During the first six years of Barack Obama's presidency, meanwhile, 36 percent of judicial appointments were filled by ethnic and racial minorities. His appointment of openly gay judges should also be noted. This diversity in appointments by the Obama administration has been warmly received by minority and women's groups seeking greater representation in positions of leadership and influence in the U.S. legal system (see Toobin 2014; Goldman 1997; Abraham 1990).

According to the National Women's Law Center (March 2016):

By the nominations he has made, President Obama has taken an important step towards increasing the representation of women, including women of color, on the bench. He has nominated 164 women to fill federal judicial vacancies and 46 percent of his nominees to the federal Courts of Appeals have been women. He successfully appointed 7 women to federal Courts of Appeals and 17 women to District Courts where no female judges had previously served. In addition, he has appointed more than twice the number of women of color to the federal bench than any previous President, many of whom have similarly broken barriers on the courts on which they now sit.

Religious Affiliation

Although 19th-century presidents occasionally considered a nominee's religious affiliation, and many appointed Catholics to the bench, beginning with Roger Taney as chief justice of the Supreme Court in 1836, religious considerations were not a major factor in judicial appointments until the 20th century. In 1916, Louis Brandeis became the first Jewish judge appointed to the Supreme Court. At that time, his religion worked against him because it was a negative factor in his confirmation fight. However, discriminatory treatment and bigotry against non-Protestants declined markedly in American life and culture during the 20th century, and it is no longer regarded as remarkable for religious minorities, especially Catholics and Jews, to be well represented on the federal bench.

Since Woodrow Wilson appointed Brandeis, there was at least one Jewish judge on the Supreme Court until 1969, when Richard Nixon replaced Abe Fortas with a Protestant. There was then no Jewish member of the High Court until Clinton appointed Ruth Bader Ginsburg in 1993 and Stephen Breyer in 1994. Similarly, during the 20th century, there have routinely been Catholic justices on the Supreme Court. After Taney's death in 1864, no Catholic was appointed to the High Court until William McKinley appointed Joseph McKenna in 1898. Since then, there has been at least one Catholic on the Court, and, in 2015, there were six—Antonin Scalia, Anthony Kennedy, Clarence Thomas, John Roberts, Samuel Alito, and Sonia Sotomayor.

For much of America's history, Democratic presidents tended to appoint more non-Protestants than did Republicans. During the Republican era in the 1920s, 82 percent of judicial appointees were Protestant, 3.8 percent Catholic, and 3.8 percent Jewish. Under Franklin Roosevelt, those numbers changed dramatically: only 67 percent were Protestant, while over 26 percent were Catholic. The percentage of Jewish judges remained about the same at 3.6 percent. Even more of Truman's appointees were Catholics (33 percent for district court judges and 23 percent for the courts of appeals) and Jewish (11 percent for the district courts and 7.7 percent for the courts of appeals), reflecting the growing influence of these religious groups in the Democratic Party. From Truman until Reagan, the percentages of Protestant judges nominated by Republican presidents has been in the 70 percent range, while it was less than 60 percent for Democrats. Catholics represented about 25 to 30 percent of Democratic appointees, and Jews represented about 10 percent. For Republican presidents, the percentage of Jewish appointees remained about the same as it was for Democratic presidents, but the proportion of Catholics appointed to the bench was generally under 20 percent

With Reagan, this changed. Reagan's presidential papers suggest that his administration considered ethnicity as one factor in appointments, using patronage to reward members of different groups who had joined his new Republican coalition. Thus, the percentage of Protestants appointed by this Republican president dropped to 62.5 percent. Reflecting the increasing number of Catholics joining the Republican Party, almost 30 percent of Reagan's judicial appointees were Catholics, while only 8.3 percent were Jewish. Reagan was also the first president to take credit publicly for the appointment of an Italian American to the Supreme Court when he appointed Scalia in 1986. Further, when he appointed Italian Americans to lower federal court judgeships, he publicized their selection in the relevant communities (see Goldman 1997).

Socioeconomic Background and Status

Like their 19th-century predecessors, 20th-century lower federal court judges generally had at least middle-class and often upper-middle-class or elite social origins. Only 4 percent of Carter's district court appointees fell into the latter category. The percentage climbed to 23 percent during the Reagan years, then to 32.4 percent for Bush Sr., and to 34.5 percent for Clinton. The same pattern was seen for appellate court judges. Only 10.3 percent were millionaires at the time of their appointment by President Carter. The number rose to 18.2 percent for Reagan and then jumped dramatically to 43.2 percent for Bush Sr. and 50 percent for Clinton appointees. Similarly, the number with a net worth of less than $200,000 at the time of their appointments declined fairly steadily. For district court appointees, the highest percentage was during Carter with 35.8 percent, declining to a low with Bush Sr. of 10 percent, and then rising again to 15 percent with Clinton. For circuit court judges, the pattern was the same, with a high of 33 percent during the Carter years and a low of 5.4 percent under Bush Sr., with a slight rise to 6.3 percent for Clinton. Furthermore, judges differed from the general population in family occupational backgrounds. Both district and appellate judges tended to come from families with a tradition of judicial and public service. Some came from families with four or more generations of attorneys, judges, or politicians.

The trend toward wealthier federal judges has continued to grow in the early 21st century. Whereas 35.8 percent of district court judges had a net worth of less than $200,000, the percent of such judges at that level after the first two years of Obama's first term was only 2.3 percent. By contrast, the percentage of district court judges worth more than $1 million soared from 4 percent during the Carter years to nearly 70 percent by 2012. Even accounting for inflation, those figures indicate a significant rise in the affluence of federal judges. Ironically, both conservatives and liberals have cited stagnant pay for federal judgeships as a key factor in the rise of millionaire judges. In 2006, conservative Chief Justice John Roberts even described Congress's failure to raise judicial salaries as a constitutional "crisis" because it was narrowing the likely field of interested and qualified candidates. He warned that low judicial salaries—especially in comparison to lucrative positions in private practice—made it increasingly difficult for men and women of modest financial means to consider pursuing judgeships (see Goldman et al. 2013; Greenhouse 2007).

Progressive legal groups such as the Alliance for Justice (AFJ) have echoed this criticism. Moreover, these groups have expressed dismay with the narrowing of "professional diversity" among judges, noting that Republicans have been particularly stingy in confirming Obama administration judicial nominees with work histories in public defenders' offices or with public interest groups. They charge that this element of GOP obstructionism has influenced the Obama administration's selection of nominees, leading it to shy away from nominees who have worked for public interest organizations (only 3 percent of all district and circuit court nominees, according to the AFJ) and toward nominees whose backgrounds are primarily with corporate or business clients (more than 70 percent of all district and circuit court nominees). From the Alliance for Justice (2016):

> Professional diversity is . . . essential to maintain the public trust in our justice system. When individuals suffer injustice . . . they need to feel like they'll get a fair shake—that their arguments will be seriously considered and understood, and their claims resolved without bias or favor. But if the judiciary is devoid of judges with prior experience representing civil rights plaintiffs or otherwise advocating for the public interest, it will appear as though the deck is stacked in advance, and public confidence in the courts— the belief that all litigants truly can have their day in court—will erode.

Education

The trend over time has been for judges to have formal undergraduate and legal education, reflecting educational developments in society overall; the impact of this trend, however, was not seen until well into the 20th century. Indeed, in the early 20th century, fewer judges had college degrees than those appointed in the antebellum era. Between 1900 and 1930, only 40.7 percent of lower federal court judges held such degrees. During the Franklin D. Roosevelt administration, educational patterns gradually changed. Overall, almost 31 percent of Roosevelt's appointees had no undergraduate education. However, there was a change during his presidency. Of those he appointed to district court judgeships during his first term, 40 percent had no college education, and 17.1 percent had no law school education. By Roosevelt's third term, however, only 23.3 percent of his appointees had no college education, and 13.9 percent had no legal education. As has been typical since the creation of courts of appeals judgeships, Roosevelt's appellate court appointees were better educated than his district court judges, with only about 14 percent with no undergraduate education and about 10 percent with no formal legal education. Furthermore, many of Roosevelt's appellate court judges had attended Ivy League schools either as undergraduates or as law students. By the Nixon administration, all federal judicial appointees had received undergraduate degrees, and this has remained the case ever since.

While the percentage of those graduating college gradually increased, fewer attended elite Ivy League schools compared to judges in the 19th century. This perhaps reflects the increasing prestige and distinction of many public and other private institutions. The percentage of judges who have attended Ivy League schools has not varied much since the administration of Ronald Reagan, with the percentage of each succeeding administration ranging roughly between 50 and 60 percent. The change in formal legal training is even more dramatic, but this is much more a reflection of changing times than class origins. By the mid-20th century, virtually every judge had graduated from law school. In addition, the type of school they attended reflected their elite backgrounds. Almost half attended costly Ivy League schools or other private universities for either their undergraduate or law degrees. And, unlike the case of undergraduate institutions, there is no correlation between political party and the prestige of the law school (see Goldman 1997).

Historically, courts of appeals judges have tended to come from more "elite" institutions than those appointed to district courts. From the 1960s through 1979, for the Second, Fifth, and District of Columbia Circuit Courts, 40 percent of the judges had graduated from Harvard, Yale, or Columbia law schools, while another 15 percent went to other prestigious law schools, including Cornell, Georgetown, Michigan, and Northwestern. From the Reagan through Obama administrations, meanwhile, the percentage of appeals court appointees with private or Ivy League undergraduate educations ranged from 55 to 87 percent (see Goldman et al. 2013; Howard 1981).

Judicial Experience

Lower court Article III federal judges appointed before the 20th century generally had more extensive judicial experience before joining the federal bench than did their counterparts named since 1900, but the numbers have been steadily climbing. In the early 20th century, presidents tended to look more to those with prosecutorial rather than judicial experience for district court appointments, but this has been gradually changing, with the turning point occurring during the Carter administration. The percentage of district court judges appointed by presidents from Franklin Roosevelt through Eisenhower with prior judicial experience ranged from 32.5 percent to 36.8. The number jumped to almost 41 percent in the Kennedy-Johnson administrations and then declined slightly to 37 percent during the Nixon-Ford years. However, the numbers rose after that, with 54 percent of Carter's, over 46 percent of Reagan and Bush Sr.'s, and 51 percent of Clinton's district court appointees having prior judicial experience. More recently, 46 percent of Obama's district court nominees during his first seven years in office—and 53 percent of his circuit court nominees—were state or federal judges prior to nomination (Alliance for Justice 2016).

With the increase in those having prior judicial experience, one also sees a decline in those with prosecutorial experience, but the decline has not been dramatic. Between 48 and 52 percent of appointees from Roosevelt through Eisenhower had such experience, but since then, the percentage has remained below 50 percent. During the first seven years of the Obama administration, for example, 42 percent of district court nominees had been state or federal prosecutors, while 37.5 percent of circuit court nominees has served prior as prosecutors.

Even with the numbers having prior judicial experience rising for district court appointees, there is a significant difference when comparing this group to appellate court judges. For the higher court overall since the days of Franklin D. Roosevelt, 60 percent had judicial experience before assuming their positions, many being promoted from federal district court judgeships. Roosevelt and Carter selected the smallest proportion with prior judicial experience at about 54 percent; no other president through 2000 had under 60 percent. The percentage with prosecutorial experience has ranged from about 28 percent to 40 percent (see Alliance for Justice 2016; Goldman 1997).

Office Holding and Activist Experience

Unlike 19th-century jurists, who had often held elective office before their appointments to the bench, the proportion of lower federal court judges in the 20th century who held political or government positions at the time of appointment, excluding judicial or prosecutorial posts, has steadily declined. This is especially true for the number who had served in Congress. Whereas in the antebellum period, 29 percent of district court judges had served in Congress before they became federal judges, only 13 percent of Franklin D. Roosevelt's appointees had been members of Congress. After Roosevelt, the numbers decline dramatically; only 7.2 percent of Truman's appointees had been members of Congress, and since Truman, the percentage has never risen above 3 percent.

Similar patterns are evident in the percentages of those who have held any elective office. Reaching a 20th-century high of 20 percent during the Truman administration, it has never been more than 10 percent since. Thus, presidents have turned to many who have spent their careers in the private rather than the public sector. Of those who had been in the private sector as attorneys before appointment, the type of law they practiced generally varied based on party affiliation: Democratic presidents tended to appoint solo practitioners or those in small-to-medium-sized firms, while Republicans favored those in larger law firms. Here, too, there are exceptions. Reagan appointed the most judges from large law firms at 17.9 percent, but Bill Clinton was second at 15.7 percent. Law professors have accounted for fewer than 5 percent of the appointees in any administration since Roosevelt. From 2009 to 2015, for example, only 4.1 percent of Obama's nominees for federal district and circuit court judgeships had experience as law professors.

Despite their comparative lack of experience as elected nonjudicial officials, 20th-century jurists have been as much political appointees as their counterparts in the 19th century. Not only have the overwhelming majority, as we have seen, been members of the same party as the nominating president, but most have been politically active, although perhaps not as much as 19th-century jurists. Approximately 58 percent of all district court appointees and over 65 percent of courts of appeal judges had a record of political activism. In the 1960s and 1970s, for example, 70 percent of those who became judges of the Second, Fifth, and District of Columbia Circuit Courts had either been candidates for political office or in other ways actively served their party before appointment. Over one-third had run for office, most commonly for the state legislature, for law enforcement positions, or for state judgeships. Others had served as public defenders, prosecutors, and lawyers for governmental agencies. Still others had donated both their time and their money to campaigning for others. Because of their activities, many had developed close political relationships with either the appointing president or the senator making the recommendation to the president (see Alliance for Justice 2016; Goldman 1997; Howard 1981).

ARTICLE I JUDGES

In addition to Article III judges, two classes of Article I judges (who by contrast do not receive life tenure) play a major role in the federal judicial system. Beginning in 1898, district judges appointed referees to oversee the administration of bankruptcy cases in the district courts. But the increasing number of bankruptcy cases led to calls for reform. In 1978, President Carter signed the Bankruptcy Reform Act, which established the position of bankruptcy judge and required bankruptcy cases to be filed in bankruptcy courts rather than in federal district courts. Judges of the court of appeals for each circuit appoint these judges to their circuits for renewable 14-year terms after merit selection committees recommend nominees to them. Although appeals are still taken to district courts, and many contested matters may be removed from bankruptcy to district courts, most bankruptcy cases are now handled entirely by bankruptcy judges.

U.S. magistrate judges have become essential to the smooth working of the district courts. Congress created these positions in 1968, replacing the old commissioner system. In the 1790s, Congress authorized circuit judges (changed in 1896 to district court judges) to appoint persons "learned in the law" as commissioners to admit persons accused of a federal crime to bail. Throughout the 19th century, Congress expanded the duties of the commissioners while reducing the qualifications necessary for the position. From 1812 on, commissioners needed no legal background at all. Still, their duties were extended to taking bail and affidavits, taking depositions of witnesses in civil cases, and issuing warrants for arrests of individuals charged with violating federal statutes. Under the Fugitive Slave Act of 1850, they became an integral part of the enforcement of what many Northerners considered an odious law, being authorized to act concurrently with district court judges in granting certificates to take the individual who owed service (i.e., the alleged runaway slave) into custody. In the Civil Rights Act of 1866, Congress gave commissioners the power to arrest, imprison, and bail any offender who violated this statute. In the 1890s, Congress granted commissioners the power to try those who violated the Chinese Exclusion Act of 1888, again concurrently with district court judges. During and after World War I, commissioners helped enforce wartime statutes. All these powers went to men without legal training who were compensated through a fee system. This led to numerous complaints that commissioners issued warrants without justification simply to increase their income.

Since Congress abolished the office of commissioner and created the magistrate judge system in 1968, it has enacted several statutes that have increased the magistrates' role. Appointed by the district court judges of their district to eight-year terms, removable before the expiration of their terms only for "good cause," magistrate judges are required to be members of the bar and are paid a fixed salary. Although the salary was only $22,000 when the office was first created, by the end of the 20th century, the salary had increased to $142,324, only $12,000 less than the salary earned by district court judges. Magistrate judges are, at least in theory, appointed by a consensus of all the district court judges in the district where the vacancy has occurred or the new positions have been authorized. In some districts, however, judges rotate the prerogative of appointment. In others, where judges sit in more than one city, the judges in the city where the magistrate judge will serve in reality make the decision.

Generally, the position is not political, and judges of one party often appoint a magistrate politically affiliated with a different party.

Magistrate judges perform those functions needed in their particular districts within the guidelines established by the Federal Magistrate Acts of 1968, 1976, and 1979. With the consent of the parties involved, they may conduct all the proceedings in a jury or nonjury civil matter, including trials, and enter a judgment in the case. They also may conduct criminal trials of persons accused of misdemeanors committed within their district, provided the defendant consents. While magistrate judges function differently in different districts, depending on the inclination of the judges and the types of cases heard in their area, a study conducted in the early 1990s of nine federal district courts revealed that magistrates were generally used in one of three ways. In some, they served as additional judges, hearing and deciding their own civil caseloads. In others, judges used them as specialists who heard and then recommended action on some special aspect of the law, especially Social Security and prisoner habeas cases. Finally, some district judges have magistrate judges act as case managers, hearing all pretrial matters and then determining when the case is ready for the district judge to take over. With the continually increasing federal docket, the responsibilities of magistrate judges continue to increase, as do the numbers Congress has authorized.

Originally, district court judges appointed their former law clerks as magistrate judges, even though they had little if any experience as attorneys. During the Carter administration, a merit selection process was instituted in which district court judges had to establish merit selection panels that would then advertise vacancies, evaluate candidates, and then submit a list of five candidates to the judges. In addition, the Magistrates Act of 1979 required that magistrate judges have five years of legal experience before appointment. By the 1980s, these changes began to have the desired effect on the type of people selected as magistrate judges. Increasingly, they were former state judges and law professors (see Smith 1990).

SUPPORT STAFF IN THE FEDERAL JUDICIARY

Law clerks also play an increasingly influential role in the federal court system (Peppers and Ward 2013). In 1875, Horace Gray, then chief justice of the Massachusetts Supreme Court, became the first American judge to use a law clerk, employing his appointee at his own expense. When Gray became a justice of the U.S. Supreme Court in 1882, he brought a law clerk with him. Oliver Wendell Holmes, who like Gray served as a former chief justice of the Massachusetts Supreme Court, annually hired an honor graduate of Harvard Law School to serve as his clerk. Felix Frankfurter, later a Supreme Court justice himself, procured law clerks for Holmes. William Howard Taft, a former law professor at Yale University, worked through the dean of the Yale Law School to hire his law clerks after Taft became chief justice of the U.S. Supreme Court. Soon it became established tradition for Supreme Court justices to hire top graduates from the best law schools to serve as clerks. Congress, however, did not authorize Supreme Court justices to hire clerks until 1922. In 1930, it empowered each circuit judge to appoint a law clerk, contingent upon the approval of the attorney general. In 1936, it extended the same privilege for district court judges, although it limited the total number throughout the United States to thirty-five. It was not until 1945 that each district court judge who wanted one was permitted to hire a clerk, and even then, the proposed clerk needed certification by the senior circuit judge.

By the mid-20th century, clerks had become commonplace at all levels in the federal court system. They serve district, circuit, and Supreme Court judges as well as bankruptcy and U.S. magistrate judges. Each Supreme Court justice has four clerks; each court of appeals judge has three. District court judges have one each, except for the chief judge, who might have two. Given the heavy federal dockets of the late 20th and early 21st centuries, many judges claim they can no longer function effectively without their law clerks. Supreme Court justices select their clerks from among those who have clerked for lower federal court judges. Lower federal court judges hire their clerks from applicants who have graduated from the top law schools or have distinguished themselves during their law school careers.

As with magistrate judges, the duties of law clerks vary by judge. In district courts, they are primarily research assistants, examining various motions filed in civil and criminal cases, delineating the issues and the positions of the parties, and researching the important points raised in motions. They also prepare written memoranda for the judges and may be involved in the initial drafting of opinions. At the appellate level, law clerks become involved first by researching issues of law and fact presented by the appeal and then are an integral part of the screening process to help differentiate between those cases that can be handled quickly and those that require more research and more time. Clerks also help judges prepare for oral arguments. After decisions are reached, law clerks frequently participate in writing the order accompanying the decision. Often they draft preliminary opinions or orders. Supreme Court law clerks generally perform the same role as do appellate law clerks, but they play a more crucial role in helping the justices decide which cases will be heard. Since the 1970s, some courts of appeals and district courts have hired staff law clerks who work for the entire court rather than for a particular judge. They are used largely to handle criminal pro se petitions (petitions from prisoners representing themselves that challenge their convictions).

The Judiciary Act of 1789 established other federal officials to aid the federal courts in their work. Federal marshals and district attorneys were appointed by the president while the clerk of court was appointed by the district court judge. Until the end of the 19th century, all were paid by fees rather than salary. Today, federal marshals and U.S. attorneys have important decision-making powers that affect the agenda of the federal courts. In the area of criminal law, for example, the U.S. attorneys decide who will be prosecuted and, under the Federal Sentencing Guidelines, largely determine what the sentence range will be for those convicted. In the civil area, they determine which federal laws will be vigorously enforced. So, for example, they can have an important influence on how vigorously environmental, antitrust, or affirmative action statutes are implemented. Marshals enforce court orders and handle many financial aspects of the court's work.

Although the Judiciary Act did not specify who would appoint the marshal, acting under his plenary constitutional power of appointment, Washington assumed that function, and the president's authority to do so thereafter has never been challenged. He appointed one marshal for each judicial district. That official serves a four-year term, but he can be removed by the president for any reason before the expiration of that term. The marshal's duty is to support the federal courts in their judicial district by carrying out all the orders issued by the judges, Congress, or the president. Originally, marshals and the deputies they appointed also served subpoenas, summonses, writs, warrants, and other processes issued by the courts; made all the arrests; and handled all the prisoners. They also disbursed the money of the court, paying the fees and expenses of the court clerks, U.S. attorneys, jurors, and witnesses. Early on, it was even their responsibility to rent courtroom and jail space and hire the bailiffs, criers, and janitors. In addition, the federal marshals served the president and Congress by representing the federal government in regions that normally had little contact with federal authority beyond the post office. Until 1890, they were in charge of taking the national census every 10 years. They also distributed presidential proclamations and collected a variety of statistical information when requested by Congress or the president. Before the Civil War, perhaps their most controversial duty was to enforce the fugitive slave laws by capturing and returning alleged fugitives to their owners and arresting others who violated the statute. During the Cold War, they arranged the details of swapping spies with the former Soviet Union.

As of 2016, there were more than 3,700 deputy U.S. marshals and criminal investigators serving the 94 judicial districts plus the District of Columbia Superior Court (US Department of Justice 2016a). Involved in virtually every federal law enforcement initiative, these men and women work nationwide in a variety of law enforcement activities that include the protection of federal judicial officials (i.e., judges, attorneys, and jurors); the capture of federal fugitives as well as fugitives wanted by foreign nations and believed to be in the United States; the protection of witnesses, especially those risking their lives testifying for the government in cases involving organized crime (includes the supervision of the witness protection program that relocates and provides new identities for witnesses needing this heightened protection); the housing of unsentenced federal prisoners in federal, state, and local jails; transporting federal prisoners and criminal aliens between judicial districts, correctional institutions, and foreign countries; and enforcing injunctions issued by the courts in, for example, labor disputes and civil rights actions. They continue to serve some processes as directed by the district court judges and manage some of the financial aspects of the work in the judicial districts. For example, federal marshals manage and dispose of all seized and forfeited properties acquired by those convicted of illegal activities. In the early 21st century, that amounted to managing over $1 billion worth of property. The proceeds from the sale of this property go to a variety of law enforcement initiatives.

Federal marshals also continue to carry out special missions ordered by the president and Congress. For example, specially trained deputy marshals provide security and law enforcement assistance to the Department of Defense and the U.S. Air Force when Minuteman and Cruise missiles are moved between military facilities (U.S. Department of Justice 2016b).

The Judiciary Act of 1789 also provided for the appointment in each judicial district of a person "learned in the law" to prosecute federal crimes and to represent the United States in all civil actions to which it was a party. The title of these judicial officials has changed over the years, but today they are known as U.S. attorneys. Initially, U.S. attorneys received their instructions from the secretary of state, but Congress changed that structure in 1861, when it authorized the attorney general to direct their duties and required the U.S. attorneys to report their official proceedings to the attorney general. Like U.S. marshals, they are appointed by the president with the advice and consent of the Senate for four-year, renewable terms; the U.S. attorneys then appoint their own assistants to help them, although the number of assistants authorized is controlled by the attorney general's office. Their primary responsibility is to prosecute suits on behalf of the federal government. The U.S. attorneys are really the gatekeepers of the judicial system, determining whom the government will sue or prosecute for violations of federal law. By the end of the 20th century, there were 94 U.S. attorney's offices, one for each federal judicial district, but these offices vary in size from small ones with only one assistant to others, especially in large urban areas, with many more.

The position of U.S. attorney, like that of U.S. marshal, is a patronage position, and they are usually members of the appointing president's party. Thus, it is customary for the U.S. attorneys to submit their resignations when a new president from the opposing party is elected. The recruitment of U.S. attorneys is similar to that of lower court judges. The Department of Justice, specifically the

Executive Office for U.S. Attorneys, screens candidates recommended by senators and state and local party leaders of the appointing president's party. Federal district court judges may also play an influential role based on their authority to fill a vacancy on a temporary basis.

Those appointed generally have strong roots in their locality, most having been born in the state in which they serve and a majority having attended undergraduate college or law school in their home state. Most also have a history of political activism and have prior governmental experience, especially in positions as public prosecutors. Since the late 20th century, about 20 percent have been promoted from the assistant U.S. attorney ranks. The majority, however, are still drawn from those who were in private practice at the time of their appointments. As is the case with judges, most U.S. attorneys are Protestant—primarily from high-status Protestant denominations—particularly those serving in the South, as one might suspect based on demographics of that region. Many U.S. attorneys see their appointment as a potential route to a federal judgeship (see Department of Justice 2016c).

The Judiciary Act of 1789 also provided that each district court judge appoint a clerk to record the orders, decrees, judgments, and proceedings of the court. The clerk also informs attorneys as to proper court procedures and what papers need to be filed when. Until 1839, the clerk served both the district and circuit courts. Since then, there have been separate clerks for each court, although often the same individual has held both positions. From early in the courts' history, the clerks kept essential records, entering all orders and actions of the courts each day in a minute book. They also recorded all other official proceedings, including naturalizations. Clerks were not paid a fixed salary until 1919 (Messinger 2002).

"Activist" Judges

Railing against activist judges is nothing new in American politics. The nation's judicial wars occur infrequently, but when they do, they erupt with painful intensity. From 1800 through 1805, the two major parties of the day—the Federalists and Jeffersonian Republicans—engaged in a tug-of-war over the federal judiciary and the proper role of judges in a republic. In the first half of the 19th century, northern and southern judges faced attack, as they found themselves caught up in the middle of the debate over slavery. Ultimately, the national furor over the Supreme Court's decision in *Dred Scott v. Sandford* (1857) helped push the nation into civil war. Liberal politicians and legal commentators still demonize the *Lochner* era Supreme Court (1890–1910) and the conservative Court of the 1930s (because the ruling protected conservative business interests); and, Democrats have expressed deep frustration with the conservative-leaning court under Chief Justice John Roberts, who has led the Court since 2005. Meanwhile, conservative and right-wing critics still surge with resentment when they think of the Warren Court (1953–1969).

Yet for all its historical familiarity, the current uproar against the federal courts has proven to be particularly active, long-lived, and troublesome. For the past three decades, conservative defenders of the status quo both within and outside government have thundered against "liberal activist judges." As they see events, the courts have repeatedly overstepped their constitutional roles as courts of law and instead have become soapboxes for left-wing judges to promote such goals as establishing same-sex marriage, protecting abortion on demand, and waging a secular war against religion by such means as censoring the Ten Commandments and prohibiting prayer in school. "This is making law, not interpreting it!" they cry. Worse yet, they continue, this "lawmaking" is aimed at what the conservative Right deems to be the express will of the people. In their estimation, arrogant, elitist federal judges are the Left's shock troops in the culture wars. Not only have these judges ignored the plain meaning of the law's texts—they have also forced new "rights" and legal concepts and visions of morality on the American people while undermining traditional American values and corrupting American democracy in the process. They insist that, by contrast, a judge should be like an umpire in baseball, calling balls and strikes, not rewriting the rules of the game.

Liberal and leftist critics argue a mirror-image case. In their view, an increasingly arrogant and conservative federal bench has brushed aside legitimate congressional claims of power to make laws for the general good and squelched legitimate claims of individual rights. These judges are embracing, in the name of traditional values, judicial supremacy over the Constitution and laws of the United States, over the elected representatives of the people and over the people themselves. Judges who claim to be committed to conservatism, these critics maintain, instead are acting like embittered radicals, waging war on more than half a century of settled constitutional law, the ultimate goal being to undo by judicial fiat the great judicial victories for individual liberty, political and social equality, and social justice of the past several decades.

Thus beset from all sides, defenders of the judiciary have some reason to feel besieged. Taking up the baseball analogy, they point out that umpires, whether on the field or on the bench, have to make a call on every pitch that comes at them—and sometimes, just calling a strike requires the umpire to apply the rules in new ways. Not every constitutional or legal question has a clear answer, these defenders continue. In fact, most great constitutional issues are hard issues, requiring judges to apply existing constitutional or legal doctrines to new fact patterns, sometimes to the extent of reshaping the principles to give them new focus and direction. If judicial activism is the problem, what form of judicial activism is even more of a problem? That of the late 19th and early 20th centuries, in which courts repeatedly struck down laws enacted by significant legislative majorities enjoying major public support, or that of the late 20th and early 21st centuries, in which courts claiming to be conservative and restrained struck down more federal laws than in any comparable historical period? It appears that one side's judicial activism is another side's responsible judging.

If we set aside these arguments as unresolvable, we must confront a basic fact about judging. Judging involves reasoned choice. Choice, in turn, implies following the lead of the law wherever it might take the judge or court that is making the choice. If, in the process, the judge or court has to modify the way a law is viewed, such is the cost of choice. Someone has to make such choices when dealing with actual legal cases and controversies, and the Constitution gives the federal courts the job.

One result of these battles over judicial activism and restraint is that over time, when a member of the U.S. Supreme Court dies or retires, the battle to choose his or her successor has become increasingly bitter and partisan. When, it seems, the conveyor belt of American constitutional law ferries every great issue to the Supreme Court, the Court's membership is of vital national concern. And, when the Court is as divided as it has been in recent years, with one or two members becoming pivotal "swing" justices, the fights to choose those justices' successors become grudge matches.

Federal court workloads have evolved over time. From a small, contested, and somewhat inauspicious beginning to today, the federal judiciary has grown steadily in size, resources, and prestige. It has also grown in the scope of its jurisdiction, the authority of its mandate, and the impact of its rulings. Originally hearing mostly private law matters and enforcing a small corpus of narrowly drawn federal statutes, the federal courts over the course of the 19th and 20th centuries developed into a major force in establishing and articulating national policy and values through cases posing vital issues of private and public law. Today the federal trial and appellate courts hear more than 400,000 cases of all kinds each year; and while numbers of filings rise and fall from year to year in response to changes within society and the law, it is unlikely that the federal courts' workloads will decline significantly in the future (Administrative Office of U.S. Courts 2016).

As the size and complexity of the federal courts' workloads increased, so too did the courts' duties. Originally, federal courts served largely as courts of dispute resolution, providing answers to conflicts under the Constitution, federal law, or state laws involving citizens of different states. With the growth of the nation—and of the federal government's powers—came new roles to play. One was that of norm enforcement. Mostly associated with criminal law but also incorporating public civil suits, norm enforcement means maintaining the rules and values that govern society. The federal courts have performed this function by providing the federal government a convenient forum to which federal authorities can bring to justice those who have broken the laws of the nation. A second, more significant role was that of policymaker. Centered mostly in the appellate courts and in the U.S. Supreme Court in particular, the policymaking powers of the courts have grown over time until many have viewed the courts as overstepping their proper bounds as courts of law.

ROLES, FUNCTIONS, AND POWERS OF STATE COURTS

State courts and judges perform a variety of functions for state governments and their citizens. State courts resolve private economic disagreements such as contract or tort disputes, as well as personal disputes such as divorce and child custody cases. State courts also mediate public disagreements, including school funding claims, procedures for criminal defendants, and other state constitutional issues. To carry out these functions, state courts are invested with specific political, legal, and constitutional powers. The courts in each state use these powers to enforce their rulings, as well as to shape the state's political landscape. However, state courts do not exist in a vacuum. State judges must navigate a complex legal environment that includes federal courts and federal law, state constitutional and statutory restrictions, mandates, and sometimes even international law. As a result, state courts and judges must make and enforce their decisions while respecting other political institutions and competing bodies of law by using the specific and limited powers at their disposal.

The power and authority of state courts comes from state constitutions, legislative statutes, common law, and in some cases, federal law. State courts perform different tasks than federal courts. State courts spend much more of their resources dealing with issues such as torts, contract law, family law, and local issues (e.g., traffic violations, petty crime, and small claims). However, state courts must also deal with issues of public law such as death penalty appeals, statutory interpretation, and constitutional interpretation. State judges have a variety of powers at their disposal to ensure that their rulings are enforced. These include, but are not limited to, issuing writs of enforcement, garnishing wages and property, empowering special masters (officials appointed by the court to carry out investigative and administrative tasks for the court), invalidating state laws, and directing state law enforcement officers to carry out legal orders.

Judicial Federalism

State courts coexist with other jurisdictions. Federal and international law, as well as the rulings from other state courts, impact the discretion and authority of state judges. The interaction of state courts with federal courts is called vertical judicial federalism, which can be a complex relationship. The federal

Constitution's supremacy clause requires that state courts enforce federal law. Yet, at the same time, state supreme courts are the final arbitrators of state law. Therefore, in some cases, state courts must obey federal courts, but in other cases, state courts are free to develop their own bodies of law independent of federal courts.

State courts interact with courts from other states. This relationship is called horizontal judicial federalism. Sometimes, state courts use precedents issued by other state courts to decide cases. At other times, because of the U.S. Constitution's full faith and credit clause, state courts are required to enforce decisions issued by other state courts. State courts have a host of functions to perform and a variety of powers to enforce their decisions. However, in conjunction with these functions and powers, other institutions and legal jurisdictions impose a number of boundaries.

THE FOUNDATIONS OF STATE COURT AUTHORITY

The authority of state courts comes from several different sources. Primarily, state courts get their authority from state constitutions. Constitutional grants of authority can be supplemented by legislative statutes that are authorized by state constitutions. State courts also have federal sources of authority. The U.S. Constitution is an indirect source of state authority and therefore, an indirect source of authority for state courts. The supremacy and the full faith and credit clauses, as well as the Tenth Amendment, carve out roles for state courts in America's federalist system. Both federal and state constitutions, as well as state legislatures, establish limits to state court authority.

Constitutionalism

Constitutionalism is the idea that the powers of government should be limited by certain fundamental principles. Typically, these principles are established in a written document, or constitution. A constitution declares the limits of government power and sometimes establishes the rights of citizens that cannot be violated by government.

State Constitutions and Federalism

Students of law typically assume that all state constitutions were drafted in the early stages of our history. In fact, this is not always true. The Montana State Constitution was rewritten in 1972 when more than 80 delegates met in Helena. The Montana Constitution is considered one of the most progressive constitutions in the United States. It contains an extensive bill of rights that includes a "right to participation," a "right to know," a "right to privacy," and a "right to a clean and healthful environment." In 1999, the Montana Supreme Court began enforcing the clean and healthful environment clause by issuing several rulings that preemptively limited the ability of mining companies to pollute.

Constitutionalism grew out of the Enlightenment but has roots in history prior to that period. During the Middle Ages, the notion of the divine right of kings meant that monarchs ruled as the representative of God. Therefore, there were no limitations on the political power of the monarch. However, the Magna Carta of 1215 established written limitations on the powers of the English king. During the Enlightenment, political writers such as Thomas Hobbes and John Locke further explored the idea of constitutionalism. They argued that monarchs and government were limited by a social contract between the rulers and the ruled.

In the United States, constitutionalism gained greater prominence after the American Revolution. While America was a colony of the British Empire, ultimate sovereignty rested with the Crown. However, after severing all political and legal ties to Britain, America's leaders needed a new source of ultimate authority. On a theoretical level, Americans decided to place ultimate sovereignty in the people. Constitutions were drafted to represent the will of the populace. After the Revolution, constitutions became more than simply rules by which citizens and legislators had to abide. Instead, state constitutions became the embodiment of popular sovereignty.

The authority of American courts is closely tied to the concept of constitutionalism. Both the United States and every individual state have written constitutions that delineate the powers and limitations of the government. More important, the existence of constitutions highlights the fact that governments are not the highest form of authority. Instead, the will of the people, as expressed in the written constitutions, supersedes the will of government officials. Therefore, courts can limit the acts of government officials by establishing that those acts are forbidden by the state or federal constitution. In a constitutional system, courts are responsible for insuring that governments do not violate the constitutional rights of individuals or exercise powers not granted to them in the given constitutions. The courts act to ensure the governments stay within the established constitutional bounds. Because each state court has the power to enforce the written provisions of its state constitution, state courts have considerable authority to dictate to the elected and administrative branches of their state.

State Constitutions

All state courts, with varying degrees, get their authority from state constitutions. Either the state constitution establishes the entire judicial system, including minor bureaucratic details, or the state constitution establishes general guidelines and grants of power while leaving the details to the state legislature to establish. The Washington State Constitution exhibits characteristics of both. In terms of the state supreme court, the Washington Constitution prescribes specific details about its jurisdiction and powers. Article IV, Section 4 of the Washington Constitution, in part, states:

> The supreme court shall have original jurisdiction in habeas corpus, and quo warranto and mandamus as to all state officers, and appellate jurisdiction in all actions and proceedings, excepting that its appellate jurisdiction shall not extend to civil actions at law for the recovery of money or personal property when the original amount in controversy, or the value of the property does not exceed the sum of two hundred dollars ($200) unless the action involves the legality of a tax, impost, assessment, toll, municipal fine, or the validity of a statute. The supreme court shall also have power to issue writs of mandamus, review, prohibition, habeas corpus, certiorari and all other writs necessary and proper to the complete exercise of its appellate and revisory jurisdiction.

In comparison, the establishment and the allocation of power for lower courts is left to the state legislature by the Washington Constitution. Section 12 of Article IV simply reads, "The legislature shall prescribe by law the jurisdiction and powers of any of the inferior courts which may be established in pursuance of this Constitution."

It is important to realize that state constitutions tend to be much longer than the federal Constitution. Article III of the U.S. Constitution establishes the power and jurisdiction for the U.S. Supreme Court. Yet, Article III is one of the shortest articles in the Constitution and speaks with sweeping generalities. Furthermore, the federal Constitution was constructed primarily, although not entirely, as a document of limited government. That is, the purpose of the federal Constitution was to limit the federal government's scope of power. Therefore, much of the U.S. Constitution addresses what the federal government cannot do. Finally, it is very difficult to amend, and therefore it is hard to add clauses to the federal Constitution. Despite thousands of attempts, Americans have only been able to add 27 clauses to the U.S. Constitution in more than 200 years.

For a variety of reasons, state constitutions, in contrast, are very long and detailed documents. State constitutions are comparatively easy to amend. As a result, state constitutions can include relatively mundane clauses. The Alabama Constitution, for example, has a prohibition against taxing wharfs. The Colorado Constitution has a clause banning the general assembly from prescribing textbooks for high schools. The Missouri Constitution has a provision mandating a department of mental health.

Dinan (2006) argues that there is a reason why state constitutions dedicate so much text to seemingly mundane legislative areas. He notes that state legislatures have plenary power. This means that laws passed by the state legislature are assumed to be constitutional unless there is a specific proscription against such authority in the state constitution. In contrast, the federal Congress can only legislate in areas in which the federal Constitution specifically authorizes them to do so. Therefore, state legislators have a much freer hand than members of Congress. Because state legislatures are less constrained, drafters of state constitutions spend much more effort detailing specific limitations of authority for their legislatures.

In addition to constitutional clauses limiting state legislative power, state constitutions cover more policy areas and include affirmative grants of power that are absent in the U.S. Constitution. For example, many state constitutions mandate that the state guarantee a free, public, and adequate education. Likewise, many state constitutions establish fundamental guarantees of privacy, equal rights for women ("little ERAs"), and environmental quality. Such provisions empower state governments to pursue certain policies. There are no similar clauses in the federal Constitution.

Policy analysts often overlook the fact that such constitutional guarantees also expand the scope of state judicial power. Consider the case of educational funding. Both federal and state governments contribute to the funding of education. However, state courts have much more power to impact state funding of education than federal courts have to impact federal or state spending. The reason for the disparity in power is that federal courts cannot point to any provision in the U.S. Constitution that establishes jurisdiction over education funding. There are no federal guarantees to a public education. As such, plaintiffs unhappy about federal education funding cannot claim that any of their federal rights have been violated. State constitutions and, therefore, state courts, do not face such a dilemma. Because most state constitutions promise their citizens a public education, state citizens can go to state court and claim their state constitution is being violated. The existence of state constitutional education provisions gives state courts the authority to ensure minimum levels of education spending and an equal distribution of education spending across the state (see Banks and O'Brien 2015, Chaps. 9 and 10).

The preceding scenario is not just a legal hypothesis. In 2003, the Nevada Supreme Court ordered the Nevada legislature to fund education at higher levels. The Nevada legislature faced a variety of procedural hurdles before enacting such a law, however. The legislature must balance the budget but cannot raise taxes unless there is a two-thirds vote. Due to these dual requirements, the legislature was unable to agree on an appropriations bill for the state school system. In response, the governor sued the legislature in the Nevada Supreme Court. Because Article 11, Section 6, of the Nevada Constitution "compels the Legislature to support and maintain the public schools," the Nevada court ordered the legislature to ignore the two-thirds vote provision and "fulfill its obligations under the Constitution of Nevada by raising sufficient revenues to fund education while maintaining a balanced budget" (*Guinn v. Legislature of Nevada,* 2003). Because the Nevada Constitution explicitly requires the funding of education, the Nevada courts had the power to order the legislature to raise taxes and then require that the funding be spent on education. Federal courts, lacking such specific authoritative grants of power, do not have the ability to influence public policy so directly.

Judicial Gatekeeping

The power of state courts is also enhanced by liberal standing requirements established in most state constitutions. *Standing* is the judicial requirement that individuals show they have been directly harmed before gaining access to the courts. The federal requirements for standings are relatively high. For example, federal taxpayers cannot challenge federal statutes simply because they are taxpayers. Many state constitutions, however, do not limit their court's jurisdictions to cases where plaintiffs meet federal standing requirements. In fact, many state constitutions explicitly provide for suits by taxpayers. Tarr and Porter (1988) note that the majority of states provide for taxpayer suits against the state government, and almost all states allow for suits against local governments.

Liberal standing criteria enhance the power of state courts because they provide state courts with a venue to impact state policies. If state courts are unable to hear cases because plaintiffs lack standing, those state courts cannot issue rulings that will alter state policy. However, if it is easy to access state courts, state judges will be able to hear all types of cases covering all areas of policy and subsequently issue rulings that alter those policies.

State courts also have the authority to issue common law decisions. Common law is established through judicial rulings, not legislative enactments (statutory law) or constitutional amendments (constitutional law). Common law relies on precedents to bind lower courts to previous decisions handed down by higher courts. The purpose of common law is to fill in the gaps of vaguely written statutory law. Some well-known examples of federal common law include the Miranda rights, the exclusionary rule, and even privacy rights that ensure abortion rights. State judges also have the power to craft common law by issuing decisions that interpret state statutes or constitutions. The power to fashion common law comes from state constitutions. When state courts are granted jurisdiction by state constitutions, those courts also acquire the inherent and concurrent authority to issue rulings regarding their areas of jurisdiction, and such rulings become part of common law.

At the state level, significant amounts of property, contract, and tort law, as well as corporate and criminal law, are created by common law. The power to craft common law is tantamount to the power to craft legislation. Even though state constitutions only grant state courts judicial power, the reality of common law is that state courts have the power to act like legislative bodies and write their own laws through judicial decision-making.

How State Courts Make Laws

Some of America's most well-known laws were never enacted by the U.S. Congress or any state legislature; instead, they were written by judges. Most Americans who have watched a TV show about police officers know that citizens must be read their rights before being interrogated. These rights, which include "the right to remain silent," are known as Miranda rights. In *Miranda v. Arizona* (1966), the Supreme Court issued a ruling that all police officers must read defendants a list of rights. If the police failed to do so, the courts could throw out defendants' incriminating testimony.

Previously, in the 1961 case *Mapp v. Ohio*, the Supreme Court created a new common law known as the exclusionary rule. The exclusionary rule requires police officers to obtain a legitimate warrant before collecting evidence against a defendant. If a warrant is not obtained, the courts may exclude the incriminating evidence from being presented at trial.

State Statutes

State constitutions are not the only source of law within a state. State legislatures, as empowered by state constitutions, have the authority to draft statutes. In fact, an overwhelming majority of all laws are statutory laws, not constitutional laws. Legislative statutes may be as mundane as establishing speed limits or as complicated as regulating property rights. All state statutes, regardless of complexity, have the force of law and therefore are enforceable by state judges.

State statutes outline the basic rules by which citizens live. As such, statutes form the basis for almost all judicial decisions. Courts are responsible for ensuring that laws are fairly applied and that punishments are distributed if laws are broken. Furthermore, state statutes can be as general as some constitutional provisions. Whenever statutes are drafted in vague terms, courts must employ their interpretive methods to apply the law to individual circumstances. Other than rare federal and state constitutional grants of authority, all state judicial power flows from legislative statutes.

For example, the primary role of the legislature is to write the statutes that the courts must interpret and enforce. Therefore, judges cannot simply punish individuals who engage in objectionable behavior. They must confine themselves to enforcing the laws the legislature has passed. In the early 1980s, state courts were powerless to punish individuals for the act of stalking. Despite the fact that many women were being terrorized by ex-spouses and obsessed strangers, the courts had no power to prevent such behavior because, at the time, antistalking statutes did not exist. From the early 1990s through the 2010s, however, many states drafted new antistalking criminal statutes empowering state judges to intervene on behalf of women who were victimized.

The Federal Constitution

State courts and judges also obtain authority from the U.S. Constitution and federal common law. When the Constitution was written in 1787, the states that participated in the process jealously guarded their sovereignty. Many framers sought to delegate as few powers to the federal government as was necessary to conduct foreign affairs, regulate interstate commerce, and maintain domestic stability. The result was a Constitution that limited the powers of the federal government to the 18 enumerated powers identified in Article I, Section 8, of the U.S. Constitution. All other powers were reserved for the states. The concept of reserved powers for the states was formalized with the passage of the Tenth Amendment two years after the ratification of the Constitution. The reserved powers for the states include police powers, which typically encompass the authority to regulate all criminal behavior; domestic relations such as marriage and family law; and business relations within a state such as contract, tort, and corporate law.

Over time, at the expense of state authority, the federal government has expanded the scope of its authority to address the challenges of various economic and military crises. Despite the gradual encroachment of federal power, the U.S. Supreme Court continues to protect the authority of state governments and state courts to adjudicate significant areas of public policy. For example, in *United States v. Lopez* (1995) and *United States v. Morrison* (2000), the U.S. Supreme Court rejected attempts by federal authorities to intrude on traditional state areas such as police powers and criminal law. The impact of these cases was to maintain state power and, concurrently, the power of state courts.

Both the *Lopez* and *Morrison* cases limited the scope of Congress's ability to interfere with state police powers. The *Lopez* decision invalidated sections of the Gun-Free School Zone Act. The congressional act made it a crime to possess a gun within a school zone. However, the Supreme Court ruled that firearm regulation was traditionally a state responsibility and Congress's commerce powers did not include the power to regulate internal state criminal codes. A few years later, the U.S. Congress passed the Violence Against Women Act, which allowed victims of sexual assault to sue their assailants in state civil courts. The Supreme Court rejected this part of the law with the same reasoning as *Lopez*.

The indirect result of the supremacy clause is that state courts have the power of judicial review over any state law that is accused of violating the U.S. Constitution. Judicial review is the ability to invalidate laws that conflict with constitutional law. Thus, state courts have the power to reject the laws passed by their state legislatures if they determine those laws conflict with the U.S. Constitution or any other federal laws.

In 1995, for example, the California Supreme Court used the supremacy clause to reject state legislation regarding credit card interest rates. In *Smiley v. Citibank*, the Court ruled that certain California rules relating to interest rates were invalid because they conflicted with federally mandated rules about interest rates. Eight years later, in *White v. Davis*, the same court ordered the California state government to pay all its nonexempt employees despite its failure to pass an appropriations bill.

Fearing the Power of the Federal Courts

In 1788, after the Constitution was drafted in Philadelphia, the document was sent out to the respective states for ratification. During the ratification debates, a group of citizens known as the Anti-Federalists was opposed to the adoption of the new constitution. The supremacy clause was one of many reasons the Anti-Federalists opposed the Constitution because they believed it would be used by the U.S. Supreme Court to overrule the decisions made by state courts. Robert Yates, writing under the pseudonym "Brutus" claimed:

> The powers of these [federal courts] are very extensive. It is easy to see, that in the common course of things, these courts will eclipse the dignity, and take away from the respectability, of the state courts. These courts will be, in themselves, totally independent of the states . . . they will swallow up all the powers of the courts in the respective states. (Constitution Society 2016)

While Yates' fears about the impact of such a development are open for debate, it cannot be denied that federal courts have used the supremacy clause to contravene the will of state courts.

Grants of Jurisdiction

Jurisdiction is the power to hear and determine a case. State courts are granted jurisdiction by either state constitutions or state statutes. Without jurisdiction, courts have no legal authority to compel parties to carry out any action or any authority to interpret statutes. There are several types of jurisdiction, and each type confers a specific amount of authority.

In Personam

In personam jurisdiction is based on geography. Courts have in personam jurisdiction over a party to a case simply as a result of that party's physical presence in the state. For example, Montana state courts have jurisdiction over Montana residents because those residents live in Montana. In personam jurisdiction also includes nonresidents who have met the "minimum contacts" test. The minimum contacts doctrine states that if an individual has had sufficient contacts with entities within a state, even if the person does not live in that state, that person is under state jurisdiction. Common actions that establish minimum contacts are doing business within a state, advertising within a state, or accepting insurance payments from a state. Individuals can also establish in personam jurisdiction through their own consent. Residents of one state may choose to file suit in another state. By choosing to file in a state in which one is not a resident, the law assumes that one has consented to that jurisdiction. And, finally, in personam jurisdiction can be established through long arm statutes. Long arm statutes establish jurisdiction over nonresidents if the cause of action affects local plaintiffs. The most common use of long arm statutes is to give local courts jurisdiction over parties to lawsuits from other states who have been involved in local auto accidents.

In Rem

State courts also have in rem jurisdiction. The court obtains in rem jurisdiction as a result of property being located within its state. Individuals may live in one state but own property in another. In these and other cases, state courts have in rem jurisdiction over such local property regardless of the residency of the owner. State courts often use their in rem jurisdiction to issue liens, foreclose property, or garnish income.

Legal Culture and Approaches to Interpretation

State constitutions and state statutes grant state courts their jurisdictions and powers of enforcement. However, individual justices interpret those grants of power differently. The way a judge interprets a grant of power will affect the level of authority state courts possess. Some judges prefer to interpret their powers very narrowly and limit their use of judicial power. Other judges prefer to take a broad interpretation of their grants of authority and wield their judicial power more comprehensively.

Judicial Restraint

Judges who impose a self-limitation on their use of judicial power follow a philosophy of *judicial restraint*. Judges who adopt this interpretive philosophy believe that courts should try to limit their roles in governance. They feel that democratically elected representatives have the primary responsibility for creating laws in their state. Judges who believe in judicial restraint will only interfere in the lawmaking process if a state legislature has clearly violated its own constitution, or written a law so vaguely that judges must interpret it for the law to have any effect. Additionally, judges who believe in judicial restraint feel that judges should interpret the law, but not write the law. Therefore, they refrain from drafting common law. Courts create common law when they establish new legal requirements in their written opinions. Finally, judges who follow judicial restraint fervently believe in the concept of separation of powers and therefore try to avoid imposing their judicial will on the other branches of government.

Judicial Activism

In contrast, judges who assume a greater role in the governing process advocate a philosophy of *judicial activism*. Although the issue of judicial activism is most highly publicized at the federal level, as decisions handed down by appeals courts and the U.S. Supreme Court impact large regional populations or even the entire nation, it is also heavily debated at the state level.

Proponents of judicial activism argue that judges need to assert themselves into the political process in three ways. Activist courts are more likely to invalidate legislation (judicial review), write their own laws (common law), and create new constitutional rights such as privacy. State judges who adopt an activist approach to legal interpretation, however, sometimes suffer electoral reprisals at the hands of voters. Whereas federal judges are appointed for life, most state constitutions have recall provisions and require judges to face periodic retention elections. In 1986, California voters recalled three sitting supreme court justices, including the Chief Justice Rose Bird. The voters were reacting to a variety of activist decisions, the most salient of which were repeated refusals to implement the state's death penalty statutes and support for allegedly "onerous" business regulations. The successful recall had a direct impact on the way the California Supreme Court applies the death penalty. After the recall, the new judges were much more likely to uphold death penalty sentences. Three decades later, supreme court justices at the state level still risk the wrath of voters—and the interest groups that rouse those voters to action—when they make rulings on controversial issues. In 2010, for example, three Iowa Supreme Court justices lost re-election after declaring in a unanimous opinion that Iowa's state constitution protected the right of gay couples to marry. The successful drive to remove those justices from the Iowa Supreme Court bench was attributed in considerable measure to campaign spending from national interest groups opposed to gay marriage, such as the National Organization for Marriage. Such incidents show that expensive political advertising and campaigns for and against prospective and sitting justices and judges can have an impact on state judicial systems.

Activist judges reject the notion that only legislatures should write law. Activist judges believe that constitutions outline broad goals and visions, but courts must craft specific details and legal procedures when they issue written opinions.

Activist judges may also create new rights that are not expressly delineated in the state constitution. For example, many courts have declared that individuals have a right to privacy even though their state constitutions do not specifically register a "right to privacy" anywhere in the text. Some activist judges use judicially created common law to grant other rights. For instance, the Massachusetts Supreme Court established the right of homosexuals to marry. The court did this by interpreting, very broadly, the text of its constitution, in addition to previously established common law.

Limits of State Court Authority

Just as state constitutions, the federal Constitution, and state legislatures empower state courts, they also serve to limit the power of state courts. State legislatures limit the discretion of judges, state constitutions limit the jurisdiction of state courts, and the U.S. Constitution mandates that state courts enforce federal law.

Legislative Limits on State Courts

State legislatures are typically responsible for determining the basic nuts-and-bolts aspects of state courts. Legislatures determine how many judges will make up a court, the judges' salaries, and the structure of the public defender system.

Judges are also limited in the punishments they can dispense. Whereas judges have considerable discretion over what types of evidence and testimony can be heard in their courtrooms, state legislatures have more control over the punishment phase of trials. Legislatures, not courts, have the power to determine which crimes are classified as misdemeanors or felonies. Misdemeanors carry smaller punishments than felony convictions. Concurrently, legislatures determine the range of punishments that are available for judges to impose on the guilty. State judges have some latitude when it comes to punishment, but the upper and lower limits are set by the legislature.

During the 1990s, state legislatures and citizens have moved to limit further the discretion of courts in the punishment phase of trials. Many state legislatures, or citizen ballot measures, imposed mandatory minimum sentencing laws. These laws require that judges impose a certain level of punishment regardless of what the trial judge thinks. By 1995, 24 states had added three-strikes laws to their criminal statutes. Many state judges objected to mandatory minimum sentences. They argue that judges are sometimes forced to impose unfair sentences and that court dockets and state prisons are becoming overwhelmed. In the 2010s, these criticisms have gained increased traction with both liberal and conservative lawmakers, activists, and voters who have expressed concern that the era of "mass incarceration" that began in the 1990s has been too destructive of families and communities, and costs far too much. As a result, sentencing mandates have come under particular scrutiny in the general push for prison sentencing reforms.

Federal Limitations on State Courts

The federal government also imposes limitations on state court power. The most fundamental limitation is the requirement that state judges enforce federal law. In this respect, the supremacy clause is a double-edged sword. From one standpoint, the clause empowers state judges to invalidate state laws. However, the supremacy clause also mandates that state judges abide by constitutional standards and federal statutory law. Such a requirement inherently limits the discretion of state courts. For example, in the late 1950s—before the U.S. Supreme Court began using the incorporation doctrine to apply rights' protections of the Fourth, Fifth, and Sixth Amendments against the actions of state governments—many state courts and judges had considerable latitude on issues such as admission of evidence and testimony, providing counsel to defendants, sanctioning interrogation techniques, determining the makeup of juries, and other criminal procedures. However, with landmark cases such as *Mapp v. Ohio* (1961), *Gideon v. Wainwright* (1963), and *Escobedo v. Illinois* (1964), the Warren Court established new mandates on criminal procedures that state courts were required to enforce. At the time, many state judges criticized the federal court for intruding on state court prerogatives. Despite some initial resistance, all state courts now accept these federal mandates. The interaction between federal and state courts is called *judicial federalism*.

Federal law can also limit the power of state courts through a doctrine known as *preemption*. Preemption doctrine states that when the U.S. Congress passes legislation, that legislation takes precedence over, or preempts, state law on the same topic. Therefore, when state law conflicts with federal law, federal law triumphs. Another way to view preemption doctrine is to see it as a seizure of jurisdiction. As noted earlier, one of the sources of state court power is the constitutional grant of jurisdiction. Preemption is the federal government taking jurisdiction away from state courts. Therefore, every time the federal government enacts laws that preempt state laws, state courts lose the jurisdiction to resolve claims that fall under the scope of that legislation.

Supreme Court's Defendants' Rights Rulings Gain Local Acceptance

In *Gideon v. Wainwright* (1963), the Supreme Court ruled that not only are defendants entitled to an attorney, but that the state must provide attorneys to defendants who cannot afford to pay for one. In *Escobedo v. Illinois* (1964), the Supreme

Court went a step further and mandated that states must make attorneys available to defendants as soon as the interrogation process begins, as opposed to after a defendant is formally indicted. At the time, both of these decisions attracted the ire of many state supreme courts. However, today, these cases are generally accepted as fundamental tenets of criminal due process.

Two other areas in which preemption doctrine has limited the power of state courts are labor law and medical law. In terms of labor law, many plaintiffs file suit in state court when they feel their labor rights have been violated. Often, there are specific state statutes that encourage plaintiffs to file in state court. However, Congress's passage of the National Labor Relations Act (NLRA) and its subsequent amendments has preempted much labor law away from states and therefore state courts. In *Burton v. Covenant Care* (2002), an employee filed suit in a California court after she was fired for discussing her wage information with other employees. However, the California appellate court refused to rule on the case because it had no jurisdiction to do so. The NLRA had preempted that authority away from state courts.

The same situation has confronted state suits regarding medical care provided by health maintenance organizations (HMOs) and managed care organizations (MCOs). Many of these suits are rejected by state courts because they lack the authority to hear such cases. The Employee Retirement Income Security Act (ERISA) of 1974 shifted the jurisdiction for these types of cases to federal court. Therefore, when plaintiffs attempt to sue for malpractice in state courts, HMO defendants usually move the case to federal court under the preemption doctrine.

THE ROLE OF STATE COURTS AND JURIES

There are many different types of state courts. Some state courts, called limited jurisdiction courts, deal only with specific issues. For example, there are traffic courts, probate courts, small-claims courts, and juvenile courts. Hawaii even has a water court to hear cases just about water rights. Each of the aforementioned courts adjudicate only those disputes that fall within their jurisdictions and areas of law. In contrast, other state courts, called general jurisdiction courts, hear all types of cases. In addition, general jurisdiction courts address larger issues such as the interpretation of state statutes and the state constitution.

State court systems also rely on juries to help adjudicate conflicts. In some courts, such as small-claims courts, judges rely on their own judgment to determine the outcome of a case. However, in other courts, judges rely on juries to determine the guilt or innocence of a defendant. As there are different types of courts, there are also different types of juries, each serving different legal purposes. State courts use both grand juries and petit juries. Grand juries decide whether the state has enough evidence against a defendant to issue an indictment, but petit juries decide questions of fact, such as the guilt or innocence of a defendant.

Courts of Original Jurisdiction

Legal disputes are heard in the first instance in courts of original jurisdiction. These courts admit evidence and hear testimony from participants in the case. It is said that courts of original jurisdiction hear questions of fact not questions of law. This means that original jurisdiction courts decide issues such as the following: Is the defendant guilty? Who should have custody of the child? Who is responsible for the property damage, and how much should they pay? Courts of original jurisdiction do not entertain questions such as the following: Is this law constitutional? How should this vague statute be interpreted? Does the governor have the power to do that? These are questions of law that are left to courts with appellate jurisdiction.

State court systems typically have two types of original jurisdiction courts. Limited jurisdiction courts only hear certain types of cases. As noted earlier, traffic courts only hear cases involving traffic accidents. They do not hear child custody cases or corporate tort cases. Their jurisdiction is limited to traffic cases. Many states also have general jurisdiction courts. These courts hear all types of cases, from criminal cases to tort cases to family law cases. As long as the issue deals with a question of fact, a general jurisdiction court has the authority to adjudicate the case.

Courts of Appellate Jurisdiction

Appellate courts entertain questions of law. In other words, they accept as true all the issues of fact that have been determined by courts of original jurisdiction. Appellate courts accept appeals from lower courts only if there is a question about the validity or interpretation of statutory law or constitutional law. For example, criminal suspects are found guilty or not guilty in a court of original jurisdiction. The defendant's innocence or guilt is a question of fact. On appeal, a convicted defendant can raise issues of law but may not revisit questions of guilt or innocence. An appellant may challenge a lower court's interpretation of a statute or the constitutionality of a statute. An appellant may argue that Fourth Amendment or other procedural rights were violated. These questions do not address the guilt or innocence of the defendant; they simply question the validity of the law or its interpretation.

Typically, legislatures draft generally worded or even vague statutes. Legislators cannot foresee every circumstance for which the law may need to apply. Vague or general statutes may not be specific enough to provide sufficient guidance to courts that are asked to apply such statutes to specific circumstances.

The role of appellate courts is to draft common law that will provide specific ways to interpret vague statutes. For example, many states require that special education students be educated in the least restrictive environment. However, many lower court judges have a difficult time determining what constitutes a "least restrictive environment." It is the role of appellate courts to create specific criteria to determine what schools need to provide to create a least restrictive environment. The common law developed by appellate courts is then implemented by lower courts of original jurisdiction. In a legal sense, appellate courts write the rules and original jurisdiction courts enforce the rules.

Appellate courts can also invalidate statutes passed by the legislature by using the power of judicial review. Original jurisdiction courts do not have the power of judicial review. Lower courts must enforce statutes as they are written. However, appellate courts may nullify laws in their entirety or just selective provisions of the law. Some states, such as Alabama and Tennessee, have two appellate court systems—one for criminal appeals and a second for civil appeals. Such a system allows judges to specialize in one field of law.

State Supreme Courts—The Courts of Last Resort

Every state has a supreme court, also sometimes known as a court of last resort (COLR). Supreme courts are so termed because there are no further appeals after a case is heard in a COLR. Not all states refer to their COLR as a supreme court. For example, Maryland simply refers to its highest court as the court of appeals. In Oklahoma, there are two supreme courts: one for criminal appeals and one for civil appeals. Supreme courts are a special type of appellate court (supreme courts have limited original jurisdiction in select areas of law). If a defendant or plaintiff loses a case in a lower appellate court, that party to the case can appeal to the state supreme court. Other than being the highest court in the state, supreme courts function just like other appellate courts.

State supreme courts have either mandatory jurisdiction or discretionary jurisdiction. Supreme courts with mandatory jurisdiction must accept and adjudicate appeals cases. In cases where the court's jurisdiction is discretionary, it has the option of refusing to hear the case. In general, state supreme courts have mandatory jurisdiction in some areas of law and discretionary jurisdiction in other areas of law. Although the rules regarding mandatory and discretionary jurisdiction change from state to state, some general patterns exist. Typically, smaller states, where the volume of cases is low, have supreme courts with mandatory jurisdiction. In larger states, where the case volume is higher, mandatory jurisdiction usually is reserved for civil cases exceeding a certain value, death penalty appeals, felony convictions, and administrative agency decisions. Supreme courts often have discretionary jurisdiction over appeals from cases dealing with small claims, minor criminal offenses, and many types of juvenile cases.

When studying state court systems, it is important to remember that no two states conduct their judicial affairs exactly alike. States take different approaches to creating limited jurisdiction courts, appellate jurisdiction courts, and courts of last resort. The structure of the state court system influences what roles and functions the different types of courts perform. In states with limited jurisdiction courts, judges can specialize in one field of law. Because states create both original and appellate jurisdiction courts, some judges concentrate on questions of fact while other judges concentrate on questions of law.

In states with mostly discretionary jurisdiction, courts have the ability to set the legal agenda. Courts with discretionary jurisdiction can refuse to hear some cases but select others. The ability to set the legal agenda is often an underestimated power of courts. Agenda-setting power is the ability to determine which political and legal issues the state will focus on. Courts can signal to politicians, attorneys, and potential litigants which issues the court considers important and which issues it does not. For example, a court may refuse to hear business regulation cases but accept civil rights cases. In doing so, the court sets the agenda. The court signals to society at large that certain issues will command the court's attention while others will not. As a result, it is possible that some litigants will elect not to bring their cases to court, but other will when they see that the court has signaled its interest in a specific field of law. In this way, the court can serve as a catalyst for pushing some areas of law and atrophying others.

Grand and Petit Juries

The American legal system uses two different types of juries. The petit jury is the most familiar to the casual legal observer. Petit juries determine issues of fact in criminal and civil proceedings. Simply put, petit juries declare the guilt or innocence of criminal defendants or determine the liability or lack of liability for civil defendants. In some states and in some cases, petit juries impose sentences on guilty defendants. In other states, juries may only recommend sentences but the presiding judge makes the final determination. In civil trials, petit juries can impose damages.

Grand juries serve a different legal purpose by determining whether the state has the legal authority to issue indictments. Grand juries serve as a check on the discretion of state prosecutors and police officials. In the American legal system, police officers collect evidence and turn that evidence over to a prosecuting attorney. The prosecuting attorney decides if there is enough evidence to justify a trial. However, in cases when a more serious crime has been committed, the prosecuting attorney may not make that decision alone. The prosecuting attorney must present the evidence before a grand jury and request an indictment. The grand jury examines the evidence and even hears witnesses.

If, after hearing the state's evidence, the grand jury decides there is enough evidence to justify a trial, it will issue an indictment. Issuing an indictment does not indicate that the grand jury believes the defendant is guilty. It simply indicates the grand jury felt there was enough evidence to merit a trial with a petit jury.

Petit Juries

Petit juries typically consist of 12 members of the community who are required to sit for the duration of one case. In some rare cases, state judicial systems allow 6-person juries. To find a defendant criminally guilty, almost all states require that the jury be unanimous. However, the U.S. Supreme Court has held nonunanimous jury verdicts constitutional.

Grand Juries

Grand juries are so called because they impanel more jurors; typically, 23 people compose a grand jury. Grand juries meet and hear evidence in secret for several reasons: (1) to ensure that individuals whose indictment is being considered will not flee; (2) to prevent subornation of perjury or tampering with the witnesses who may testify before the grand jury and later appear at the trial of those indicted by it; (3) to encourage honest disclosures by witness; and, (4) to protect the reputations of innocent individuals when the grand juries refuse to indict them.

The Fifth Amendment to the U.S. Constitution mandates that grand juries be used in the federal legal system. The Fifth Amendment states, "No person shall be held to answer for a capital or otherwise infamous crime, unless on a presentment or indictment of a Grand Jury, except in cases arising in the land or naval forces, or in the Militia, when in actual service in time of War or public danger. . . ." However, unlike most provisions in the Bill of Rights, the grand jury provision has never been incorporated to the states. Therefore, state court systems are not required by the Constitution to use grand juries, but most do.

THE WORK OF STATE COURTS

In the United States, the federal courts, especially the U.S. Supreme Court, get most of the attention. The national media tend to focus on issues that affect all Americans, and legal decisions handed down in one state rarely qualify. The reality, however, is that state courts do most of the heavy lifting in America's legal system. State courts hear more cases, hand down more decisions, and adjudicate a wider field of legal questions than federal courts.

To begin with, the sheer size of the state court system dwarfs the federal system. State courts have more judges and hand down more decisions. In 2012, the federal courts employed 677 district judges, 179 appeals court judges, 9 U.S. Court of International Trade justices, and 9 Supreme Court justices for a total of 874 judges. Each year, those judges receive as many as 3 million filings. However, that pales next to the number of legal filings processed by state courts every year. According to the Court Statistics Project (CSP 2010), a total of 31,134 state judges and justices (including 356 sitting on courts of last resort; 1,013 in intermediate appellate courts; 11,860 in general jurisdiction courts; and 17,905 in limited jurisdiction courts) processed 103.5 million cases in 2010. About 2 out of 3 of those cases—68 million—were heard in limited jurisdiction courts, while 35 million were processed in general jurisdiction and single-tiered courts.

Not only is the sheer size of the state court systems larger than the federal court system, state courts adjudicate a wider range of legal issues. State courts deal with private conflicts such as torts, contracts, death penalty appeals, attorney discipline, custody hearings, small claims, probate, divorce applications, criminal trials, and juvenile trials. To better understand state court systems, it is helpful to categorize state court workloads into four general divisions. State courts adjudicate criminal proceedings, civil proceedings, family law, and appeals. In recent years, the overwhelming number of private disputes has led courts to encourage alternative methods for resolving disputes. Therefore, a complete study of state courts includes an examination of alternative dispute resolution (ADR) methods, which are discussed later in this chapter.

State courts do more than just hear private disagreements. State courts also hear public law cases. Public law is an area in which the courts must rule on the law itself, not a citizen's violation of the law. For example, state courts can use their powers of judicial review to invalidate legislative acts, interpret vague clauses in state laws, and even write new laws known as common law. State courts can use these same powers to invalidate or interpret laws passed by the people themselves. Many state constitutions allow for direct democracy where citizens can write state ballot measures enacting their own laws. Just like legislative acts, state courts must interpret these new laws. Every time a state court invalidates a law, interprets a law, or writes new common law, it makes public policy.

Criminal Proceedings

Criminal law is predominantly the responsibility of state courts. Because the federal Constitution was designed to impart only specific and enumerated powers to the national government, states were left relatively undisturbed in the area of criminal law. Beginning with the New Deal and accelerating during the civil rights movement, the federal government started using its commerce clause powers as a vehicle to create federal police powers. Despite these trends, state courts still adjudicate most criminal law.

Criminal law can be subdivided into two categories: felonies and misdemeanors. A felony is a more serious crime than a misdemeanor. Felonies typically include crimes such as murder, rape, robbery, and arson. One cannot be charged with a felony unless a separate grand jury allows the prosecutor to file charges. Those convicted of a felony usually serve serious prison terms. Misdemeanors are lesser crimes and typically include petty crimes that inflict less than a certain dollar amount of damage. Prosecutors can file misdemeanor charges without the approval of a grand jury. Sometimes crimes once identified as misdemeanors become felonies. Many states once listed driving under the influence (DUI) as a misdemeanor, but after drunk driving became more widely recognized as a serious issue, states increasingly began to classify DUIs as felonies.

Judges within a state criminal court system are responsible for a variety of functions. Criminal proceedings usually begin with a preliminary hearing or a grand jury indictment. Absent a grand jury indictment, state judges can hold preliminary hearings to decide if there is enough evidence to warrant a trial. If the judge decides there is enough evidence to warrant a trial, the defendant is arraigned. At the arraignment, defendants are informed of charges against them, and the judge asks for a plea. After entering a plea, judges either set bail or remand the defendant to jail to await trial.

Before the trial begins, judges entertain pretrial motions. During this stage of a criminal proceeding, attorneys can make discovery motions and move that evidence be suppressed, and defense attorneys inform the judge of their defense strategy, such as insanity, self-defense, or some other legal defense.

After a trial begins, judges serve as an umpire between the prosecution and defense attorneys. They ensure that all evidence is submitted according to the rules of law. They rule on objections from attorneys. They make sure witnesses are only asked questions that conform to the rules of evidence. After all the evidence and testimony have been introduced, it is the judges' role to inform the juries about the nature of the law. Judges instruct juries on what criteria must be met in order to return a guilty verdict. If juries become deadlocked, the judge will work to overcome the stalemate without directly participating in the deliberations.

If the jury returns a guilty verdict, the judge is responsible for imposing a sentence. In some cases, the judge is solely responsible for the punishment phase of the trial. In other cases, juries recommend sentences to the judge.

Criminal law consumes more time and resources from state courts than civil matters because criminal defendants are guaranteed certain procedural rights in state and federal constitutions. For example, criminal defendants are guaranteed attorneys, jury trials, and an appeals process. Civil litigants do not have such procedural guarantees. One of the ways state courts overcome the burden of criminal trials is to use a procedure called plea bargaining.

Plea bargaining is a process in which attorneys for the defendant and the state compromise on charges and penalties. Typically, the attorney for the state or city offers to reduce the charges and promises to seek less serious penalties in return for a guilty plea from the defendant. If the defendant pleads guilty, a jury trial is not needed, and the process can move directly to the penalty phase. Only a small fraction (less than 5 percent) of all criminal cases actually end up before a jury. The vast majority of cases are either decided by plea bargains or evaporate with the dismissal of charges.

The turn toward plea bargaining has accelerated in recent years. The National Center for State Courts (2015) reported that in a study based on states that account for roughly a third of the country's overall population, the percentage of state felony cases that resulted in trials dropped from 8 percent in 1976 to 2.3 percent in 2009. The Center also reported that although total caseloads tripled during that time, the overall number of criminal trials (both jury trials and trials with judges determining guilt or innocence) only increased a small amount. These trends have been corroborated by the U.S. Bureau of Justice Statistics (Rosenmerkel and Durose 2010), which reported that 94 percent of all convictions in state felony cases are due to guilty pleas. As Matt Clarke (2013) of *Prison Legal News* noted:

> Federal data also indicated a sharp reduction in the percentage of cases that were dismissed or ended in acquittals. In 2009, nine of ten cases resulted in a plea bargain while one in twelve ended in dismissal. From 1979 to 2009, the acquittal rate dropped from one acquittal per 22 guilty pleas to one in 212 guilty pleas.

According to Clarke, legal experts say that these trends show that prosecutors who determine whether to press or dismiss charges against defendants have become more powerful than ever before: "Judges have lost discretion, and that discretion has accumulated in the hands of prosecutors, who now have the ultimate ability to shape the outcome," stated University of Utah law professor (and former prosecutor) Paul Cassell. "With mandatory minimums and other sentencing enhancements out there, prosecutors can often dictate the sentence that will be imposed."

Civil Proceedings

Civil proceedings are analogous to criminal proceedings. However, civil proceedings employ different legal standards and impose different sanctions. Because civil proceedings do not deal with criminal statutes, there are no arraignments, grand juries, and bail proceedings. Instead, civil proceedings begin with commencing a lawsuit and filing court documents that are called pleadings. During the pleading stage, parties to the lawsuit inform the court of the nature of their dispute. The plaintiff in the case issues a complaint, and the defendant offers an answer, or reply.

Similar to criminal proceedings, civil proceedings have pretrial motions where attorneys seek information about the case and try to end it by making discovery requests, indicating whom they plan to depose as witnesses, and moving for summary judgments. After the trial begins, civil trials are similar to criminal trials. Witnesses are called, evidence is introduced, and judges make rulings on the appropriateness of each. At the end of the trial, a judge or jury will decide the case.

A significant difference between criminal and civil proceedings is that civil proceedings have a much lower burden of proof standard. Criminal juries are required to find defendants guilty beyond a reasonable doubt. However, civil juries are held to lower standards. They may find a party responsible for damages simply based on a preponderance of the evidence. Second, civil juries do not impose prison sentences; they award monetary damages.

Tort Cases

When individuals or businesses claim they have suffered harm by another individual or business, they can file a lawsuit seeking compensation. Typically, these types of lawsuits are called tort cases. Tort cases are civil filings that seek monetary damages, not criminal punishment. In the past decade, national and state politicians have turned their attention to the tort system in America. A few high profile cases, in which large damages were awarded for seemingly trivial accidents, have made America's tort system a political issue.

Because the national and local media often highlight astronomically high tort awards, or frivolous cases, it is commonly assumed that state courts are overburdened by tort filings. The data, although not comprehensive, suggests qualified support for this contention. One contributing factor to the increase in tort filings was the liberalization of standing requirements. Courts require that a plaintiff have standing before filing a lawsuit. Prior to the 1970s, litigants had to show that they had personally suffered direct harm before they could file a suit. Such a standard prevented taxpayers or special interest groups from suing the government over public policy. Thereafter, however, many states, by statute, constitutional amendment, or court decision, eased their standing requirements to allow more legal suits.

In addition, in the 1970s, courts began to liberalize the use of punitive damages. Before the 1970s, punitive damages were only awarded for intentional torts. These were torts where the defendant intentionally harmed another individual. Eventually, the courts lowered the standard to gross negligence. Under this standard, plaintiffs did not have to prove a tort was intentionally committed; they only had to show that defendants acted without regard for others. When the legal standard was lowered, the number of tort filings began to increase.

Calls for state tort reform often follow high-profile cases in which juries have awarded seemingly astronomical awards for trivial actions. One of the most notorious of these cases took place in 1992, when 79-year-old Stella Liebeck of Albuquerque, New Mexico, spilled a cup of McDonald's coffee in her lap while riding in her grandson's sports car (Banks and O'Brien 2015, 233; Haltom and McCann 2004). Claiming the coffee was too hot, she successfully sued the restaurant for $200,000 in compensatory damages and an additional $2.7 million in punitive damages. Critics argued that Liebeck was responsible for spilling the coffee on herself, and, regardless of fault, the award was too high. The story was picked up by the national media and repeated so often that it has become part of American pop culture. Such high-profile cases are clearly a driver of dissatisfaction with state tort systems, especially within the business community and among pro-business lawmakers.

Since the mid-1990s, statistical data indicate that tort filings have shown a modest decline. Many scholars attribute the decline to the host of tort reform measures, most of them crafted and supported by the GOP (Republican Party), that swept into the states in the early 1990s. In fact, in a study of 30 states between 1992 and 2001, there was an average decline in tort filings by 15 percent. One of the reasons people sometimes misinterpret the tort filing data is that they fail to take into account an increase in population over time. Simply totaling the number of medical malpractice suits between 1992 and 2001 shows a 24 percent increase. However, if population increases are accounted for, the number of malpractice filings per 100,000 citizens actually fell. These trends continued through the G. W. Bush administration as well. According to the National Center for State Courts (2015), tort case filings decreased by 25 percent from 1999 to 2008 in 13 general jurisdiction courts examined by the NCSC, even as contract cases in those same courts increased by 63 percent.

Overall tort costs, meanwhile, leveled off or even decreased for much of George W. Bush's second term and Barack Obama's first term. According to a 2011 study by Towers Watson, a business investment and consulting firm, the average annual increase in tort costs in the United States exceeded 13 percent in both 2001 and 2002; however, from 2005 to 2009, the average annual increase never exceeded 2.1 percent (and in two of those years, tort costs actually decreased). While this trend was interrupted in 2010 by a 5.1 percent increase in U.S. tort costs, the study explained that the uptick was misleading: "The increase is attributable to the April 2010 Deepwater Horizon drilling explosion and resulting oil spill in the Gulf of Mexico. Absent the costs from this event, tort costs would have shown an overall decrease of 2.4 percent in 2010."

A 2015 study by the National Center for State Courts, meanwhile, found that:

High-value tort and commercial contract disputes are the predominant focus of contemporary debates . . . collectively they comprised only a small proportion of the [caseloads in its study]. In contrast, nearly two-thirds (64 percent) were contract cases, and more than half of those were debt collection (37 percent) and landlord/tenant cases (29 percent). An additional 16 percent were small claims cases involving disputes valued at $12,000 or less, and 9 percent were characterized as 'other civil' cases involving agency appeals and domestic or criminal-related cases. Only *7 percent were tort cases* [emphasis added] and only one percent were real property cases. (iii)

Contracts

Contracts are promises, or a set of promises, between two participants in which both participants agree to fulfill certain obligations. Contracts can be written or oral. People who write and sign contracts devote considerable effort to ensuring that contracts anticipate every possible contingency. Despite that effort, there are unforeseen circumstances that contracts do not anticipate. When that happens, judges must interpret contracts and decide which parties to the contract bear certain obligations.

In other circumstances, the guidelines of the contract are perfectly clear, but one or more parties to the contract refuse to meet their obligations. In such cases, when asked, judges step in and require that delinquent parties meet their obligations. Sometimes, this might require a judge to seize property or other assets to compensate individuals who have entered into a contract.

State courts are also called on, in appropriate cases, to declare contracts void. In certain instances, contracts can be entered into without the legal consent of one of the parties. Courts have held that consent is absent when one of the parties was under duress or undue influence. Courts also void contracts where one of the parties was subject to fraud or misrepresentation.

Family Law

Family law is different from criminal law in that the main purpose of family law is neither to punish nor to award damages. Family law is more concerned with overseeing the legal aspects of marriage, mediating family disputes, and insuring that family members are protected. Judges involved in family law grant marriages and divorces, award child custody after divorce, regulate adoptions, and decide paternity responsibilities.

Domestic Relations

Domestic relations include most of the laws that regulate relationships between families. In fact, many people refer to domestic relations law as family law. State courts deal with many different types of domestic relations' legal matters. Courts grant divorces between married couples, decide custody issues when the parties to the divorce have children, resolve paternity claims, establish child support payments, and regulate adoptions. Paternity hearings are the most common type of domestic relations case.

Juvenile Cases

Juvenile courts are limited jurisdiction courts that adjudicate cases in which a minor has committed a crime or when a minor needs protection from abusive or neglectful guardians. Usually, anyone under the age of 17 is eligible for juvenile court. In most cases, juvenile records are kept sealed until the minor reaches adulthood, at which point, they are expunged. The rationale is to allow children who have committed crimes to have a fresh start when they enter adulthood. However, as it has become more common for minors to commit serious offenses such as murder, many states have lowered the age at which a person can be considered an adult. Deciding when a child should be considered an adult and prosecuted in adult courts has thus become an enormously controversial issue in many states.

Judges who work for juvenile courts often take a greater interest in the background and environment of the child than they would if they were overseeing an adult case. Many juvenile court judges see their role as different from judges in criminal courts. Juvenile court judges rely heavily on officers of the court, such as probation officers, doctors, and psychologists, for information about the juvenile case before them. Juvenile court judges often use the information to craft a ruling designed to rehabilitate the child and direct them into a more positive direction. For most nonviolent crimes, juvenile courts are less interested in punishment (though that is part of the equation) than they are in forms of intervention designed to steer offenders onto a more law-abiding and productive path. For example, it is common for juvenile court judges to require defendants to write letters of apology or earn money to compensate the victims of their crimes. Sentences often include community service or mandatory counseling, with incarceration reserved for more serious crimes such as rape, assault, robbery, drug offenses, and murder.

Over the past half century, juvenile court delinquency caseloads have undergone dramatic changes, with the years from 1960 to 1997 seeing rapid and steady increase, and the years 1998 to 2013 experiencing a similarly steady downturn. All told, state courts with juvenile jurisdiction handled an estimated 1.058 million delinquency cases, according to the National Center for Juvenile Justice's *Juvenile Court Statistics 2013* (delinquency offenses are acts committed by juveniles that would have qualified for criminal prosecution if committed). According to one report by the National Center for Juvenile Justice, U.S. courts processed about 1,100 delinquency cases a day in 1960. Fifty-three years later, juvenile courts handled approximately 2,900 such cases each day. Much of that increase came after the 1960s, though. In fact, between 1991 and 2013, the number of cases decreased for all juvenile offense categories, including crimes against property (by 59 percent), crime against persons (35 percent), public order crimes (29 percent), and drug-related crimes (26 percent) (Hockenberry and Puzzanchera 2015).

Juvenile status offense cases—cases in which the law is violated only because the person engaged in the activity is a minor, such as drinking alcohol, truancy, curfew violations, or running away from home—also have declined from the mid-1990s and afterward. The National Center for Juvenile Justice reported that in 2013, U.S. courts with juvenile jurisdiction petitioned and formally disposed of an estimated 109,000 status offense cases, a 13 percent decrease from 1995 (Hockenberry and Puzzanchera 2015).

State Appeals Courts

Like the federal court system, state court systems include appellate courts that entertain questions of law and not facts. Tort, contract, criminal, domestic, and juvenile cases are heard in trial courts that only entertain questions of fact. However, participants in trial courts often disagree with the rulings or procedures as they were conducted in the trial court. Such individuals can seek a remedy in appellate court by filing appeals. Appellate court judges review lower court trials and decide if the participants' procedural rights were protected. If they find errors by the lower courts, appellate courts can craft remedies and refer the cases back to the trial courts. Appellate court judges also reexamine how lower court judges have interpreted statutes or constitutional provisions. If an appellate court disagrees with the way a lower court has interpreted a statute, it can remand the case to the lower court. The remand usually comes with instructions on how the lower courts should have interpreted the statute or constitutional provision.

Appellate courts hear both mandatory and discretionary appeals. Appellate courts must accept mandatory appeals but can elect not to hear discretionary appeals. All death penalty appeals are mandatory appeals. The composition of these appeals cases depends on the type of appellate court. Civil cases make up about 47 percent of the cases intermediate appeals courts (appeals courts one level below supreme courts) hear, and criminal cases make up an additional 40 percent. Other administrative cases and writs for habeas corpus make up the rest of the caseload. Habeas corpus writs ask courts to determine the legality of a detainee's confinement. If courts find that an individual has been illegally detained, they can issue such a writ demanding that the individual be released (see National Center for State Courts 2016).

State Supreme Courts

Although a state supreme court is just a special type of appellate court, these courts deserve special attention because they are courts of last resort. In addition, it is valuable to compare the workload of the federal Supreme Court with the workloads of state supreme courts.

State supreme courts are the final arbitrators of questions dealing with state law. The U.S. Supreme Court can only review a decision by a state supreme court if the case addresses some type of federal constitutional question. State supreme courts hear many more cases that the U.S. Supreme Court, but state supreme courts have much less discretion over their dockets.

Unlike state supreme courts, the U.S. Supreme Court has almost complete control over the cases it decides to hear. Therefore, the U.S. Supreme Court can grant or deny certiorari. Most state supreme courts have mandatory jurisdiction and, therefore, must grant an appeal to a variety of cases.

Three factors contribute to higher caseloads for state supreme courts. State statutes and constitutions may require mandatory jurisdiction for many types of cases. In contrast, after passage of the Judiciary Act of 1925 and subsequent amendments in 1988, the U.S. Supreme Court has very few mandatory cases. Therefore, state supreme courts are required by state law to hear more cases than federal law requires of the U.S. Supreme Court. In addition, all states grant mandatory jurisdiction in death penalty cases. Therefore, states that have the death penalty also tend to have supreme courts with higher caseloads. Lastly, most states give their supreme courts original jurisdiction in a variety of cases. For example, Colorado, like many other states, gives its supreme court original jurisdiction over any controversies arising from reapportionment. Almost all states grant original jurisdiction in cases of attorney discipline. And, many other states, such as Ohio and Kansas, grant their supreme courts original jurisdiction in quo warranto, mandamus, and habeas corpus proceedings (see Ostrom and Hanson 2001).

Alternative Dispute Resolution

The evidence is overwhelming that state courts perform a significant amount of work for state governments. They adjudicate millions of legal claims and disputes each year that cover an extensive range of public policy issues. However, on many levels, state courts are becoming overburdened by the amount of filings they face each year. As a consequence of their workloads, fewer and fewer legal conflicts are resolved by an actual trial.

As court systems become clogged with so many cases, judges look to other ways to resolve conflicts. Often, judges encourage attorneys to reach out-of-court settlements so a trial will not be necessary. State prosecutors offer plea bargains to criminal defendants to avoid the need for a trial. To reduce the caseload further, courts have begun to encourage the use of alternative dispute resolution (ADR). ADR is a mechanism available for the resolution of a conflict without using the court system. ADR includes mediation, voluntary or mandatory arbitration, and settlement conferences.

Mediation is the process of using a neutral third party (a mediator) to assist differing parties in finding a resolution. Mediators have no formal power; they can only suggest options and help facilitate communication between parties. *Arbitration* is similar to mediation, except that the neutral third party (an arbitrator) has the power to enforce, or bind, the parties to his or her decision. Parties that elect to use arbitration engage in it voluntarily. Parties that are required to use arbitration, either by a signed contract or a state statute, engage in mandatory arbitration. *Settlement conferences* are also similar to mediation except that arbitrations typically convene and administer a settlement conference.

Not all state courts view ADR with the same degree of approval. While most courts accept that ADR reduces caseloads and is a cost-efficient method of conflict resolution, there is no consensus on the appropriate role of ADR as a replacement for legal proceedings. Most of the concern has focused on the legality of mutual arbitration agreements, sometimes called *cram down arbitration*. In response to increasing litigation costs, many employers require that new employees sign contracts in which employees waive their rights to resolve employment disputes in court. Instead, the employee agrees to mandatory arbitration. The U.S. Supreme Court, in *Gilmer v. Interstate/Johnson Lane Corp* (1991), upheld mandatory arbitration agreements in age discrimination cases. Some state supreme courts have followed the U.S. Supreme Court's lead. For example, the New Jersey Supreme Court held that disability discrimination suits were subject to mandatory arbitration agreements. The Texas Supreme Court also ruled that employers must accept mutual arbitration agreements and that the decision of the arbitrator carries the same weight as a court's legal decision. However, other state supreme courts have been more skeptical. California courts, for example, have shown some resistance to mandatory, or cram down, arbitration. In several cases, the California courts have ruled that certain cram down arbitration agreements are unconscionable and, therefore, unenforceable. Because ADR is relatively new to state courts, there will most likely be an adjustment period in which state legislatures and state courts craft a body of law that both promotes efficiency and protects individuals' civil rights.

State Courts Make Public Policy

Discussions about public policy typically focus on the role of the legislative and executive branches. Legislatures are most visible when they are drafting, debating, and enacting legislation. Governors are most prominent when they are signing bills into law or using their veto power to reject legislation. However, state courts also play a significant, but sometimes more subtle, role in crafting public policy. The two main avenues by which state courts create public policy is through the power of judicial review and the right to develop common law.

Judicial Review

Judicial review is the power of courts to invalidate any law enacted by the state if the court finds the law conflicts with the state constitution or U.S. Constitution. The power of judicial review gives courts the ability to act as a check on the power of other elected officials. However, courts cannot use the power of judicial review indiscriminately. First, courts must wait for a citizen to challenge a law before they may invalidate it. Because state courts with the power of judicial review have only appellate jurisdiction, they can only invalidate a law after it has become subject to a constitutional challenge. Governors, on the other hand, may veto a bill before it becomes a law. Second, governors may veto a law for any reason, including a simple dislike for the proposed legislation. Courts, however, are supposed to invalidate only those laws that expressly violate the state constitution or federal Constitution. Courts are not supposed to use their personal dislikes for a law as grounds for invalidating it. When courts invalidate laws quite frequently or use their own values to reject legislation, they are often called judicial activists.

Political debates in the United States about judicial activism are as old as the republic. Ever since Chief Justice John Marshall established the use of judicial review in American federal courts, there have been debates on how courts should use such power. Some argue that courts should defer to the legislature because the legislature is elected by the people. Individuals who advocate that position promote the concept of judicial restraint. Judicial activists believe that courts need to protect civil and other rights by invalidating any law that seems unjust, even if there are no specific provisions in the state constitution or federal Constitution that are violated. These arguments were outlined previously in the "Legal Culture and Approaches to Interpretation" section.

Despite the longstanding debate about the legitimacy of federal judicial review, state courts adopted the practice of judicial review early in American history and without much controversy. In the 1780s, the same decade the U.S. Constitution was ratified, five state courts confronted issues of judicial review. In four of those cases, the state supreme courts ruled they had the power to invalidate unconstitutional state legislation. By 1820, state supreme courts in 10 of the original 13 colonies had invalidated acts of their legislatures. One reason state courts may have been more comfortable with the process of judicial review was their history as royal or charter colonies of the British Crown. Prior to the American Revolution, legislative acts of a colonial legislature could be repealed by an act of Parliament, the king, or even a Privy Council. If colonial legislatures became too rebellious, the king or Parliament could revoke their colonial charter. Therefore, state legislatures had ample experience with judicial review prior to the establishment of post-revolutionary state constitutions or the drafting of the federal Constitution. In many ways, state supreme courts simply replaced English Privy Councils but maintained their same function (see Emmert 1988, 1992).

Despite early historical debates about judicial review, today, all courts use the power of judicial review to eliminate laws. Such an act has a profound effect on public policy. In the past, state courts have invalidated death penalty statutes, tort reform measures, changes to the criminal justice system, school funding legislation, restrictions on gay rights, and many other laws.

Common Law

There are two aspects of common law. First, courts are needed to interpret vague or undefined constitutional provisions. Legislatures cannot address every possible area of potential conflict. They need judges to follow general directives set forth by the legislature and fill in the gaps on their own. Second, courts are needed to create new law when they encounter a controversy without any statutory, administrative, or constitutional guidelines to follow. Sometimes issues arise that need to be adjudicated immediately, but the court has no guidance from the typical sources: precedent, statutes, and the state constitution. Sometimes judges need to be judicial innovators.

Interpretation of Statutes and Constitutions

State courts also have the authority to interpret all state statutes and constitutional provisions. Yet, constitutional clauses and legislative statutes often include vague terminology. Legislatures cannot foresee every possible conflict that may arise. For example, what is a *reasonable* search and seizure? What exactly constitutes *cruel and unusual* punishment? What type of behavior must one commit to be guilty of *gross negligence*? All these terms lack specific criteria. As a result, courts must issue judicial opinions that clarify vague terms.

The power to interpret laws is akin to the power to write laws. A constitutional provision may require "adequate spending" on education, but courts would then have the power to determine what exactly constitutes adequate spending. Under such a provision, courts would have the power to interpret such a law and then require specific levels of funding either per school district or per pupil. A legislature may pass a law holding contractors liable for injuries caused in work that is "inherently dangerous," but the state courts will decide which types of work qualify as inherently dangerous.

Judicial Innovation

Common law is a system of jurisprudence that is based on judicial precedent rather than statutory laws. Sometimes, however, courts encounter controversies in which there is little to guide them to a legal solution because the legislature has not anticipated the issue, administrative agencies have not drafted any rules concerning the issue, or courts have never created any precedent on the issue. These types of cases are often called cases of first impression. In cases such as this, courts need to draft their own laws.

An example of judicial innovation is the Massachusetts Supreme Court's ruling legalizing gay marriage. In 2001, several homosexual couples in Massachusetts applied for marriage licenses but were denied. The existing marriage statutes in Massachusetts were silent on the issue of gay marriage. The statutes simply establish minimum standards for obtaining a license, such as health and age, as well as banning marriage between relatives and those who are already married. However, the statute did not explicitly mention that marriage was only between a man and a woman, nor did the statute expressly forbid issuing a license to people of the same gender. Furthermore, the Massachusetts Supreme Court had no precedent from the state body of common law directly relating to gay marriage. Therefore, the court had to examine the state constitution and craft new law from scratch. The court, citing general constitutional clauses and some tangential precedents, decided that marriage between people of the same sex was protected by the Massachusetts Constitution.

Advisory Opinions

State supreme courts sometimes offer advisory opinions to state legislatures. There are times when a state legislature does not know if a proposed statute will comply with the state's constitution. In such a case, the legislature will ask the court to give its opinion as to whether a yet unpassed law would be upheld if it were subjected to a constitutional challenge. Legislatures seek advisory opinions to save time and anticipate the possible objections of the state supreme court. For example, in 2003, the Massachusetts Supreme Court held unconstitutional the state practice that only authorized marriage licenses for heterosexual couples. In confronting this ruling, the Massachusetts legislature was unsure if a new law that allowed civil unions, but not marriage licenses, for homosexual couples would comply with the court's ruling.

State Courts and Direct Democracy

Twenty-six U.S. states have some form of *direct democracy*, which is generally understood to mean one or more of the following: the right to draft and vote on ballot measures (initiatives), recall elected officials (recalls), and ratify or reject legislative bills (referendums). American states first started experimenting with direct democracy during the Populist era of the late 1800s, but the movement gained wider acceptance during the Progressive Era of the early 1900s. Therefore, many western states, which joined the Union after the Populist era, have some form of direct democracy as part of their constitutions. Eastern states gradually followed suit, and now some states in every region of the country have some form of direct democracy (see National Conference for State Legislatures 2016).

Direct democracy presents unique issues for state courts. Political activists who use direct democracy have to follow different rules than legislators. To qualify an initiative for the ballot, activists must collect signatures, draft ballot titles, and follow specific guidelines unique to the initiative process. Supreme courts almost never interfere with the internal mechanisms of a legislature, but state courts frequently oversee the initiative process. For example, most states require that ballot measures only address a *single subject*. This means that ballot measures may not change both the tax system and a completely unrelated criminal statute. Like other legal terms, single-subject is prone to many interpretations. It is very common for opponents of ballot measures to appeal to state courts claiming that a ballot measure addressed two subjects and then demand that the measure be invalidated.

Furthermore, many state ballot measures challenge basic civil rights that are protected by state constitutions or common law. For example, ballot measures have sought to limit rights related to abortion, homosexuality, immigrants, and criminal defendants. Most state courts are very protective of civil rights. Therefore, state courts nullify a much greater percentage of ballot measures than legislative statutes.

THE ENFORCEMENT POWER OF STATE COURTS

In *Federalist Papers*, No. 78 (1788), Alexander Hamilton described the U.S. Supreme Court as having "no influence over either the sword or the purse." Hamilton was suggesting that because the Court lacked an army or the power to tax and spend, it would be the "least dangerous branch" of government (Yale Law School 2016). To some extent, Hamilton was right, and his comments about the U.S. Supreme Court are equally applicable to state courts. However, if courts lack any real power, as Hamilton suggested, then they would have a difficult time enforcing their decisions. Yet, citizens have considerable faith in the court system to bring about justice, both in criminal and civil cases. Though Hamilton was right when he said that the courts lacked an army and spending power, it would be incorrect to assume that state courts lack any form of coercive and financial power. Every day, state courts issue rulings, and those rulings are enforced. In truth, state courts have considerable power to use the police powers of their state to enforce their directives, whether those take the form of imprisonment, financial penalties, or some other judgment.

In some respects, in fact, state courts do have the power of the "sword." State judges can use the services of law enforcement officers in their state. Judges can order police officers to seize individuals and property, and to carry out other types of judicial orders. Courts can also hold law enforcement officers at bay by withholding search or arrest warrants. Hamilton may have been right when he argued that courts do not have an army, but state courts definitely have armed individuals at their disposal. Additionally, state judges have the power to seize money and property from defendants. Through a variety of legal procedures, discussed in the following sections, state judges can transfer wealth from one party to another. Again, state courts may not have the power of the purse, but they do have the power to seize financial assets and transfer those assets to other individuals.

Judicial Orders

Before addressing the specific powers courts have to enforce their decisions, it is important to understand the types of orders judges issue. Judges issue temporary or permanent orders, and self-executing or nonself-executing orders.

Temporary and Permanent Orders

The difference between temporary and permanent orders is intuitive. *Temporary orders* impose some type of restraint on an individual for a limited amount of time. For example, a judge may issue a temporary injunction or a temporary restraining order. A temporary injunction or restraining order is a judicial order that temporarily bars a legal party from doing or continuing some type of action. A *permanent injunction*, on the other hand, would ban such actions permanently. Judges usually employ temporary orders to buy the court some time. Often, courts intervene in the middle of an ongoing process. If courts are forced to conduct an entire trial before taking any action, harmful behavior could continue. For instance, an individual being illegally evicted needs immediate relief from the court. It would not benefit society to allow illegal acts to proceed and then, afterward, declare them illegal. Temporary orders allow the court to hear evidence and testimony and then make a decision. After a final decision has been reached, the court will issue a permanent order.

Self-enforcing and Nonself-enforcing Orders

Some orders by state courts are self-enforcing, but others need external police power to carry them out. Judges do not personally seize assets or take people to jail. They need the assistance of police officers or other state-empowered officials. Judges grant damages to plaintiffs by simply issuing defendants a piece of paper. The paper itself does not facilitate the transfer of funds. A state officer must physically seize the defendant's assets. Orders such as these are *nonself-enforcing*. In contrast, some judicial orders take effect simply because the judge issues an order. These types of orders are *self-enforcing*. Sometimes participants in a political or legal conflict do not know their rights. They may seek a declaratory judgment from a court. A declaratory judgment simply explains an issue of law or indicates what rights exist for individuals. There is no need for an official of the state to enforce this type of decision.

Political Remedies

State courts essentially have two types of powers: they can seize money and assets from defendants, or they can order a defendant to cease a certain type of behavior. It is helpful to think of the first type of action as a civil remedy and the second type of action as a political remedy. Political remedies take many forms. The following sections identify and detail the most common political remedies.

Extraordinary Writs

There are two types of extraordinary writs: writs of mandamus and writs of prohibition. A *writ of mandamus* is a legal command from a court that orders a government official to fulfill his or her official duties properly. In fact, mandamus is Latin for "we command." Courts issue a writ of mandamus to compel an official to carry out some ministerial act that the court recognizes as an absolute duty. Often, administrative or elected officials have a certain amount of discretion as to how they perform their duties. Courts may order officials to carry out specific tasks with a mandamus order. Writs of mandamus are also used by higher courts to order lower courts to take some type of action. In very rare cases, defendants cannot wait for the appeals process. Instead, they need a higher court to order a lower court to engage in some proceeding prior to the lower court making its final decision.

A *writ of prohibition* is similar to a writ of mandamus. Instead of ordering a specific action, a writ of prohibition bars a specific action. Writs of prohibition can be issued by judges to prevent, for example, the state from suspending someone's driver's license or liquor license, to prevent a city council or county commissioner's ordinance from going into effect, and even to dismiss another judge from hearing a case if there is evidence he or she may be biased against the defendant.

Declaratory Judgments

A *declaratory judgment* is a ruling by a court that establishes the rights of parties engaged in a legal dispute, or expresses the opinion of a court about a question of law. Declaratory judgments simply inform; they do not order any specific action. Often, parties who are bound by a legal contract or subject to a state statute do not know their rights or responsibilities under the contract or statute. In such a case, they can appeal for a declaratory judgment. The court will then examine the contract or statute and deliver an opinion regarding the demands of the statute or contract.

The court also informs each party of its duties or rights. For example, the Maine statute on declaratory judgments states:

> Courts of record within their respective jurisdictions shall have power to declare rights, status and other legal relations whether or not further relief is or could be claimed. No action or proceeding shall be open to objection on the ground that a declaratory judgment or decree is prayed for. The declaration may be either affirmative or negative in form and effect. Such declarations shall have the force and effect of a final judgment or decree. (Maine Revised Statutes 2016)

The purpose of a declaratory judgment is to address disputes before they require further legal action. Often, legal disputes result from the fact that contracts or statutes are vague or fail to address an unforeseen event. In such a case, parties simply do not know what is required of them, or there is a disagreement between parties as to the obligations of each. Declaratory judgments can clarify the law before the need for further legal action.

Contempt Citations

One of the most powerful tools state courts have is the ability to hold individuals in contempt of court, or to issue contempt citations. Courts can hold individuals in *direct* contempt if they resist a court order while in the presence of that court. Courts can hold individuals in *constructive* contempt if individuals fail to comply with a court order while outside the actual courtroom. Individuals can be held in *civil* contempt if they fail to abide by a court's order to remedy some financial debt. Typically, in civil cases, the losing party is ordered to pay the winning party some type of damages. If the losing party fails to pay, it can be held in civil contempt. Courts can also hold people in *criminal* contempt. People who obstruct the administration of justice can be held in criminal contempt.

The penalties for contempt are either a fine or imprisonment. Courts can imprison those held in contempt for an indefinite period. The purpose of contempt imprisonment is to compel an individual to carry out a court-ordered action. For example, a state judge may order an individual to testify or turn over evidence to a court. If the individual refuses, that person can be held in contempt and then be imprisoned until there is compliance. But contempt imprisonment cannot be perpetual. Judges may only use contempt imprisonment to coerce individuals to act, not to punish. After it becomes clear that the imprisonment will not result in an acceptance of the court's demands, the defendant is freed. Judges have wide discretion in determining when such a time arrives.

Injunctions

Injunctions are the courts' method of preventing or interrupting damaging or illegal activities. An injunction is similar to a writ of prohibition. The purpose of an injunction is to prevent or guard against future injuries. Most of the time, courts award damages after an injury has already been committed. Courts can use injunctions to prevent such injury from ever occurring.

Courts can issue temporary and permanent injunctions. A *temporary* injunction, sometimes called an *interlocutory* injunction, prevents any further action until a trial court can make a final determination. Because court proceedings can be lengthy, courts may want to prevent an action while the hearing is taking place. Otherwise, the offending party would be able to continue its harmful actions while the court carried out its business. A temporary injunction halts potentially harmful action until the court can decide if the action is, in fact, harmful. If the court determines the action was not harmful, the temporary injunction is lifted, and the defendant is allowed to resume his or her business. A *permanent* injunction is issued after a trial court has reached a final decision. The permanent injunction enforces the will of the court. Those who violate injunctions can be held in contempt and imprisoned.

One reason injunctions are such powerful tools is that there are almost no limitations on how a judge may use an injunction. A judge can use an injunction to prevent any behavior the judge is inclined to stop. The only way to overturn an injunction is for a higher court to overrule the injunction imposed by the lower court, but this rarely happens.

During the late 1800s, when the labor movement was gaining influence, state courts regularly used injunctions to prevent strikes and protests, claiming they violated conspiracy and antitrust laws. When workers ignored the courts and proceeded with their strike plans, they were held in contempt and jailed. Furthermore, after courts had issued injunctions and held workers in contempt, they also facilitated the participation of governors and other police officials to enforce the injunction. Therefore, acting on the authority of the courts, many governors would call out state militias to break up strikes and protests. After the passage of the Wagner Act in 1935, courts could no longer use their injunction powers to prevent collective action by unions.

Judicial Review of Administrative Decisions

Just as state courts have the power of judicial review to invalidate state laws, courts also have the power to invalidate administrative decisions. As with any governmental system, elected officials rarely administer the programs or laws they enact. Bureaucratic officials manage the day-to-day business of the state. Administrative agencies make decisions about unemployment compensation, marriage licenses, environmental rules, welfare benefits, and much more. State courts have the power to overturn most administrative decisions. Moreover, state courts have the power to direct administrative agencies to take specific actions. As a result, state courts have considerable influence over how state benefits are distributed and how rules are enforced.

Special Masters

Special masters, sometimes called masters in chancery, are officials appointed by the court to carry out investigative and administrative tasks for the court. Many appellate courts need information before they can administer the law. Special masters can be directed to collect testimony, investigate conflicts, and then report their findings back to the court. Special masters can also be used to investigate civil cases by computing damages, determining the holdings of a defendant, auditing individuals and firms, and taking affidavits. In family courts, judges often appoint special masters to act as custodial referees. In this role, the special master interviews children and parents, visits the home, and arbitrates family conflicts. The special master then refers the findings to the court where a final decision is made.

Special masters enhance the power of courts by enforcing judicial decrees. It is one thing for a court to order that a defendant declare assets. It is quite another for a court to order a special master to determine those assets. Often courts suffer from the principle-agency dilemma, which arises from the fact that courts must often rely on a party to the case to carry out the decision or order of the court. Many times, the preferences of the party so ordered are at odds with the court's commands. Therefore, courts are often faced with ordering the fox to watch the chicken coop. Special masters alleviate this problem. Special masters also ensure that information given to the court is impartial.

In addition to collecting information, special masters can oversee the enforcement of a judicial decree. Judicial decisions often impose a variety of restrictions on a party or impose a variety of commitments. Special masters are given the power to ensure that those commitments are met. For example, a judge may issue a ruling demanding that an administrative agency reduce the amount of toxic materials in a public waterway. A judge may not have the ability to direct the day-to-day events of the administrative agency. Instead, judges can empower a special master to oversee the enforcement of the decree.

Quo Warranto

Quo warranto is Latin for "by what authority." State attorneys general can file writs of quo warranto when an elected official usurps a power that he or she does not legally possess. In a quo warranto proceeding, a state supreme court asks the following of an elected official: By what authority do you take this action? If the state officer cannot legally justify the action, the court can order the official to stop. Quo warranto proceedings can also challenge the actions and authority of a corporation within a state. Quo warranto proceedings are very rare.

Civil Remedies

In addition to arbitrating conflicts in the political arena, state courts also arbitrate civil disputes. When adjudicating civil disputes, the most versatile tool state courts have is the power to award and collect damages. State courts can award many different types of damages and have a variety of methods at their disposal to collect those damages. Awarding and collecting damages is the state court's "power of the purse."

Compensatory Damages

State courts award three types of damages: compensatory, punitive, and nominal. Compensatory damages are awarded to compensate a plaintiff for such things as property damage, personal injury, pain and suffering, mental distress, loss of wages, and injury to reputation. The purpose of compensatory damages is to award plaintiffs enough to return them to the situation they were in before they suffered harm by the defendant. In some cases, perfect disgorgement is easy to compute. If a plaintiff has suffered $2,000 in damage to an automobile, then the court will award $2,000 and sometimes attorney fees. However, in a case such as mental anguish or physical deformity, it is more difficult to establish a monetary figure that represents perfect equity. To succeed, plaintiffs must prove to the court that they have suffered some harm due to the tortuous conduct of a defendant.

Punitive Damages

In some situations, state courts can award punitive damages (sometimes referred to as exemplary damages). Punitive damages are designed to go beyond merely making the plaintiff whole; they are intended to punish. In addition to punishment, punitive damages have two other functions. They serve as a deterrent against future misconduct, and high punitive awards are one way juries express their outrage at a defendant who shows disregard for others. For example, corporations may not be deterred from producing products with a known defect if the only consequence is paying compensatory damages. However, if additional punitive damages are awarded, a financial incentive is created to correct its reckless or deliberate misbehavior. Punitive damages create incentives not only for the current defendant but also for potential future defendants. Punitive damages can range from a few thousand dollars to several billion dollars. Textbook legal theory suggests to succeed in winning a punitive award, plaintiffs must show that the defendant acted deliberately to cause harm or in such a way that the misbehavior was likely to cause harm.

Achieving equity can be complicated when there is more than one defendant or when the plaintiff bears some of the blame. For example, in car accidents involving multiple cars, a plaintiff may sue several defendants who caused the wreck and an automaker who sold a car with a defective braking system. At the same time, the plaintiff may bear some blame for exacerbating the injury by failing to wear a seat belt.

Intentional Torts

To win monetary damages in a civil case, a plaintiff must prove that the defendant acted in a sufficiently egregious manner as to be liable for the damages. However, legislatures and courts have established different standards that plaintiffs must prove in order to receive damages. The legal standard that must be met is typically identified in the statute.

An intentional tort occurs when someone purposefully injures another party. To recoup damages from an intentional tort, the plaintiff must prove, in court, that the defendant intended to cause harm. For example, in assault and battery cases, the plaintiff can usually prove that the defendant intended to cause harm.

In other torts, the plaintiff does not have to prove that the defendant intentionally caused harm. Instead, the plaintiff is held to a lower standard and must only prove that the defendant acted with negligence. For example, in most personal injury lawsuits, including medical malpractice and car accidents, a plaintiff can prove negligence if he or she simply shows the defendant acted in a manner counter to how a reasonable person would act. It typically falls to the jury to decide how a reasonable person would act.

In some cases, statutes require that a plaintiff prove that the defendant acted in a reckless manner. This standard of proof is slightly harder to prove. In such a case, the plaintiff must show that the defendant acted more than just carelessly but in a manner that showed a conscious disregard of substantial and unjustified risk. To be reckless, a defendant needs to be conscious of the danger associated with his or her actions and follow through with those actions anyway.

To win punitive damages, plaintiffs typically need to show the defendant acted in a willful and wanton manner, which is a slightly higher standard of proof than recklessness. A wanton action is usually described as acting with extreme carelessness that exhibits a reckless disregard for the rights of others. When someone acts in a willful and wanton manner, he or she knows that the actions will result in harm to others. Awards can be adjusted to account for the proportion of injury the plaintiff allowed to occur by not exercising sufficient care.

Nominal Damages

When compensatory and punitive damages are inappropriate, courts award nominal damages. Nominal damages are awarded when a defendant breaches a legal duty, but the plaintiff suffers no damages. In such a case, courts cannot award compensatory damages because there is no harm to compensate. Nominal damages are often awarded when someone's rights have been violated. For example, if one's privacy rights are violated, it is difficult to monetarily quantify the harm inflicted. If punitive damages are not legally permitted, the court can award nominal damages.

In state courts, judges rarely determine the amount of damages a plaintiff receives. Juries typically perform that duty. However, state judges do have the power of additur and remittitur. When judges feel the damages awarded by a jury are insufficient, courts can add to the award by granting an additur. This increases the damage award. Conversely, if the trial judge or appellate court feels the award is too high, courts can grant a remittitur and lower the award value. In high-profile tort cases, appellate judges often grant a remittitur. Although it is common for the media to highlight extremely high punitive damage awards, they rarely publicize subsequent remittiturs that lower the award significantly.

After courts award damages, they have several means to collect those damages. The following sections discuss methods state courts use to collect damages. It is important to remember that the following methods consist of more than simply issuing a piece of paper. The issuance of these orders empowers state police officers to enforce them.

Writs of Attachment and Execution

A writ of attachment is a process by which the court seizes the property of a defendant. The attached property can be sold so that damages awarded by the court can be paid, or the court can hold property until the damages are paid, after which the property is returned. At one time, courts could attach property during judicial proceeding on the chance that the plaintiff might prevail. However, the U.S. Supreme Court has limited the practice, and courts must provide due process before they seize property prior to a judgment.

Writs of execution are similar to writs of attachment. They empower police officers to seize property from someone who has been directed to pay damages. However, writs of execution can be general or specific. A general writ of execution instructs an officer to seize property without identifying any particular property. A specific writ of execution instructs an officer to seize a particular or set of particular items.

Garnishments and Liens

Judges do not always seize property. Damages can be collected by garnishing wages. Courts can issue a writ of garnishment that gives the court the authority to seize a percentage of a defendant's salary. States do not allow courts to seize an entire paycheck but only a limited percentage. Each state has different rules about the maximum percentage that can be garnished.

Garnishments apply to a third party. Writs of attachment take property from the person who actually owes a fine or court-ordered damages. Garnishments seize property or money from a third party who owes the debtor. The most common use of a garnishment occurs when courts order an employer (third party) to turn over funds that were destined for the debtor. Instead, those funds are rerouted to the plaintiff who was awarded the damages. The most well-known form of wage garnishment is associated with court orders to ensure that child support or alimony payments are made.

A lien does not immediately seize property. Instead, a lien declares that after a piece of property is sold, the owner is not entitled to the funds acquired. Rather, after the property is sold, the lien holder has the first rights to the profits. If there is any money left over, then the owner of the property gets to keep the remaining funds. For example, if a homeowner refuses to pay required association dues, the courts can put a lien on the home. When the home is sold, the court seizes the payments and allocates the appropriate funds to the homeowner association. The remaining funds are then granted to the owner of the house. Liens are typically placed on property; however, courts can also place liens on tax returns and business inventories.

Receivership

State courts can appoint a person (a receiver) to act as a custodian for contested property during the length of the trial. Receivership serves civil disputes in the same manner that temporary injunctions serve political disputes. The court appoints a receiver to ensure that no harm comes to the property or either party to the suit during the length of the trial. In most cases concerning property, the owner of the property maintains ownership until the court decides the legal controversy. Such an arrangement leaves the nonowners of the property vulnerable to the acts of the owner while the trial proceeds. For example, legal disputes sometimes challenge the way a pension plan is being administered. There can be charges of embezzlement or fraud. During the length of the trial, the embezzlement or fraud can continue. To prevent that from occurring, courts can appoint a receiver to manage the pension fund while the trial takes place. If it turns out no tortuous activity was proven, the receiver returns control of the property to its rightful owner.

Rescission and Reformation

Rescission and reformation typically apply to contract law. There are times when individuals enter into a contractual agreement but due to ambiguous language, mistakes, or outright fraud, the contract does not reflect the agreement of the two parties. In such cases, courts can use their powers of reformation to rewrite parts of the contract to bring the contract in line with the intended agreement.

Rescission occurs when a court simply invalidates a contract. There are times when parties use coercion, such as threats or other types of illegal pressure, to make people sign contracts, or, one party simply lies about the nature of the contract. Rather than rewrite the contract, a court will declare it void.

Vertical Federalism

State supreme courts are the final arbitrators and interpreters of state law. Federal courts cannot dictate to state courts how to interpret their own state constitutions or state statutes unless those laws interfere with federal laws. The concept that federal courts will not interfere in a state court's interpretation of its own law was established by two U.S. Supreme Court decisions, *Rooker v. Fidelity Trust Co.* (1923) and *District of Columbia Court of Appeals v. Feldman* (1983), and has come to be known as the Rooker-Feldman doctrine. The Rooker-Feldman doctrine is fundamental to protecting the autonomy of state courts. Because of the doctrine, federal courts cannot meddle in the affairs of state law unless those laws explicitly violate the U.S. Constitution or other federal statutes.

The Rooker-Feldman doctrine was an issue in the historic case of *Bush v. Gore* (2000), which arbitrated the disputed presidential election of 2000. Lawyers for then Governor George W. Bush challenged the State of Florida's vote-counting procedures. When appealing to the Supreme Court, Justice O'Connor's first question was, "Why are we here?" Justice O'Connor asked that question because voting procedures are covered by state constitutions and state law, and the Supreme Court of Florida had already issued a ruling. To many court observers, the Rooker-Feldman doctrine should have applied, and the federal Supreme Court should have refused to hear the case. However, lawyers for Governor Bush claimed that the voting procedures established by the Florida Supreme Court violated the Fourteenth Amendment of the U.S. Constitution. The Rooker-Feldman doctrine does not apply if state laws or state supreme court decisions violate the U.S. Constitution or other federal laws.

If the U.S. Supreme Court in *Bush v. Gore* had not agreed that there was a federal legal question presented to the Court, it would have been unable to hear the case. Furthermore, after the Supreme Court agreed to hear the case, it was limited to adjudicating only the federal Fourteenth Amendment questions. It was not allowed to revisit the Florida Supreme Court's interpretation of the Florida statutes regulating election procedures. The U.S. Supreme Court could only rule as to whether those election statutes or Florida court decisions violated federal law.

It is worth noting, however, that in 2006, the Supreme Court ruled in *Lance v. Dennis* that "The *Rooker-Feldman* doctrine does not bar actions by nonparties to the earlier state-court judgment simply because [. . .] they could be considered in privity with a party to the judgment." In other words, the Rooker-Feldman doctrine did not preclude plaintiffs from pursuing legal remedies in federal court in cases where they were not the parties in a state court proceeding.

The supremacy clause empowers federal courts to dictate to state courts in areas of federal law. However, even when state courts are legally required to comply with federal courts, state courts are not powerless to frustrate the will of federal judges. Civil rights law has been one area that has historically led to tensions and disagreements between state and federal courts.

Beginning in the 1950s, federal courts started taking a leading role in the protection of civil liberties. *Brown v. Board of Education* (1954) was the most notable of many cases that started the process of insuring civil rights to African Americans. Numerous other cases expanded the rights of the accused. In a series of decisions by the Warren Court, defendants were guaranteed attorneys, interrogation protections, Miranda rights, search and seizure protections, and much more. The Warren Court was in the process of selective incorporation.

Selective incorporation is the process of applying particular amendments in the Bill of Rights, or even particular clauses from one amendment, to state governments. Ever since the 1833 decision in *Barron v. Baltimore*, state governments had not been bound by the restrictions of the Bill of Rights. In his last decision, Chief Justice John Marshall reasoned that because the First Amendment states that *Congress* "shall make no law respecting . . ." that the Bill of Rights only applied to the federal government. Following the Civil War, however, Congress passed, and the states adopted, the Fourteenth Amendment, which limited the autonomy of state lawmaking by barring state legislatures from passing laws that "deprive any person of life, liberty, or property, without due process of law; nor deny to any person within its jurisdiction the equal protection of the laws." After states were prevented from denying any of its citizens liberty without due process, the Supreme Court eventually determined that "liberty" included the provisions of the Bill of Rights.

Slowly, between the 1920s and the 1970s, the U.S. Supreme Court reversed the *Barron* decision and required that state lawmakers respect the mandates of the Bill of Rights. However, in the process of incorporating the Bill of Rights against the actions of state governments, the Court met resistance from state supreme courts. The Warren Court was characterized by critics as an activist court, and not all of the rulings handed down by the Warren Court were popular at the time. States with a more conservative ideology did not like many of the Warren Court incorporation cases.

In response, many state supreme courts took actions to resist mandates from federal courts. In some cases, state supreme courts simply ignored federal rulings. In other cases, state supreme courts used the ambiguous or vague language of federal decisions to carve out legal exceptions in their states. In the same manner, state supreme courts could use vague language to argue that the federal precedent did not apply to their particular states' laws. David and Francine Romero (2003) have shown that state courts remained very hostile to civil rights for African Americans even after *Brown* was decided. After *Brown*, 74 percent of all federal court civil rights rulings supported the protection of civil rights for African American citizens. However, in comparison, only 31 percent of state supreme court decisions protected civil rights for African Americans. State courts also resisted the expansion of rights for criminal defendants.

Romans (1974) examined how state supreme courts resisted the mandates of *Escobedo v. Illinois* (1964) and *Miranda v. Arizona* (1966). Both *Escobedo* and *Miranda* were U.S. Supreme Court decisions that expanded the rights of criminal defendants. However, most criminal defendants are tried in state courts, not federal courts. Romans (1974) shows that although the state supreme courts were bound by federal precedent, many state supreme court justices took the narrowest possible view of federal decisions to maintain long-standing state law enforcement practices.

New Judicial Federalism

Surprisingly, following personnel changes on the U.S. Supreme Court in the 1970s and 1980s, the tension between state supreme courts and the U.S. Supreme Court reversed itself. When the U.S. Supreme Court was dominated by liberal appointees in the Warren Court, the federal courts were seen as the primary defenders of civil liberties. However, with the retirement of Earl Warren and the appointment of his successor, Warren Burger, the U.S. Supreme Court began to hand down a new line of civil rights cases. In many cases, the Burger Court rescinded or narrowed the application of many of the Warren Court decisions. As a result, many state supreme courts began to rely on their own state constitutions to protect civil rights that were no longer protected by federal precedent. Scholars have referred to this movement as new judicial federalism. Although it is no longer new, the term highlights the fact that federalism provides multiple access points to the political system. If proponents cannot get what they want at one level of government (federal level), they are free to try at a different level of government (state level). Now, when litigants attempt to secure more rights in state courts than are recognized by the federal Supreme Court, it is known as relying on independent state grounds.

State supreme courts can rely on independent state grounds because each state has its own constitution and therefore its own set of civil liberties protections. Because of vertical judicial federalism, state courts cannot offer fewer protections of civil rights than the federal courts mandate. However, the reverse is not true. State supreme courts are free to offer greater protections than offered by federal precedent. As the Burger Court began to rein in the precedents of the Warren Court, state supreme courts responded by expanding protections of civil liberties by relying on state law instead of federal law.

For example, Tarr (1998) points out that the U.S. Supreme Court reversed course in 1973 and declared that illegally obtained confessions can still be introduced in court for the purposes of impeaching witnesses. To many legal activists, this decision was seen as a rollback of Fourth Amendment protections. However, in response to the 1973 decision, four state supreme courts declared that their state constitutions forbid the introduction of illegally obtained confessions. Thus, what the U.S. Supreme Court took away, several state supreme courts returned. Many times, the conflict between federal and state courts is a function of ideology. When the U.S. Supreme Court is dominated by liberal appointees, supreme courts from conservative states try to resist the mandates of the federal court. When the U.S. Supreme Court is dominated by conservative appointees, supreme courts from more liberal states try to use their own state constitutions to go beyond what the federal court has mandated.

The ideologically driven nature of new judicial federalism fuels much of the criticism of this doctrine. Some judicial scholars have objected to judicial federalism because it appears to be opportunistic rather than theory driven. Critics argue that using state constitutions to thwart the decisions of the U.S. Supreme Court is typically an ends-driven policy rather than a sincere interpretation of state constitutions. As such, judges appear to be playing politics and imposing their personal values as much as fairly interpreting state law.

However, state supreme courts often sincerely disagree with the precedents set by federal courts. In some cases, state judges reason the federal courts have gone too far and try to impede the will of federal courts. In other instances, state supreme court justices determine the federal courts have not gone far enough and seek to use state constitutions to offer more protections to their citizens. The following cases provide recent examples illustrating how the process of vertical judicial federalism works both ways.

In 1976, the U.S. Congress passed the Hyde Amendment, which restricted the use of federal tax dollars for abortions. A year later, the U.S. Supreme Court, in *Maher v. Roe* and *Beal v. Doe*, upheld the congressional policy and further ruled that state governments are not required to fund abortions. Having lost the battle at the federal level, many abortions rights organizations focused their attention on state governments and state courts. Eventually, several state supreme courts ruled contrary to the U.S. Supreme Court. The states of Massachusetts, New Jersey, California, Vermont, and Connecticut all declared that their state constitutions required the state funding of abortions as part of state medical plans.

In *Lawrence v. Texas* (2003), the U.S. Supreme Court faced a sodomy case involving a same-sex couple. Texas statutes criminalized sodomy, but the plaintiffs argued the Texas law violated their rights of privacy. The U.S. Supreme Court agreed and invalidated the sodomy statute. However, the Court did endorse the privacy rights, and, in doing so, it overruled *Bowers v. Hardwick* (1986), a case that rejected homosexual rights. *Lawrence* only implied a right to marry for gays, something that Justice Antonin Scalia railed against in his dissent. Later in 2003, the Massachusetts Supreme Court, citing the *Lawrence* precedent and relying on the Massachusetts Constitution, declared that homosexuals did have the constitutional right to marry, at least in Massachusetts.

The case of *Zelman v. Simmons-Harris* (2002) arbitrated a disagreement over the use of school vouchers. Opponents argued that vouchers violated the establishment clause of the First Amendment. Supporters argued they were permissible under the First Amendment. The U.S. Supreme Court ruled that school vouchers did not violate the concept of separation of church and state and were therefore constitutional and permissible. However, a year later, courts in both Florida and Colorado ruled that vouchers violated their state constitutions' prohibitions against mingling church and state. Therefore, even though the U.S. Supreme Court authorized the use of vouchers, two separate state courts barred their implementation.

Using the doctrine of independent state grounds, state supreme courts have been willing to challenge the rulings of the U.S. Supreme Court. In some cases, state supreme courts have expanded the rights of individuals beyond what the federal courts require. In other cases, they have further limited the options of individuals. In 1983, the U.S. Supreme Court intervened to establish rules for when courts may use the doctrine of independent state grounds. In the case of *Michigan v. Long* (1983), the U.S. Supreme Court ruled that if state supreme courts want to rely on independent state grounds to contravene federal precedents, they must use only state legal precedents.

Prior to *Michigan*, state supreme courts were using federal precedent to support the rejection of federal precedents. State courts were arguing that state constitutions protected individual rights beyond those protections established by the federal Supreme Court, but were then using federal precedents to buttress their cases. The *Michigan* ruling rejected that process. After *Michigan*, state courts must clearly indicate that they are relying on "bona fide separate, adequate, and independent grounds" and, in doing so, must only cite state common law to buttress their decisions. State supreme courts can still mention federal law and precedents, but they must include a plain statement clause ensuring the U.S. Supreme Court that the decision was based on state law. For example, in a Montana case, the Montana Supreme Court noted:

> While we have devoted considerable time to a lengthy discussion of the application of the Fifth Amendment to the United States Constitution, it is to be noted that this holding is also based separately and independently on [the defendant's] right to remain silent pursuant to Article II, Section 25 of the Montana Constitution. (*State v. Fuller,* 1996)

By including such a statement in the decision, the Montana court signaled that the decision was based solely on Montana constitutional law and therefore is beyond the review of the U.S. Supreme Court. In contrast, the U.S. Supreme Court has made it clear that if "a state court decision fairly appears to rest primarily on federal law, or to be interwoven with the federal law" (*Michigan*, 1983), the U.S. Supreme Court can take jurisdiction and contravene the state court's decision.

The development of the independent state grounds doctrine does not necessarily mean that state courts universally offer greater civil rights protections than federal courts. Often, state courts are seen as too responsive to local politics. During the initial stages of the civil rights movement, state courts regularly ignored the rights of African Americans. Their only recourse was to appeal to federal courts.

Horizontal Federalism

Horizontal judicial federalism is the manner in which state courts interact with other state courts. Some of the interaction is voluntary. Courts can elect to use precedents from other states to help them resolve disputes in their own states. Some of the interaction is mandatory. The U.S. Constitution's full faith and credit clause mandates some cooperation between state judges.

Diffusion

Diffusion is the process by which a precedent developed in one state court is adopted by courts in other states. State courts are not bound by any decision or ruling in other states. However, at times, state courts voluntarily adopt, as precedent, rulings that come from other state supreme courts. Gregory Caldeira (1985) has studied the process of judicial diffusion and found that diffusion was a function of geography, the size of a state's caseload, and the prestige of the court. State supreme courts are more likely to adopt precedents from other states if they are geographically close. Second, the number of cases a supreme court decides impacts how often that court will be cited by other state courts. Last, some state supreme courts have a higher level of prestige. Because some state courts are more respected than others, they are also more likely to be cited. Research shows that the California, New York, and New Jersey courts have the highest reputation among all the other supreme courts. Wyoming, South Dakota, and Hawaii have the lowest reputation scores. Having a low reputation score does not mean a court makes bad decisions; it simply means their rulings do not have the same impact on other jurisdictions as other courts.

A recent example of judicial diffusion is the Oregon Supreme Court's *Armatta v. Kitzhaber* (1998) decision. In *Armatta*, the Oregon court ruled that state ballot measures voted on by the people may only amend one clause in the Oregon Constitution. The court reasoned that without the *Armatta* separate vote rule, ballot measure drafters could change multiple parts of the constitution with only one vote. Soon after the *Armatta* case was decided, the supreme courts of Montana and Washington adopted the separate vote rule. Despite the fact that neither the Montana nor Washington constitutions required a separate vote, nor were there any in-state precedents supporting such a decision, both supreme courts accepted the Oregon ruling as binding in their respective states.

Full Faith and Credit Clause

Because each state has jurisdiction over its own laws under federalism principles, no state is bound by the constitutions or statutes of other states. Such a legal environment invites problems. Defendants could escape the judgments of state courts by fleeing to other states. A couple married in Virginia who moved to New York could be denied marital status. In response to these possibilities, the framers drafted the full faith and credit clause, in Article IV of the U.S. Constitution, which reads:

> Full faith and credit shall be given in each state to the public acts, records, and judicial proceedings of every other state. And the Congress may by general laws prescribe the manner in which such acts, records, and proceedings shall be proved, and the effect thereof.

According to Justice Harlan Stone in *Milwaukee County v. M. E. White Co.* (1935), through the full faith and credit clause, the framers:

> . . . altered the status of the several states as independent foreign sovereignties, each free to ignore obligations created under the laws or by the judicial proceedings of the others, and to make them integral parts of a

single nation throughout which a remedy upon a just obligation might be demanded as of right, irrespective of the state of its origin.

The full faith and credit clause is often used to enforce child support decisions and extradition rulings, and to make sure civil damages are paid to successful plaintiffs even if the defendant moves to another state. The clause also prevents defendants from forum shopping. After litigants have reached a judicial settlement in one state, they may not move to another state and relitigate the same conflict.

CONCLUSION

Although the judicial branch is the smallest of the three branches of government in the United States, the courts play a key role in the operation of our constitutional system of government. With the power of judicial review, these courts have a significant say in the shaping of public policy. Given this power, therefore, the perspectives, capabilities, and backgrounds of those people who preside over these courts—and by implication the ways they are appointed to serve—have a large impact on the shaping of public policy and daily life in the United States.

We cannot and should not expect judges to perform their functions and roles with more than human wisdom or detachment, for that expectation would collide with the reality that federal and state courts are human institutions, just as the Constitution and the laws are crafted by human hands. At the same time, we can ask judges to rise as much as possible above merely rubber-stamping their personal predispositions, biases, or prejudices into the evolving body of federal or state judicial precedent. For example, the greatest moments in the history of the federal judiciary are those in which federal judges identify and give voice to the best and highest aspirations of the constitutional system. If, at times, this means that they must set aside the habits of thought and feeling shaped by a lifetime of experience, many of our greatest jurists have proved that such transcendence is not beyond human reach. At the same time, some of the worst moments in the history of the judiciary have come from authorities who succumb to fears, prejudices, and shortsighted rationalizations in carrying out and interpreting American law.

Charles L. Zelden, Sean O. Hogan, and Ginny Hollinger

Further Reading

Abraham, Henry J., Griffin B. Bell, Charles E. Grassley, Eugene W. Hickock, John W. Kern, Stephen J. Markman, and William Bradford Reynolds. 1990. *Judicial Selection: Merit, Ideology, and Politics.* Washington, D.C.: National Legal Center for the Public Interest.

Administrative Office of U.S. Courts. 2016. "Judicial Caseload Indicators, 12-Month Periods Ending June 2006, 2011, 2014, and 2015." June 30. http://www.uscourts .gov/statistics-reports/analysis-reports/federal-judicial-caseload-statistics.

Advisory Council to the U.S. Court of Appeals for the Federal Circuit. *United States Court of Appeals for the Federal Circuit: A History: 1990–2002*. 2004. Washington, D.C.: U.S. Court of Appeals for the Federal Circuit.

Alliance for Justice. 2016. *Broadening the Bench: Professional Diversity and Judicial Nominations*. Washington, D.C.: AFJ. http://www.afj.org/wp-content/uploads/2014/11 /Professional-Diversity-Report.pdf.

Atkins, Burton, and Henry Glick. 1976. "Environmental and Structural Variables as Determinants of Issues in State Courts of Last Resort." *American Journal of Political Science* 20 (February): 97–115.

Banks, Christopher P., and David M. O'Brien. 2015. *The Judicial Process: Law, Courts, and Judicial Politics*. Thousand Oaks, CA: CQ Press.

Banks, Christopher P., and John C. Blakeman. 2012. *The U.S. Supreme Court and New Federalism: From the Rehnquist to the Roberts Court*. Lanham, MD: Rowman & Littlefield.

Banks, Christopher P., David B. Cohen, and John C. Green, eds. 2005. *The Final Arbiter: The Consequences of Bush v. Gore for Law and Politics*. Albany, NY: SUNY Press.

Barrow, Deborah J., and Thomas G. Walker. 1988. *A Court Divided: The Fifth Circuit Court of Appeals and the Politics of Judicial Reform*. New Haven, CT: Yale University Press.

Barrow, Deborah J., Gerard S. Gryski, and Gary Zuk. 1996. *The Federal Judiciary and Institutional Change*. Ann Arbor: University of Michigan Press.

Baum, Lawrence. 1994. "What Judges Want: Judges' Goals and Judicial Behavior." *Political Research Quarterly* 47(3): 749–768.

Baum, Lawrence. 2006. *Judges and Their Audiences: A Perspective on Judicial Behavior*. Princeton, NJ: Princeton University Press.

Beiser, Edward. 1974. "The Rhode Island Supreme Court: A Well-Integrated Political System." *Law and Society Review* 8(1): 167–186.

Bermant, Gordon, and Russell R. Wheeler. 1995. "Federal Judges and the Judicial Branch: Their Independence and Accountability." *Mercer Law Review* 46: 835–861.

Birkly, Robert H. 1983. *The Court and Public Policy*. Washington, D.C.: CQ Press, 462.

Brandenburg, Bert. 2012. "Beating Back the War on Judges." *Slate*, November 12. http:// www.slate.com/articles/news_and_politics/jurisprudence/2012/11/judicial_elec tions_in_2012_voters_rejected_the_politicization_of_the_courts.html.

Breyer, Stephen. 2015. *The Court and the World: American Law and the New Global Realities*. New York: Knopf.

Buehler, Cheryl, and Jean Gerard. 1995. "Divorce Law in the United States: A Focus on Child Custody." *Family Relations* 44(4): 439–458.

Cahan, Richard. 2002. *A Court That Shaped America: Chicago's Federal District Court from Abe Lincoln to Abbie Hoffman*. Evanston, IL: Northwestern University Press.

Caldeira, Gregory. 1983. "On the Reputation of State Supreme Courts." *Political Behavior* 5(1): 83–108.

Caldeira, Gregory. 1985. "The Transmission of Legal Precedent: A Study of State Supreme Courts." *American Political Science Review* 79(March): 178–193.

Canon, Bradley. 1972. "The Impact of Formal Selection Processes on the Characteristics of Judges—Reconsidered." *Law and Society Review* 13: 570–593.

Canon, Bradley. 1973. "Reactions of State Supreme Courts to a U.S. Supreme Court Civil Liberties Decision." *Law and Society Review* 8(1): 109–134.

Carp, Robert A., and C. K. Rowland. 1983. *Policymaking and Politics in the Federal District Courts*. Knoxville: University of Tennessee Press.

Carp, Robert A., and Ronald Stidham. 1998. *The Federal Courts*. 3rd ed. Washington, D.C.: CQ Press.

Champagne, Anthony, and Judith Haydel, eds. 1993. *Judicial Reform in the States*. Lanham, MD: University Press of America.

Chase, Harold W. 1972. *Federal Judges: The Appointing Process*. Minneapolis: University of Minnesota Press.

Clark, Mary L. 2004. "One Man's Token Is Another Woman's Breakthrough? The Appointment of the First Women Federal Judges." *Villanova Law Review* 49: 487–550.

Clarke, Matt. 2013. "Dramatic Increase in Percentage of Criminal Cases Being Plea Bargained." *Prison Legal News*, January 15. https://www.prisonlegalnews.org/news/2013/jan/15/dramatic-increase-in-percentage-of-criminal-cases-being-plea-bargained/.

Clayton, Cornell W., and Howard Gillman, eds. 1999. *Supreme Court Decision-Making: New Institutionalist Approaches*. Lawrence: University Press of Kansas.

Cohen, Jeffrey, and Charles Barrilleaux. 1993. "Public Opinion, Interest Groups, and Public Policy Making: Abortion Policy in the American States." In *Understanding the New Politics of Abortion*, edited by Malcolm Goggin. Newbury Park, CA: Sage Publications.

Constitution Society. 2016. "Antifederalist Papers: Brutus No. 1." http://www.constitution.org/afp/brutus01.htm.

Court Statistics Project. 2010. "Number of Authorized Justices and Judges in State Courts." http://www.courtstatistics.org/~/media/Microsites/Files/CSP/SCCS/2010/Number_of_Authorized_Justices_and_Judges_in_State_Courts.ashx.

Court Statistics Project. 2012. "Examining the Work of State Courts: An Analysis of 2010 State Court Caseloads." http://www.courtstatistics.org/other-pages/~/media/microsites/files/csp/data%20pdf/csp_dec.ashx.

Dinan, John J. 2006. *The American State Constitutional Tradition*. Lawrence: University Press of Kansas.

Ellis, Richard. 1971. *The Jeffersonian Crisis: Courts and Politics in the Young Republic*. New York: W. W. Norton.

Emmert, Craig. 1988. "Judicial Review in State Supreme Courts: Opportunity and Activism." Paper presented at the Midwest Political Science Association Meeting, Chicago.

Emmert, Craig. 1992. "An Integrated Case-Related Model of Judicial Decision Making: Explaining State Supreme Court Decisions in Judicial Review Cases." *Journal of Politics* 54(2): 543–552.

Esler, Michael. 2003. "Federal Jurisprudence, State Autonomy: *Michigan v. Long*: A Twenty Year Retrospective." *Albany Law Review* 66(March): 835–856.

Fallon, Richard H., Jr., John Manning, Daniel Meltzer, and David Shapiro. 2015. *The Federal Courts and the Federal System*. 7th ed. St. Paul, MN: Foundation Press.

Feeley, Malcolm M., and Edward Rubin. 2000. *Judicial Policy Making and the Modern State: How the Courts Reformed America's Prisons*. Cambridge, UK: Cambridge University Press.

Forer, Lois. 1992. "Justice by the Numbers." *Washington Monthly* (April): 12–14.

Frankfurter, Felix, and James Landis. 1927. *The Business of the Supreme Court: A Study in the Federal Judicial System*. New York: Macmillan.

Freyer, Tony A. 1979. *Forums of Order: The Federal Courts and Business in American History*. Greenwich, CT: Jai Press.

Glick, Henry. 1991. "Policy Making and State Supreme Courts." In *The American Courts: A Critical Assessment*, edited by John Gates and Charles Johnson. Washington, D.C.: CQ Press.

Glick, Henry, and Kenneth Vines. 1969. "Law-Making in the State Judiciary: A Comparative Study of the Judicial Role in Four States." *Polity* 2(1): 142–159.

Glick, Henry, and Kenneth Vines. 1973. *State Court Systems*. Englewood Cliffs, NJ: Prentice-Hall.

Goggin, Malcolm, and Christopher Wlezien. 1993. "Abortion Opinion and Policy in the American States." In *Understanding the New Politics of Abortion*, edited by Malcolm Goggin, 190–202. Newbury Park, CA: Sage Publications.

Goldman, Sheldon. 1997. *Picking Federal Judges: Lower Court Selection from Roosevelt through Reagan*. New Haven, CT: Yale University Press.

Goldman, Sheldon, Elliot Slotnick, and Sara Schiavoni. 2009. "W. Bush's Judicial Legacy: Mission Accomplished." *Judicature* 92(6): 258–288.

Goldman, Sheldon, Elliot Slotnick, and Sara Schiavoni. 2013. "Obama's First Term Judiciary." *Judicature* 97(1) (July/August): 7–47.

Greenhouse, Linda. 2007. "Chief Justice Advocates Higher Pay for Judiciary." *New York Times*, January 1.

Grossman, Joel B., and Austin Sarat. 1975. "Litigation in the Federal Courts: A Comparative Perspective." *Law and Society Review* 9(Winter): 321–346.

Guide to the Federal Courts: An Introduction to the Federal Courts and Their Operation: Includes Explanation of How a Case Is Litigated. 1984. Washington, D.C.: Want Publishing.

Hall, Kermit. 1975. "The Civil War Era as a Crucible for Nationalizing the Lower Federal Courts." *Prologue* 7(Fall): 177–186.

Hall, Kermit. 1976. "Social Backgrounds and Judicial Recruitment: A Nineteenth-Century Perspective on the Lower Federal Judiciary." *Western Political Quarterly* 29(June): 243–257.

Hall, Kermit. 1979. *The Politics of Justice: Lower Federal Judicial Selection and the Second Party System, 1829–1861*. Lincoln: University of Nebraska Press.

Hall, Kermit. 1980. "The Children of the Cabins: The Lower Federal Judiciary, Modernization, and Political Culture, 1789–1899." *Journal of Negro History* 18(October): 423–470.

Hall, Kermit, ed. 1987a. *The Courts in American Life: Major Historical Interpretations*. Vol. 4 of *United States Constitutional and Legal History*. New York: Garland Publishing.

Hall, Kermit, ed. 1987b. *The Judiciary in American Life: Major Historical Interpretations.* Vol. 5 of *United States Constitutional and Legal History.* New York: Garland Publishing.

Hall, Melinda. 2014. *Attacking Judges: How Campaign Advertising Influences State Supreme Court Elections.* Palo Alto, CA: Stanford Law Books.

Haltom, William, and Michael McCann. 2004. *Distorting the Law: Politics, Media, and the Litigation Crisis.* Chicago: University of Chicago Press.

Handberg, Roger. 1978. "Leadership in State Courts of Last Resort: The Interaction of Environment and Procedure." *Jurimetrics* 19: 178–195.

Hellman, Arthur D., ed. 1990. *Restructuring Justice: The Innovations of the Ninth Circuit and the Future of the Federal Courts.* Ithaca, NY: Cornell University Press.

Henderson, Dwight F. 1985. *Congress, Courts, and Criminals: The Development of Federal Criminal Law, 1801–1829.* Westport, CT: Greenwood Press.

Heydebrand, Wolf, and Carroll Seron. 1990. *Rationalizing Justice: The Political Economy of Federal District Courts.* Albany: State University of New York Press.

Hockenberry, Sarah, and Charles Puzzanchera. 2015. *Juvenile Court Statistics 2013.* National Center for Juvenile Justice, July. http://www.ojjdp.gov/ojstatbb/njcda/pdf/jcs2013.pdf.

Hoffer, Peter Charles, Williamjames Hull Hoffer, and N. E. H. Hull. 2016. *The Federal Courts: An Essential History.* New York: Oxford University Press.

Howard, J. Woodford, Jr. 1981. *Courts of Appeals in the Federal Judicial System: A Study of the Second, Fifth, and District of Columbia Circuits.* Princeton, NJ: Princeton University Press.

Howard, Robert M., and Amy Steigerwalt. 2011. *Judging Law and Policy: Court and Policymaking in the American Political System.* New York: Routledge.

Hutcheson, Joseph C., Jr. 1929. "The Judgment Intuitive: The Function of the 'Hunch' in Judicial Decision." *Cornell Law Quarterly* 14: 274–288.

Johnson, Molly Treadway. 1995. *Studying the Role of Gender in the Federal Courts: A Research Guide.* Washington, D.C.: Federal Judicial Center.

Kagen, Robert, Bliss Cartwright, Lawrence Friedman, and Stanton Wheeler. 1977. "The Business of State Supreme Courts, 1870–1970." *Stanford Law Review* 30(1): 121–156.

Kahn, Paul. 2016. *Making the Case: The Art of the Judicial Opinion.* New Haven, CT: Yale University Press.

Keck, Thomas M. 2014. *Judicial Politics in Polarized Times.* Chicago: University of Chicago Press.

Levi, Edward H. 2013. *An Introduction to Legal Reasoning.* Chicago: University of Chicago Press.

Logan, James K. 1992. *The Federal Courts of the Tenth Circuit: A History.* Denver, CO: U.S. Court of Appeals for the Tenth Circuit.

Los Angeles Times Editorial Board. 2016. "Senate Republicans Refusal to Consider Merrick Garland's Supreme Court Nomination is Dangerous Obstructionism." *Los Angeles Times,* March 16.

Lyles, Kevin L. 1997. *The Gatekeepers: Federal District Courts in the Political Process.* Santa Barbara, CA: Praeger.

Maine Revised Statutes. 2016. "Declaratory Judgments Act." Section 5953. http://www.mainelegislature.org/legis/statutes/14/title14sec5953.html.

Marcus, Maeva, ed. 1992. *Origins of the Federal Judiciary: Essays on the Judiciary Act of 1789*. New York: Oxford University Press.

McCloskey, Robert G. 2016. *The American Supreme Court*. 6th ed. Chicago: University of Chicago Press.

McConkie, James. 1976. "Decision-Making in State Supreme Courts." *Judicature* 59 (February): 337–343.

Miller, Ken. 1999. "The Role of Courts in the Initiative Process: A Search for Standards." Paper presented at Annual Meeting of the American Political Science Association, Atlanta, Georgia.

Morris, Jeffery. 1987. *Federal Justice in the Second Circuit: A History of the United States Courts in New York, Connecticut, and Vermont, 1787–1987*. Washington, D.C.: Second Circuit Historical Committee.

Murphy, Walter. 1964. *The Elements of Judicial Strategy*. Chicago: University of Chicago Press.

National Center for State Courts. 2015. *The Landscape of Civil Litigation in State Courts*. Williamsburg, VA: NCSC. http://www.ncsc.org/~/media/Files/PDF/Research/Civil JusticeReport-2015.ashx.

National Center for State Courts. 2016. "Appellate Caseloads." October 8. http://www .courtstatistics.org/Appellate.aspx.

National Conference of State Legislatures. 2016. "Initiative and Referendum." October 9. http://www.ncsl.org/research/elections-and-campaigns/initiative-and-referendum .aspx.

National Women's Law Center. 2016. "Women in the Federal Judiciary: Still a Long Way to Go." March 16. http://nwlc.org/resources/women-federal-judiciary-still-long-way-go/.

Nelson, William. 1972. "Changing Conceptions of Judicial Review: The Evolution of Constitutional Theory in the State, 1790–1860." *University of Penn Law Review* 120: 1166–1185.

Neubauer, David W., and Stephen Meinhold. 2012. *Judicial Process: Law, Courts, and Politics in the United States*. 6th ed. Belmont, CA: Wadsworth Publishing.

"The Obama Judiciary at Midway." 2011. Roundtable, Midwest Political Science Association, 69th annual conference, Chicago, Illinois, April 1.

Orfield, Gary, and Erica Frankenberg. 2014. "Brown at 60: Great Progress, a Long Retreat, and an Uncertain Future." The Civil Rights Project/Proyecto Derechos Civiles, May 15. https://civilrightsproject.ucla.edu/.

Ostrom, Brian, and Roger A. Hanson. 2001. "Caseload and Timeliness in State Supreme Courts." *Caseload Highlights: Examining the Work of State Courts*, December. http://cdm16501.contentdm.oclc.org/cdm/ref/collection/appellate/id/89.

Ostrom, Brian, Neal Kauder, and Robert LaFountain. 2002. *Examining the Work of State Courts, 2001: A National Perspective from the Court Statistics Project*. Williamsburg, VA: National Center for State Courts.

Peppers, Todd C., and Artemus Ward. 2013. *In Chambers: Stories of Supreme Court Law Clerks and Their Justices (Constitutionalism and Democracy)*. Charlottesville: University of Virginia Press.

Phillips, Thomas. 2003. "State Supreme Courts: Local Courts in a Global World." *Texas International Law Journal* 38(3): 557–568.

Posner, Richard A. 1996. *The Federal Courts: Challenge and Reform*. Cambridge, MA: Harvard University Press.

Posner, Richard A. 2016. *Divergent Paths: The Academy and the Judiciary*. Cambridge, MA: Harvard University Press.

Presser, Stephen. 1983. *Studies in the History of the United States Courts of the Third Circuit*. Washington, D.C.: Bicentennial Committee of the Judicial Conference of the United States.

Purcell, Edward A. 1992. *Litigation and Inequality: Federal Diversity Jurisdiction in Industrial America, 1870–1958*. New York: Oxford University Press.

Purcell, Edward A. 2000. *Brandeis and the Progressive Constitution: Erie, the Judicial Power, and the Politics of the Federal Courts in Twentieth-Century America*. New Haven, CT: Yale University Press.

Romans, Neil. 1974. "The Role of State Supreme Courts in Judicial Policy Making: *Escobedo, Miranda* and the Use of Judicial Impact Analysis." *Western Political Quarterly* 27(1): 38–59.

Romero, David, and Francine Romero. 2003. "Precedent, Parity, and Racial Discrimination: A Federal/State Comparison of the Impact of *Brown v. Board of Education*." *Law and Society Review* 37(4): 809–827.

Rosenmerkel, Sean, and Matthew Durose. 2010. *Felony Sentences in State Courts, 2006 Statistical Tables* (revised Nov. 22, 2010). http://www.bjs.gov/content/pub/pdf/fssc06st.pdf.

Rowland, C. K., and Robert A. Carp. 1996. *Politics and Judgment in Federal District Courts*. Lawrence: University Press of Kansas.

Segal, Jeffrey A., and Harold J. Spaeth. 1991. *The Supreme Court and the Attitudinal Model*. New York: Cambridge University Press.

Slotnick, Elliot. 1977. "Who Speaks for the Court: The View from the States." *Emory Law Journal* 26(1): 107–147.

Songer, Donald, and Susan Tabrizi. 1999. "The Religious Right in Court: The Decision Making of Christian Evangelicals in State Supreme Courts." *Journal of Politics* 61(May): 507–526.

Staszak, Sarah. 2015. *No Day in Court: Access to Justice and the Politics of Judicial Retrenchment*. New York: Oxford University Press.

Surrency, Erwin C. 2002. *History of the Federal Courts*. New York: Oceana Publications.

Symposium. 1994. "The Supreme Court and the Attitudinal Model." *Law and Courts Newsletter* (Spring): 3–12.

Tachau, Mary K. Bonsteel. 1978. *Federal Courts in the Early Republic: Kentucky, 1789–1816*. Princeton, NJ: Princeton University Press.

Tarr, Alan. 1998. *Understanding State Constitutions*. Princeton, NJ: Princeton University Press.

Tarr, Alan, and Mary Porter. 1988. *State Supreme Courts in States and Nations*. New Haven, CT: Yale University Press.

Toobin, Jeffrey. 2014. "The Obama Brief: The President Considers His Judicial Legacy." *The New Yorker*, October 27.

Topf, Mel. 2001. "State Supreme Court Advisory Opinions as Illegitimate Judicial Review." *Detroit College of Law at Michigan State University Law Review* 1(1): 101–137.

Towers, Watson. "U.S. Tort Cost Trends: 2011 Update." http://www.casact.org/library/studynotes/Towers-Watson-Tort-Cost-Trends.pdf.

U.S. Department of Justice. 2016a. "U.S. Marshals Service, Facts and Figures." April 29. https://www.usmarshals.gov/duties/factsheets/facts.pdf.

U.S. Department of Justice. 2016b. "U.S. Marshals Service Fact Sheets." March. https://www.usmarshals.gov/duties/factsheets/index.html.

U.S. Department of Justice. 2016c. "History of U.S. Attorneys." June 8. https://www.justice.gov/usao/history.

Walker, Thomas G. 1999. "Perspectives on the Selection of Federal Judges: Commentary on the Selection of Federal Judges." *Kentucky Law Journal* 77: 635.

Walsh, Joseph. 2003. "The Evolving Role of State Constitutional Law in Death Penalty Adjudication." *New York University Annual Survey of American Law* 59(2): 341–353.

Wasby, Stephen L. 2012. "Legal Scholarship Highlight: Interaction of the Supreme Court and the Courts of Appeals." *SCOTUSblog.* March 14. http://www.scotusblog.com.

White, Penny. 2003. "Legal, Political, and Ethical Hurdles to Applying International Human Rights Law in the State Courts of the United States." *University of Cincinnati Law Review* 71(Spring): 937–975.

Wilson, Steven Harmon. 2002. *The Rise of Judicial Management in the U.S. District Court, Southern District of Texas, 1955–2000.* Athens: University of Georgia Press.

Yale Law School, The Avalon Project. 2016. "The Federalist Papers: No. 78." http://avalon.law.yale.edu/18th_century/fed78.asp.

Yarbrough, Tinsley E. 1987. *A Passion for Justice: J. Waties Waring and Civil Rights.* New York: Oxford University Press.

Zelden, Charles L. 1993. *Justice Lies in the District: The U.S. District Court, Southern District of Texas, 1902–1960.* College Station: Texas A&M University Press.

Zeldon, Charles L. 2007. *The Judicial Branch of Federal Government: People, Process, and Politics.* Santa Barbara, CA: ABC-CLIO.

Cases

Brown v. Board of Education. 1954. 347 U.S. 483.
Dred Scott v. Sandford. 1857. 60 U.S. 393.
Gideon v. Wainwright. 1963. 372 U.S. 335.
Mapp v. Ohio. 1961. 367 U.S. 643.
Marbury v. Madison. 1803. 5 U.S. 137.
McCulloch v. Maryland. 1819. 17 U.S. 316.
Miranda v. Arizona. 1966. 384 U.S. 436.

On the Web

Administrative Office of the U.S. Courts, http://www.uscourts.gov
Federal Judicial Center, http://www.fjc.gov
Judicial Branch, http://www.4uth.gov.ua/usa/english/politics/judbranc.htm
National Center for State Courts, http://www.ncsc.org
Supreme Court Historical Society, http://www.supremecourthistory.org

CHAPTER THREE
STRUCTURE AND PROCESS

Courts are institutions created by the government and given the authority to resolve disputes through the application of the laws and rules of a society. In the United States, the exact nature of federal judicial authority—what types of cases the courts can hear, how they are structured, what substantive laws they apply—is set by Congress under the dictates of the Constitution. The Constitution sets outside limits on the range of issues that federal courts can affect and the remedies that they can provide. Courts are reactive institutions. They do not reach out and choose the issues or controversies on which they will rule; rather, they act only when someone files a suit requesting their help and that suit fits within the constitutional and legal limits on the court's jurisdiction. Limiting a court's jurisdiction limits its reach; expanding its jurisdiction expands its ability to affect people and policymaking.

When courts take a case, the objective is to provide litigants (both private and public) a level playing field in which to work out the disputes, problems, and crises of everyday life. In doing this, courts serve to preserve order and provide predictability in society, to provide for the general welfare, and to protect individuals and property.

Like their British ancestors, American courts pay respect to tradition. The American legal culture has developed rigid expectations about actors in the court system. These traditions have evolved into formal rules, which have ramifications for court decisions. This culture affects how a case is discussed, which reasons and evidence are persuasive to the decision-making process, and who is entitled to plead a case. The sections that follow discuss these cultural characteristics.

POLITICS AND THE FEDERAL COURTS

Politics affects the federal courts in more ways than just the naming of judges. The courts are major political players in our governmental and political systems. As Alexander Hamilton noted in *Federalist* No. 22, "Laws are a dead letter without courts to expound and define their true meaning and operation" (Yale

Law School 2016a). Yet in the process, these decisions also have major political and policymaking consequences. From limiting or expanding the congressional and presidential ability to impose economic or social regulation, to judicial proclamation of expanded civil liberties' protections, the federal courts are institutions as political as the more officially "political" branches of the government.

This political influence of the federal courts, their ability to shape public policy by reference to the ideas or sometimes the whims of the judges and justices sitting on the courts, also suggests the influence of politics *on* the federal courts. Federal judges and justices are political actors operating within the social, cultural, and economic assumptions of their historical era. It is rare for them to rule in ways that are at odds with the general lawmaking majorities in the United States—at least for extended periods. Rather, federal judges provide a legitimating political function by giving a stamp of constitutionality to popularly supported policies and objectives. Still, we can take this view too far. Judges' decisions as to the fundamental values needing protection—and the extent that these values match those held by the political leadership of the other branches of government—impose limits on the range of public policy choices, emphasizing some while diminishing or even erasing others. As two Supreme Court watchers noted, "the Court may be a legitimator . . . but it is also a significant wielder of power" (Handberg and Hill 1980, 321). Therefore, although the political rhetoric of the United States emphasizes the important power of political majorities to make public policy choices through the election process and through petitioning or otherwise influencing their elected representatives, the federal judiciary may well have the last word on many public policies.

THE STRUCTURE OF THE FEDERAL COURT SYSTEM TODAY

The basis for our federal court system is found in Article III of the U.S. Constitution. As noted in more detail later, Congress first moved to create the federal court system in the Judiciary Act of 1789, which has been amended and expanded on numerous occasions since. The structure of this system is usually described as pyramidal, with the federal district courts—the trial courts—creating the broad base of the triangle. The courts of appeals form an intermediate appellate step, and the U.S. Supreme Court sits at the apex as the highest court in the nation.

United States District Courts

There are more than 95 federal district courts, which are the trial courts of the federal judicial system. There is at least 1 federal district court for every state and territory of the United States, and some states have as many as 4 district courts. No district court crosses a state line, and the federal code requires that the personnel who operate these courts—judges, U.S. attorneys, marshals, and juries—be residents of that federal judicial district. The Constitution and Congress establish the jurisdiction of the district courts. Congress has established the subject matter jurisdiction of the district courts (i.e., what cases can be heard in these courts) to include all cases in law or equity that can be brought under the Constitution and the laws or treaties of the United States. This grant of authority is established by statute and cannot be created by agreement or collusion among the parties to the action. There must be a real conflict involving real wrongs for federal subject matter jurisdiction to apply. In addition, the nature of these wrongs has to fall within the express limits set by federal statute.

Federal criminal actions, for example, must arise from federal statutes. In the federal system, there are no common-law crimes. Judges cannot rule against an act simply because it is dangerous or unwelcome. Congress must make these choices and place them into a specific criminal statute. The district courts simply apply these criminal rules to specific situations.

In civil cases, the subject matter jurisdiction of the federal courts extends to two types of cases: federal questions and diversity of citizenship cases. Federal-question jurisdiction is found in cases that involve legal claims based on the U.S. Constitution, U.S. laws, or U.S. treaties. Admiralty, trademark, or copyright cases, for example, are included here, as are cases brought by the United States to enforce federal regulations, tax codes, and procedures. As with federal criminal law, the district courts are limited to applying only those laws, rules, or rights found in the Constitution, federal codes, or federal treaties.

Diversity of citizenship jurisdiction exists in cases that have as parties citizens of different states (or a citizen against a foreign party) and where the amount in controversy is believed in good faith to exceed $75,000. State citizenship relates to domicile, the place at which one has a principal residence and intends to reside. If a person has a home in Florida but works out of state for a season, that person remains a citizen of Florida for diversity of citizenship purposes if he or she intends to return to live there. As currently applied, diversity jurisdiction requires that no plaintiff and defendant can be citizens of the same state, no matter how many other states' citizens may be involved in the lawsuit. This means that even in a case where there are more than 100 plaintiffs and 100 defendants, if 1 plaintiff and 1 defendant are from the same state—even if no other plaintiff or defendants share state residencies—the case cannot be heard in federal court under diversity jurisdiction.

Yet where full diversity of citizenship exists, this jurisdiction allows plaintiffs (the party filing the action) a choice as to whether to bring a civil action in a state or a federal court. This decision may be based on issues of convenience for the parties or their witnesses. It may revolve around the reputation of some courts for greater or lesser awards by courts and juries. The plaintiffs may want to avoid a particular court where their reputation is tarnished or may want to select that court because the defendant's reputation at that court is poor. It could also be as simple as the likely speed with which their case would be heard in a federal as opposed to a state court. Finally, diversity jurisdiction also affords some plaintiffs the ability to avoid trying the action in a state court in the defendant's home state, for fear of prejudice in favor of the defendant in that state court.

In addition, can businesses have citizenships? Corporations are a legal fiction—a company made up of many people treated by the law, as if it were a single individual. Hence, corporations—like individuals—can be said to have a home state. A corporation is deemed in law to be a citizen both of the state in which it is incorporated and of the state where it has its principal place of business. If a business is incorporated in Florida, for example, but has its principal place of business in Georgia, the company would be deemed a citizen of both states. Consequently, diversity of citizenship would not exist in an action where an opposing party was a citizen of either Florida or Georgia.

In addition to having subject matter jurisdiction, the court must also have jurisdiction over the parties to the action, the property that is the subject of the lawsuit, or both. By filing the lawsuit, the plaintiff submits himself to the court and consents to the court's personal (in personam) jurisdiction. To issue a judgment that is binding on the defendant, however, the court must have personal jurisdiction over the defendant as well. To claim jurisdiction over a defendant, our judicial system operates on a basic consideration of fairness. A defendant must have sufficient "minimum contacts" with the state in which the action is being filed so that he or she might reasonably expect to be subject to a court's jurisdiction there. A defendant from Florida who has never been to California, never done business there, nor had other forms of contact with the state would not be subject to its courts' jurisdiction based on a lack of "minimum contact" with California, for example. On the other hand, a Florida resident who does business in Mississippi most likely would be subject to the latter state's authority. The facts of each case must be examined in determining whether such contacts are sufficient.

Federal courts obtain personal jurisdiction in various ways. Service of a summons (an order from the court, noting that the defendant is being sued by the plaintiff and demanding a response within a set time) within the state where the federal court sits may be sufficient. Alternatively, a defendant who appears before the court to defend the case on the merits may subject the defendant to the personal jurisdiction of the court. (The logic here is that if one is willing to argue the merits of a case, then one should also be willing to have the court handle the matter. Where defendants want to challenge the jurisdiction of the court, they can file a "special appearance" in the court without subjecting themselves to personal jurisdiction.) Federal courts can also take advantage of "long-arm" statutes in effect in the state where the federal court is located. Under these statutes, the state legislature has already defined what minimum contacts will support personal jurisdiction; the statute also provides methods for the service of summons on the defendant in another state. If the defendant is served under a long-arm statute, he or she must appear and defend or risk losing the case by default.

How does the court obtain in personam jurisdiction over a business? As a condition of doing business in the state, most states require that corporations appoint an agent to accept service of legal papers relating to litigation arising out of the corporation's activities conducted in the state. Some states require that state officials be designated as the agent for the corporation. In either case, the exact meaning of "doing business" in a state is set by statute and is based on the type of business done in the state. Soliciting business or executing contracts in a state may be sufficient "contact" to hold that a corporation is doing business in a state. Simply sending an order into the state from time to time may not be sufficient to establish a corporate "presence" in the state.

Some court actions have as their goal a judgment directed at an item of property, for example, to settle a dispute over ownership of the property. This property may be real property, such as land or a building, or it may be personal property, such as a car, bank account, or furniture. In either case, the court may exercise jurisdiction over property that is within the state where the court sits. This is called in rem jurisdiction, jurisdiction over the "thing" as opposed to jurisdiction in personam, jurisdiction over the person. What differentiates an in rem proceeding from an in personam one is that the decision is directed at the property itself instead of being directed at a person, such as an order for a person to pay money damages. Property title disputes—who owns what—are often decided as cases in rem. Federal forfeiture suits by the government to seize illegal property are also generally handled as in rem proceedings.

Plaintiffs may bring a case in any state or federal court that has jurisdiction. They are not required to bring their actions in federal court just because the federal court would have jurisdiction. Nor are they barred from turning to the federal courts just because a state court could also hear the case. In a unique aspect of federal jurisdiction, defendants against whom an action has been brought in a state court can "remove" that case from state to federal court (say, to avoid having the case tried in the plaintiff's "home court") if a federal district court has jurisdiction. Generally, if the suit could have been filed initially in federal district court, it is "removable." That is to say, where all of the requirements for subject matter jurisdiction of the district court are met (i.e., there must be claims under federal law, treaties, or the U.S. Constitution, or there must be diversity of citizenship in the case, with the damage claim requirement met), the case is removable. If there are no "federal questions" and no diversity of citizenship, the case may not be removed.

District courts hearing cases under diversity operate under a unique set of circumstances. Although they are federal courts, they are applying state laws. Yet what does it mean "to apply state laws"? What are state laws, statutes, judicial precedents, and rules of procedure? Historically, the answer was statutes alone. In the case of *Swift v. Tyson* (1842), Justice Joseph Story held that federal judges were bound to follow only the black-letter law of a state in applying diversity jurisdiction; state judicial precedents and procedures could be ignored in favor of federal ones. In 1938, however, the Supreme Court in the case of *Erie Railroad Co. v. Tompkins* ruled that both the statutes and judicial precedents governing state matters bound a federal district court. Whereas the rules of procedure would remain federal, the laws applied and the precedents governing the application of those laws would be set by the states themselves. In this way, the Supreme Court assured that rulings arrived at under diversity jurisdiction would have the same outcomes whether they were heard in state or federal courts.

Circuit Courts of Appeals
Civil Matters

Under the Judiciary Act of 1789, the circuit courts had limited powers of judicial review of cases from the district courts. Appeals from the district courts in admiralty and revenue cases were most common. For admiralty cases, the value in dispute had to exceed $300. In civil cases in district courts, review of cases where the sum in controversy exceeded $50 could be sought in circuit court on a writ of error. Reviews by the Supreme Court of the decisions of circuit courts could be sought by a writ of error or a writ of appeal. These writs differ procedurally, but the distinction between the two steadily eroded over the first century of the American courts to the point where the differences hardly mattered.

The writs of appeal that were used to bring matters from the district court to the circuit court had their beginnings in the English courts that dealt with civil law, where the writs of error had been used by the common-law courts. Common-law courts kept limited records aside from pleadings filed, and admiralty courts preserved testimony in depositions. The difference between the two writs revolved around the extent of the record from the lower court that went to the reviewing court. Writs of error were ordinarily more limited because the record did not include all matters heard by the court below; it consisted mostly of the pleadings. Where the writ of appeal was used, the record of testimony before the court was more complete. The Judiciary Act of 1789 required that the method of proof by examination of witnesses be the same in all courts of the United States, reducing the distinction, in practice, between the two writs, but not ending it.

The application of the two writs distinguished them. On a writ of appeal, with all evidence and testimony from the trial court before the reviewing court, issues of both fact and law arising from the record were examined, and the review was broader. On a review of a writ of error, the circuit court examined the record for an error of law on the face of the written pleadings and more limited record. The writ of error did not reach matters within the discretion of the trial judge or such matters as a new trial request. To cure the limited record, lawyers asked for material to be incorporated into the trial record with a bill of exceptions. Lawyers could object to evidence, give grounds for the objections, and then "take exception" to the court's ruling and have it all included in the record of the court to be reviewed by a writ of error. Without the bill, these matters were left out of the court record.

During the course of the 19th century, the use of court stenographers became common. As a complete transcript of proceedings became available, the need for the bill of exceptions to preserve particular matters diminished. As laws and court rules referred generically to the "record" of proceedings, the transcript displaced the need for the bill of exceptions. The bill of exceptions was finally eliminated from court rules in the mid-20th century. Statutes and rules for the courts had long referred to "transcripts" being needed for appeals, and the phrase "transcript of record" became the commonly used term. After 1911, this phrase described the record on appeal for the circuit courts of appeals, as well as the Supreme Court.

At the beginning of the 20th century, the distinction between the writ of error and the writ of appeal had been lost to such a degree that some lawyers brought cases on both writs to avoid having their case dismissed because they had selected the wrong writ. In 1916, Congress acted to solve the problem by telling courts to ignore the mistake of bringing the wrong writ. In 1928, Congress did away entirely with the writ of error and ordered that relief be sought by a simple appeal.

Cases appealed to the circuit court from the district court on a writ of error were subject to the limited review described earlier, and the circuit court decision originally was final between the parties. Later, the Supreme Court was given the jurisdiction to review cases taken to the circuit by writ of error just as it examined other cases. In the 19th century, various requirements were imposed on the jurisdictional amount of circuit court judgments necessary for those judgments to be reviewed by the Supreme Court. After the establishment of the circuit courts of appeals in 1891, these monetary limits were repealed, and cases were considered depending on the nature of the case and not the amount in dispute.

In the early days of the circuit courts, two judges sat to hear the appeals from district court and to try cases of their own. Justices of the Supreme Court would sit in the circuit court with a district court judge. From time to time, these judges would split on decisions about the legal principles involved in a case. A procedure was used that allowed the judges to certify to the Supreme Court the question over which they had divided to have the Supreme Court settle the matter. When the circuit courts of appeals began operation in 1891, their judges could certify questions to the Supreme Court for guidance in their decisions. The Supreme Court later instructed the courts of appeals to decide these issues for themselves, and the practice became defunct.

Criminal Matters

When Congress created the federal courts in 1789, it did not create a method of appeals in criminal cases. Such appellate review, for the most part, did not exist in the English courts or those of the colonies. Instead, new trials were often granted to the defendant as a means of providing relief. In 1802, Congress took action to address the issue of appellate review in criminal cases by allowing circuit court judges to certify questions to the Supreme Court for guidance in their rulings in the trial of criminal actions when the two judges did not agree. Recall that the circuit court was the principal federal trial court for criminal offenses at the time, not the district court, and that district courts had only one judge, so a disagreement could not occur.

The Supreme Court itself limited the extent of this 1802 "appeal" provision by restricting itself to only those questions certified to it by the circuit court and not conducting any broad inquiry into the other circumstances and law of the case. In fact, early in its life, the Supreme Court opined that it could not hear criminal cases on writs of error or writs of appeal. The Court interpreted congressional enactments as allowing certain writs in the appeal of civil actions only, so that it could not hear criminal appeals on a writ of error; rather, the Court could only determine questions certified to it when a split of opinion occurred in the circuit court, and then only on the particular issue of law sent to the Court.

Other avenues of appeal were attempted in criminal actions. One was by a writ of habeas corpus, a method frequently used in the 20th and 21st centuries. This writ was infrequently used in the 19th century except for prisoners in federal custody. The writ ordered the person having custody of the prisoner to produce him or her in court and show legal cause for the detention of that individual. The writ was not to determine guilt or innocence, but only whether the person was being held according to law—in other words, whether the person was being accorded due process of law. The few cases that came to the Supreme Court prior to the Civil War did not call for the examination by the Court of varied issues of criminal law akin to the appeal of a case.

A second avenue employed was Section 25 of the Judiciary Act of 1789, which authorized the Supreme Court to review the decision of a state's highest court when the decision denied the validity of a federal statute or a provision of the Constitution. Claims by defendants that their rights under the Fifth and Sixth Amendments of the Constitution had been violated by a state's actions were turned away by the high court, which decided that these amendments did not apply to the states. The Court strictly adhered to the requirement that there be a division in the lower court's opinion in order to have a question certified to the Supreme Court. The Court denied that it had appellate power in criminal cases because Congress had not allotted it that power. Congress attempted to grant all parties a "split of opinion" certification right from final circuit judgments in 1872, but the statute endured only two years.

It was not until 1879 that Congress enacted a general law that allowed appeals in federal criminal cases. The law allowed appeals by writ of error from the district court to the circuit court in cases involving sentences of imprisonment, a certain level of fines imposed, or both. This was a limited right, and appeal to the Supreme Court was still restricted to the cases of divided opinions at the circuit court.

In 1874, an act was passed that allowed limited appeals of certain limited criminal matters from the Supreme Court of the Territory of Utah to the Supreme Court, but it was not until 1889 that a statute gave defendants the right to appeal to the Supreme Court, and that right was limited to defendants sentenced to death. This appeal was taken by a writ of error. The right of appeal was extended two years later to cases involving "other infamous crimes," a term later defined by the Supreme Court as including offenses punishable by imprisonment in the penitentiary. The filing of the writ stayed (suspended) proceedings in the lower courts, and the writs were to be heard expeditiously.

The circuit courts of appeals were set up in 1891 with some limited jurisdiction to review criminal cases, but the right of appeal to the Supreme Court in capital cases and those "other infamous crimes" was left intact. This left a large number of cases on the high court docket. Six years later, such appellate review was limited to capital cases, with the other matters to be taken up by the circuit courts of appeals. In 1911, the direct appeal to the Supreme Court was ended, and all criminal appeals were to be directed to the circuit courts of appeals. They could then be heard by the Supreme Court if the Court was willing to issue a writ of certiorari. The right of appeal to the Supreme Court from the circuit courts of appeals today continues to exist where a state statute has been struck down as contrary to federal law, treaty, or the U.S. Constitution.

The rules for appeals of criminal cases by the U.S. government are somewhat more restricted. Shortly after the Criminal Appeals Act of 1889 was passed, a federal district attorney (the previous title of U.S. attorneys) brought a writ of error to the Supreme Court, contesting a circuit court decision. The Supreme Court held that the government was not entitled to bring such a writ—the government could not correct errors of the trial court, even when those errors were obvious to all observers. When a similar situation arose that threatened a federal indictment, President Theodore Roosevelt pressed Congress to change the law, which it did with the Criminal Appeals Act of 1907. This act allowed limited government appeals of criminal case decisions, especially of pretrial orders.

In 1911, the government extended the right to obtain review by certiorari of cases where the district court ruling was upheld by the court of appeals, a situation where the high court had previously denied any further claim for review by the government. The circuit courts of appeals also retained the power to certify questions to the high court, a procedure that could aid either party. This tool is seldom used. Today, most criminal appeals are heard by way of grants of certiorari by the Court, rather than by habeas corpus proceedings or certification of questions.

The Supreme Court

The Constitution, it should be noted, created only the Supreme Court and left the establishment of other courts in the hands of the national legislature. The Constitution gives appellate jurisdiction to the Supreme Court under the laws to be passed by Congress. This means, essentially, that the Court's appellate jurisdiction is limited, and it is restricted to that approved by Congress. The Constitution provided that the Supreme Court would have original jurisdiction in some cases—notably suits affecting ambassadors and public ministers, and where a state is a party. This means that such actions would be filed in and first heard by the Supreme Court. Indeed, the early Court presided over cases that were heard by juries, although that ended in the first decade of the Court's existence. In that same decade, the Eleventh Amendment to the Constitution revoked the Court's jurisdiction in suits against states brought by citizens of other states.

Since the passage of the Eleventh Amendment, the Supreme Court's remaining exercise of original jurisdiction has been principally in suits by one state against another, regarding, for example, state boundaries. The Court has ordinarily referred such matters to a master appointed by the Court to hold hearings and prepare findings on the issues before him or her. The Court then approves those findings.

The Court's original jurisdiction in matters involving ambassadors and public ministers was a shared jurisdiction, as the Judiciary Act of 1789 gave this jurisdiction to the circuit courts as well. As a result, the cases involving ambassadors and public ministers have ordinarily been left to the lower federal courts.

Early on, the Supreme Court's ability to hear appeals was determined by what monetary amount was involved in the matter and by what writ was used to take the appeal. The Judiciary Act of 1789 required that the amount in controversy exceed $2,000. Cases that did not involve money issues, say, the liberty of an individual, would not be heard on appeal. The Court required that there be a certain pecuniary value established to hear the appeal.

Two writs were employed to take appeals—the writ of error and the writ of appeal. If a circuit court had heard an appeal from a district court on a writ of error, the Supreme Court held that determination to be final and would hear no further appeal. If the case traveled from the district court to the circuit court by a writ of appeal, however, the Supreme Court did not deem the circuit court decision as final. In 1830, a statute abolished the distinctions, and appeals by writs of error could be taken from the circuit to the Supreme Court.

The best-known and most disputed authority for the appellate jurisdiction of the Supreme Court was Section 25 of the Judiciary Act of 1789. This gave to the Court the ability to hear appeals from the highest court of a state in matters involving the "validity of a treaty or statute" of the United States ruled on in a state court or the validity of a state statute or an action by a state that is claimed to violate the Constitution, a treaty, or a law of the United States. Furthermore, it gave the Supreme Court appellate jurisdiction in cases involving the interpretation of the U.S. Constitution, a treaty, or a federal statute. In the early years of the United States, many states opposed allowing the Supreme Court to review the decisions of their highest state courts, and the validity and application of Section 25 was frequently called into question by states in appeals of judgments. Attempts were made in the national legislature to repeal Section 25. The Supreme Court repeatedly upheld the validity of that section, and Congress defeated attempts to repeal this provision. It should be noted that under Section 25, if the claim of a federal right was upheld by a decision of the state's highest court, no appeal to the Supreme Court was authorized by the statute. In 1914, this was changed so that decisions upholding or denying federal rights claims could be appealed from a state's top court to the Supreme Court.

Between the passage of the Judiciary Act of 1789 and the Civil War, the Supreme Court's jurisdiction was largely unaltered. At the same time, the United States grew tremendously in size and population, and so the number of trial courts grew apace. The explosion in the number of trial courts resulted in an increased load for the appellate courts. While the circuit courts had some appellate review of the district courts, the Supreme Court was the only general appellate court for the nation. During this time, Congress enacted statutes granting judicial review in some matters regardless of the pecuniary amount involved, expanded removal jurisdiction of actions against federal officers brought in state courts, provided for appeals in certain patent and copyright actions, allowed for direct appeals to the Court from district court in some land claim cases, and mandated Supreme Court review in some limited and special cases. The Civil Rights Acts of 1866 and 1871, which intended to provide federal protections for the rights of the newly freed slaves, also authorized appeals to the Supreme

Court and did not require proof of a pecuniary loss of a certain amount. Some maritime statutes authorized appeals. Congress, controlling the appellate jurisdiction of the Supreme Court according to the provisions of the Constitution, steadily increased the rights of litigants to take an appeal to the highest court of the United States. Between 1870 and 1880, the number of cases on the Supreme Court's docket almost doubled.

Under the Evarts Act of 1891, Congress created the circuit courts of appeals to relieve some of the burden of the Supreme Court. The law provided that most appeals from district or circuit courts would be taken to the circuit courts of appeals. Some issues, however, were considered by Congress to be so important that direct appeals from the trial court to the Supreme Court were authorized. These included disputes over jurisdiction of the court, convictions in "infamous crime" or capital cases, and cases involving interpretation of the Constitution or the constitutionality of a law.

Decisions of the circuit courts of appeals in some cases were defined as "final" in order to lower the number of cases that could be appealed. These cases included some equity cases, some criminal matters, and various others. The Supreme Court could review such cases, however, by the use of a writ of certiorari. This writ required a lower court to provide a higher court with the record of a case that the higher court wants to review. Thus, any circuit court of appeals case could be reviewed if the Supreme Court wanted to grant the review. This marked the expanded use of the writ in appellate practice of the Court. The Court set its own rules regarding when the writ could be issued. One area of increased use was where the circuit courts of appeals reached different results on the same legal issue. Throughout the 20th century, the Court developed rules to govern the exercise of "judicial discretion" that is reflected in the granting of the writ. The Court determined that one area in which the writ should be granted is to reconcile the conflicting decisions of the circuit courts of appeals.

Another intention of the Evarts Act was to establish a time period within which an appeal by writ of error or writ of appeal could be taken. The Judiciary Act of 1789 had allowed as much as five years for the action, which was then limited to two years by Congress in the 1870s. The 1891 law provided that writs to the court of appeals had to be taken within six months, and appeals or writs to the Supreme Court had to be taken within a year. While no time period was prescribed for writs of certiorari, the Court itself applied a one-year time period.

Direct appeals from the trial court to the Supreme Court were often authorized by Congress. The Evarts Act attempted to divert some matters to the circuit courts of appeals, but the direct appeals statutes persisted. Over the years, matters that had been directly appealable were shunted to the circuit courts for final resolution. So-called infamous crimes (those punishable by time in a penitentiary) were directed to the circuit courts of appeals in the late 1880s, and even capital cases, previously routed directly from the trial court to the Supreme

Court, were diverted to the circuit courts in the early 20th century. Throughout the century, the Court asked Congress to limit cases that could be directly appealed to the Supreme Court, and Congress complied. In 1988, Congress ended most direct appeals.

Procedures of the Supreme Court

The Judiciary Act of 1789 outlined some of the procedures for seeking an appeal to the Supreme Court by way of certain writs (e.g., writ of error or writ of appeal). These writs created a method for the Court to review the proceedings of a lower court. In utilizing the writs, the Court looked to the practice of the English courts, wherein these writs had been employed for years. This writ system of appeal remained basically unchanged into the 20th century.

The Judiciary Act of 1789 gave review jurisdiction over circuit court decisions via the writ of error. The process required that the amount in dispute meet the jurisdictional requirement ($2,000) and that the judge certify that security for damages and costs are provided. The writ had to include a transcript of the record in the court below; a listing of the errors asserted to have been committed requiring review; a request for reversal of the judgment; and notice to the other party, with an opportunity for it to respond to the writ. The writ did not act to halt all proceedings, so the security was needed to cover damages awarded below as well as costs incurred. The security was not originally meant to cover costs incurred at the Supreme Court. This was changed in the early 19th century, when a bond to cover costs at the Supreme Court was required, and this continues to be the practice of the Court.

The use of a writ of error to take a case from the highest state court to the Supreme Court was similar in procedure. A petition stating the matters for review was written, along with a request for review and the posting of a sufficient bond as approved by the state judge.

In circuit court writs and state court writs, a similar process was followed to prepare the matter for the Supreme Court's review. The clerk of the lower court would send the documents necessary for the review to take place to the clerk of the Supreme Court. These included a transcript of the proceedings in the lower court and copies of whatever documents filed in the case were needed for the Supreme Court to understand the legal issues and to provide full review of them. These papers are referred to collectively as the *return*. The Supreme Court provided time limits within which all of these documents had to be provided; if these limits were not adhered to, the matter could be dismissed on motion of the opposing party. If a party believed that the record submitted was incomplete, methods were provided to cure the omission of documents and complete the record. The Court would decline to hear a case with an incomplete record.

In its early use of review on a writ of error, the Supreme Court was limited in its ability to reverse a lower court decision. The Court could not act on errors in facts, for example. In matters within the discretion of the lower court judge, the Supreme Court refrained from reviewing the issues, leaving them in the lower court's hands. Matters were returned to the lower court for final judgment rather than having the judgment issue from the Supreme Court.

The same Judiciary Act of 1789 that provided for the writ of error also provided for the writ of appeal. Early on, this writ was used in admiralty and maritime cases. Over time, as has been previously noted, the two writs lost their distinctness, and review of cases from the circuit or state courts could be brought by either writ.

Another method of bringing a matter before the Supreme Court was by certification of a question to the Court. This method was created to solve a problem that could arise in the circuit courts. These courts had two judges. From time to time, they disagreed in their opinions, and Congress approved a method of settling these disagreements by allowing the circuit judges to ask the Supreme Court to settle their differences. Congress provided that in a split of opinions, the circuit judges would certify the issue in question for submission to the Supreme Court, if the parties in the case so requested. The matter was argued before the Court and the decision sent back to the circuit court. The cases in which certification could be used included criminal as well as civil cases. In these cases, the proceedings of the circuit court would be halted until the response of the high court was received.

Not all issues could be certified to the Supreme Court for decision. Just as in the case of writs of error, matters that were in the discretion of the lower court were not to be considered on certification. In addition, certification was a limited action. The whole case was not taken up to the high court by certification; the Court considered only the points where there was a division of opinion in the lower court. The rest of the case remained in the hands of the circuit court.

Over time, the provisions for certifying questions changed. Apparently concerned about the fact that certification delayed the conclusion of cases in which it was employed, Congress provided that the opinion of the presiding judge would be the circuit court's opinion, basically eliminating a possibility of a split in the opinion. After the case was concluded, however, the judges could notify the Supreme Court of their divided opinions, and the parties were always free to seek review by writ of error or writ of appeal. This seeming attempt to limit certifications was in contrast to a later law (after the establishment of the circuit courts of appeals in 1891) that seemed to broaden the ability of circuit judges to certify questions to the high court without regard to a division of opinion of the judges. This did not matter. The practice was discouraged by the Supreme

Court, and the number of certified questions has steadily diminished over the past century. Certification is practically extinct today.

As noted earlier in this chapter, the differences between the writs of error and appeal steadily eroded as the Supreme Court convinced Congress to restrict appeals via these writs and by way of direct appeal. The Court steadily moved to the use of the writ of certiorari, which allowed appeals at the discretion of the Supreme Court. In 1925, the use of the writ of error and the writ of appeal was further restricted by statute, and the writ of certiorari became the primary vehicle for review by the Court. This continues to the present day.

A word should be offered about the method of appeal, which involves the record, briefs, and arguments before the Court. The record basically consists of copies of the documents filed in an action in the lower court. It includes the transcript of proceedings, all filings in the case, motions, rulings, and the evidence submitted to the court, among other items. Without a complete record, the Supreme Court will not proceed with a case. Preparation of the record is the responsibility of the clerk of the court.

Simply stated, briefs contain the arguments of counsel in a case; the position of counsel on points of law in the case; and the statement of facts, laws, pleadings, and other materials on which counsel relies in his or her claim before the Court. The brief should include all matters that counsel intends to present in oral argument before the Court, with references to the matters of record on which counsel intends to rely. The Supreme Court, in its rules, describes the contents and length of the briefs, as well as their style and structure. These rules set the time, place, and manner for submission of the briefs of counsel to the Court and opposing counsel as well. The Court itself sets the rules for admission to practice before the Supreme Court.

It should be noted that in 19th-century practice, it was possible for counsel to submit a matter to the Supreme Court based solely on its briefs, without arguing the matter before the Court. It was up to counsel to decide whether to proceed in this fashion. Up to the end of the 19th century, this was a fairly common practice. In the 20th century, the practice fell into disfavor, with the Court preferring that matters be orally argued before submission.

The rules for oral arguments have evolved over time, and limiting their length has been a prime issue. For about the first 100 years, no time limits were set for oral arguments. Some arguments went on for days, especially in cases involving numerous attorneys, each wanting to be heard. As limits were developed on the number of attorneys who could argue in a given matter, the arguments were reduced in time. In the mid-19th century, counselors were given a couple of hours apiece for argument. In the 20th century, the time allotted was steadily diminished, first to 99 minutes, then to 1 hour, and finally to 30 minutes. The Court may always extend this time at its discretion, and as counsel is frequently asked numerous questions by the Court during its argument, time can be extended to allow counsel to finish his or her remarks. The Court often reminds counsel that the Court has reviewed the briefs of counsel, so counsel should not simply repeat what was provided in the brief.

The Judiciary Act of 1789 allowed the Supreme Court, as well as the other federal courts, to create rules to govern their operation. These rules could not expand the Court's jurisdiction or violate laws, but otherwise the law gave the Court power to govern its business. In the early years of the Supreme Court, the rules it created were not organized, leading to some questions about which rules governed which particular procedures or motions. In the mid-19th century, the rules were collected and organized to do away with the confusion. Many matters were dealt with in the rules: procedures before the Court, contents of briefs, rules governing the clerk, Court fees, and other items. In the 20th century, the Supreme Court established rules governing practice before the high court. The Court also established rules regarding the review of cases by writ of certiorari. In the early 1950s, sweeping rule changes were made by the Court, including the eventual creation of an advisory committee to review and change the Court's rules. Since then, the Court has revised time periods for completion of appeals procedures and the nature of documents submitted to it as well. The point to be made is that the Court has taken and exercised control over its own business.

Specialized Courts

When we think about the federal court system, we commonly envision it as a three-level pyramid, with the trial courts (federal district courts) at the bottom, the intermediate appellate courts (the circuit courts of appeals) at the second level, and the U.S. Supreme Court at the top. This neat and simple diagram of the national court system is incomplete, however. A number of national courts have a limited area of concern; that is, they are restricted to considering only certain special types of cases in limited areas of the law. These are courts created by Congress under the statutory authority of Article I rather than the power vested in Congress by Article III to create federal courts. These courts exist for specific purposes, and some have expired as their purposes were fulfilled. Here are some examples of these specialized courts.

Court of Claims

From time to time, persons and entities make claims against the national government, some for reimbursement for property taken, for services rendered, or for payments promised by representatives. In the early Republic, these claims were presented to Congress by petition and considered by committees of

Congress; then, Congress would decide whether or not to honor the claim by passing a bill in the ordinary course of congressional business. In other words, the ordinary legislative process was followed, through and including the president's signing the bill into law. This process was cumbersome and slow and allowed politics to enter into the process for consideration of the payment of claims.

In the mid-19th century, Congress changed this system by passing legislation to create a Court of Claims for hearing matters based on claims against the national government and other matters sent to the court by Congress. It was a three-judge court, and its findings were forwarded to Congress. Congress could then pass a bill to fulfill the judgment of the court. Congress, however, continued to hold its own hearings on the Court of Claims findings and to decide for itself about the validity of the claim. This prevented the process from moving forward rapidly, and Congress soon modified the law to make the Court of Claims findings a final judgment, to provide for a method of appeal to the Supreme Court, and to establish a method for paying the claims out of national funds.

The Court of Claims operated in a way that was different from other federal courts. The court, from the mid-19th century, employed commissioners to gather information about the claims that it received. As the number of claims increased, the court divided, with the commissioners acting as triers of fact, and the court acting as an appeals bench. Later the commissioners were allowed to make decisions on issues of law as well as finding facts. In appeals to the Supreme Court, that Court limited itself to considering issues of law and not whether the claim was deserving of compensation. The Court of Claims also had the power to certify questions of law to the Supreme Court, as the courts of appeals could, and when the Supreme Court began to use certiorari as the main vehicle for appeal, this was also applied to appeals from the Court of Claims.

In the early 1980s, the Court of Claims was combined with the Court of Customs and Patent Appeals to constitute the Court of Appeals for the Federal Circuit. The commissioners of the trial division became trial judges in a newly established U.S. Claims Court, later denominated as the United States Court of Federal Claims. The jurisdiction of the court is broad, covering matters of salvage claims, tax claims, property "takings," and numerous matters involving American Indian tribes. It is also concerned with almost all claims involving contracts with the federal government. It is not, however, involved with tort claims against the government.

Customs Court

The major source of income for the early U.S. government was customs duties. Congress enacted various laws setting the level of duties on imports. Frequently, disputes arose on the assessment placed on goods, and claims would be made for the overpayment of customs duties. In the early Republic, the manner of settling such claims was to bring an action in the district court. This process was slow and could lead to different decisions being reached in the different courts that were geographically associated with different ports.

In 1890, a law was passed to modify the method for reviewing tariff disputes. A Board of General Appraisers was created to hear challenges made by merchants about the classification and appraisal of goods. The procedure was informal, mainly based on the classification of goods into different categories with different duties applied. In many cases, the duty claimed by the Customs Service officer would be challenged by the importer in an action before the board. The hearing was without a jury, and cases moved swiftly. The board's findings were deemed final, and a provision was made for appeal to the circuit court of appeals. It is called a "final order" because appeals can only be taken from orders that are final, as opposed to proposed orders or interim orders. The circuit court, however, did not just review the board's findings—it conducted a new trial of the entire matter, both as to law and facts.

In the 1920s, an issue arose as to the judicial nature of the board. Some foreign governments were hesitant to allow evidence to be gathered by a U.S. board in their country. To rectify this problem, Congress changed the title of the Board of General Appraisers to the Customs Court. The new court's jurisdiction was the same as that of the old board, but certain additional federal court powers were allowed it, including the power of compelling attendance of witnesses and production of evidence along with contempt of court powers. In 1980, the Customs Court was given even greater jurisdiction in international trade matters and was renamed the U.S. Court for International Trade.

Most appeals from the Board of General Appraisers were heard by the circuit courts of appeals. Decisions could vary among the circuits. In 1909, this changed with the creation of the Court of Customs Appeals, which would hear all appraisal appeals. This court reviewed the facts and the law regarding the duties charged. It was made up of a presiding judge and four associates appointed by the president. Appeals from the newly denominated Customs Court were made to the circuit courts of appeals as well.

In 1929, the mission and jurisdiction of the Court of Customs Appeals was changed as it was now authorized to hear appeals from decisions of the Patent Office regarding patents and trademarks. The court then became the Court of Customs and Patent Appeals. Later changes further expanded the jurisdiction of the court in trade matters. In the early 1980s, this court was abolished, and its powers were transferred to the U.S. Court of Appeals for the Federal Circuit along with the powers of the Court of Claims.

Tax Court

Soon after its establishment by law in 1913, the U.S. government came to rely on the income tax as a valuable source of revenue. The tax code became increasingly complex, and a need arose for a body to hear appeals from the decisions of the commissioner of internal revenue. In 1924, the Congress created the Board of Tax Appeals. Previously, taxpayers had to pay the whole tax assessment and pursue a case before the Court of Claims or district court if they claimed an inaccurate assessment. The Board was established to allow for consideration of the commissioner's decisions and to create a uniform standard for taxpayers. It could review the commissioner's decision, but its findings were not final and could be taken to district court by either party. Provisions were also made for direct appeals to the court of appeals in certain matters. The board members were commissioners, not judges.

In the early 1940s, the Board of Tax Appeals was renamed the Tax Court, and the former commissioners were made judges. Over the years, a number of proposals have been entertained in Congress to alter the Tax Court, but most have not been enacted. In 1969, the powers of the Tax Court were expanded to resemble those of a district court. A separate division was created to deal with tax claims of less than $1,000, a sort of small claims court of taxes. Its decisions are not appealable, but cases can be reconsidered on motion. Most legal issues regarding taxes continue to be determined in appeals to the circuit courts of appeals, however, and not the Tax Court.

Veterans' Claims

The Veterans Administration (VA; established in 1930) makes decisions on the nature and extent of benefits to be awarded to U.S. military veterans. Health, education, disability, and support payments are determined by the VA. In 1933, the Board of Veterans Appeals was created in an attempt to shield the decisions of the VA from appeal, but in the late 1980s, Congress created the Court of Veterans Appeals to provide review of VA decisions involving either a denial of benefits or the level or type of benefits approved.

The court has a chief judge and six associates. Authorized to sit anywhere in the United States, it screens cases for hearings, conducts full-blown hearings before a panel of judges, and considers issues of both law and fact. It is empowered in much the same way as a district court to carry out its decisions. The final decision of this court is appealable to the Court of Appeals of the Federal Circuit. To avoid confusion with a similarly named division of the Veterans Administration, the name of the court was changed to U.S. Court of Appeals for Veterans Claims in the late 1990s.

OVERVIEW OF THE AMERICAN LEGAL SYSTEM
Some Fundamental Issues in Understanding State Courts

To understand state courts, it is helpful to start by introducing some of their basic aspects. Among the most important qualities of state courts that need to be introduced at the outset are the distinctions among judges, courts, and law. *Courts* are governmental institutions that have legal and constitutional authority to resolve disputes between two or more competing parties over matters of law, rights, or compliance with law. As institutions, they are staffed by personnel with specific roles to play in the organization. As a branch of government, courts are viewed by most people as having legitimate authority to issue decisions that the parties involved should obey or be forced to obey by governmental power.

A *judge* is an individual who has power, by virtue of their place in the institution of the court system, to hear evidence, resolve arguments over points of law, make binding judgments in those cases, and see that the judgment is enforced. The court of law is the forum from which the judge issues a decision. It is also the governing body that puts the judge's decision into effect. A judge's decision is supposed to stem from the law and available evidence in particular cases. When decisions do not stem from these sources, appellate courts may overrule lower court decisions, and, in some cases, errant judges may be disciplined or removed from office through some institutional process. While the judge's institutional role entitles the judge to make certain decisions about policy and behavior, the institution conditions the judge's choices.

Another term worth taking some time to clarify is *law*. One may define *law* as the body of formal rules, rights, and regulations that people expect government to protect and enforce through the exercise of coercive power. One element of this definition is the threat of governmental coercion, or *force*. Not all legal scholars agree that the threat of force is a necessary component of law. Some find a law exists when individuals feel compelled to behave in some way, with or without the threat of force. This approach encompasses morality, cultural norms, courtesy, and other social pressures that regulate individual behavior. These forces certainly are important in society, but unless there is an expectation that government will enforce a behavior, it is beyond the scope of this discussion. Of concern is the collection of rights and norms of behavior that come through governmental channels and that will be enforced by government officials.

Law: Its Origins, Authority, and Nature

To help analyze law, it is helpful to try to categorize types of law that seem to have common attributes, much the way biologists try to sort plants into categories of kingdom, phylum, genus, and species. In the same spirit, law can be organized into classifications by its distinguishing features.

The Sources of Law

There is considerable debate about the sources of authority that permit courts to rule as they do. It is important for readers to understand the sources of authority cited in U.S. courts. Not all laws are created equally. There is a pecking order in the American system that determines which law should prevail if two legal principles come into conflict. This discussion gives an overview of how competing legal authority is typically prioritized.

Natural Law

Some theorists, particularly those interested in the philosophy of law, turn to the study of nature to find parallels with the ultimate origins of law. *Natural law* is often associated with theological concepts, but not always. In short, the natural law theory suggests that a natural or divine source instilled in the human imagination creates certain norms of behavior that cause most people to respect the dignity of themselves and others without legislation having to insist on it. This same ultimate source of human behavior instills in individuals a common sense of certain self-restraints or duties. To natural law scholars, law that is common to all societies can be observed through appropriate scientific methods, just as the use of appropriate scientific tools allows one to observe chemical or biological phenomena. Much of human behavior, in this school of thought, is a natural occurrence.

Natural law scholars find that almost all societies oppose incest and killing other humans, and that most individuals have a sense of self-preservation and act in their self-interest. Therefore, at some minimal level, a divine or natural force makes some rules common to all societies, regardless of culture, climate, or dominant religion. In the United States, much has been made about the phrase in the *Declaration of Independence* that all people are "endowed by their Creator with certain unalienable rights" to argue that natural rights-natural law reasoning is at the core of American political philosophy. Many natural law theorists would agree with the sentiment among the American revolutionaries that when the laws of a government are unjust, reasoning people have no moral obligation to conform, a precept of natural rights thinking.

Positive Laws: Laws Made by People

Many political scholars are interested in natural law theory, but in general, its relevance to understanding the day-to-day work of American state courts is limited because U.S. courts rely on written civil authority to justify rulings. Without written civil authority, a judge's decision-making would be seen as arbitrary or pressing up against the constitutional separation of church and state. Rather, the laws enforced by government are referred to as positive law. Here, the word *positive* means that a government-asserted regulatory authority is needed to put rules into words and then into force, regardless of what is motivating them to do so.

Seven main types of positive regulations make up the law that is enforced by American courts: constitutional laws, statutes, ordinances, regulations, executive orders, common-law rulings, and contracts. There are two main factors that help differentiate the types of laws. The first is the authorship of the law. Each type of law or rule is written by a different authority. The second is the order of importance of these laws and rules.

Constitutions in the U.S. tradition are the highest form of law. Any act of government found to be in conflict with the U.S. Constitution or that state's constitution must be ruled invalid. Among the state and federal courts, the federal Constitution is supreme. In the states, however, courts show similar respect for their constitutions that the U.S. Supreme Court shows to the national charter.

A constitution's principal function is to establish a government, determine who in that government should make which decisions, set out the process of making binding rules, and resolve disputes within a society. Just as noteworthy, constitutions in each of the states say there are certain things government cannot do, such as prohibit religious worship, limit the expression of political opinions, and keep people from traveling. Some state constitutions severely limit certain taxing powers, or limit the number of terms of office for some leaders, protect important industries, and, recently, prohibit same-sex and polygamous marriages.

Because of the number of amendments addressing local concerns, state constitutions can be quite wordy. Alabama's runs 315,000 words and has more than 740 amendments. California voters, for example, are quite fond of the voter initiative, where ordinary citizens put proposed constitutional amendments to a vote on statewide ballots. Constitutional rules can make the amendment process quite easy or very difficult. Due to the weight of numerous amendments, 40 states introduced new constitutions after 1960 (see Council of State Governments 2016).

Constitutions at the federal and state levels refer primarily to procedural aspects of law. That is constitutional law dictates how decisions should be made, who should make them, and, in general terms, how a society will choose its political leaders. The U.S. Constitution requires that each of the states have a *republican* government, or one in which elected leaders make decisions, usually by majority rule.

Procedural aspects of constitutions can be contrasted with the substantive elements of constitutions. Substantive features of law refer to specific rights or duties. For this reason, some law is ruled invalid because it was passed in an invalid way, not necessarily because the law itself violated some fundamental right of a citizen. For example, many state constitutions have single-subject rules that require each bill coming through the legislature to deal with only one topic. Congress, by contrast, often finds it necessary to pass omnibus bills that carry many subjects to please many audiences. State courts have struck down otherwise valid laws because they violate their state's single-subject clause.

Statutes, also referred to as *acts*, are rules enacted by legislatures. Ordinances are similar to statutes, but the term generally refers to the acts established by local legislatures such as city councils and county boards. Statutes and ordinances become law primarily through deliberative bodies, though some states and cities allow voters to enact legislation directly through what is called the initiative process.

Regulations, which are rules made by regulatory agencies, have the same force as statutes. Agencies, however, cannot create regulations of their own volition. Rather they must find statutory authority to create particular rules. In other words, a statute will authorize an agency to create specific regulations to achieve some general goal. For example, a state legislature may authorize the state natural resources department to regulate airborne pollutants for the public good. In doing so, the legislature delegates to the agency's scientific and legal staff the responsibility to define "pollutant" and "public good." This then leads to the limits on the fumes that cars or factories can emit into the atmosphere. As legislatures can grant authority to create rules, they also can limit the scope and process of bureaucratic rulemaking.

Executive orders are rules or commandments issued by the governor, a mayor, or the heads of bureaucratic agencies to inferior administration agents. This may be the case when the governor orders a hiring freeze or cancels travel during financial crises. Formally, the executive order is thought of as an internal issue between the boss and subordinate, but the effects may be felt outside the agency.

Case law, also called common law, is the reasoning consistently applied by courts in the resolution of disputes. Case law finds its origins in the courts. It not only creates a command; it also provides a way of thinking about a problem so that similar situations can be addressed with similar legal logic. For example, in the absence of statute, superior courts have developed standards to be used by lower courts when they hear cases. Supreme courts in each state have established standards regarding the responsibility of different parties when an injury occurs in a workplace or elsewhere, which the trial judges must consider when ruling in personal injury cases. In this way, courts devise reasoning about how to handle responsibility when people claim they were hurt while on the job, when using a manufactured product, or in other situations.

The individual may claim the injury was caused because of reasonable use (e.g., the injured party stood on a chair to change a lightbulb). The character of the case, however, may require that the judge consider a higher standard of intended use of the product. In this way, the higher court creates a rule that gives rise to outcomes by governing the decision-making process and the selection of what items are worthy of consideration in a hearing.

Only some of what is written in a constitution is straightforward. Courts are left to give meaning to high-minded phrases such as "equal protection" or "high-quality education" because constitutional authors seldom define these expressions in the text of a state charter. Although state constitutions provide the foundation for constitutional law, state courts must give meaning to ambiguous terms. State supreme courts issue decisions related to the powers of government, decision-making processes, civil rights and liberties, and other concerns incorporated into the constitutions.

Contracts are enforceable agreements by which individuals or organizations submit to rules of their own creation and by their own volition. This type of law is the work of parties who freely choose to submit to the terms of the contract to receive the benefits of the duties performed by the other party. Government's coercive power comes into effect only when courts are called on to enforce these agreements. In some cases, courts are bypassed altogether in favor of alternative dispute systems such as arbitration. (Alternative dispute resolution is discussed in Chapter 2.) State law, federal law, and court decisions place some restrictions on the content of contracts, but, in general, contracts represent a distinct type of rule in the sense that they only directly affect the people who entered into the agreement.

A Hierarchy of Law

Law can be organized according to a hierarchy or by order of importance. It is very much a part of the American legal tradition that some sources of political power outweigh others, and the law from one source can outweigh another.

For those who subscribe to the ideas of natural law, God's law or the laws of nature have precedence over all other types of law. This approach is advocated not only by religious scholars, such as Thomas Aquinas, but secular observers such as Sir William Blackstone, whose treatise *Commentaries on the Laws of England* is cited quite widely today in American courts. Blackstone argues the following:

This law of nature, being coeval with mankind and dictated by God Himself, is of course superior in obligation to any other. It is binding over all the globe, in all countries, and at all times. No human laws are of any validity, if contrary to this; and such of them as are valid derive all their force, and all their authority, mediately or immediately, from this original. But in order to apply this to the particular exigencies of each individual, it is still necessary to have recourse to human reason; whose office it is to discover, as was before observed, what the law of nature directs in every circumstance of life; by considering, what method will tend most effectually to our own substantial happiness. (Yale Law School 2016b)

Even if one does not subscribe to the ideas of natural law, there still remains a hierarchy of laws within states' political systems. When one legal obligation or right is in conflict with another, the superior source of authority prevails. In general, the hierarchy of American law ranges from the U.S. Constitution at the top to local ordinances and contracts at the bottom. From the supremacy clause of the U.S. Constitution, the national charter acquires power superior to all other positive law at work in the United States. Because local governments acquire their power from state legislation, local rules and regulations are lower in authority.

Within individual states, state constitutions have a place analogous to the federal Constitution. This allows state courts to overturn state statutes when the statutes are contrary to the state's constitution. Statutes are next in importance. Bureaucratic regulations, case law, and executive orders can be modified or reversed by an act of the legislature. Local ordinances can be overridden by state authorities because under the U.S. system, state government authority is sovereign, with local governments existing as instruments of the states. Contracts have the least authority because they are instruments between private parties, and the public good usually outweighs individual need.

The Public and Private Nature of Law

Public law refers to the rules that affect the prerogatives of governmental officials and the rights of citizenship. Like their colleagues on the federal courts, state judicial officers are presented with demands to consider issues related to the government's role in society, its power to tax, spend money, and control behavior. They determine the scope of individual rights under federal and state constitutions. Public law includes questions about voting, public speech, legislative deliberations, and the monetary value of court awards. They also review the work of state regulatory agencies. Public law, in short, is concerned with making public policy, citizenship, society, and the relationship between government and the individual. An individual court decision that affects the law governing the conduct of public affairs is a decision in public law.

Within this genus of public law are various species. Constitutional law is the body of doctrines that define the meaning of the federal or state constitutions, the rights guaranteed to individuals, or the powers granted to government through these documents. Another species of public law is criminal law, which deals with violations of law, enforcement powers, arrest processes, and investigation, prosecution, and punishments that may be meted out as a result of conviction.

Another form of public law is administrative law. This is a complex area of law that is concerned with the authorities of bureaucratic agencies, ranging from their powers to develop regulations to the rights of agency staff in relation to their employer. Because many agencies have executive enforcement powers as well as quasi-legislative rulemaking power and quasi-judicial powers, administrative law contains a hybrid of other forms of public law.

Private law refers to cases between individuals, corporations, or other non-government entities. In private suits, parties seek peaceful resolution of a quarrel between the parties at hand, and the suits have no immediate implications for public affairs. Within the confines of private law, one can find tort law, which is more often than not related to personal injuries. Another type is contract law, which deals with the agreements that individuals freely make with each other and the extent to which courts can, or will, enforce them. Family law deals with marriage, children, adoption, and the like. State courts determine private issues such as adoption and child custody, personal injury claims, conflicts over contracts, property ownership, and the organization of businesses. By dealing with private law, state courts determine ownership of a disputed piece of property, including creative works and other intellectual property. In this way, courts can bring a nonviolent solution to private conflict.

Although called private law, state supreme courts play a vital function in shaping the rules by which individuals resolve their disputes. Even in cases that are not contested, the lawyers advising clients in private negotiations are familiar with the boundaries set by state supreme courts. With this in mind, it becomes evident that when negotiating a contract or making amends for personal injury, informed parties are influenced by the decisions already made by local and state level courts.

Criminal and Civil Law

In the American judicial system, broadly speaking, two types of cases are heard: criminal and civil. Criminal law governs individual conduct with a set of rules enforced by the government. The primary objective is the maintenance of social order. Criminal law does this job by punishing what society perceives as deviant behavior and, in so doing, sets standards of proper behavior by which it can define and discourage antisocial behavior. There are different levels of severity in criminal offenses—infractions, misdemeanors, and felonies—dealt with by progressively more severe punishments. Criminal law makes the government a party to the action as the representative of the entire society. Most criminal law actions take place in state courts, but the federal criminal caseload has grown with the increase in federal criminal laws.

Civil cases are those that relate to the conduct of and relationship between individuals or business enterprises. People who think that they have suffered a loss at the hands of a business or another individual represent themselves in the action. Litigants in civil cases usually seek compensation for a loss or the return of something valuable that was taken from someone. The government does not act as representative of the society for the loss suffered by an individual. Rather, the courts serve as impartial forums for private dispute resolution. Civil law judges serve a similar role to that of umpires or referees in sports. While they have no personal interest in the outcome, it is their job to see that the process goes smoothly and that the interests of the wider audience (in the case of the law, the people) are protected.

Most cases in the American judicial system never get to trial. Trials are expensive, time-consuming, and unpredictable. Most civil cases are accordingly settled by the agreement of the parties themselves outside a courtroom on the basis of their lawyers' expectations as to the likely outcome should the case go to trial. In criminal actions, pleas, plea bargains, and diversion programs account for the failure to go to trial.

The judicial system in the United States consists of both a federal court system, established under the U.S. Constitution, and the judicial systems of each of the 50 states. Civil and criminal cases are heard in both of these systems, and both are basically systems with three levels or tiers. For both systems, the bottom level consists of trial courts, where actions are first filed and litigated. One step up from that, in the middle tier, are the intermediate appellate courts of the states and the courts of appeals in the federal court system. On top sits the highest court of the respective systems, most often named by states as the supreme court (though some states use other names), while in the federal system, it is called the U.S. Supreme Court.

It is not a misnomer to talk about 51 American court systems as opposed to simply *the* American court system. Although there are many similarities between the various state and federal courts, their rules—both substantive and procedural—vary widely. The differences tend to be greatest at the level of content (rules). The structures by which these courts are organized, in terms of both procedures and organization, are much more similar than they are different.

To hear and decide a case, for instance, the court (state or federal) must have jurisdiction to do so. This means they must have the legal authority to hear and grant relief in particular cases. This authority is usually conferred by either the statutes or constitution that apply to each court system, or both. In the federal system, jurisdiction is governed by federal law and the U.S. Constitution. There are two basic types of jurisdiction: original and appellate.

Original jurisdiction refers to the ability of a court to hear a case as a trial court. This usually refers to the court that hears the case first in the judicial system. Under original jurisdiction, a court will hear and determine the facts of a case, in addition to applying the law to the facts of the case. Trials can take two forms: trial by jury or a trial by a judge. In a trial by a judge (called a "bench trial"), the judge has control of all aspects of the trial; that is, the judge determines the facts of the case and then applies the law to those findings. In a jury trial, there is a division of tasks between the judge and the jury. The judge will rule on issues of law (e.g., admissibility of evidence) and provide the jury with instructions on the law that it is to apply. The jury hears the witnesses and evaluates the evidence to determine what facts have been successfully proven. The jury resolves conflicts in the testimony of witnesses and determines who is to be believed. It assigns weight to different items of evidence and testimony, and then applies the law given in the judge's instructions to the facts it finds. The jury reaches a verdict favoring one side or the other in the case.

After a trial, an unsatisfied party may request a review of the finding of the trial court by appealing the trial court decision. Appellate jurisdiction is a court's ability to review and alter the decision of a trial court. Usually, the appellate court will limit its review to the application of the law in the trial court and not conduct a review of the record of facts found in the lower court. The appellate court decides whether the trial court properly applied the correct law in the case or whether an error was committed. There is no jury in the appellate court, and no witnesses are heard. The court's review is limited to the facts and legal theories developed in the trial court by the parties to the case. No new arguments or proof are allowed at the appellate level; the court relies on the record of proceedings sent to it by the trial court and the briefs of legal arguments submitted by the parties. (The record of proceedings is a complete file containing all of the pleadings and documents filed in the case, as well as a transcript of the trial itself.) If, after an appeal is heard and decided, a party is still unsatisfied with the decision on the appeal, he may have the right to take a further appeal to the highest appellate court in the state or federal system.

Generally, in both state and federal systems, litigants are guaranteed only a single appeal on the merits of their case. This guaranteed appeal is usually provided by the intermediate courts of appeals, such as the federal circuit courts of appeals. Appeals beyond this level—in the federal system, to the U.S. Supreme Court—are at the discretion of the court. Only those cases deemed most important get a second hearing by an appellate tribunal (more on this later in this chapter).

The Nature of Law: Process and Substance

There are two other categorizations of law: procedural law and substantive law. Procedural law is concerned with the rules of the court decision-making system. Procedural law controls how law is to be enforced, understood, argued, made, or changed—in other words, the rules of the game.

Substantive law refers to the actual right, responsibility, or norm of behavior that is in dispute. In the U.S. system, a procedural rule is that our courts use an adversarial system where opposing lawyers argue before a neutral judge. The substantive argument may be over whether Jones owes Johnson money. The procedure may be friendlier to the debtor, or the creditor, by requiring that creditors file claims within very tight or very relaxed deadlines, which in turn affects how long someone has to make the substantive claim to money.

Structure of Court Systems

It may be appealing to think of courts in the hierarchical structure of the federal judicial system. As stated earlier, the general structure of the federal judicial system is drawn to look like a pyramid with trial courts at the foundation, appellate courts in the middle, and a court of last resort (COLR) at the apex. Thinking of the state courts in these terms, however, would be a serious mistake. Only a handful of states have this type of three-step judicial system: trial court of general jurisdiction, an intermediate court of appeals, and a single COLR. Each of the remaining 46 states has its own variety of courts of limited jurisdiction. Oklahoma and Texas, for example, have more than one COLR. The states with courts of limited jurisdiction have distinct appeals processes, sometimes requiring more steps between the trial court and court of final appeal than is the case in the federal system. Some state court systems do not have the intermediate appellate court, which means that appeals of trial court decisions proceed directly to a COLR (see National Center for State Courts 2016a).

All of this is to say that no one diagram accurately describes the structure of state court systems. Rather, it is more accurate to think of the variety of court systems that exist. Despite the variety of structures, the Fourteenth Amendment of the U.S. Constitution insists on some characteristics of *due process* that make some of the procedures and structures common to all states. One of the most important due process features that affects structure is the principle that a trial decision may be reviewed by an appeals court. In other words, in every state, no matter how simple or complex in structure, there is a court of origin in which cases are initially filed (originates) and where trials are held. There is also at least one court of review, or a court of appeals, which is authorized to accept, reject, or require modifications to the legal decisions made in lower courts. This section begins with an explanation of the courts most narrow and limited authority. It then progresses to a discussion of trial courts with general authority and finally moves through the appeals process.

Courts of Limited Jurisdiction

Courts of limited jurisdiction are those trial courts authorized to resolve cases of a special and focused nature. This contrasts with courts of general jurisdiction, in which any type of case, with any level of significance, can be filed.

Organized either by a state constitution or by an act of legislation, courts of limited jurisdiction may have geographic jurisdiction. A common type of limited jurisdiction court is a municipal court, which serves the needs of an individual city. In other cases, these courts are limited by subject matter, such as drug courts, family courts, and in some western states, water courts. Some are limited by the gravity of the issues that may be brought before them, such as small-claims courts, which are limited by the dollar value of the awards they can issue.

It is perhaps the limited jurisdiction courts that distinguish the state judicial systems from one another. In the United States, there are roughly 14,000 to 16,000 limited jurisdiction courts (Cornell 2012). What makes the judicial systems so distinctive is that there are so many types of limited jurisdiction courts across the nation. Moreover, even when states have the same type of limited jurisdiction courts, there can be important differences in how these courts function and the work they do. New York and Georgia, for example, have 8 separate limited jurisdiction courts. Some of these courts may have jury trials, while others are not allowed to use juries. Some of the limited jurisdiction courts are active in specific locations, such as Atlanta or New York City, while others are found in every part of these states.

Massachusetts, for example, has six types of limited courts. In Massachusetts one special court, *probate and family court*, deals with divorce and adoptions, while the *juvenile court* handles other domestic matters such as domestic battery. New Jersey has a tax court, where residents are able to contest local tax bills. Other states have specific duty courts to deal with the environment, water rights, wills, or children. Despite these important differences, there are eight main types of limited jurisdiction courts. These are described in the following sections.

Administrative Agency Courts

Administrative agency courts are designated to hear cases emerging from disputes with particular governmental bureaucracies or on narrowly defined subject matter. Administrative courts are independent from the executive branch of government. Before accepting cases, these courts typically require that all avenues for resolving the conflict through commissions and agencies have been attempted. It is only when the bureaucracy has failed to find a resolution that is satisfactory to the parties involved in the dispute that the court will take up a particular case. Selection of judges, their terms of service, and qualifications for office vary by state. Appeals of the decisions made by administrative agency courts go directly to intermediate appeals courts, or in some states, to the highest court.

There are different types of administrative courts across the nation. The development of particular administrative courts is closely connected to the particular culture, history, industry, and natural environment of individual states. For example, there are water courts in arid western states, such as Montana and Colorado, which are often subject to drought and forest fires. The water courts allocate access rights to rivers, lakes, and underground aquifers. In Arizona, where many residents prefer limited governmental intervention, there is a special *tax court* to review complaints about property tax assessments.

Chancery Courts

Chancery courts are judicial offices where chancellors rather than judges are empowered to substitute equity for law in rendering a decision. The point of a court of equity is to afford a *fair* ruling when the common law might render a harsh verdict.

A decision in equity often takes the form of commandment for some party to act or stop performing some act. These injunctions and orders typically attempt to balance financial considerations with other values not easily understood in the common-law tradition. Common-law traditions would care only about the ownership of some property, ignoring the historic, natural, sentimental, or spiritual value of that property to nonowners. For example, a real estate developer with a proper deed to land may discover that he is building on an ancient Native American burial ground. The sentimental and spiritual value of this parcel to a Native American tribe may be argued in a court of equity. The tribe may seek *equitable* relief, or an order to refrain from upsetting holy ground, without any demand for money to change hands.

As venues for resolving dispute, *courts of equity* handle disputes that are concerned with business, finances, tax, contracts, shareholders, and property. In some states, such as Arkansas and Mississippi, chancery courts have jurisdiction in civil areas such as wills, family, juvenile, and insanity cases.

Chancery courts have existed in Europe since feudal times. Chancellors hear cases either alone or on panels that usually consist of three people. Although the United States inherited many English legal traditions, the importance of chancery courts in the United States has diminished over time. The clear distinction between law and equity has faded, and the two principles may be pleaded in the same court. Through adoption of the U.S. Constitution in 1789, federal courts were authorized to hear both law and equity cases. Most states followed suit and abandoned the use of a distinct chancery court. However, Delaware, Tennessee, Mississippi, and, to a lesser extent, New Jersey, maintain distinct chanceries in their state court systems.

Originating as clerical offices of European monarchs, chanceries eventually gained from the Crown the power to waive common-law judgments. The ancient chanceries were organized to provide ministerial support, maintain official records, and provide formal communications for European kings, princes, and bishops. Chancellors later were given power to resolve disputes outside common-law systems.

Today some chanceries still perform support functions by providing notary services and record keeping.

Drug Courts

Drug courts are among the most recent types of limited jurisdiction courts in the nation and have become one of the busiest. The creation and growth in drug court activity reflects changes in laws during the 1980s. At that time, the "war on drugs" meant state and federal officials tightened laws against the trafficking and possession of illegal substances. Many misdemeanor offenses were reclassified as felonies, drug laws were enforced more rigorously, and punishments became more severe. With stricter laws, the caseloads of the state trial courts swelled. In 1997, more than 33 percent of the nation's prison population was made up of individuals who had been convicted on drug offenses. This compares with about 7 percent in 1980 (Garrison 2002). With this burgeoning activity in court, states established special venues to handle the traffic in drug cases.

These courts are unique in that they generally have broader geographic jurisdiction than most state trial courts. Where most state courts have geographic jurisdiction boundaries, drug courts operate without these to avoid questions about *venue*, or where a trial must be held. Drug courts also are encouraged to refer cases to federal courts when federal penalties are higher or when a case involves interstate drug trafficking.

Drug courts rely on traditional punishment as well as rehabilitation, counseling, and education programs to discourage offenders from using drugs in the future. In states with drug courts, a special division of the local court system receives most drug cases. Drug case judges receive additional training and have social service agencies in close contact but remain in the general jurisdiction court systems.

Family Courts

Family courts, sometimes called *domestic relations* courts, deal strictly with family matters. Only a few states have formal family courts. In these courts, a specially trained family law judge hears domestic abuse, juvenile delinquency, and divorce cases. Family law concerns adoptions, incest, domestic violence, juvenile delinquency, disposing of wills, divorce, institutionalization of someone mentally unfit to care for himself or herself, and paternity-child custody issues.

Family-court judges are afforded additional personnel and liaisons with social service agencies uniquely suited to dealing with the sensitive domestic issues beyond the typical scope of the legal dispute. Family courts have extra latitude to look at social rehabilitation in addition to incarceration and penalties when criminal behavior is involved. In some states, such as Delaware, judges are required to have specialized training and practice in domestic law matters prior to serving as a family court judge, while most other states do not formally recognize family law as a subspecialty.

Justice of the Peace Courts

Justice of the peace courts may be best known for providing civil marriage ceremonies. Once a fixture in every state, justices of the peace (JPs) serve in only a handful of states today as magistrates in petty criminal offenses and small-claims civil cases, notaries, and administrators of oaths of office. Several other states continue to select JPs but do not grant them any formal court authority. Rather, in states such as Vermont, JPs serve on local election commissions, hear tax abatement petitions, and preside at weddings. Unlike other judicial officers, JPs advertise their wedding services and earn income this way. JPs usually are chosen in local elections and are not required to have a law license. The idea of justice of the peace courts came to colonial America from England. British monarchs appointed JPs to serve a variety of local judicial and administrative purposes in rural government. Most of the early JPs in America were volunteer judges and police officers and were not trained in law.

Juvenile Courts

In recent decades, the juvenile courts in many states have been absorbed into family courts. Where they are active, juvenile court is another name for family court. Juvenile courts began in Chicago in 1899 and service two types of youths: abused and neglected children, and young criminal suspects. The reason for special juvenile criminal courts is threefold. First, some crimes, such as truancy and curfew violations, apply only to youths. Second, U.S. society generally has come to accept the idea that young offenders should be given a second chance at a career and social life without the baggage of an adult criminal record, so teens may be tried in a specially designated juvenile court. Third, juvenile courts are often equipped to coordinate traditional legal intervention with social and developmental resources to modify the behavior of young offenders and to place abused or neglected children in foster care.

The use of juvenile courts provides states with a means to address these concerns. Moreover, the use of these courts also helps keep the names of juvenile offenders secret and the court proceedings closed to the public. By concealing juvenile offenders in this manner, it helps protect the juveniles' reputation and the reputations of their families, which can help reduce recidivism. Abused children similarly benefit from this type of discreet court system.

Juvenile court processes often automatically trigger evaluations of a young person's needs for education, substance abuse treatment, or family counseling, whereas adult criminal courts do not necessarily do so. During the late 1980s and 1990s, however, a rash of gang-related violence prompted prosecutors to bring teenagers charged with violent and serious drug crimes to adult courts, where they would be punished as adults rather than as children. Today, some states require that older teens charged with violent crimes be processed in adult courts. The specific age at which teens are now being charged as adults depends on the state, but it ranges from ages 15 to 17. In other jurisdictions, a court order is required to try teens in adult court. Nationally, for every 1,000 formal delinquency cases, an average of 8 were waived to adult criminal court between 1989 and 1998 (Puzzanchera 2001). The number of waived cases has declined since 1994 to 1.2 percent of all juvenile criminal cases.

Municipal Courts

Municipal courts (city courts and alderman's courts) typically have jurisdiction over cases involving local regulations. These courts decide local liquor-license issues, complaints about land-use violations, city ordinance violations, misdemeanor traffic and parking violations, and other minor complaints. In many states, such as Delaware, local elected officials, including the mayor or city council members, preside over these courts as part of their official duties. In Montana, the municipal courts have jurisdiction in small claims, with maximum awards ranging from $3,000 to $15,000. The Montana courts often include a jury. Meanwhile, municipal courts in Arkansas and New Jersey have no juries, but presiding officers handle initial felony appearances. The existence and particular powers of these courts vary, even within individual states (see National Center for State Courts 2016a).

Small-Claims Courts

Small-claims courts are those with jurisdiction to hear cases with very limited financial implications, generally valued up to $15,000, or with a maximum as low as $5,000. Small-claims courts generally have less rigorous procedures, and they are venues that encourage individuals to represent themselves, without the assistance of a lawyer. In many instances, the small-claims courts have been absorbed into municipal courts where a magistrate assists the trial court by setting bond and still satisfying demands for justice claimants of modest means.

Courts of General Jurisdiction

Moving up the judicial ladder are courts of general jurisdiction. Unlike courts of limited jurisdiction, courts of general jurisdiction exist in every state. However, like limited jurisdiction courts, these courts are designed as trial-level courts. The general jurisdiction courts are the first step in the judicial process for felonies and larger civil disputes in all states, even if there is a limited jurisdiction court for the cases of lower financial value or criminal gravity. Their jurisdiction is called *general* because there are very few limitations on the nature of the cases that may come to their attention.

They have authority to try facts and apply law in both civil and criminal affairs, regardless of their magnitude. In states using courts of limited jurisdiction, the general jurisdiction courts serve dual roles. Their first role is to serve as the trial court for most felonies and civil cases with higher amounts of money at issue. A second role for general jurisdiction courts is to hear appeals from limited jurisdiction courts. Discussions of both these functions follow.

Courts of general (superior) original jurisdiction are trial-level courts that hear a wide range of criminal and civil cases, from misdemeanors to felony offenses and from small-claims cases to large-sum civil suits. In less populated communities, an individual judge will hear a broad array of case types, while in court systems in heavily populated areas, such as the Cook County Circuit Court in the Chicago area, judges are assigned either to a civil or criminal court, but not both.

These courts go by various names. In California, New Jersey, and Rhode Island, they are called *superior* courts; in Illinois, Kentucky, and Michigan, *circuit* courts; and in Iowa, Louisiana, and Montana, *district* courts. In New York, the supreme court is the general jurisdiction trial court and the court of appeals is the COLR, but the court structure is even more complicated than this. The supreme court in New York City hears both criminal and civil complaints, but in the rest of the state, the supreme court hears only civil suits, while the county court hears criminal cases.

Indiana has both superior courts and circuit courts, with almost identical duties. However, Indiana's superior courts are created by the state legislature and circuit courts by the constitution. The selection process of superior court judges varies from place to place within the state. Indiana's circuit courts, however, were created by the state constitution; the state circuit judges are chosen by election.

Powers of General Jurisdiction Courts

In addition to their role in hearing these types of cases, general jurisdiction courts frequently are the first level in the appellate process in states with limited jurisdiction courts. Land-use cases contested in municipal courts often are good candidates for rehearing in the more rigorous superior courts. After a case has been decided in a limited court, the dissatisfied party may seek review in the general court. A single judge, assigned randomly in most cases, will preside during the presentation of arguments and reexamination of evidence.

Courts of general jurisdiction have the authority to set bail. In states where a limited jurisdiction court initially sets bail, the general jurisdiction court can modify the bail. In many jurisdictions, judges can modify jury sentences and remedies. These courts have power to determine which evidence may be excluded from trial, stop a lawyer from posing particular questions, or rule that an argument is not germane to the trial. These courts also have power to weigh the value of that evidence. Courts of general jurisdiction also have authority to review the actions of other coequal branches of government and set those actions aside if they do not meet with principles of the state or federal constitutions. This is a power called *judicial review*, which was described in detail in Chapter 2.

Finally, these courts have authority to make binding judgments. Sides are obliged by law to comply with the orders of a court of general jurisdiction. The decisions of trial courts rarely are set aside and usually never come to review. Statistics from the National Center for State Courts (2016b) indicate that barely 262,000 final trial decisions are challenged with an appeal.

Intermediate Appellate Courts

The American legal tradition favors the idea that, in law, each party is entitled to a fair trial and a fair review of that trial. The next step in that ladder, in all but eight states and the District of Columbia, is an intermediate court of appeals. These courts exist to ensure that each side has an adequate opportunity to present its case, to challenge opposing evidence, and to get a ruling from a decision maker with no stake in the outcome. A three-judge panel usually makes the decisions for the appellate courts.

Appellate courts are not designed to retry cases. Evidence is not presented, and witnesses are not called to testify. Instead, appellate judges assume that lower courts correctly decided the *facts* of the case, and only those facts presented at trial can be discussed on appeal. What is of interest to the appeals court is the legal meaning that the lower court gave to the facts. Rather than trying to prove guilt or innocence, lawyers filing an appeal usually try to prove there was an error in the trial process, that the law was not properly applied, or that the law itself is illegitimate. Appellate courts assume the trial was conducted fairly. However, if the process or the law was in error, the case outcome should be reversed on appeal.

When bringing a case to appeal, the process shifts the burden of proof to the one pressing the appellate case, no matter his status at trial. Appellate courts presume the lower court's verdict was correct; that the trial court properly applied the law, and that it met the constitutional requirements for ensuring that the defendant's due process rights were protected.

Among the primary justifications for the creation of appellate courts is to reduce the workload on COLRs and to afford parties dissatisfied with the trial outcome an opportunity for a higher court to review the lower court's ruling. Tennessee, Texas, and Oklahoma have separate intermediate courts for criminal and civil matters. Delaware, Maine, Montana, Nevada, New Hampshire, North Dakota, Rhode Island, Vermont, West Virginia, and Wyoming do not have separate intermediate appellate courts. However, their courts of general jurisdiction can review the decisions of lower limited jurisdiction courts. When the general jurisdiction courts of these states are the court of origin, appeals are made directly to the COLR.

In 10 jurisdictions, only a trial court and a final court, with no intermediate court, make up the judicial process. In Oklahoma, criminal cases can be appealed to the court of criminal appeals, which is the final state court for a criminal case. However, there is a middle-tier court of civil appeals. In other words, only civil cases get an intermediate level of review. This again demonstrates that the duties and structures of appellate jurisdiction can be as varied among the states as are the courts of origin (see National Center for State Courts 2016a).

The Powers of Appellate Courts

While quite varied, typical powers of appeals courts include issuing or rescinding restraining orders or injunctions. In rare cases, they can decide to reject an appeal. More likely, they may set aside a final trial decision or exercise judicial review.

The authority of the intermediate appellate courts is established by state law and varies considerably. State constitutions and statutes determine which court may receive appeals or whether appellate courts have discretion in taking cases. State law establishes whether intermediate courts can issue various types of orders to individuals and governmental agencies. Laws and constitutional provisions establish whether appellate courts may alter a lower court's judgment on criminal sentences or civil remedies. Law and custom decide whether these courts will remand a case—that is, to return it to the trial court for new proceedings—or whether the outcome for the parties is determined at the appeal level.

Courts of Last Resort

As stated earlier, at the end of the judicial system in each state is a court of last resort (COLR). This is the final court in a state's judicial system and the one empowered with the greatest authority to give meaning to the law in each state. Most commonly, these courts are called the state supreme court. In some states, however, they go by other names. In New York, the highest court is the court of appeals. In Oklahoma and Texas, there are two final courts: one for criminal appeals and another for civil decisions. Almost all final courts sit en banc, but in Connecticut, Mississippi, Montana, Nebraska, Nevada, and New Mexico, three- to five-member panels of the COLR review cases from the lower courts (see National Center for State Courts 2016b).

Membership in the COLRs ranges between five and nine justices, with all final courts having an odd number of justices to avoid tied decisions. When there is a vacancy causing an even number of judges on the COLR, ties may occur. In such a case, the lower court ruling would stand. As stated previously, COLRs sit en banc—all the judges on the court, not just a panel, hear cases. As is the situation with trial and appellate courts, the final courts in U.S. states differ in their structure, size, and authorities.

COLRs are reviewing panels and almost never hear trials. In some situations, they are authorized to do so, but, in general, they delegate trial duties to lower courts or to an especially appointed master. The COLR, then, reviews the evidence and written decision of the master.

Because these courts usually are not reviewing facts, the questions from judges focus more on how the law applies. This type of hearing is almost identical to that of the intermediate appeals court process. The process of these hearings is described in the coming pages.

A complete discussion of appellate powers, explored in Chapter 2 and the present discussion, makes it important to recall ways in which those powers emerge from the COLR's place in the American judicial process. In certain cases (e.g., death penalty cases), the COLR may be forced into the process, whereas in other areas of law, it may have a choice to withhold judgment. Unlike the intermediate and trial courts, COLRs have significant control over their dockets.

Often state COLRs are required to hear *certified questions*, in which lower court judges ask the higher court for clarification on matters of law or procedure needed to allow a trial to proceed. State constitutions also force high courts to hear cases involving judicial review, budget matters, or separation-of-power cases. Supreme courts may also find themselves authorized to try cases of mandamus, where the court is asked to order an office holder from another branch of state government to fulfill some official responsibility. Additional powers of these courts may include the discipline of wayward lawyers, setting rules of procedure for all courts in the state, filling certain judicial vacancies, and handling other administrative matters. However, their most important power is serving as the state's final authority in the judicial process. These courts decide matters of federal and state constitutional law, death penalties, and rules that affect millions of dollars at stake in civil litigation.

Arbitration

In arbitration, a neutral decision maker called an arbitrator takes information and recommends a solution. The arbitrator may take testimony or make a decision after only reading documents. If there is a hearing, the setting can be informal and closed to the public, unlike a trial. Arbitration can be binding or advisory. A mediator is like an arbitrator but gives only advisory opinions, while an arbitrator's decisions are said to have more binding power.

Begun principally as a means of resolving labor disputes, arbitration is increasingly used in real estate, insurance, and other contract cases. Some

35 states have laws that govern arbitration, as does the federal government. Though arbitrators are not government officials, state laws frequently give them limited power to issue subpoenas and to render binding decisions. State law also sets out the rights of parties to have an attorney, fees arbitrators can charge, how they must communicate their rulings, and the appeals process. States also decide what parts of an arbitration's record can be presented in court. Usually, laws state that arbitrators themselves cannot be questioned in court, and evidence is shielded from use in the judicial process.

Arbitration begins when there is a dispute, and one party files an *arbitration claim* with the arbitrator. The arbitrator notifies the other side and informs both sides of hearing dates. Arbitration can relax some of the trial procedures, rules of evidence, or witness questioning. However, most states insist that evidence is shared before hearings, much like a discovery. Law usually requires both parties to have an opportunity to be heard and to cross-examine adverse witnesses. Where judges are prohibited from meeting with only one side of a dispute, in arbitration this can be different. Arbitrators are not necessarily licensed lawyers, and they do not necessarily follow the tradition of consulting written legal opinion to support their decisions. Better arbitration services make known their rules of procedure and the principles on which their arbitrators should make judgments.

Some law firms specialize in this type of practice, rather than the more conventional practice of giving advice and advocacy. Fees for this service, and which party must pay for the service, are set out in a contract. There is neither a uniform standard of qualifications to act as an arbitrator, nor is there a national association of career arbitrators. Because there is no professional association of arbitrators, little is known for certain about the amount of arbitration, the variety of cases handled, or the number of arbitrators in practice.

Judicial Process

The structure of the court system itself implies a process. In this process, fewer and fewer cases are brought up to higher levels of authority for review. Only after another decision has been made can a case go up the hierarchy for further review. The judicial process in the United States is intended to ensure fairness, although it can be somewhat mystifying. Essential elements of this process are explained in the following sections.

Types of Claims

When an injury or a crime is to be presented to a court for a decision, the first step is to make the complaint known to a court. Filing a claim, or synonymously a petition, initiates the judicial process. A criminal claim often is called a *complaint* or a *charge*. The party who feels injured by the other party files the claim. The responding party files an *answer.*

Before going further, it is important to distinguish between two types of claims: civil and criminal cases. Civil and criminal complaints carry with them different procedures and expectations. A thorough examination of the distinctions between civil and criminal proceedings can be better understood after the nature of civil and criminal activity is explained.

Although the purpose of both civil and criminal law is to bring order to social behavior, the distinction between the two is substantial. From the often-subtle distinctions flow very important expectations about precisely the type of behavior the court is asked to help control, who is involved in the judicial process, and the tools available to the court for accomplishing social control. The criminal-civil distinction affects who may bring a case, the rigor applied to the process, and the nature of the court's response to behavior. As is explained in further detail, if one is responding to a suit, this distinction indicates whether the government seeks to label someone a criminal and penalize a suspect as such or whether one is being called on to repay a debt or perform a promised service. The distinction suggests whether one can require the government to hire the respondent an attorney (if unable to pay) or whether one must rely on his or her own resources to get legal advice. It also determines whether the court has authority in law to sentence the defendant to prison or merely order the defendant to comply with the terms of a contract.

Criminal Cases

A criminal act is considered a disruption to the community as a whole, not just to the individual victim. As a consequence, only the government, acting on behalf of the community as a whole, can file criminal cases. Our society has given limited authority to government to use regulated violence to impose the community's will. Acting on behalf of their respective communities, the 2,341 state and local prosecutors' offices across the United States file their criminal complaints in the name of such parties as "the state of Arizona" or "the people of the state of Illinois." More than 17.4 million criminal cases were filed in state courts during 2013, according to the National Center for State Courts annual caseload statistics (2016b). While the government alone files criminal cases, the government itself is never the suspect in a crime. Still, all too often governmental officials are charged with crimes because they personally abused the authority society loaned to them. When this happens, they are prosecuted through the same system in the name of the community.

General Characteristics of Criminal Law

The key features of criminal law are that the government forbids an act, government enforces and prosecutes violations, and the law sets the terms of punishments. These punishments may include probationary periods, fines, prison terms, and even death. For an act to be considered criminal, it first must have been forbidden by an act of the legislature. Under the U.S. Constitution's ex post facto provision, the act must have occurred while a law forbidding the action was in effect. Horrible as some act might be, someone cannot be prosecuted for a crime unless a law was in existence to make that act illegal. Similarly, even with illegal acts, the Constitution prevents government from increasing the level of punishment after the act has taken place. In the U.S. tradition, foreknowledge of the punishment should deter criminal behavior or at least allow ordinary people a way to weigh the risks of performing an illegal act before they commit it.

Felonies and Misdemeanors

Within the criminal justice system, two levels of offense are prosecuted: felony and misdemeanor. The process of each is very similar, but there are a few notable differences. To understand this, it is necessary to clarify the difference between criminal and misdemeanor events.

The most offensive crimes are called felonies. This category of serious crime includes offenses such as homicide, arson, rape, large-scale drug distribution, treason, and so on. Official FBI statistics refer to many of these as index crimes. Punishments in these types of cases usually require heavy monetary fines and can remove convicts from general society by placing them in a state penitentiary for more than a year or by putting them to death.

Misdemeanors are minor offenses such as traffic violations, minor drug possession, littering, or various boisterous behaviors. Though not as morally offensive as felonies, misdemeanors upset public peace, so they are prosecuted by the government's law enforcement agencies. Misdemeanor punishments usually require the payment of smaller fines, detention in a local jail for less than a year, or the performance of some community service.

Violent Crimes, Property Crimes, and Victimless Crimes

Criminal acts can be divided into categories of violent crimes, property crimes, and victimless crimes. Violent crimes are those acts that involve real or threatened physical harm to a person. Some 5.7 million violent crimes were estimated to have occurred in 2001, according to the DOJ Crime Victimization Survey (2005). However, that number has decreased since then. In 2015, the number of violent crimes reported by law enforcement was 1.19 million (U.S. DOJ 2016).

Crimes are quantified in the FBI's Uniform Crime Report, which summarizes criminal activity made known to state and local police agencies. These two reports—the Crime Victimization Survey and the Uniform Crime Report—show different levels of crime occurring. The difference between these two reports is that some crime, including violent crime, goes unreported to law enforcement agencies but gets picked up in the Crime Victimization Survey. This is a household survey, in which an interviewer asks respondents about crimes committed against him or her.

Property crimes involve either stealing or damaging something that belongs to someone else. More than three-quarters of the 24 million crimes reported to the DOJ were property crimes. A third category, victimless crimes, includes those unlawful acts where the parties most immediately involved have given their consent. For example, prostitution, sodomy, illegal gambling, and drug possession are considered illegal in many jurisdictions. Opponents of these behaviors have argued successfully that society is diminished by these actions and should prohibit them.

Civil Cases

Where criminal law requires recognition of an act of the state legislature, only some of the civil law draws its authority from legislation. Courts have a greater hand in defining civil law. Another important difference is in the variety of cases. In criminal law, there are felonies and misdemeanors. In civil law, there are many, many types of cases, and a simple scale of severity such as misdemeanor and felony cannot be applied in civil law.

Civil law finds its origins in Imperial Rome and relies on edict, legislation, and other written regulations. The lion's share of modern civil law is intended to provide a means of peacefully resolving disputes when private individual parties believe they have been wronged. Unlike criminal cases, private parties initiate the vast majority of civil cases, and a civil violation may take place even where there is no legislation to label an act illegal. Though legislatures may (and often do) create types of civil actions, courts themselves declare behaviors a violation of some interest. Even individuals can create their own expectations that civil courts can enforce, as is the case in contracts law, for example. Rather than meting out punishment to offenders, the aim of a civil action is to give to each his own.

General Characteristics of Civil Law

This is a much more active area of law than is criminal law, even when traffic tickets are added to the equation. Most civil cases advance private interests, but this body of law covers a huge variety of cases, including divorce, child custody, personal injuries, rights to property, and contractual obligations. Civil cases generally are separated into these categories: torts, property, probate (or succession), family law, equity, contracts, and constitutional law.

Though civil cases are initiated to advance the narrow interests of an individual or firm, they may advance larger social interests as well. A civil case can advance a social interest when it is used to change the scope of the government's authority or the balance of power between various levels of government. Civil suits also can affect whole societies by ruling on matters related to the quality of life in a neighborhood, land development, constitutional rights, pollution, and the like. Similarly, they can affect the larger society when private suits cause big interests such as hospitals, drug companies, equipment makers, and other firms to modify the way they conduct business under the threat of liability suits.

Civil law may be distinguished from common law, which originated in English social customs. In the common-law tradition, judges make law. Rather than referring to legislation, common-law rulings were based on widely held expectations about relations between common, or ordinary, people. English common-law judges would explain their reasoning to establish a precedent. This precedent made explicit some social expectation and established logic that would give lawyers a basis for advising their clients. The precedent would provide other judges with principles to guide their thinking in later cases. In the American legal experience, many common-law doctrines come under the umbrella of civil law. In modern law, however, the common law is considered a subset of the civil law.

Level of Proof

While the level of proof needed in criminal law is beyond a reasonable doubt, in civil law it is typically the preponderance of the evidence. Though a reasonable doubt is a flexible term, the government must put to rest any doubt that the juror of ordinary intelligence could have before there can be a finding of guilt. Though not mandatory, unanimous jury decisions have indicated the lack of a reasonable doubt. Even if the evidence is strong, if there is a small but reasonable doubt about the evidence, the doubt should decide. In civil law, the preponderance of the evidence standard allows a reasonable juror to have doubts about the evidence, but to still find for the plaintiff when the weight of the evidence seems to point in favor of the plaintiff's case.

Findings and Judgments

Another important distinction between criminal and civil law is that in a criminal case, a suspect is either guilty or not guilty. There is no in-between with criminal case outcomes. Civil cases, on the other hand, are not either-or propositions. Rather, civil courts often try to resolve the degree to which someone has a right, an obligation, or a liability. This way, courts decide the amount of time and conditions surrounding visits between noncustodial parents and their children, rather than assigning exclusive custodial rights to one parent. In personal injury cases, a civil court can assign each of several drivers in a traffic accident some degree of liability for the injury suffered. This way, a jury can assign some degree of fault to a plaintiff for not fastening her seat belt, as well as a proportional share to the other drivers.

A further distinction is in the outcome of a case. While maximum criminal sentences are fixed in law, civil remedies, including financial payments, often are much more flexible. A court might require the liable party to pay a fair share to repair damaged property, to replace a defective product, or to stop doing something. In this way, a judgment may go up or down depending on the degree of harm proven by the plaintiff. In criminal law, the corresponding court order is to label someone guilty, and the penalty is usually fixed by statute. This choice of words indicates a greater degree of social indignation toward the guilty criminal than with the liable civil party. Moreover, a guilty party pays his or her debt to society; whereas with civil liability, the wrongdoer pays a private party.

Overlapping Boundaries between Civil and Criminal Law

There is plenty of overlap between criminal and civil law, and so a single event may be the genesis of both a criminal indictment and a civil complaint. An example might help bring clarity. Former football star O. J. Simpson was tried in Los Angeles for the murder of his estranged wife and another man who was with her at the time. The police arrested Simpson and developed the information used against him at trial. In the criminal proceedings, the county prosecutor sought to convict him. This is punishable by death or prison under California law. The court returned a verdict of not guilty, and he was released from the government's custody.

After the criminal process ended, his wife's family initiated civil proceedings against Simpson for his wife's wrongful death. The family's lawyers, rather than the government, were responsible for assembling the information to be presented to the court this time. They claimed, among other things, they endured great emotional despair because he brought about her untimely death. This contrasts with the government's interest in protecting society from murderers. In the civil process, Simpson was found liable and ordered to compensate the family in cash for their grief.

Making a Claim

Regardless of whether a claim is civil or criminal, a case does not exist until one is filed with the right court. A claimant, or plaintiff, is the party that files a civil case with a court, claiming that he or she suffered some type of injury. In criminal law, the claimant is referred to as the prosecution, or the state.

Courts of Origin

The first stage of a case is with a court of origin, commonly called the trial court, which is where a case originates. The complaints are written by a lawyer, or law clerk, and filed in the office of the local court clerk. Nonlawyers may prepare some small-claims and no-fault divorce cases by using preformatted documents available in a number of office supply stores. In criminal cases, the local prosecutor's staff files after approving of the police evidence. Once filed, the court clerk's assistants decide if the written complaint is accompanied by appropriate filing fees and whether it meets requisite formatting. If it is properly filed, then it is given an identification number and random lot; the assistant then assigns it to a judge for the next phase.

For a case to be filed properly, the plaintiff must identify the party who caused the harm. In criminal cases, a defendant is usually a person. In civil cases, the respondent is the person or institution that will answer a claim. In this way, a governmental agency can be accused of a civil violation such as exceeding the authority the state assembly granted to it or denying a person his or her constitutional rights.

Very early in the process, courts will decide whether the parties have standing. To have standing, the plaintiff must show that he or she has in fact suffered some injury or has other authorization to file. In addition, the plaintiff must show that the government recognizes the injury, or crime, as something a court can act on. Finally, a plaintiff must usually demonstrate that the respondent, or defendant, is a potential source of the injury. In both civil and criminal cases, the party who initiates the case bears the burden of proving these things.

The Criminal Trial Process

Whether an infraction is major or minor, when it comes to trial, the U.S. Supreme Court has ruled that certain requirements are fundamental to saying the suspect has been afforded his or her constitutional rights to due process of law. Following is the fundamental outline:

The right to be informed of the charges
The right to legal representation
The right to know and challenge the government's evidence, including the
    right to cross-examine adverse witnesses
The right to a neutral decision maker
The right to an appeal

The burden of proof is on the government. In addition, elements of the Bill of Rights (for this discussion Fourth, Fifth, Sixth, and Eighth Amendments) are incorporated into state trial procedure through the Fourteenth Amendment's due process clause. These requirements include the defendant's right to keep evidence gained from unwarranted searches out of the process, the right to be free from coerced confessions, the right to be free from torture while in custody, the right to legal representation, and the like.

Misdemeanor Process

Criminal cases begin with the infraction, followed by an investigation and arrest. Courts define an arrest as the point at which police restrict a person's movements, even if this restriction is implied and not explicitly announced (see *United States v. Martinez-Fuerte,* 1976 and *Terry v. Ohio,* 1968). The restriction may come by creating an environment where a reasonable individual would feel no alternative but to stay. Following an arrest, a suspect often will be released on a signature bond, which means he or she promises to attend the court hearing. In other misdemeanor cases, bail is made by surrendering a driver's license or a small sum of cash until the hearing is held or the fine is paid.

In minor cases, there is no bond hearing in court. Rather, the arresting officer receives the signature bond, driver's license, or some down payment. With more serious misdemeanors, such as drunken driving or weapons violations, a suspect may be jailed until bail is paid or a judge orders the release. At the bond hearing, the suspect is informed of dates for future hearings. With traffic citations, there is an arrest and a trial, with no other intervening hearings.

With higher misdemeanors, suspects follow judicial processes much more like the felony process. These include various types of hearings. The first is the preliminary hearing, at which the judge decides if prosecutors have enough evidence to continue pressing charges. For the sake of efficiency, the preliminary hearing usually combines other elements of the judicial process, such as the arraignment and bond hearing, into a single visit.

At arraignments, the suspect may enter a plea, which is to claim to be guilty, not guilty, or in some jurisdictions nolo contendere, meaning "no contest." If the suspect pleads not guilty, the case proceeds; otherwise, the judge accepts or rejects the plea and then issues a sentence. If a judge thinks the suspect is incapable of understanding his or her legal rights at this time, the court may temporarily reject a guilty plea until the suspect can consult with a lawyer.

By this point, most misdemeanor and felony cases are resolved. When the prosecutor and defendant want to negotiate the outcome, they ask the judge to ratify their plea agreement. Plea agreements require the suspect to enter a guilty plea, while prosecutors may reduce a charge to a lesser offense or ask for mercy in sentencing. Plea agreements are entered because they benefit both parties. Both sides avoid the uncertainty of the trial or sentencing process. Defendants and their families avoid the embarrassment from public attention, and law enforcement can move on to other cases.

If the case has not been resolved, the next step for lawyers is to file *motions*, or requests of the courts. Motions seek permission for additional time to collect and analyze data, to suppress some evidence, or to reconsider previous decisions. Motions may ask the court to order someone to turn over information or demand that a witness testify. If someone objects to a motion, the judge may hear arguments on the issue.

There may be a period of *discovery* in which sides exchange information and the names of witnesses that will form the evidence for a trial. This process of discovery can be quite extensive, especially in white-collar crimes, where prosecutors must sift through volumes of business documents, financial records, correspondence, and other sorts of information to find relevant papers. With more serious cases, the attorneys may seek a pretrial conference with the judge to discuss whether a plea bargain is an option and the various sentencing guidelines. If the case goes to trial, there could be hearings for the selection of jurors.

In many jurisdictions, associate judges, JPs, or magistrates will decide minor criminal cases. These judges serve shorter terms of office, and their job is to take the burden off trial-level judges who have somewhat higher responsibilities. In some states (e.g., Illinois), elected trial court judges from a local jurisdiction appoint the associate judges or magistrates to fill these short-term appointments. Magistrates and JPs in many jurisdictions do not have law school training or a license to practice law.

Plea Bargains

Courts will not automatically accept plea bargains. Judges still must be sure that there is a reasonable basis for the charges. In addition, courts need to be assured that the defendant entered the guilty plea voluntarily and without threats or delusions about the reduced sentence a judge might, or might not, issue. Finally, the defendant needs to understand the consequences of the plea and understand the evidence against him or her. All the while, the defendant is entitled to the advice of an attorney.

Some states do not make formal distinctions between its misdemeanor and felony courts. Other states do delegate misdemeanor cases to courts of limited jurisdiction. In Delaware, for example, these courts may hear only certain types of cases, such as drug or local ordinance violations. Low-level courts may also accept guilty pleas or hand down sentences in related felony cases. In some jurisdictions, these courts may issue search warrants and arrest warrants. With more serious and complex legal proceedings, judges with higher stature than magistrates will preside at trial and decide if evidence should be admitted to the trial process. However, in misdemeanor cases, the court of limited jurisdiction hears the trial, issues a verdict, and, if necessary, sentences a guilty party usually in a single hearing.

Felony Process

In felony cases, more stringent procedures are followed, even before the arrest. However, if a law enforcement officer witnesses a criminal event, he or she must attempt to make an arrest on the spot. In addition, if a law enforcement officer has probable cause that someone committed a crime, the officer may make the decision to arrest. Otherwise, the investigating officers seek an arrest warrant. To do this, the officers present their evidence first to the local prosecutor's office, which works with police to present the evidence to a judge who will either approve the warrant or reject it.

In most jurisdictions, a local prosecutor may file charges, which is to say the prosecutor reviews the evidence and decides whether someone's behavior fits the definition of a crime. This decision may rest on witness testimony, documents, videotapes, or physical evidence (e.g., fingerprints or a weapon). In many serious and very complex criminal cases, prosecutors instead may call for grand jury hearings before pressing charges.

A grand jury is a committee of citizens (usually 15 to 25) that examines testimony and evidence from the government's side only. In many jurisdictions, defense lawyers or a suspect are not present, except when called to give testimony. The grand jury holds hearings in secret to shield the reputations of innocent subjects and to avoid disrupting the work of detectives.

The grand jury holds these hearings to decide if law enforcement agencies have enough evidence to proceed with a full trial; it is not asked to decide guilt. If the grand jury finds there is enough evidence to charge a suspect with a crime, it says so in a formal document called an *indictment* or a *true bill*; the opposite finding is announced in a *no bill*. At that point, the grand jury is finished investigating an individual for a particular offense. Even after a no bill, the grand jury may continue investigating the same person and other people for related offenses. The grand jurors' term of service and compensation are set in each state by law.

The modern grand jury hearing is a part of the judicial process in that it checks the power of prosecutors. The grand jury screens cases before they go to trial. At the same time, an investigation is part of the prosecutorial process. Grand juries investigate passively, relying on career law enforcement agents to do the work. Grand juries can issue court orders, for example, subpoenas, which demand witness testimony, or the submission of digital or written documents, photographs, or sound recordings. In effect, they help build cases for law enforcement agents this way.

The origins of the grand jury come from 12th-century England, where local informants reported to the king about crimes and who committed them. When a grand jury refused to indict the enemies of King Charles II, it was seen as able to protect the ordinary people against the strength of the government (Kadish 1996). The grand jury concept was imported to the United States through the Fifth Amendment of the U.S. Constitution. This requires that "No person shall be held to answer for a capital, or otherwise infamous crime, unless on a presentment or indictment of a Grand Jury. . . ." This requirement applies to the U.S. government, and most local jurisdictions follow this model.

When charges are filed, warrants issued, and a suspect is in custody, the process continues with hearings much like the misdemeanor. There is opportunity for a bond hearing and preliminary hearings, which may combine several procedural steps into a single appearance. If the prosecutor's charges come to court without the grand jury's involvement, a judge will hold a preliminary hearing to determine whether there is enough evidence to continue charging someone with a crime. The arraignment, or advisement, is the point of the process when the judge informs the suspect of the charges and likely penalties. The judge also asks if the suspect understands the charges and whether he or she can afford a lawyer, or if the court should appoint one. States usually check someone's finances to be sure that person is eligible for a public defender.

The felony bond hearing is the same procedurally as in misdemeanor court, but the stakes are higher. Most commonly, the bond requires a cash deposit with the court. The bail is the amount deposited and is a fraction (typically 10 percent) of the bond. The full bond is forfeited if the suspect flees justice before the end of the trial. Bond is higher, and out of reach for many suspects, when an accused is at a high risk for fleeing. Judges may also issue no-bond orders if convinced that a suspect is likely to flee.

Discovery Phase

The discovery phase has several parts. Discovery begins with an exchange of written questions and sworn answers called *interrogatories*. Parties can press each other to make their answers more specific. Each side may also require witnesses to participate in formal face-to-face interviews, called *depositions*. The deposition is recorded and typically takes place in a lawyer's office.

Depositions can be collected from anyone the parties want, and interrogatories are collected from the parties named in a suit. Lawyers may also consult with clients as they prepare responses to either. Though depositions may have a broad focus, a trial judge should limit courtroom use of transcripts to witnesses and statements central to the trial issues.

Because these are sworn statements, if a witness dies or is incapacitated before trial, courts can accept relevant passages, as though the witness was in court. The honesty of a witness will be challenged if he or she gives trial testimony conflicting with his or her deposition or interrogatory. Some courts allow lawyers to hire actors to sit in the witness stand and read the deposition answers of absent witnesses while the lawyers repeat their questions.

As with misdemeanor processes, there is opportunity for pretrial hearings, motions, discovery, and plea bargains. In fact, 95 percent of felony convictions in state courts during 2000 came by a plea rather than a trial (Durose and Lanagan 2003).

Prior to the trial, defendants will inform the court that they want a jury or a bench trial, where a judge alone decides both the facts and the law. If a defendant wants a jury, a pool of prospective jurors, called the venire, is selected from the local adult population. Court clerks usually draw prospective jurors at random from names on voter registration and driver's license records. Once called, prospective jurors are screened for eligibility and interviewed by lawyers during a process called voir dire.

Various states have stipulations about who may opt out of service due to such conditions as age or occupation. In the voir dire process, lawyers look for indications that a prospective juror is predisposed to decide the verdict in some way, and they then seek that person's exclusion from the jury. If this is the case, lawyers can ask the court to dismiss an unlimited number of prospective jurors if there is cause. Lawyers also get a limited number of peremptory challenges, which allow them to disqualify a juror without explanation. More typically, they try to find statements from a prospective juror suggesting that he or she has begun to form opinions about the case.

Lawyers also consider various traits such as race, religion, gender, age, or occupation that they think may be correlated with certain sympathies. However, the U.S. Supreme Court has ruled repeatedly that it is a violation of the Constitution to exclude jurors by using race alone as a crude indicator of attitude. In capital cases, it may be necessary to ask prospective jurors if they could be fair to a defendant of another race (see, e.g., *Powers v. Ohio,* 1991 and *Ristaino v. Ross,* 1976).

Defense lawyers also may suggest that pretrial news coverage has affected opinions of the pool of jurors. If this is the case, defense attorneys may ask for a change of venue, so the trial is held out of town, where prospective jurors are less likely to have come across inflammatory news coverage of the case. This also imposes additional costs to prosecuting the case. Even when there is a lot of pretrial news coverage, local courts have a great deal of latitude in deciding whether the trial needs to leave town to get jurors who are not predisposed (see, e.g., *Mu'min v. Virginia,* 1991 and *Aldridge v. United States,* 1931).

After jurors and substitutes (called alternates) are chosen, the trial begins. If there is a jury, jurors decide which testimony and evidence to believe. Meanwhile, the judge rules on which principles of law and procedure apply. During the trial, judges admonish jurors to avoid discussing the proceedings with anyone, especially the press or people involved directly in the case. There are standing orders for jurors to avoid paying attention to news coverage of the case during trial. In cases with extremely high levels of news coverage, judges can sequester juries, which is to put them up in a hotel during the course of the trial so the court can manage their access to news coverage and other outside influences.

Coroner's Inquest

Another pretrial investigating hearing is the coroner's inquest. In many, but not all, jurisdictions, the local coroner's office is the agency that provides the medical evidence needed to determine the cause of an unnatural, or suspicious, death. A coroner's inquest produces a legal determination, rather than a scientific one, about whether the cause of death was due to an illness or an unnatural source such as suicide or homicide.

Coroners are the chief administrator of the office, and staff medical examiners perform autopsies. Once the work of morticians, autopsies today are conducted by scientists trained in medical schools. The autopsy is a process of examining the body, organs, and blood for evidence of the cause of death. An autopsy report is presented publicly at a coroner's inquest. A jury reviews the coroner's evidence, listens to testimony, and votes to determine the cause of death.

The Trial Begins

The trial begins with an introduction from the prosecution's attorney and the defense attorney. The government is obliged to present a case, which is its evidence, witnesses, and rules of law supporting the accusations against the defendant. The defendant, in the U.S. legal system, has the right, but not the obligation, to present a case.

The government's case usually involves direct questioning, during which the government's lawyers pose questions to witnesses hoping to get answers supporting their argument. Witnesses may be eyewitnesses who personally watched an event. They may be expert witnesses, including detectives, medical examiners, handwriting analysts, and crime scene technicians who collect and evaluate evidence. The defense has an opportunity to cross-examine these witnesses, hoping to draw out testimony weakening the government's arguments. In civil cases, expert witnesses are called because of their knowledge of some relevant issues.

After the government's case is presented, defense lawyers have an opportunity to ask for a directed verdict. This is a motion that asks the judge to declare that the state's evidence is too weak to continue charging the accused. Normally, this is not successful, and the defense attorney then may bring in witnesses supporting the defendant. At this time, the defense poses the direct questioning, and the state cross-examines the defendant's witnesses. This is followed with the summation, also called closing arguments, from each side. Opposing lawyers typically summarize the high points of the testimony and evidence presented to the judge or jury and then ask for a verdict favoring their side.

If there is a jury, the judge presents directions for the jury. Typically, both sets of lawyers give the judge recommended instructions, which the judge can modify. The jury instructions tell the jurors the basic rules of law, the weight of evidence that they should consider, and the possible verdicts they can return. The instructions typically tell jurors that it is up to them to decide whether a piece of evidence or testimony is believable, but that they are not to decide the fairness, or the constitutionality, of the law itself. In this way, judges decide law, and jurors decide facts.

Thereafter, the jury retires to a room in which all deliberations take place. There they select a foreperson, who serves as a chairman of the committee, records the jury's votes, and formally communicates with the judge. During deliberations, various forms are provided to the jury. These forms are prepared in advance, so the jury can return any one of the possible decisions that it may reach.

During deliberations, jurors can ask questions of the judge. These questions are made known to attorneys for both sides, and the judge may give some additional guidance. Judges have discretion in how long they will allow a jury to deliberate before ruling that a hung jury cannot reach a decision. Judges may ask the foreperson if he or she thinks the jury is making progress toward a verdict. An inability to decide will prompt the judge to declare a mistrial, which means the jury is dismissed, and the process goes back to the pretrial motions. The verdict is the finding that the defendant is guilty or not guilty on any or all of the possible charges. In felony cases, the jury usually must agree unanimously to the outcome of each charge.

When a verdict is reached, the jury foreperson announces the verdict or passes the verdict papers to the judge to announce in court. Defense attorneys may elect to poll the jury, that is, to ask each juror to restate in public his or her vote on each charge.

Post-Trial Proceedings

When a suspect is found guilty at trial, the next step is to decide on a punishment. If the suspect is found not guilty, his or her release from the charges comes with a formal declaration from the judge, usually on the same day. Following a guilty verdict, the judge, or sometimes jury, must decide what punishment to impose. To persuade the court, the prosecutor will present aggravating evidence, which is intended to demonstrate how horrible the crime is and how society has suffered from it. This often involves testimony from loved ones of a murder victim, for example. Most states require an opportunity for victims to give impact statements that become part of the decision-making process.

The defense attorney will present mitigating evidence, which is intended to show there may have been grounds for committing an evil offense. This is done without challenging the guilty verdict. Mitigating factors might involve showing that a crime victim was not entirely innocent. The victim may also have been a competing drug dealer or may have previously hurt or threatened the defendant.

Discrimination and the Courts

Before concluding that lawyers cannot discriminate in their peremptory challenges, the Supreme Court had to break barriers that local court systems put in
the way of minorities (see *Carter v. Jury Commission,* 1970) and women (see
Taylor v. Louisiana, 1975) ever becoming part of the venire.

Now, there is a more contemporary and philosophical debate over whether
it is better that a jury be impartial or representative. In other words, is it better
to have a jury that is neutral or to have a jury that resembles the racial, religious,
and income characteristics of the community?

The U.S. Supreme Court held that the juries are "instruments of public justice [and] that the jury [should] be a body truly representative of the community" (*Smith v. Texas,* 1940). However, the Court refined the cross-section
requirement by applying it only to the venire. "The fair cross-section requirement
is a means of assuring, not a representative jury [which the Constitution does not
demand], but an impartial one [which it does]" (*Holland v. Illinois,* 1990).

In capital cases, the jury is called on to make two separate choices. The first
is to determine whether the nature of the crime makes the defendant eligible
for the death penalty, and second whether the jury actually recommends a death
sentence. While the guilty or not-guilty verdict must be unanimous, the sentencing decision does not require unanimity, although many state laws make
this a requirement.

Following the jury's sentencing deliberations, it formally announces the decision, and the judge ratifies it at a later time. When there is a suggestion that the
jury was improperly influenced, a judge may set aside the verdict and sentence.
Without a jury, and at some time soon after trial, a sentencing hearing is the
formal announcement of the sentence. In every state, death penalty sentences
are automatically appealed to the state's highest court (see Von Drehle 1995).
These courts alternatively review the sentence alone or the entire court process.
In lesser offenses, defendants have an opportunity to appeal to a reviewing court.

The Civil Trial Process

As with criminal cases, civil cases can be organized by the nature of claims.
Civil matters, however, are far more complex than criminal matters. Due to the
complexity of civil cases, many states offer more courts of limited jurisdiction
in civil matters than they do for criminal ones. Unlike criminal cases, the Sixth
Amendment does not guarantee a speedy trial in civil cases. Instead, with more
than millions of civil cases processed in the state courts each year, civil trials
typically take more than two years to complete. Many additional claims are settled without a suit being filed.

The civil trial process is similar to the criminal process. However, there is
nothing in the civil process akin to the grand jury process, and there is no bond

hearing. During the 1980s and 1990s, however, with complaints of rapidly increasing numbers of personal injury cases, some state legislatures put up hurdles to frivolous claims. Often this involved review of cases by a panel of experts to advise courts whether there was evidence that a person in a responsible position lapsed in judgment.

There may be steps that a plaintiff must go through before filing suit in court. In a case where an individual is challenging a decision by a government body, such as terminating welfare benefits, expelling a student from school, or a disciplinary process for a governmental employee, courts may require the plaintiff to show he or she has used all appeals available in the administrative process before filing suit. A growing number of contract and insurance cases are expected to be resolved through arbitration. In this alternative dispute resolution, arbiters other than judges hear cases in a quasi-judicial, but private, setting to resolve civil complaints out of court. Contractual provisions in insurance policies or employment agreements frequently require alternative dispute resolution processes.

The Sentencing Phase

As in the verdict phase, the sentencing phase involves jury instructions that can be a bone of contention. Jurors need to know what will happen to the convicted defendant if they decide against death (see *Kelly v. South Carolina,* 2002). They also need to be able to give effect to mitigating circumstances, that is, the jury forms must allow them to vote against the death penalty (see *Penry v. Lynaugh,* 1989). In addition, the Court has held that it violates the cruel and unusual provision of the Eighth Amendment to apply the death penalty to mentally disabled defendants (*Atkins v. Virginia,* 2002) but not to minors.

Appealing Decisions

After the decision is made, the unhappy party has the opportunity for an appeal. Generally, this opportunity comes after a final disposition, meaning the conclusion of the trial. In several situations, the decisions of trial courts may be appealed when a court is asked to decide a procedural question that would affect the outcome, such as the admission of evidence, or have long-lasting effects, such as the placement of children during custody hearings.

The process of trying to overturn a trial decision is done through the appellate courts. The process of presenting arguments on appeal is very different from the trial process. In fact, many outstanding trial lawyers will turn over cases to colleagues better versed in presenting appellate cases. The decision-making process of a trial is most rigorous for felony-criminal processes, holding the prosecution to a standard of proving guilt beyond a reasonable doubt. Somewhat less stringent are misdemeanor processes. The civil process, while very rigorous, holds the plaintiff to a standard of the preponderance of the evidence. At the conclusion of the trial, it is generally presumed that the defendant/respondent has been afforded due process of law. Thus, the burden of overcoming the decision of a trial court rests with the party asking for review in the appellate court.

After the trial, the losing party has the opportunity for a case to be reviewed and overturned. Perhaps it is better to say, the dissatisfied party has the opportunity to appeal those parts of the trial that may have been conducted in error. By appealing the case to a higher court, the unhappy party can hope to reverse a trial judgment or at least some part of it. The civil and criminal processes in appeals courts virtually are indistinguishable, except in states such as Oklahoma and Texas, which separated the two very formally at the appellate stages. More routinely, the formal process is the same, though deadlines may be altered to accommodate the needs of time-sensitive cases. For purposes of this discussion, criminal and civil appeals processes are not distinguished.

Appellate Process

When arguing about the rules of the game, parties can ask reviewing courts to intercede from the outset. Trial courts must make decisions about relocating high-publicity trials to ensure suspects have an unbiased jury. Trial courts must decide whether to freeze bank accounts during financial cases and whether to permit progress on demolition of a building when neighborhood or preservation societies contest the plans. These are intermediate decisions that can affect the course of a trial and have long-lasting effects on parties if a trial takes an extended period of time. Consequently, parties argue fiercely about such decisions and appeal these intermediate court rulings.

Appeals courts routinely take interlocutory appeals, which are hearings made during the course of trial proceedings. This is often one of the first times an appeals court will come to know of a specific trial case. Interlocutory hearings go before the appeals court on short notice because they challenge a trial judge's temporary, rather than final, court orders. They challenge the rules of the trial, suppression of evidence, allowing a witness, exclusion of a juror, and so on, rather than the final outcome such as a finding of guilt.

Interlocutory appeals also are made to challenge temporary restraining orders (TROs), which are used during the judicial process to prevent a party from doing something that would be irreversible. A typical TRO orders a party to wait until the court's final order is issued to spend money, receive a nonemergency medical procedure, remodel an historic building, or alter the natural environment. Parties argue over whether waiting for a trial outcome to continue with some activity is a great burden.

Other short-term decisions are challenged on interlocutory appeal. These affect children or wards of the state. Their concerns are often appealed on an expedited basis. These often involve custody of children during divorce or involuntary hospitalization of the mentally ill. The admission of evidence or witnesses may be challenged prior to the trial process also. If judicial processes drag on, temporary orders can have long-term consequences. Thus, they are afforded instant decisions.

In the interlocutory appeals process, all parties are bound to very strict deadlines. These deadlines apply first to the party wanting to contest the trial court's order and the opponent's reply. Second deadlines apply to the appeals court itself. Once filed, an appellate court is under guidelines to hold a hearing, typically within 3 to 5 business days of the filing. This pushes aside other tasks on the desks of judges, and pushes the interlocutory appeal ahead of others on the agenda. With interlocutory appeals, the reviewing court is almost always under deadlines to provide rapid feedback. This type of deadline varies across the states, but usually a decision is due in a business week, or at the most 30 days. Failure to do so could cause further delays in a trial, seriously burden parties to the trial, or render moot one of the parties' cases.

Review of Final Orders

It may be more customary for news consumers to read or hear about an appeal on a final order. The process of appellate review typically begins after a trial court gives its final decisions in a case. Then the losing party (the appellant) may seek review in the higher court. It is common for some lawyers to first file a motion with the appeals court. The first is the petition for a stay of judgment, which puts on pause the trial court's remedy until the appeal is completed. This is then followed with the formal petition to the appellate court to review the decision.

More often than not, state appellate courts have little choice but to accept a case for review. When they do use discretion, appeals courts can accept the case by issuing an order to lower court officers requiring them to send the case record to the higher court. Most appeals come through a petition for leave to appeal (PLA). This is the formal request made by the appellant for review of a trial decision. On the other hand, when a court has discretion, it may deny the petition usually without explanation. If granted, parties are free to reach negotiated settlements before the higher court hears the case or announces a ruling.

When the losing party files the PLA and any court fees, the opposing party is formally notified with a copy of the PLA and is given time to file an answer. Each state has deadlines and strict format guidelines for filing PLAs and answers. These format requirements ensure that certain statements are made on the cover to identify the case and the author of the document. Format guides give details for maximum length of the document and the rules for making a table of contents and table of cases. They also might require certain font style and size for print, color, and size of paper, and may even demand certain colors for the cover page so judges can identify documents by the color codes. A set number of stapled photocopies are acceptable in some jurisdictions, while other places have fancier duplication and binding requirements.

Closer to the substance of the issues before the court, a PLA must explain the jurisdictional authority (or duty) of the court to take the case, cite precisely the legal authority being questioned in the appeal, explain how specific trial errors adversely affected the client, and state how the appellate court should respond. Appellate courts will reject appeals that do not cite specific trial errors for review. It is not enough for a party only to be dissatisfied. Appellate courts routinely reject cases unless they claim both that there were errors in trial court judgment and that those errors led to an adverse outcome. They also reject cases when they are outside the court's authority.

Appellate Case Processing

In most states, the appellate court clerk's office first examines the appellate filing to make sure it conforms to rules about length and formatting specifications. The clerk's office also collects any filing fees and verifies that the responding party gets a copy of the PLA. After that is verified, the clerk's office sends the PLA to a panel of three judges. All of the appellate judges in a jurisdiction constitute the court. In most appeals, however, a panel of three judges is chosen by lot from all the available appellate judges in that jurisdiction to review the case. On occasion, all of the judges in an appellate court will sit en banc (when all members of the court hear the case at one time) to decide the case. Courts sit en banc after two different panels from the same court have reached conflicting opinions on some topic.

This system of randomly assigning cases serves four purposes. First, it averts judge shopping by lawyers, who might hope to know in advance whether they will have a sympathetic or hostile panel. Second, random assignment minimizes specialization on the appeals courts. Many judges resist specialization on their courts out of fear that they would get cozy with litigants frequently before a specialized court. Third, it is expected that the random selection method keeps the law more coherent because judges participate in deciding cases across many areas of law, rather than only in a specialized field. Finally, it helps distribute the workload more evenly among all judges in a jurisdiction. This way the chief judge cannot keep all the glamorous cases for himself while sending an overwhelming number of dull cases to a disfavored colleague.

In many jurisdictions, the lottery will further assign one of the judges on the panel to be the case administrator. In other jurisdictions, the judge with the greatest number of years of service will be the presiding judge for the case. The administrator will make sure there is proper communication with parties and superintend the scheduling of hearings and announcement of a decision. This judge-administrator is involved in the decision.

If accepted for appeal, a new set of briefs will be filed with the court. Appellate judges want lawyers to summarize only those trial elements that they claim are in serious error, and successful lawyers are skilled at explaining trial errors and appropriate law succinctly. Appellate courts may be reviewing dozens of cases at a time and almost never have the time to review a case in its entirety. The whole case transcript and documents, however, may go to the court for reference.

After the appellant files a case, the opposing party is notified formally of the appeal and may file its own answer to the briefs. After both are filed, judges begin reviewing the documents. In some cases, the judges may write to both parties and ask them to revise their documents and address, or to avoid discussing, certain legal authority or theory.

A judge's law clerks play a vital role at this point as well. Law clerks are advanced law students or lawyers early in their careers who assist judges in their legal research and writing. These individuals must be distinguished from court clerks who are administrators, responsible for the accurate keeping of vital court documents. Law clerks analyze the case formally and informally for their employers. Law clerks will prepare memoranda verifying lawyers' interpretation of prior court decisions, examine case records, and do other research under the direction of a judge. Law clerks find out how or if other appellate courts in the state or in neighboring states deal with similar issues. In this way, clerks help the judge understand how an individual case fits into the overall landscape of the law.

Oral Arguments and Decisions on the Records

Most appellate decisions are made by reviewing briefs and case records without any discussion from lawyers. This is customary, and most lawyers expect, and often ask for, no oral hearing. When novel legal issues are brought up, or when lawyers request it, appeals courts will invite lawyers to give short question-and-answer presentations called oral arguments. Judges at this level do the questioning, and lawyers are the ones who answer. This is quite to the contrary of the trial experience where lawyers do questioning while judges have a relatively more passive role.

By the time of oral arguments, judges have reviewed the case and have become aware of legal developments on the point. Therefore, they probably have formed some initial opinions. At minimum, they have formed opinions about whether the lawyers have focused on the interesting issues or have made compelling written arguments. Judges want oral arguments to be focused discussions, but oral arguments give judges an opportunity to clarify issues by posing hypothetical situations about the consequences of legal innovations (Hogan 2000). Judges listen for direct, complete, logical, and thorough answers to their questions. Floundering and illogical answers indicate uncertainty in a lawyer's argument or at least a lack of preparation. Oral arguments generally last about an hour or less.

Oral arguments take place before the three-judge panel. Each lawyer has an opportunity to present arguments. Their time is limited and consumed with the questions of judges. Lawyers must be thoroughly prepared because judges are free to ask any question about the case, its facts, or any element of law any of the three judges thinks needs explanation. Judges may be energetic in this questioning or may sit passively and listen to arguments. This is a matter of a judge's personality and the nature of the case before the court.

Scholars say that lawyers should be cautious in reading a judges' questioning for clues about a case outcome. Judges variously use questioning to get lawyers to say something that will influence other judges on the panel, to gain information central to their own decision-making, to play devil's advocate, and to unmask weaknesses about their own tentative decisions. The precise questioning may depend greatly on the nature of the case. When the court is asked to review novel issues, courts may be animated, and judges may interrupt with frequent questions. With more mundane issues, a cold court might sit passively as lawyers deliver oral arguments.

Oral arguments make up a relatively small amount of the appeals judge's working day. In geographically large states, judges and lawyers may have to travel for hours to reach the courthouse, so oral hearings are scheduled well in advance. Courts in these states may hear oral presentations for a few weeks during each season of the year and then return to their hometowns to write opinions and read newly filed cases. In smaller states, it is easier for appeals judges to hold court more frequently.

Forming Decisions

After the oral presentations, judges on the panel hold a conference to discuss the case in private. If there are no oral arguments, judges can deliberate either in person, by conference phone call, through e-mail, or through memoranda. Even before the conference, judges have read the lawyers' material and conducted independent research. This allows them to form some initial impressions about the case. During deliberations, however, judges also have the opportunity to persuade each other, analyze the case, and gain additional information. Usually an impression vote indicates a judge's views on a case, but this vote is not binding until the decision is made public.

Decisions require a majority vote to modify or overturn the trial court's decision. Unlike a lone trial judge, judges on appellate courts must reach conclusions by building consensus both in terms of which party should win and in terms of the reasons for the outcome. To do this, appellate judges must work in close consultation with each other to make rulings. As a result, judges learn the thought processes of their colleagues, they learn to persuade one another, they learn to accommodate one another, and they learn to debate and negotiate satisfactory outcomes with each other. They learn to swallow disagreements, and they learn to express their disagreements so that they can continue to work together in a professional environment.

Judges discuss cases immediately after each oral argument or after the full day's oral arguments are done. In private, the case administrator may summarize the issues and open the topic for discussion. After the discussion, if there is any, judges will take an impression vote.

If the case supervisor is in the minority, he or she will trade writing responsibilities with a colleague who will write the majority opinion. Otherwise, the vote is recorded with the basic rationale each judge thinks important to supporting the decision. Typically, the judge-administrator for the case writes the ruling. During the decision process, judges compose their written opinions with the aid of their law clerks. Drafts are distributed usually through a secure e-mail system and then shared with the rest of the panel. Colleagues on the panel will give the author input. Colleagues may ask for spelling corrections, or they may request substantial changes in rationale, construction, statements of relevant facts, or citations.

Judges may change their minds after making an impression vote, and deliberations may continue over the course of several days. Votes count only when the court's decision is announced to the parties. However, Marvell (1978) estimates that judges change their minds between the initial vote and the announcement in fewer than 15 percent of the cases. Hogan (2000) found judges who said this is rare, but it does happen.

Sources of Information

In addition to the formal filed paperwork and oral arguments of litigators, judges have several sources of information to help them decide cases. Along with the formal processes, judges may encounter news coverage, friends, or staff members who have something to say about a case. Only some of those informal sources are discussed here. There are far too many potential sources to cover them all; moreover, the means by which state appellate judges arrive at decisions is just beginning to be explored.

The Role of Law Clerks in the Decision Process

In the process of writing opinions, law clerks play an important role. There may also be a legal research staff appointed by the court; however, the clerks work under the direction of and are the employees of individual judges. The extent to which the work of law clerks finds its way into the formal opinion of the court varies from case to case and from judge to judge. H. W. Perry's book *Deciding to Decide* illustrates the vital role law clerks play in drafting opinions for the U.S. Supreme Court. Marvell (1978) and Hogan (2000), meanwhile, see much more diversity in the way that state appellate judges apply the work of law clerks.

As a case enters the court system, law clerks may be asked to prepare bench memos, which further reduce the central questions, authority, and issues, before the court decides to take an individual case. Clerks also frequently discuss cases with their employers as they prepare for oral arguments. Finally, clerks play varying roles in the preparation of the court's final orders.

At one extreme is the law clerk who has little role in the substance of the outcome. This clerk finds citations for a judge and checks his or her punctuation. At the other extreme is the clerk whose memoranda become the court's opinion. The typical law clerk will not draft memoranda during the first few months on the job. When they do, judges may dictate the memo. In other situations, the judge may tell the clerk what rationale to use and which cases to cite but leave the writing to the clerk. Other clerks will have more latitude, depending on the confidence the judge has in them. All the while, it is the judge, not the clerk, who has decision-making power. Some judges fear becoming lazy or dependent on law clerks for their reasoning, while others prefer to delegate.

Law clerks also serve other informative roles. By discussing cases, clerks may debate outcomes with their supervisors. As lower employees, the clerks may bring to light relevant side issues that do not get into the published opinion. In addition, clerks may help write speeches for the judge, keep the judge's personal law library and subscriptions current, or act as a chauffeur. In any event, law clerks provide research, ideas, and services judges would not otherwise get.

Consultation with Other Legal Professionals

In addition to the prescribed routines of holding oral arguments and reviewing official case documents, judges have told researchers that they may turn to outside sources of information when deciding a pending case. Marvell (1978) said this type of consultation is the exception. Similarly, Hogan's (2000) research found that, on rare occasions, an appeals judge might consult with fellow judges who are not on the same appeal panel. Marvell writes that judges looking for some guidance prefer to direct clerks to discreetly contact their professors about points of law. Otherwise, a judge may discuss the case, in the abstract, with a trusted friend or relative about the practical implications of some decision. However, it is taboo for judges to discuss the specifics of any pending litigation.

Seeking outside information does not give parties to the litigation opportunity to challenge it. For this reason, judges tell Marvell (1978) that they find it unfair to receive input this way. Judges who might seek consultation typically couch these discussions in abstract, or hypothetical, form. Alternatively, they may ask about where to go for further information to avoid revealing details or their thoughts of a case before them.

Consultation with Party and Interest Group Leaders

When contacted by party officials about charged cases, judges told Hogan (2000) that they quickly change the subject. Even among elected judges who attend party functions, none admitted to discussing pending litigation with state or local legislative or executive officials. In addition, none acknowledged with certainty that any colleagues shared information on pending litigation. This custom is so strict that one Illinois Appellate Court judge with whom Hogan spoke said her husband (also a lawyer) learned that she had decided a high-profile case only by reading about her opinion in the local newspaper. Local professional culture and the court's customs will dictate the extent to which judges feel free to consult with outside sources, but it is forbidden to forward third parties case outcomes or the leanings of a court prior to formal announcement.

Some public officials and interest groups may attempt vicariously to communicate with judges about pending litigation. Holding a press conference to discuss cases may have this effect. However, many lawyerly publications decline to publicize news related to pending cases. It is more customary, and acceptable, for elected officials and interested third parties to communicate with judges by filing formal friend of the court briefs. In this way, public officials and policy advocates legitimately can communicate political information through the judicial process.

Announcing Appellate Decisions

When a majority is satisfied with the written opinion (both a decision and, if needed, a dissent), it is announced through the court clerk's office. In most jurisdictions, the appellate court is expected to announce rulings within a fixed time frame. Because these rulings represent a binding governmental decision, appeals courts issue written rulings following standardized and formal writing routines. Like the lawyers' briefs, court opinions adhere to conventional writing techniques to easily identify case parties, issues under consideration, legal authority, and the court's final ruling.

Setting Precedence

Unlike trial courts, appellate courts are much more likely to issue rulings that explain the court's reasoning in writing. For more routine issues, decisions are issued in memoranda sent only to the affected parties. When there are more issues of larger concern, decisions can be made public by being published in a volume called a reporter and, more recently, on the Internet. The importance of written opinions is to set precedence, which is to establish reasoning that gives guidance to other courts deciding a case on the same point of law. This tradition of following precedence, also called stare decisis, requires that lower courts within a reviewing court's jurisdiction abide by that reasoning until it is modified or rejected by a higher court. Only a few appellate decisions have precedential, or law-making, value. No statistics are kept, but most rulings merely decide disputes and are of little interest except to the parties (Marvell 1978).

Many times, appellate-level judges want to see precedent overturned. Some appeals judges have devised strategies to impress upon higher courts the urgency for this. Appellate judges may use what Fish (1999) calls the rhetoric of regret in which they write that despite their own misgivings, duty binds them to apply a cruel law (Fish 1999). Hogan's (2000) interviews with Illinois Appellate Court judges revealed that on selected cases, appeals judges work together to form a majority opinion applying current law as it is, but they will also help a colleague write an even more compelling dissent to urge Illinois Supreme Court reconsideration of some issue.

Judges are intelligent readers of current events about their colleagues but do not tend to reverse higher court rulings until given formal direction to do so. Some judges and scholars have tried to anticipate changes in state supreme courts and U.S. Supreme Court direction by counting each justices' public statements, as opposed to the opinions, to estimate whether the state supreme court or U.S. Supreme Court was ready to reverse precedent. In the U.S. Supreme Court's decision *Agostini v. Felton* (1997), justices both changed policy and reminded readers that they should not jump to conclusions that a decision is overruled based on writings justices make outside the Court:

> The statements made by five Justices . . . do not, in themselves, furnish a basis for concluding that our (First Amendment) jurisprudence has changed. . . . The views of five Justices that [a] case should be reconsidered, or overruled cannot be said to have effected a change in [the] law.

Supreme Court Process

The last stop in a state's judicial system is with its COLR, as mentioned earlier. The only possible venue after the state supreme court is the U.S. Supreme Court, which will refuse cases that do not have a claim made in federal law. The decision process of the state supreme courts is very similar to that of intermediate appeals courts. Differences are highlighted in the discussion that follows, though the section on intermediate appeals courts offers helpful insights to the process of preparing for, hearing, and deciding appeals.

The process for bringing a case to COLRs typically follows one of two paths. When filing a petition to appeal, lawyers must be careful to identify which of these avenues they want to pursue and explain in a few words why this is the correct legal path to the high court.

The first route is by petitioning for leave to appeal as a mandatory appeal, which says the court is obliged to review the lower court's decision. The other is through a writ of certiorari, also called a discretionary appeal, in which the court accepts the case as a matter of choice. All states require their high courts to hear some types of cases. The most commonly used mandatory appeal is the automatic right all states grant criminals who have been sentenced to death. In addition, many state constitutions require high courts to review decisions related to the use of a writ of mandamus, certain budget cases (namely those where a trial court has declared a tax or budgetary item in violation of the state constitution), and cases where public officials are expelled from office through the judicial process.

Filing Process

As with other courts, the state supreme court has a court clerk who receives the case and advises the parties about whether it was filed within deadlines and according to appropriate format requirements. In most states, cases meeting proper deadline and format requirements are screened to see if any of the justices have a conflict of interest in the case.

After the case is approved by the clerk's office, in most states, the case is randomly assigned to a justice to usher the case through the court. This justice summarizes the case and puts it on an agenda with other cases that the court will consider for review. If accepted, this judge usually is the author of a written decision. The judge discusses whether there are any legal merits to reviewing the case, and the court decides as a group if the case is ready, or worthy, for court review. Given that hundreds of cases are brought to high courts for review in any year, justices find that they can only do a good job by taking those with the most important legal matters at hand. In a vast majority of cases, the supreme courts will decline to take discretionary cases.

Courts will reject cases if there is no showing that a lower court was in error. Courts also reject cases if the case has resolved itself or has been settled before oral hearings (*moot*). Supreme courts will decline cases if the court finds no novel legal issues at stake or that a litigant is challenging a law that has not gone into effect (these are considered *not ripe*). Less commonly, the court may find out during oral arguments that a case they accepted was not what they expected.

If this is the case, the court can declare the case dismissed as improvidently granted without issuing an opinion. This leaves the lower court decision intact.

After the court accepts a case, it is placed on its docket for review. Review may be by private discussion among judges or with oral arguments. When justices grant oral arguments, lawyers will be given information about when the case will be heard, and they will be told how much time will be allotted to present cases. During oral arguments, lawyers very often will be interrupted with pointed questions from the court. This can be unnerving to inexperienced lawyers. Again, as a reviewing court, there will be no witnesses or evidence presented. Rather the case facts are accepted as the trial court found them. The higher courts use the real case facts as real-world examples of how the law is being applied. This gives them feedback to make adjustments to earlier supreme court rulings or to decide whether an act of the legislature is in violation of the constitution.

Deciding to Accept a Case

Though dramatic to lay observers, death penalty cases have in some respects become routine for state supreme courts. This is because the core legal questions have been resolved. On the other hand, serious doubts recently have been raised about the death penalty process in states such as Illinois.

Through the petition for writ of certiorari, the court uses its own discretion to take a case. In this process, lawyers must be more persuasive. Using this process, courts accept cases when lawyers succeed in raising more serious questions about the meaning of a law or by arguing that a constitutional principle is being looked at in a new light. Evidence that the court needs to resolve a case is seen clearly when lower state courts express confusion over the proper interpretation of a Supreme Court decision.

Two examples might help explore this point. In some cases, several appeals panels may have examined the same legal question with a similar fact set but have reached opposing decisions. Clearly, then, the law cannot be applied fairly when reasonable people come to wildly different conclusions about the meaning of a law. In this way, there is unfairness in the law when the same case is getting different outcomes.

Another indicator of confusion comes in an individual case when the trial court judge and one appellate judge see the rule of law one way, but the other two appellate judges think differently. These types of cases indicate to Supreme Court justices that legal experts are confused about how they should decide court cases. With this sort of situation, a state supreme court can be persuaded that it needs to put its authority behind one way of thinking, so lower courts can apply a uniform standard to future cases.

Making Rulings

There is nothing in the current literature on state courts that would distinguish the process of preparing for and holding oral arguments in a supreme court with an intermediate appeals court. Readers are referred to the "Oral Arguments and Decisions on the Records" section of this chapter for discussion of preparing for and holding oral arguments. The process of engaging in conference deliberations and impression votes is very much the same.

Much more is known about small group consensus building on the U.S. Supreme Court. However, some scholars think much of that knowledge can be translated to the state courts. The knowledge, intellectual capacity, sense of humility, desire to "do the right thing," and sense of humor of individual judges has helped propel courts during tense moments. Within state final courts, personality of judges is a subject of some interest. Glick, in interviewing a variety of state supreme court judges, found that many judges learn to bite their tongues to preserve a friendly work environment: "Such things as arrogance, pride and a loss of temper were condemned" (Glick 1991).

How Does the Difference in Court Structure Matter?

The structure of a court and its size play important roles in several aspects of its internal function and decision-making routines. Generally, smaller courts with special functions attract lawyers with particular specialties. These attorneys, in turn, gain valuable insight to the thinking of judges and court routines simply by having regular contact there. This type of intimacy would frustrate outside lawyers trying to win decisions there. Meanwhile, more formalized and bureaucratic court systems are built for efficiency, uniformity, and lawyers who are able to thrive in a more formalized work environment.

Consolidated Courts

Satisfaction among court personnel is seen as being higher in consolidated courts than in multiple limited jurisdiction courts, according to Mikeska (2000). Remember that consolidated courts are those structured in the same way as the federal court system. They have a simple structure with a single trial-level court, though the trial court may hold sessions in many locations. In comparing local court structure, Mikeska (2000) found that staff in consolidated courts reported greater levels of teamwork, fewer political pressures, less interpersonal conflict, and a fairer distribution of workloads than the staffs in multiple special jurisdiction systems. In exploring resistance to efforts to move to consolidated forms, court clerks in limited jurisdiction venues voiced fears of greater political influence, loss of their own influence or prestige, and heavier work burdens.

Part of the efficiency courts gained through consolidation came through combining numerous bank accounts used to collect and distribute funds. This simplified record keeping. Furthermore, consolidated courts had more standardized operating procedures in the clerical, personnel, and financial departments. This made operations easier to follow for users who had business in the courts. Under consolidation, rules for case filing, accepting payment by check, decisions about disclosing court records to the public, and the rates charged for certain types of court services did not vary from court to court within a single county as they did in local judicial systems of multiple limited jurisdiction courts. This undermined the value of insider knowledge.

The consolidated system can be more approachable for ordinary users because an individual may look at many cases as a single case, when they stem from one event. For example, a court could assign components of a case separate case numbers and court dates for a domestic battery case (felony court), child custody case (juvenile court), and divorce case (another civil court). Meanwhile, the individuals involved may regard the three cases as having arisen from a single family and the same event. Many individuals will find it frustrating to work through the idiosyncrasies of three limited jurisdiction courts.

Consolidated courts make tracking case progress easier for court users with a one-stop-shopping sort of approach. Unified courts may also find it easier for judges to share information across cases, when they can be flagged as being related. However, some jurisdictions in Oregon and Delaware tried overcoming this by creating liaisons that alert judges when a single family may have relevant cases in several divisions of the local court system. This allows some families with overlapping litigation to bundle their cases into a single case.

Small Jurisdictions

Small jurisdictions, meanwhile, have some interesting qualities of their own. On one hand, a study of Fulton County, Georgia's juvenile court system found that the system's two full judges could work collaboratively and share authority well (Klaversma and Hall 2003). To accomplish this, the two judges revealed high degrees of confidence in each other's decision-making abilities. However, much of their time was divided between managing the day-to-day administration of the court system and resolving disputes. Associate judges, who had less institutional authority, also lacked resources such as legal research and secretarial staff and could not be counted on to alleviate the administrative burdens of the full judges.

Large Jurisdictions

Large jurisdictions tend to have more bureaucratization and specialization. These districts, such as the Cook County Circuit Court surrounding Chicago, has multiple locations and hundreds of judges, clerks, and other staff. They have many institutional resources such as libraries and record-keeping facilities. For judges in these systems, division of labor is highly rigorous. The judges of the civil division do not hear criminal cases, unless they seek reassignment. This occurs despite the fact that Illinois has a unified, or consolidated, court system. Functions, by necessity, are distributed. Appointed associate judges in these large court systems may do little more than hear traffic violations all day long, while senior judges are swamped in complex and challenging litigation.

Differences in Selection

Differences in selection remain a matter of controversy. Some think that elected supreme court justices will be interested in the separation-of-power questions if they are appointed by governors and approved by legislatures. This is because these judges depend on other actors for their jobs. On the other hand, judges who are elected directly will connect the law to popular demands and be sensitive to the policy implications in preparation for future elections (Comparato 2003).

The jury is still out, so to speak, on the implications of judicial selection and policy implications. At the same time, there is no real consensus on the effects of selection on representation in the courts. Women, Latinos, and African Americans are underrepresented in the courts; that is, there are more white men sitting as judges (Alozie 1990). What has yet to be determined is the degree to which selection methods best meet prevailing social sentiments (ideological representation) or whether there is advantageous group representation for underrepresented groups to be had by greater numbers of female and minority judges.

Party Control

Party control of state government affects the latitude judges may feel. Where the governor and legislature are divided over a policy, courts may enjoy more latitude. Where both of the other chambers of government are in unison on a policy, they may bring resources, cooperate with interest groups in filing friend of the court (amicus curiae) briefs, and bring public pressure on courts to rule a certain way.

Courts with greater resources of their own and a tradition of independence may shrug off this sort of pressure. *Institutionalism* has to do with the resources of a branch of government and its members. Institutionalism or partisanship within other branches of government provide courts an opportunity to carve out a middle ground, or even take sides, while finding at least some support from a peer institution of state government (see, e.g., Langer 2003). On the other hand, where both of the political branches are of one mind, the potential for retribution against the courts is high. In such cases, judges have an incentive to suppress their true policy goals and avoid costly political battles.

Major Topics in Studying State Courts

Courts may hold power in defining the meaning of provisions in their state constitutions, but they depend on other branches of government for enforcement and authority to render judgment in other areas. They also depend on others to bring cases to the courts. Unlike state legislators who bring issues before the legislature, judges depend on litigants, often state officials, to bring cases and to define the issues that judges are to decide. Courts also depend on other branches of government for their funding, which has important implications for staffing, record keeping, research facilities, and other resources that allow judges to make "independent" decisions.

Within a state's governing apparatus, the courts can play a critical role in shaping policy and checking the powers of the legislative or executive branches of government. Some observers think state courts act more aggressively in this respect than the federal courts do toward Congress, federal agencies, or the president. Baar (1982) recounts an instance where one colorful judge in Wayne County, Michigan, called the county commissioners into court. He was angered over a lack of funding for the local judiciary. Those who supported the court's budget requests were dismissed, while the others were held in contempt of court.

Courts also are using their powers beyond the garden-variety exercise of judicial review. Normally, courts striking down statutes stop when they have identified the constitutional violation. More recently, some have advocated particular policies within their rulings and offered specific advice on how to draft the law. For example, a Wisconsin Supreme Court's decision included a page in which justices wrote to "urge the legislature to thoughtfully examine . . . the possibility of a license or permit system for persons who have good reasons to carry a concealed weapon" (*State of Wisconsin v. Hamdan*, 2003).

This chapter has tried to explain some of the fundamental aspects of state courts that are helpful for understanding the role, structure, and character of these courts. The chapter has also provided background on the historical development of these courts and important judicial trends. Yet there is far more to state court politics, which will be explored in Chapter 4.

State Court Structures

One of the most important characteristics of courts is their basic structure. The state court culture values positions of authority in addition to expertise. This culture also respects hierarchy. Some states have fairly simple structures, with only two layers, but more typical is three tiers. In either structure, one court has higher authority than another to review and resolve arguments. This lends certainty to decisions. The culture also thrives on percolation, or the opportunity for many lower courts to disagree with each other on a point of law before the higher court has to choose from competing ideas.

The hierarchical structure of courts encourages this idea vetting. The first tier in the structure is the trial court, which is authorized to hear all manner of trials from complex civil litigation, to heinous felony trials, to small claims. Above the trial court is an appeals court, which reviews trial cases for errors in legal judgment. At the apex is the COLR, usually called the supreme court. This three-layer model, where cases pass from low to middle to high court, is often called a unified court system. In more complex systems, there are multiple, limited jurisdiction courts. Each of these courts has jurisdiction over a focused type of case, such as traffic court or juvenile court. In two states, there are multiple supreme courts, authorized to review either criminal or civil cases. In these courts, the route of an appeals case is state-specific. Court structure is important because it affects a judge's breadth of knowledge and expertise, with the more complex systems allowing judges to develop legal specialties. The court structure also affects the workload of courts and the ease with which cases reach higher levels of judicial review. In each structural framework, judges and lawyers consider the opportunity for appeal and the likelihood of success. The structure of the court system either helps encourage or limit litigation, which, in turn, affects the judges' time to consider a case.

Cases and Controversies

Institutional norms of behavior are also important in determining whether a case will ever come before a judge at all. One such custom is the adversarial structure of a trial. This means there are no friends in court. Instead, opposing sides bring forward a case or controversy for the judge to resolve. In this way, courts avoid being bogged down resolving academic legal questions or testing hypothetical situations. Similarly, the court will not hear a case until after an injury has occurred—a legal doctrine called *ripeness*. If an issue is resolved elsewhere, it is considered moot by the court. Finally, many courts shy away from political questions, which are better left to the legislative or executive branches of government to resolve. The political-question criterion is very ambiguous. The following are general rules.

Inputs to Court Decisions

In the other branches of government, the elected and appointed officials are very open about which issues they choose to bring up for a decision. The character of state court politics is different from the policy-making habits of the other branches. In the courts, litigants choose the arguments to put before the courts. For this reason, courts are called the passive branch of government. While judges may decide that some evidence is irrelevant to the decisions they have to make, it is the lawyers who do the most important legwork in providing the information that goes into making a ruling. On the other hand, governors and state legislators are expected to be policy leaders by identifying problems and then advocating the policy outcomes they favor.

Lawyers play a key role in determining the nature of the input on which courts will make rulings. Unlike the lobbyists in other branches of government, the culture of state courts presumes that formal legal training is a requirement for preparing an effective presentation in court. As with other lobbyists, attorneys are skilled in understanding the mechanics of how decisions are made in the branch of government they stand before. Ordinary people usually can represent themselves in court (after overcoming some hurdles to show they are capable), but few laypersons can match a licensed attorney's familiarity with methods of questioning witnesses or ability to efficiently comb through documentary evidence. Nor will a layperson have the mastery of the regulations governing the way evidence is to be presented and the lawyer's grasp of what points must be raised at trial to preserve rights to appeal.

After the case is in court, all parties have to be before a judge when any information is presented. It is illegal for individuals to attempt ex parte communication, which is communication between the judge and only one side in the case. Lobbyists cannot privately persuade judges during the decision-making process, as they would when lobbying a legislator. While the First Amendment's right to petition government protects this type of lobbying of legislators, it can be grounds for a contempt-of-court citation when the judge is the target. Courts are duty bound to involve all parties in all communication that is presented to the court. Judicial tradition expects to produce decisions based on the record of facts and arguments presented in trial.

Announcing Decisions

Judges announce their decisions only after all the evidence is presented. Governors and legislators, meanwhile, are free to predispose themselves in public before, during, and after legislative debate. This same type of action by a judge brings scorn from all angles of the legal profession. For example, Supreme Court Justice Antonin Scalia in 2004 was pressured into recusing himself from a gay-rights case because he delivered a speech to the Philadelphia Urban Family Council, an "anti-gay" organization, even though the organization was not represented in the case, and he did not even mention the case or legal theory at work in it. The organization, which Scalia praised, was actively opposing a domestic-partnership ordinance the Philadelphia City Council had been considering (Serrano and Savage 2004).

Only after both sides rest their cases do judges announce decisions, and usually this is done in writing. The customs of court do not approve of holding press conferences to explain judicial decisions. One decision-making process is not better than another. The culture of the courts has somewhat different expectations of its decision makers.

In the public eye, judges are regarded poorly unless they act, write, and speak like judges, that is, appearing dispassionate in their relation to the parties, scholarly in their writing, and certain of their decisions. For this reason, judges often seem stoic, even when presiding over very emotionally charged cases. Displays of emotion may be fine for a governor, for example, when he or she reveals humanity or concern. However, the norm of judicial restraint, or the exercise of strict self-control, advises judges to conceal their emotional reactions, to choose their words with care, and to apply the law as it is written, no matter how they personally feel about it.

Growing Workload in State Courts

Two important trends are occurring in criminal courts. One of them is the growing use of negotiated settlements to resolve cases, and the other is the growing number of criminal cases being filed. The vast majority of the millions of felony case handled in the United States go through state court systems, and some of the most rapid growth in felony filing rates comes from the midwestern states.

What happens to these cases after they enter the court system? In general, the legal culture of the states encourages negotiated settlements over trials. Plea agreements are negotiated settlements between the parties and affirmed by a judge. In a plea agreement, the judge remains a neutral third party, free to accept or reject the settlement. The trend toward more plea agreements is true, even in states in which there is greater public opposition. Various studies on state courts have found a fairly constant trend in the proportion of cases being settled across the nation, despite some public outcries.

Court observers often believe negotiated settlements eliminate uncertainty for both the prosecutor and the accused. Settlements are defended as a way to bring a case efficiently through an otherwise expensive and seemingly endless system of trial and appeal. The interdependence between regular actors in the court system fosters shared local ideas about which cases should be tried and which should be settled. That is, defense attorneys often know the going rate that a defendant will see in minimized punishment in exchange for a guilty plea. Attorneys may find it in their personal interest, as well as that of the client, to urge some suspects to accept or reject a settlement given the current economy for a guilty plea.

Despite the tendency of the states to look for negotiated settlements, the workload of the criminal courts has been growing since the mid-1980s. This increased burden has been attributed to stricter law enforcement in the areas of domestic violence, illicit drugs, and gang-related crimes. In addition, teenagers accused of serious crimes increasingly were processed in adult criminal, rather than juvenile, court systems.

Civil Case Workload

While criminal activity may garner much of the space in news coverage about state and local courts, the bulk of the courts' work falls under the civil category. In 2013, roughly 34 percent of the work in state trial courts of general jurisdiction was devoted to civil actions, as opposed to 21 percent that was concerned with criminal allegations (National Center for State Courts 2016b). These civil cases are relevant because they often involve large sums of money, rights of tenants, claims of unfair treatment in the workplace, and the authorities of local units of government.

In one of the most closely watched political dramas in history, the Florida Supreme Court was drawn into a high-stakes election-law dispute with the presidency of the United States hanging in the balance. Between November and December of 2000, the Florida court system was forced to decide the meaning of a handful of ballots, where the voters' choices in the 2000 presidential election (between Democrat Al Gore and Republican George W. Bush) was obscured by "dimpled" or "hanging" chads. The outcome of the presidential election was a virtual tie, and Florida was a critical "swing state." With the country's eyes on Florida, the presidency would be decided on the meaning that the state court would give to fewer than 400 disputed ballots.

On a second appeal, the U.S. Supreme Court ultimately agreed to take up the central issues of the case, which reversed the outcome of the state court (see *Bush v. Palm Beach County Canvassing Board,* 2000 and *Bush v. Gore,* 2000), but not until the Florida Supreme Court sat for a time at the center of national politics. Civil filings rarely are as dramatic as that particular case, and the growth rate in this area is not as rapid as the change in criminal court filings.

JUDGES AND OTHERS: PEOPLE WHO OPERATE THE COURTS

Judges, like other governmental actors, make choices when issuing their decisions. Like other citizens, judges have individual policy preferences. The impulse for judges to act solely on these policy preferences when making choices is kept in check by institutional expectations and by the knowledge that they are being watched by their peers and the larger legal profession. The language of relevant law and political pressure help shape how judges rule. These pressures include such factors as elections, prevailing policy preferences among lawyers, and the persuasiveness of legal argument.

Even though there are constraints on how they act, judges do have some discretion when making decisions. New and novel cases are frequently brought to the courts, whether they are about life-prolonging medical treatment, gay marriages, or something else. In these cases, judges are forced to think and rethink how the law applies. In some cases, the law has not been tested, and judges must resolve a specific problem for the first time. In these and other situations, a judge may be able to shape the direction of future legal interpretations. For example, one interesting question being raised today relates to the nature of the Internet. Judges are being asked if an individual buys a product over the Internet, then did that transaction take place on the buyer's home computer or on the seller's computer? A court's answer to that question could have important implications for which state gets to impose a sales tax. The logic applied here could then be transferred to other legal and illegal activity.

Judges
Federal Judges

Who are the people who make up the federal courts? The federal courts are human institutions, just as the Constitution and the laws are human things. We cannot and should not expect judges to perform their functions and roles with more than human wisdom or detachment, for that expectation collides with reality. At the same time, however, we can and do ask judges to rise as much as possible above rubber-stamping their personal predispositions, biases, or prejudices onto the evolving body of federal judicial precedent. Such is the dilemma at the heart of the federal judiciary.

The greatest moments in the history of the federal judiciary are those in which federal judges identify and give voice to the best and highest aspirations of the constitutional system. If, at times, in rising to this level, judges must set aside habits of thought and feeling shaped by a lifetime of experience, many of our greatest jurists have proved that such transcendence is not beyond human reach. At the same time, some of the worst moments in the history of the federal judiciary have resulted when those judges who aspire to greatness yield to the fears, prejudices, and shortsightedness that they claim to have set aside. In either case, the actions and inactions of these courts are based in large part on the people who serve within them. So who are the people who make up the federal courts, and what how do they meet the conflicting needs we impose upon them?

How judges are selected and by whom depends on the judgeship to be filled, the influence of the president and the other potential decision makers (including presidential advisers and members of the Senate), and the responses of whatever professional associations or interest groups regard the nomination as important. Different procedures are followed for nominations to the Supreme Court, to the circuit courts of appeals, and to the district courts. Further, these procedures have changed over time, as the nation's political climate and political culture have changed. Nevertheless, in every era, judicial appointments are the result of a complex political process that includes many players.

Generally, four key factors shape the selection and appointment of a federal judge. The first is the drive to appoint candidates who share the president's political and judicial philosophy. The second grows out of the tendency of presidents to select one candidate over another based on the needs of his party or his political future, for example, the need to maintain political unity or to further the interests of important factions. The third is the need to balance representation, be it geographical or ethnic, and in so doing, to strive for a representative bench. Last, there is merit. Although objective merit has not generally been the decisive factor in determining a final selection, occasionally there have been candidates who have been such prominent jurists that they became the obvious choice despite their political affiliation, place of residence, ethnic background, or other traditional factors.

Then there is the complex process of Senate confirmation. The president may name the judge, but the U.S. Senate has the right to dispute and to reject the president's choice. Here, politics, both ideological and practical, plays an important role, as does geography. Under a process known as senatorial courtesy, senators have a very large say in the choosing of district and circuit judges to sit in their states. In fact, when the senator and the president are of the same party, the senator is often the real force behind the nomination of a district judge and sometimes behind that of a circuit judge.

This appointment process produces a judiciary whose members are more alike than they are different. Though variations do exist, most federal judges tend to come from the same kind of families, go to the same universities and law schools, and belong to churches (or synagogues), clubs, and societies that uphold similar values. The vast majority of federal judges have, in fact, been white males whose social origins are firmly rooted in the top three-quarters of the social order. Most, in fact, are drawn from the top quarter of society. Federal judges tend to grow up in families with a tradition of legal, judicial, and public service. Most are drawn from the district or circuit in which they serve. In terms of prior employment, between one-third and one-half of all federal judges had some prior experience on the bench. The same numbers held for former federal prosecutors.

Limited in both numbers and diversity of backgrounds, yet extensive as to the duties they perform, the people who make up the federal judicial branch face a difficult task. The smallest of the three federal branches of government, the federal courts play key roles in the operation of our constitutional system. Wielding the power of judicial review, these courts have a significant say in the shaping of public policy. In light of this power, we can safely say, therefore, that the makeup and backgrounds of those people who staff these courts—and by implication the ways that they are appointed to serve—have a large impact on the shaping of public policy in America.

State Judges

Political scientists view the application of governmental authority as an act of politics. Consequently, the use of judicial power is by definition a political issue. On a more basic level, state court judges in all cases come into contact with other political actors, such as the governors who appoint them, the parties that support their elections, or the voters who select them. These facts of life place burdens on judges to account for political considerations because they are explicitly brought into the reasoning in rulings, because the case is highly charged and permeates the background of the decision, or because the decision affects voting, campaign finances, and other political activities.

One of the most prominent forces influencing the judges are the bar associations, which are the professional association for attorneys in each state. These groups have special status in the politics of judging in a number of ways. First these associations establish guides and codes of conduct for lawyers and judges. They are vocal when structural reform efforts, such as the merit selection of judges, are discussed. Bar associations assert themselves in framing legislation that affects the discretion of judges. Bar associations also take a very keen interest in who gets appointed or elected to the courts. Almost always, prominent members of bar associations are appointed to serve on the commissions that help select judges in states that use the merit plan. In states where judges are elected, the bar associations publicly announce their ratings of the judicial candidates. These associations are also influential in shaping rules of procedure for courts and in setting licensing standards for prospective lawyers.

Other groups are also important in judicial politics. Manufacturers and physician associations have led civil reform efforts to limit personal injury litigation. Interest groups petition courts to file amicus curiae or friend-of-the-court briefs to influence the decisions rendered by COLRs. Other interest groups sponsor litigation. Though they do not often have the right to sue in their own name, interest groups identify parties who themselves have a right to sue. Then interest groups influence courts by providing their clients with the legal representation and technical support to move issues through the courts.

Selection of Judges: Some General Criteria

Many states have requirements for service as a judge. These typically involve age and residency requirements, and certain career experience. One of the first criteria for being selected as a judge is education. To be a judge in the state courts of the United States, one must be a licensed lawyer, which generally means that one has graduated law school. The one exception to this is some JPs and judges in courts of limited jurisdiction who are required to have at least a high school education. If one of these nonlawyer judges hears a case, the parties involved must have the opportunity to have the case reheard in front of a law-school-trained judge if they are unhappy with the first trial's outcome.

The necessary qualifications to be a judge are discussed in state law or the state constitutions. Generally, states require that judges be licensed lawyers. The Supreme Court ruled in the 1970s that if a judge is not a lawyer, due process requirements are met only if an individual has the right to a later trial in front of a judge who is trained in the law. Often, states also require that judges have been a member of the state bar for a certain number of years and require that judges be citizens of the United States and residents of the state, and possibly the jurisdiction in which they would preside. Many states also have mandatory retirement ages, requiring that judges can only serve until the age of 70. Beyond being qualified, an individual must also be selected to be a judge. In the state courts of the United States, there are five methods of judicial selection: appointment by governor, appointment by state legislature, merit selection, nonpartisan election, and partisan election.

Appointment by Governor

During the founding era (1776–1830s), state judges were either chosen by state legislatures or by the governor. There are currently four states that use appointment by governor as their primary method of judicial selection: California (supreme court and court of appeals judges only), Maine, New Hampshire (also requires approval by a five-member executive council), and New Jersey. It is worth noting that in most states using partisan or nonpartisan elections, interim vacancies generally are filled through gubernatorial nomination. In many states, judges reach the bench of at least some courts through gubernatorial appointment (Institute for the Advancement of the American Legal System 2016).

One of the criticisms of appointment by governor is that the governor is likely to select individuals who have been active in the governor's political party—not necessarily a glowing recommendation for a judge. The concern is that these individuals are chosen to serve as a judge not because they are qualified to be a judge, but rather as a political favor. Pinello (1995) found when looking at state supreme courts that gubernatorial-appointed judges were more likely to prefer business over the individual and the states, and to prefer the individual over the state.

Appointment by Legislature

As was mentioned previously, selection by state legislature was one of the ways that state court judges were chosen during the founding era. Currently two states, South Carolina and Virginia, have state judges chosen by state legislatures. Since 1997, South Carolina's general assembly has used a 10-member nominating commission to screen judicial candidates. The South Carolina General Assembly can only select candidates found qualified by the Merit Selection Commission (American Judicature Society 2005). Virginia's legislature does not use a nominating commission, but the governor can make recess appointments when the legislature is not in session.

One of the criticisms of appointment by legislature is that state legislatures tend to turn to former members of the legislature when appointing judicial candidates (Carp et al. 2004). The concern is that individuals are appointed to trial and appellate courts because they have friends and colleagues in the state legislature, rather than being appointed because of ability. When looking at state supreme courts, Pinello (1995) found that legislatively selected judges tended to favor government.

Partisan and Nonpartisan Elections

Election of judges became popular during the time of Andrew Jackson's years as president, an era when his supporters sought to make the political process more democratic. By 1860, 24 of the 34 states elected some or all of their judges, and every new state admitted into the country from 1846 to 1912 elected some or all of its judges (Lozier 1996). Unfortunately, strong (and often corrupt) "political party machines" in many large urban areas had "party bosses" selecting incompetent party members for judicial positions (Lozier 1996). Because the party machine controlled elections, the result was an incompetent judiciary in many parts of the country. Today, partisan elections are used in fewer states than nonpartisan elections. In a partisan election, judicial candidates must be endorsed by a political party (unless they are running as independents), and the candidate's party affiliation appears on the ballot during the general election. States that select judges in this manner include Alabama, Arkansas, Illinois, Pennsylvania, Texas, and West Virginia. States that select some of their judges in this manner include Indiana, Kansas, Missouri, and Michigan.

States that use nonpartisan elections hold judicial elections but do not allow party affiliation to appear on the ballot or to appear in campaign materials. It is difficult to say exactly how many states use partisan elections because many states use more than one method to select their judges. There are approximately 12 states that use nonpartisan elections to choose judges, and an additional 8 states that use nonpartisan elections to choose some of its judges, or as one stage in their selection processes (see Banks and O'Brien 2015, 103).

For example, though Michigan has nonpartisan elections of judges at the general election stage, judicial candidates are chosen during partisan primaries. In addition, the state of California chooses its supreme court and court of appeals judges through appointment by governor but chooses its superior court judges through nonpartisan elections.

Prior to the 1970s, judicial elections were generally uncontested. A judge running for reelection (in Pennsylvania, Illinois, Indiana, and New Mexico, elected judges face a retention election after serving their first term) was often not running against another candidate. This has changed in recent decades, which has caused concern. Judicial candidates are spending money to win elections, and increasingly, it is lawyers who are making contributions to these campaigns (Carp et al. 2004). Critics say the problem with lawyers contributing to campaigns is twofold. First, some fear that lawyers contribute to campaigns in hopes that a judge will treat them more favorably. The second concern focuses on judges soliciting contributions from lawyers. If a sitting judge approaches a lawyer for a campaign contribution, lawyers may feel pressured to contribute to the judge's campaign.

There are additional concerns surrounding the financing of judicial elections. One source of campaign funds is interest groups. As much as there is concern that a lawyer contributing to a campaign will receive favorable treatment from the bench, there is concern that interest groups making contributions will receive similar benefits. By putting judges in a position where they have to solicit campaign contributions, some suggest that judges are placed in a position that threatens their ability to be impartial decision makers. Groups supporting various economic interests or social causes have the resources to make large contributions to judicial candidates, and this worries some observers.

One way around campaign contributions is to have candidates use their own money, or public funding, to pay for campaign expenses. The downside to this is probably obvious. If we begin to expect candidates to pay for their own campaigns, we are restricting judgeships to those who have the personal resources to pay for publicity and can afford to take time off of work to campaign. If it is publicly funded, then state treasuries are forced to provide scarce funds for candidates or parties. Moreover, many taxpayers object to seeing their taxes support the messages of candidates and causes with which they may disagree.

An additional criticism of nonpartisan elections is that voters are not likely to be familiar with candidates running for judicial office. Press coverage of judicial races is far less intense than for executive or legislative races, so the lack of party identification on the ballot will leave voters with one less clue about the candidate. Voters will be left to decide not to vote in that particular race, or to vote for the candidate with the most familiar sounding name. Such strategies are not in concert with selecting the most qualified candidate in the judicial race or the one who is most sympathetic to a voter's interests.

In a state with partisan elections, there is a strong likelihood that voters will select the candidates endorsed by their favorite party, even though they know little or nothing about the judicial candidate (Anderson 2004). In addition, if a state uses partisan elections, and one of the political parties dominates the state, the majority of judges will probably be members of that party. This is a problem in West Virginia, a state that uses partisan elections and is predominantly made up of Democrats. It is estimated that at any given time, 80 percent of judges in West Virginia are Democrats. Pinello (1995) found, when examining state supreme courts, that elected judges were more likely than other judges to be influenced by public opinion; more likely to favor the state over individuals and business; and in cases where the state is not a party to the suit, to favor individuals over business.

Merit Selection

The most common method of judicial selection in the state courts is merit selection. Merit selection, also referred to as the Missouri Plan, is a three-step judicial selection process. It involves a nominating committee (or commission), the governor, and the voters. The first step involves a nominating commission or committee. The makeup of the committee is determined by the state constitution or by state law. The nominating commission typically is comprised of lawyers and nonlawyers appointed by the governor. Law may place a limit on how many commission members can be from any one political party. Law may also dictate that members of the commission must come from certain geographic parts of the state.

Commission members typically serve set terms, with a few commissioner terms coming up each year. When a judicial vacancy occurs, it is the job of the commission to review potential judges and to forward to the governor a list of the candidates they feel are best qualified. The governor is then required to select a name on that list and to appoint one of those individuals to the judicial vacancy. After individuals have been appointed to the bench, they serve for at least one year, and then during the next scheduled general election, they are put up for a retention vote. The retention vote involves putting the judge's name on the ballot and asking the voters to essentially vote yes, retain the judge, or no, don't retain the judge. Typically, if judges receive a majority vote, they serve a set term (determined by individual state law), and at the end of that term, once again face a retention election.

Merit selection is supported by many scholars because it is believed that this method of selection produces the best qualified judges. Opponents of merit selection argue that the members of the nominating commission are often friends of the governor and that this method does not differ significantly from gubernatorial appointment.

Critics also point out that in most states using this method, judges almost always survive the retention election—possibly because voters are not informed enough about them to vote them out of office. Additional criticisms of the merit selection system include that it takes away the right of citizens to elect government officials, that the nominating commissions do not represent the entire community, that voters do not understand retention elections, and that those chosen as judges do not represent a cross-section of the community.

Arguments in favor of merit selection include research indicating that it is beneficial for women and minorities trying to get on the bench. Eight states that use merit selection have provisions providing for diversity of applicants, and 10 states (including 2 of the previous 8) have rules against discrimination (American Judicature Society 2005). Those in favor of merit selection also argue that in states where it is used, more highly qualified judges have been the result. In addition, several states that use merit selection for some courts and elections for others have found that judges selected through the merit selection method are much less likely to face disciplinary charges than judges chosen through election (Lozier 1996). Many argue that in addition to giving us a more diverse judiciary, merit selection gives us the best of both worlds: a judge chosen based on merit and retained in office through the votes of the citizens.

Becoming a Judge

After an individual has been appointed or elected, he or she needs to make the transition from lawyer to judge. For many years, it was assumed that judges would be able to do this on their own. The belief was that lawyers had seen what judges did while arguing cases in the courtroom so that was sufficient training. Increasingly, states are now requiring additional education for their judges. This may be as simple as a judicial orientation course to a requirement for continued education if an individual wants to continue to serve as a judge. The National Center for State Courts and many law schools provide training for first-time judges and continuing educational seminars for experienced judges.

One resource that has been very useful for states is the Federal Judicial Center, which offers courses for both federal and state court judges. Courses cover topics ranging from jury selection to criminal practice to torts. In addition to training judges on substantive areas of law, many training programs also cover technological advances, case management, security, and personnel management. The not-for-profit National Association of State Judicial Educators was formed in 1975 and is entirely devoted to the education of state court officials. Many states also offer their own judicial education programs. For example, Vermont has shifted from using nationally offered programs for education of state court judges to offering its own one-week judicial college (Morse et al. 1997). By providing its own program, it is able to address issues specific to Vermont courts.

Judge Compensation and Tenure

Salaries for state judges vary by state and by judicial position. At the bottom of the pay scale are JPs, whose entire income comes from fines collected or fees charged to perform weddings. At the other end of the pay scale are state supreme court justices in the more populous states. A survey conducted by the National Center for State Courts (updated in 2016) found that, on average, state supreme court chief justices earn $167,000 per year, associate supreme court justices earn $160,000, intermediate appellate court judges earn $159,000, and trial court judges earn $146,000.

Although these salaries may seem high at first glance, for many lawyers, becoming a judge, even at these salaries, involves taking a pay cut. In Minnesota, the salary for a district court judge is $138,318; however, first-year associates in Minnesota law firms are generally paid around $160,000. In Texas, Chief Justice Wallace B. Jefferson's 2005 "State of the Judiciary" message mentioned that Texas was losing good judges because of the relatively low salaries earned by judges. A Texas court judge who returns to private law practice was likely to double or triple his or her salary. Those who chose to go into education or move on to the federal bench were likely to see a 40 percent increase in pay. However, in 2013, the state legislature voted to increase district and appellate judge salaries by 12 percent, that is, from $125,000 to $140,000. And, counties could supplement judge salaries with an additional $18,000.

After an becoming a judge, there is a very high likelihood that the individual will remain a judge for as long as he or she wants to serve in that position. Supreme court justices and court judges serve terms ranging from 4 years to 14 years, to life. Mandatory retirement at age 70 may be the only way to remove a judge, depending on which state he or she is in. The terms of office between states can vary quite dramatically. An individual on the Kansas Court of Appeals has a term of 4 years, while an individual on the Massachusetts Supreme Court or court of appeals is appointed for life, with mandatory retirement at age 70. At the trial court level, judges are typically looking at terms of 4 to 12 years. At the end of their terms, judges who were appointed by a governor or a state legislature must be reappointed, judges selected through partisan or nonpartisan elections must be reelected, and judges chosen through merit selection must stand for another retention election.

Leaving the Court

Judges can leave the court in a voluntary or involuntary manner. Some judges at the end of their terms, or even in the middle of their terms, decide that they no longer want to be judges. Some choose not to stand for retention. They resign from their judicial positions and are replaced by others. Many states also have mandatory retirement ages for judges. In these states, a judge is required to resign when he or she reaches that age. In some states, judges may complete their terms of office after reaching the retirement age.

Judges may also leave the bench against their will. This typically happens when a judge is found guilty of illegal activity (e.g., accepting a bribe), abuse of power (e.g., using one's power as a judge to issue a warrant when evidence does not support the warrant), or found to be incapable of doing the job due to incompetence or senility. Many states hope that a mandatory retirement age will reduce the number of cases where age leads to senility or loss of stamina needed for the job.

There are two major avenues by which judges are forced out of office. One is by impeachment by the state legislature. The other is through a hearing, typically involving a state judicial disciplinary board and the state supreme court. Almost all state constitutions allow legislatures to intervene by impeaching a judge by vote of the state legislature. If the legislature finds against a judge, he or she may be removed from office by a vote of the state senate. This approach is rarely used.

More commonly, if a judge abuses his or her power or commits an illegal act, someone will file a claim with a state judicial disciplinary commission. There are variations among the states, but all states follow some combination of these general guidelines. The agency or commission will investigate the complaint. Staff investigators will compile a file and present the data. Appointed officers, who make up the voting members of the commission, will first decide if the complaint is valid. If the complaint is valid, the commission holds a formal hearing. At the end of that formal hearing, if the commission finds the judge guilty of the charges, the judge will be disciplined either by the commission or by the state supreme court. Discipline can involve anything from a formal reprimand to removal from the court.

Attorneys

Judges are just one group of actors found within state court systems. Another group of actors is attorneys, which includes attorneys who represent the state government as well as attorneys who represent individuals and nongovernmental institutions such as businesses or nonprofit agencies.

In Britain and Ireland, the lawyers who practice in courtrooms are called barristers, while those who provide legal advice outside the courtroom are called solicitors. In the United States, there is no such formal distinction, but there are some lawyers who specialize as a matter of preference.

Attorneys for the State

The companion volume *The Executive Branch of State Government* provides complete details about the workings of attorneys general and local prosecuting attorney offices. Because these agencies work so closely with the courts, it is essential that their role be mentioned here as well. Each state has an attorney general who acts as the chief legal official for the state. The attorney general's job is to see that the laws of the state are enforced. This individual, who is an elected official in most states, manages an office of attorneys who handle civil cases and statewide criminal cases involving the state. The office of the attorney general can participate in statewide criminal investigations, institute civil suits, represent state agencies, and handle criminal appeals. This office defends state laws when they are questioned on constitutional grounds. Most state attorneys general offices also employ many additional attorneys. Of greater interest in the area of courts is the role of the prosecutor. Prosecutors include state prosecutors, district attorneys, county attorneys, and assistant and deputy county and district attorneys.

District attorneys (often called county attorneys or state's attorneys) typically are locally elected. The job of a district or county attorney involves prosecuting cases on the government's behalf. Jurisdiction is determined by law and may involve anything and everything from traffic tickets to capital murder, to advancing a county's interests in civil proceedings. State's attorneys' offices usually have civil divisions that acquire property for road projects, defend the county's land-use policies, or respond to tort claims against the county. The job of a prosecutor involves reviewing evidence, pertinent court decisions, laws, polices, and regulations, and then deciding whether there is sufficient evidence for indictment and prosecution. Things that go into the prosecutor's decision of whether or not to prosecute can include the chance of winning the case in front of a jury, the nature of the evidence against a suspect, and whether resources exist to support prosecution of the case. The decision to prosecute also includes the decision concerning which charges to pursue and the applicable law.

The prosecutor also has discretion concerning whether a defendant can enter into a negotiated outcome, such as a plea agreement. As this is an elected position in most states, voters can remove a district or county attorney if they do not agree with his or her decision concerning the prosecution of a case. In cases including eminent domain, land use, and civil rights, state law determines whether the attorney general acts alone, whether county attorneys act alone, or whether the two work together. For example, in Minnesota, the attorney general acts in conjunction with county attorneys in cases involving the use of public lands.

Assistant county attorneys, deputy county attorneys, assistant district attorneys, and deputy district attorneys work for the county or district attorney. These are not elected positions. These individuals are trial attorneys and prosecute cases as assigned. They do not have discretion as to whether to bring charges in a case, and they typically need the approval of the county or district attorney to enter into a plea agreement. The prosecutor is responsible for participating in preliminary hearings, probation hearings, bench trials, and jury trials. This includes the need to interact with the public, identify and question witnesses, and understand relevant laws and policies.

Attorneys for Activists

Many activist groups use the courts to bring about social change, and there are lawyers who specialize in these types of cases. Scheingold and Sarat (2004) call this "cause lawyering." They see this group of lawyers as including everyone from property rights lawyers to right-to-life lawyers to environmental lawyers. Lawyers take cases in these and other fields not by accident but because they have an intent to bring about change in some particular policy area. Groups that come to mind when one thinks of cause lawyers include the American Civil Liberties Union (ACLU) and the National Association for the Advancement of Colored People (NAACP). These groups hire lawyers and provide legal services for parties in cases related to the cause supported by the group.

These groups rarely are listed as the plaintiff or respondent in their most profound suits. Rather, they provide legal or financial support to the people or groups who are named in a case. For example, though the NAACP was not the litigant, it provided the legal staff that succeeded in desegregating the Topeka, Kansas, schools in *Brown v. Board of Education*.

Attorneys for Criminal Defendants

In 1963, in a case called *Gideon v. Wainwright*, the U.S. Supreme Court ruled that the Sixth Amendment right to an attorney included an attorney at the expense of the state if a criminal suspect could not afford an attorney on his or her own. In 1972, in *Argersinger v. Hamlin*, the Supreme Court ruled that an individual cannot be sentenced to jail if he or she had not been provided with the opportunity to have an attorney. If an individual can afford to hire an attorney, there are many attorneys available in most communities who specialize in defending individuals in criminal cases. Private defense counsel is available either for an hourly fee or for a set amount of money for a certain type of case. Although paying for an attorney can be a hardship for some, unless defendants can show that they are indigent (destitute and in need of help from others), they must pay for an attorney on their own. On the other hand, if individuals are indigent and cannot afford an attorney, one is provided for them by the state.

The first step taken by an individual who cannot afford an attorney typically is an application for indigent defense services. Individuals can prove that they are indigent by showing that they do not have property that can be converted into cash, showing that they have excessive debt, or by demonstrating through past and present financial history that they do not have the resources necessary to hire an attorney. The judge then makes a ruling on whether an individual is indigent. It is also possible for an individual's status of indigence to change over the course of a trial. If individuals are indigent, legal assistance will be provided for them in the form of assigned counsel or a public defender.

States and localities provide indigent defendants with defense attorneys. Some local governments turn to private attorneys who take cases for indigent defendants. These assigned counsel attorneys are paid by the government to do this as part of their regular work. Some states have entire agencies dedicated to defending the poor. Public defenders are government lawyers outside the attorney general's chain of command who represent poor criminal defendants at trial and on appeal. Most states use a combination of assigned counsel and public defenders, with assigned counsel being more common in rural areas, and public defenders more common in urban areas. Lawyers may or may not have a choice as to whether they will serve as assigned counsel, and if assigned to a case, lawyers must accept the compensation set by state law, even if that compensation is less than they would receive through private practice. For example, although attorneys may typically charge $100 per hour for their legal services, they may only get compensated $50 per hour on a case where they are an assigned counsel.

There are multiple criticisms of the system of assigned counsel. Some argue that states place cost containment above quality. There is also concern that attorneys are assigned to cases that they may not be well qualified to deal with. Some states offer incentives to lawyers who plead a case rather than take the case to trial, and some states conduct little or no monitoring of assigned counsel. In states that contract out for indigent defense services, some reward low bids, placing more emphasis on hiring an inexpensive, rather than highly qualified, legal service. Critics do acknowledge that some states do a better job with assigned counsel than others. States that have effective systems related to assigned counsel are more likely to require minimum attorney qualifications, offer compensation in line with local fees, and provide some type of oversight mechanism. The state of Indiana, for instance, has a Public Defender Council, a state agency whose responsibility is to be a support center for assigned counsel.

Approximately 25 percent of states use a public defender system to provide counsel for all indigent parties, and many other states use it to provide counsel for some indigents. With a public defender system, a state agency hires attorneys to defend indigent criminal defendants. For example, in Maryland, all indigent suspects who are involved in a criminal case carrying a possible jail sentence or a fine greater than $500 can be provided with an attorney through the public defender's office. Although there are states that use just public defenders, a more common situation is a state such as Ohio that uses both public defenders and assigned counsel. The office of the public defender in Ohio both provides legal representation in the form of public defenders and oversees appointed counsel in its county courts. Ohio has an interesting division of responsibilities in that it uses primarily assigned counsel at the trial level and public defenders at the appellate level. In some parts of California, assigned counsel is used, while more populous counties such as Orange County have public defenders.

Some of the criticisms of public defender systems include the complaint that lawyers work with very heavy caseloads but lack the experience or resources necessary to compete with staff and resources of the state's attorney's office, especially in death penalty cases. States have been responding to these criticisms, successfully in many cases. Public defenders in Maryland now must have at least five years prior experience in litigating criminal cases. Alaska also has a statewide public defender system, with 65 public defenders employed in 13 offices throughout the state. Finally, Colorado is another state that has a public defender's office that serves the entire state. Colorado has separate trial and appellate public defenders. In addition, Colorado has trial-level public defenders that specialize in death penalty cases. Most individuals hired as public defenders in Colorado are hired directly out of law school, although many have clinical or clerking experience (see Langton and Farole 2010).

Attorneys for Civil Defendants

The Sixth Amendment right to have an attorney provided if one cannot afford an attorney is applicable only in criminal cases. The Constitution does not discuss the right to an attorney in a civil trial. As a rule, if an individual desires to have an attorney in a civil trial, that person must pay for an attorney. In most civil cases, if an individual cannot afford an attorney, that person must proceed without an attorney. This may not seem significant, unless civil cases include divorce and custody issues. There are, however, three developments that have made an attorney in a civil case more affordable to a middle-class litigant.

The first of these is flat fees. There are some lawyers who offer basic legal services, such as an uncontested divorce, for a flat fee. The second advancement is prepaid legal services. Individuals are enrolled in prepaid legal services typically through their employer as part of a benefit package or through a plan offered with a credit card, credit union, or other similar entity. Basically, a job benefit or credit union benefit might be a set number of hours of legal assistance in a given year. The plan normally provides a list of attorneys that an individual must choose from. A third development that has made legal assistance more accessible for the middle class is the use of contingency fees. The way that contingency fees work is that an attorney will agree to take a case on contingency, meaning that his or her compensation in the case is based on the amount of the settlement. If the attorney loses the case, the individual pays nothing; but if the attorney wins the case, he or she is sometimes reimbursed for expenses, and then also receives some percentage (typically around 33 to 50 percent) of the remaining settlement.

In some states, such as Wisconsin, contingency fees are limited by law (Kritzer 2002). In his 1995 study of contingency-fee practitioners, Kritzer found that contingency fees did not have the negative impact on the legal practice feared by many scholars. He found that contingency fees are adequately governed by the market, that contingency fees are generally competitive, and that although there are some extremely large contingency fees paid to lawyers, as a general rule, they are reasonable (Kritzer 2004). Furthermore, Coben (2004) finds that over the past 30 years, there is no real evidence that contingency fees have been harmful to the public.

Free Legal Services for the Poor

Legal services for the poor in civil cases are difficult for many to find. It is primarily provided in three ways: as pro bono work, through legal clinics provided by law schools, and through legal services programs. Pro bono work refers to legal services provided by an attorney for free. The American Bar Association's *Model Rules of Professional Conduct* suggests that attorneys have an obligation to perform pro bono work. Some attorneys satisfy this obligation by representing poor individuals in civil cases. Law schools often provide clinical experiences for their third-year students. Although clinics exist in many legal fields, clinics focusing on issues such landlord-tenant disputes and family law can provide affordable legal assistance for the poor. Legal services programs, historically funded by federal, state, and local funds, involve setting up offices in cities and neighborhoods to provide legal services for indigent clients. Funds went to pay attorneys providing the legal services. Recent budget cuts at the state and federal level have resulted in a reduction in legal services programs.

Support Staff

State trial courts and appellate courts cannot function without court clerks, law clerks, and other support staff. These are the individuals who assist judges in carrying out their duties, as well as taking care of the administrative responsibilities involved in a smoothly functioning court system. Some of these individuals are elected, some are appointed, and some are hired. Some serve terms set by state law or the state constitution, while others serve at the pleasure of the individual who hired them. Without these support personnel, the state courts would come to a grinding halt.

Court Clerks

The clerk of a court is an elected or appointed official. A court clerk is responsible for docketing cases, arranging jury selection, maintaining court records, and collecting court fees. This is the individual who handles the day-to-day functions of the court.

Court clerks are different from a judge's law clerks, who assist judges in their legal research. A clerk of a court will frequently have responsibility for one or more courtrooms while the court administrator may run an entire courthouse. Appointed clerks frequently serve at the pleasure of the individual or court who appointed them, while elected clerks typically serve terms of two-, four-, or six years and are accountable to the voters, rather than judges of the court. Appointed clerks may be appointed by the court, a chief judge, a county board, some other local governing body, or the governor. In Hawaii, the clerks of trial courts actually have civil service tenure.

Appellate Court Clerks

Clerks play an important role in appellate courts and are provided for either by state law or in the state constitution. The majority of clerks of appellate courts are appointed by the judge(s) of the court that they are working for. In Indiana, Montana, and Ohio (court of appeals only), they are elected. In Rhode Island, they are appointed by the governor. Most clerks serve at the pleasure of the court; however, in some states, such as Arkansas, Indiana, and Kansas, clerks of appellate courts serve set terms. Clerks of appellate courts frequently have staffs who work for them.

Responsibilities of the clerks' offices in the appellate courts include day-to-day operations of the court's physical plant, management of the court's docket, oversight of the state bar, and support for the judges of the court. These functions include accounting, accounts payable, administrative meetings, oversight of the state bar, budget preparation, oversight of commissions and boards, maintenance of court statistics, data processing, facility management, legal research, liaison with state legislature and other courts, payroll, property control, purchasing, records management, planning, and technical assistance to lower courts. It is their responsibility to keep the court operating in every manner imaginable. In many states, there is no minimum qualification to serve as the clerk of an appellate court, but, in some, an individual must be a lawyer and admitted to the state bar, and, in others, an individual must have experience in court operations (Rottman and Strickland 2004).

Trial Court Clerks

The clerk of court for a trial court differs significantly from a clerk of court for an appellate court. Whereas the majority of clerks of court for appellate courts are appointed by the court, many clerks of court for trial courts are elected, in either partisan or nonpartisan local elections. Legislation typically provides a clerk of court for each court, so it is not uncommon within a given state for there to be more than 100 clerks of court. Much like clerks of appellate courts, clerks of trial courts often have staffs who work for them. Responsibilities of trial court clerks are set by law. In some states, such as Minnesota, clerks of the court are called court administrators. Clerks of trial courts are responsible for the day-to-day operation of that particular court. Every state now has something resembling an administrative office of the courts. This agency performs a variety of administrative tasks, including judicial education, budgeting, research, personnel management, facility management, and public information.

Responsibilities of the administrative office of the courts in a trial court can include day-to-day operations of the court's physical plant, management of the court's docket, oversight of the state bar, and support for the judges of the court. These functions include accounting, alternative dispute resolution, assignments for sitting and supplemental judges, alternative sanction programs, budget preparation, facility management, foster care review, judicial education, law libraries, legal research, representation and general counsel, legal services, liaison with the state legislature, oversight of adult and juvenile probation, public information, purchasing, research and planning, and technical assistance to the courts (Rottman and Strickland 2004).

As an example, the Trial Court Services Division of the Alabama Administrative Office of the Courts provides assistance for Alabama trial courts in the areas of court automation, case management and time standards, jury management, judge case assignments, education support, municipal courts, uniform traffic ticket complaints, the unified judicial system magistrate program, and municipal court clerk and management certification. For instance, in the area of judge assignment, this division handles all temporary judge assignments. In the area of case management and time standards, this division monitors the processing of cases in all state trial courts and works with individual court staff to more efficiently schedule cases and utilize court staff.

The National Center for State Courts (NCSC) is a research and training resource for both court clerks and for trial court administrators. One of NCSC's functions, carried out through its Institute for Court Management, is providing education and training for court personnel, with the goal of helping courts to better serve the public. NCSC offers a Court Executive Development Program and a Court Management Program. In addition to participating in one of the two programs previously mentioned, state court clerks and state trial court administrators can take courses in person or online on topics covering everything from managing court financial resources, to introduction to case flow, to emergency management and court security. NCSC offers a course corresponding to most of the functions mentioned previously.

Law Clerks

The use of law clerks at the appellate court level has allowed appellate courts to increase their efficiency in handling their caseloads. State law typically provides that each supreme court justice or appellate court judge has one to three law clerks. Law clerks are different from court clerks in that law clerks provide legal assistance while court clerks are administrative assistants. These individuals have legal backgrounds, work for a specific individual justice, and may be a short-term or long-term employee. In addition, state law may provide for some number of the central law staff for a court. Central staff attorneys typically have a legal background, work for the appellate court as a whole, have limited ties to individual justices, and often work in the office of the clerk of the court. This individual may be referred to as a research attorney, a commissioner, a staff law clerk, or may have another title. Law clerks are either individuals still in law school or are individuals with a law degree.

When one thinks of law clerks working in the appellate court environment, the function that initially comes to mind is that these individuals assist judges and justices in preparing their opinions in cases that the court has considered. Law clerks assist the court in many more ways as well. Law clerks can assist the court by helping conduct and manage settlement conferences, and they can assist in handling cases by helping with screening, preparing memoranda, scheduling the case for oral argument, or performing other aspects of case management. They can also assist the court by helping train new staff, conducting research on motions and writs, and preparing memoranda on discretionary petitions. Functions performed by law clerks can also include developing databases, tracking information, indexing cases, and making recommendations to a judge concerning questions that should be asked during oral argument. Any work that can be handled by a law clerk frees up a judge or justice's time to focus on other more important tasks.

Law clerks also play a role at the trial court level. Trial court law clerks may assist judges by helping in legal research and court management, processing motions, attending conferences, mediating small-claims cases, and summarizing information for the judge.

Court Reporters and Courtroom Deputy

Court reporters are courthouse staff who create word-for-word transcripts of what occurs during legal proceedings. Often using stenography equipment to take transcriptions, it is their responsibility to make sure there is a complete and accurate record of the trial. This is important because the transcript of the trial created by the court reporter is the record on which any appeal is built. In addition to providing a transcript of a trial, court reporters may also take pretrial depositions from witnesses involved in a case or take transcripts during other hearings in the process. The National Court Reporters Association provides training for court reporters. Depending on the type of certification required, this training, on average, takes two to four years.

The courtroom deputy position is one that goes by many names—deputy clerk, bailiff, deputy sheriff—but whose function is the same: courtroom security. Specific job functions differ from one courtroom to the next, but, essentially, the bailiff is responsible for maintaining order and security in the courtroom and for ensuring the protection of judges, juries, and courtroom participants. This individual announces the entrance of the judge and jury, prevents persons from entering the courtroom while a judge is instructing a jury, escorts the judge outside of the courtroom when necessary, and removes individuals who disrupt court proceedings. When a jury is sequestered, bailiffs may escort jurors to restaurants and to their hotels. Individuals who work as bailiffs typically have police academy training, have arrest authority, and often are employed through a sheriff's department.

Jurors and the Jury

Although there are tens of millions of felonies and misdemeanors in the United States each year, only 300,000 cases or so are actually decided by a jury. Although an individual is guaranteed a jury trial in the U.S. Constitution's Sixth Amendment, many individuals waive that right and opt for a bench trial (a trial in front of a judge) rather than a jury trial. Despite this low number, the jury (also called *trial jury* or *petit jury*) plays an important role in the American judicial system. The jury system as it is used here in the United States is a legacy of our English common-law tradition. The right to a jury trial dates back to antiquity, and the jury trial as we understand it has been part of the Western tradition since the Magna Carta. In the United States, an individual has the right to request a jury trial if he or she faces a sentence of more than six months in jail.

The first step in jury selection involves the creation of a master jury list, which includes a representative cross-section of the community. States use multiple sources in creating these lists. States may use city or county directories, driver's license lists, motor vehicle registrations, telephone directories, tax rolls, lists of utility customers, voter registration lists, or some combination of these. Most states allow a person to serve on a jury on reaching the age of 18, although Alabama and Nebraska require that a potential juror be at least 19, and Mississippi and Missouri require that potential jurors be at least 21 years of age. Many states disqualify convicted felons from serving on juries, and some require that a potential juror has been a resident of the jurisdiction for some amount of time, although residency requirements are not to exceed a year (Rottman and Strickland 2004). The U.S. Supreme Court has ruled that women (*Taylor v. Louisiana,*

1975), blacks (*Strauder v. West Virginia,* 1880), and Mexican Americans (*Castaneda v. Partida,* 1977) cannot be systematically kept off juries simply due to race or gender. This is one valuable legacy of the civil rights and women's movements. Women and blacks, who were systematically kept off of juries for years, are now allowed to serve.

The next phase in jury selection is venire, or the drawing of a jury pool from the master jury list. Clerks of the court randomly select a group of names from the master list and send a survey to those individuals asking questions concerning their eligibility to serve on a jury. Some states exempt potential jurors who are senior citizens.

States may also exempt a person from serving on a jury if that person is in a specified profession, including judicial officer, public official, elected legislator, physician, or attorney. If people are in an exempt category, they will not be allowed to serve on a jury, even if they want to.

In addition, some states will excuse potential jurors if serving on a jury would pose undue hardship or extreme inconvenience, or if public necessity or physical or mental disability should preclude this person from serving on a jury (Rottman and Strickland 2004). These include cases where a person's absence from work or family would adversely affect public health, safety, welfare, and interest. For example, some state law makes it easy for lawyers, public officials, police officers, and news reporters to be excused from jury service. Potential jurors who are not exempted or excused will eventually receive a summons directing them to appear at the courthouse on a given date to possibly serve on a jury.

Voir dire is the final step in jury selection. Potential jurors are asked questions concerning their ability to be an impartial juror in a particular trial. The complexity of this process is often influenced by the nature of the case involved. At one end of the spectrum was the O. J. Simpson case where 250 potential jurors were asked to complete a 79-page, 294-question questionnaire. At the other end would be a misdemeanor state trial where a jury of six can be selected in an hour or two. For example, if an individual was charged with writing a forged check in California, it would be a misdemeanor offense, and that person would be facing up to a year in jail, giving him or her a right to a jury trial. Chances are that a jury would be chosen rather quickly.

Jury selection in a capital (death penalty) case differs from jury selection in general in two ways. First, the defense may be provided with additional peremptory challenges. When a defendant's life is at risk, and his attorney has a "gut feeling" that a particular juror may be hostile to the defendant, the attorney is able to use a peremptory challenge to keep that person off of the jury. An additional difference is something referred to as *death qualification* of a jury. The prosecution is allowed to ask potential jurors whether they feel that they could impose a death sentence if the defendant is found guilty. Asking this type of question is not seen as a method of creating a jury that is pro-death penalty.

Instead, it is a way of ensuring that if a person is on the jury, he or she can fairly apply the law to the case at hand.

Increasingly, attorneys are using scientific jury selection, where professional jury consultants are brought in to pinpoint the type of juror who is most likely to side with their client. In addition to assisting attorneys during jury selection, professional jury consultants can also assist attorneys in developing trial presentations targeted at the specific types of individuals on the jury.

Jury size and the number of votes required to reach a verdict also differ by state. The U.S. Supreme Court has ruled that a jury in a state trial can have as few as 6 members (*Williams v. Florida,* 1970), that the vote of the jury need not be unanimous (*Johnson v. Louisiana,* 1972), but that in order to allow a nonunanimous vote, the jury must have at least 12 members (*Burch v. Louisiana,* 1979). The one exception to this rule is Oregon, which has a 5 of 6 rule concerning juries of 6 in some of its courts. States have been moving away from requiring a unanimous jury verdict. If one requires a 5 of 6 or a 9 of 12 vote, there is less likelihood of a hung jury than if unanimity is required.

Most states require a jury of 12 in felony cases, but Alabama, Connecticut, Florida, Indiana, Massachusetts, and Utah allow for juries of 6 or 8 members in some or all noncapital felony cases. All states, with the exception of Louisiana and Oregon, require a unanimous vote by the jury in a felony case. Louisiana will allow a 10 of 12 vote in cases where punishment is hard labor, and Oregon allows a 10 of 12 vote in all cases not involving a murder. Jury size for cases involving misdemeanors also varies by state. In civil cases, jury sizes range from 6 to 12 jurors, with some states requiring that a judgment be unanimous, some states employing a 5 of 6 rule, and others employing a 3 of 4 rule (Rottman and Strickland 2004).

The Grand Jury

Although the Fifth Amendment of the U.S. Constitution provides "[N]o person shall be held to answer for a capital, or otherwise infamous crime, unless on a presentment or indictment of a Grand Jury," this has never been interpreted as applying to the states. As a result, not all states require grand jury indictment in felony cases. Some states require a grand jury indictment for all felonies, some states require a grand jury indictment only if the death penalty and/or a life sentence is being requested, and some states use the grand jury primarily for criminal investigations. In many states, grand jury indictment has been replaced by a document called criminal information that is drawn up by the prosecutor and presented directly to a magistrate or judge. An *information* is essentially a legal document that lays out the evidence that the prosecutor has that a crime has occurred. An information is a more efficient method of processing a criminal complaint, but for complex criminal problems such as public corruption and fraud, the grand jury is still the preferred route. If the judge or magistrate believes there is probable cause that an individual has committed a crime, the judge will issue the necessary search and/or arrest warrant.

The grand jury functions very differently from a trial jury. The job of the grand jury is not to determine guilt or innocence; rather, it is to determine if there is sufficient evidence to arrest an individual and to bring him or her to trial. A grand jury is convened when a prosecutor has a case he or she wants the grand jury to review. The prosecutor presents the state's case, and then witnesses are called to testify in front of the grand jury.

The accused and his or her attorney are not present in the room, and suspects are often not aware that they are the target of the investigation. In many states, the only individuals allowed in the grand jury chamber are the jurors, the prosecutor, and a single witness who has been called to testify. The individuals testifying can have their attorneys outside the room, and they can consult with their attorneys whenever they feel the need. Some states also allow the judge to be present during testimony, and, in some states, witnesses are allowed to have their attorney present during testimony. In addition to the prosecutor asking questions of the witness, jurors are also allowed to ask questions.

Witnesses who have testified in front of a grand jury are prohibited from discussing their grand jury testimony with others. The grand jury investigation is kept secret so that the grand jury can faithfully do its job without risk that witnesses will be tainted, witnesses will be threatened by the targets of the investigation, or that the investigation itself will be compromised.

If a grand jury believes that the state has a compelling case, the grand jury issues an indictment, which allows the state to bring charges against an individual. Unanimity is not required to issue an indictment; most states allow for a majority, two-thirds, or three-fourths vote. In some states, grand juries are primarily employed to help conduct criminal investigations. A single grand jury may hear evidence in more than a single case, unlike a petit jury that dissolves at the end of the individual trial for which it was assembled.

Selection of grand juries has many similarities with selection of trial juries. The same master list is used, and venire is often the same. At this point, there is not questioning by attorneys or use of peremptory challenges, as one would see at the voir dire stage with a trial jury. Instead, the judge will empanel those for whom service on a grand jury would not pose an undue hardship. One significant difference between trial juries and grand juries is that in many states, grand jurors may be asked to serve as long as 18 or 24 months, and during that period of time, the grand jury may hear multiple cases.

Grand jury sizes range from a low of 5 to 7 jurors in the state of Virginia to a high of as many as 23 in 11 states. Due to the hardship faced by jurors serving terms of up to 2 years, in some states, grand juries can conduct business with a quorum (Kansas requires a grand jury of 15 members but has set a quorum at 12), and some states, such as Pennsylvania, have alternate jurors. Individuals serving on a grand jury are not sequestered. In addition, the grand jury generally meets from 9:00 a.m. to 5:00 p.m., allowing jurors to go home at night, and generally does not meet every day, allowing jurors to go to their jobs. In some states, grand jurors serve a set term, while in others, the grand jury is convened to address a particular case and is dismissed by the judge when that task is complete (Rottman and Strickland 2004).

Jury Compensation and Characteristics

Jury compensation varies by state. Some states require an employer to continue to pay a juror while on jury duty, while the majority of states compensate jurors. Some states provide for jury compensation through state law, while in other states, jury compensation is a local or county matter. Compensation ranges from as little as $40 per day for federal jurors to as much as $50 per day (or more if jurors' employers must pay them while on jury duty) after serving on a grand jury for at least 45 days. In some cases, jurors may also receive compensation for mileage, parking, and other expenses.

Financial hardship is often offered as a reason that people do not want to serve on juries. On a national level, roughly 1 in 10 jurors summoned for jury service are excused from serving as jurors, but in some states, the rate is as much as 20 percent (Center for Jury Studies 2016).

There is concern that juries are not representative of the population at large. A study of juries in Vermont revealed that people selected for jury service tend to be wealthier, older, more often white collar, and better educated than the community at large (Nelson 2016). This stands to reason because these same characteristics apply to those who vote most regularly, and voter rolls are an important source of juror selection lists. This raises concern over groups that are systematically kept off of juries. As mentioned in the discussion of venire, groups that may be exempted from jury duty include convicted felons, judicial officers, public officials, elected legislators, physicians, and attorneys.

Some states will also keep members of additional groups off of juries (through excusal) if serving on a jury would pose an undue hardship on the individual or the community. These groups include schoolteachers, hospital employees, firefighters, police officers, those active in the military, and those who do not read and write in English (Rottman and Strickland 2004). The exemption and excusal of large groups of people might result in the tacit denial to a defendant the jury of his or her peers, as guaranteed in the Sixth Amendment.

An additional concern is that low compensation for jurors is also keeping many potential jurors off of juries. In states where jury compensation is low, compensation may not even be enough to cover gas, parking, and lunch, let alone enough to make up for wages that a person will not receive from their employer for that day or days spent serving as a juror. Very few states require employers to pay jurors their regular salary while serving as a juror. Scholars examining the jury system in Florida found that individuals with good paying jobs were likely to ask to be excused from jury service. In addition, they found that Florida courts often excused professionals and parents with child care expenses, as well as laborers and salespersons (Rebein et al. 2003). They found that those who typically remained in the jury pool, after excusal for hardship, were those who were not employed and those whose employers continued to pay their salaries while they served on a jury. Increasingly, a jury of one's peers has become a jury of the retired and unemployed (Schwartz et al. 2003), creating concern as to whether defendants are truly being judged by a jury of their peers.

Charles L. Zelden, Sean O. Hogan, Ginny Hollinger

Further Reading

Abraham, Henry J. 1998. *The Judicial Process.* 7th ed. New York: Oxford University Press.

Alozie, Nicholas O. 1990. "The Distribution of Women and Minority Judges." *Social Science Quarterly* 71(7): 315–325.

American Bar Association. 2016. "Lawyer Demographics." http://www.americanbar.org /content/dam/aba/administrative/market_research/lawyer-demographics-tables-2016 .authcheckdam.pdf.

Anderson, Brian P. 2004. "Judicial Elections in West Virginia: 'By the People, for the People' or 'By the Powerful, for the Powerful?' A Choice Must Be Made." *West Virginia Law Review* 107 (Fall): 235–259.

Baar, Carl. 1982. "Judicial Activism in State Courts: The Inherent Powers Doctrine." In *State Supreme Courts: Policy Makers in the Federal System*, edited by Mary Cornelia Porter and G. Alan Tarr. Westport, CT: Greenwood Press.

Banks, Christopher P., and David M. O'Brien. 2015. *The Judicial Process: Law, Courts, and Judicial Politics.* Thousand Oaks, CA: CQ Press.

Banks, Christopher P., and John C. Blakeman. 2012. *The U.S. Supreme Court and New Federalism: From the Rehnquist to the Roberts Court.* Lanham, MD: Rowman & Littlefield.

Barrow, Deborah J., and Thomas G. Walker. 1988. *A Court Divided: The Fifth Circuit Court of Appeals and the Politics of Judicial Reform.* New Haven, CT: Yale University Press.

Barrow, Deborah J., Gary Zuk, and Gerard S. Gryski. 1996. *The Federal Judiciary and Institutional Change.* Ann Arbor: University of Michigan Press.

Carp, Robert A., and C. K. Rowland. 1983. *Policymaking and Politics in the Federal District Courts.* Knoxville: University of Tennessee Press.

Carp, Robert A., and Ronald Stidham. 1996. *Judicial Process in America.* 3rd ed. Washington, D.C.: CQ Press.

Carp, Robert A., and Ronald Stidham. 1998. *The Federal Courts.* 3rd ed. Washington, D.C.: CQ Press.

Carp, Robert A., Ronald Stidham, and Kenneth L. Manning. 2004. *Judicial Process in America*. 6th ed. Washington D.C.: CQ Press.

Center for Jury Studies. 2016. "Jury Manager's Toolbox: Best Practices for Excusal Policies." http://www.ncsc-jurystudies.org/~/media/Microsites/Files/CJS/Toolbox /Best%20Practices%20for%20Excusal%20Policies.ashx.

Champion, Dean J., and Richard D. Hartley. 2011. *Criminal Courts: Structure, Process, and Issues*. Upper Saddle River, NJ: Pearson.

Coben, Larry E. 2004. "Contingency Fees: If It's Not Broken, Why Fix It?" *Arizona Attorney* 41(September): 44.

Comparato, Scott A. 2003. *Amici Curiae and Strategic Behavior in State Supreme Courts*. Westport, CT: Praeger.

Cornell, James G. 2012. "Limited Jurisdiction Courts: Challenges, Opportunities, and Strategies for Action." In *Future Trends in State Courts (2012): Special Focus on Courts and Communities*, edited by Carol R. Flango, Amy M. McDowell, Deborah W. Saunders, Nora E. Sydow, Charles F. Campbell, and Neal B. Kauder, 67–70. Williamsburg, VA: National Center for State Courts.

Council of State Governments. 2016. *The Book of the States* (Chapter 1, State Constitutions, Table 1.1., General Information on State Constitutions, as of January 1, 2010). http://knowledgecenter.csg.org/kc/system/files/Table_1.1_1.pdf.

Cushman, Clare. 2015. *Of Courtiers and Kings: More Stories of Supreme Court Law Clerks and Their Justices*. Charlottesville: University of Virginia Press.

Durose, Matthew R., and Patrick A. Lanagan. 2003. "Felony Sentences in State Courts, 2000." *Bureau of Justice Statistics Bulletin* (June): 1–12.

Fish, Stanley. 1999. *The Trouble with Principle*. Cambridge, MA: Harvard University Press.

Flango C. E., V. Flango, and H. Rubin. 1999. *How Are Courts Coordinating Family Cases?* Williamsburg, VA: National Center for State Courts.

Frankfurter, Felix, and James Landis. 1927. *The Business of the Supreme Court: A Study in the Federal Judicial System*. New York: Macmillan.

Garrison, A. H. 2002. "Drug Treatment Programs: Policy Implications for the Judiciary." *Court Review* 38(4): 24–35.

George, James P. 2002. *The Federal Courthouse Door: A Federal Jurisdiction Guide*. Durham, NC: Carolina Academic Press.

Gillman, Howard, Mark A. Graber, and Keith E. Whittington. 2012. *American Constitutionalism: Volume I: Structures of Government*. New York: Oxford University Press.

Glick, Henry. 1991. "Policymaking and State Supreme Courts." In *The American Courts: A Critical Assessment*, edited by John B. Gates and Charles A. Johnson. Washington, D.C.: CQ Press.

Handberg, Roger, and Harold F. Hill, Jr. 1980. "Court Curbing, Court Reversals, and Judicial Review: The Supreme Court Versus Congress." *Law and Society Review* 14(2): 309–322.

Heydebrand, Wolf V., and Carroll Seron. 1990. *Rationalizing Justice: The Political Economy of Federal District Courts*. Albany: State University of New York Press.

Hogan, Sean O. 2000. *Continuity and Change in the Common Law: Illinois Tort Law 1971–1996* (unpublished Ph.D. diss., University of Illinois at Chicago).

Institute for the Advancement of the American Legal System. 2016. "Judicial Appointments by State Governors." http://iaals.du.edu/quality-judges/judicial-appointments-state-governors.

Jefferson, Wallace B. 2005. "The State of the Judiciary in Texas." http://www.texasweekly.com/documents/SOTJ2005.pdf.

Jonakait, Randolph N. 2003. *The American Jury System*. New Haven, CT: Yale University Press.

Kadish, Mark. 1996. "Behind the Locked Door of an American Grand Jury: Its History, Its Secrecy and Its Process." *Florida State University Law Review* 24 (Fall): 1–77.

Klaversma, Laura G., and Daniel J. Hall. 2003. *Organizational and Administrative Review of the Fulton County, Georgia, Juvenile Court*. Williamsburg, VA: National Center for State Courts.

Kritzer, Herbert M. 2002. "Seven Dogged Myths Concerning Contingency Fees." *Washington University Law Quarterly* 80 (Fall): 739–785.

Kritzer, Herbert M. 2004. "Advocacy and Rhetoric vs. Scholarship and Evidence in the Debate over Contingency Fees: A Reply to Professor Brickman." *Washington University Law Quarterly* 82 (Summer): 477–507.

Langer, Laura. 2003. *Judicial Review in State Supreme Courts: A Comparative Study*. Albany: State University of New York Press.

Langton, Lynn, and Donald Farole, Jr. 2010. *State Public Defender Programs*, 2007 (September). http://www.bjs.gov/content/pub/pdf/spdp07.pdf.

Lozier, James E. 1996. "Is the Missouri Plan, a/k/a Merit Selection, the Best Solution for Selecting Michigan Judges?" *Michigan Bar Journal* 75 (September): 918.

Lyles, Kevin L. 1997. *The Gatekeepers: Federal District Courts in the Political Process*. Santa Barbara, CA: Praeger.

Marvell, Thomas B. 1978. *Appellate Courts and Lawyers: Information Gathering in the Adversary System*. Westport, CT: Greenwood Publishing.

Messinger, I. Scott. 2002. *Order in the Courts: A History of the Federal Court Clerk's Office*. Washington, D.C.: Federal Judicial Center.

Mikeska, Jennifer. 2000. *Court Consolidation: Reinventing Missouri State Courts*. Williamsburg, VA: National Center for State Courts.

Morse, James L., Stephen B. Martin, Lee Suskin, and Marna Murray. 1997. "The Vermont Experience: A Small State's Story in Educating Judges." *Vermont Bar Journal and Law Digest* 23 (April): 35.

National Center for State Courts. 2016a. "State Court Structure Charts." http://www.courtstatistics.org/Other-Pages/State_Court_Structure_Charts.aspx.

National Center for State Courts. 2016b. "Examining the Work of State Courts: An Overview of 2013 Caseloads." http://ncsc.contentdm.oclc.org/cdm/ref/collection/ctcomm/id/86.

Nelson, William A. 2016. *Vermont Criminal Practice*. Salem, VT: Butterworth Legal Publisher.

Neubauer, David W., and Henry F. Fradella. 2016. *America's Courts and the Criminal Justice System*. 12th ed. Boston: Cengage Learning.

Neubauer, David W., and Stephen S. Meinhold. 2012. *Judicial Process: Law, Courts, and Politics in the United States*. 6th ed. New York: Harcourt Brace.

O'Connor, Karen, and Larry J. Sabato. 1997. *Essentials of American Government, Continuity and Change*. 3rd ed. Boston: Allyn & Bacon.

Peckham, Robert F. 1981. "The Federal Judge as a Case Manager: The New Role in Guiding a Case from Filing to Disposition." *California Law Review* 69(3): 770–805.

Perry, H. W., Jr. 1991. *Deciding to Decide: Agenda Setting in the United States Supreme Court*. Cambridge, MA: Harvard University Press.

Pinello, Daniel R. 1995. *The Impact of Judicial-Selection Method on State-Supreme-Court Policy: Innovation, Reaction and Atrophy*. Westport, CT: Greenwood.

Puzzanchera, Charles M. 2001. "Delinquency Cases Waived to Criminal Court, 1989–1998." *OJJDP Fact Sheet* 35(September). Washington, D.C.: Office of Juvenile Justice and Delinquency Prevention, U.S. Department of Justice.

Rebein, Paul W, Victor E. Schwartz, and Cary Silverman. 2003. "Jury (Dis) Service: Why People Avoid Jury Duty and What Florida Can Do About It." *Nova Law Review* 28 (Fall): 143–156.

Rottman, David B., and Shauna M. Strictland. 2004. *State Court Organization 2004*. August. http://www.bjs.gov/content/pub/pdf/sco04.pdf.

Scheingold, Stuart A., and Austin Sarat. 2004. *Something to Believe In: Politics, Professionalism, and Cause Lawyering*. Stanford, CA: Stanford University Press.

Schubert, Frank A. 2000. *Introduction to Law and the Legal System*. 7th ed. New York: Houghton Mifflin.

Schwartz, Victor E., Mark Behrens, and Cory Silverman. 2003. "The Jury Patriotism Act: Making Jury Service More Appealing and Rewarding to Citizens." American Legislative Exchange Council. https://www.alec.org/model-policy/jury-patriotism-act/.

Serrano, Richard A., and David G. Savage. 2004. "Scalia's Talk to Anti-Gay Group Spurs Ethics Debate." *Boston Globe*, March 8. http://archive.boston.com/news/nation/articles/2004/03/08/scalias_talk_to_antigay_group_spurs_ethics_questions/?page=full.

Smith, Christopher E. 1990. *United States Magistrates in the Federal Courts: Subordinate Judges*. Santa Barbara, CA: Praeger.

Soule, George W. 2005. "Protecting an Independent and Qualified Judiciary." *Bench and Bar of Minnesota* 62(April): 34.

Surrency, Erwin C. 2002. *History of the Federal Courts*. 2nd ed. New York: Oceana Publications.

Symposium. 1995. "The Death Penalty in the Twenty-First Century." *American University Law Review* 45: 239–352.

Tarr, G. Alan. 2003. *Judicial Process and Judicial Policymaking*. 3rd ed. Belmont, CA: Thomson-Wadsworth.

Texas Politics. 2003. "Profiling Texas Judges." University of Texas at Austin. https://texaspolitics.utexas.edu/archive/html/just/features/0403_01/judges.html.

U.S. Department of Justice. 2003. *Performance and Accountability Report of 2002*. Office of the Attorney General. https://www.atf.gov/resource-center/docs/2002-accountability-report-tocpdf/download.

U.S. Department of Justice. 2005. "Crime Victimization Survey." Bureau of Justice Statistics, Washington, D.C. http://www.bjs.gov/content/pub/pdf/cv05.pdf.

U.S. Department of Justice. 2016. "Crime in the United States, 2015." https://ucr.fbi.gov /crime-in-the-u.s/2015/crime-in-the-u.s.-2015/offenses-known-to-law-enforcement /violent-crime.

Wheeler, Russell R., and Cynthia Harrison. 1994. *Creating the Federal Judicial System.* 2nd ed. Washington, D.C.: Federal Judicial Center.

Yale Law School, The Avalon Project. 2016a. "The Federalist Papers: No. 22." http:// avalon.law.yale.edu/18th_century/fed22.asp.

Yale Law School, The Avalon Project. 2016b. "Blackstone's Commentaries on the Laws of England: Introduction." http://avalon.law.yale.edu/18th_century/blackstone_intro .asp#1.

Cases

Agostini v. Felton. 1997. 521 US 203.

Aldridge v. United States. 1931. 283 U.S. 308.

Argersinger v. Hamlin. 1972. 497 U.S. 25.

Atkins v. Virginia. 2001. 533 U.S. 976.

Batson v. Kennedy. 1986. 476 U.S. 79.

Burch v. Louisiana. 1979. 441 U.S. 130.

Carter v. Jury Commission. 1970. 396 U.S. 320.

Castaneda v. Partida. 1977. 430 U.S. 482.

Gideon v. Wainwright. 1963. 372 U.S. 335.

Holland v. Illinois. 1990. 493 U.S. 474 at 480.

JEB v. Alabama ex rel. T.B. 1994. 511 U.S. 127.

Johnson v. Louisiana. 1972. 406 U.S. 356.

Kelly v. South Carolina. 2002. 534 U.S. 246.

Mu'min v. Virginia. 1991. 500 U.S. 514.

Penry v. Lynaugh. 1989. 492 U.S. 302.

Powers v. Ohio. 1991. 499 U.S. 400.

Ristaino v. Ross. 1976. 424 U.S. 589.

Smith v. Texas. 1940. 311 U.S. 128.

Strauder v. West Virginia. 1880. 100 U.S. 303.

Taylor v. Louisiana. 1975. 419 U.S. 522.

Terry v. Ohio. 1968. 392 U.S. 1 at 20.

United States v. Martinez-Fuerte. 1976. 428 U.S. 543.

Williams v. Florida. 1970. 399 U.S. 78.

On the Web

Administrative Office of the U.S. Courts, http://www.uscourts.gov

Federal Judicial Center, http://www.fjc.gov

Judicial Branch, http://www.4uth.gov.ua/usa/english/politics/judbranc.htm

National Center for State Courts, http://www.ncsc.org

Supreme Court Historical Society, http://www.supremecourthistory.org

CHAPTER FOUR

POLITICAL ISSUES AND CONTROVERSIES OF THE JUDICIAL BRANCH

Part I: Constitutional Politics and Democratic Principles

JUDICIAL REVIEW

All judges sitting on state or federal courts are bound to uphold the U.S. Constitution because it is the highest law of the land. In reviewing cases, judges exercise the power of judicial review to determine if laws passed by the legislature or actions taken by the executive branch are consistent with the Constitution. If they are not, state or federal courts may use their authority to strike down laws or executive actions that are contrary to their respective constitutions. As the exercise of judicial review gives courts the power to nullify laws and actions from the political branches, it vests the judiciary with considerable authority to make law and social policy. Judicial review therefore remains politically controversial because some critics say it empowers judges to use their political preferences and attitudes to create law that is not derived from constitutions, the democratic process, or majority will. As a result, judicial review is sometimes characterized as being counter-majoritarian, or an anti-democratic, power. As Alexander Bickel, who clerked for Justice Felix Frankfurter and later became a Yale University law school professor, colorfully explains, the reality of judicial review is a "different kettle of fish" because it "thwarts the will of representatives of the actual people of the here and now; it exercises control, not on behalf of the prevailing majority, but against it" (Bickel 1962, 17).

The Origins and History of Judicial Review

The idea that courts could invalidate acts of the legislature can be traced back to early English common law. In *Dr. Bonham's Case* (1610), Chief Justice Coke struck down an act of Parliament that disciplined a person who was practicing medicine without a license on the grounds that it violated common right or reason. This case and other early federal and state court decisions in the United States suggested that judicial review was acknowledged to be an ordinary part of the judicial function (Mendelson 1992, 133–134). Even so, it is doubtful that the founding generation fully anticipated how the concept of judicial review would work in practice in future cases.

For these reasons and others, the historical evidence as to whether the framers of the U.S. Constitution originally intended for the courts to have the power of judicial review is inconclusive. The related question of whether judicial review should be a normal function of how courts decide constitutional issues is also subject to debate. What remains clear is that the framers did not specify in the Constitution that the Supreme Court be empowered to use judicial review to decide legal cases. In fact, Article III said nothing about the exercise of judicial power; it only created the U.S. Supreme Court, and it assigned to the First Congress the task of establishing lower federal courts. Moreover, the political circumstances of the time did not make judicial review a significant issue because the nation's first charter of government, the Articles of Confederation, did not give to the federal judiciary many powers that would interfere with state governments or their laws. The onset of the Constitutional Convention in 1787, though, and subsequent political events changed that reality. Anti-Federalists, or those who favored only amending the Articles and not necessarily replacing them with a new Constitution, grew concerned that the national government would become too powerful and effectively destroy state governments. Federalists, or the supporters of a strong, centralized national government, countered that the new government under the proposed Constitution would be limited in its powers and operate to work in harmony with state governments (Storing 1981).

Against this background, the issue of judicial review in the federal courts became more relevant once the framers proposed to use the Constitution to replace the Articles and create a strong national government and federal judiciary. In theory, the Anti-Federalists were afraid that the federal courts would use their powers to displace state courts and state laws. Even though subsequent landmark legislation, such as the 1789 Judiciary Act that created the basic structure of lower federal courts, did not identify whether courts were vested with the power of judicial review, Anti-Federalists remained suspicious and fearful of the role that federal courts would play in the new constitutional system (Storing 1981). As a result, when the new Constitution was put before the states for ratification, the issue of judicial review became the focus of the published commentary of Anti-Federalists (who opposed ratification) and Federalists (who supported ratification).

Robert Yates, writing under the pseudonym of *Brutus*, asserted the Anti-Federalist position by claiming that the proposed Constitution would give to the federal courts, and the federal government generally, almost unlimited powers that would be used to destroy the states. In response, Alexander Hamilton, a Federalist, wrote in *Federalist Papers*, No. 78, that the federal judiciary was the least dangerous branch in the political system because it did not possess legislative or executive powers (Yale Law School 2016). It only had the power of judgment under a rule of law. In other words, federal judges could only decide cases by remaining faithful to the terms of the written Constitution. Consequently, federal courts lacked the authority to make or administer the law because the Constitution specifically assigned those powers only to the legislative and executive branches. Hamilton's understanding of the judicial function is significant because it suggests that courts must have the power of judicial review in order to check the political branches when they act beyond the legitimate scope of their constitutional authority. Thus, under the Hamiltonian view, judicial review is an essential part of the constitutional framework in a political system that respects principles of limited government (that government cannot act in excess of its powers under law), separation of powers (between the legislative, executive, and judicial departments), and checks and balances (which allows different branches of government to check the actions of the others in order to maintain a balanced system of governmental power).

The Political Significance of *Marbury v. Madison* (1803)

Hamilton's defense of judicial authority was later etched into constitutional law in *Marbury v. Madison* (1803). *Marbury* is a landmark ruling that declared that the Supreme Court is the final arbiter of the Constitution's meaning. Notably, the dispute that led to the Court's decision was heavily influenced by the politics of the day, and the decision itself is highly political in scope and application. In the 1800 election, Thomas Jefferson defeated the Federalist Party's presidential incumbent, John Adams, and the control of Congress switched from the Federalist Party to the incoming president's Jeffersonian Republican party. Shortly before being ousted from power, the Federalist-dominated legislature enacted the Judiciary Act of 1801, sometimes colloquially referred to as the Midnight Judges Act. Its purpose was to keep the Federalist Party's influence in politics by placing many Federalists in political and judicial offices at a time when the Jeffersonian Republicans remained in control of the federal government. Working against a midnight deadline on the day before President Jefferson would assume office, outgoing President Adams and his secretary of state, John Marshall, prepared paperwork that would have given William Marbury, a Federalist, a commission for a justice of the peace appointment in the District of Columbia—but in his haste Marshall failed to deliver it properly. Although the commission was signed by President Adams, Marshall decided to let the next secretary of state, James Madison, in the Jefferson administration deliver it—but once in office President Jefferson forbade Madison from delivering Marbury's commission. As a result, Marbury did not receive his judicial appointment, and he sought to get it back by commencing an original action in the Supreme Court. Specifically, Marbury argued that congressional legislation, or section 13 of the 1789 Judiciary Act, authorized the Supreme Court to issue a writ of mandamus that would force James Madison as secretary of state to give him his appointment. These basic facts positioned the Court to announce in *Marbury* that the federal judiciary has the sole power to use judicial review to decide the Constitution's final meaning.

Ironically, after his service as secretary of state had ended, John Marshall (1755–1835) was appointed as Chief Justice of the Supreme Court, and he wrote the Court's opinion in *Marbury v. Madison* in 1803. In his opinion, Marshall reviewed three legal issues:

1. Did Marbury have a legal right to the commission?
2. If Marbury had a legal right to the commission, did he also have a legal remedy?
3. If Marbury had a legal remedy, did the Supreme Court have the power to grant a writ of mandamus?

Writing for a unanimous Court, Marshall reasoned that Marbury had a legal right to the commission and also that the law provided him with a remedy because the commission was not delivered properly. On the critical third question, however, the Chief Justice used the power of judicial review to strike down Section 13 of the 1789 Judiciary Act because Congress exceeded its power in giving the Supreme Court the jurisdiction, or authority, to issue a writ of mandamus. Section 13, in other words, conflicted with Article III of the U.S. Constitution, the only true source that defined the scope of the Court's jurisdiction to decide legal cases. More importantly, Marshall announced that the Supreme Court was the sole institution in the political system that had the power to determine the Constitution's final meaning. As Marshall flatly declared, "It is emphatically the province and duty of the judicial department to say what the law is." Marshall's ruling thus denied Marbury his judicial appointment while establishing the basis for the enduring principle that the Supreme Court has the power to use judicial review to strike down legislation or executive acts that conflict with the U.S. Constitution. How the case was resolved was also politically adept: denying a Federalist a judicial appointment pleased the Jeffersonian Republicans while simultaneously agreeing with the Federalist position that Marbury's legal rights had been violated and there was a legal remedy.

Chief Justice Marshall's ruling in *Marbury v. Madison* has become a powerful symbol of the Court's authority. By legitimizing the principle of judicial review, it established that the Supreme Court was an equal co-branch of the federal government, on par with Congress and the President. As the nation grew and history unfolded, the Supreme Court and state courts of last resort have exercised the power of judicial review to act as final arbiter of contemporary public policy disputes that originate from the political branches in the federal government and the states. As an agent of legal change and social policy, the Supreme Court especially has been at the forefront of determining the civil rights and liberties of citizens in a variety of controversial areas of law, including the death penalty, health care, affirmative action, school integration, abortion, and same-sex marriage. While some court watchers have applauded and defended the Court's use of judicial review to create law and public policy, others have questioned it by arguing that the Court's role is simply to declare the law, and not make it. In other words, the Court's proper role is to respect and apply the laws enacted by the majoritarian democratic process through elected representatives. Under this view, judicial review enables the courts to become anti-democratic and therefore politically illegitimate.

Christopher P. Banks

See also: Abortion Restrictions; Affirmative Action; The Affordable Care Act; Capital Punishment; Constitutional Interpretation; Defendants' Rights; Gay Marriage; Judicial Activism and Restraint; Racial Discrimination

Further Reading

Bickel, Alexander. 1962. *The Least Dangerous Branch: The Supreme Court at the Bar of Politics*. Indianapolis, IN: Bobbs-Merrill Company.

Corwin, Edward S. (with a new introduction by Matthew J. Franck). 2014. *The Doctrine of Judicial Review: Its Legal and Historical Basis and Other Essays*. New Brunswick, NJ: Transaction Publishers.

Hall, Kermit L., ed. 2000. *The Supreme Court in American Society: Equal Justice Under the Law*. New York: Garland Publishing.

Levy, Leonard W., ed. 1967. *Judicial Review and the Supreme Court: Selected Essays*. New York: Harper & Row.

Mendelson, Wallace. 1992. "The Judiciary Act of 1789: The Formal Origin of Federal Judicial Review." *Judicature* 76: 133–136.

Nelson, William E. 2000. *Marbury v. Madison: The Origins and Legacy of Judicial Review*. Lawrence: University Press of Kansas.

Newmyer, R. Kent. 2001. *John Marshall and the Heroic Age of the Supreme Court*. Baton Rouge: Louisiana State University Press.

Otter, Ronald, and C. Den. 2009. *Judicial Review in an Age of Moral Pluralism*. Cambridge, MA: Cambridge University Press.

Storing, Herbert J. 1981. *What the Anti-Federalists Were For: The Political Thought of the Opponents of the Constitution*. Chicago: University of Chicago Press.

Whittington, Keith. 2007. *Political Foundations of Judicial Supremacy: The Presidency, the Supreme Court, and Constitutional Leadership in U.S. History*. Princeton, NJ: Princeton University Press.

Yale Law School, The Avalon Project. 2016. "The Federalist Papers: No. 78." http://avalon.law.yale.edu/18th_century/fed78.asp.

Cases

Dr. Bonham's Case. 1610. 8 Co. Rep. 114.
Marbury v. Madison. 1803. 5 U.S. (1 Cranch) 137.

CONSTITUTIONAL INTERPRETATION

Federal and state appellate court judges declare legal rights and create public policy by interpreting the meaning of constitutions. While the U.S. Constitution is the touchstone for constitutional interpretation for federal courts, state courts use state constitutions to establish legal rights and public order. In general, constitutional interpretation remains controversial because the method by which judges derive constitutional meaning is often a reflection of a controlling legal philosophy that gives judges the opportunity to use their personal preferences and translate them into law. Although judges use various theories of constitutional interpretation, many judges have adopted two broad methodologies or approaches for deciding constitutional law cases: interpretivism and noninterpretivism. The ongoing debate and political controversy surrounding these two general methodologies centers on the role that appellate courts of last resort play in trying to strike an appropriate balance between respecting democratic majority rule and protecting individual rights.

Article III of the U.S. Constitution provides the Supreme Court with the power of constitutional interpretation by stating that its authority "shall extend to all cases, in law and equity, arising under this Constitution, the laws of the United States, and the treaties made, or which shall be made. . . ." Similar provisions are found in state constitutions. Notably, constitutional interpretation by federal or state appellate courts is a critical part of the power of judicial review. Under judicial review, courts have the authority to invalidate laws or executive actions that are incompatible with the Constitution. For example, in *Marbury v. Madison* (1803) the U.S. Supreme Court used the power of judicial review to nullify part of Congress's 1789 Judiciary Act on the grounds that it violated Article III by improperly giving the Supreme Court jurisdiction to decide if a Federalist judicial appointment, which was not finalized by the end of the Adams administration, must be honored by the incoming Jeffersonian-Republican president, Thomas Jefferson.

The importance of constitutional interpretation and judicial review is highlighted further by the concept of judicial supremacy, or the Supreme Court's position as the final arbiter on all constitutional issues. As a result, the Court has had an enduring impact on a variety of controversial political issues, such as abortion, affirmative action, and same-sex marriage. Similarly, the highest courts of last resort in the states exert considerable influence by interpreting their own constitutions to influence criminal law, environmental law, and educational funding policies, among others. In either context, the exercise of judicial review by federal and state appellate courts underscores the political nature of judicial decision-making, which in turn, intensifies ongoing debates relating to judicial selection. In other words, decisions are often shaped by the judicial philosophies of jurists who are appointed or elected to the bench. Accordingly, how these appellate judges interpret their respective constitutions becomes highly significant in the development of the law and public policy.

Theories of Constitutional Interpretation

Various theories have been developed in order to explain constitutional interpretation. However, each can be described in terms of one of two general approaches known as interpretivism or noninterpretivism. Broadly speaking, the primary difference between them is the extent to which justices consult sources other than the text of the Constitution. Whereas interpretivist judges are more confined to construing meaning from the "four corners of the document," noninterpretivist judges are more apt to go beyond the text to interpret constitutional language in light of prevailing cultural norms, social values, or personal preferences. Although neither approach directly corresponds to a particular political philosophy, conservative justices are often thought to be interpretivists and their liberal counterparts are typically labeled noninterpretivists. To illustrate, in the Roberts Court (2006–present) conservative Justices Antonin Scalia and Clarence Thomas have been known to use textualist or plain-meaning interpretivist approaches when they decide constitutional law cases. In contrast, liberal Justice Stephen Breyer is widely considered a noninterpretivist judge who construes the Constitution as a living document that should reflect modern society and contemporary values.

Interpretivism

Although interpretivism restricts judges to the texts of constitutions, it also allows for the historical context surrounding the ratification of provisions to be taken into account. Typically, interpretivists have been portrayed politically as judges who exercise judicial restraint because they simply declare, and do not make, law. Thus, the methods by which judges engage in constitutional interpretation become highly significant in the political arena. Political candidates who are campaigning for office typically accuse the Supreme Court of judicial activism because its decisions create law in controversial areas of public policy whenever rulings deviate from a literal reading of the Constitution. For example, in the late 1960s, and in response to progressive Warren Court (1954–1969) decisions that expanded the rights of the criminally accused during a time of political and social unrest, Republican presidential nominee Richard Nixon announced that he would only fill Supreme Court vacancies with strict constructivists. Packing the Court with strict constructionists therefore limits the justices' capacity to legislate from the bench and create new constitutional rights because only the text of the Constitution is consulted during constitutional interpretation. However, strict constructivism may have significant political and social consequences. Historically, Chief Justice Roger Taney used this approach in *Dred Scott v. Sandford* (1857) to declare that blacks were not citizens of the United States, which accelerated the development of the Civil War that was fought largely over the issues of slavery and racial equality.

Using a strict constructivist approach is controversial, in part because the methodology does not recognize that all judges must make subjective value choices during constitutional interpretation. For instance, in religious freedom cases justices must choose between resolving disputes by interpreting either the First Amendment's free exercise clause or establishment clause. The lack of guidance strict constructivism provides is also demonstrated by the different methodological approaches the Warren and Burger (1969–1986) Courts took in the adjudication of Fourth Amendment search and seizure cases. Whereas the progressive Warren Court relied on the amendment's warrants and probable cause clauses to expand criminal defendants' constitutional rights, the conservative Burger Court often supported the police and the prosecution of criminal defendants by focusing on what would constitute an unreasonable search and seizure. A related criticism is that strict constructionism is difficult to use because many of the terms and phrases in the Constitution are not defined and provide little insight into the intent of the framers. As critics argue, it is impossible to know if signs and banners are protected forms of free speech under the First Amendment or whether the Eighth Amendment's cruel and unusual punishment clause includes the death penalty.

The Theory of Originalism

In response to such criticisms, an alternative interpretivist theory, originalism, was developed that allows justices to consider the framers' intent behind each provision and amendment of the Constitution. Still, this approach envisions the Constitution as purposively embodying nonexhaustive general principles so that the amendments in the Bill of Rights can be applied to a variety of circumstances. In other words, the Constitution has what legal philosophers call "open texture" (Hart 1961). This less restrictive view of the Constitution, in conjunction with the option to refer to the intent of the framers, provides justices with more choices and guidance during constitutional interpretation than strict constructivism. However, originalism is not problem-free and there are still limitations to how the theory applies in practice to cases.

The two primary weaknesses of originalism are identical to those found in strict constructivism, namely determining who the framers are and what their intent is behind each constitutional provision. With respect to who is a framer, it is unclear whether originalism refers only to those who signed the Constitution or also includes delegates who left the Constitutional Convention without signing the document or were sent to the 13 state ratifying conventions. In light of this interpretative difficulty, it is problematic to determine the framers' intent. Complicating the issue is that first, the Constitutional Convention was conducted in secrecy so records are either incomplete or unreliable. Second, disagreements regularly arose over the language of the provisions and amendments, so the Constitution can only be viewed as the result of considerable compromise among the framers. Consequently, discovering intent is a subjective endeavor and can only lead to conflicting interpretations. Not surprisingly, this has led some legal scholars to question whether the framers envisioned their intent serving as guidelines for constitutional interpretation.

In light of these criticisms, many interpretivists subscribe to a related theory, termed textual originalism, by Justice Antonin Scalia. Instead of intent guiding constitutional interpretation, the "original understanding" or "original meaning" of constitutional language is considered by the justices. Under this view, justices must interpret the Constitution in a way that corresponds with how the framers envisioned each provision and amendment being applied at the time of the Constitutional Convention in 1787. Thus, textual originalism perceives the Constitution as representing a set of principles that are derived from the framers' political philosophies. Rather than limiting constitutional interpretation to the framers' intent, justices may also consult relevant historical texts.

For critics, textual originalism provides no insight into how constitutional provisions may apply to specific cases raising contemporary issues of constitutional law. Additionally, textual originalism can lead to idiosyncratic interpretations of constitutional provisions that are based mostly on personal preferences but appear justifiable by a justice's legal philosophy. For instance, Justice Scalia admitted that as a justice living in the 20th century he would find public flogging (i.e., whipping or lashing) to be a cruel and unusual punishment under the Eighth Amendment even though it was considered acceptable to the framers. However, Scalia's "vision of constitutional human dignity" does not extend to also concluding that the death penalty is always unconstitutional as Justices William Brennan and Thurgood Marshall maintained in *Furman v. Georgia* (1972) and subsequent cases. For Justice Brennan and other noninterpretivist judges, capital punishment was categorically unconstitutional because it violated contemporary norms of civilized behavior and evolving standards of decency. Regardless, proponents of originalism argue that it is a better alternative and a "lesser evil" than subscribing to the legal philosophy of noninterpretivism (Scalia 1989). Under this view, textual originalism is a limitation on the power of judicial review by decreasing the likelihood that decisions to invalidate legislation are based on the political preferences of the justices. By focusing instead on the text and meaning of the Constitution, judges can avoid the temptation to engage in activist and countermajoritarian judicial decision-making—a description of judicial behavior that asserts that unelected justices are going beyond the law to overturn democratically enacted legislation in an effort to pursue individual political agendas.

Noninterpretivism

In contrast, noninterpretivist approaches advance broad interpretations of the principles underlying the text of the Constitution by allowing justices also to take into account a variety of nontextual factors, such as history, social science, or natural law. Beginning with history, a noninterpretivist approach would consider economic, technological, and political changes that have occurred since the time that the framers ratified the Constitution. Consequently, the Constitution is viewed as a living document that must reflect the values of modern day society. For example, in *Roe v. Wade* (1973) the Burger Court (1969–1986) interpreted the Fourteenth Amendment's due process clause as embracing a woman's right to have an abortion because pregnant mothers have a constitutional right of privacy that gives them the liberty to make choices relating to reproductive freedom. Similarly, in *Brown v. Board of Education* (1954) a unanimous Warren Court used social science and psychological studies as evidence to conclude that the Fourteenth Amendment's equality principles rejected the long-standing discriminatory "separate but equal" doctrine in favor of racial integration in public schools.

Drawing upon natural law or philosophy during judicial decision-making also elicits criticism because it allows the Court to conceive of constitutional provisions in a way that advances the justices' political preferences. Natural law is a legal philosophy that maintains that some rights are natural or inalienable and cannot be given or taken away by the government, such as the freedoms of "life, liberty, and the pursuit of happiness" that are included in the Declaration of Independence. Justice Felix Frankfurter's creation of the "shocks the conscience test" as a legal doctrine that is used to determine when police and other government officials violate the Fourteenth Amendment's due process clause in *Rochin v. California* (1952) is illustrative. There, Justice Frankfurter reasoned that the natural law principles of decency and fairness, which are "so rooted in the traditions and conscience of our people as to be ranked as fundamental," prevented the police from using a stomach pump to collect evidence of illicit drug use. Similarly, the Supreme Court's broad interpretation of the Fourteenth Amendment and norms of public morality in *Obergefell v. Hodges* (2015) granted same-sex couples the legal right of marriage across all 50 states.

Arguably, constitutional interpretation may result in counter-majoritarian decisions that reflect the Court's political philosophy. As a result, some noninterpretivist theories, such as process-oriented judicial review and prag-matism, have been introduced over time in an effort to mitigate such concerns. Under process-oriented judicial review, constitutional interpretation focuses on safeguarding the integrity of democratic political processes and enabling the participation and representation of minority political interests. Still, this theory has been criticized for impeding the Court from protecting civil rights and lib-erties and providing little guidance on how to decide cases involving presiden-tial power and federalism. Similarly, pragmatism, or consequentialism, requires justices to consider the practical implications of a decision. In *District of Colum-bia v. Heller* (2008), dissenting Justice Stephen Breyer criticized the Court's deci-sion declaring that the Second Amendment includes a right to gun ownership for the purpose of self-defense within the home on the grounds that it "threat-ens to leave cities without effective protection against gun violence." Conse-quently, the ruling can only result in negative consequences for the district and society.

Lisa Hager

See also: Abortion Restrictions; Capital Punishment; Gay Marriage; Gun Owner-ship Rights and Restrictions; Judicial Activism and Restraint; Judicial Review; Racial Discrimination

Further Reading

Balkin, Jack. 2011. *Living Constitutionalism*. Cambridge, MA: Harvard University Press.

Berger, Raoul. 1977. *Government by Judiciary: The Transformation of the Fourteenth Amend-ment*. Cambridge, MA: Harvard University Press.

Breyer, Stephen G. 2005. *Active Liberty: Interpreting Our Democratic Constitution*. New York: Knopf.

Federalist Society. 1986. *The Great Debate: Interpreting Our Written Constitution*. Wash-ington, D.C.: The Federalist Society.

Hart, H. L. A. 1961. *The Concept of Law*. Oxford: Clarendon Press.

O'Brien, David M. 1980. "Seduction of the Judiciary: Social Science and the Courts." *Judicature* 64: 8–21.

O'Brien, David M. 2014. *Constitutional Law and Politics: Civil Rights and Civil Liberties*. 9th ed., vol. 2. New York: W. W. Norton.

Powell, H. Jefferson. 1985. "The Original Understanding of Original Intent." *Harvard Law Review* 98: 885–948.

Scalia, Antonin. 1989. "Originalism: The Lesser Evil." *Cincinnati Law Review* 55: 849–865.

Scalia, Antonin. 1997. *A Matter of Interpretation: Federal Courts and the Law*. Princeton, NJ: Princeton University Press.

Whittington, Keith. 1999. *Constitutional Interpretation: Textual Meaning, Original Intent, and Judicial Review*. Lawrence: University Press of Kansas.

Cases

Brown v. Board of Education. 1954. 347 U.S. 483.
District of Columbia v. Heller. 2008. 554 U.S. 570.
Dred Scott v. Sandford. 1857. 60 U.S. 393.
Furman v. Georgia. 1972. 408 U.S. 238.
Marbury v. Madison. 1803. 5 U.S. 137.
Obergefell v. Hodges. 2015. 135 S.Ct. 2584.
Rochin v. California. 1952. 342 U.S. 165.
Roe v. Wade. 1973. 410 U.S. 113.

JUDICIAL ACTIVISM AND RESTRAINT

The judicial behavior of state and federal courts may be characterized as either activist or restrained in terms of how courts interpret the law in controversial areas of social policy, such as abortion, gun rights, or same-sex marriage politics. *Judicial activism* assumes that courts are result-oriented and decide cases by going beyond a law's plain meaning. In this light, activist courts use their own policy preferences to reach legal outcomes that may contradict the original intent of the law. In contrast, courts acting with *judicial restraint* do the opposite. Courts decide cases by exercising self-restraint: they follow what the law was intended to mean when it was created by the political branches or constitutional framers. Notably, but mistakenly, courts that are thought to be ideologically conservative are often praised as courts that act with judicial restraint; whereas, liberal courts are routinely criticized as being activist. In reality, the labels of restraint or activism are not very useful in describing judicial decision-making because there are many historical and contemporary examples of conservative judicial activism and liberal judicial self-restraint, and vice-versa. As a result, the exact meaning of judicial activism or judicial restraint remains unclear because it typically varies with the prevailing political climate (Canon 1982/1983, 237–239).

The Political Debate and Criticisms of Judicial Activism and Restraint

The criticism that courts engage in activist behavior has a long-standing history in American politics. A frequent target is the U.S. Supreme Court, in part because of the Anti-Federalist fear that a national judiciary would usurp the powers of elected representatives, state courts, and the states themselves. In *Federalist Papers*, No. 78, Alexander Hamilton (1788) responded to these concerns by arguing that the courts would only use their authority to declare, and not make, the law. Even so, shortly after the U.S. Constitution's ratification, the Jeffersonian-Republican Party sharply accused the Court, which was dominated by justices aligned with the Federalist Party, of abusing its powers by overturning congressional prerogatives and violating the people's civil rights and liberties. The Jeffersonian-Republican criticism was grounded in the belief that the Court was an anti-democratic political institution: its justices, which were unelected and served for life, could use activism to strike down congressional legislation and thereby expand its own judicial powers without being checked by the people. Early landmark rulings by Chief Justice John Marshall, such as *Marbury v. Madison* (1803), which struck down part of the 1789 Judiciary Act and confirmed that the judiciary had the sole and final authority to interpret the Constitution's meaning through its power of judicial review, only intensified the Anti-Federalist and Jeffersonian-Republican apprehension of a politically unaccountable and activist federal judiciary.

Subsequent rulings over the next generations illustrate that the Supreme Court increasingly used its authority to generate social change in major political controversies through allegedly activist decisions. As the nation struggled with the issue of slavery in the 19th century, Congress enacted the Missouri Compromise of 1820, legislation that prohibited slavery from the territories. But in *Dred Scott v. Sandford* (1857), Congress's legislative attempt—the so-called Missouri Compromise of 1820, which in part banned slavery from being extended into the northern portions of the Louisiana Territory—was struck down by a judicial opinion written by Chief Justice Roger Taney, a southerner who favored keeping the institution of slavery intact. Taney's opinion declared that Congress did not have the power to prohibit slavery and that Dred Scott, a runaway slave who lived in a free state, did not have the constitutional right to sue for his freedom in federal court since he was not a U.S. citizen. "On the contrary," Taney declared, slaves were never intended to become part of the political community at the time the Constitution was adopted because "they were at the time considered as a subordinate and inferior class of beings, who had been subjugated by the dominant race, and whether emancipated or not, yet remained subject to their authority, and had no rights or privileges but such as those who held the power and the government might choose to grant to them." In what many consider an activist ruling, Taney's strict construction of the Constitution's text repudiated Congress's attempt to resolve the political problem of slavery and helped propel the nation into a bloody and costly Civil War. The infamous *Dred Scott* ruling badly tarnished the Supreme Court's reputation as a neutral and impartial arbiter of the law.

In the early 20th century, the Supreme Court's activism reflected support for conservative business interests, a sentiment aligned with a *laissez-faire* (i.e., the government that governs least, governs best) philosophy that represented the social fabric of the times. *Lochner v. New York* (1905) overturned a New York law (the Bake Shop Act) that limited the maximum number of hours that bakery employees could work per day and per week. At the time, urban bakeries were oppressively hot and unsanitary because they were located in underground cellars with dirt or wooden floors, and not well-ventilated. The working conditions were made worse because coal-fired ovens were used in the baking process, exposing workers to not only vermin, but also coal and bakery products' dust. The law's purpose was to protect the workers since breathing in bakery fumes under such conditions posed a serious health threat. Still, Justice Rufus Peckham's majority opinion struck down the New York law by reasoning that it violated the Fourteenth Amendment's due process clause on the grounds that it interfered with the liberty of bakery employers and employees to establish an employment contract. As the Constitution's Fourteenth Amendment due process clause does not contain any textual language that specifies such a liberty to contract, *Lochner* is widely seen as an activist ruling because the Supreme Court overturned legislation by creating a right that was not explicitly part of the framers' intent (Justice 2012, 44). Moreover, as Justice Oliver Wendell Holmes argued in his dissent in *Lochner*, the Court's activism allowed the case to be decided in favor of business interests and the *laissez-faire* economic principle that limits government's power to regulate private labor relationships.

Allegations of judicial activism also surfaced in the New Deal politics of the 1930s. In response to the high rate of unemployment and the virtual collapse of the nation's banking system brought on by the Great Depression, President Franklin Delano Roosevelt (FDR) and Congress tried to stabilize the economy by a series of progressive reforms and legislative programs known as the New Deal. The New Deal, however, greatly expanded the federal government's power over the economy. Hence, several laws passed by Congress as reform measures were repeatedly struck down by a conservative Supreme Court that favored free market capitalism and less governmental interference with the private economic marketplace. In the aftermath of his landslide, re-election in 1936 but with his economic recovery package in jeopardy, in February, 1937 FDR introduced his controversial court-packing plan to counter the Supreme Court's conservative activism. The court-packing proposal sought to neutralize the Supreme Court politically by giving the president the power to appoint a new justice for every justice that was over the age of 70, thus replacing up to at least six conservative justices with progressives that would uphold, instead of strike down, vital New Deal legislation (Lindquist and Cross 2009). While the plan was never enacted into law, shortly thereafter Justice Owen Roberts, who in prior cases regularly joined with a four-justice bloc of conservative justices to nullify key New Deal legislation, voted in *West Coast Hotel v. Parrish* (1937) to uphold the constitutionality of a state law that forced employers to pay minimum wages for women and children. Shortly thereafter, Roberts abandoned the bloc of conservative justices again in *National Labor Relations Board v. Jones & Laughlin Steel Corporation* (1937), thereby affirming the constitutionality of the National Labor Relations Act, another key part of New Deal legislation that allowed the federal government to regulate unfair labor practices. Justice Roberts' behavior and key votes, collectively referred to as the famous "switch-in-time-that-saved-nine," made the court-packing plan irrelevant; but, more importantly, it signaled that the Supreme Court would vote in later cases to ratify the New Deal's constitutionality, thus creating the legal foundation for a long period of judicial self-restraint by the Supreme Court that would greatly expand the federal government's regulatory powers over the economy.

After the New Deal and World War II, the Supreme Court's activism—or lack of judicial self-restraint—wrote into constitutional law new rights that cut across liberal and conservative ideological lines in abortion, gun control, and same-sex marriage cases. In *Griswold v. Connecticut* (1965), Justice William Douglas's majority opinion interpreted the Fourteenth Amendment's due process clause and provisions of the Bill of Rights as embracing a right to privacy that was violated because a Connecticut law restricted the distribution of contraceptive information and medical advice to married couples who wanted it for family planning purposes. As binding precedent that was decided by a liberal Supreme Court under the leadership of Chief Justice Earl Warren, *Griswold* became a legal basis for a conservative Supreme Court, then under the leadership of Warren's successor, Chief Justice Warren Burger, to announce in *Roe v. Wade* (1973) that a Texas law that imposed criminal penalties on doctors who performed abortions violated the Fourteenth Amendment's due process clause and a mother's right of personal autonomy to make intimate medical decisions. Notably, in *Planned Parenthood of Southeastern Pennsylvania v. Casey* (1992), a conservative Supreme Court under Chief Justice William Rehnquist's leadership chose not to overturn *Roe* as binding legal precedent because it feared that reversing it threatened the rule of law and the Supreme Court's interest in preserving its judicial integrity as an impartial arbiter of legal controversies.

The Roberts Court's Judicial Activism

Under the leadership of Chief Justice John Roberts Jr., the Supreme Court is reputed to be a conservative court that consistently rules in favor of business interests. Even so, its jurisprudence affecting some contentious areas of social policy illustrates its conservative and liberal activism, or a lack of judicial self-restraint. In *District of Columbia v. Heller* (2008), Justice Antonin Scalia's decision for the Court struck down the District of Columbia's gun control ordinance by interpreting the Second Amendment as encompassing a personal right to keep weapons in the home as a matter of self-defense. *Heller* is controversial because in *McDonald v. City of Chicago* (2010) the Court extended the right to all 50 states under the Fourteenth Amendment's so-called incorporation doctrine. As a result, states and localities across the nation must now write their gun control laws in a way that does not violate the Second Amendment's fundamental right to keep and bear arms in the interest of personal safety. Consequently, liberal critics assert that *Heller* is an activist ruling that overturns legislation while inventing a new right that is not explicitly found in the Second Amendment's textual language.

From the other side of the ideological spectrum, conservative critics have assailed the Roberts Court's activism in declaring that same-sex couples have the fundamental right to marry in the landmark case of *Obergefell v. Hodges* (2015). Drawing off the Fourteenth Amendment's due process and equality principles, by a 5–4 vote the Court ruled that states must license and recognize same-sex marriages performed in their own states and in others. *Obergefell* was decided at a time when there were a growing number of state supreme courts that recognized the right of same-sex marriage. Still, a few states, including Kentucky, Michigan, Ohio, and Tennessee, legally defined marriage as a union between a man and a woman, and the federal courts of appeals were split on the issue. In striking those laws down, the Court reasoned that same-sex marriage is a fundamental right that cannot be denied by the states. The dissenters, Chief Justice Roberts and Justices Antonin Scalia, Clarence Thomas, and Samuel Alito, accused Justice Anthony Kennedy, who wrote the opinion of the Court that was joined by Justices Stephen Breyer, Ruth Bader Ginsburg, and Sonia Sotomayor, as engaging in the worst sort of judicial activism because five unelected members of the federal judiciary took away the power of the states to define through the democratic and legislative process that marriage can only be defined as a heterosexual union. For the first time during his tenure as chief justice, Roberts took the symbolic and powerful step of reading his dissent from the bench to signal his profound disagreement with the Court's ruling. In casting aside the commitment to judicial self-restraint, Roberts declared that the Court's majority "seizes for itself a question that the Constitution leaves to the people" and wrongly "enacted their own vision of marriage as a matter of constitutional law."

Christopher P. Banks

See also: Abortion Restrictions; Constitutional Interpretation; Gay Marriage; Gun Ownership Rights and Restrictions; Incorporation Doctrine; Judicial Review

Further Reading

Canon, Bradley C. 1982/1983. "Defining the Dimensions of Judicial Activism." *Judicature* 66: 236–247.

Halpern, Stephen C., and Charles M. Lamb, eds. 1984. *Supreme Court Activism and Restraint*. Lexington, MA: Lexington Books.

Hamilton, Alexander, James Madison, and John Jay. (1787–88) 1999. *The Federalist Papers*, edited by Clinton Rossiter. New York: Mentor.

Justice, William Wayne. 2012. "The Two Faces of Judicial Activism." In *Judges on Judging: Views from the Bench*, 4th ed., edited by David M. O'Brien. Thousand Oaks, CA: CQ Press.

Keck, Thomas M. 2004. *The Most Activist Supreme Court in History*. Chicago, IL: University of Chicago Press.

Kens, Paul. 1998. *Lochner v. New York: Economic Regulation on Trial*. Lawrence: University Press of Kansas.

Lindquist, Stefanie A., and Frank B. Cross. 2009. *Measuring Judicial Activism*. New York: Oxford University Press.

Peretti, Terri Jennings. 1999. *In Defense of a Political Court*. Princeton, NJ: Princeton University Press.

Wilkinson, Harvie J., III. 2012. *Cosmic Constitutional Theory: Why Americans Are Losing Their Inalienable Right to Self-Governance*. New York: Oxford University Press.

Cases

District of Columbia v. Heller. 2008. 554 U.S. 570.

Dred Scott v. Sandford. 1857. 60 U.S. 393.

Griswold v. Connecticut. 1965. 381 U.S. 479.

Lochner v. New York. 198 U.S. 45.

Marbury v. Madison. 1803. 5 U.S. 137.

McDonald v. City of Chicago. 2010. 561 U.S. 3025.

National Labor Relations Board v. Jones & Laughlin Steel Corporation. 1937. 301 U.S. 1.

Obergefell v. Hodges. 135 S.Ct. 2584.

Planned Parenthood of Southeastern Pennsylvania v. Casey. 1992. 505 U.S. 833.

West Coast Hotel v. Parrish. 1937. 300 U.S. 379.

JUDICIAL FEDERALISM

Judicial federalism in the United States reflects the dual court system created under the U.S. Constitution: one federal court system, and 50 separate state court systems. The federal and state judicial systems are distinct and independent of each other, yet are also interrelated. The courts at the federal level represent the United States and primarily adjudicate disputes concerning constitutional and federal law, and the courts of the 50 states primarily adjudicate state law disputes. State courts are the workhorses of the legal system and adjudicate the vast majority of civil and criminal cases in the United States. In contrast, federal courts have more limited authority, and decide far fewer cases. The division of authority between federal and state courts is enshrined in the Constitution of the United States, and over the course of more than 200 years of constitutional development judicial federalism has been in a state of change.

The U.S. Constitution creates the federal government and establishes federalism, which is the basic relationship between the national government and the states. Several provisions of the Constitution create the basic outline of judicial federalism, which is part of the larger doctrine of federalism. First, Article III of the Constitution creates a national judiciary in the form of the Supreme Court of the United States and lower courts to be established by Congress. The creation of a national judiciary was controversial, as noted in the following section, because under the existing constitution—the Articles of Confederation— there was no national judiciary, and many saw one as unnecessary and unwise. Second, Article III defines the foundation for federal court power, and indicates that national courts will have jurisdiction over cases concerning the Constitution, federal law, treaties, admiralty and maritime law disputes, cases in which the United States is a party, and cases in which a citizen of one state sues a citizen of another state. Third, Article VI of the Constitution declares that the Constitution and all federal laws and treaties are the supreme law of the land and also specifies that state courts must accept the supremacy of the Constitution and federal laws and treaties. By implication federal court decisions interpreting national law or the Constitution are likewise supreme, and especially so when decided by the U.S. Supreme Court. Fourth, the rights and liberties contained in the Bill of the Rights, as interpreted by the U.S. Supreme Court, have been extended to the states through the process of incorporation, and state courts are bound to follow the Court's decisions. Fifth, and finally, the Constitution is silent about the roles, functions, and jurisdictions of state courts. Thus, the presumption is that each state defines the powers and organization of its own court system.

Federalist/Anti-Federalist Debate

The dual system of state and federal courts proposed in the new Constitution was contentious, and during the debate over ratifying the Constitution, two clear camps emerged: the Federalists and the Anti-Federalists. The Federalists advocated for the new Constitution and for the creation of a national judiciary. The Anti-Federalists in contrast opposed the Constitution and the creation of a national judiciary. Alexander Hamilton was the primary Federalist promoter of the judiciary, and in his *Federalist Papers*, Nos. 78–82, (1788) he argued that the federal judiciary was a key institution in the Constitution as it could offer impartial judgment, unlike state courts, which generally seek to protect the interests of their state government and citizens (Yale Law School 2016). Moreover, for Hamilton, the judiciary would be the "least dangerous branch" when compared with the other two national branches—Congress and the Presidency—thus states had nothing to fear from it. Counter to Hamilton the Anti-Federalists, chiefly through Robert Yates who wrote a series of articles under the pen name Brutus, argued that the federal judiciary would gradually usurp power from state courts and state governments, so that over time state courts would become less important. Indeed, some Anti-Federalists feared that the national judiciary would simply eradicate state judiciaries over time. The contours of the debate over judicial federalism were established by the Federalists and Anti-Federalists and remain to this day. The Federalist legacy lies with those who see the federal judiciary as instrumental, and indeed necessary, to a functioning, sovereign, national government. The Anti-Federalist legacy lies with those who, while not opposed to the national judiciary, are at least very suspicious of it and decisions by the U.S. Supreme Court that affect critical state policy areas such as criminal justice, education, social welfare and public health.

Vertical and Horizontal Judicial Federalism

Judicial federalism fosters a relationship between federal courts and state courts, and a relationship among state courts themselves. The federal-state judicial relationship is defined as vertical judicial federalism, whereas the relationship among state courts is referred to as horizontal judicial federalism. *Vertical judicial federalism* is most evident when state courts adjudicate cases that directly or indirectly concern the U.S. Constitution or federal law. A good illustration concerns criminal law. State governments are in charge of their own criminal justice systems, and state courts adjudicate state criminal cases. Yet, state law must adhere to certain federal constitutional guidelines often defined by the U.S. Supreme Court. For example, state courts must follow the famous Supreme Court case *Miranda v. Arizona*, decided in 1966, in which the Court interpreted the Fifth Amendment to require all law enforcement officers to inform criminal suspects of their constitutional rights. The *Miranda* case illustrates that the Supreme Court's power to interpret the Constitution is far-reaching, and also highlights the vertical—or top down—relationship between it and lower state courts.

In comparison, *horizontal judicial federalism* concerns the relationship between courts of different states. A good instructive case here is *Lake v. Wal-Mart* (1998), in which the Minnesota State Supreme Court decided that the common law tort invasion of privacy would become part of Minnesota's tort law system. The Minnesota court considered the jurisprudence of other state supreme courts and recognized that all states but three, including Minnesota, had decided to create the same tort, or cause of action, for their own citizens. Thus, the Minnesota court "borrowed" legal precedent from other states to change Minnesota's civil tort law. In this sense, state supreme courts exist on the same plane as each other and are free to consult and adopt decisions by other state supreme courts when needed. Horizontal judicial federalism leads to a more collaborative relationship among state supreme courts, whereas vertical federalism leads to a subordinate relationship in which state courts must generally follow U.S. Supreme Court decisions in certain areas of the law.

New Judicial Federalism

Beginning in the early 1970s a new aspect of judicial federalism developed. Termed the "New Judicial Federalism," it was a movement among state supreme courts and their justices to rely more on state constitutions, instead of the federal Constitution, when deciding civil rights and civil liberties cases. The New Judicial Federalism was prompted by a conservative shift on the U.S. Supreme Court that was reflected in the Court's narrowing of civil liberties decisions from the 1950s and 1960s. It was also encouraged by Supreme Court Justice William Brennan, who argued that states should look to their own constitutional traditions to protect rights and liberties, a view that was supported by state supreme court judges who showed more awareness of the richness and veracity of their own constitutional traditions. A state case that illustrates the new federalism is *Commonwealth of Kentucky v. Wasson*, decided in 1992, in which the Kentucky state supreme court struck down Kentucky's law criminalizing certain homosexual conduct, even though the U.S. Supreme Court declared in the case *Bowers v. Hardwick* in 1986 that the federal Constitution did not stop states from criminalizing certain types of homosexual conduct. In deciding *Wasson,* the Kentucky court relied on the Kentucky Constitution's guarantee of the right to privacy and equal protection of the law and ruled that in Kentucky at least those rights protected homosexual couples from criminal prosecution. The decision showed two key trends of the New Judicial Federalism. First, even if a state law is constitutional under the U.S. Constitution, it might be unconstitutional under a state's own constitution. Second, state supreme court judges are willing to depart from U.S. Supreme Court precedents and use their own constitutional principles and traditions to adjudicate disputes concerning rights and liberties. This latter issue shows that the vertical relationship inherent in judicial federalism is not necessarily a hard and fast connection between state courts and federal courts. That is, at least when state supreme courts are concerned, state judges can depart from federal court decisions as long as they do not violate those decisions. In criminal justice, for example, U.S. Supreme Court decisions have long articulated the basic rights that individuals have when they encounter police officers or other government agents in a criminal justice investigation. Those rights stem from the Fourth, Fifth, and Sixth Amendments to the Constitution, and the Court's interpretations of those rights establish a constitutional minimum that state courts must uphold. However, state supreme courts are free to use their own constitutions to expand the rights of criminal defendants in a state's criminal justice system. To illustrate, the Supreme Court has declared that under the Fourth Amendment illegally seized evidence must generally be excluded from trial. The exclusionary rule has been moderated by the "good faith exception," however, so that evidence seized by police acting in good faith, yet still in violation of the Fourth Amendment, can be used in a criminal trial. Many state supreme courts have chosen not to follow that good faith exception, thereby maintaining more stringent protections for criminal defendants.

Judicial federalism is an artifact of the U.S. Constitution. The Constitution establishes the federal judiciary and leaves it to the states to create and maintain their own separate and distinct judicial systems. State courts predominantly adjudicate state law disputes, and federal courts deal primarily with disputes concerning federal law and the Constitution. A vertical relationship exists between state courts and federal courts, and due to the supremacy clause in Article VI of the Constitution state judges are bound to follow federal law and, by implication, the U.S. Supreme Court's decisions interpreting the Constitution. State courts exist in a horizontal relationship with each other too, in that state supreme courts will often look to each other for guidance on legal issues, and will borrow from each other. Finally, under New Judicial Federalism, state supreme courts retain autonomy to develop state law based on their own state constitutions. To be sure, judicial federalism is a dynamic, changing relationship that ebbs and flows with larger political, legal, and constitutional changes. As federal and state courts have proceeded through eras of political and legal change, whether the expansion of the constitutional rights of criminal defendants in the 1960s or the articulation of same-sex marriage in the 2000s, these courts have subtly and continuously altered the dynamics of judicial federalism through their policymaking.

John C. Blakeman

See also: Constitutional Interpretation; Defendants' Rights; Gay Marriage

Further Reading

Abraham, Henry J. 1998. *The Judicial Process: An Introductory Analysis of the Courts of the United States, England, and France.* 7th ed. Oxford: Oxford University Press.

Brennan, Justice William H. 1977. "State Constitutions and the Protection of Individual Rights." *Harvard Law Review* 90: 489–503.

Canon, Bradley C., and Charles A. Johnson. 1999. *Judicial Politics: Implementation and Impact.* 2nd ed. Washington, D.C.: CQ Press.

Kaminski, John P., and Richard Leffler, eds. 1998. *Federalists and Anti-Federalists.* 2nd ed. Madison, WI: Madison House Publishers.

Tarr, G. Alan. 1997. "The Future of State Supreme Courts as Institutions as Institutions in the Law: the New Judicial Federalism in Perspective." *Notre Dame Law Review* 72: 1097–1118.

Tarr, G. Alan, and Mary Cornelia Aldis Porter. 1988. *State Supreme Courts in State and Nation*. New Haven, CT: Yale University Press.

Zimmerman, Joseph F. 1992. *Contemporary American Federalism*. New York: Praeger.

Cases

Bowers v. Hardwick. 1986. 78 U.S. 186.

Commonwealth of Kentucky v. Jeffrey Wasson. 1992. 842 S.W.2d 487.

Lake v. Wal-Mart. 1998. 582 N.W.2d 231.

Miranda v. Arizona. 1966. 284 U.S. 436.

STATE BALLOT INITIATIVES AND REFERENDUMS

The power of ordinary citizens to create or amend laws through state ballots and initiatives is a form of direct democracy that is increasingly significant in contemporary American politics. While ballot initiatives are not a characteristic of the federal political system, they are widely available as part of the state lawmaking process. Different types of electoral measures, ranging from recall, to legislative or popular referenda, and citizen ballot initiatives, let citizens actively participate in, and sometimes even entirely bypass, the legislature whenever popular preferences and interests are not fully represented by elected officials in the democratic process (Anderson et al. 2005). Through state ballots and initiatives, the people directly set, or influence, the legislative policy agenda and the substance of laws. For that reason, laypersons, and not professional politicians, are positioned to challenge the inherent authority that legislatures have to make laws and set public policy. Still, since state ballots and initiatives transfer legislative power to the people, they are controversial and remain prone to legal challenges in court. Consequently, by exercising their judicial authority courts play a key role in determining if certain types of state ballots and initiatives, such as those legalizing same-sex marriage or others seeking to protect the environment, actually become public policy at the state or local level. Even the specter of future court challenges of state ballots and initiatives is important. To illustrate, although the state courts ultimately did not have to decide the issue, in Ohio's 2015 elections voters refused to pass a citizen and special interest-led ballot initiative that would have legalized marijuana for medicinal and recreational purposes; but, simultaneously, voters passed an initiative that the Ohio legislature placed on the ballot that prevented business monopolies from being created in the sale and distribution of marijuana. Had the legalization of pot ballot initiative also passed, arguably a constitutional crisis would have been created and the only way to resolve it would have been for the Ohio courts to decide the legality of conflicting ballot initiatives that supported legalization while also preventing the distribution of marijuana.

The Political Evolution of State Ballots and Initiatives

State ballots and initiatives have evolved with the democratic political landscape. American constitutionalism is founded on the principles of representative government and a careful array of checks and balances in a system of separation of powers. The founders believed that this structure of limited government is the best method to control majority factions that would exert their influence on the legislature to enact laws that favored themselves, thereby harming minorities that also seek political representation. As the nation grew, so did the power of elite special interests and the wealthy who used the legislative process to their advantage. Thus, beginning in the late 19th century, progressive reformers sought to change state politics with proposals favoring direct democracy (Cain 2015). The reforms aimed to create democratic mechanisms that returned political power back to the people instead of allowing it to rest exclusively with professional politicians that were either corrupt or under the sway of special interests.

Underlying the spirit of the reforms is the need for politicians to represent the people better. If citizens can actively participate in creating laws and public policy, the people can check the actions of elected officials and make them more directly accountable to popular will. Over time, many states have adopted several forms of direct democracy in their state constitutions, including the recall of public officials, legislative or popular referenda, and citizen ballot initiatives. To varying degrees, these devices permit citizens to vote directly on key issues of public policy, such as tax or budget proposals, legislation, or constitutional amendments. Once a proposal is on the ballot, in most instances a simple majority vote will put it into law.

Types of State Ballots and Initiatives

The types of ballots and initiatives used in the states determine how much influence citizens will have in the lawmaking process. *Recalls* enable citizens to petition for an election to decide if an elected official should be removed from office before their term of service ends. Nearly half the states permit the recall of state officials. More typically, cities or towns allow for the removal of elected officials on local councils or school boards. Similarly, legislative or popular referenda are another type of democratic check on governmental power. A *legislative referendum* allows the legislature to place a proposal on the ballot for voter approval. A *popular referendum* is different because it goes on the ballot through a voter petition process. Either way, referenda give citizens the authority to vote in favor of, or against, a law that is being proposed, or one that is already enacted by the legislature. In contrast, the *initiative* permits citizens to use petitions to propose, and then vote on, laws that they create and put on the ballot (National Conference of State Legislatures 2015).

Used in 24 states, initiatives are most commonly petitions that propose new legislation, although a few states permit constitutional amendments to appear on the ballot. Although initiatives are used nationwide, today many of them are a routine part of Oregon, California, Colorado, Washington and Arizona politics. Moreover, the actual process of getting initiatives on the ballot varies considerably. Whereas some states allow initiatives to go directly on the ballot without input from the legislature, other states let elected officials have an opportunity to evaluate the initiative and reject, change, or ignore it before it is put before the voters (National Conference of State Legislatures 2015).

Of the different mechanisms, citizen initiatives are the most politically significant because they allow popular majorities to circumvent the normal democratic process that vests lawmaking power in the state legislatures. As Theodore Roosevelt once remarked, "I believe in the initiative, which should be used not to destroy representative government, but to correct it when it becomes misrepresentative" (McCrath 2011, 612). They affect a wide breadth of legal topics and public policies, including abortion, campaign financing, criminal justice, gambling, redistricting, sports stadium funding, the legalization of marijuana, and taxes, among others (Anderson et al. 2005). Consequently, they draw the most controversy. While supporters claim that citizen initiatives encourage more direct participation in the democratic lawmaking process, critics counter that they produce bad laws that are put into effect without the careful deliberation of elected officials. Another powerful criticism is that the electoral process has been captured by the wealthy or special interest groups that use their money and lobbying influence to generate petitions and laws that they ideologically favor. At bottom, the debate over the wisdom of allowing citizens to have a direct influence on legislative policy is essentially over whether it is best to have a direct or representative democracy.

The Judicial Ratification of State and Local Ballots and Initiatives

By evaluating the legality of state ballots and initiatives in litigation challenging their use, the judiciary plays a vital role in determining whether they become enforceable laws in contentious areas of social policy. In that respect, the judiciary is an important, and sometimes the only check, on the people (Miller 2009). In *Pacific States Telephone and Telegraph Company v. Oregon* (1912), the Supreme Court established the constitutionality of state ballots and initiatives by holding that they do not violate the federal government's obligation to guarantee to every state in the Union a republican form of government under Article IV, Section 4 of the U.S. Constitution. In dismissing an Oregon corporation's claim that Oregon could not use the initiative process levy a tax on its business operations, the justices reasoned that the issue was a political question, and one that the judiciary lacked the power to decide. Apart from the review of constitutional issues, both federal and state courts routinely have been called upon to assess if state ballots and initiatives have met all of the procedural requirements to be put before the voters, such as whether they have the correct number of signatures, or if they violate bans against using paid solicitors, and the like (Zimmerman 2015). Regardless of the type of challenge to their legal validity, the judiciary has been at the forefront of determining if the people have the basic right to represent their own interests and create or shape laws apart from the legislature.

Although ballot initiatives are not useful to propose new federal legislation, increasingly they are an integral part of state politics because they raise crucial policy issues, such as government spending and borrowing, affirmative action programs, stem cell research, and immigration reform (National Conference of State Legislatures 2015). Moreover, state ballots and initiatives are the stimulus for kick-starting a national political conversation that begins in the states but sometimes is finished or dramatically shaped by judicial oversight. The hotly contested politics surrounding the legalization of same-sex marriage is a good illustration. In the aftermath of the Hawaii Supreme Court's ruling in *Baehr v. Lewin* (1993), which held that outlawing same-sex marriages violated the state constitution, Hawaiian legislators responded by using a ballot measure to amend the state constitution to permit the legislature to enact a law that defined marriage as a heterosexual union between a man and a woman. After voter approval, several other state assemblies, including Alaska, California, Nebraska, and Nevada, followed Hawaii's lead and enacted similar ballot measures with voter consent. Following the Massachusetts Supreme Court's decision in *Goodridge v. Department of Public Health* (2004), which interpreted the state constitution as permitting same-sex marriage, even more states used the ballot process to ban same-sex marriage, either through statutes or by constitutional amendment. While the issue was being politically debated and intensely litigated across the country, California's Proposition 8, which overturned the state Supreme Court's decision to uphold same-sex marriages by constitutional ballot amendment in *In re Marriage Cases* (2008), reinstated the ban by a majority of the popular vote. Ultimately, the California litigation became the center of rulings by the U.S. Supreme Court that not only struck down a federal "Defense of Marriage Act" law that discriminated against same-sex couples in *Windsor v. United States* (2013), but also established same-sex marriage as a fundamental constitutional right in *Obergefell v. Hodges* (2015).

Although ballot initiatives on crucial issues of state law are an ingrained feature of electoral politics, they are also used on the local level. Courts thus have evaluated the legality of citizen initiatives that try to ban oil pipelines, or natural gas exploration though hydraulic fracturing ("fracking"), in the interest of environmental protection. As with state issues, the litigation is often fought in pitched battles between well-resourced and experienced public interest and business-led advocacy organizations in addition to citizens themselves. In Ohio, several realtors sought to put on the November 2015 ballot proposals to adopt charters in three counties that banned fracking operations. Opposition to the charter petitions came from other citizens and several business advocacy groups that represented the oil and gas industry and the state chamber of commerce. Although the respective board of electors certified the petitions, the Ohio secretary of state invalidated them on the grounds that the charter proposals conflicted with the state of Ohio's exclusive powers to regulate oil and gas activities within the state. On appeal, in *State ex rel. Walker v. Husted* (2015) the Ohio Supreme Court upheld the secretary's decision to disqualify the petitions because they did not technically comply with the requirements that defined what a charter initiative was under Ohio law. However, in an important caveat, the justices also declared that the secretary did not have unlimited authority to determine if the ballot proposals were substantively legal or not. In limiting the secretary's discretion to act as the sole arbiter of a ballot measure's legality, the Ohio Supreme Court reaffirmed the people's basic power to change the local laws through referenda and initiatives, a principle that is often at the heart of identical ballot and initiatives' litigation in many other states.

Christopher P. Banks

See also: Abortion Restrictions; Affirmative Action; Constitutional Interpretation; Gay Marriage

Further Reading

Anderson, Christopher J., Andre Blais, Shaun Bowler, Todd Donovan, and Ola Listhaug. 2005. *Losers' Consent: Elections and Democratic Legitimacy.* Oxford: Oxford University Press.

Biggers, Daniel R. 2014. *Morality at the Ballot: Direct Democracy and Political Engagement in the United States.* New York: Cambridge University Press.

Cain, Bruce E. 2015. *Democracy More or Less: America's Political Reform Quandary.* New York: Cambridge University Press.

Cronin, Thomas E. 1989. *Direct Democracy: The Politics of Initiative, Referendum, and Recall.* Cambridge, MA: Harvard University Press.

Ellis, Richard J. 2002. *Democratic Delusions: The Initiative Process in America.* Lawrence: University Press of Kansas.

Griffen, Stephen M. 2015. *Broken Trust: Dysfunctional Government and Constitutional Reform.* Lawrence: University Press of Kansas.

Lewis, Daniel C. 2013. *Direct Democracy and Minority Rights: A Critical Assessment of the Tyranny of the Majority in the American States.* New York: Routledge.

Magleby, David B. 1998. *Direct Legislation: Voting on Ballot Propositions in the United States.* Baltimore: Johns Hopkins University Press.

Manweller, Mathew. 2005. *The People versus The Courts: Initiative Elites, Judicial Review and Direct Democracy in the American Legal System.* Bethesda, MD: Academica Press.

Matsusaka, John G. 2004. *For the Many or the Few: The Initiative, Public Policy, and American Democracy.* Chicago, IL: University of Chicago Press.

McGrath, Robert J. 2011. "Electoral Competition and the Frequency of Initiative Use in the U.S. States." *American Politics Research* 39: 611–638.

Miller, Kenneth P. 2009. *Direct Democracy and the Courts.* New York: Cambridge University Press.

National Conference of State Legislatures. 2015. "Initiative and Referendum." http://www.ncsl.org/research/elections-and-campaigns/initiative-and-referendum.aspx.

Zimmerman, Joseph F. 2015. *The Initiative: Citizen Lawmaking.* 2nd ed. Albany: State University of New York.

Cases

Baehr v. Lewin. 1993. 852 P.2d 44.

Goodridge v. Department of Public Health. 2003. 798 N.E.2d 941.

In re Marriage Cases. 2008. 183 P.3d 384.

Obergefell v. Hodges. 2015. 135 S.Ct. 2584.

Pacific States Telephone and Telegraph Company v. Oregon. 1912. 223 U.S. 118.

State ex rel. Walker v. Husted. 2015. Slip Opinion No. 2015-Ohio-3749.

Windsor v. United States. 2013. 133 S.Ct. 2675.

Part II: Judicial Access, Independence, and Accountability

PUBLIC ACCESS TO COURTS

Federal and state courts play a crucial role in our political system, as well as in the everyday lives of ordinary Americans; therefore, it is essential that Americans be able to access the court system, regardless of whether they are criminal defendants, civil plaintiffs, civil defendants, witnesses, jurors, or citizens who want to use the courts to influence public policy. However, using the judiciary can be expensive, difficult, and forbiddingly complex; consequently, the issue of improving public access to courts is critical to achieving a just society. There are three key aspects of public access to courts: the representation of lower-income litigants; the judiciaries' efforts to make their systems easier to use; and, organized groups using the courts on behalf of ordinary citizens to influence public policy.

Indigents' Access to Legal Representation: Criminal Cases

One aspect of public access to courts concerns poor people's ability to obtain representation in the judicial system. Representation is crucial because legal precedents, rules, and procedures are extremely complex; therefore, litigants need representation by well-trained, accredited attorneys, especially for criminal defendants who could lose their property, liberty, or life without effective representation. However, quality representation is expensive, and although the Sixth Amendment to the U.S. Constitution guarantees the right the counsel, it does not explicitly guarantee that courts must provide counsel for litigants who cannot afford an attorney. For much of American history most states and the federal government did not provide attorneys to needy criminal defendants. However, in *Johnson v. Zerbst* (1938), the U.S. Supreme Court ruled that the Sixth Amendment right to counsel compels federal district court judges to appoint attorneys for federal criminal defendants who could not afford one; but, significantly, this ruling did not cover state courts. In the Court's opinion Justice Hugo Black wrote that the Sixth Amendment "embodies a realistic recognition of the obvious truth that the average defendant does not have the professional legal skill to defend himself when brought before a tribunal with the power to take his life or liberty."

The story of providing indigent criminal defendants access to state courts is more complex. In the early 1930s the U.S. Supreme Court began to require states to supply adequate counsel. *Powell v. Alabama* (1932) involved nine African American males, known as the Scottsboro Boys, who were convicted of raping two white girls, and eight of them were sentenced to death. The Alabama courts forbid the defendants from consulting with attorneys until immediately before their trials, when it was too late to mount an effective defense. The U.S. Supreme Court, however, overturned their convictions arguing that denying these defendants effective counsel, particularly given that these were capital cases, was a violation of the Fourteenth Amendment's due process clause, which applied the Sixth Amendment right to counsel provision to the states. However, one decade later the U.S. Supreme Court ruled in *Betts v. Brady* (1942) that the U.S. Constitution does not require states to appoint counsel for indigent noncapital defendants who could not afford an attorney. In this case Betts was convicted of robbery in Maryland after representing himself because he could not afford an attorney, and the court would not appoint one. Under Maryland law, the court appointed attorneys only in capital cases.

In the 1960s the U.S. Supreme Court increased access in criminal cases with the landmark case of *Gideon v. Wainwright* (1963). Clarence Gideon, who was indigent, was convicted of felony breaking-and-entering after the trial judge refused to appoint an attorney for him. Gideon appealed his case to the U.S. Supreme Court, which overturned the *Betts* precedent and ruled that the Sixth Amendment right to counsel is so fundamental to civil liberties that under the Fourteenth Amendment's due process clause states must provide felony defendants with an attorney if they cannot afford one. Justice Hugo Black wrote in the Court's opinion that, ". . . in our adversary system of criminal justice, any person haled into court, who is too poor to hire a lawyer, cannot be assured a fair trial unless counsel is provided for him." In *Miranda v. Arizona* (1966), the Court required that arresting officers need to inform suspects of their right to have a court-appointed attorney if they are unable to afford their own. Finally, in *Argersinger v. Hamlin* (1972) the Court extended access by requiring that courts appoint attorneys in misdemeanor cases that could result in jail time. These rulings undoubtedly expanded access to court for criminal defendants. Most jurisdictions have established public defender systems that consist of government-employed attorneys who represent poor defendants, but there is considerable debate over whether public defenders provide a sufficiently effective defense.

Indigents' Access to Legal Representation: Civil Cases

Public defenders provide access for criminal defendants, but they do not represent the underprivileged in civil cases, which also involve issues central to people's lives, such as foreclosures, landlord-tenant disputes, divorce, custody battles, and consumer protection. One key barrier to access concerns fees that are required to file a civil suit or appeal a lower court decision. In 1892 Congress passed a statute that allowed indigent litigants to file or appeal federal court cases under in forma pauperis ("in the form of a pauper"). This law requires federal judges to waive filing fees for indigent defendants, unless the legal filing is frivolous. This in forma pauperis law has greatly expanded access to federal courts. For example, Clarence Gideon's appeal to the U.S. Supreme Court (discussed in the preceding section) was filed in forma pauperis.

Another barrier to access in civil cases concerns the quality of representation. Without help, poor and working-class litigants cannot afford attorneys to represent them in civil cases; consequently, they lack access to courts. Legal aid societies in local areas provide help for lower-income litigants in civil cases, but these organizations historically relied on charitable donations, which were often not sufficient to grant full public access to the courts. In 1965 the federal government addressed this problem by creating the Legal Services Program (LSP). The Office of Economic Opportunity, the executive agency that implemented President Lyndon Johnson's "War on Poverty" programs, established the LSP to dispense grants to local legal aid societies, which then used the money to represent poor people in civil cases.

The federal government disbanded the LSP during the early 1970s and replaced it in 1974 with the Legal Services Corporation (LSC). Unlike the LSP, the LSC is an independent government corporation run by a board of directions that consists of both Republicans and Democrats who are appointed by the president and confirmed by the Senate. Its mission is to "promote equal access to justice in our Nation and to provide high quality legal assistance to low-income people" (Legal Services Corporation 2015). Similar to the LSP, the

LSC receives federal funding to disseminate grants to nonprofit local legal aid organizations in localities throughout the nation. These organizations provide free legal assistance to people who are at or below 125 percent of the poverty line. Specifically, the LSC provides legal assistance in cases concerning domestic violence victims (to obtain restraining orders and gain custody of children), divorce law, foreclosures, landlord-tenant disputes, consumer protection, employment law, government services, and veterans issues. The LSC also works with the Red Cross and the Federal Emergency Management Agency (FEMA) to help victims of disasters with their legal issues. In short, the LSC significantly increases public access to courts.

Courts' Efforts to Facilitate Public Access

In addition to providing representation for lower-income litigants, the issue of public access to courts also concerns making it easier for all participants (litigants, attorneys, witnesses, and jurors) to engage in the judicial process, regardless of their economic status. Judicial procedures can be exceedingly complex, which can limit access to court. According to its recently published Strategic Plan, the federal judiciary has sought to streamline its processes by adopting a number of strategies, such as decreasing costs and delays, transferring much of its work from paper to electronic formats, and improving the publication of rules and procedures. It has also increased opportunities for alternative dispute resolution, in which the parties involved in a civil case try to arrive at a solution outside of the trial setting. Additionally, the federal judiciary has made the judicial process more understandable for all participants in court, including litigants, attorneys, witnesses, and jurors. To implement this strategy, federal courts are providing interpreters for non-English speakers and making it easier for litigants who represent themselves. The federal courts are also seeking to lessen the burden of serving on juries.

Many state courts have also adopted policies to make it easier to use their court systems. The National Center for State Courts (NCSC), which is a nonprofit organization that works with state judges and court administrators throughout the United States to enhance state court management, has developed ways to improve public access to state courts. Specifically, the NCSC created the Center on Court Access to Justice for All (CCAJA), which collaborates with state courts to make filing forms easier, increase electronic filing opportunities, and enhance litigants' ability to represent themselves. The CCAJA also promotes unbundling, in which attorneys provide low-income clients with behind-the-scenes help without formally representing them. This limited involvement gives litigants assistance at a reduced cost, thus increasing access to courts. Private companies, such as LegalZoom, provide similar unbundling (of legal) services, but the CCAJA works on a nonprofit basis. In short, CCAJA's efforts have undoubtedly increased public access to state courts.

Public Access through Interest Group Litigation

Public access to courts is also significant because the judiciary affects public policy. Courts have the power to interpret laws and even overturn laws that judges deem unconstitutional; therefore, they play a key role in deciding public policy questions, particularly in the areas of civil rights, civil liberties, and economic regulation. Given the importance of the courts as policymakers, organized interest groups sponsor cases with the ultimate goal of the judicial branch issuing a decision that influences public policy in their favor. Sponsoring cases entails an interest group providing the financial and intellectual support that is needed to sustain a litigation campaign from its planning stages until it achieves an important victory in court.

The most well-known example of an organized interest group accessing the judiciary to influence public policy is the National Association for the Advancement of Colored People Legal Defense Fund (NAACP-LDF), which has focused on improving civil rights for racial and ethnic minorities since the early 20th century. From its inception, the NAACP-LDF has focused on school segregation, in which many state laws required that whites and African Americans attend separate schools—with the African American schools receiving far fewer resources. The segregation laws were the product of state legislatures and school boards that were dominated by white supremacists, and because African Americans were disenfranchised at that time, they lacked the political power needed to convince these institutions to end segregation. Consequently, the NAACP-LDF concentrated on litigating in federal court, where judges serve life terms and are immune from political pressure. Attorneys and other staff employed by the NAACP-LDF worked for more than a decade on crafting a legal strategy, which culminated in *Brown v. Board of Education* (1954)—the landmark court case in which the U.S. Supreme Court unanimously ruled that the equal protection clause of the Fourteenth Amendment to the U.S. Constitution prevented states from segregating by race. In short, by accessing the courts, the NAACP-LDF was instrumental in establishing a major victory in civil rights policy that affected millions of Americans and changed the course of American history.

Based on the NAACP-LDF's success, other interest groups have accessed the courts in order to influence public policy. Specifically, organized interest groups have accessed the judiciary to increase civil rights for women, religious minorities, the LGBT community, and even nonhuman animals. In fact, some of the LSP (as discussed earlier in this chapter) cases that were litigated on behalf of poor clients eventually resulted in U.S. Supreme Court decisions that influenced poverty policy (Lawrence 1990). In short, public access to the court through organized interest groups has exerted a significant impact on public policy.

Steven C. Tauber

See also: Defendants Rights; Incorporation Doctrine; Racial Discrimination

Further Reading

Feldman, S. M. 1985. "Indigents in the Federal Courts: The In Forma Pauperis Statute—Equality and Frivolity." *Fordham Law Review* 54: 413–437.

Greenberg, J. 1994. *Crusaders in the Courts: How a Dedicated Band of Lawyers Fought for the Civil Rights Revolution.* New York: Basic Books.

Lawrence. S. E. 1990. *The Poor in Court: The Legal Services Program and Supreme Court Decision Making.* Princeton, NJ: Princeton University Press.

Legal Services Corporation. 2015. "About LSC." http://www.lsc.gov/about-lsc.

National Center on State Courts. 2015. "Center on Court Access to Justice for All." http://www.ncsc.org/atj.

Tauber, S. C. 2015. *Navigating the Jungle: Law, Politics, and the Animal Advocacy Movement.* New York and London: Routledge.

United States Courts. 2015. "Strategic Plan: Issue 5 Enhancing Access to the Judicial Process." http://www.uscourts.gov/statistics-reports/issue-5-enhancing-access-judicial-process.

Cases

Argersinger v. Hamlin. 1972. 407 U.S. 25.

Betts v. Brady. 1942. 316 U.S. 455.

Brown v. Board of Education. 1954. 347 U.S. 483.

Gideon v. Wainwright. 1963. 372 U.S. 335.

Johnson v. Zerbst. 1938. 304 U.S. 458.

Miranda v. Arizona. 284 U.S. 436.

Powell v. Alabama. 1932. 287 U.S. 45.

CAMERAS IN THE COURTROOM

A critical issue for state and federal courts is how well they provide a readily accessible forum for members of the public who need to use them to resolve legal disputes. For ordinary citizens, and even for many lawyers, courts can be unfamiliar and intimidating places. In fact, anyone who uses a court, whether it is a citizen, a lawyer, a witness, or a juror, may not understand how courts work, or what is necessary to participate fully and competently in the legal process. In recognizing this difficulty, federal courts have established the principle that securing fair access to courts is a core value of the judiciary (Administrative Office of U.S. Courts 2015a). Many judicial leaders in state courts also endorse the commitment that all citizens are granted equal access to the legal system (Lippman 2015). In this light, an ongoing, but largely unresolved, controversy is whether cameras ought to be put into courtrooms in order to increase transparency and to educate the public about what courts actually do. Even so, historically the judiciary has been reluctant to put cameras in the court and, in fact, has routinely banned them through court rules and ethical prohibitions. In response, legislators, court reform activists, and scholars continue to insist that cameras will increase judicial access and that more will be lost rather than gained in courts that prohibit public broadcasting. The rapid growth of Internet, computer, and digital technologies has only intensified calls for reform that seek increased media or public access to courts. Accordingly, federal and state courts have begun to experiment with the idea by modifying court bans and instituting pilot projects that permit the public to see what is going on inside courtrooms. In addition, the judiciary is adapting to evolving technologies by taking alternative steps to increase public access to courts, such as improving their websites, employing public information officers, and providing audio files and transcripts of oral arguments and court proceedings.

The Debate over Cameras in the Courtroom

Advocates for increased access to the courts argue that allowing cameras in the courtroom permits the judiciary to become more responsive to court users, which, in turn, helps educate citizens about the judicial process while preserving the First Amendment's right to free speech and press. Achieving the goals of guaranteeing individual rights, open transparency, judicial accountability, and providing better education to citizens is part of the vital mission of courts because it builds public confidence and establishes judicial legitimacy. In contrast, opponents of cameras in the courtroom cite historical precedent, and the need to protect a defendant's Sixth Amendment right to a fair trial, for claiming that putting cameras into courtrooms transforms judicial proceedings into unsavory public spectacles that diminish courtroom decorum, embarrasses litigants, and undermines fairness. A commonly referenced example is the famous Lindbergh baby kidnapping and 1935 murder trial of defendant Bruno Hauptmann, which drew national attention from the media and public spectators who, in turn, got out of hand and arguably disrupted the trial proceedings (Kielbowicz 1979). In more contemporary times, the sensationalism of O. J. Simpson's murder trial in 1995, or the criminal prosecution of pop star Michael Jackson on child molestation charges in 2005, raised identical concerns. Among other things, for anti-camera advocates these trials and others like them only show that the pressure of the public spotlight causes judges to lose control of the proceedings. In addition, the participants in the trial process, namely lawyers, witnesses, jurors, and the litigants themselves, actually change their behavior to the point where fairness is compromised and impartiality is lost because they are intimidated by the presence of cameras. As Alex Kozinski, a federal judge on the Ninth Circuit, and his former law clerk observe, such criticisms are based on the conclusion that "Cameras poison the atmosphere inside the courtroom, and they distort the public's view outside of it" (Kozinski and

Johnson 2010, 1108). For these reasons and others, the established legal community, led by the American Bar Association (ABA), has registered long-standing objections to allowing broadcasting, television, and photography in courtrooms (Kozinski and Johnson 2010, 1107–1109).

The Federal Judiciary and Cameras in the Courtroom

Beginning in the 1960s, the U.S. Supreme Court has weighed in on the permissibility of cameras in the courtroom by sending mixed signals about whether courts should permit television broadcasting in the court houses across the country. In *Estes v. Texas* (1965), the Court overturned the conviction of a swindler who bilked investors because the extensive camera coverage of his trial proceedings violated his constitutional rights to have a fair trial and due process. However, in *Chandler v. Florida* (1981) the justices refused to interpret *Estes* as a precedent that imposed a flat constitutional ban on television broadcasting in the trial of two Florida cops who were accused of committing burglary offenses. Instead, the Court upheld the convictions after finding that there was little empirical evidence to show that having cameras in the courtroom unduly prejudiced the defendants' right to a fair trial. For some scholars, *Chandler* had the dual effect of encouraging the states to experiment with permitting cameras in the court while also softening and adding flexibility to the ABA's anti-camera stance (Cohn and Dow 1998, 23–24). Even so, many years later, in *Hollingsworth v. Perry* (2010)—a high-profile civil case that tested the constitutionality of a California ban on same-sex marriage—the Court overturned a district court judge's decision to amend the court's local rules to allow live streaming video of the trial under a federal court pilot program permitting cameras in the courtroom. While *Hollingsworth* did not address the constitutional validity of broadcasting trial court proceedings, the justices suggested that a key issue in future cases will be whether the parties claiming that cameras ought to be banned from the courtroom have any empirical or social science evidence to prove that public broadcasting of court activities has a harmful effect on the adversary judicial process or individual constitutional rights (Lambert 2013, 26–33).

Significantly, the U.S. Judicial Conference, the official policymaking body of the federal courts, has followed the direction of Supreme Court precedent by showing a great reluctance to broadcast federal court proceedings. Beginning in 1946, taking photographs or broadcasting judicial proceedings was banned in criminal cases under federal rules. In 1972, the Judicial Conference extended the prohibition to criminal and civil cases by modifying the rules governing judicial ethics. In 1991, however, the Federal Judicial Center, an administrative body that provides research support for federal courts, began a three-year pilot program that allowed cameras to broadcast the proceedings of several federal trial courts and two federal circuit appellate courts. The study concluded that the presence of cameras in courtrooms did not dramatically diminish courtroom decorum or negatively change the behavior of trial participants. Nevertheless, in 1994 the Judicial Conference declined to follow an internal committee's recommendations to let cameras air the proceedings of district court trials and appellate proceedings in civil cases (Administrative Office of U.S. Courts 2015a).

Shortly thereafter, and following another internal study from a pilot program that reached an opposite conclusion from what the 1991 study concluded—that witnesses and jurors were in fact intimidated by the presence of cameras in federal courtrooms—in 1996 the Judicial Conference took more aggressive action by adopting a firm policy of opposing public broadcasts. It then urged the lower courts to ban them as well through their local rules. Even so, the Judicial Conference continues to study the issue and create new possibilities for reform. In 2011, it authorized a three-year pilot project that allowed, with the consent of the presiding judge and parties, the public broadcasting of civil trials in 14 district courts. After the pilot study ended, the Ninth Circuit Judicial Council, with the Judicial Conference, let three districts in the Ninth Circuit that participated in the pilot study continue in order to gather more information about whether the official policy banning cameras in the courtroom in civil cases should continue to be followed (Administrative Office of U.S. Courts 2015a). According to Supreme Court Justice Steven Breyer's own estimate, if the federal courts do in fact opt to change their policy, they will be joining nearly all of the states that already give to judges the authority to broadcast nonjury trials in civil cases if they so choose (*Hollingsworth* 2010). At least for some observers, the movement toward allowing at least some camera access in federal and state courts is proof that having cameras in the courtroom does not adversely distract lawyers, jurors, or witnesses from performing their adversarial or judicial roles (Kozinski and Johnson 2010, 1112–1114).

Informational Technologies and Public Access to Courts

The debate over whether cameras should be in the courtroom has been complicated by the growth of Internet, cell phone, computer, and digital technologies. As public institutions, courts also have a responsibility to keep their doors open for the public to visit and witness first-hand their proceedings. While some courts still ban video cameras and photographs from being taken in court, increasingly others are revamping their webpages to give the public more access to court documents, judge profiles, calendar information, and general historical facts about the court's origin and what type of legal services it provides in resolving cases. Another trend is increasing the availability of oral arguments and written transcripts, especially in high profile litigation having significant public policy consequences, such as same-sex marriage, abortion, affirmative action, or death penalty cases. Many courts employ public information officers (PIO) as well. As representatives of the courts, PIOs serve as a buffer between the court and the public by answering citizen inquiries and educating the general public about the court and the community it serves. While ordinary citizens are still barred from seeing what courts do in private conferences or in judicial chambers to resolve legal disputes, the various forms of public outreach act in lieu of cameras in the courts because they supply important insights about how courts function and deliver legal services.

Another important issue relating to the cameras-in-the-courtroom debate relates to the growth of computer technologies and personal handheld devices. Citizens and journalists are increasingly equipped with sophisticated but relatively unobtrusive laptops, tablets, and smart phones that are easy to use. Unless there is a specific court policy against the practice, the ubiquity of those devises and the rapid expansion of social media outlets, such as Twitter, Instagram, Facebook, You Tube, Flickr, and blogs, present special challenges for courts because the new media makes it easy for anyone to record court proceedings and disseminate them to anywhere in the world instantly (Click 2011). The pervasive use of digital computer technologies by citizens and journalists has been also accompanied by persistent and ongoing legislative proposals that purport to remove the barriers on using cameras in the courtroom under so-called "Sunshine in the Courtroom Acts" that have been regularly introduced in the U.S. Congress in recent years. The pressure for courts to adapt to rapidly evolving technological advancements means the judiciary will continue to wrestle with the issue of cameras in the courtroom for the foreseeable future.

Christopher P. Banks

See also: Abortion Restrictions; Affirmative Action; Defendant's Rights; Gay Marriage; Judicial Independence; Public Access to Courts

Further Reading

Administrative Office of U.S. Courts. 2015a. "Cameras in Courts." http://www.uscourts.gov/about-federal-courts/cameras-courts.

Administrative Office of U.S. Courts. 2015b. "Strategic Plan for the Federal Judiciary." http://www.uscourts.gov/statistics-reports/strategic-plan-federal-judiciary.

Click, Laura. 2011. "From Sketch Pads to Smart Phones: How Social Media Has Changes Coverage of the Judiciary." In *Future Trends in State Courts (2011)[Special Focus on Access to Justice]*, edited by Carol R. Flango, Amy M. McDowell, Charles F. Campbell, and Neal B. Kauder, 46–50. Williamsburg, VA: National Center for State Courts.

Cohn, Marjorie, and David Dow. 2002. *Cameras in the Courtroom: Television and the Pursuit of Justice*. Lanham, MD: Roman and Littlefield.

Kielbowicz, Richard B. 1979. "The Story Behind the Adoption of the Ban on Courtroom Cameras." *Judicature* 63: 14–23.

Kozinski, Alex, and Robert Johnson. 2010. "Of Cameras and Courtrooms." *Fordham Intellectual Property, Media & Entertainment Law Journal* 20: 1107–1134.

Lambert, Paul. 2013. *Television Courtroom Broadcasting Effects: The Empirical Research and the Supreme Court Challenge.* Lanham, MD: University Press of America.

Lippman, Jonathan. 2015. *The State of the Judiciary 2015 (Access to Justice: Making the Ideal a Reality).* http://www.nycourts.gov/ctapps/news/SOJ-2015.pdf.

Cases

Chandler v. Florida. 1981. 449 U.S. 560.

Estes v. Texas. 1965. 381 U.S. 532.

Hollingsworth v. Perry. 2010. 558 U.S. 183.

JUDICIAL SPECIALIZATION

Although lawyers are generalists, specialization is widespread in legal practice and across federal and state judicial systems. The trend toward specialization has been met with resistance by the organized bar that has traditionally disfavored the commercialization of legal practice. Even so, the Supreme Court has generally invalidated disciplinary rules that prevent attorneys from holding themselves out as specialists on free speech grounds. As a result, many states have increasingly permitted lawyers to become certified as specialists in a limited number of areas of legal practice. In addition, federal and state courts are vested with the jurisdiction to decide specialized cases at both the trial and appellate court level. Typically, judicial specialization consists of having courts or judges review cases in a narrow or particular set of cases or areas of the law, such as bankruptcy, intelligence surveillance, tax, domestic relations, or personal injury. While there are many federal courts with limited jurisdiction that handle specialized dockets, a growing trend in state courts is to adopt problem-solving courts that assist offenders suffering from drug addiction, mental health, or veteran disabilities.

The Increasing Specialization of the Legal Profession

Lawyers typically are considered to be generalist practitioners of law as a result of their legal training, licensing requirements, and ethical rules. While attending law school, law students learn their craft by acquiring an expertise to perform legal analysis in broad areas of public and private law that incorporate certain legal subject matter, such as consumer protection, environmental, bankruptcy, criminal, labor, contract, family, or tort law. After graduating from law school, students are professionally licensed by passing the bar examinations in states that test a mastery of a wide range of legal subjects. As generalists, a newly minted lawyer can advise a client on how to get a divorce (family law), write a will (probate law), defend a criminal prosecution (criminal law), create a binding legal agreement (contract law), or sue a negligent defendant for causing personal injuries (tort law). The generalist training in law is consistent with the traditional if not romanticized notion that attorneys can hang out their own shingle and be a country lawyer with a general practice (Ariens 1994, 1005–1006).

In reality, though, most lawyers engaged in private practice develop an expertise in specific concentrations or fields of law. Beginning in the 1950s, the growing complexity of law led to increasing demands for lawyers to put limits on their professional competencies so that they could serve their clients' needs better. By holding themselves as truly experts within a field of law, lawyers gain the business and confidence of clients seeking the delivery of a narrow set of legal services, such as solving tax problems with the Internal Revenue Service, or filing bankruptcy, worker's compensation, and personal injury claims. Even so, critics assert that the reputation of the legal profession is diminished with legal specialization because the practice of law becomes more like a business rather than a profession. When asked about his opinion on lawyer advertising, Chief Justice Warren Burger said that one must "never engage the services of a lawyer who finds it necessary to advertise in order to get clients" (Burger 1994, 7). Under this view, lawyers are more likely to let profit motives and business interests drive their behavior. In other words, attorneys with specialized law practices are more likely than general practitioners to not only make more money, but also survive in an increasingly competitive marketplace.

The legal, political, and social controversies surrounding the issue of professional specialization raise other regulatory and ethical concerns. Traditionally, legal practice is largely regulated by the professional rules and norms set by lawyers themselves. Under this regulatory framework, many state bar associations created disciplinary rules to prohibit lawyers from holding themselves out as specialists in any field of law. The state bar rules were patterned on ethical canons from the ABA that historically disfavored the solicitation of clients and the commercialization of law practice. In light of these ethical constraints, lawyers seeking to advertise themselves as specialists have challenged the rules by claiming they are unconstitutional burdens to commercial free speech. In response, the Supreme Court loosened the ethical restrictions in favor of protecting the rights of lawyers who wish to specialize and advertise their wares in a way that attracts a larger client base. In *Bates v. State Bar of Arizona* (1977), the Supreme Court declared that the First Amendment protects the commercial speech of attorneys who advertised their fees and rates in an attempt to drum up the business of low-income clients needing help with routine matters of legal practice, such as uncontested divorces, adoptions, or simple bankruptcies. Likewise, in *Peel v. Attorney Registration and Disciplinary Commission of Illinois* (1990), the Supreme Court held that the First Amendment invalidated a state bar's ethical rule that stopped an attorney from representing himself as a trial specialist in civil litigation under a certification issued by the National Board of Trial Advocacy. Not surprisingly, the *Bates* and *Peel* rulings have encouraged many state bar associations to reform their disciplinary rules to allow lawyers to become certified as specialists in certain areas of legal practice. Since the mid-1990s, the number of lawyers holding specialty certifications has steadily grown, especially in the areas of civil or criminal trial advocacy, family law, probate law, and personal injury.

Specialization in Federal and State Courts

There are many examples of specialized courts in the federal and state judicial systems. While the organizational structure of courts and the authority by which judges can decide specialized cases varies considerably, both courts and judges uniformly perform specialized duties. A court may consist of a large concentration of individual judges that decide cases in respect to one specific area of law. In contrast, only a few judges may act as specialists in a particular type of court. For example, federal bankruptcy courts are organized to let a large number of judges review only bankruptcy cases; but, in the specialized U.S. Foreign Intelligence Surveillance Court (FISC), only a few federal district court judges have the statutory authority to decide wiretap authorization petitions in national security prosecutions by the U.S. government on a part-time basis. In this regard FISC judges serve in a dual capacity. As part-time FISC judges, they adjudicate wiretap cases; but in their capacity as full-time district court judges they review a wide range of legal matters in nonspecialized areas of civil and criminal law. These two examples illustrate that judicial specialization is best understood as generally giving courts, or judges, the power to hear a limited range of cases that affect a specific area of legal policy (Baum 2011, 6–10).

The federal judicial system is characterized by specialized appellate or trial courts that require judges to perform a variety of limited judicial duties. Organized under Article I of the U.S. Constitution, the U.S. Tax Court is a trial court that hears tax cases against the federal government. As an Article I court, U.S. Tax Court judges only serve 15-year terms even though they are selected for service by presidential appointment and confirmation by the U.S. Senate. On the other hand, the U.S. Court of Appeals for the Armed Forces is an Article I court staffed by five civilian judges that serve for 15-year terms in reviewing appeals in military justice cases. In contrast, the U.S. Court of International Trade is organized as a trial court under Article III of the U.S. Constitution, which means that its judges serve for life while adjudicating international trade disputes involving the federal government. Or, as mentioned earlier, the U.S. Foreign Intelligence Surveillance Court is a trial court that uses 11 federal district court judges who are appointed by the chief justice of the U.S. Supreme Court to decide wiretap petitions brought by the federal government in national security cases. Notably, appeals from the U.S. Foreign Intelligence Surveillance Court are heard in the U.S. Foreign Intelligence Court of Review by three federal district court or court of appeals judges that hold five-year terms.

An identical, but even more complex diversity is found in specialized courts in state judicial systems. Interspersed across all 50 states, judicial specialization differs from state to state and remains formally or informally distinctive in terms of legal subject matter, court organization, and staffing. Depending upon the state, judges adjudicating specialized legal subject matter may be appointed by the legislature or governor's office, popularly elected by the voters, or placed on the bench by a combination of appointive and elective methods at both the trial and appellate court level. Another important characteristic of state judicial specialization is that it is far more prevalent at the trial level as opposed to the appellate court level. Alabama, Oklahoma, and Texas each use courts that are officially designated to hear only criminal appeals. In two of those states (Oklahoma and Texas), the specialized courts operate as the court of last resort (COLR) for criminal appeals (Baum 2011, 18). In addition, at the trial court level, many states assign judges and subordinate magistrates or referees to dispose of legal disputes in a particular set of legal subject matter. As a result, state trial judges routinely adjudicate caseloads in a limited number of legal fields, such as traffic, small claims, juvenile, or domestic relations law.

It is also common for states to create limited jurisdiction courts at the trial court level that only handle cases in a specific area of law that affects a narrow set of litigants. Known as problem-solving courts, these specialty courts are often patterned after the success of the nation's first drug court that was instituted in Miami-Dade County, Florida in the late 1980s. A drug court is distinctive because it operates differently than typical trial courts. In problem-solving drug courts, judges work with court staff and community drug treatment professionals to rehabilitate, and not just punish, offenders that suffer from drug addiction. With careful screening and by using diversionary programs that place defendants under intensive monitoring and supervision by the court and community professional services, drug courts try to solve the underlying drug problem of addicts in an attempt to prevent them from re-offending. After treatment and going through employment training sessions offered through the drug court, offenders become drug-free and do not have to be incarcerated which, in turn, gives them a chance to become productive members of society.

A growing trend in the states has been to extend the drug court model to other specialized public policy areas or fields of law, such as mental health, domestic violence, homelessness, or veteran disabilities, among others. Community courts are another type of problem-solving court, and they are designed to provide justice for communities that are faced with the problem of how to deal with low-level offenders that cannot break the cycle of crime. In 1993, in Manhattan a Midtown Community Court was created in prevent misdemeanor offenders, such as prostitutes and minor drug users, from being routinely returned to the street after their prosecution in the regular criminal courts. Unlike criminal courts, the Midtown Community Court offers supervised treatment programs and alternative sentences based in restitution to allow offenders the chance to pay back the community by performing manual labor, such as cleaning public toilets and local parks, or painting over graffiti. Similarly, in 2008 the nation's first Veteran's Treatment Court was set up in Buffalo, New York to give veterans the help they need with substance abuse or mental health problems that contribute to their criminal behavior. Under a court-supervised program, veterans that are being prosecuted are placed under an intense system of mandatory treatment—a program that, if successfully completed, allows for the possibility that their criminal charges will be dismissed or reduced and thereby avoid or minimize jail time. For example, California's Combat Veterans Court has a highly structured eligibility screening process and treatment program to help veterans who break the law while suffering from post-traumatic stress disorder, brain injuries, substance abuse problems, or psychological disorders. After requiring that veterans accept responsibility and plead guilty to the charges at the beginning of the program, for a minimum of 18 months veterans regularly meet with an array of judicial, legal, military, and mental health professionals who collaborate with each other to devise and implement a treatment plan before each court session. California's court is unique, though, because it enlists the help of appeals court judges who sit on other California courts but also have a military background to serve as mentors to the Combat Veterans Court. If the veteran successfully completes the program, oftentimes the criminal record is expunged and jail time is avoided.

Christopher P. Banks

See also: Constitutional Interpretation; Defendants' Rights; Freedom of Speech; Judicial Federalism

Further Reading

Ariens, Michael. 1994. "Know the Law: A History of Legal Specialization." *South Carolina Law Review* 45: 1003–1061.

Baum, Lawrence. 2011. *Specializing the Courts.* Chicago: University of Chicago Press.

Berman, Greg, and John Feinblatt (with Sarah Glazer). 2005. *Good Courts: The Case for Problem-Solving Justice.* New York: The New Press.

Burger, Warren E. 1993. "The Decline of Professionalism." *Tennessee Law Review* 61: 1–7.

Casey, Pamela M., and David B. Rottman. 2005. "Problem-Solving Courts: Models and Trends." *Justice System Journal* 26: 35–56.

Lanni, Adriaan. 2005. "The Future of Community Justice." *Harvard Civil Rights-Civil Liberties Law Review* 40: 359–404.

Moore, Eileen C. 2012. "A Mentor in Combat Veterans Court: Observations and Challenges." In *Future Trends in State Courts 2012 (Special Focus on Courts and Community)*, edited by Carol R. Flango, Amy M. McDowell, Deborah W. Saunders, Nora E. Sydow, Charles F. Campbell, and Neal B. Kauder, 39–43. Williamsburg, VA: National Center for State Courts.

Nolan, James L., Jr. 2001. *Reinventing Justice: The American Drug Court.* Princeton, NJ: Princeton University Press.

Sulmasy, Glenn M., 2009. *The National Security Court System: A Natural Evolution of Justice in an Age of Terror.* New York: Oxford University Press.

Cases

Bates v. State Bar of Arizona. 1977. 433 U.S. 350.

Peel v. Attorney Registration and Disciplinary Commission of Illinois. 1990. 496 U.S. 91.

ADVERSENESS AND ADVISORY OPINIONS

Federal and state courts can only hear legal disputes that are properly before them for judicial resolution. Before they can render a legal decision, courts must have the power, or jurisdiction, to preside over cases involving controversies that are legitimately adverse and directly pertain to concrete issues that are justiciable, or appropriate for judicial review. Under Article III of the U.S. Constitution, federal courts are only permitted to adjudicate "cases" or "controversies" that involve issues of federal law. While some state constitutions may have similar jurisdictional requirements, many do not. Thus state courts have more flexibility in resolving cases or legal issues that the federal courts are barred from hearing because of the constraints imposed by Article III. In addition, other legal doctrines, such as the rule that prevents courts from rendering advisory or nonbinding legal opinions, have been developed by the judiciary to limit its review of cases. Even so, while federal courts have traditionally followed the advisory opinion prohibition as a rule of judicial abstention, state courts have been more receptive to giving advice about legal issues that greatly impact the political administration of state government, public policy, and justice.

The "Cases" or "Controversies" Requirement

Article III of the U.S. Constitution specifies that federal courts can only adjudicate "cases" or "controversies." As Chief Justice John Marshall suggested in the landmark decision of *Marbury v. Madison* (1803), the Court's power to exercise judicial review is conditioned on the fact that the judiciary first must have appropriate jurisdiction to hear cases or controversies. Under this requirement, the judiciary has no authority to hear a dispute, or case, unless the controversy clearly involves opposing legal interests that are not hypothetical in nature or nonadverse between the disputing parties. While the text of Article III is straightforward, its application to legal disputes remains ambiguous and subject to the exercise of judicial discretion. For example, in *Aetna Life Insurance Company v. Haworth* (1937) an insurance company refused to pay disability benefits to a policyholder because the insured's illness prevented him from continuing to make payments under his insurance premium, causing the policy to lapse. In rejecting the claim that the policyholder's lawsuit seeking disability coverage was nonjusticiable because of nonpayment, the Supreme Court ruled that the lawsuit's underlying merits could be reviewed because the parties' differences over the meaning and application of the insurance contract presented a live controversy that was definite, concrete, and adversarial in nature. Had the Court ruled differently, the insured would have been left without a remedy to enforce his contractual rights because the case was not nonjusticiable or capable of judicial resolution. In this light, the case or controversy requirement enables the judiciary to act like a gatekeeper that permits, or denies, litigants access to courts.

Significantly, the Article III cases or controversies' requirement is a rule of judicial discretion that sits at the base of many other legal doctrines of justiciability that similarly vest courts with the authority to choose which cases it opts to hear. These principles, famously described by law professor Alexander Bickel as the judiciary's "passive virtues," include the doctrines of standing, mootness, ripeness, and political questions (Bickel 1961). Under the standing doctrine, federal courts will abstain from reviewing a case unless the party bringing a lawsuit can establish a personal stake in the outcome. Mootness and ripeness, on the other hand, are threshold determinations by courts that a case is either brought too late (mootness) or too early (ripeness) for judicial resolution. Under the political question doctrine, a court will refuse to decide a case if the subject matter is inherently political in nature, which means that the executive or legislative branches, and not the courts, are the proper forum to resolve the issue.

When any of these passive virtues, or discretionary rules of judicial abstention, are applied in a dispute, the reviewing court will refrain from deciding the lawsuit's legal merits, even though the litigant was initially permitted to file a claim at the courthouse. The court's decision to remain passive, therefore, has enormous consequences for litigants seeking favorable results in their own legal matters but also in trying to effectuate legal and public policy change. Litigants that are permitted to press their substantive arguments in lawsuits in litigation have unique opportunities not only to win on a personal level but also to change the general direction and content of the law relative to the development of public policies that affect American political society. Parties to a lawsuit that are turned away from the court are not so lucky or fortunate.

While federal courts are obliged to follow Article III's jurisdictional requirements, many state constitutions do not have identical language or proscriptions.

Consequently, state courts have considerably more discretion to permit or deny access to the courts to litigants seeking individual remedies or broader legal and public policy change from the judiciary. With more flexibility than what federal courts possess, state courts can grant standing, hear potentially unripe or moot cases, or decide inherently political disputes that federal courts simply have no power or jurisdiction to decide. In this regard state courts remain at the vanguard of "policy formation, government accountability, and social participation in the passionate issues of the day" (Hershkoff 2001, 1839). Notably, the different approaches federal and state courts take in making threshold determinations about which cases they will hear more fully on the merits extends to whether courts are fit to render advisory opinions about how the law will apply to the facts of any given case.

Advisory Opinions

Under Article III, federal courts will refuse requests from government officials or private citizens to give advice about the law or how it applies in hypothetical or abstract cases. As with other justiciability doctrines, the constitutional ban on advisory opinions is grounded in part on a separation of powers' rationale. Under the theory of separation of powers, federal courts sit apart from the political branches so they can only act within the authority granted to them under Article III. As a result, federal courts cannot offer advice about the law to political officials because doing so would improperly enlarge the judicial function by taking it into the legislative or executive sphere. In one of the first applications of the nonadvisory ban, in 1793 the Supreme Court refused Secretary of State Thomas Jefferson's request to advise the Washington administration on various legal questions pertaining to the U.S. policy of neutrality in a war between Great Britain and France. In its refusal, the justices asserted that rendering legal advice "extra-judicially" would improperly cross the "Lines of Separation" that required the different departments of government to remain in proper balance (Anonymous Note 2011, 2067).

Since 1793, federal courts have strictly adhered to the nonadvisory ban and its corollary principle that the judiciary lacks the power to rule on abstract, hypothetical, or nonadverse cases. In articulating this notion of judicial restraint, Justice Felix Frankfurter once remarked that advisory opinions "are ghosts that slay" because they permit courts that render them to undermine the legislature's duty to make the laws and contravene democratic values (Frankfurter 1927, 1008). By contrast, state courts in several states—among them Alabama, Colorado, Florida, Massachusetts, Michigan, Oklahoma and South Dakota—are empowered by either the state constitution or statutory law to give advice to political officials upon request. Although each state's advisory practice is different, typically the courts field questions on a broad range of topics that relate to some issue of public financing, such as determining the legality of a proposed tax; or they may render advice on other issues that explore how constitutional or statutory provisions apply to the general administration of government in specific situations, such as exploring if a governor has the power to commute a death sentence, or whether the legislature is following the correct procedures in creating a reapportionment or redistricting plan. Moreover, the courts' practice of advising political officials is generally constrained by other norms and commonsense principles that prevent the judiciary from treating the advisory opinions as binding legal judgments; rather, they are more characteristically described as merely establishing broad guidelines that political officials can follow and rely upon in the course of deciding how to administer government powers, duties, and rights under the law (Hershkoff 2001, 1844–1852).

The flexibility of state court justiciability practice extends not only to rendering advice but also to other areas of the law that facilitate greater access to courts. Whereas federal courts generally are reluctant to grant standing to citizens or groups that question how taxpayer monies are being spent on federal projects or programs, state courts routinely permit citizens to sue as taxpayers on the grounds that they have a direct interest in the consequences of official regulatory actions affecting public funds. Similarly, in contrast to federal courts, state courts are less likely to dismiss a case on the grounds of mootness or ripeness in litigation raising significant matters of public interest that implicate constitutional freedoms, such as the right to die, public school financing, property or land use rights, and the termination of parental rights. Moreover, at least in some states the judiciary has shown a tendency to wade into the political thicket more so than the federal courts on certain issues. To illustrate, on questions relating to the legality of municipal boundaries, such as annexation, state courts are not inclined to use the political question doctrine as a basis to avoid hearing the lawsuit (Hershkoff 2011, 1852–1867). In general, therefore, the diversity of justiciability practices in the states implies that state courts may enjoy more autonomy than Article III federal courts in exercising the judicial function and granting review of certain types of cases that are uniquely linked to state or local political governance. In doing so, the state judiciary may have more opportunities to strike an appropriate balance in meeting the goals of not only facilitating access to justice but also retaining their judicial independence in a political system organized under federalism and separation of powers principles.

Christopher P. Banks

See also: Constitutional Interpretation; Judicial Federalism; Judicial Review; Jurisdictional Doctrines and Procedures; Political Restraints on Judicial Power; Public Access to Courts

Further Reading

Anonymous. 2011. "Advisory Opinions and the Influence of the Supreme Court Over American Policymaking." *Harvard Law Review* 124: 2064–2082.

Barak, Aharon. 2008. *The Judge in a Democracy*. Princeton, NJ: Princeton University Press.

Bickel, Alexander M. 1961. "The Passive Virtues." *Harvard Law Review* 75: 40–244.

Bickel, Alexander M. 1962. *The Least Dangerous Branch: The Supreme Court at the Bar of Politics*. Indianapolis, IN: Bobbs-Merrill Company.

Brilmayer, Lea. 1979. "The Jurisprudence of Article III: Perspectives on the "Case or Controversy" Requirement." *Harvard Law Review* 93: 297–321.

Chemerinsky, Erwin. 2012. *Federal Jurisdiction*. New York: Wolters Kluwer Law & Business.

Frankfurter, Felix. 1924. "A Note on Advisory Opinions." *Harvard Law Review* 37: 1002–1009.

Hershkoff, Helen. 2001. "State Courts and the 'Passive Virtues': Rethinking the Judicial Function." *Harvard Law Review* 114: 1833–1940.

Pushaw, Robert J., Jr. 1994. "Article III's Case/Controversy Distinction and the Dual Functions of Federal Courts." *Notre Dame Law Review* 69: 447–532.

Cases

Aetna Life Ins. Co. v. Haworth. 1937. 300 U.S. 227.
Marbury v. Madison. 1803. 1 U.S. 137.

JURISDICTIONAL DOCTRINES AND PROCEDURES

The judiciary may resolve legal disputes once it has jurisdiction to act and the matter before the court is fit for judicial resolution. The legal determination of jurisdictional fitness is left to federal and state judges that must make a preliminary decision in the early stages of litigation that the court has the authority to hear the legal dispute or controversy. Courts can only review cases and controversies if they are legally justiciable, or capable of judicial resolution. The legal doctrines of justiciability are part of the technical rules of jurisdiction and procedure that empower courts to accept or deny cases that raise substantive legal issues. Justiciability doctrines include the doctrines of standing, mootness, ripeness, and political questions. In addition, all federal and state courts have rules of procedure that litigants must follow in filing the lawsuit and keeping it on the court's docket. Like doctrines of justiciability, the rules of procedure that courts create and administer in the delivery of justice gives the judiciary considerable discretion to keep or remove cases from the docket. In this fashion, jurisdictional doctrines and procedures are key elements to facilitating or retarding judicial access to courts. Consequently, how federal and state courts exercise their judgment in applying rules of jurisdiction and procedure to cases and controversies has significant consequences for litigants and other interested parties or groups that seek to use the courts as agents for legal and public policy change.

Justiciability Doctrines

Courts and judges have discretion to avoid deciding cases or controversies under a variety of legal doctrines that have evolved with the development of the common law, or judge-made precedent. The inherent logic behind these rules is to limit the judiciary's exercise of judicial review, the authority written into the constitutional law by *Marbury v. Madison* (1803). Under *Marbury*, courts are the final arbiters of the meaning of constitutional text, which gives them the raw power to nullify legislative or executive actions that are enacted through the democratic political process. Although state appellate courts of last resort are composed of judges that serve for a term of years, they still retain the basic authority to interpret the constitutionality of laws in a manner analogous to life-tenured federal appeals court judges. As a result, justiciability doctrines give either federal or state courts the power to refuse to decide the legal merits of cases that already have been filed in court for possible legal resolution.

Under the standing doctrine, the judiciary abstains from reviewing a case unless the litigant bringing the lawsuit can establish that there is a personal stake in the outcome. The decision to grant the threshold justiciability issue of standing necessarily dictates whether the case's legal merits are ultimately determined in contentious and significant areas of public policy. Two cases, *Bond v. United States* (2011) (*Bond* I) and *Bond v. United States* (2014) (*Bond* II), are illustrative. In the *Bond* litigation, federal officials prosecuted defendant Bond for violating a federal chemical weapons ban after she poisoned her husband's mistress with toxic chemicals. In challenging the federal prosecution, Bond claimed that she could only be prosecuted in state court under principles of federalism and the Tenth Amendment. The federal government countered that Bond lacked standing to raise that defense because she was a private citizen and not a state official. In *Bond* I, the Supreme Court rejected the federal government's position and granted Bond standing. Still, the legal merits of her principal defense—that she could not be prosecuted under federal law under constitutional principles of federalism and the Tenth Amendment—went unresolved, so the case was sent back to the lower court for review. After the Third Circuit affirmed Bond's conviction, subsequently in *Bond* II the Supreme Court addressed the substantive merits of her defense and ruled in her favor, holding that the federal government lacked the power to prosecute her under a federal law that was designed to implement the terms of an international treaty banning the use of weapons of mass destruction. In reversing Bond's conviction, Chief Justice John Roberts reasoned that the federal chemical weapons ban had no connection to a local crime that took place in the states, a criminal act that he dryly characterized as a misguided and "amateur attempt by a jilted wife to injure her husband's lover."

In contrast, mootness and ripeness are essentially timing doctrines that operate to dismiss cases that are factually either brought too late (mootness) or too early (ripeness) for judicial resolution. Under either doctrine, whether a case is mooted or deemed unripe is dependent upon how the specific facts of the case are applied to the law. In *Campbell-Ewald Co. v. Gomez* (2016), the Supreme Court applied the mootness doctrine to a class-action lawsuit brought by Gomez, a person whose cell phone was placed on a telemarketer's automatic-dialing call list without his consent in violation of federal law. Before the class action was certified, the telemarketing company made a proposal to Gomez to settle his own claim, which Gomez ignored. Thereafter, the company moved to dismiss the case on the basis that the offer of settlement mooted Gomez's individual claim in a class action raising similar complaints. In rejecting the company's argument, the Supreme Court held that Gomez's individual claim was not erased or mooted by an unaccepted offer of settlement because the controversy itself remain live and adverse between the disputing parties. The operation of the ripeness doctrine is similar. In *Renne v. Geary* (1991), a lawsuit was brought by voters against elected local officials on the grounds that they were allegedly deleting political endorsements from voting pamphlets during nonpartisan elections. But, there were no facts showing that the officials actually engaged in that behavior. As a result, the Court used the ripeness doctrine to dismiss the lawsuit because it did not raise a live controversy that needed judicial resolution.

Under the political question doctrine, a court will refuse to decide a case if the subject matter raises a political issue that is best resolved in the legislative or executive branches and not the courts. The doctrine itself originates from *Marbury v. Madison* (1803) when Chief Justice John Marshall declared that "Questions in their nature political, or which are, by the constitution and the law, submitted to the executive, can never been made in this court." As a general rule, the federal courts apply justiciability principles such as the political question doctrine more strictly because they are obliged to do so under the jurisdictional constraints imposed by Article III and its cases or controversies requirement. Still, in the last few decades even federal courts have shown a willingness to decide matters relating to political campaigns and elections that were once thought to be unreviewable. Perhaps the best example is the Supreme Court's decision to review in *Bush v. Gore* (2000) whether the vote-counting procedure performed by election officials in a few Florida voting districts violated the Fourteenth Amendment's equal protection clause in the highly contested presidential contest. In a controversial 5–4 decision, the Court ignored the dissenters' plea to use the political question doctrine to avoid deciding the case. For the dissenters, the Twelfth Amendment and other federal statutes vested in Congress, and not the courts, the power to decide contested presidential elections. Instead, the Court ruled that the standards used by election officials in counting the votes manually violated equal protection because it was impossible to determine what the voters intended to do when they cast their ballots. By rendering a decision in the case, the Supreme Court demonstrated that it, and not Congress, was the final arbiter of the Constitution's meaning, an outcome that delivered the presidency to George W. Bush.

Procedural Rules

An important but often overlooked feature of the judicial process is the impact that technical procedural rules have on litigants seeking access to court and justice. Procedural rules of court are created and periodically revised by judicial committees that consist of judges and are led by court leaders that have the responsibility to set policies that govern court operations. The rules govern the process by which cases are commenced and managed on court dockets. They set the requirements that litigants and attorneys must follow if they wish to start a legal action and keep it on the court's docket for final judicial resolution.

For federal courts, the Federal Rules of Civil Procedure provide guidance on how to start and maintain civil actions seeking compensatory or other relief from courts. The Federal Rules of Criminal Procedure perform a similar function for criminal prosecutions by establishing the procedures for punishing defendants that break the law. Both sets of rules detail specific requirements for filing court pleadings and motions that procedurally move legal actions that are on the docket to trial or final judgment. They set the procedural guidelines for commencing legal actions, completing the discovery process (where information is exchanged between parties to narrow the legal issues and to prepare for trial), holding pretrial conferences, and conducting jury or bench (judge-only) trials. In addition, a myriad of other rules pertain to different federal courts or areas of law that govern the federal judicial process. These include the Federal Rules of Appellate Procedure, the Federal Rules of Bankruptcy Procedure, and the Federal Rules of Evidence, among others. Analogous sets of rules exist to guide the judicial processes of state courts. Significantly, the failure to comply with procedural rules runs the risk that the legal action will be dismissed or taken off the docket as a final resolution even if that outcome is not the most desirable result for litigants or interested parties.

In theory, procedural rules are in place because they supply key information to litigants and attorneys about how to start and keep legal actions on the docket. In practice, however, the uneven development of the rules of judicial procedure in individual federal and state courts across the country has unintentionally transformed them into significant barriers to judicial access because they are complex, confusing, and ambiguous for anyone who tries to apply them. Accordingly, litigants wishing to use the courts to resolve their legal disputes may be shut out of the judicial process because it is too costly, time-consuming, or complicated in litigation to comply properly with rules of process. Moreover, even if the procedural rules are understood and applied correctly to legal actions, courts and judges retain the discretion to decide their scope and application in legal disputes. By exercising their discretion courts and judges not only manage their dockets, but they also may determine as a threshold matter whether courts have the jurisdictional authority to resolve their legal affairs in various stages of the litigation contest. As a consequence, jurisdictional rules greatly affect whether litigants can successfully settle their own legal matters but also use the courts as agents for creating significant legal and public policy change.

Christopher P. Banks

See also: Adverseness and Advisory Opinions; Constitutional Interpretation; Judicial Activism and Restraint; Judicial Review; Public Access to Courts

Further Reading

Barak, Aharon. 2008. *The Judge in a Democracy.* Princeton, NJ: Princeton University Press.
Bickel, Alexander M. 1961. "The Passive Virtues." *Harvard Law Review* 75: 40–244.
Bickel, Alexander M. 1962. *The Least Dangerous Branch: The Supreme Court at the Bar of Politics.* Indianapolis, IN: Bobbs-Merrill Company.
Chemerinsky, Erwin. 2012. *Federal Jurisdiction.* New York: Wolters Kluwer Law & Business.
Doyle, Kelly R., ed. 2015. *Constitutional Inquiries: The Doctrine of Constitutional Avoidance and the Political Question Doctrine.* New York: Novinka.
Hershkoff, Helen. 2001. "State Courts and the 'Passive Virtues': Rethinking the Judicial Function." *Harvard Law Review* 114: 1833–1940.
Mourtada-Sabbah, Nada, and Bruce E. Cain, eds. 2007. *The Political Question Doctrine and the Supreme Court of the United States.* Lanham, MD: Rowman & Littlefield Publishers.

Cases

Bond v. United States (Bond I). 2011. 564 U.S. 211.
Bond v. United States (Bond II). 2014. 134. S.Ct. 2077.
Bush v. Gore. 2000. 531 U.S. 98.
Campbell-Ewald Co. v. Gomez. 2016. 136 S.Ct. 663.
Marbury v. Madison. 1803. 1 U.S. 137.
Renne v. Geary. 1991. 501 U.S. 312.

JUDICIAL INDEPENDENCE

An indispensable feature of the American constitutional system of government is preserving the judiciary's capacity to render impartial legal judgments without fear of retribution or retaliation by the political branches. The concept of judicial independence, which is crucial to sustaining judicial sovereignty and respect for the rule of law, was built into the constitutional framework by the framers at the time of the nation's founding. As the power and influence of the judiciary has grown through its exercise of judicial review, the reality is that neither the federal nor state courts can remain completely independent or free from political pressures. Most federal judges are appointed to the bench, so their tenure is not dependent upon the vagaries of popular elections. Also, because of certain constitutional protections federal judges are better situated to withstand political attacks from the legislative or executive branches. Even so, the independence federal courts enjoy is complicated by the problems caused by so-called *counter-majoritarian difficulty*—most federal judges are not directly accountable to the people through elections because they are appointed for life. In contrast, most state judges are elected into office and face a *majoritarian difficulty* (Kermit 2005, 64). In other words, state judges have less judicial independence because they are always mindful of the electoral connection and the need to please a majority of the voters. In this regard, state judges are more accountable to the people, but they are also more susceptible to external political pressures, which, in turn, diminish their capacity to make independent judgments in law that might strike down popular, but ill-conceived, legislation or executive action. Accordingly, the degree of independence federal and state courts have is tied to how judges are selected for service and how much political opposition they face when they make unpopular rulings. In this light, courts are always vulnerable to political attacks on their judicial independence because they invariably encounter political pressures to remain judicially accountable in the political system whenever they make or shape public policy through their judicial decision-making.

The Historical Evolution of Judicial Independence

Historically, the issue of judicial independence is centered on principles of judicial impartiality and judicial accountability. Before the American Revolution the colonies became increasingly distrustful of judges who were appointed by colonial governors that were acting under royal authority. Indeed, the growing concern that courts or judges were being dominated by the executive was cited as a grievance by Thomas Jefferson in the Declaration of Independence. After the American Revolution, most states and citizens expressed more faith in the legislature, although concerns remained about its growing dominance in the political system. Even so, most early state constitutions permitted the legislature to appoint judges because the popularly elected branch was thought to be a repository of the people's will (Tarr 2012, 9–10). Furthermore, the nation's founding document was structured in a way that would prevent the new federal judiciary from becoming too dependent upon either the executive or legislative branches. This institutional arrangement was distinct from the English model because Great Britain's constitutional system did not have any meaningful division of governmental authority: the king was sovereign, so parliament and the courts were subordinate to the Crown. In contrast, under Articles I, II, and III of the U.S. Constitution, government departments were separated into distinct political institutions that detailed the source and limitations of legislative, executive, and judicial powers. Accordingly, the separation of powers principle remains the cornerstone of judicial independence in the American constitutional republic.

Federal Courts and Judicial Independence

Judicial independence and impartiality is secured by several interlocking constitutional specifications and principles. Under the separation of powers principle, Article III establishes that the federal judiciary is to remain independent as a department from the legislative and executive branch, thus preventing it from being directly controlled by either. Also, under Article II most federal judges are put on the bench by presidential appointment and confirmation after two-thirds of the Senate gives its advice and consent. After Senate confirmation, under Article III federal judges serve for life, and their salaries cannot be diminished for any reason, including making unpopular rulings. As well, federal judges cannot be removed by impeachment if they exhibit good behavior; rather, they can only be impeached for illicit behavior (committing "treason, bribery, or other high crimes and misdemeanors" under Article II) by a majority vote by the House of Representatives, and only then removed after a separate trial and conviction by the Senate.

While the constitutional protections afforded federal judges enhance judicial impartiality, they also have the effect of making the federal judiciary less accountable to the people because its judges are not subject to the constraints imposed by elections. The lack of direct electoral accountability makes federal judges easy targets for politicians who disagree with their judicial rulings. For example, in 2012 presidential candidate and former speaker of House Newt Gingrich (R-GA) referred to federal judges as dictators because they decided cases that weakened religious freedom and national security. Likewise, in his campaign for the presidential nomination in 2016 former Republican Arkansas Governor Mike Huckabee condemned the U.S. Supreme Court for legalizing same-sex marriage. Notably, the attacks on courts come from both sides of the political spectrum. In his State of the Union addresses and in several stump speeches, Democratic President Barack Obama has assailed the conservative Roberts Court (2006 to present) for not only taking cases that threatened to overturn his landmark health care insurance program under the Patient Protection and Affordable Care Act, but also for deciding cases that undermined voting rights or increased the power of corporations to spend money during campaigns and elections (Eshbaugh-Soha and Collins 2015, 634). The political rhetoric by conservatives and liberals poignantly illustrates the criticism that it is inherently anti-democratic, and counter-majoritarian, to permit life-tenured federal judges to make policy decisions in controversial areas of social policy because they are beyond the reach of the people.

State Courts and Judicial Independence

Like the federal Constitution, at the time of the founding, several state constitutions included good behavior requirements and impeachment provisions. Over time, those restrictions on judicial tenure were replaced or put into relative disuse by other provisions that narrowed judicial service to a set term of years. Also, until the mid-19th century most states used appointment or legislative election as the preferred manner of judicial selection. Thereafter, a majority of the states switched to holding partisan, or contested, elections as the primary means to select judges because of rampant political corruption in state legislatures and in political parties. As a reform measure, using partisan elections increased judicial independence because it gave the people, and not corrupt politicians, the ability to determine the membership of state courts. In reality, though, replacing judicial appointments with contested elections had an opposite effect because state judges realized they had to campaign for office, which, in turn, made them more susceptible to external political pressures and the lobbying of well-funded special interest groups.

By the beginning of the early 20th century and with the increasing support of the organized bar and the legal profession, many states sought to increase judicial accountability and rein in the courts by once again revising their judicial selection methods. Many states chose either to adopt nonpartisan elections or so-called merit plans in an effort to take the politics out of judicial selection. With nonpartisan elections, judicial candidates are not identified by party label on the ballot, which then permits voters to make judicial choices that are only based on the candidate's merit and not the candidate's party identification. Similarly, under merit plans, a commission made up of citizens, lawyers, and politicos compile a short list of judicial candidates and present it to the governor to let the executive appoint judges into service. After serving a term of years, at the next general election voters decide if the judge should remain on the bench. Merit plans, in theory, are less political because the governor does not have the sole discretion to appoint state judges, and the people weigh in on the governor's choice during a retention election that positively or negatively evaluates the judge's judicial performance and record while in office.

Whether the use of nonpartisan elections or merit plans is effective, and whether they increase judicial independence or judicial accountability, remains unclear because of the increasing politicization of state judicial politics. Much of the political turmoil is rooted in the attacks waged by politicians and special interest groups that ask the voters to replace state court judges because they use their power to legislate from the bench in controversial areas of social policy, such as same-sex marriage, abortion, or death penalty cases. For retired Supreme Court justice Sandra Day O'Connor, the ensuing "national war on state courts" is a growing threat to the judicial independence of state courts (Jackson 2013). While several states hold nonpartisan elections, the process by which judicial candidates get on the ballot is inherently political. Also, the use of merit plans is increasingly criticized. Under this view, the judicial commissions that give the executive a short list of candidates for appointment are heavily biased in favor of political elites from legal profession and members of the organized bar. Another problem is that judges facing retention elections after their initial appointment only rarely face any serious opposition; and, even if they do, voters cannot exercise a meaningful vote because they are politically apathetic, or they do not have enough information to make informed choices about who should remain on the bench. For critics, then, the way merit plans work in practice is flawed because they are infused with politics, and they only increase the likelihood that state judges, who are sitting as incumbents in retention elections, will always get re-elected and stay on the bench indefinitely, or for life.

Moreover, like federal appellate courts, state courts of last resort have the power to make social policy with rulings that affect many controversial political issues, such as same-sex marriage, health care, capital punishment, public education funding, environmental protection, and voting rights. The growing role that state courts play as agents of legal and political change has been matched by the rising influence of special interest groups in states holding judicial elections. These trends have been greatly affected by the Supreme Court's ruling in *Citizens United v. Federal Election Commission* (2010). With *Citizens United*, Congress's ability to enact meaningful regulations on campaign financing was significantly weakened when the Court ruled that corporations and labor unions can spend unlimited amounts of money under the First Amendment in federal elections. In response, many states removed their restrictions on judicial campaign spending, which encouraged special interest groups with an ideological agenda to spend large sums of money on negative attack ads against their opponents. For critics, the infusion of unregulated special interest group money into judicial campaigns weakens judicial independence because it works in favor of the political interests of wealthy donors and groups that seek to change the membership and corresponding judicial policymaking of state courts. On the other hand, supporters counter that judicial candidates are not only protected by the First Amendment, but also that judicial elections and campaigns strengthen the values underlying democratic and judicial accountability. To be sure, the debate about whether it is better to have judicial independence or judicial accountability is intimately related to the majoritarian difficulty and the problem of trying to retain judicial impartiality and respect for the rule of law amid a growing and pervasive politicization of state judicial campaigns and elections.

Christopher P. Banks

See also: Court Curbing; Freedom of Speech; Impeachment and Removal of Federal Judges; Judicial Activism and Restraint; Judicial Campaigns and the First Amendment; Judicial Federalism; Partisan Judicial Elections and Political Money; Political Restraints on Judicial Power

Further Reading

Eshbaugh-Soha, Matthew, and Paul M. Collins, Jr. 2015. "Presidential Rhetoric and Supreme Court Decisions." *Presidential Studies Quarterly* 45(4): 633–652.

Gibson, James L. 2012. *Electing Judges: The Surprising Effects of Campaigning on Judicial Legitimacy.* Chicago: University of Chicago Press.

Greytak, Scott, Alicia Bannon, Allyse Falce, and Linda Casey. 2015. *Bankrolling the Bench: The New Politics of Judicial Elections 2013–2014.* Washington, D.C.: Justice at Stake, Brennan Center for Justice, and National Institute on Money in State Politics. http://newpoliticsreport.org/app/uploads/JAS-NPJE-2013-14.pdf.

Hall, Kermit L. 2005. "Judicial Independence and the Majoritarian Difficulty." *The Judicial Branch*, edited by Kermit L. Hall and Kevin T. McGuire, 60–85. New York: Oxford University Press.

Hamburger, Philip. 2008. *Law and Judicial Duty.* Cambridge, MA: Harvard University Press.

Jackson, Jay L. 2013. "The Siege on State Courts." *ABA Journal* 99: 54–61.

Peabody, Bruce, ed. 2011. *The Politics of Judicial Independence.* Baltimore: John Hopkins University Press.

Shugerman, Jed Handelsman. 2012. *The People's Courts: Pursuing Judicial Independence in America.* Cambridge, MA: Harvard University Press.

Tarr, G. Alan. 2012. *Without Fear of Favor: Judicial Independence and Judicial Accountability in the States.* Stanford, CA: Stanford University Press.

Cases

Citizens United v. Federal Election Commission. 2010. 558 U.S. 310.

COURT CURBING

The judicial decisions of appellate federal and state courts have a substantial effect on public policy. In many controversial issue areas, judicial rulings have led to widespread societal, political, and legal change by permitting abortions, racially integrating public schools, instituting affirmative action programs, supporting environmental regulations, and expanding health care coverage. Still, the impact of judicial policymaking, or the ability of a court to create or alter public policy through a judicial decision, is contingent upon whether government officials follow and implement the ruling. Moreover, the politics underlying judicial policymaking often involve attempts by the elected branches to limit the power of courts to make or change policy by introducing court-curbing legislation. While there are multiple types of policies used to curb the courts, in practice the bills rarely become law or succeed at substantially limiting judicial power. Even so, the proposals may have an effect in changing the way courts operate within the political system. The introduction of court-curbing legislation serves as a potent reminder to courts that they run the risk of diminishing their institutional legitimacy, or authority and public standing, if they make unpopular judicial decisions that stray too far from prevailing democratic norms and public opinion.

Although there are many ways to diminish the impact of unpopular judicial decisions, it is important to note that courts lack the ability to control how decisions are interpreted and enforced. Therefore, an important limit on judicial power is for government officials and lower courts to simply ignore or refuse to comply with rulings. Another alternative is to attempt to reverse judicial decisions with ordinary legislation or constitutional amendments. Since overriding decisions is time consuming and requires agreement from numerous legislators, individual lawmakers may opt for the tactic of sponsoring court-curbing legislation. Due to its importance as a source of national political change, the U.S. Supreme Court is a frequent target of political attacks and court-curbing proposals (e.g., Blackstone 2013). Court-curbing bills, therefore, attempt to restrict judicial power by altering the Supreme Court's procedures (i.e., how it operates), jurisdiction (i.e., the types of cases it can hear), or composition (i.e., the number of justices on the bench and/or their length of service on the bench).

The Types of Court-Curbing Bills

Scholars studying court-curbing legislation directed at the Supreme Court have classified the proposals into six different categories: judicial review, composition, procedure, jurisdiction, remedy, and other (Clark 2011, 37–42). First, judicial review court-curbing bills try to limit or remove the Court's power of judicial review—the ability to strike down laws or governmental actions that conflict with the Constitution. Most often the bills attempt to completely strip the Court of this power while others would require a supermajority of justices to agree before legislation could be invalidated or provide Congress with an automatic opportunity to override decisions that deemed a law unconstitutional.

Second, composition court-curbing bills are designed to alter the number of justices on the bench. A well-known example is President Franklin D. Roosevelt's "Court-Packing Plan" that would allow him to appoint up to six additional justices to the Supreme Court in an effort to avoid more New Deal legislation being declared unconstitutional in the 1930s (Clark 2011; Leuchtenburg 1966).

The third type of court-curbing bill is introduced to alter judicial procedures, or the way the Court manages its caseload (Clark 2011). For instance, some procedure-altering proposals would change the process for appealing a case to the Supreme Court or institute requirements for judicial recusal, or the method of forcing justices to remove themselves from a case because of a conflict of interest or other ethical concerns that would make it difficult to decide the case in an unbiased manner (Clark 2011).

The fourth and fifth types of court-curbing bills seek to dictate the cases that appear on the Court's docket and the content of decisions (Clark 2011). Jurisdiction court-curbing bills are introduced with the purpose of limiting or entirely eliminating the Court from hearing certain types of cases or those over specific areas of the law. Usually these bills would prohibit the Court from hearing cases relating to specific Acts of Congress or controversial issues, such as flag burning or same-sex marriage (Clark 2011). Remedy court-curbing bills restrict how the Court can resolve a dispute in the case. Congress introduced these bills during the 1970s in an effort to forbid the Court from allowing forced busing in school desegregation cases (Clark 2011). Lastly, court-curbing bills that do not fit into any of the aforementioned categories are labeled as other. These bills do not target judicial power per se, but instead voice displeasure with a specific decision or behavior exhibited by the Court, such as citing foreign law in judicial opinions or not allowing cameras in the courtroom (Clark 2011).

The Politics of Court-Curbing Bill Sponsorship

Despite these various types of court-curbing bills, it's rare for legislators to seriously consider or enact these proposals (e.g., Clark 2011; Engel 2011; Rosenberg 1992; Nagel 1965). Since it does not appear that legislatures are pursuing actual changes to the judiciary's jurisdiction, composition, etc., it appears that legislators sponsor court-curbing bills for political reasons. Most often, the bills are used to help the legislator get re-elected and/or influence the ideological content of judicial decisions (liberal or conservative).

Representing Constituents

Legislative officials are often concerned about their chances of getting re-elected, so they tend to continue campaigning even while in office. With this in mind, an unpopular or ideologically adverse judicial ruling becomes an opportunity for political posturing. Thus, a court-curbing bill is introduced for the strategic purpose of alerting the constituency of the unpopular ruling and signaling that some action is being taken to counter its policy effect. In instances when the public is already aware of the decision because it was highly publicized by the media, these bills also allow legislators to respond to constituent disagreement with the ruling. Generally speaking, the proposal to limit the court's power is done as a position-taking endeavor—a publicly visible action that members can point to while campaigning to demonstrate that they have actively represented constituent interests (Clark 2011; Mayhew 1974). Republican Senator Ted Cruz (R-TX) opted for this strategy when conservatives in Texas and across the country disapproved of the Supreme Court's decisions to uphold tax credit provisions of the Affordable Care Act in *King v. Burwell* (2015) and legalize same-sex marriage in *Obergefell v. Hodges* (2015). Cruz stated that these decisions were "the latest in a long line of judicial assaults on our Constitution and Judeo-Christian values that have made America great," as the Supreme Court "has now forced the disaster of a health care law called Obamacare on the American people and attempted to redefine an institution that was ordained by God" (Zeizima 2015). In response, Cruz sought to restrict the Supreme Court's power by introducing a constitutional amendment that would establish retention elections for the justices. If enacted, the court-curbing proposal would allow Americans to remove justices from the bench for decisions that go against public opinion.

Although court-curbing bills rarely receive a committee hearing (or let alone pass), they remain important signals to constituents that their representatives are committed to checking a court's authority whenever judicial decision-making is out of step with prevailing majority preferences or perceived to be activist. In other words, the court is seen as making political decisions that advance its own ideological policy preferences rather than handing down rulings with sound legal or constitutional arguments. Another reason that legislators commonly respond to judicial decisions with court-curbing legislation is because they will not be punished at the polls for failing to enact the bills. Instead, constituents tend to blame the legislature as a whole (e.g., Clark 2009, 2011; Parker and Davidson 1979).

Pursuing Public Policy Goals

In addition to using court-curbing legislation as a way to create a public track record of representing constituent interests after courts hand down rulings, many legislators use the bills to pursue their own ideological policy preferences. For example, conservative members of Congress, such as representatives John Hostettler (R-IN) and Dan Burton (R-IN), who oppose the legalization of same-sex marriage introduced the Marriage Protection Act throughout the 2000s, which sought to strip the federal courts of jurisdiction over constitutional challenges to the Defense of Marriage Act (DOMA), in an effort to avoid judicial policymaking that would expand gay rights. Similarly, Republican Governor Sam Brownback of Kansas signed into law legislation backed by Republican state legislators to remove the power to select trial court judges and set court budgets from the Kansas Supreme Court in 2014. The law serves as retaliation for a Kansas Supreme Court ruling earlier that year that declared the state's educational funding system unconstitutional and attempts to ensure future decisions that reflect the preferences of the elected braches. As these examples suggest, court-curbing proposals that are used by legislators to pursue their policy agendas occur most often during periods of ideological divergence with the judiciary or when there is a substantial difference between the preferences of the policymaker and the judicial branch.

Judicial Responses to Court-Curbing Legislation

While it is important to understand the motivations and political strategies behind the introduction of court-curbing legislation, an equally important question is how courts respond to political attacks on their judicial independence. In theory, federal or state courts might perceive these bills as limiting judicial power and threatening the ability of the judges to rule on cases in a manner that is consistent with their view of the law or their preferred policy preferences. As a result, some scholars have argued that courts may change the way in which they decide cases because they are concerned about losing their capacity to translate their policy preferences into law, or more broadly, having political attacks undermine their institutional legitimacy (e.g., Clark 2009, 2011; Handberg and Hill 1980; Marshall et al. 2014; Nagel 1965; Rosenberg 1992). Studies of the Supreme Court indicate that court-curbing legislation does not consistently constrain the justices from pursuing their personal political agendas (e.g., Handberg and Hill 1980; Clark 2009, 2011; Segal et al. 2011). However, the Court does tend to respond to the bills to protect its institutional legitimacy (Clark 2009, 2011; Marshall et al. 2014; Rosenberg 1992). Discovering that courts are fearful of losing their authority and public standing in the political system is significant. Moreover, this concern is warranted as government officials may not comply with implementing judicial decisions on the grounds that they are inconsistent with public opinion. In other words, courts that fail to respond to court-curbing legislation by making controversial judicial decisions can intensify political conflict and run the risk of losing judicial independence by seriously diminishing the judiciary's institutional legitimacy (Murphy 1964; Rogers 2001).

Lisa Hager

See also: Judicial Activism and Restraint; Judicial Independence; Political Restraints on Judicial Power

Further Reading

Blackstone, Bethany. 2013. "An Analysis of Policy-Based Congressional Responses to the U.S. Court's Constitutional Decisions." *Law & Society Review* 47: 199–228.

Clark, Tom S. 2009. "The Separation of Powers, Court Curbing, and Judicial Legitimacy." *American Journal of Political Science* 53: 971–989.

Clark, Tom S. 2011. *The Limits of Judicial Independence.* New York: Cambridge University Press.

Engel, Stephen. 2011. *American Politicians Confront the Court: Opposition Politics and Changing Responses to Judicial Power.* New York: Cambridge University Press.

Epstein, Lee, and Jack Knight. 1998. *The Choices Justices Make.* Washington, D.C.: CQ Press.

Handberg, Roger, and Harold F. Hill, Jr. 1980. "Court Curbing, Court Reversals, and Judicial Review: The Supreme Court versus Congress." *Law & Society Review* 14: 309–322.

Leuchtenburg, William E. 1966. "The Origins of Franklin D. Roosevelt's 'Court-Packing' Plan." *The Supreme Court Review* 1966: 347–400.

Marshall, Bryan W., Brett W. Curry, and Richard L. Pacelle, Jr. 2014. "Preserving Institutional Power: The Supreme Court and Strategic Decision Making in the Separation of Powers." *Politics & Policy* 42: 37–76.

Mayhew, David R. 1974. *Congress: The Electoral Connection.* New Haven, CT: Yale University Press.

Murphy, Walter. 1964. *Elements of Judicial Strategy.* Chicago: University of Chicago Press.

Nagel, Stuart S. 1965. "Court Curbing Periods in American History." *Vanderbilt Law Review* 18: 925–944.

Parker, Glenn R., and Roger H. Davidson. 1979. "Why Do American Love Their Congressmen So Much More Than Their Congress?" *Legislative Studies Quarterly* 4: 53–61.

Rogers, James R. 2001. "Information and Judicial Review: A Signaling Game of Legislative-Judicial Interaction." *American Journal of Political Science* 45: 84–99.

Rosenberg, Gerald N. 1992. "Judicial Independence and the Reality of Political Power." *Review of Politics* 54: 369–398.

Segal, Jeffrey A., Chad Westerland, and Stefanie A. Lindquist. 2011. "Congress, the Supreme Court, and Judicial Review: Testing a Constitutional Separation of Powers Model." *American Journal of Political Science* 55: 89–104.

Zezima, Katie. 2015. "Ted Cruz Calls for Judicial Retention Elections for Supreme Court Justices." *Washington Post*, June 27. http://www.washingtonpost.com/blogs/post-politics/wp/2015/06/27/ted-cruz-calls-for-judicial-retention-elections-for-supreme-court-justices/.

Cases

Brown v. Board of Education. 1954. 347 U.S. 483.
King v. Burwell. 2015. 135 S.Ct. 2480.
Obergefell v. Hodges. 2015. 135 S.Ct. 2584.

POLITICAL RESTRAINTS ON JUDICIAL POWER

Judicial decisions greatly impact specific litigants as well as society as a whole. Federal and state courts possess the raw authority to resolve legal actions commenced by individuals, organized groups, and government officials. Under the power of judicial review, the judiciary can use its discretion not only to declare the law but also to make it in key areas of social policy such as affirmative action, LGBT rights, or capital punishment. As a result, those who disagree with the substantive content of judicial decision-making routinely seek to limit judicial power by using the democratic process to counter unpopular rulings. In the American political system, various institutional mechanisms impose political restraints on the exercise of judicial power. These internal and external restraints are typically a function of how federal and state courts operate in a political system characterized by a separation of powers, checks and balances, and a commitment to democratic values. Whereas courts internally constrain the exercise of judicial discretion through the operation of informal norms and professional ways of working, the political branches impose external limitations on the judiciary by several stratagems, including constitutional amendments, legislation, and judicial recruitment methods. In addition, courts are ultimately constrained by, and accountable to, the people in the constitutional republic.

After *Obergefell v. Hodges* (2015), incumbent conservative politicians and like-minded candidates on the campaign trail condemned the Court's decision to extend LBGT rights by making same-sex marriage a fundamental right as a matter of due process and equal protection. Conservatives criticized the decision as a counter-majoritarian, activist ruling that undercuts the people's right to enact state laws that banned same-sex marriage through the operation of democratic politics. Apart from *Obergefell*, similar denunciations have been a part of the criticism of the Supreme Court by liberals in the aftermath of *District of Columbia v. Heller* (2008), a ruling expanding gun rights under the Second Amendment, and *Citizens United v. FEC* (2010), a decision permitting corporations and labor unions to spend large sums of unregulated money in political campaigns and elections under the First Amendment. Such political attacks are not confined to the federal judiciary. In *Gannon v. State* (2014), the Kansas Supreme Court invalidated the state's system of public educational financing on the grounds that it violated equality principles under the state's constitution. The ruling unleashed a series of political attacks by conservatives in the legislature and the governor's office, including one that threatened to defund the entire judiciary if the Kansas Supreme Court struck down a law that removed the Court's power to appoint chief judges in Kansas's judicial districts. Apart from the political rhetoric assailing courts, the political branches are institutionally equipped with several mechanisms that work to limit judicial authority through the democratic process. In addition, courts impose a number of self-imposed restraints on their own discretion during the administration of justice.

Internal Limitations

By virtue of their legal training, lawyers and judges are socialized into the profession by learning the norms, traditions, and ethical obligations that accompany being a legal professional. For lawyers that become judges, several powerful informal ways of working operate as internal limitations on how judges perform their judicial role and decide cases in a collegial and professional environment. One important constraint is the obligation to follow the rule of law—not personal feelings—in construing the law's meaning in any given case. A well-respected law lord in Great Britain observed that the rule of law concept captures Greek philosopher Aristotle's maxim that "It is better for the law to rule than one of the citizens' . . . so even the guardians of the laws are obeying the laws" (Bingham 2011, 3). This duty is ingrained into judges by the symbolic act of taking a judicial oath to remain faithful to the law. It is also reinforced by individual conceptions of judicial philosophy that emphasize deference to respecting long-standing judicial norms, traditions, procedures, and principles that are an inherent part of the judicial and decision-making process. Moreover, a potent internal restraint on the judiciary is the judge's keen interest in gaining the respect and "esteem of audiences that are important to them," including other lawyers, bar associations, and fellow judges (Baum 2008, 22). A judge that strays too far from conventional understandings or applications of mainstream precedents risks the scorn of other judges, courts, and colleagues who might conclude that the judge is deviating from the basic obligation to follow the rule of law. The impulse to conform to the ideal of the rule of law is a compelling internal restraint on judicial authority.

External Limitations

Within the political system, the judiciary is externally constrained by forces in the political environment that exert pressure on courts. These include legislative acts, executive judicial recruitment decisions, the ideological litigation strategies of organized and special interest groups, and public opinion. Often, the constraints are imposed on courts for political reasons that are masked under the pretext of trying to enact reforms that purport to improve judicial administration and the delivery of justice to those who need it. In the late 1990s, conservative Republicans that targeted the liberal decision-making of the Ninth Circuit tried to enact court reform legislation that would have divided the circuit into different geographical regions on the grounds that reform was required because the court was too large and was delaying justice in administering its caseload. The actual motivation for reform, though, was the partisan expectation that changing the court's jurisdiction would alter its ideological decision-making in certain controversial areas of the law, including criminal law, environmental protection, and religious freedom (Banks 2000). In other instances, political attempts to limit judicial authority are more directly con-nected to reversing specific unpopular decisions or the potential that a court may continue to make them if the court's jurisdiction or membership is not adjusted. In recent years, well-funded organized groups in several states, includ-ing California and Iowa, have spearheaded electoral efforts to convince voters to remove judges from courts that did not decide capital punishment and abor-tion cases in the ideological fashion that they favored (Banks and O'Brien 2015, 322–324).

Federal and state legislatures across the country have proposed court-curbing initiatives aimed at reducing the impact of judicial decisions. Legislatures may introduce bills or constitutional amendments that modify the jurisdiction and size of the judiciary or that change the amount of funding they receive in their judicial budgets. Before the Supreme Court's *Obergefell* ruling, almost a major-ity of the states had successfully amended their constitutions to ban same-sex marriage through state ballots and initiatives. While amending constitutions may be the best tactic to use in successfully curbing court power, it is a time-consuming and difficult step to take in reversing offending court decisions. For that reason, on the federal level, the U.S. Constitution has been amended suc-cessfully only a little more than a handful of times even though thousands of amendments have been introduced since the nation's founding (Banks and O'Brien 2015, 322–325). Although state constitutions are amended more often as a matter of traditional constitutional practice, rarely, if at all, do they appear to be put in place to reverse unpopular judicial opinions (Sturm 1982).

A principal strategy that the executive branch uses to shape and alter the impact of court decisions is controlling the judicial selection process to deter-mine who sits on the bench. While Article II of the U.S. Constitution requires that life-tenured judges are appointed by the president with the advice and con-sent of the Senate, a majority of state court judges are selected for service after an election is held. In states with merit plans, governors pick judges from a short list of nominees that are vetted through a judicial commission of politicos, lawyers, and citizens. After gubernatorial appointment, in the next general elec-tion, incumbent judges are subjected to a noncompetitive contest that asks the voters the single question of whether the judges should be retained and stay on the bench. Still, in some states the legislature or the executive has the power to appoint judges without electoral oversight; and, even in merit plan states, there is a growing trend to give either the legislature or the governor more control over the judicial selection process. Regardless if the appointment power is lodged in the U.S. president's office or in the governor's office, astute executive offi-cials are well aware that they ought to pack the courts with judges that share their ideological vision and political goals. Perhaps the best example of this cog-nizance is President Franklin Delano Roosevelt's (FDR) ill-fated court-packing plan in 1937. The plan was in response to the frustration FDR was experiencing in having a conservative bloc of Supreme Court justices repeatedly strike down key parts of the New Deal during the economic crisis precipitated by the Great Depression in the 1930s. Under the court packing plan, FDR proposed to Congress that he should be able to replace the bloc of anti–New Deal conservatives with progressives that supported the New Deal. While the court-packing plan was never implemented, it shows that presidents will go to great lengths to use their executive authority to shape the bench's membership in an effort to control judicial decision-making when it is politically warranted or advantageous.

Moreover, federal and state courts will always be accountable to the people. While it is important for courts to remain independent from political pressures, the judiciary is responsive to the political will of dominant majority coalitions that are a part of the democratic process (Dahl 1957). A strong pull on the decision-making of courts is being sensitive to what the people want in exercising the judicial function. One example is *Schuette v. Coalition to Defend Affirmative Action* (2014). In response to two Supreme Court affirmative action decisions that were interpreted by Michigan officials to sanction the limited use of race-based preferences in the public schools' admission process, Michigan voters approved a 2006 ballot measure that amended the state's constitution to ban affirmative action programs in public employment, public education, and public contracting settings. In rejecting a legal challenge claiming that the ban deprived minorities of their constitutional rights to equality, the Supreme Court upheld the right of Michigan voters to ban affirmative action programs by amending the state's constitution. As Justice Anthony Kenney put it in speaking for the Court, "This case is not about how the debate about racial preferences should be resolved." Instead, "it is about who should resolve it." Consequently, the Court had to respect the decision of Michigan voters "to enact laws as a basic exercise of their democratic power."

Christopher P. Banks

See also: Constitutional Interpretation; Court Curbing; Freedom of Speech; Judicial Activism and Restraint; Judicial Federalism; Judicial Independence; Judicial Review; Merit Plans

Further Reading

Banks, Christopher P. 2000. "The Politics of Court Reform in the U.S. Courts of Appeals." *Judicature* 84: 34–43.

Banks, Christopher P., and David M. O'Brien. 2015. *The Judicial Process: Law, Courts, and Judicial Politics.* Thousand Oaks, CA: CQ Press.

Baum, Lawrence. 2008. *Judges and Their Audiences: A Perspective on Judicial Behavior.* Princeton, NJ: Princeton University Press.

Bingham, Tom. 2011. *The Rule of Law.* London: Penguin Books.

Clark, Tom S. 2011. *The Limits of Judicial Independence.* New York: Cambridge University Press.

Dahl, Robert. 1957. "Decision-Making in a Democracy: The Supreme Court as a National Policy-Maker." *Journal of Public Law* 6: 279–295.

O'Brien, David M. 2014. *Storm Center: The Supreme Court in American Politics*. New York: W. W. Norton.

Sturm, Albert L. 1982. "The Development of American State Constitutions." *Publius* 12: 57–98.

Williams, Robert F. 2009. *The Law of American State Constitutions*. New York: Oxford University Press.

Cases

Citizens United v. FEC. 2010. 558 U.S. 310.

District of Columbia v. Heller. 2008. 554 U.S. 570.

Gannon v. State. 2014. 298 Kan. 1107.

Obergefell v. Hodges. 2015. 135 S.Ct. 2584.

Schuette v. Coalition to Defend Affirmative Action. 2014. 134 S.Ct. 1623.

Part III: The Politics of Judicial Selection and Removal

State Courts

MERIT PLANS

Unlike the federal judiciary, each state has a distinct method of selecting its judges for service on the bench. In general, most states use appointments, elections, or some combination of these to select judges. While state judicial selections methods have evolved over time, most states require that state judges have to run for office or retain their seats through some type of election process. The fact that judges are elected raises questions of judicial independence and judicial accountability because it is difficult for judges to be impartial in their decision-making if they are also required to campaign for office like ordinary politicians. A significant movement to take the politics out of judicial selection is the development of merit plans in the states. Merit plans are a hybrid appointment and election process that tries to minimize political influences in the initial appointment of judges while insuring that they are held democratically accountable by elections continuous judicial service. While there are a variety of different types of merit plans in the states, increasingly they are subject to criticism and growing legislative scrutiny or reform.

The Historical Development of Merit Plans

The issue of judicial selection in state courts has been debated since the nation's founding. Of utmost concern in these discussions is to find qualified candidates for judicial service that are committed to preserving individual rights, limiting government powers, and respecting the rule of law. At the time of the American

Revolution, the colonists argued that royal judges were despotic because they were too dependent on the king's will. Thus, in the Declaration of Independence, the corrupt administration of royal justice is listed as a grievance against the king. The colonists' position, which sought to separate the judiciary from the influence of the monarch, is grounded on the principle of judicial independence, or the need to keep judges independent from politics in order to preserve their impartiality. At the same time, the colonists realized that judges had to remain accountable to the people, a core democratic value that gives citizens a basic right to control government. The struggle to strike an appropriate balance between judicial independence and judicial accountability has been at the forefront of the evolution of state judicial selection processes.

After the Revolution, the states generally staffed the courts through an appointment process that gave the legislature the power to appoint judges; less often, governors had the authority to choose judges if the legislature closely monitored the appointment process. It was not until the onset of Jacksonian Democracy in the 1830s—a populist reform movement that sought to give the people more control over governmental institutions—that many states replaced the appointment system with popular elections. Still, moving from appointments to elections led to problems caused by political corruption. Judges facing elections became less independent because they had to campaign for office and increasingly were put under the sway of the affluent, political parties, and special interest groups. Another difficulty related to the electorate was that voters who were making judicial selections were ill-informed or ignorant about the candidates they were putting on the bench. As result, after the Civil War, many states decided to change their judicial selection processes again. While several states began to use nonpartisan elections—elections that omit the partisan affiliation of judges running for office from the ballot—many others adopted merit plans as the method to install judges. These reforms have predominately defined the diversity of how states staff their courts in the modern era. Today, while most states use elections (partisan or nonpartisan) or merit plans, a few still permit either the governor or the legislature to appoint judges.

The movement to reform the state judicial selection process was inspired by progressives in the early 20th century who were alarmed by the growing corruption of courts and judges due to contestable elections. A leader for reform was Roscoe Pound, a law professor and future dean of the Harvard Law School. In a 1906 speech to the ABA, Pound warned against the dangers of the judiciary losing its independence if courts went into the political thicket and judges were forced to campaign as politicians. Pound stated, "Putting courts into politics and compelling judges to become politicians in many jurisdictions has almost destroyed the traditional respect for the bench" (1906). Pound's clarion call prompted the legal profession, academics, and other nonprofit groups to experiment with selection methods that were distinct from contestable elections.

The idea of introducing a merit plan—similar to the civil service reform in the Progressive Era, which stressed that hiring practices in administrative agencies must be based on a candidate's merits instead of political connections—took root in the American Judicature Society (AJS). Founded in 1913, the AJS was a nonpartisan group composed of judges, lawyers, and citizens who were interested in achieving the fair administration of courts and justice by improving state judicial selection methods. (For a variety of reasons, the AJS was dissolved in 2014.)

In the early 20th century, Professor Albert Kales, a cofounder of the AJS and one of its directors, proposed that state judges be selected through a procedure he called a nonpartisan court plan. The nonpartisan court plan gave elected chief justices the power to appoint lower court judges from a list of candidates recommended by a judicial council or commission (typically made up of a mixture of lawyers and judges). After serving on the bench, the appointed judges would then run in unopposed, noncompetitive elections to retain their seats. The appointed judges continued their service if they won a majority of the votes from the people in retention elections. In theory, nonpartisan court plans aimed to increase judicial independence and promote job security, which, in turn, would create a bench that was attractive to serve on and filled with legal experts. They also had the advantage of letting the people ratify judicial choices in elections. In practice, though, they reduced judicial independence because giving chief justices the sole authority to appoint lower court judges led to political corruption as the appointed judges were obliged to do the partisan bidding of the chief judges who were responsible for their selection.

While the facet of allowing chief judges to appoint judges in the initial selection process fell into disfavor over time, the element of using judicial commissions to nominate candidates remained popular as states continued to experiment with merit plans. An important and growing influence in those experiments was the role that the organized bar played in reforming judicial selection, which concluded that it was better to develop a professionalized bench with legal experts. Lawyer elites were also critical of holding judicial elections because they were thought to produce political corruption and reward voter incompetence. In 1934, California, which before then had switched to nonpartisan elections, became the first state to incorporate merit into the selection process by using judicial commissions. Under the California plan, the governor had the initial authority to appoint judges, but thereafter a commission made up of judges and the attorney general would review and then confirm the governor's choice. After the commission's ratification of the governor's appointment, the judge would begin service and then run for office in a retention election in the next general election. In the retention election, voters would be asked one question: Should the judge be retained? If a majority of voters thought so, then the judge would remain in office for a 12-year term.

A critical aspect of the California plan was using the judicial commission as a board that ratified the governor's choice after the governor initially nominated the judge for service (Shugerman 2012, 185–186). Although California governors were given considerable authority to shape the state bench with their appointments, the California system was unique in setting an established term limit for judicial service. Even so, shortly after the California plan was instituted, the ABA officially endorsed the AJS's merit format, which used judicial commissions to prepare lists of candidate for judicial service before (and not after) gubernatorial appointment. Following the ABA's lead, other states began to devise their own judicial selection methods that required judicial commissions to take a leading role, not a subordinate role, in nominating judges to the state bench. In 1940, Missouri adopted a process of judicial selection that was styled as a non-partisan court plan even though it was, later on, widely referred to as the Missouri plan. Increasingly, other states developed their own merit-based formats that typically used some combination of judicial commissions, gubernatorial appointments, and retention elections to staff the state courts.

The Characteristics of Merit Plans

Although there is a wide diversity among the types of merit plans used in the states, they generally share a number of basic features. All states with merit plans use a judicial commission to evaluate the merits of prospective nominees for the bench. Typically, judicial commissions consist of a mixture of lawyers and citizens; whereas attorney members are elected as commissioners by state or local bar associations, citizens are put into service by gubernatorial appointment (but sometimes only after legislative confirmation). After the judicial commission makes its assessment, it prepares a short list of qualified individuals and gives it to the governor for appointment. While several states limit the governor's authority by using judicial commissions to prepare a short list of nominees before the governor has a chance to make an appointment, other states restrict the appointment power further by requiring that the legislature confirm the governor's selection. Moreover, another common characteristic of merit plans is that they allow the people to weigh in on the governor's choice after the judges begin their service and have built a judicial record of performance. During the next general election that occurs following a judge's appointment to the bench, voters decide in a retention election if the sitting judges (who run unopposed on the ballot) should remain in service.

The diversity of state judicial selection processes and the use of merit plans register the difficulties in creating methods that best shield the judiciary from political influences that diminish its impartiality or judicial independence. Consequently, the continued use of merit plans is subject to ongoing debates and criticisms that invite increasing legislative scrutiny and possible reform.

For supporters of merit-based plans, the use of judicial nomination commissions in advance of gubernatorial appointment lets lawyers and citizens make informed and objective evaluations about who is best qualified to serve as a judge. The commissions, by and large, employ systematic evaluations using written rules and established procedures to screen and vet judicial candidates. In addition, the use of retention elections enhances democratic participation in a selection process that minimizes political cronyism and corruption. On the other hand, opponents of merit plans assert that they are ineffective because the electorate cannot make informed choices about sitting judges who run unopposed in retention elections. As a result, incumbent judges serve for life because they are never removed from the bench by the voters. Another common criticism is that merit plans are infused with political bias by lawyer elites who play a dominant role on judicial commissions. Accordingly, these controversies have caused some states to entertain reform measures that permit the legislature or governor to play a larger role in the selection process. While some states have considered giving the governor the power to change the composition of judicial commissions by adding or removing seats, other states have introduced proposals that require a sitting judge to repeat the entire merit review process (i.e., undertaking evaluation by a judicial commission and gubernatorial reappointment) before a retention election is held (Raftery 2013).

Christopher P. Banks

See also: Judicial Campaigns and the First Amendment; Judicial Independence; Partisan Judicial Elections and Political Money; Political Restraints on Judicial Power

Further Reading

Caufield, Rachel Paine. 2012. *Inside Merit Selection: A National Survey of Judicial Nominating Commissioners.* Des Moines, IA: American Judicature Society, the Opperman Center at Drake University. http://www.judicialselection.us/uploads/documents/JNC_Survey_ReportFINAL3_92E04A2F04E65.pdf.

Epstein, Lee, Jack Knight, and Olga Shvetsova. 2002. "Selecting Selection Systems." In *Judicial Independence at the Crossroads: An Interdisciplinary Approach*, edited by Stephen B. Burbank and Barry Friedman. Thousand Oaks, CA: Sage Publications.

National Center for State Courts. 2015. "Judicial Selection in the States." http://www.judicialselection.us/.

Pound, Roscoe. 1906. "The Causes of Popular Dissatisfaction with the Administration of Justice." *Annual Report of the American Bar Association* 29: 395–417.

Raftery, William. 2013. "Judicial Section in the States." http://www.ncsc.org/sitecore/content/microsites/future-trends-2013/home/Monthly-Trends-Articles/Judicial-Selection-in-the-States.aspx.

Shugerman, Jed Handelsman. 2012. *The People's Courts: Pursuing Judicial Independence in America*. Cambridge, MA: Harvard University Press.

Tarr, G. Alan. 2012. *Without Fear of Favor: Judicial Independence and Judicial Accountability in the States*. Stanford, CA: Stanford University Press.

PARTISAN JUDICIAL ELECTIONS AND POLITICAL MONEY

Since the founding, the U.S. Constitution has provided for a singular method of placing judges on the federal bench that requires the nomination by the president and confirmation by the Senate. The states, however, have been free to adopt any method of judicial selection appropriate to the social, political, and economic needs or wishes of the community. Over the nation's history, states have experimented with an assortment of approaches, including an appointment process (that often mirrored that of the federal level), elections (both partisan and nonpartisan), and merit systems. Partisan judicial elections, which allow voters to choose among candidates for the bench who are affiliated with political parties, were at one time considered a preferred reform that would end rank political cronyism that had eroded trust in the judicial process. Advocates for this change argued that elections would enhance democracy by making judges directly accountable to the public. Critics contend that elections have the opposite effect, eroding trust in an institution that has become beholden to well-placed interests rather than acting as an independent voice for law and justice. The debate between supporters of an independent judiciary and those who desire judicial accountability is central to the contemporary discussion over partisan elections and their continued utility.

History of Judicial Selection in the States

In the period after the signing of the Declaration of Independence, states drafted the earliest versions of their constitutions by relying heavily on the appointment of judges by either the legislature or governor. Alexander Hamilton promoted the process of judicial appointment during this period in his essay *Federalist Papers*, No. 78, defending the insulation of the arbiters of the law from the influence of politics and the power of the public through the ballot (Hamilton [1788] 1961). While the process of appointing federal judges has survived unchanged for more than two centuries, citizens in the states began to expand democratic processes related to the courts as early as the first decade of the 19th century. Mississippi became the first state to empower voters to elect judges in all trial and appellate courts in 1832, following the lead of Georgia and Indiana, which had permitted limited electoral control more than a decade earlier. In the eight decades that passed after New York adopted the practice of partisan judicial elections in 1846, every state that joined the union—19 in total—opted for this approach (Tarr 2012, 40–45). There are a number of explanations for this transformation. First, the rise of Andrew Jackson as president during the 1820s created a political revolution that promoted heightened democracy and greater control of government institutions by the public. As one proponent of judicial elections argued during the debate over the original Wisconsin state constitution in 1847, appointment of judges contravenes "the genius of the people" whose votes inspire confidence in an impartial and efficient judiciary" (Quaife 1919, 288). Second, supporters of the change hoped to end what they perceived to be the partisan and corrupt influence of legislative appointments that led to the placement of incompetent or biased judges on the bench. Substituting elections for appointments created a judiciary independent of the political and economic interests of the legislature and created a direct check by the public.

Support for partisan judicial elections began to wane during the early years of the 20th century. Critics noted that many of the complaints levied against the appointment of judges were evident in partisan elections, including the influence of political parties that often promoted candidates who served the needs of special interests rather than the public. Two alternative methods slowly began to displace partisan elections as the dominant approach for judicial selection. The first was the use of nonpartisan elections in which the partisan affiliation of the candidate for the bench was absent from the campaign process as well as the ballot. Typically, voters would select among a number of candidates during a nonpartisan primary. The two individuals who received the greatest number of votes would vie for office in a nonpartisan general election.

A second reform came with the introduction of the merit selection system, promoted by early 20th-century thinkers who wanted to eliminate legislative, gubernatorial, and popular control of judicial selection. This approach, first adopted in Missouri in 1940, relies on a judicial commission that is responsible for selecting competent candidates for judicial office. A list of qualified individuals is transmitted to the governor of the state who is then empowered to select among the roster created by the commission. Judges who gain their positions in this manner face periodic retention elections at which time the public may vote to retain or remove the judge from the bench. This injects the public into the process by allowing a measure of accountability reminiscent of partisan and nonpartisan electoral processes. Advocates for this change argued that eliminating a reliance on elections and appointments would free judges from fealty to a particular constituency—whether voters, a political party, or a branch of government—thus heightening judicial independence.

Contemporary Partisan Judicial Election Practices

Today, only a handful of states retain some form of partisan elections for the selection of judges. Four states (Alabama, Louisiana, Texas, and West Virginia) select all judges in trial and appellate courts via partisan contests. To retain their seat in these states, incumbent judges run for re-election in subsequent partisan contests. In Illinois and Pennsylvania, candidates compete in partisan elections for open seats. At the end of their terms, incumbents run in retention elections that require voters to either re-elect or remove the sitting judge, but the judges face no opponent. New Mexico preserves an element of the partisan process in the system it reformed in 1988. The governor of the state is empowered to appoint individuals to vacancies on the bench from a list of candidates generated by the judicial nominating committee. Newly appointed judges are then required to compete in a partisan contest to maintain the position at the next general election. All subsequent contests in New Mexico are retention elections. Finally, two additional states, Ohio and Michigan, use nonpartisan systems to elect judges but only after nominees for the general election are chosen through partisan primaries, creating what are effectively de facto partisan elections (Bonneau and Gann Hall 2009, 3–10).

Partisan elections in these holdout states have survived a recent trend toward reform that saw more than a dozen states substitute either merit systems or nonpartisan elections. The pressure to end the practice has come from scholars and legal practitioners alike who argue that systems of partisan elections are unable to attract qualified and competent candidates to run for available positions; undermine the independence of those who sit on the bench; and fail to serve the public in its attempt to control the content or direction of legal policy (DuBois 1980, 20). One of the most powerful contemporary voices on this issue, former associate justice of the U.S. Supreme Court Sandra Day O'Connor, maintains that judicial elections have the effect of undermining a fair and impartial process (O'Connor 2010; O'Connor 2007). She also argues that the legitimacy of courts is likely to suffer as a result of a political and electoral environment that is dominated by ever-increasing levels of partisanship.

Judicial Campaigns, Free Speech, and Political Money

Changes to the environment in which judicial races are contested have developed, in part, from a number of recent U.S. Supreme Court decisions addressing disputes regarding how judicial elections are conducted. In 2002, a divided Supreme Court announced its decision in *Republican Party of Minnesota v. White*. The case involved a First Amendment challenge to a section of the Minnesota Code of Judicial Conduct that prohibited candidates for a judicial office from announcing a position on issues related to judicial or political questions. The majority held that the restriction interfered with the speech rights of those seeking a place on the bench, striking down the Minnesota ethical regulation and those like them that silenced judicial candidates who hoped to express a position on political or legal controversies. While certainly not a mandate for those running for the bench, court-watchers worried that in the scrum of a partisan contest, incumbents and challengers alike would be compelled to voice their positions on myriad issues. Many feared the impact of the decision would erode the legitimacy of the courts by creating the perception that judges were no longer unbiased arbiters of the law but merely an extension of the partisan political process with predetermined outcomes for judicial controversies.

This concern was exacerbated by the 2010 decision by the Supreme Court in *Citizens United v. Federal Elections Commission*. In another split decision, the justices overturned a section of the 2002 Bipartisan Campaign Reform Act (commonly known as McCain-Feingold) that had prohibited campaign communications and expenditures by not-for-profit organizations during certain periods of federal campaigns. The thrust of the opinion had no direct connection to judicial campaigns and elections in the states. However, the loosening of the purse strings on independent expenditures suggested that judicial campaigns would become a target for increased ideological spending that would further complicate the maintenance of an independent judiciary and create the impression that judges were beholden to supporters who had expended significant amounts of money on their behalf.

According to data collected by the Brennan Center for Justice, the worry was well-founded. Since the decision in *Citizens United*, interest groups have poured money into judicial elections (partisan, nonpartisan, and retention) by spending more than $10 million in state supreme court races during the 2013–2014 campaign cycle—constituting 29 percent of all dollars expended in those elections. If spending by political parties is included, the total rises to 40 percent of total dollars spent, just shy of the record of 42 percent set during the 2011–2012 election year. In six states, more that $28 million dollars was spent across races for 17 seats to state high courts averaging more than $1.6 million per contested judicial position, more than double the average spent in similar elections in 1990. Significantly, much of the money that is raised and expended comes from donors whose identity is not known to voters, limiting the ability to know to whom judges may be accountable for their election to the bench.

A pair of recent holdings by the Supreme Court, however, indicates a willingness by the justices to recognize the potential impact of unregulated campaigns for judicial seats. In *Caperton v. Massey Coal Company* (2009), the justices reviewed a decision of the West Virginia Supreme Court that voided a trial court award of $50 million against the Massey Coal Company over contract disputes with the petitioner. After the trial verdict, Don Blankenship, the president and chairman of Massey, contributed more than $2.5 million to an organization created to support the candidacy of Brent Benjamin in a partisan contest to unseat the incumbent Supreme Court Justice Warren McGraw. Benjamin went on to defeat McGraw and proved a pivotal vote to overturn the award against Blankenship's company. Writing for the majority, Justice Anthony Kennedy held that the Fourteenth Amendment's due process clause demands that judges recuse themselves from cases in which "the probability of actual bias on the part of the judge or decision maker is too high to be constitutionally tolerable." For the Court, Blankenship's contributions to the election of Justice Benjamin appeared to unduly and inappropriately influence the outcome of the case.

In 2015, the Supreme Court again addressed the effect of money on judicial elections when it ruled in the case of *Williams-Yulee v. Florida Bar*. Rules established under the Florida Code of Judicial Conduct prohibit those seeking an elected position on the bench from personally soliciting campaign contributions. Williams-Yulee, a candidate in a nonpartisan race for trial court judge, sent a letter to local voters that solicited donations to her campaign. The Florida Bar disciplined Williams-Yulee for ignoring the Code, fining her $1,860 and issuing a public reprimand for her actions. She challenged the ruling by arguing that it violated her First Amendment speech rights. A majority of the justices held that the Code and sanction from the Florida Bar was justified to help maintain the integrity of the judicial branch, and to generate public confidence in the institution. *Williams-Yulee*, along with *Caperton*, appears to counter-balance the Court's previous holdings that created an environment of nearly uncontrolled campaign communications and spending. The justices used these cases to establish outer limits for the activity in which judicial candidates might engage. In establishing boundaries on the process of campaigning for office, the Supreme Court has suggested that the value of independence is necessary for the continued legitimacy of judges and the judicial branch.

The Supreme Court's decisions over the past dozen years expose the problems that reformers have criticized for more than a century. The judiciary is often considered a unique branch of government that is intended to avoid the political and partisan fray typical among legislative or executive electoral processes. Partisan judicial elections may create the impression that judges are biased toward particular interests that supported their candidacies or beholden to constituencies that were instrumental to their election. The tension registered by the holdings of the Court that stress the need for accountability to the electorate while fostering the desire for an independent and unbiased judiciary continues to fuel the debate over the utility of partisan election of judges.

Charles F. Jacobs

See also: Campaign Finance; Judicial Campaigns and the First Amendment; Judicial Independence; Merit Plans

Further Reading

Bonneau, Chris W., and Melinda Gann Hall. 2009. *In Defense of Judicial Elections*. New York: Routledge.

DuBois, Philip L. 1980. *From Ballot to Bench: Judicial Elections and the Question for Accountability*. Austin: University of Texas Press.

Gibson, James L. 2012. *Electing Judges: The Surprising Effects of Campaigning on Judicial Legitimacy*. Chicago: University of Chicago Press.

Greytak, Scott, Alicia Bannon, Allyse Falce, and Linda Casey. 2015. *Bankrolling the Bench: The New Politics of Judicial Elections 2013–14*, edited by Laurie Kinney. New York: Brennan Center for Justice at New York University School of Law. http://newpoliticsreport.org/report/2013-14/.

Hamilton, Alexander. (1787–88) 1961. "Federalist Paper 78." *The Federalist Papers*, edited by Jacob E. Cooke. Middletown, CT: Wesleyan University Press.

National Center for State Courts. 2015. "Judicial Selections in the States." http://www.judicialselection.us/judicial_selection/.

O'Connor, Sandra Day. 2007. "Fair and Independent Courts: Remarks by Justice O'Connor." *Georgetown Law Journal* 95: 897–898.

O'Connor, Sandra Day. 2010. "Choosing (and Recusing) Our State Court Justices Wisely." *Georgetown Law Journal* 99: 151–156.

Quaife, Milo M., ed. 1919. *The Convention of 1846: Wisconsin Historical Society Constitutional Series, Volume II*. Madison, WI: Democrat Printing Company.

Tarr, G. Alan. 2012. *Without Fear or Favor: Judicial Independence and Judicial Accountability in the States*. Stanford, CA: Stanford University Press.

Cases

Caperton, et al. v. A.T. Massey Coal Co., et al. 2009. 556 U.S. 868.

Citizens United v. Federal Election Commission. 2010. 558 U.S. 310.

Republican Party of Minnesota, et al. v. White, Chairperson, Minnesota Board of Judicial Standards et al. 2002. 536 U.S. 765.

Williams-Yulee v. Florida Bar. 2015. 135 S.Ct. 1656.

JUDICIAL CAMPAIGNS AND THE FIRST AMENDMENT

Under Article II of the U.S. Constitution, federal judges are placed on the bench after presidential nomination and confirmation by the Senate, that is, after it gives its "advice and consent." In contrast, state judges are predominately recruited to serve after the voters have weighed in on their acceptability as judicial officers in elections. At least 39 states elect trial or appellate judges to serve in state judiciaries. Whereas many states have merit plans—a hybrid method of judicial selection that combines gubernatorial appointment with retention elections—other states hold either partisan or nonpartisan election contests to staff the judiciary. Under this framework, a significant issue in law and politics is whether judges campaigning for office violate constitutional principles or their ethical obligations by either asking for campaign contributions or by expressing their political or legal viewpoints about current issues of the day during judicial campaigns. Complicating the constitutional issue is whether the legal rules that permit donors or organized groups to make largely unregulated expenditures or contributions in political campaigns apply with the same force to judicial campaigns. Striking an appropriate constitutional balance between preserving judicial independence and protecting rights to free speech are the focus of U.S. Supreme Court cases that try to set legal guidelines for aspiring judges to follow in state judicial elections.

Are Judges "Politicians in Black Robes?"

A growing issue in law and politics is whether state judges should be evaluated by the same legal and ethical standards that apply to politicians who seek elected office in the legislative or executive departments of government. Especially in the aftermath of the controversial U.S. Supreme Court's rulings in *Citizens United v. FEC* (2010) and *McCutcheon v. FEC* (2014), wealthy donors and special interest groups with an ideological agenda are permitted under the First Amendment to contribute (and spend) large sums of money to political campaigns without significant legal restrictions or penalties. The infusion of largely unregulated money into the political system has also substantially affected how judicial elections in the states are conducted. The lack of legal constraints has encouraged well-funded individuals and groups to target judicial candidates or electoral contests in key state appellate courts that threaten, or facilitate, vested ideological interests. In the 2013–2014 election cycle, a study from a coalition of nonpartisan law and policy institutes reported that more than $34.5 million was spent in 19 states holding state supreme court elections (Greytak et al. 2015). Of that total, roughly $10 million (29 percent) was spent by outside special interests that are not legally obliged to disclose their donors or their expenditure amounts. As with ordinary political contests, a large proportion of the spending is directed at paying for TV advertisements that either praise or attack judicial candidates on certain policy or legal issues (Greytak et al. 2015). To illustrate, a common theme of judicial elections is to portray judges as either being too tough or too soft on crime, resulting in ads from conservative and liberal interests that accuse candidates of fighting to "protect sexual predators," being "sympathetic to rapists," or having a track record of refusing to prosecute sex offenders (Shepherd and Kang 2014). Political attack ads are not confined to one ideological theme or political party, however. Often they originate from the respective political positions of conservatives who seek to protect business or insurance interests and liberals who work on behalf of labor unions and trial lawyers on contentious issues of tort reform, government overreach, environmental protection, family values, and criminal punishment issues, among others.

The increasing politicization of the state judicial selection process has transformed judicial elections and campaigns into contests that are "nastier, nosier, and costlier" in recent decades, replete with judges that arguably are being reduced to merely "politicians in black robes" (Schotland 1998; Geyh 2003). While some scholars suggest that judicial elections reinforce important principles of democratic participation and judicial accountability, other critics, including prominent judges, assert that they are destructive because they undermine principles of judicial independence and judicial impartiality, which, in turn, diminishes public confidence in the courts. Whereas retired Supreme Court Justice Sandra Day O'Connor has long argued that the politicization of judicial elections seriously threatens judicial impartiality, sitting Supreme Court Justice Ruth Bader Ginsburg has denounced *Citizens United* because it has led to the political system "being polluted by money" (O'Connor 2013; Holpuch 2015). The issue of whether state judicial candidates are merely acting like politicians in black robes thus raises important questions about how their campaign speech or conduct in raising money complies with First Amendment principles of free speech and ethical codes of conduct established by the legal profession.

Republican Party of Minnesota v. White

In *Republican Party of Minnesota v. White* (2002), a sharply divided Supreme Court invalidated Minnesota's announce clause—an ethical prohibition enacted by the state bar association that put strict limits on what judicial candidates could say in announcing their positions on controversial legal and political issues. In holding that the announce clause was a content-based restriction that violated the First Amendment, Justice Antonin Scalia and four other justices, Chief Justice William H. Rehnquist and Justices Anthony Kennedy, Sandra Day O'Connor, and Clarence Thomas, reasoned that judicial elections cannot be differentiated from political campaigns in terms of the protections guaranteed by the First Amendment. As a result, judges, as well as politicians, enjoy the freedom to announce their positions in electoral contests, a traditional forum for expressing and discussing ideas about public policy issues within a democracy. In contrast, a forceful dissenting opinion, written by Justice Ruth Bader Ginsburg and joined by Justices John Paul Stevens, David Souter, and Stephen Breyer, maintained that the bar association's rule must be upheld under an assumption that judges are fundamentally different from ordinary politicians. Unlike politicians, who serve as representatives of the people and remain acutely responsive to popular will and desires, judges have an ethical duty to render impartial justice that is not tainted with the temptation of political bias or favors. As Justice Ginsburg put it, "Judges . . . are not political actors" because "they do not sit as representatives of particular persons, communities, or parties" (*Republican Party* 2002, 806). Accordingly, Minnesota's announce clause is constitutional because it reasonably sought to insure that judges would stay impartial in their decision-making, a virtue that strengthens judicial legitimacy.

Post-*White* Limitations on Free Speech in Judicial Elections

In general, the decision to expand the free speech rights of judges in elections
is an extension of the Roberts Court's commitment to guaranteeing the expression of controversial speakers, such as for antihomosexual protesters that picket
a fallen soldier's funeral (*Snyder v. Phelps* 2011), sellers of violent video games to
children (*Brown v. Entertainment Merchants Association* 2011), distributors of videos
depicting animal cruelty (*U.S. v. Stevens* 2010), and liars that claim they earned
esteemed military awards and honors (*U.S. v. Alvarez* 2012) (Howe 2015). Still,
other decisions, such as *Caperton v. Massey Coal Company* (2009) and *Williams-
Yulee v. Florida Bar* (2015), indicate that the Supreme Court is willing to enforce
ethical rules against judges if they engage in election and campaign activity that
present conflicts of interest or otherwise threatens judicial impartiality. In *Caperton*, the justices established a standard of recusal that requires judges to disqualify or remove themselves from court proceedings that are likely to create a
serious risk of actual bias on the part of judicial decision makers. The *Caperton*
principle was announced in light of facts showing that the president of a coal
company donated more than $2.5 million of campaign cash to the opponent of
a Supreme Court justice that voted to disallow a large damage award in favor
of the coal business. After the targeted Supreme Court justice was defeated in
the election, the justice who won the partisan contest was instrumental in subsequently voting to reinstate the damage award, thus prompting the Supreme
Court to announce its recusal standard as a constitutional principle.

Whereas *Caperton* was based on a rationale that prevents judges from being
embroiled in conflicts of interest, *Williams-Yulee* was directed at precluding
judges from making personal campaign solicitations in judicial elections. As in
many other states, Florida ethical canons let campaign committees engage in
fund-raising activities in judicial elections; but it also prohibited judicial candidates from making personal solicitations for contributions. Even so, in an effort
to win a position on a county court, Williams-Yulee sent a letter to local voters
asking for contributions to help fund her candidacy. After she lost the primary
election, Williams-Yulee challenged the Florida bar's decision to initiate a disciplinary action against her on the grounds that it violated her First Amendment rights. In upholding Florida's personal solicitation ban, the Supreme Court
ruled in a 5–4 decision that the bar association had a compelling interest
in preserving judicial impartiality and integrity through its ethical rules. In
announcing the judgment, Chief Justice John Roberts and Justices Ruth Bader
Ginsburg, Stephen Breyer, Sonia Sotomayor, and Elena Kagan all agreed that
the rule reasonably protected the principle of judicial integrity by fostering the
impartiality of legal decisions, which ultimately fostered public confidence in
the judiciary. Unlike what the Court intimated in *Republican Party*, the justices
in *Williams-Yulee* differentiated judicial candidates from ordinary politicians in
the First Amendment context of whether judges should be allowed to make personal solicitations in their own campaigns. As the Court flatly declared, judges

"are not politicians, even when they come to the bench by way of the ballot" (*Williams-Yulee v. Florida Bar* 2015). In dissent, the author of the controlling opinion in *Republican Party*, Justice Antonin Scalia, along with Justices Samuel Alito, Anthony Kennedy, and Clarence Thomas, maintained that it was inconsequential that the speakers in a political election happened to be judges. Instead, the dissenters asserted that the Florida canon operated to stifle the free speech rights of judicial candidates who merely sought to communicate their political messages to the voters, a core value underlying the constitutional principles of democratic participation and governmental accountability.

Christopher P. Banks

See also: Campaign Finance; Freedom of Speech; Judicial Campaigns and the First Amendment; Judicial Independence; Judicial Recusal; Merit Plans; Partisan Judicial Elections and Political Money; Presidential Appointments and Court Packing

Further Reading

Geyh, Charles Gardner. 2003. "Why Judicial Elections Stink." *Ohio State Law Journal* 64: 43–79.

Gibson, James L. 2012. *Electing Judges: The Surprising Effects of Campaigning on Judicial Legitimacy.* Chicago: University of Chicago Press.

Greytak, Scott, Alicia Bannon, Allyse Falce, and Linda Casey. 2015. *Bankrolling the Bench: The New Politics of Judicial Elections 2013–2014.* Washington, D.C.: Justice at Stake, Brennan Center for Justice, and National Institute on Money in State Politics. http://newpoliticsreport.org/app/uploads/JAS-NPJE-2013-14.pdf.

Holpuch, Amanda. 2015. "Ruth Bader Ginsburg: I Would Overturn Supreme Court's Citizens United Ruling." *The Guardian*, February 4. http://www.theguardian.com/law /2015/feb/04/ruth-bader-ginsburg-supreme-court-citizens-united.

Howe, Amy. 2015. "In Plain English: Justices Finally Find Speech They Do Not Like— and It's by (Would-Be)." *SCOTUSblog*, April 29. http://www.scotusblog.com/2015/04 /in-plain-english-justices-finally-find-speech-they-do-not-like-and-its-by-would-be -judges/.

O'Connor, Sandra Day. 2013. "Retired U.S. Supreme Court Justice Sandra Day O'Connor's Speech at NCSL's 2013 Legislative Summit." *National Conference for State Legislatures* (Video), August 12. http://www.ncsl.org/research/civil-and-criminal-jus tice/general-session-sandra-day-oconnor-video.aspx.

Schotland, Roy A. 1998. "Comment." *Law and Contemporary Problems* 61: 149–155.

Shepherd, Joanna, and Michael S. Kang. 2014. "Skewed Justice: Citizens United, Television Advertising and State Supreme Court Justices' Decisions in Criminal Cases." *Skewed Justice.* http://skewedjustice.org/.

Shugerman, Jed Handelsman. 2012. *The People's Courts: Pursuing Judicial Independence in America.* Cambridge, MA: Harvard University Press.

Tarr, G. Alan. 2012. *Without Fear of Favor: Judicial Independence and Judicial Accountability in the States.* Stanford, CA: Stanford University Press.

Cases

Brown v. Entertainment Merchants Association. 2011. 131 S.Ct. 2729.

Caperton v. A.T. Massey Coal Company, Inc. 2009. 556 U.S. 868.

Citizens United v. FEC. 2010. 558 U.S. 310.

McCutcheon v. FEC. 2014. 134 S.Ct. 1434.

Republican Party of Minnesota v. White. 2002. 536 U.S. 765.

Snyder v. Phelps. 2011. 562 U.S. 443.

U.S. v. Alvarez. 2012. 132 S.Ct. 2537.

U.S. v. Stevens. 2010. 559 U.S. 460.

Williams-Yulee v. Florida Bar. 2015. 135 S.Ct. 1656.

JUDICIAL RECUSAL

Americans expect judges to be impartial arbiters of the law; therefore, judges should not be biased for or against one of the parties that appear before them. Because judges settle private disputes and issue decisions that affect public policy, it is essential that the public have confidence that the decisions of judges are based on neutrality and fairness and not infused with partiality toward or prejudice against one of the litigants. In short, there should be no conflict of interest between a judge and a litigant, and even if judges can be impartial when such a conflict exists, they need to avoid the appearance of bias to ensure public confidence in judicial decisions. Accordingly, when judges have a favorable or unfavorable bias toward one of the parties in a case (or counsel representing a party), they should not hear the case; that is, they should recuse themselves, or voluntarily step down from a case. If judges suspected of bias do not recuse themselves, then litigants can move to disqualify them. The issue of voluntary judicial recusal, or involuntary disqualification, seems straightforward—judges should not hear cases if there is a conflict with one of the litigants or attorneys. Nevertheless, recusal is a complex issue because one cannot easily determine whether a particular relationship between a judge and a litigant is severe enough to warrant disqualification. Many rules and controversies surround judicial disqualification. There is a long-standing history underlying the concept of recusal, and it has been practiced routinely in federal and state courts. More recently, the growing importance of state judicial elections have raised ongoing controversies concerning judicial disqualification.

History of Judicial Disqualification in Federal Court

The issue of judicial disqualification dates back nearly 700 years to the early years of the English common law. Initially, litigants could insist that judges be disqualified by merely suspecting that that the judge harbored bias; however, by the 18th century, England tightened its recusal laws so that judges would be disqualified only if they had a financial relationship with one of the parties in a case. Upon the founding of the United States, Congress adopted a similar recusal policy for federal judges that applied only when a judge had a financial interest in one of the parties in a case. Throughout most of the 19th century, Congress retained this standard, only expanding the recusal requirement in a few cases, such as a judge's familial association with one of the parties.

By the late 19th century and early 20th century, Congress passed statutes that expanded reasons for judicial disqualification. For example, in 1891, Congress forbade federal appellate judges from deciding cases in which they had issued a ruling from a lower court. In 1911, Congress expanded recusal to include cases in which a judge was a material witness and, more importantly, in instances where a judge exhibited bias toward one of the litigants. The latter reason for disqualification was relevant in the U.S. Supreme Court decision in *Berger v. United States* (1921). In this case, the Court overturned Berger's criminal conviction because the presiding federal judge, Kenesaw Mountain Landis, refused to recuse himself after expressing blatant prejudice against Germans—Berger was an Austrian immigrant. Nevertheless, the Court did rule that federal judges enjoy a significant amount of discretion to decide whether there is sufficient reason to remove themselves from cases in which a litigant asks for their disqualification.

The recusal controversy resurfaced in the 1960s after the U.S. Senate rejected Clement Haynsworth's nomination to the Supreme Court because, among other reasons, he had not disqualified himself in an appeals court case despite having a financial interest in one of the parties. In 1972, the ABA, the trade association regulating lawyers, established the Code of Judicial Conduct to regulate the ethical behavior of judges. This code required judges to recuse themselves whenever there was a "reasonable" concern about their impartiality. In 1974, Congress amended statutes governing judicial recusal by essentially adopting the ABA's recusal requirement.

Currently, the primary federal statute regulating judicial disqualification is 28 U.S.C. § 455. Title 28 of the U.S. Code covers rules of judicial procedure, and § 455 focuses specifically on judicial disqualification. This law requires that all federal judges (district court, appeals court, and Supreme Court) and magistrates must recuse themselves in any case in which their "impartiality might be reasonably questioned." The statute lists specific examples of bias, including personal prejudice, association with the case prior to assuming the current judicial position, and personal or familial financial interest in one of the parties. The statute mandates that judges be familiar with their personal or familial relationships with any party that might appear before them. Moreover, the statute requires disqualification not only for actual bias but also for the appearance of bias. The existence of this statute might lead people to believe that recusal is common, but judicial ethics also require federal judges to hear cases to which they are assigned, unless one of the specified items of bias has been violated. Judges cannot use recusal as a pretext to avoid challenging or distasteful cases.

Judicial Recusal in State Courts

In addition to federal courts, state court judges are also subject to disqualification rules, but unlike the uniform regulations for the federal judiciary, each state makes its own rules governing judicial disqualification. Nevertheless, all states employ the same general rules as the federal government—disqualification is required when judges have a financial or personal interest in one of the parties or attorneys appearing before them. Moreover, the U.S. Supreme Court has required state judges to disqualify themselves because of the Fourteenth Amendment's due process clause, which requires that states provide all citizens with due process of law. Biased judges will subvert the application of "due process of law." For example, in *Tumey v. Ohio* (1927), the U.S. Supreme Court overturned Tumey's conviction for possession of alcohol (during the Prohibition era) because his case was decided by mayor of the Village of North College Hill, Ohio, who, along with other law enforcement personnel, were allowed to keep a portion of the fines they collected from convictions in prohibition cases. As Chief Justice William Howard Taft wrote in the Court's opinion, "It certainly violates the Fourteenth Amendment, and deprives a defendant in a criminal case of due process of law, to subject his liberty or property to the judgment of a court the judge of which has a direct, personal, substantial pecuniary interest in reaching a conclusion against him in his case." Similarly, in *Ward v. Village of Monroeville* (1972), the U.S. Supreme Court overruled a practice in Monroeville, Ohio that allowed the mayor to hear traffic cases, even though the mayor is responsible for the finances in the city. Writing for the majority, Justice William Brennan argued that this system does not guarantee a neutral arbiter because the city derives much of its revenue from traffic fines; therefore, the policy violates the defendants' due process rights. Justices William Rehnquist and Byron White dissented, stating that, "To justify striking down the Ohio system on its face, the Court must assume either that every mayor-judge in every case will disregard his oath and administer justice contrary to constitutional demands or that this will happen often enough to warrant the prophylactic, per se rule urged by the petitioner. I can make neither assumption. . . ."

Judges' actions prior to assuming the bench can also raise recusal issues, particularly in state courts. For example, prior to serving on the Pennsylvania Supreme Court, Justice Ronald D. Castille was the district attorney of Philadelphia, and, in that capacity, he sought the death penalty for a defendant named Terrance Williams. Williams was sentenced to death, but a judge vacated the sentence after ruling that the prosecutors failed to reveal evidence that Williams's victim sexually abused him. Pennsylvania prosecutors appealed the ruling, and Justice Castille sided with the other justices in overturning the lower court judge's decision and reinstating the death sentence. Justice Castille did not recuse himself, despite the role he played in Williams's sentencing. In 2016, in *Williams v. Pennsylvania*, the U.S. Supreme Court directed the supreme court of Pennsylvania to reconsider the defendant's claims of prosecutorial misconduct in light of the Fourteenth Amendment due process requirement that judges recuse themselves in situations where there is a "significant, personal involvement" in the prosecution.

Judicial Elections and Recusal

The fact that many state judges are elected presents an additional disqualification issue. Whereas federal judges are appointed by the president, confirmed by the senate, and serve life terms (unless they are impeached and removed from office for misconduct), many states use elections to select their judges. The suitability of elected versus appointed judges is the subject of considerable debate, but the judicial elections pose an additional controversy because attorneys and business leaders are often very active in judicial elections. Therefore, many legal observes suspect that elected judges favor litigants or attorneys who supported their campaigns and are biased against litigants or attorneys who supported their opponents.

Furthermore, campaign contributions play a major role in judicial elections, which creates significant controversy in light of judicial disqualification. Over the past couple of decades, campaign contributions to judicial candidates have increased significantly, and there is considerable debate over the propriety of raising money for judicial races in general. In fact, the American Bar Association's Model Code of Judicial Conduct Canon 5C(2) prohibits judicial candidates from directly raising money for their campaigns. Instead, judicial candidates must establish separate committees that raise money on their behalf. By separating campaign finance from the judicial candidate, this regulation presumably limits campaign contributions from biasing judges. However, states also require public disclosure of all campaign contributions, even for judicial elections; consequently, judges are undoubtedly able to discover who contributed to their campaigns and who contributed to their opponents. Thus, there is still a possibility that judges could be biased, favoring attorneys and litigants who contributed to their campaigns, or they could be prejudiced against litigants and attorneys who contributed to opponents. At a minimum, contributions to judicial campaigns suggest the appearance of impropriety.

The U.S. Supreme Court has provided some guidance on settling the controversy of disqualification and campaign finance in *Caperton v. Massey Coal Company* (2009). This case began in 2002 when a West Virginia jury awarded Hugh Caperton $50 million in a civil suit against Massey Coal because of Massey's fraudulent actions to destroy Caperton's business. As Massey appealed this verdict to the Supreme Court of Appeals—West Virginia's highest court—its

CEO and president Don Blankenship donated money to Supreme Court of Appeals candidate Brent Benjamin, who was challenging incumbent Justice Warren McGraw. In addition to contributing the maximum $1,000 to Benjamin's campaign committee, Blankenship donated $2.5 million to an independent committee that supported Benjamin and opposed McGraw, and he spent $500,000 on separate advertisements in support of Benjamin and against McGraw. In fact, Blankenship was by far the most dominant contributor to Benjamin's campaign. Benjamin won the race; therefore, when the West Virginia Supreme Court of Appeals was about to hear the appeal of the verdict, Caperton petitioned to disqualify Justice Benjamin, arguing that the magnitude of Blankenship's contributions was sufficient evidence of Justice Benjamin's bias. Claiming that he was impartial, Justice Benjamin refused to recuse himself. In 2007, Justice Benjamin provided the deciding vote in a 3–2 decision that overturned the $50 million verdict.

Caperton appealed this decision to the U.S. Supreme Court, arguing that Justice Blankenship's refusal to recuse himself violated his Fourteenth Amendment due process rights because Blankenship's involvement in Justice Benjamin's campaign prevented Caperton from receiving a fair and impartial hearing. Recognizing that none of the recusal precedents addressed election contributions, Justice Anthony Kennedy, who wrote for the five-justice majority, noted that Justice Benjamin's benefit in this case was analogous to the mayor's direct benefit in *Tumey*. Justice Kennedy argued that the Court did not need to find tangible evidence of bias to require disqualification; rather, he employed a standard of "probability of bias." Kennedy concluded that, "Not every contribution by a litigant or attorney creates a probability of bias that requires a judge's recusal, but this is an exceptional case." Conversely, Chief Justice John Roberts wrote for the four dissenters arguing that, "the standard the majority articulates—'probability of bias'—fails to provide clear, workable guidance for future cases." The *Caperton v. Massey* case concerned major financial contributions to a judicial candidate; consequently, it reflects an extreme case. The Supreme Court ruling has not provided any guidance on whether more modest contributions should require disqualification; consequently, the bulk of the controversy over campaign contributions and judicial disqualification remains undecided.

Steven C. Tauber

See also: Partisan Judicial Elections and Political Money; The Politics of Judicial Selection and Removal; The Role of the American Bar Association

Further Reading

American Bar Association. 2015. "Model Code of Judicial Ethics: Canon 5." http://www .americanbar.org/groups/professional_responsibility/publications/model_code_of _judicial_conduct/model_code_of_judicial_conduct_canon_5.html.

Flamm, R. 1996. *Judicial Disqualification; Recusal and Disqualification of Judges*. Boston: Little Brown & Company.

Geyh, C. G. 2010. *Judicial Disqualification: An Analysis of Federal Law*. 2nd ed. Washington, D.C.: Federal Judicial Center.

Cases

Berger v. United States. 1921. 255 U.S. 22.

Caperton v. Massey Coal Company. 2009. 556 U.S. 868.

Tumey v. Ohio. 1927. 273 U.S. 510.

Ward v. Village of Monroeville. 1972. 409 U.S. 57.

Williams v. Pennsylvania. 2016. 136 S.Ct. 1899.

Federal Courts

PRESIDENTIAL APPOINTMENTS AND COURT PACKING

The federal judiciary, especially the Supreme Court, plays a key role in shaping public policy, so a variety of political factors influence the selection of judges. At the forefront are the nominee's ideological policy preferences—liberal or conservative—because judicial decisions can impact the president's policy agenda. Additionally, these judges are uniquely positioned to continue representing the president's preferences, even after leaving the White House. For example, calls for Justice Ruth Bader Ginsburg to retire before President Barack Obama left office were motivated by the desire for a Democrat to name her successor in the event a Republican won the 2016 election. Additional factors, such as the nominee's qualifications, party loyalty, and personal characteristics that could diversify the bench, are also taken into consideration. Presidents emphasize each of these factors differently based upon the court on which the nominee would serve and the amount of opposition expected from the Senate during the confirmation process (O'Brien 2003). Despite these differences, presidents use different criteria in the judicial selection process, but all methods are inherently political in nature.

Judicial Selection Criteria

Article II of the U.S. Constitution bestows the power to appoint "judges of the Supreme Court and all other offices of the United States" to the president "with the advice and consent of the Senate. . . ." Because Article III provides members of the federal judiciary with life tenure, judicial appointments quickly became a way for presidents to protect their legacy and have a lasting impact on public policy once out of office. As a result, presidents attempt to pack the courts with ideologically like-minded nominees. However, to ensure that nominations will be confirmed by the Senate, presidents must also consider the candidate's qualifications, or objective merit (Abraham 1983). Suitable nominees have an educational background or training in the law, professional legal expertise and competence, a personality suited for the bench, and excellent written and oral communication skills. In other words, a nominee's credentials must demonstrate that they have the knowledge and ability to serve as a federal judge or Supreme Court justice. However, because nearly all candidates can be deemed worthy of being nominated based on their credentials, presidential nominations are best explained as motivated by ideology.

In addition to a nominee's ideology and qualifications, presidents also consider party loyalty and demographic factors that could add diversity to the courts. When nominations are based on political patronage, presidents typically nominate personal friends or political associates. For example, President Lyndon B. Johnson nominated Abe Fortas, a close friend, to the Supreme Court in 1968 (O'Brien 2003), and President Obama nominated the solicitor general, Elena Kagan, in 2010.

Although presidents assess how a nominee can diversify the bench, the federal judiciary is composed of mostly white, Protestant males. Starting with the Carter administration, more women have been appointed to the federal bench, and, in 1981, President Ronald Reagan nominated the first woman, Sandra Day O'Connor, to serve on the Supreme Court. She would later be joined by Ruth Bader Ginsburg during the Clinton administration and Sonia Sotomayor and Elena Kagan, both nominated by President Obama.

Less progress has been made with respect to racial, ethnic, and religious diversity. Since the 1950s, roughly 8 out of 10 federal judges are white, even though African Americans and Hispanics comprise a substantial portion of the American population. In regards to the Supreme Court, only two African Americans (Thurgood Marshall and Clarence Thomas) and one Latina (Sonia Sotomayor) have served on the bench. The religious composition of the federal judiciary has remained roughly stable since the Kennedy administration with 50 to 60 percent of judges identifying as Protestant, 25 to 30 percent Catholic, and 10 to 15 percent Jewish (Banks and O'Brien 2015).

Patterns of Judicial Selection

The apparent lack of diversity in the federal courts underscores how some presidents place a different emphasis on each of these four selection criteria: ideology, merit, partisanship, and diversity. For example, President Obama has filled judicial vacancies with women, minorities, and gays and lesbians. A focus on how a nominee can add diversity to the court is a characteristic of trying to fill the bench with candidates that will be more acceptable to senators across the ideological spectrum. In addition to President Obama, Republican presidents Dwight D. Eisenhower and Gerald Ford and Democratic presidents Jimmy Carter and Bill Clinton used this approach to selecting nominees. Although representative factors are important, these presidents have emphasized the nominee's qualifications while also taking into account party loyalty. Objective merit, instead of ideological compatibility, has been the primary consideration for these presidents in appointing judges to the federal bench.

Conversely, a nominee's ideology has been of utmost importance for certain Republican presidents because they view judicial selection as an opportunity to exert power over the federal judiciary and to pursue political policy agendas. Richard Nixon first took this approach when he refused to nominate so-called activist judges and those who would not support his law and order policy agenda. Subsequent Republican presidents—Ronald Reagan, George H. W. Bush, and George W. Bush—also prioritized ideology in an effort to ensure that the ideological content of decisions, particularly those made by the Supreme Court, remained conservative. For example, Ronald Reagan nominated Antonin Scalia to the Supreme Court and elevated William Rehnquist to Chief Justice after the retirement of Warren Burger. Similarly, after Chief Justice Rehnquist's death, President George W. Bush also sought a conservative replacement and nominated John Roberts.

Rather than selecting nominees based on ideology and willingness to support the president's policy agenda, other presidents have prioritized party loyalty. Under this approach to judicial selection, presidents Franklin D. Roosevelt, Harry Truman, John F. Kennedy, and Lyndon B. Johnson viewed nominations as essentially a reward for party patronage. Presidents also take into account the candidate's qualifications and whether the nominee can serve as a symbolic representation of an underrepresented demographic on the Supreme Court or other circuit courts of appeals. For example, President Lyndon Johnson nominated the first African American, Thurgood Marshall, to the Supreme Court in 1967. Regardless of how presidents approach judicial selection, numerous individuals can be deemed qualified to fill a vacancy within the federal judiciary. As a result, the nomination process involves identifying and vetting candidates with much attention paid to whether the candidate will likely be confirmed by the Senate.

The Nomination Process

Notably, and beginning with the Carter administration, judicial selection increasingly has been delegated to attorneys from the Department of Justice (DOJ) and White House counsel and advisors with the expectation that selections agree with presidential legal policy preferences. In an effort to receive recommendations that would diversify the federal bench, President Jimmy Carter created nominating or merit commissions composed of lawyers and nonlaw-yers with diverse backgrounds. In contrast, the Reagan administration elimi-nated the use of nominating commissions and created another judicial selection body, the Federal Judicial Selection Committee, which was composed of executive branch attorneys who would work with the DOJ's Office of Legal Policy to identify and screen potential candidates. Following Reagan, all presi-dents thereafter have relied upon this committee because of the time-consuming nature of the vetting process that involves examining the nominee's qualifi-cations, finances, health, professional experience, judicial philosophy, and writ-ten record (e.g., academic writing in law reviews and judicial opinions). Some, but not all, presidents also accept input from interest groups, such as the ABA, which rates candidates as well qualified, qualified, or not qualified based on their merits in an attempt to minimize the political nature of judicial selection. However, President George W. Bush refused to accept input from the ABA because he deemed their ratings as unacceptable as they were from what he thought was a liberal organization that "takes public positions on divisive political, legal, and social issues that come before the courts" (Gonzales 2001).

The Role of the Senate

The Senate also participates in the nomination process, which can provide insight into whether the nominee will be confirmed, through the traditions of senatorial courtesy and the blue slip process. Senatorial courtesy entails the president discussing the nomination with the senators from the nominee's home state. If they object, the Senate's confirmation vote will reflect these preferences, and a nominee is not likely to be confirmed. This process has the most impact on federal district court nominations because jurisdictions are limited to one state while a circuit court's jurisdiction spans multiple states; however, sena-tors are increasingly requesting to be consulted when filling these vacancies because they want their political preferences to be respected by the president.

The blue slip process formalizes senatorial courtesy and occurs after the pres-ident has submitted his official nomination to the chair of the Senate Judiciary Committee (SJC). In turn, the chair of the SJC sends a form on blue paper to both of the home-state senators requesting their opinion on the nominee. Sen-ators can either return the blue slip and support the nomination or keep it and essentially veto the nomination because the SJC chair waits until both blue slips have been returned before scheduling confirmation hearings. Consequently, senators can also use blue slips as a way to delay the confirmation process. Although this process appears to provide senators with considerable power over judicial selection, blue slips are simply a tradition that can be used and honored at the discretion of the SJC chair. For example, Senator Orrin Hatch (R-Utah) allowed home-state Republicans to use blue slips to delay confirmation hearings or block nominations during the Clinton administration, but when George W. Bush was president, hearings were held, even if home-state Democrats did not return their blue slips. This example also highlights the political nature of the judicial selection process in which the SJC chair can use blue slips in a way to aid or impede the president from packing the courts (Banks and O'Brien 2015).

Confirmation Hearings

After all the blue slips are returned, the SJC will evaluate the nominee's merits and hold confirmation hearings. The nominee's educational background, professional qualifications, ABA rating, and written record are again compiled and evaluated by committee members. During the confirmation hearing, nominees can respond to questions relating to their credentials, legal viewpoint, or their general approach to judicial decision-making. Hearings for district court nominees are relatively short—sometimes five minutes or less—while those for Supreme Court Justices can take multiple days. The length of hearings has continued to increase, as this is the opportunity for SJC members to expose and attack the nominee's ideological preferences (Banks and O'Brien 2015).

After the confirmation hearing, the SJC reports the nomination out of committee and includes a recommendation of whether the Senate should confirm or reject the nomination. The floor vote is another opportunity for senators to influence judicial appointments and hamper presidential court packing. Most often, senators filibuster (continuously debate) the nomination to prevent the vote from taking place. Other tactics include altering floor rules relating to cloture (the procedure used to end filibusters) and holds (official requests to party leaders to delay or prevent action on the nomination) (Binder and Maltzman 2009).

The Politics of Judicial Appointments

Although almost all federal judiciary nominations are confirmed, senatorial obstruction and delay has become relatively common due to the prevalence of divided government and party polarization. This phenomenon is underscored by the amount of time it takes to confirm judges. In the past, from the Carter to the Clinton administrations, it took roughly 71 days for district court nominees to be confirmed. In contrast, during the Obama administration, it took 190 days for district court nominees and 220 days for circuit court nominees to be confirmed (Banks and O'Brien 2015). President Obama also faced unprecedented levels of opposition from the Republican-controlled Senate when he nominated D.C. Circuit Court judge Merrick Garland to the Supreme Court after the death of Associate Justice Antonin Scalia. Prior to the nomination, Senate

Majority Leader Mitch McConnell and SJC Chair Charles Grassley announced that hearings would not be held because the Republicans believed that the public should have a voice on the issue, and therefore, that the winner of the 2016 presidential election should select a nominee to fill the vacancy on the bench (Everett and Bresnahan 2016). Even after Garland's nomination was announced, Senate Republicans remained steadfast in their refusal to consider Scalia's replacement during the 114th Congress (Demirjian 2016).

The political nature of the judicial appointment process highlights the role of the courts in public policymaking. However, this elicits concern from court watchers who argue that the current process stands to decrease judicial legitimacy. Regardless of reform proposals that would decrease the amount of time taken to fill vacancies (e.g., putting time limits on the SJC) and emphasize the nominee's merits over ideology, the process is inherently political. However, criticism levied against the judicial selection process can also be juxtaposed against President Obama's record of filling more than 200 judgeships. In the end, most presidents extend their legacy by the success they have in packing the court with nominees they favor. Nevertheless, the increased polarization and partisan gridlock that characterizes presidential and congressional relations only impedes the judicial selection process and inhibits the president's ability to pack the federal judiciary.

Lisa Hager

See also: Blue Slips; Filibusters of Presidential Nominations to the Federal Bench; The Role of the American Bar Association; Supreme Court Confirmation Hearings

Further Reading

Abraham, Henry J. 1983. "A Bench Happily Filled: Some Historical Reflections on the Supreme Court Selection Process." *Judicature* 66: 282–295.

Banks, Christopher P., and David M. O'Brien. 2015. *The Judicial Process: Law, Courts, and Judicial Politics.* Thousand Oaks, CA: Sage/CQ Press.

Binder, Sarah, and Forrest Maltzman. 2009. *Advice and Dissent: The Struggle to Shape the Federal Judiciary.* Washington, D.C.: Brookings Institution.

Demirjian, Karoun. 2016. "Republicans Refuse to Budge Following Garland Nomination to Supreme Court." *Washington Post,* March 16. https://www.washingtonpost .com/news/power post/wp/2016/03/16/republicans-refuse-to-budge-following-gar land-nomination-to-supreme-court/.

Epstein, Lee, and Jeffrey Segal. 2007. *Advice and Consent: The Politics of Judicial Appointments.* New York: Oxford University Press.

Everett, Burgess, and John Bresnahan. 2016. "McConnell: No Hearings or Meetings with Supreme Court Nominee." Politico, February 23. http://www.politico.com/story /2016/02/senate-gop-supreme-court-219661.

Gerhardt, Michael J. 2000. *The Federal Appointments Process: A Constitutional and Historical Analysis*. Durham, NC: Duke University Press.

Goldman, Sheldon. 1989. "Reagan's Judicial Legacy: Completing the Puzzle and Summing Up." *Judicature* 72: 318–330.

Goldman, Sheldon. 1997. *Picking Federal Judges: Lower Court Selection From Roosevelt Through Reagan*. New Haven, CT: Yale University Press.

Goldman, Sheldon, Elliot E. Slotnick, and Sara Schiavoni. 2011. "Obama's Judiciary at Midterm: The Confirmation Drama Continues." *Judicature* 94: 262–303.

Gonzales, Alberto R. 2001. "Letter from Alberto R. Gonzales, Counsel to the President to Martha W. Barnett, President, American Bar Association," March 22. http://abcnews.go.com/US/story?id=93754.

Kimel, T. J., and Kirk A. Randazzo. 2012. "Shaping the Federal Courts: The Obama Nominees." *Social Science Quarterly* 93: 1243–1250.

McElroy, Lisa T., and John Cannan. 2012. "Obama's Second Term and the Federal Courts." *Judicature* 96: 99–107.

O'Brien, David M. 2003. "Federal Judgeships in Retrospect," In *The Reagan Presidency: Pragmatic Conservatism and Its Legacies*, edited by W. Elliot Brownlee and Hugh Davis Graham, 327–354. Lawrence: University Press of Kansas.

Teter, Michael. 2014. "Rethinking Consent: Proposals for Reforming the Judicial Confirmation Process." *Ohio State Law Journal* 73: 287–342.

THE ROLE OF THE AMERICAN BAR ASSOCIATION

The American Bar Association (ABA) plays a significant role in the process of selecting federal judges. Historically, the ABA's advisory function was based on an assumption that the organized bar's evaluations of federal court nominees must be grounded upon a candidate's objective merit and not political considerations. The ABA's presence as an important institutional actor in the federal judicial selection process has grown over time, even though the U.S. Constitution does not give the ABA any sort of advisory role. In fact, Article II of the U.S. Constitution only specifies that the president has the power to appoint federal judges with the advice and consent of the Senate. Even so, the ABA has assumed an important place in rendering advice on the acceptability of federal bench nominees. Despite its claim that it is providing politically neutral advice on nominees, the ABA's interest in judicial selection often stems from trying to advance nominations that are aligned with its own institutional and political interests on matters that affect the legal profession, lawyers, or courts. For analogous reasons, presidents and the Senate have used partisanship as a basis to either consider or ignore the ABA's input during the nomination and confirmation process. While many presidents and the Senate have traditionally accepted the ABA's role in federal judicial selection, the ABA has had to defend itself against long-standing criticisms that its evaluations are ideologically biased.

The Origins of the ABA's Interest in Federal Judicial Selection and Its Growing Impact

The ABA was first organized in 1878. In 1908, it began to assess the professional qualifications of federal judges. At that time, the organization's Committee on Professional Ethics declared that the selection of judges was a critical canon of professional ethics. Under this proclamation, the ABA perceived that the organized bar had an ethical duty to insure that judicial candidates had the requisite qualities of fairness and impartiality before they would be allowed to serve on the bench (Grossman 1965, 49–50). At first, the ABA's involvement was expressed through the pressure it put on political leaders, or local bar groups or committees, to respond to prevailing political issues or reform movements that threatened the interests of the judiciary or the legal profession. Before 1932, the ABA directed most of its advocacy efforts on the activities of state judiciaries, in part because the federal courts and the Supreme Court were mostly conservative and therefore more sympathetic with the ABA's political and social interests than state courts, which were deemed too liberal. However, with the onset of the New Deal in the mid-1930s, the ABA began to combat the liberal decisional trends of federal courts that largely favored expansive government regulation. As a result, it quickly turned its institutional attention to trying to influence federal judicial selection at the confirmation and then the nomination stages (Grossman 1965, 52–58).

The sum of these efforts culminated in the creation of the ABA's Committee on the Judiciary in 1946. For the next two decades—at first through an invitation by the Senate Judiciary Committee's (SJC) chairman to let the ABA weigh in on nominee qualifications either by direct testimony or formal recommendation—the ABA and the SJC started what has now has become a long-standing practice of working together in assessing the merits of nominees that were called to service in the federal courts. The evolving relationship would increasingly give the organized bar a predominant voice in the nomination and confirmation of federal judges. The liaison between the ABA and the Senate progressed to working also with the attorney general of the U.S. Department of Justice (DOJ), a key player representing the president's interests in staffing the bench.

In 1949, the ABA Committee on the Judiciary was given permanent status as a standing committee that was charged with the sole task of assessing the selection and removal of federal judges. A few years later, a political accommodation that was reached by the ABA and the attorney general's office further reinforced the group's growing role in the politics of judicial selection. Under the agreement, the attorney general let the ABA make an informal preliminary assessment of each nominee in a secret screening process that occurred before the ABA made its formal recommendation to the Senate on the candidate's merits. Simultaneously, the Standing Committee adopted a rating system that evaluated the candidate's qualifications on a four-point metric that permitted the

ABA to rate nominees as either being "exceptionally well qualified," "well qualified," "qualified," or "not qualified" (Grossman 1965, 64–76). While the ratings system has changed slightly, both innovations establish the foundation for how the ABA operates today in giving the president and the Senate its advice about who should serve on the federal bench.

The ABA Standing Committee on the Federal Judiciary

Today, the Standing Committee on the Federal Judiciary is staffed with 15 members appointed by the ABA's president. With the exception of the Ninth Circuit, which has two members, the remaining 12 federal circuits are represented by one member each, and one member serves in an at-large capacity. Each member holds staggered three-year terms; so a member cannot serve more than two terms. Traditionally, those appointed to the Standing Committee are typically renowned as professional leaders that have earned a high degree of success and stature within the legal community (American Bar Association 2014, 1; Grossman 1965, 82–92).

The committee's stated mission is to evaluate the professional qualifications, namely the integrity, professional competence, and judicial temperament, of candidates appointed to the federal bench by the president, without regard to the nominee's political affiliation or views. The committee reviews a candidate's personal character and general reputation in the legal community in making a judgment about the nominee's integrity. In addition, it weighs a nominee's professional competence by evaluating the scope of the candidate's legal experience in light of the person's intelligence, judgment, and analytical abilities. In assessing judicial temperament, the committee considers whether the nominee has certain character traits, such as compassion, patience, open-mindedness, and a belief in the principle of equal justice (American Bar Association 2014, 3).

In performing its role, the committee distinguishes between making assessments for trial and middle-tier appellate court nominees with evaluations that are made of Supreme Court nominees. Although the same basic standards and procedures are used in each instance, Supreme Court nominees are held to a higher standard because the committee expects them to possess exceptional professional qualifications. In addition, all members of the committee are vested with the duty of performing evaluations (American Bar Association 2014, 10). For most federal judges, the evaluation progress begins after the officials from the White House or DOJ send to the committee's chair the name of an appointee that the executive branch would like to see fill a vacancy on the bench. Upon receipt, the chair assigns the task of evaluation to the relevant committee member who represents the circuit in which the vacancy arose. To trigger review, candidates are first required to complete a Personal Data Questionnaire (PDQ) and waiver forms that seek the release of personal information and disciplinary or other miscellaneous records. After the completed PDQ and waiver forms are received by the committee, the circuit member conducts an in-depth review of the nominee's professional written record in conjunction with holding interviews with colleagues, law school personnel, bar and group leaders, and the like. Near the end of the evaluation process, the nominee is interviewed as well. After the circuit member's evaluation is completed, the evaluator prepares an informal report and sends it to the committee for further assessment. After the informal report is discussed with the White House, the president asks the committee to prepare a formal report if the White House requests that a rating be provided (American Bar Association 2014, 4–7).

After its evaluation work is done, the committee rates nominees by designating them well qualified, qualified, or not qualified. The highest rating—*well qualified*—is earned if the committee believes the nominee is at the highest level of the profession in terms of legal ability, experience, and reputation. A *qualified* rating is issued if nominees merely satisfy the requisite criteria of integrity, competence, and judicial temperament. *Not qualified* means the committee has concluded that at least one of the three metrics of integrity, competence, or temperament is not fulfilled. In all nonunanimous votes, the committee discloses its rating by revealing that the nominee achieved a substantial majority (10–13), majority (8–9), or minority vote (American Bar Association 2014, 7).

The Politics of ABA Judicial Evaluations

The ABA's role in federal judicial selection generates political criticism for a variety of reasons. For cynics, the ABA should not be given a special status or place in advising the president or Senate on federal nominees because, at its core, the ABA is a private group that seeks to advance its members' goals through advocacy in the political process. Shortly after its inception, in 1916, the ABA opposed the nomination of Louis D. Brandeis to the Supreme Court because he was thought to be too liberal in his decision-making. Nearly 75 years later, the ABA was criticized by conservatives for not issuing its full support for Robert Bork's 1987 ill-fated Supreme Court nomination, even though he had strong legal credentials to hold the position (Banks and O'Brien 2015, 117–118). The growing institutionalization of the ABA's advisory role in judicial selection has also been accompanied by sporadic changes in the group's evaluation criteria, which implies that nominees will be assessed by criteria that do not remain centered on an impartial examination of professional qualifications. In addition, skeptics critical of the ABA's institutionalized role in judicial selection like to point out that the group has not hesitated to adopt firm advocacy positions on the most controversial political topics of the day, including abortion, religious freedom, criminal justice reform, and affirmative action (Hatch 1996, 2–3).

Many of these concerns were aired in a 1996 congressional hearing investigating the ABA's role in judicial selection. For Orrin Hatch (R-Utah), the chairman of the Senate Committee on the Judiciary, the investigation was warranted to determine if it was "time to pull the plug on the American Bar Association's preeminent role in judicial selection and reclaim for this committee its full place in the advice and consent function with respect to judges" (Hatch 1996, 1). At the hearing, former Attorney General Richard Thornburgh recounted that up until 1977, the ABA was committed to evaluating candidates on the basis of their competence, integrity, and judicial temperament; but, in 1980 and then later in 1988, the Standing Committee expanded its scope of review to put more emphasis on weighing a nominee's political or ideological views. Shortly thereafter, the ABA agreed to eliminate that criteria and return to its traditional practice of evaluating only the candidate's objective merits (Thornburgh 1996, 6–7). Still, as Thornburgh and other witnesses testified in the 1996 hearing, a number of other concerns were raised by skeptics who questioned the ABA's neutrality in the selection process. For example, Ninth Circuit Court judge Diarmuid O'Scannlain objected to the group's practice of issuing statements on high profile matters of social policy; and he also took issue with the ABA's increasing tendency to file third-party "friend of the court" amicus briefs in federal litigation on similar controversial legal issues. For O'Scannlain, these activities inherently raised important questions about the ABA's capacity to remain impartial in the judicial selection process (O'Scannlain 1996, 14). In response to these criticisms, supporters of the ABA's role countered that the advice the ABA gives is sent on a voluntary basis; so, the president, individual senators, or the Senate as a whole can choose to consider or ignore it. In this light, the ABA cannot assume a greater role in the selection process. Rather, the ABA is simply another source of information that may provide important insight as to a candidate's professional qualifications if the president or senate opts to consider its ratings and heed the ABA's recommendations (Feingold 1996, 70).

Regardless of these contrasting views, since the 1950s, most presidents have afforded the ABA at least some place in vetting federal court nominees. Even so, because the informal practice of allowing the ABA to monitor judicial candidates is more akin to an executive privilege instead of a constitutional obligation, some presidents have opted to diminish the ABA's influence by removing it from the White House's assessment of judicial nominees. In 2001, President George W. Bush decided to eradicate the ABA's role from White House deliberations on judicial selection on the grounds that the group is one among a score of others that press a liberal agenda. Bush's policy decision was quickly reversed when President Barack Obama seized the White House in 2008. In addition, before the Obama presidency, the ABA's special place in the federal judicial selection process has been diminished somewhat by the growing role that the Federalist Society for Law and Public Policy Studies, a conservative organization, began to play in advising conservative presidents and analogous ideological groups about the acceptability of federal court nominees. While it has not adopted a formal rating system, there is little doubt that the Federalist Society is and will remain a dominant player in the judicial selection process in the event that a conservative president is elected to office after the Obama presidency, especially if Republicans continue to retain control of the Senate.

Christopher P. Banks

See also: Blue Slips; Filibusters of Presidential Nominations to the Federal Bench; Impeachment and Removal of Federal Judges; Presidential Appointments and Court Packing; Supreme Court Hearings

Further Reading

American Bar Association. 2014. *Standing Committee on the Federal Judiciary: What It Is and How It Works.* Chicago: American Bar Association. http://www.americanbar.org /content/dam/aba/uncategorized/GAO/Backgrounder.authcheckdam.pdf.

Banks, Christopher P., and David M. O'Brien. 2015. *The Judicial Process: Law, Courts, and Judicial Politics.* Thousand Oaks, CA: Sage/CQ Press.

Feingold, Russell D. 1996. U.S. Congress. Senate. Committee on the Judiciary. "The Role of the American Bar Association in the Judicial Selection Process (May 21, 1996)." 104th Congress, 2d sess. S. Rept. S. Hrg. 104–497.

Grossman, Joel. 1965. *Lawyers and Judges: The ABA and the Politics of Judicial Selection.* New York: John Wiley and Sons.

Hatch, Orrin G. 1996. U.S. Congress. Senate. Committee on the Judiciary. "The Role of the American Bar Association in the Judicial Selection Process (May 21, 1996)." 104th Congress, 2d sess. S. Rept. S. Hrg. 104–497.

Martinek, Wendy L., Mark Kemper, and Steven R. Van Winkle. 2002. "To Advise and Consent: The Senate and Lower Federal Court Nominations, 1977–1998." *Journal of Politics* 64: 337–361.

O'Scannlain, Diarmuid F. 1996. U.S. Congress. Senate. Committee on the Judiciary. "The Role of the American Bar Association in the Judicial Selection Process (May 21, 1996)." 104th Congress, 2d sess. S. Rept. S. Hrg. 104–497.

Thornburg, Richard. 1996. U.S. Congress. Senate. Committee on the Judiciary. "The Role of the American Bar Association in the Judicial Selection Process (May 21, 1996)." 104th Congress, 2d sess. S. Rept. S. Hrg. 104–497.

FILIBUSTERS OF PRESIDENTIAL NOMINATIONS TO THE FEDERAL BENCH

Under Article I of the U.S. Constitution, Congress is structured as a bicameral institution that divides lawmaking authority between the House of Representatives and the Senate. Under Article II, the Senate must give its advice and consent on, and confirm, presidential appointments to the federal courts. In exercising its constitutional powers to make the laws, Congress uses a complex array of legislative norms, rules, procedures, and traditions that are designed to facilitate open discussion among our nation's elected representatives about the wisdom of enacting legislation and executive appointments. Analogous rules and customs affect the Senate's deliberation over presidential appointments to the federal judiciary whenever the Senate discharges its constitutional duty to render advice and consent. Two parliamentary mechanisms, the filibuster and the rule of cloture, have been used in the Senate to extend, through filibuster, or to end, by invoking a rule of cloture, legislative discussions about presidential appointments to the bench. The political evolution and application of these rules has become highly significant in a heightened era of political polarization because the party with minority status in the Senate can theoretically use the filibuster as a strategic weapon to delay or prevent up-or-down votes on presidential judicial appointments that are favored by the Senate majority or the president. As a procedural tactic of delay and obstruction, the minority party's use of the filibuster has caused the Senate majority or the president to respond in kind with an array of other political tactics, including recess appointments or Senate rule changes, to force the Senate to deliver an up-or-down vote on presidential appointments that are being delayed or obstructed by filibusters.

The Origins of the Filibuster

One of the key institutional aspects of Congress is the democratic principle that representatives and senators must enjoy the freedom to engage in full discussion and deliberation on matters affecting legislation and executive appointments to the bench. Another important characteristic of legislative behavior is to manage the terms of the debate by the use of procedural rules and institutional norms or traditions. The use of the filibuster, a term that originates from the Dutch word *vrijbuiter*, meaning a pirate or freebooter, is one of those procedural stratagems (Arenberg and Dove 2015, 22). While the term itself is not defined by formal rules, it is generally understood to be a legislative tactic that elected representatives or senators use to delay, block, or prevent a proposed law from coming to a vote (Beth and Heitshusen 2014, 1). As applied to the Senate's advice and consent function under Article II, a senator can turn to the filibuster as a partisan strategy to continue debate on disfavored presidential appointments that, in turn, works to delay or obstruct the confirmation of the president's choices by not giving the Senate the chance to deliver a formal up-or-down vote.

The adoption of institutional rules to manage legislative discussions on the floor of either the House or Senate can be traced to the nation's founding. As Congress's membership in the House of Representatives grew as the country's population expanded, the House promulgated rules to restrict debate on the floor (U.S. Senate 2016). In the Senate, a much smaller body, the absence of similar rules traditionally has put fewer limitations on senators to restrict how long senators can debate, or stop discussion, on items of legislative business (Beth and Heitshusen 2014, 1). In addition, other rules, such as the previous question rule, permitted debate to be cut off in the House of Representatives but not in the Senate. Instead, senators brought discussion to a close by reaching an agreement to do so by consensus behind closed doors. Because of its disuse, the Senate eliminated the previous question rule in 1806. Thereafter, in 1917, the year in which the Senate adopted Rule XXII, or the rule of cloture, debate in the Senate was virtually unlimited by rule or practice for more than 100 years (Arenberg and Dove 2015, 19–20). As originally conceived, the rule of cloture could be invoked by a two-thirds majority vote, which, in practice, is hard to muster. In 1975, the two-thirds requirement was reduced and replaced by an easier, but still somewhat difficult to obtain, threshold barrier of obtaining a supermajority vote of 60 out of 100 senators. If cloture is invoked, the debate is refocused procedurally, which guarantees the Senate will curtail debate and eventually vote on the legislative matter or executive appointment at hand (U.S. Senate 2016; Beth and Heitshusen 2014, 13).

For much of its early history, there was little need in the Senate to have an institutional process in place to limit or stop an extended debate because the practice of filibustering bills did not gain significant traction until the 1840s. At that time, one of the nation's first filibusters arose over a patronage battle that pitted opponents against each other regarding whether local printers should be employed to publish official records of Congress, a dispute that almost led to a duel between Whig senator Henry Clay and Democratic senator William King of Alabama. Later, in the throes of war fever and whether the United States should maintain its neutrality during the World War I, a minority of isolationists staged a 23-day filibuster on the issue of whether U.S. merchant ships should be armed in light of Germany's decision to engage in unrestricted submarine warfare. In defending the right of the Senate to consider the issue of whether the nation should thrust itself into the emerging worldwide conflict, Senator George Norris of Nebraska, a protagonist of the filibuster, was said to have quoted Woodrow Wilson in exclaiming, "It is the proper duty of a representative body to look diligently into every affair of government and to talk much about what it sees" (Arenberg and Dove 2015, 23).

The Partisan Use and Abuse of the Filibuster in Judicial Appointments

The filibuster and the Senate's right to cut off full deliberation on matters of legislation or executive judicial appointments have become increasingly controversial in recent decades. Empirical studies report that the rate of filibusters has risen sharply since the 1960s, a time when it affected only about 8 percent of legislative matters. Between the 1970s and 1980s, it was a factor in 27 percent, and then later in the 1990s and early 2000s, 51 percent of legislative deliberations. Similarly, as of the mid-1960s, cloture had only been tried a total of 37 times and was rarely successful in actually ending a Senate debate; but, thereafter, its invocation steadily increased to unheard of proportions after the Carter presidency. During the Reagan years in the 1980s, at least 202 cloture petitions were filed, 139 cloture votes were taken, and cloture was invoked to close off debate a total of 91 times (Arenberg and Dove 2015, 29–31). These trends reflect the intense partisanship that has become almost a routine part of determining whether presidential appointments to the federal bench are successful or not in the modern era, particularly in the George W. Bush and Obama administrations. In fact, much of the political vitriol surrounding the contemporary judicial appointment process has its roots in the struggles Bush and Obama endured in getting their judicial choices confirmed in the face of strident Senate minority ideological opposition.

Early in Bush's second term, several of the president's appellate court nominees were filibustered by the Democratic minority opposition in the Senate, led by Minority Leader Harry Reid (D-Nev.). The filibuster was mounted by Democrats because they thought the appointments were out of the ideological mainstream, and at least two of the seven appointments at issue were leading candidates to serve eventually on the Supreme Court. One conservative nominee, Janice Rogers Brown, was slated to fill a vacancy on the D.C. Circuit, an appeals court often characterized as the nation's second most influential court because of the dual role it plays deciding federal agency appeals and in grooming future Supreme Court appointments (Banks 1999). In response, President Bush warned that he would use his constitutional authority to place nominees on the bench with recess appointments that constitutionally do not need Senate approval whenever the Senate is out of session. Moreover, Bill Frist (R-Tenn.), the Senate's Majority Leader at that time, also threatened to change the Senate rules with "the constitutional option," a move that would end filibusters by allowing a simple majority (51) and not a supermajority (60) vote to invoke cloture. Democrats labeled the threat a "nuclear option," as it would incinerate long-standing traditions of unrestricted debate and give the minority party at least some voice in legislative deliberations (Goldman et al. 2007, 264–267).

The nuclear option scenario was averted by a last-minute bipartisan "Gang of 14" compromise that was forged by 7 moderate senators from each side of the political aisle. Under the pact, 7 Democratic senators agreed to give an up-or-down vote on some of the filibustered nominees and promised only to filibuster other nominees in undefined "extraordinary circumstances." In return, the Republican signatories would not vote to rewrite Senate rules, an agreement that implied that the president would refrain from making any more recess appointments (Wawro and Schickler 2006, 271). Any binding force that the pact had on keeping the supermajority cloture rule in place evaporated when the Democrats captured control of the Senate in the last year of Bush's presidency and with Obama's 2008 election. In Obama's first term, Republicans, now in minority status, exacted political revenge by using the filibuster to block several of Obama's executive and judicial appointments to the federal courts. Partisan tensions came to a head in 2013 when the Republicans, led by Minority Leader Mitch McConnell (R-Ky.), used the filibuster to prevent up-or-down votes on three of Obama's nominations that were destined to tip the ideological balance in favor of the liberals on the influential D.C. Circuit. Confronted by Republican obstructionism, Democrat Reid, now the Senate Majority Leader, pulled the trigger on the nuclear option and eliminated filibusters for executive appointments and all judicial nominations except to the Supreme Court. Under the new Senate rules, legislative proposals could still be filibustered, but extended debates on executive and most judicial appointments were now ended with a simple majority vote, an unprecedented step that represented a sharp break with the past and parliamentary rules that had remained intact for more than 40 years. In defending the change, Democrat Reid justified the move by calling it a way to fix a broken Senate; but, in condemning it, Republican McConnell called it a "sad day in the history of the Senate" and one that Democrats will in time come to regret (Kane 2014; Arenberg and Dove 2015, 192).

After the midterm 2014 elections that swept the Republicans into power with significant majorities in both the House and the Senate, McConnell's words were prophetic, especially after the untimely death of conservative Supreme Court Justice Antonin Scalia in early 2016. For his part, Majority Leader McConnell and the Chairman of the Senate Judiciary Committee, Charles Grassley (R-Iowa), quickly announced that Obama's appointment of Judge Merrick Garland to the D.C. Circuit in the last year of his presidency—which, in theory, would alter the Court's ideological composition in favor of the liberals for decades into the future—would not get a hearing until after the results came in from the 2016 presidential election (Fabian 2016). In staking their claim to have the people weigh in on whether a Republican or Democratic president should make the appointing choice after Obama picked Garland, who is widely seen as a nominee that both Republican and Democratic senators can support, the hardball political tactics surrounding the presidential appointment process is not likely to end any time soon (Demirjian 2016). Likewise, there is little doubt that rewriting the filibuster rules through the nuclear option similarly demonstrates that extreme partisanship and majoritarian politics will dominate the success or failure of presidential appointments. Unless the filibuster rules are changed again, the party that controls the Senate will enable the majority to let the executive pack the federal bureaucracy and federal courts with its ideological preferences without any significant constraints imposed by the minority opposition (Cohen 2013).

Christopher P. Banks

See also: Blue Slips; Impeachment and Removal of Federal Judges; Presidential Appointments and Court Packing; Supreme Court Hearings

Further Reading

Arenberg, Richard A., and Robert A. Dove. 2015. *Defending the Filibuster: The Soul of the Senate.* Bloomington, IN: Indiana University Press.

Banks, Christopher P. 1999. *Judicial Politics in the D.C. Circuit Court.* Baltimore: John Hopkins University Press.

Beth, Richard S., and Valerie Heitshusen. 2014. "Filibusters and Cloture in the Senate." *Congressional Research Service (RL30360),* December 24, 2014. Washington, D.C.: Congressional Research Service.

Cohen, Tom. 2013. "5 Ways Life Changes in the Senate after the Nuclear Option on Filibusters." *CNN Politics,* November 23. http://www.cnn.com/2013/11/22/politics/senate-nuclear-option-5-things/.

Demirjian, Karoun. 2016. "Republicans Refuse to Budge Following Garland Nomination to Supreme Court." *Washington Post,* March 16. https://www.washingtonpost.com/news/powerpost/wp/2016/03/16/republicans-refuse-to-budge-following-garland-nomination-to-supreme-court/.

Fabian, Jordan. 2016. "Obama to Meet McConnell, Grassley to Discuss Supreme Court Vacancy." *The Hill,* February 25. http://thehill.com/homenews/administration/270767-obama-to-meet-mcconnell-grassley-to-discuss-supreme-court-vacancy.

Goldman, Sheldon, Elliot Slotnick, Gerard Gryski, and Sara Schiavoni. 2007. "Picking Judges in a Time of Turmoil: W. Bush's Judiciary During the 109th Congress." *Judicature* 90: 252–283.

Kane, Paul. 2013. "Reid, Democrats Trigger 'Nuclear' Option; Eliminate Most Filibusters on Nominees." *Washington Post,* November 21. https://www.washingtonpost.com/politics/senate-poised-to-limit-filibusters-in-party-line-vote-that-would-alter-centuries-of-precedent/2013/11/21/d065cfe8-52b6-11e3-9fe0-fd2ca728e67c_story.html.

U.S. Congress. Senate. 1996. Committee on Rules and Administration. "Examining the Filibuster (April 22, 2010; June 23, 2010; July 28, 2010; September 22 and 29, 2010)." 111th Cong., 2d sess. S. Rept. S. Hrg. 111–706.

U.S. Senate. 2016. "Senate History: Filibuster and Cloture." http://www.senate.gov/artandhistory/history/common/briefing/Filibuster_Cloture.htm.

Wawro, Gregory J., and Eric Schickler. 2006. *Filibuster: Obstruction and Lawmaking in the U.S. Senate.* Princeton, NJ: The Princeton University Press.

BLUE SLIPS

Under Article II, Section 2 of the U.S. Constitution the president is vested with the power to make federal judicial appointments subject to the Senate's advice and consent. The Senate's role in rendering its advice and consent thus affects the appointments of federal district court, circuit court, and Supreme Court nominations from the president. In discharging its duties, traditionally the Senate has been afforded the discretion to influence the president's attempt to pack the lower federal courts with nominees who share his ideological views through the norms of senatorial courtesy and the practice of issuing blue slips. The blue slip procedure is an extension of the courtesy norm and has been an institutionalized practice in the Senate since the early 20th century (Sollenberger 2003b, 3). Regardless of their party affiliation, after a nomination, home-state senators are sent forms on blue paper from the Senate Judiciary Committee (SJC). Returning the blue slip signals a senator's approval; withholding or returning it with negative feedback registers disapproval. The blue slip's political significance rests with the capacity of individual senators to disrupt or block the president's judicial appointments to the lower federal courts in conjunction with the chairperson of the SJC's political discretion to use the blue slip upon receipt of an objection from a home-state senator. In highly polarized political times, the blue slip is thus one of the procedural devices or tactics the Senate can use to deny or obstruct a presidential appointment to the federal bench.

History and Evolution of the Blue Slip Procedure

The senatorial courtesy norm dates back to the founding and the George Washington administration. Under courtesy, home-state senators from the president's party are given the authority to derail a nomination for any reason. According to the *American Congressional Dictionary*, the courtesy evolved as a customary practice which signifies that a senator finds the president's nominee to be personally obnoxious or objectionable (Sollenberger 2003b, 2). In the 1930s, President Franklin D. Roosevelt's nominee, Floyd Roberts, who was slated to fill a Virginia district court vacancy, was denied on these grounds after one Virginia senator declared that the president's choice was "personally obnoxious to me, as to my colleague" (Epstein and Segal 2007, 76). The rationale for extending the courtesy is wholly political in nature. In this respect, senators have a vested interest in showing to their constituencies back home that they play a significant role in the presidential nomination process, thus positioning themselves to take credit for good appointments. Conversely, giving home-state senators the chance to band together and voice their opinion about a nomination protects senators from the embarrassment of being ignored by a president during the selection process, a circumstance that might be even more painful if the president's choice is politically obnoxious to individual senators (Sollenberger 2003b, 2).

Although there is some scholarly disagreement about when the blue slip practice began, one congressional researcher uncovered archival evidence that found blue slips in operation for every Congress beginning with the 65th Congress (1917–1919) (Sollenberger 2003b, 3–5). The practice evolved, even though it is not codified in the Senate rules; it remains merely a creature of Senate tradition and custom. While the precise reasons for using it remain unclear, the blue slip is widely seen as a mechanism that formally institutionalizes the norm of senatorial courtesy, in large part because it permits the chairperson of the SJC to show deference to the views and advice of home-state senators.

The institutionalization of the blue slip procedure has significant consequences on the politicization of the judicial selection process for lower federal court nominees. Because a blue slip is given to home-state senators regardless of their party affiliation, senators that remain ideologically opposed to the president are afforded the same amount of influence as senators from the president's party who could use the senatorial courtesy norm to block or obstruct judicial appointments. In fact, under the blue slip, *any* senator, regardless of party affiliation, holds a trump card to block or delay presidential appointments at any given time. Thus, in periods of divided government—a time when the party that controls the White House is different from the one that controls the Senate—the president's ideological opponents (or supporters) can use the blue slip to stop or block a president's nominations. Or, in periods of unified government—a time when the same party controls the presidency and the Senate—senators in the minority party (or majority party) can express their ideological disagreement with a president's choice by not returning a blue slip or delivering it with objections, a process that is likely to delay a nominee's confirmation.

Home-state senators from the Republican Party have frequently procrastinated in handing back blue slips during the Obama administration: Arizona senator John McCain and then Arizona senator John Kyl delayed Senate consideration of Rosemary Marquez's nomination to a district court in Arizona by holding onto their blue slips for more than a year and a half (McElroy and Cannan 2012, 101). In addition, whereas senatorial courtesy represented a norm of deference that informally signaled dissent, the written "paper trail" of submitting and returning a blue slip today openly documents home-state senators' formal objections. As a result, senators from either side of the political aisle can point to the blue slip and exert considerable pressure on their Senate colleagues to follow and respect the opposing senators' views about a judicial nominee, regardless of whether or not they come from the president's party (Binder and Maltzman 2009, 35–37).

The Political Use of Blue Slips by the Senate

Senatorial courtesy and, ultimately, the blue slip practice have somewhat reduced influence in the selection of circuit court of appeals' vacancies because those courts exert authority over several states. Because district or trial courts are within a single state's jurisdiction, showing deference to the views of home-state senators is more important with respect to filling district court vacancies. Even so, senators are not immune from trying to wield more influence over the selection of appeals court judges. For example, when President Barack Obama was elected to his first term, the Republican caucus (which was then in the Senate minority) sent him a letter stating in unmistakable terms that Republicans would unite to block his judicial confirmations if Republican home-state senators were not duly consulted. The letter's implicit purpose was to convey the threat that the blue slip procedure would be invoked as a partisan tool to stop President Obama from packing the lower federal courts with his favored nominees (Goldman et al. 2011, 267).

The politicization of the blue slip process manifests itself in how the chairperson of the SJC interprets the governing rules and practices of senatorial advice and consent. Upon receiving a negative blue slip, in theory, the chairperson can act upon it by doing the following: (1) stopping all committee hearings and proceedings; (2) moving ahead with the nomination but giving extra consideration to the negative feedback or opposing senators' views; or, (3) moving the proceeding along with notice of the negative feedback or opposing senators' views (Sollenberger 2003b, 4). In practice, whether the president's nominations are fully considered by the Senate and successfully confirmed thus depends on whether the Senate chairperson manipulates his blue slip authority to achieve political gains. In this respect, the blue slip can be used as an offensive or defensive tool or tactic to advance or obstruct the president's choices to the federal bench. Although in its early history, the blue slip was more or less the means for the Senate chairperson to learn about whether a president's choice was going to offend personally a home-state senator without necessarily stopping Committee proceedings, "it has evolved into something like a veto power" over time (Toobin 2013; Palmer 2009).

Different SJC chairpersons vary the blue slip policy in accordance with their political will. In 1956, Chairperson James O. Eastland (D-Miss.) eliminated the information-gathering function of the blue slip and replaced it with a policy that halted all action on a nomination whenever a home-state senator registered a negative objection by using the blue slip procedure. In 1979, Chairperson Edward Kennedy (D-Mass.) gave the full committee the option to vote on whether action on the nomination should proceed in the event a home-state senator failed to return a blue slip (Sollenberger 2003a, 4–5). During the Clinton administration and when the Republicans controlled the Senate, Orrin Hatch (R-Utah) sanctioned the practice of letting home-state Republicans obstruct and delay confirmation hearings on disfavored Clinton appointees. However, in response to Democratic opposition to President George W. Bush's nominations, Hatch reversed his policy as SJC chairperson by disregarding the blue slip procedure altogether, thus opting instead to hold hearings, even in situations when Democratic home-state senators had not returned favorable blue slips. For some court watchers, the policy of ignoring objections from the minority opposition is more likely to gain traction in highly polarized political environments (Binder and Maltzman 2013, 53).

In contrast, when the Democrats controlled the Senate during the Obama presidency, Democratic Chairperson Patrick Leahy (D-Vt.) opted to honor the blue slip practice by electing to hold confirmation hearings only when they were returned by each home-state senator. Leahy acted with mixed political motives. Although his policy was in part based on having traditional respect for the blue slip practice, he also reasoned that Obama's judicial choices would stand a better chance of being confirmed if he secured Republican preclearance. As Leahy explained, "I assume no one will abuse the blue slip process like some have abused the use of the filibuster to block judicial nominees on the floor of the Senate." Thus, he continued, "As long as the blue slip process is not being abused by home-state senators, then I will see no reason to change that tradition." Still, Senator Leahy's posture vested Republicans with a unilateral power to deny President Obama's judicial selections and that authority has been used to limit the president's authority in filling vacancies in the lower federal courts for an unprecedented length of time (Toobin 2013; Binder and Maltzman 2013, 50).

Christopher P. Banks

See also: Filibusters of Presidential Nominations to the Federal Bench; Impeachment and Removal of Federal Judges; Presidential Appointments and Court Packing; Supreme Court Hearings

Further Reading

Binder, Sarah A., and Forrest Maltzman. 2009. *Advice & Dissent: The Struggle to Shape the Federal Judiciary.* Washington, D.C.: Brooking Institution Press.

Binder, Sarah A., and Forrest Maltzman. 2013. "New Wars of Advice and Consent: Judicial Selection in the Obama Years." *Judicature* 97: 1–56.

Denning, Brannon P. 2002. "The Judicial Confirmation Process and the Blue Slip." *Judicature* 85: 218–226.

Epstein, Lee, and Jeffrey A. Segal. 2007. *Advice and Consent: The Politics of Judicial Appointments.* New York: Oxford University Press.

Goldman, Sheldon. 1997. *Picking Federal Judges.* New Haven, CT: Yale University Press.

Goldman, Sheldon, Elliot Slotnick, and Sara Schiavoni. 2011. "Obama's Judiciary at Midterm: The Confirmation Drama Continues." *Judicature* 94: 262–301.

McElroy, Lisa T., and John Cannan. 2012. "Obama's Second Term and the Federal Courts." *Judicature* 96: 96–107.

Palmer, Betsy. 2009. "Evolution of the Senate's Role in the Nomination and Confirmation Process: A Brief History." *Congressional Research Service (RL31948)* May 13, 2009. Washington, D.C.: Congressional Research Service.

Sollenberger, Mitchel A. 2003a. "The Blue Slip Process in the Senate Committee on the Judiciary: Background, Issues, and Options." *Congressional Research Service (RS21674)* November 21, 2003. Washington, D.C.: Congressional Research Service.

Sollenberger, Mitchel A. 2003b. "The History of the Blue Slip in the Senate Committee on the Judiciary, 1917–Present." *Congressional Research Service (RL32013)* October 22, 2003. Washington, D.C.: Congressional Research Service.

Toobin, Jeffrey. 2013. "Blue-Slip Battle: The Senate Obstructionists' Secret Weapon,"
The New Yorker, November 26. http://www.newyorker.com/news/daily-comment
/blue-slip-battle-the-senate-obstructionists-secret-weapon.

SUPREME COURT HEARINGS

The process of judicial selection in the 50 states is a crazy quilt of alternative
approaches that includes both partisan and nonpartisan elections, merit-based
selection systems, appointment by governors and legislators, and several hybrid
systems that incorporate elements from more than one of these schemes. The
landscape of state judicial selection has changed over time because of the pressures created by various social and political movements that have sought to
increase the accountability of judges to the electorate, improve the quality of
judges and judging, or establish greater independence by insulating courts from
the thickets of partisan politics. One fixed star in the constellation of American judicial selection, however, has been the approach employed at the federal
level since the time of the founding. The Constitution crafted in Philadelphia
in 1787 specified a practice in Article II that endowed the president with the
power to make all nominations to the Supreme Court and other inferior courts
created by Congress. As a check on unlimited executive authority, the framers
provided the Senate with the power of advice and consent, which allows the
chamber to signal its approval or disapproval of the president's selection by voting to accept or reject the nominee. While this basic two-step method of judicial selection has remained unamended since the ratification of the Constitution
in 1789, the process of confirming nominees to the federal bench has been influenced by the adoption of a variety of institutional practices by the Senate, as
well as by extra-institutional forces that have sought to sway the outcome of the
confirmation process for political purposes. This change has been most evident
in the confirmation of those picked to fill vacancies on the U.S. Supreme Court.
Nominees to the high court face a gauntlet of scrutiny by the public, the press, the
president making the selection, and, in particular, the Senate Judiciary Committee (SJC) that conducts days-long hearings that investigate candidates for
the bench. These hearings not only serve to satisfy the Senate's duty of advice
and consent but also provide an opportunity to evaluate the personal, professional, and political qualifications of those who will serve on the Supreme Court.
A review of this set of qualifications also assists in creating a measure of democratic accountability through the vetting of potential justices by elected officials (Batta et al. 2012, 7).

Early Senate Review of Judicial Nominations

The Constitution establishes the basic process for the placement of federal judges on the bench. It does not, however, identify the manner in which the Senate is to gather information to exercise its duty to advise and give consent on the nominations made by the president. An initial effort to institutionalize the process came in 1816 when the Senate established the Senate Judiciary Committee, endowing it with the authority to review judicial nominees. This ended the practice of consideration of each candidate by the full Senate, even though substantial numbers of nominees continued to sidestep review by the SJC until after the Civil War when it became the body with nearly exclusive power to investigate presidential selections (Collins and Ringhand 2013, 34). Although the SJC had the power to offer a recommendation to the Senate, it often did so without holding formal hearings—a practice it did not adopt until 1873. It is unclear what information the SJC members gathered and used to evaluate nominees during hearings because the meetings and deliberations were typically conducted outside of the view of the public, as were debates in the Senate.

The first public committee hearing for a nominee to the high court did not occur until Louis Brandeis was picked by President Woodrow Wilson in 1916 to fill a vacancy created by the resignation of Joseph Lamar from the bench, although Brandeis himself did not appear to testify (Yalof 2008, 146). Public hearings would not become the norm until John J. Parker earned a nomination to the Court from President Herbert Hoover in 1930, the same year that changes to institutional rules permitted debate about nominees on the floor of the Senate (Maltese 1995, 86). Harlan Fiske Stone made the first appearance by a Supreme Court nominee before the SJC in 1925. Interestingly, the members of the committee did not delve into Stone's qualifications to serve as a member of the high court. Instead, it interrogated him about his work as attorney general. The first nominee to endure a full and wide-ranging inquisition from members of the SJC did not occur until 1939, when President Franklin Roosevelt selected Felix Frankfurter to fill a seat on the Court left empty after the death of Benjamin Cardozo. While a number of nominees to the Supreme Court appeared after the testimony by Frankfurter, it was not until after the selection of John Marshall Harlan II to the bench in 1955 that it became a fixed practice that all Supreme Court nominees would submit to questioning by members of the SJC— with the exception of those individuals whose nomination was withdrawn prior to the commencement of hearings (Ringhand and Collins 2011, 34–35).

Contemporary Supreme Court Hearings

During the slow transformation of the process for vetting nominees, elements that would become standard practice began to emerge. Initially, the hearings were conducted by only a subcommittee to the SJC. Today, candidates face review by the entire membership of the SJC. The extent of the investigation of nominees has also grown over time. For more than a century, there was little more than a perfunctory review of the president's selection, resulting in confirmation to the bench in days rather than months as has become more typical. Today, the committee may spend days questioning the nominee with additional time allotted for testimony from supporters and detractors, including organized interest groups, legal professionals, and members of Congress. This process has established the committee as an important and forceful check on the president's power to fill vacancies on the Court. In addition to the increased activity inside the Senate, there has also been a surge in the participation by actors outside of Congress, including increased involvement by the public and more intense lobbying by the White House and organized groups for the president's selection.

There is some debate among scholars concerning what triggered a conversion in the Senate from bit player in the process of judicial selection to a body more conscientious and active in its role of providing meaningful advice and consent. Some scholars point to the late 1960s, in particular, the confirmation hearings for Thurgood Marshall, when senators on the SJC significantly increased the percentage of comments and questions they offered regarding judicial decisions. Prior to the hearings convened for Marshall, few senators probed potential justices about their positions on case law, including not a single question leveled at Robert Jackson, William Brennan, or Byron White. Three other nominees, Frankfurter, Harlan, and Arthur Goldberg, fielded only a fraction of the total number of questions on the topic of legal or judicial decision-making. This behavior indicated a shift away from a review of more personal and professional qualifications toward an inquiry into both how the nominee assesses legal doctrine and how their positions might impact the development of substantive law. This transformation suggests that the Senate came to recognize the political import of the selection of members of the bench in the latter years of the leadership of Chief Justice Earl Warren during the 1960s. During this era, the Supreme Court earned the reputation as an activist institution that greatly expanded civil rights and liberties and altered long-standing interpretations of the Constitution (Batta et al. 2012).

Other scholars point to a rise not only in the type of questions posed by members of the committee but also the volume. Beginning in the early 1980s, a dramatic spike occurred in the number of comments made by individual senators tasked with investigating the nominee, an event that appears to coincide with the advent of televised hearings. After the broadcast by C-SPAN of the hearings for the first woman to be nominated to the Court, Sandra Day O'Connor, in 1981, both public and cable TV outlets began to televise gavel-to-gavel coverage of the proceedings. From 1939 until the O'Connor hearing, the nominee on average made 181 comments under questioning by senators while the members of the SJC typically made 253 comments. Beginning with the selection of Associate Justice William Rehnquist in 1986 to replace Warren Burger as chief justice of the Court and continuing through 2009, the average number of nominee comments rose to 749 and comments from senators swelled to 987—nearly a fourfold increase for both groups. The high water mark for senatorial questions came with the selection of Robert Bork by President Ronald Reagan in 1987 when the nominee faced nearly 2,000 comments from senators, a 70 percent increase over the number of comments made during the Rehnquist hearing (Ringhand and Collins 2011, 9).

Bork's hearing is notable not only for the number of questions launched at the nominee but also for the partisan battle that erupted over the potential legal and political implications of the confirmation of Reagan's choice. Although Bork merited the appointment based upon his stellar legal résumé, his interpretative approach to the Constitution, known as original understanding, paired with a very large corpus of legal writing, led to significant opposition by segments of the public. Original understanding is a method of interpretation that limits the discretion of judges who construe the Constitution to the original meaning of those who drafted the document. The effect of this interpretive method on the law, critics claim, is to limit the expansion of civil rights and liberties. In particular, opponents of Bork's nomination argued that his presence on the bench would not only limit the development of the law in areas such as privacy and equal protection but also would lead to the eradication of newly established protections for women and minorities. As an advocate of original understanding, he had little sympathy for arguments that promoted the existence of unwritten rights such as abortion. Those on the ideological left feared that Bork, who would replace moderate Justice Lewis Powell, would significantly alter the tenor of legal decision-making for years to come. The battle between conservative forces that continued to fight against the rights expansion that began during the era of the Warren Court (1953–1969) and the liberal advocates who pressed for a greater well on constitutional protections led to the mobilization of forces that both supported and opposed Bork. As a result, more than 400 interest groups sought to influence a confirmation process that became the longest in American history (Maltese 1995, 146–147). In the end, Bork was denied a seat on the Court when the Senate voted 58 to 42 to reject the appointment.

The Bork nomination appeared to many to signal a shift in the confirmation politics for the Supreme Court. SJC confirmation hearings that followed were often an attempt to discover the hidden, and potentially dangerous, ideological agenda of the nominee. This was the case with President George Bush's selection of David Souter in 1990, who was dubbed the stealth nominee for the absence of a large or clear body of legal opinion, and with more recent nominees such as Sonia Sotomayor, selected by President Barack Obama in 2009, who was questioned about her stated reliance on experiences as an ethnic minority as an influence in her decision-making. Hearing inquiries also waded more deeply into the personal lives of nominees, as was the case with Clarence Thomas, appointed by President George H. W. Bush in 1991, who answered questions regarding his relationships with female coworkers while serving as Chair of the Equal Employment Opportunity Commission.

The transformation of the federal judicial selection process over the past quarter century has led to the call for its reform. Arguably, the most radical of these proposals was the suggestion that the candidate should no longer be required to attend hearings, thus eliminating the potential for senators to grandstand for the public or media through never-ending colloquies with the nominee. Another approach sought to limit the capacity of senators to ask any questions that would press the nominee for an opinion about a legal matter or question that he or she might face when on the bench. Still another suggestion promoted the idea that nominees should be judged by their record and the evaluation of their work by legal professionals (Maltese 1995, 146–147). Despite the push for change, Supreme Court hearings operate in much the same fashion since the modernization of the process began in the latter 1960s. In the aftermath of the death of Associate Justice Antonin Scalia in early 2016, President Barack Obama faced stiff opposition from Senate Republicans regarding any candidate for the vacancy. Just hours after the announcement of Scalia's death, Senate Majority Leader Mitch McConnell suggested that the Senate should not confirm a nominee to the Court during a presidential election year, arguing that the choice should be left to the next occupant of the White House. Other Senate Republicans, including those serving on the SJC, concurred with McConnell, not only blocking hearings on Obama's nominee, Merrick Garland, but also refusing to even meet with the nominee. These actions were not particularly well-disguised attempts to thwart the replacement of the solidly conservative Scalia with the choice of a Democratic president. This most recent dustup reveals that Supreme Court nominations and the hearings that accompany them will continue to be extremely partisan political theater into the future.

Charles F. Jacobs

See also: Filibusters of Presidential Nominations to the Federal Bench; Judicial Independence; Partisan Judicial Elections and Political Money; Political Restraints on Judicial Power; Privacy Rights

Further Reading

Abraham, Henry J. 2007. *Justices, Presidents, and Senators: A History of U.S. Supreme Court Appointments from Washington to Bush II.* 5th ed. Lanham, MD: Rowman & Littlefield.

Batta, Anna, Paul M. Collins, Jr., Tom Miles, and Lorie A. Ringhand. 2012. "Let's Talk: Judicial Decisions at Supreme Court Confirmation Hearings." *Judicature* 96(1): 7–15.

Collins, Paul M., Jr., and Lori A. Ringhand. 2013. *Supreme Court Confirmation Hearings and Constitutional Change.* New York: Cambridge University Press.

Maltese, John Anthony. 1995. *The Selling of Supreme Court Nominees.* Baltimore: The Johns Hopkins University Press.

Ringhand, Lori A., and Collins, Paul M., Jr. 2011. "May it Please the Senate: An Empirical Analysis of the Senate Judiciary Committee Hearings of Supreme Court Nominees, 1939–2009." *American University Law Review* 60(3): 590–641.

Wedeking, Justin, and Dion Farganis. 2010. "The Candor Factor: Does Nominee Evasiveness Affect Judiciary Committee Support for Supreme Court Nominees?" *Hofstra Law Review* 39: 329–368.

Wittes, Benjamin. 2006. *Confirmation Wars: Preserving Independent Courts in Angry Times.* Lanham, MD: Roman and Littlefield.

Yalof, David A. 1999. *Pursuit of Justices: Presidential Politics and the Selection of Supreme Court Nominees.* Chicago: The University of Chicago Press.

Yalof, David A. 2008. "Confirmation Obfuscation: Supreme Court Confirmation Politics in a Conservative Era." *Studies in Law, Politics, and Society* 44: 141–171.

IMPEACHMENT AND REMOVAL OF FEDERAL JUDGES

Impeachment is a process for removing from office top government officials and judges. For federal officials and judges, the impeachment process is defined in the U.S. Constitution in Article II, Section 4, and in Article III. For state governors, top officials, and judges, the impeachment process is spelled out in state constitutions and statutes. Impeachment is a process, which means several constitutionally mandated steps must be followed in sequence in order to remove the officeholder.

In more than 200 years of American constitutional history, fewer than 20 federal judges have been impeached and removed from office. Impeachment has also been used as a threat against judges to force them to resign as well. With state judges, there are no detailed statistics to indicate how many have been removed from their positions by impeachment, and it is important to note that impeachment is only one of many ways that state and local judges can be forced out of their positions.

Impeachment does not lead to the criminal prosecution and imprisonment of government officials. Its purpose is not to inflict criminal punishment. Instead, it is meant as a remedial tool to remove individuals from office who because of their conduct have damaged the operation of government institutions and negatively affected the public's trust in government (Cole and Garvey 2015, 8). Thus, impeachment serves to protect government institutions and to provide for the continuity of government when faced with wrongdoing by certain officials.

The U.S. Constitution Impeachment Process and Federal Judges

Article III of the U.S. Constitution stipulates that federal judges, including Supreme Court justices, "shall hold their Offices during good Behavior." This means that judges effectively serve for life, although they can resign or retire at a time of their own choosing. The only way to remove a federal judge against his or her will is through the impeachment process specified in the Constitution in Article I, Sections 2 and 3, and Article II, Section 4. As legal scholar Raoul Berger noted, impeachment is the exclusive means for removing judges and it "bars all alternatives," which means there are no other constitutionally allowable means to remove a federal judge from office. As Berger also pointed out, because impeachment is the sole means of removal, it further serves to insulate judges from the political process and ensure their independence (1973).

The impeachment clause (Article II) states that "The President, Vice President and all civil Officers of the United States, shall be removed from Office on Impeachment for, and Conviction of, Treason, Bribery, or other high Crimes and Misdemeanors." Article I, Section 2, specifies that the House of Representatives must initiate the impeachment process, which means the House defines the impeachment charges against the official and must vote to impeach formally. Article I, Section 3, mandates that the Senate has the sole power to conduct an impeachment trial, based on the House's impeachment charges, and if the official is convicted, the sole sanction is removal from office.

Even though the impeachment clause does not specifically mention judges, Congress has historically interpreted the "all civil officers" requirement to include federal judges. Further, even though the Constitution specifies that judges serve during good behavior, Congress has historically read the Constitution to also mean that judges are impeachable for "high crimes and misdemeanors" and that the concepts of good behavior and high crimes and misdemeanors overlap. As noted in the following section, definitions of high crimes and misdemeanors are contingent on the political process, and there historically has been disagreement among legislators and legal scholars about whether high crimes should be interpreted broadly to include conduct that is not specifically criminal, or interpreted narrowly to include only conduct that is also considered criminal as defined by existing criminal codes.

Impeachment and State Judges

In contrast to federal judges who can only be forcibly removed from their positions through the impeachment process, impeachment is typically one of several different ways that state judges can be removed. The American Judicature Society (now dissolved) once noted that most states have some kind of impeachment process in their constitutions. Those processes usually mirror the federal impeachment process too, in which one house of a state legislature—typically the lower house—initiates impeachment proceedings, and the other house, often the senate, conducts a trial. State constitutions and state laws often define impeachment for reasons such as malfeasance, misfeasance, gross misconduct, gross immorality, high crimes, habitual intemperance, and maladministration. These words are as interpretable as the types of offenses that would pertain to the "high crimes and misdemeanors" clause in the U.S. Constitution.

In addition to impeachment, some states allow judges to be removed through a "legislative address" in which a majority of legislators vote for a judge's removal. A legislative address is a very broad process; unlike impeachment, which requires a legislature to address and define specific conditions for impeachment such as high crime, gross misconduct, and the like, a legislative address is a simple majority vote that does not adhere to a specific process or define a set of reasons for removal. Another means of removal is through a recall election, in which state voters cast votes in a statewide election to remove a judge. If a majority of voters vote to recall a judge, the judge is removed. In addition to recall elections, voters can exercise their power more regularly through the ballot box as well. Because most state judges are elected for set terms such as 4, 6, 7, or 10 years, state voters will often have a regular means of removing judges by not re-electing them. Finally, most states have judicial conduct commissions that review complaints filed against judges. Most commissions have the authority to recommend removal of a judge if warranted, and it may fall to a state governor, legislature, or state supreme court to act upon the commission's recommendation. Generally, though, very few state judges are ever removed through the process.

Examples of Federal Judicial Impeachment

Because impeachment is the only way to remove federal judges, key examples of judicial impeachment in American constitutional development illustrate how the process works in practice. It is important to point out that in more than 200 years of constitutional development, and with more than 3,000 federal judges appointed since 1789, only 15 federal judges have been impeached and removed from office, according to the Federal Judicial Center. Thus, the process of impeachment is rarely used to remove judges; in fact, it is rarely used to remove other federal officials as well. Other judges have resigned when faced with a serious threat of impeachment, but those instances are also rare.

The first judge impeached was U.S. District Judge John Pickering, who was removed in 1804 for charges of mental instability and intoxication while acting as a judge. More controversial than Pickering's impeachment was that of Supreme Court Justice Samuel Chase in 1805. Justice Samuel Chase, a Federalist judge appointed by President John Adams, was impeached by a House of

Representatives controlled by the Jeffersonian Republicans and Anti-Federalists who were bitterly opposed to the Federalist Party's control of the judiciary. The House of Representatives approved impeachment charges accusing Chase of partisan bias as a justice as well as questionable conduct as a trial judge in two high-profile sedition trials. The Senate acquitted Chase of the charges by a vote of 18–16, with several Jeffersonians in the Senate voting to acquit and therefore not siding with their colleagues in the House.

Other examples of federal judicial impeachment concern District Judge West H. Humphreys who was impeached by the House and convicted by the Senate in June, 1862, for refusing to hold court and for joining the Confederacy at the outbreak of the Civil War. In the late 1800s, District Judge Mark W. Delahay was impeached by the House for intoxication on the bench, and he resigned before the Senate could conduct a trial.

Several judges were impeached between 1980 and 2010 for alleged criminal conduct ranging from tax evasion and sexual assault to bribery. District Judge Alcee Hastings, appointed as a judge in 1979, was charged with bribery while a judge and found not guilty by a jury in 1983. In response, the House of Representatives voted to impeach him, and the Senate convicted him and removed him as a judge in 1989. Interestingly, Hastings ran for Congress and was elected to the House of Representatives in 1992 to represent a congressional district in southeast Florida. Another federal judge, Walter L. Nixon, was convicted for making false statements (perjury) to a federal grand jury and was sentenced to five years in a federal prison. He refused to resign as a judge and continued to collect his judicial salary while in prison until the House impeached and the Senate convicted him in 1989.

Threats of Impeachment

Rarely, presidents use the threat of impeachment to try to force a judge or Supreme Court justice to retire. One notable example concerns Justice William O. Douglas and President Richard Nixon's attempt to force him off the high court. Douglas was appointed to the Supreme Court by President Franklin D. Roosevelt, and by the Nixon administration, he had become one of the longest serving justices in American history. By the late 1960s, rumors began to develop about Douglas's personal life, including allegations of extramarital affairs and excessive drinking. He had also developed a reputation as one of the most liberal justices on the Court. The Nixon administration was hostile to the Supreme Court under Chief Justice Earl Warren, mainly because of the Court's liberal decisions in school desegregation, free speech, and criminal justice cases. As top Nixon aide John Ehrlichman noted, the Nixon White House focused its ire on Justice Douglas: "From the beginning, Nixon was interested in getting rid of William O. Douglas; Douglas was the liberal ideologue who personified everything that was wrong with the liberal Warren Court" (quoted in Murphy 2003, 429). Nixon's aides compiled a file on Douglas and sent it to Michigan Congressman Gerald R. Ford with the goal of having Ford initiate Article I impeachment proceedings in the House of Representatives against Justice Douglas. White House aides went so far as to talk about Douglas's impending impeachment with reporters in off-the-record meetings (Murphy 2003, 430). Congressman Ford started impeachment proceedings in the House in April 1970 and outlined several of the accusations against Douglas, including allegedly illegal connections with the gambling industry in Nevada, interfering with U.S. foreign policy during trips to the Dominican Republic, being "one in spirit" with "the militant hippie-yippie movement," and showing early signs of "senility" (quoted in Murphy 2003, 433). Ford also stated that an impeachment offense "is whatever a majority of the House of Representatives considers it to be at a given moment in history." Ford's definition of impeachable offenses shows the highly political nature of impeachment, and although various committees in the House of Representatives have sought to narrow the application of impeachment by defining the contexts in which it is appropriate, Ford's dictum is still relevant because impeachable offenses are essentially what a majority of the House are willing to approve.

In Justice Douglas's case, a House subcommittee voted in December 1970 to drop impeachment proceedings against him. To the Nixon administration's surprise, Douglas had refused to resign and in fact "dug in his heels," although he recognized that the impeachment proceedings were "a very serious threat" (quoted in Murphy 2003, 435). Justice Douglas served on the Court for three more years, and ironically he participated in the famous case in which the Court unanimously ordered President Nixon to turn over White House tapes to the ongoing Watergate investigation. The Court's decision in part prompted Nixon to resign the presidency.

Conclusion

Overall, impeachment is used infrequently to remove federal and state judges from their positions. For federal judges, the impeachment process is specified in the U.S. Constitution, and although the impeachment clause is not clear about the types of conduct for which judges should be impeached, the historical practice of the House of Representatives and Senate is that judges should be impeached and removed for high crimes and misdemeanors committed while serving as federal officials. This is the same standard that applies to other government officials. State-level impeachment of judges is very rare, mainly because judges are elected and can thus be voted out of office due to misconduct, or otherwise fall under state judicial conduct commissions that have authority to investigate judicial misconduct and sanction judges for wrongdoing. At either level, impeachment offers the other branches of government an added check on the judiciary. This process allows elected officials to remove from office judges who, because of their conduct, have damaged the public's trust in government institutions.

John C. Blakeman

See also: Blue Slips; Filibusters of Presidential Nominations to the Federal Bench; Presidential Appointments and Court Packing; Supreme Court Hearings

Further Reading

Abraham, Henry J. 2008. *Justices, Presidents, and Senators: A History of U.S. Supreme Court Appointments from Washington to Bush II.* 6th ed. New York: Rowman and Littlefield.

Berger, Raoul. 1973. *Impeachment: The Constitutional Problems.* Cambridge, MA: Harvard University Press.

Cole, Jared, and Todd Garvey. 2015. *Impeachment and Removal.* Washington, D.C.: Congressional Research Service, 7-5700, R44260.

Federal Judicial Center. 2015. History of Federal Judicial Impeachments. http://www .fjc.gov/history/home.nsf/page/judges_impeachments.html.

Murphy, Bruce Allen. 2003. *Wild Bill: The Legend and Life of William O. Douglas.* New York: Random House.

National Center for State Courts. 2016. Removal of Judges. http://www.judicialselection .us/judicial_selection/methods/removal_of_judges.cfm?state.

Part IV: Political Controversies in State and Federal Courts

INCORPORATION DOCTRINE

Justice Felix Frankfurter once remarked that constitutional law and its interpretation "is not at all a science, but applied politics" (O'Brien 2014, 68). In this respect, the degree to which citizens enjoy personal freedoms is closely related to the U.S. Supreme Court's exercise of its political discretion in construing the broad language of the Fourteenth Amendment's due process clause. Before the Fourteenth Amendment's ratification in 1868, the Supreme Court interpreted the Constitution and the Bill of Rights to apply against only the federal government. Until the early 20th century, the justices narrowly applied and therefore limited the Fourteenth Amendment's reach in protecting state citizens against rights' violations. Increasingly thereafter, the Supreme Court expanded the meaning of the Fourteenth Amendment's due process clause by establishing a constitutional principle to apply specific provisions of the federal Bill of Rights to the actions of state government—an interpretative process often referred to as the *incorporation doctrine*.

The incorporation doctrine enables the Supreme Court to decide what process is due each citizen and defines the limits to governmental authority. In developing the incorporation doctrine, the Supreme Court has used rival interpretative theories to nationalize the federal Bill of Rights and constrain state powers. Today, nearly all of the particular provisions of the Bill of Rights have been incorporated under the Fourteenth Amendment's due process clause, thereby affording to citizens a wide range of personal freedoms in the areas of free speech and press, religious liberty, gun rights, criminal procedure, privacy, and equal protection, among others.

The Incorporation Doctrine's Evolution

At the founding, the wisdom of adopting the U.S. Constitution as a replacement for the ineffectual Articles of Confederation was heatedly debated. Federalists—the supporters of centralized government—favored ratifying the Constitution, whereas Anti-Federalists argued that consolidating federal powers would only lead to the destruction of the states and a loss of individual liberty. A critical element of the debate pertained to whether a written Bill of Rights should be appended to the Constitution. Initially, Federalists such as Alexander Hamilton contended in *Federalist Papers,* No. 84, (1788) that the Constitution itself contained certain rights' protections. Federalist James Madison similarly agreed, asserting that a written bill of rights was unnecessary because federal government could only act through the powers delegated to it under the formal structure of the Constitution, thus leaving the states ample room to safeguard the civil rights and civil liberties of its people through their own constitutions and laws (O'Brien 1991, 131–133). Eventually, the tides of public opinion and the practical necessity of securing the people's support for the Constitution ultimately led to the ratification of 10 Amendments, the Bill of Rights, to the Constitution in 1791.

Although the Anti-Federalists legitimately claimed a victory in securing the approval of a written Bill of Rights as part of the constitutional framework, in practice, those guarantees only constrained federal government powers until the 20th century. Before then, the federal Bill of Rights did not apply against the actions of state government, a principle written into constitutional law by the Marshall Court's ruling in *Barron v. Baltimore* (1833). In *Barron*, a wharf owner complained to the Supreme Court that the improvements the City made to Baltimore's harbor (diverting streams and street paving) destroyed the wharf's profitability after large deposits of sand entered the harbor and lowered the water level, thus making the wharf economically useless because ships could not gain ingress. Barron argued that the City owed him damages for violating the Fifth Amendment, a guarantee that bars private property from being taken for public use without just compensation. In rejecting that argument, Chief Justice John

Marshall ruled that the framers clearly intended that the Bill of Rights only limit federal powers, thus exempting the states from liability under the federal constitution.

Marshall's interpretation ultimately yielded to the evolution of constitutional law principles that developed after the Civil War and the Fourteenth Amendment's ratification in 1868. The Fourteenth Amendment was enacted to give freed slaves constitutional rights' protections. It supplemented the other Civil War amendments that banned slavery (Thirteenth) and guaranteed voting rights (Fifteenth). Under Section 1 of the Fourteenth Amendment, states are prohibited from abridging the rights of citizens under the privileges or immunities clause, or denying the guarantees afforded to citizens under the due process or equal protection clauses. In regards to due process protections, the amendment declares that no state shall "deprive any person of life, liberty, or property, without due process of law."

Because the meaning of the words "life," "liberty," "property," and "due process of law" are inherently vague, federal judges have ample room to interpret the concept of due process in a way that allows the Fourteenth Amendment to absorb, or incorporate, rights contained in the Bill of Rights that protect citizens against state infringement. In addition, the extent to which other Fourteenth Amendment guarantees, such as those pertaining to the privileges or immunities clause, or the right of equal protection, remained subject to judicial interpretation. Thus, in the *Slaughterhouse Cases* (1873), the Supreme Court refused to apply the Fourteenth Amendment's privileges or immunities clause to the states when a group of butchers tried to use it to strike down a state law that gave a corporation a monopoly to run a slaughterhouse in New Orleans. In doing so, the Court set a precedent that the privileges or immunities clause cannot be the basis for extending national citizenship rights and privileges (or in theory any other Bill of Rights' protections) to the states. In subsequent cases, though, the justices incrementally answered the open question of whether the due process clause could operate to incorporate the Bill of Rights to limit state infringement.

Rival Incorporation Theories and the Expansion of Personal Freedoms

The discretion that federal judges exercise in interpreting the substantive and procedural meaning of due process has had significant consequences for the judicial development of law and social policy in the United States. Still, the proposition that the Fourteenth Amendment was intended to incorporate any or all of the Bill of Rights remains highly controversial and subject to considerable judicial and academic debate. As did Justice John Harlan's dissenting opinion in *Hurtado v. California* (1884), Justice Hugo Black argued in his dissenting opinion in *Adamson v. California* (1947) that the Fourteenth Amendment's framers intended that the due process clause incorporated all of the Bill of Rights. In a lengthy appendix in his dissent that surveyed the Fourteenth Amendment's history, Black asserted that "the original purpose of the Fourteenth Amendment" was "to extend to all the people of the nation the complete protection of the Bill of Rights." Rather than agree with the Court's majority decision to uphold a defendant's murder conviction, Black's dissent argued it should have been overturned because it was a violation of due process and the Fifth Amendment's self-incrimination clause to permit a California law to stand because it let prosecutors comment on the defendant's refusal to testify at his trial. Notably, Justices Frank Murphy and Wiley Rutledge, also dissenters in *Adamson*, advanced an even broader variation of Black's theory called *total incorporation plus*. Under this version, due process is said to embrace the total incorporation of all of the Bill of Rights *plus* any other fundamental rights that are not specified therein.

While the total incorporation and different plus theories have received support from a variety of Supreme Court justices from time to time, a competing *incorporation theory of fundamental fairness* has also garnered favor during the Court's history. In contrast to Black's total incorporation theory, in *Adamson v. California* (1947), Justice Felix Frankfurter's concurring opinion argued that the justices were obliged to use an ad hoc, or case-by-case, due process standard that determines if state laws "offend those canons of decency and fairness which express the notions of justice of English-speaking peoples even toward those charged with the most heinous offenses." In *Rochin v. California* (1952), Justice Frankfurter's majority opinion applied this formula to overturn a defendant's drug conviction because the police obtained evidence by forcibly stomach-pumping it out of the defendant's body without a warrant. For Frankfurter, such police conduct violated fundamental fairness because it "shocks the conscience" and "are methods too close to the rack and the screw."

The judicial preference of linking concepts of fundamental rights and fairness to due process has found expression in the *selective incorporation theory*, an approach that has been endorsed by a majority of justices since the late 1930s. Often linked to Justice Benjamin Cardozo's ruling in *Palko v. Connecticut* (1937), the theory enables the Supreme Court to select only those provisions from the Bill of Rights that must be guaranteed against state infringement because they are "of the very essence of a scheme of ordered liberty" and therefore part of a "principle of justice so rooted in the traditions and conscience of our people as to be ranked as fundamental." Often referred to as the "Honor Roll of Superior Rights" or the "preferred freedoms" doctrine, in conjunction with the other rival theories, the Supreme Court has selectively incorporated virtually all of the particular rights contained in the first eight amendments through the due process clause to limit state powers (Abraham and Perry 2003, 95–105).

In *McDonald v. City of Chicago* (2010) the Supreme Court used the incorporation doctrine to apply the Second Amendment's right to bear arms provision to the states, which until then remained an unresolved question in light of the Court's earlier decision in *District of Columbia v. Heller* (2008) (declaring that a District of Columbia gun control ordinance violated the Second Amendment right to self-defense and gun ownership in the home). In *McDonald*, a 5–4 ruling, Justice Samuel Alito's opinion of the Court's plurality reasoned that the right to bear arms was a fundamental freedom under the Fourteenth Amendment's due process clause. As such, it could not be denied because it is a deeply rooted principle that is part of the nation's history, tradition, and system of ordered liberty and justice. With *McDonald*, the Supreme Court added the Second Amendment to a long list of other incorporated rights that encompass free speech and press, religious freedom, and criminal procedure (rights against unreasonable searches and seizure, right against self-incrimination, right to counsel, the right to remain free from cruel and unusual punishments), among others. Accordingly, only a few personal freedoms remain unincorporated, including the Third Amendment's provision against quartering of soldiers, the Fifth Amendment's right to indictment by a grand jury, the Seventh Amendment's right to jury trial in civil cases, and the Eighth Amendment's ban on excessive fines (O'Brien 2014, 344).

Christopher P. Banks

See also: Capital Punishment; Constitutional Interpretation; Defendants' Rights; Freedom of Speech; Gun Ownership Rights and Restrictions; Judicial Federalism; Judicial Review; Religious Freedom

Further Reading

Abraham, Henry J., and Barbara A. Perry. 2003. *Freedom and the Court: Civil Rights and Liberties in the United States.* 8th ed. New York: Oxford University Press.

Amar, Akhil Reed. 1992. "The Bill of Rights and the Fourteenth Amendment." *Yale Law Journal* 101: 1193–1284.

Cortner, Richard C. 1981. *The Supreme Court and the Second Bill of Rights: The Fourteenth Amendment and the Nationalization of Civil Liberties.* Madison: University of Wisconsin Press.

Curtis, Michael Kent. 1986. *No State Shall Abridge: The Fourteenth Amendment and the Bill of Rights.* Durham, NC: Duke University Press.

Fairman, Charles. 1949. "Does the Fourteenth Amendment Incorporate the Bill of Rights? The Original Understanding." *Stanford Law Review* 2: 5–139.

Hamilton, Alexander. (1787–88) 1961. "Federalist Paper 84." *The Federalist Papers,* edited by Jacob E. Cooke. Middletown, CT: Wesleyan University Press.

Israel, Jerold H. 1982. "Selected Incorporation Revisited." *Georgetown Law Review* 71: 253–338.

Nelson, William E. 1998. *The Fourteenth Amendment: From Political Principle to Judicial Doctrine.* Cambridge, MA: Harvard University Press.

O'Brien, David M. 1991. "The Framers' Muse on Republicanism, The Supreme Court, and Pragmatic Constitutional Interpretation." *Constitutional Commentary* 8: 119–148.

O'Brien, David M. 2014. *Constitutional Law and Politics: Civil Rights and Civil Liberties.* 9th ed., vol. 2. New York: W. W. Norton.

Cases

Adamson v. California. 1947. 332 U.S. 46.

Barron v. Baltimore. 1833. 32 U.S. 243.

District of Columbia v. Heller. 2008. 554 U.S. 570.

Hurtado v. California. 1884. 110 U.S. 516.

McDonald v. City of Chicago. 2010. 130 S.Ct. 3020.

Palko v. Connecticut. 1937. 302 U.S. 319.

Rochin v. California. 1952. 342 U.S. 165.

Slaughterhouse Cases. 1873. 83 U.S. 36.

SAME-SEX MARRIAGE

In a historic and landmark decision in *Obergefell v. Hodges* (2015), the Supreme Court afforded to same-sex couples a fundamental right to marry under the Fourteenth Amendment's due process and equal protection clauses. Prior to *Obergefell*, federal and state judiciaries, as well as legislatures, grappled with the legal issue of marriage rights and related constitutional questions of privacy, personal autonomy, gender, and sexual orientation and lesbians, gay, bisexual, and transgender (LGBT) discrimination with mixed, and often conflicting, results. While *Obergefell* recognized the constitutionality of same-sex marriage, it was delivered in a 5–4 decision that generated vitriolic reactions from the dissenting justices who opposed the outcome. In addition to cultural ramifications, the legal repercussions and political implications of the Court's ruling remain unclear and far from settled. Thus, the decision and its impact on American courts and society are likely to be felt for decades to come.

Right to Marriage Cases

Although the states have historically regulated marriage rights, obligations, and benefits, the laws they create are subject to overriding constitutional limitations. Under the Supreme Court's incorporation doctrine, the Fourteenth Amendment's due process clause has been interpreted to extend most of the Bill of Rights to the actions of state governments, including an implied right to privacy. Moreover, the Fourteenth Amendment's equal protection clause has been a source of liberty protections against state interference with personal autonomy. As a result, decisions such as *Griswold v. Connecticut* (1965) and *Eisenstadt v. Baird* (1972) recognized that all citizens enjoy fundamental rights to privacy relative to the personal choices they make about intimate relationships. Whereas *Griswold* struck down a Connecticut law that infringed upon a marital privacy interest because it prohibited the use of contraceptives, *Eisenstadt* ruled that equal protection principles safeguarded unmarried persons against a ban on contraceptives that only applied to unmarried, but not married, couples.

Under this legal framework, the Supreme Court has invalidated state marriage laws because they transgress Fourteenth Amendment due process or equality values. Chief Justice Earl Warren's unanimous opinion in *Loving v. Virginia* (1967) nullified Virginia's criminal ban on interracial marriages on due process and equal protection grounds. In striking down not only Virginia's law but also the legislation of 15 other states that punished marriages based on racial classifications, the Chief Justice reaffirmed that the "freedom to marry has long been recognized as one of the vital personal rights essential to the orderly pursuit of happiness by free men," thus making marriage one of the "basic civil rights of man." The Supreme Court extended *Loving's* reasoning to overturn state laws that either prevented fathers from marrying if they could not meet their child support obligations (*Zablocki v. Redhail*, 1978) or refused to permit prison inmates to marry unless the prison superintendent sanctioned it for a compelling reason (*Turner v. Safley*, 1987). While the Court's earlier right-to-marry precedents were established in the context of heterosexual unions, gradually the justices began to entertain constitutional challenges to state and federal laws that impinged or degraded LGBT rights.

LGBT Discrimination Cases

In *Bowers v. Hardwick* (1986), Georgia's criminal prohibition against heterosexual or homosexual sodomy was upheld even though the defendant committed the act with the consent of another adult male in the defendant's bedroom. In a 5–4 decision, Justice Byron White's opinion of the Court rejected the lower appeals court's ruling that the state law ran afoul of the defendant's fundamental right to engage in homosexual activity under the Fourteenth Amendment's due process clause. Whereas Justice White reasoned that the personal choice to commit private consensual acts of sodomy is not a fundamental right because it is not part of an implicit concept of ordered liberty under the nation's history or traditions, concurring Chief Justice Burger declared that the criminalization of sodomy has "ancient roots" that are "firmly rooted in Judeo-Christian moral and ethical standards."

However, in *Romer v. Evans* (1996), the Supreme Court used the Fourteenth Amendment's equal protection clause to annul an amendment to Colorado's state constitution that prevented localities from enacting laws that protected persons who were being discriminated against because of their sexual orientation. Writing for a 6–3 Court, Justice Anthony Kennedy determined that the state's constitutional amendment, which resulted from a voter referendum, unfairly and irrationally targeted homosexuals and lesbians by taking away civil rights protections that were afforded other groups, thus violating equality principles. Thereafter, Justice Kennedy also wrote the controlling opinion in *Lawrence v. Texas* (2003), a ruling that not only overturned *Bowers v. Hardwick* but also a Texas law that criminalized sodomy by consenting, same-sex couples. In finding that the Texas law affronted substantive privacy rights and liberty interests under the Fourteenth Amendment's due process clause, Kennedy observed that sodomy laws in the states were diminishing and rarely enforced, a trend that aligned with the establishment of laws and court precedents from foreign jurisdictions that validated same-sex rights as basic human rights. In a dissent joined by Chief Justice William Rehnquist and Justice Clarence Thomas, Justice Antonin Scalia complained that the majority's decision to overrule *Bowers* "effectively decrees the end of all morals legislation." In arguing the Court exceeded its authority by striking down a sodomy ban that was created by the democratic political process and majority will, Scalia added that the Court has clearly "taken sides in the culture war" and "has largely signed on to the so-called homosexual agenda."

The Supreme Court's emerging recognition of LGBT rights was accompanied by parallel efforts to expand and restrict them in the states and by federal legislation. In the same year *Lawrence* was decided, the Supreme Judicial Court of Massachusetts granted same-sex couples the right to marry under the state constitution in *Goodridge v. Department of Public Health* (2003). Increasingly fearful that the courts would authorize same-sex marriage, in the aftermath of *Goodridge*, more than half the states enacted laws or passed constitutional amendments that restricted marriage to only heterosexuals. While some state courts struck down legal bans against same-sex marriage, others did not, and public opinion remained divided and in flux on the issue. Against this turbulent political and legal background, the Supreme Court delivered another ruling that was a harbinger of further change. In *United States v. Windsor* (2013), the Court held that the 1996 federal Defense of Marriage Act violated due process and equal protection principles by defining marriage in heterosexual terms, thereby discriminating against same-sex couples that were legally married in states authorizing those relationships. Although *Windsor* was a significant step toward the legal recognition of LGBT rights, the constitutionality of same-sex marriage remained an open question until the Supreme Court answered it in *Obergefell v. Hodges* (2015).

Obergefell v. Hodges

To challenge the legal bans against same-sex marriage in Michigan, Kentucky, Ohio, and Tennessee, in *Obergefell v. Hodges* (2015), 14 same-sex couples and

2 men whose same-sex partners had died argued that their Fourteenth Amendment due process and equal protection rights were denied either because they could not get married or their marriages were not legally binding, even if they were lawfully performed in another state. In supporting their claims, the Supreme Court in a 5–4 ruling declared, "the right to marry is a fundamental right inherent in the liberty of the person" under the due process and equal protection clauses. Justice Anthony Kennedy's opinion of the Court, which was joined by liberal Justices Ruth Bader Ginsburg, Stephen Breyer, Sonia Sotomayor, and Elena Kagan, was sharply opposed by the Court's conservative justices, namely Chief Justice John Roberts and Justices Antonin Scalia, Clarence Thomas, and Samuel Alito, who all wrote dissenting opinions.

Through Kennedy, the five-justice majority emphasized the importance of marriage, claiming it is essential to the human condition. Unlike the dissent, the majority asserted that the history of marriage reflected a pattern of continuity and change. The history of sanctioning arranged marriages and the common law doctrine of coverture (restricting legal rights and obligations of women in favor of husbands) eventually gave way to modern conceptions of marriage and legal precedents that celebrate respecting the personal dignity and autonomous choices that individuals make in an intimate marriage relationship. In this light, the Court's duty is to identify and protect the "interests of the person [that are] so fundamental that the State must accord them its respect." Undertaking this type of judicial inquiry "respects our history and learns from it without allowing the past alone to rule the present," thus enabling the Court to use its power to correct the "nature of injustice" that "we may not always see . . . in our own times." By interpreting the Constitution as a living document, Kennedy thus concludes that same-sex couples have a fundamental right to marry under the due process clause because it advances four principles and traditions that are inherent in the marriage relationship: (1) individual autonomy, (2) securing a two-person union that transcends individual interests, (3) safeguarding children and families, and (4) preserving the social order. Finding that there is a "synergy" between due process and equality, Kennedy also declared that there is a right to marry under the Fourteenth Amendment's equal protection clause.

In separate dissents, Chief Justice Roberts and Justices Scalia, Thomas, and Alito accuse the Court of hijacking the democratic process and wrongfully using its judicial power to end the ongoing political and social debate about whether the states ought to permit same-sex marriages. For the Chief Justice, the Court's decision disregards the fact that only a minority of the states endorse same-sex unions while a majority of the country outlaws it through state law. Thus, he complains that, "Five lawyers have closed the debate and enacted their own vision of marriage as a matter of constitutional law." Similarly, Justice Scalia wrote separately, "to call attention to this Court's threat to American democracy," thereafter characterizing its ruling as "a naked judicial claim to legislative—indeed, *super*-legislative—power." Justice Thomas echoes these sentiments by arguing that the lack of judicial restraint shown by the majority only "exalts the role of the judiciary in delivering social change," an approach that not only undercuts an original understanding of the Constitution's meaning but also threatens everyone's natural rights to support only heterosexual marriages. Finally, Justice Alito adds that *Obergefell* "usurps the constitutional right of the people to decide whether to keep or alter the traditional understanding of marriage," which, in turn, threatens the rule of law and degraded or marginalized the religious beliefs of "many Americans that have traditional ideas."

The internal division on the Supreme Court over the constitutional meaning and impact of *Obergefell* is not likely to dissipate soon as new claimants that oppose same-sex marriage will likely continue to challenge its scope and application in future cases that test the legal boundaries of religious freedom, LGBT rights, government benefits or obligations, and polygamist unions, among others. The future direction of the Supreme Court's jurisprudence on the issue of same-sex marriage and its related legal and political consequences will be invariably influenced by future presidential appointments to the Supreme Court and to lower federal courts. This issue is highlighted by the political turmoil surrounding President Obama's selection of D.C. Circuit judge Merrick Garland to fill the vacancy on the high court created by Justice Scalia's death in February, 2016, during a presidential election year.

Christopher P. Banks

See also: Constitutional Interpretation; Incorporation Doctrine; Judicial Activism and Restraint; Judicial Federalism; Judicial Review; Privacy Rights; Religious Freedom

Further Reading

Boies, David, and Theodore B. Olson. 2014. *Redeeming the Dream: The Case for Marriage Equality*. New York: Viking.

Brown, Cynthia, and Erika K. Lunder. 2015. "Recognition of Same-Sex Marriage: Implications for Religious Objections." *Congressional Research Service (R44244) (October 23, 2015)*. Washington, D.C.: Congressional Research Service.

Franke, Katherine. 2015. *Wedlocked: The Perils of Marriage Equality*. New York: New York University Press.

Gerstmann, Evan. 2008. *Same-Sex Marriage and the Constitution*. 2nd ed. New York: Cambridge University Press.

Kaplan, Roberta A., and Lisa Dickey. 2015. *Then Comes Marriage: United States v. Windsor and the Defeat of DOMA*. New York: W. W. Norton.

Macedo, Stephen. 2015. *Just Married: Same-Sex Couples, Monogamy and the Future of Marriage*. Princeton, NJ: Princeton University Press.

Perry, Rodney M. 2015. "Obergefell v. Hodges: Same-Sex Marriage Legalized." *Congressional Research Service (R44143) (August 7, 2015)*. Washington, D.C.: Congressional Research Service.

Pinello, Daniel R. 2006. *America's Struggle for Same-Sex Marriage*. New York: Cambridge University Press.

Cases

Bowers v. Hardwick. 1986. 478 U.S. 176.

Eisenstadt v. Baird. 1972. 405 U.S. 438.

Goodridge v. Department of Public Health. 2003. 798 N. E. 2d 941.

Griswold v. Connecticut. 1965. 381 U.S. 479.

Lawrence v. Texas. 1967. 539 U.S. 558.

Loving v. Virginia. 1967. 388 U.S. 1.

Obergefell v. Hodges. 2015. 135 S.Ct. U.S. 1039.

Romer v. Evans. 1996. 517 U.S. 620.

Turner v. Safley. 1987. 482 U.S. 78.

United States v. Windsor. 2013. 133 S.Ct. 2675.

Zablocki v. Redhail. 1978. 434 U.S. 374.

THE AFFORDABLE CARE ACT

Enacted in the first two years of the Obama administration, the Patient Protection and Affordable Health Care Act (2010) (Affordable Care Act, ACA) is a highly significant legislative accomplishment that fundamentally alters the delivery of health care for Americans in the 21st century. Even so, it remains politically controversial for ideological reasons. As a result, conservatives who oppose it have attacked it in campaigns and elections whenever politically expedient, and like-minded congressional representatives and senators have repeatedly tried to alter its main provisions or to repeal it entirely. The ACA has also been the focus of several constitutional and statutory interpretation challenges in the federal courts across the nation, including in the Supreme Court. At the state level, because it is perceived by opponents as an egregious example of federal overreaching that directly impacts the operation and independence of state governments in delivering health care, governors and state attorneys general have launched similar legislative and litigation efforts to dismantle or destroy it under federalism principles.

Although the ACA has been the center of unrelenting political attacks from the right and in the states, Congress has yet to repeal it by legislation, and the Supreme Court has largely validated its main provisions in key rulings. Unless conservatives capture the presidency and assume ideological dominance in either Congress or the states, the failure to remove the ACA from the political landscape thus suggests that President Obama's signature piece of domestic legislation will remain an enduring characteristic of his presidential legacy long after he exits the White House.

The Affordable Care Act's Bipartisan Origins and Its Main Provisions

After President Obama signed it, the ACA became law on March 23, 2010. It originated from a variety of health care proposals that had bipartisan support after Medicare and Medicaid programs were established in 1965. Since then, a central theme in the modern health care debate is finding a way to supply health care coverage for a growing number of citizens who remain uninsured (or under-insured), often simply because they cannot afford it or because they are denied due to preexisting medical conditions. Many of the solutions that ultimately were adopted by the ACA included legal mandates that used subsidies to require employers to supply, and individuals to buy, health insurance through market-places, or exchanges, that are administered by the government and the private insurance industry. For example, the 2006 Massachusetts Health Care Plan—a bipartisan initiative that was enacted into law over Governor Mitt Romney's sig-nature and with the support of liberal Senator Ted Kennedy and the conserva-tive Heritage Foundation—used mandates, subsidies, and a state-run exchange to expand health care coverage and greatly reduce the number of state residents who were uninsured (Quadagno 2014, 45).

The ACA's core provisions adopt similar provisions but also significantly increases the role that the federal government plays in conjunction with the states in providing health care to citizens. In particular, the law requires (1) most citizens to buy minimum essential health insurance (the individual mandate) or face a tax penalty; (2) employers with more than 50 full-time employees to offer health insurance to its employees and their children up to the age of 26, or face a fine (employer mandate); (3) the implementation of a nondiscrimination principle that prohibits higher rate-charging or denials of health insurance based on preexisting medical conditions; (4) the use of private health insurance exchanges—marketplaces—that are administered by the federal government or the states that permit citizens and small businesses to buy health insurance on a competitive basis; (5) the use of subsidies or tax credits that allow eligible lower-income citizens and families to buy insurance if insurance is purchased through a federal or state private health insurance exchange; and (6) the regula-tory use of federal monies to expand Medicaid health care coverage in the states for eligible nonelderly low-income individuals (Quadagno 2014, 46–49). As of March 2016, only 14 states and the District of Columbia have chosen to operate their own exchanges under the ACA, thus giving the federal government the responsibility of operating 36 exchanges that span the remaining states across the country (National Conference of State Legislatures 2016).

Political Opposition and Legal Challenges to the Affordable Care Act

The ACA remains politically controversial because opponents vigorously object to the expanded role that the federal government plays in delivering health care options to citizens in the states through private insurers. Much of the opposition comes from conservatives and libertarians in Congress or state governments that try to repeal the ACA or, alternatively, defund or delay its operation and implementation (Redhead and Kinzer 2015). While efforts to repeal the legislation outright have not been successful during the Obama administration, its ideological opponents have strategically attacked it in the federal courts.

In *National Federation of Independent Business v. Sibelius* (2012), the most controversial feature of the law, the individual mandate, was challenged on the grounds that enacting it was an unconstitutional exercise of Congress's Article I commerce or taxing and spending powers. In his opinion of the Court, Chief Justice John Roberts concluded that while the individual mandate could not be sustained under the commerce power or Article I's necessary or proper clause, it nonetheless can be justified as a tax under Congress's power to tax and spend for the general welfare. In addition, Roberts put new limitations on congressional authority by ruling that Congress exceeded its powers in requiring that states expand their Medicaid health care coverage under the threat of losing federal monies if they failed to do so. Notably, the Court was not of one mind in reaching these conclusions. The main dissenters, Justices Antonin Scalia, Anthony Kennedy, Clarence Thomas, and Samuel Alito, argued in a separate, unsigned opinion that the entire ACA should be struck down as an unconstitutional exercise of Congress's commerce and taxing authority. Nor could it be justified as an exercise of Congress's power to enact necessary and proper laws. On the other hand, Roberts crossed party lines and joined his liberal colleagues—Ruth Bader Ginsburg, Stephen Breyer, Sonja Sotomayor, and Elena Kagan—to uphold the individual mandate because Congress legitimately mandated the purchase of minimum health care coverage under its taxing powers. On the Medicaid expansion issue, two justices, Ginsburg and Sotomayor, did not agree with the rest of the Court that Congress violated its spending authority because they did not see how the ACA imposed any element of statutory coercion on the states. In spite of the fractured result, the effect of the Court's ruling is to uphold Medicaid expansion while limiting Congress's ability to withhold all federal funding unless there was compliance, thus essentially making Medicaid expansion optional in the states.

Another formidable litigation challenge tried to undercut the ACA's funding mechanism. A key element of the health care law's operation depends upon whether eligible individuals and small businesses can offset the cost of buying health insurance with the help of federal subsidies they receive if they purchase it through private health insurance exchanges. Thus, in *King v. Burwell* (2015), opponents of the ACA argued that the exact wording of the law restricted subsidy payments and the purchase of insurance to and from only an "Exchange established by the State" (ACA 2010 § 1401). If the challenge succeeded, then a majority of those seeking coverage in federally run exchanges would not be able to receive subsidies or buy health insurance because only 14 states operated exchanges. As Justice Sotomayor remarked at oral argument, endorsing the challenger's position would effectively put the ACA into a "death spiral that [the health care] system was created to avoid" (Howe 2015). However, by a 6–3 vote, the justices upheld the subsidies provision on the grounds that the statutory text cited by the challengers could not be read in isolation from the ACA's overall purpose, which was to provide more health care coverage for those who needed it by using either federal- or state-run exchanges. Justice Scalia's dissent, joined by Thomas and Alito, countered that abandoning the statute's plain meaning was nothing more than judicial activism because it wrongfully imposed a judicially created version of "SCOTUScare" on unwilling participants in a radical new system of health care.

While the *National Federation of Independent Business* and *King* rulings remain significant victories for the Obama administration, conservatives in Congress and the states have continued to use the federal courts as the means to disrupt or dismantle the ACA. A source of recurring litigation are suits arguing that certain types of nonexempt businesses or employers are not mandated under the ACA to give coverage to its employees for all FDA-approved contraceptive and sterilization procedures on the grounds that doing so violates deeply held and sincere religious convictions. In a 5–4 ruling, in *Burwell v. Hobby Lobby Stores, Inc.* (2014), the Supreme Court ruled that the so-called contraceptive mandate violated the federal Religious Freedom Restoration Act, an outcome that permitted Hobby Lobby and Conestoga Wood Specialties—as closely held for-profit corporations—to remain exempt from giving its employees contraceptive coverage under federal regulations.

While the Court in *Hobby Lobby* did not directly rule on the constitutional issue of whether the contraceptive mandate violates the First Amendment's free exercise of religion clause, it encourages future litigation that will ultimately test that issue but also generate other cases that make a claim for statutory exemptions on religious freedom grounds. Indeed, if new federal regulations that are in the planning stage actually become law, then big businesses and conservatives are likely to launch analogous litigation that will determine if the ACA's nondiscrimination rule means that employers must offer insurance plans that will cover the cost of gender transition and language translation services and procedures for employees (Alonso-Zaldivar 2016). In addition, the vacancy created on the Supreme Court in early 2016 by Justice Scalia's unexpected death and whether President Obama (or his successor) will be able to fill it with a liberal appointment before the 2016 presidential and Senate elections will go a long way in determining if conservatives will begin to win the war it is waging against the ACA in the federal courts.

Christopher P. Banks

See also: Constitutional Interpretation; Judicial Federalism; Privacy Rights; Religious Freedom

Further Reading

Alonso-Zaldivar, Ricardo. 2016. "Disputed Health Law Rule Would Broaden Transgender Rights." Associated Press. March 22. http://hosted.ap.org/dynamic/stories/U/US _HEALTH_OVERHAUL_TRANSGENDER?SITE=AP.

Banks, Christopher P., and John C. Blakeman. 2012. *The Supreme Court and New Federalism: From the Rehnquist Court to the Roberts Court.* Lanham, MD: Roman and Littlefield.

Howe, Amy. 2015. "Justices to Weigh Subsidies for Health Insurance: In Plain English." *SCOTUSblog*, February 23. http://www.scotusblog.com/2015/02/justices-to-weigh -subsidies-for-health-insurance-in-plain-english/.

Karlan, Pamela S. 2012. "Foreword: Democracy and Disdain." *Harvard Law Review* 126(1): 1–71. http://www.scotusblog.com/2015/06/symposium-a-decisive-scotus -victory-for-the-aca-that-may-bring-an-end-to-endless-aca-litigation/.

Koppelman, Andrew. 2013. *The Tough Luck Constitution and the Assault on Health Care Reform.* New York: Oxford University Press.

National Conference of State Legislatures. 2016. "Health Insurance Exchanges or Marketplaces: State Profiles and Actions as of March 1, 2016." http://www.ncsl.org/por tals/1/documents/health/health_insurance_exchanges_state_profiles.pdf.

Persily, Nathaniel, Gillian E. Metzger, and Trevor W. Morrison, eds. 2013. *The Health Care Case: The Supreme Court's Decision and Its Implications.* New York: Oxford University Press.

Quadagno, Jill. 2014. "Right-Wing Conspiracy? Socialist Plot? The Origins of the Patient Protection and Affordable Care Act." *Journal of Health Care Politics, Policy and Law.* 39: 35–56.

Redhead, C. Stephen, and Janet Kinzer. 2015. "Legislative Actions to Repeal, Defund, or Delay the Affordable Care Act." *Congressional Research Service (R43289) (November 14, 2015).* Washington, D.C.: Congressional Research Service.

Selker, Harry P., and June S. Wasser, eds. 2014. *The Affordable Care Act as a National Experiment: Health Policy Innovations and Lessons.* New York: Springer.

U.S. Government Publishing Office. 2010. P.L. 111–148: Patient Protection and Affordable Care Act. https://www.gpo.gov/fdsys/pkg/PLAW-111publ148/content-detail.html.

Cases

Burwell v. Hobby Lobby, Inc. 2014. 134 S.Ct. 2751.
King v. Burwell. 2015. 135 S.Ct. 2480.
National Federation of Independent Business v. Sibelius. 2012. 132 S.Ct. 2566.

FREEDOM OF SPEECH

The First Amendment to the U.S. Constitution reads, "Congress shall make no law respecting an establishment of religion, or prohibiting the free exercise thereof; or abridging the freedom of speech, or of the press, or the right of the people peaceably to assemble, and to petition the Government for a redress of grievances." Note that although the amendment only references Congress, it has been construed to apply to federal, state, and local governments in general. Freedom of speech is one of at least five basic rights defined by the amendment, and it is a right considered vital to freedom and democratic governance. As U.S. Supreme Court Justice Louis Brandeis noted in the early free speech case of *Whitney v. California* in 1927, the framers of the Constitution and First Amendment "believed that freedom to think as you will and to speak as you think are means indispensable to the discovery and spread of political truth." The First Amendment limits the power of government to censor and limit what people say, and over the course of the 20th century, the Supreme Court emerged as the main policymaking institution charged with policing federal, state, and local government attempts to limit freedom of speech. Thus, over time, the high court sought to define various tests, or standards, by which government regulation of speech is to be judged under the Constitution. Much of the Court's jurisprudence has sought to balance the competing interests of an individual's right to freedom of speech with the government's need to regulate speech under certain conditions. As the Court has striven to balance those competing interests, it has articulated in a series of cases when government can or cannot limit speech, and in so doing has developed the large body of constitutional law on the First Amendment's free speech clause.

The right to free speech is not absolute; it can be regulated by government under certain circumstances. To be sure, since the addition of the First Amendment to the Constitution in 1791, political institutions at the federal, state, and local level have sought both to limit and protect free speech, and it was not until 1925 that the Supreme Court began to articulate the basic constitutional doctrines protecting free speech from most government regulation. As constitutional law scholars Neal Devins and Louis Fisher note, prior to the early 20th century, "free speech was a matter decided by Congress, the president, and state and local communities," and ultimately protections for free speech resided as much in public sentiment as well as court decisions (2004, 173). However, since at least 1919, cases concerning free speech have regularly appeared on the Supreme Court's docket. As the Court has confronted government attempts to limit speech, it has articulated several "tests" or judicial standards for determining when speech is protected from the government. In addition, the Court has created categories of speech that are typically protected from government regulation and other categories of speech that are not protected.

The Clear and Present Danger Test, the Bad Tendency Test, and the Free Marketplace of Ideas

In a series of cases in 1919, soon after World War I, the Court addressed, for the first time, the meaning of the free speech clause. In one case, *Schenk v. United States*, the Court confronted the federal government's attempt to censor speech that potentially interfered with the draft. In *Schenk*, the Court defined the clear and present danger test, which is the first constitutional test for determining when government can censor or punish someone's speech. Justice Oliver Wendell Holmes crafted the test, and his opinion is worth quoting at length (*Schenk v. United States* 1919, 52):

> The character of every act depends upon the circumstances in which it is done. . . . The most stringent protection of free speech would not protect a man in falsely shouting fire in a crowded theatre and causing a panic . . . the question in every case is whether the words used are used in such circumstances and are of such a nature as to create a clear and present danger that they will bring about the substantive evils that Congress has a right to prevent.

For Holmes and the Court, the speech in question in *Schenk* sought to encourage young men to avoid the draft during World War I, and because it thus posed a clear and present threat to the government's power to wage war, the speech could be banned—it was not protected by the First Amendment.

In a subsequent case only a few weeks later, the Court ignored the clear and present danger and created what is called the bad tendency test. In the *Abrams v. United States* case, at issue was speech by a group of socialists and anarchists that advocated for a general strike of American workers to curtail production of war materials vital for U.S. forces. The speakers hoped that a general strike would force the United States to ultimately withdraw from the conflict in Europe and from potentially interfering in the Russian Revolution. Even though the general strike never happened, and the government suffered no harm, a majority of the Court still allowed the government to punish the speech because the purpose of it was to "defeat the war program of the United States" and was thus encouraged harmful or bad tendencies in society. It did not matter that the speech did not achieve its goal of interfering with the war effort; what mattered was the potential, harmful results that the speech could have (*Abrams v. United States*, 1919, 621). Justice Holmes, author of the clear and present danger test, dissented in *Abrams*, and it articulates what has become a very powerful view of the free speech clause. Holmes argued that the ultimate goal of the First Amendment is "the free trade in ideas—the best test of truth is the power of the thought to get itself accepted in the competition of the market" (*Abrams v.*

United States, 1919, 630). Holmes's free marketplace of ideas holds, essentially, that there should be very few limits on free speech. The public will determine those ideas that it values and those that it does not value in the competition of the marketplace. The public will make its preferences known, thus the government should allow a wide range of speech and ideas to flourish. Other justices and later Supreme Courts would eventually gravitate to Holmes's idea.

Fighting Words and Obscenity

The Court has defined other classes of speech that are considered outside of the First Amendment because they do not typically contribute to free exchange of ideas "and are of such slight social value as a step to truth that any benefit that may be derived from them is clearly outweighed by the social interest in order the morality" (*Chaplinsky v. New Hampshire*, 1942, 26). One class of speech—fighting words—is not normally protected by the First Amendment because they tend to cause injury and immediate breaches of the peace, and as such contribute little to public debate. However, the Court ruled in 1992 that government generally cannot prohibit hate speech directed at a person or group because of their race, color, gender, or religion. Although hate speech is insulting and can lead to violence, as the Court put it, the government cannot regulate speech "based on hostility—or favoritism—toward the underlying message expressed" (*R.A.V. v. City of St. Paul*, 1992).

Another class of speech that can be banned is obscenity. Obscene speech is also of little value, and the Court has grappled for more than 50 years with how to define obscenity. Speech that is only offensive to some is not usually obscene. In *Cohen v. California* (1968), the Court ruled that the First Amendment does not allow the government to censor or punish offensive words used in public debate. However, the Court qualified that decision in subsequent cases in which it imposed stricter limits on student speech in public schools or at school-sponsored functions. Thus, even though schoolchildren do not check their first amendment rights at the schoolhouse gate (*Tinker v. Des Moines Independent Community School District*, 1969), school administrators do have the power to limit student speech in order to maintain order and good discipline within a school. Thus in *Morse v. Frederick* (2007), the Court upheld a school principal's censorship of a student sign that read "Bong Hits for Jesus" that was displayed at a school function, even though the sign was not displayed on school property.

Finally, speech that is defamatory is not typically protected under the First Amendment either. Defamation is an old common law principle that allows individuals to sue others who use false words about them. Slander and libel are forms of defamation, and speakers who use slanderous words or who print libelous statements are not protected by the First Amendment. However, public figures, such as politicians or others who intentionally put themselves into the public spotlight, cannot collect damage awards for defamation unless they prove that the speaker intentionally lied about them in order to damage their reputation. While there are thousands of defamation cases in the United States every year, most will be decided by state courts, and very few will involve public figures.

Speech and Conduct

The Supreme Court has recognized that speech can be linked to conduct, thereby making the conduct itself expressive and protected under the First Amendment. In the very controversial case of *Texas v. Johnson* (1989), the Court ruled by a 5–4 vote that burning the American flag is a form of expressive or symbolic speech and therefore protected under the free speech clause. The free speech clause protects symbolic expression such as the wearing of articles of clothing or black armbands to protest war (*Tinker v. Des Moines*, 1969) or saluting or refusing to salute the American flag. However, the Court made clear that government can regulate certain types of conduct linked to symbolic expression, even if the regulation ends up limiting free speech. In *United States v. O'Brien* (1968), the justices ruled that the burning of draft cards to protest the Vietnam War was not protected by the free speech clause because the federal government had an overriding interest in maintaining an orderly draft system, and destroying draft cards even to send a protest message interfered with government's national security interest.

Speech and Public Safety

Speech and conduct can also be linked in disputes concerning speech taking place in public places. The Court has usually held that publicly owned spaces (but not private property) are normally open to free speech activities. Exceptions include military bases or government properties linked to national security and other areas that by their nature preclude free speech activities. The government can regulate speech in public places, but only through time, place, and manner regulations. Although the content of the speech cannot normally be regulated, the time at which it takes place, its location, and the manner in which it is done can be limited, in part for the interest of safeguarding public safety. Thus, the government must normally articulate clear and compelling reasons for time, place, and manner rules, and such reasons might include public safety (e.g., not allowing speakers to hold a rally in public spaces during highly congested times) or to preserve the tranquility of a neighborhood—so, noisy demonstrations cannot be held in public parks late at night, and related disturbances will get limited First Amendment protection.

Speech and Campaign Finance

One area of free speech that has vexed the Court since the early 1970s concerns the extent to which campaign finance, such as donations to political candidates and causes, is protected by the free speech clause. Since 1971, when Congress comprehensively regulated political contributions with the Federal Election Campaign Act, the high court has decided many campaign finance disputes often by close margins. In general, the Court has recognized that donations to political campaigns and causes are an aspect of free speech and thus invoke First Amendment considerations. In one controversial case, *Citizens United v. Federal Election Commission* (2010), the Court by a 5–4 majority ruled that political donations by corporations and unions are a form of free speech, and restrictions on those donations will generally be unconstitutional. In the aftermath of the Court's decision campaign, donations from corporations and unions and other groups increased considerably (Brennan Center 2016). Retired Supreme Court Justice John Paul Stevens, who dissented in *Citizens United*, was very critical of the Court's decision and called for a constitutional amendment that would allow Congress to regulate campaign finance more strictly. As he noted:

> Unlimited expenditures by nonvoters . . . whether made by nonresidents in state elections . . . by corporations, by unions, or by trade associations in federal elections—impairs the process of democratic self-government by making successful candidates more beholden to the nonvoters who supported them than to the voters who elected them. (2014, 78)

Conclusion

Since 1919, the Supreme Court has been the main policymaker for protecting freedom of speech under the First Amendment. Through several hundred cases, the Court has defined the basic principles of the free speech clause and the appropriate constitutional limits on the ability of federal, state, and local governments to regulate speech. The Court has made clear that the freedom of speech is not an absolute right, but it has also emphasized that it will closely scrutinize any government regulation of the freedom and that free speech is a preferred right that deserves a heightened sense of protection. There are three broad principles that the Court applies to any government regulation on speech. First, the regulation cannot be vague—it must specifically address what type of speech the government seeks to regulate. Second, government cannot regulate the underlying content of speech, although it can regulate the time, place, or manner in which the speech is delivered. Third, the regulation on speech cannot be overly broad or regulate too much speech relative to the government's objectives. Thus, the government can only control the minimal amount of speech necessary to achieve its policy goals.

The Court's decisions on free speech are complex, but over the course of almost 100 years, it has become clear that the justices value free speech and recognize its vital importance to American democracy. Most of them would agree with Justice Holmes's argument that free speech should exist in a free marketplace of ideas that is relatively free from government regulation.

John C. Blakeman

See also: Campaign Finance; Constitutional Interpretation; Incorporation Doctrine; Partisan Judicial Elections and Political Money

Further Reading

Abraham, Henry J., and Barbara A. Perry. 1994. *Freedom and the Court: Civil Rights and Liberties in the United States.* 6th ed. New York: Oxford University Press.

The Brennan Center for Justice. 2016. "Democracy Agenda: Money in Politics." February 4. http://www.brennancenter.org/analysis/democracy-agenda-money-politics.

Devins, Neal, and Louis Fisher. 2004. *The Democratic Constitution.* New York: Oxford University Press.

O'Brien, David M. 2014. *Constitutional Law and Politics: Civil Rights and Civil Liberties.* 9th ed., vol. 2. New York: W. W. Norton.

Stevens, John Paul. 2014. *Six Amendments: How and Why We Should Change the Constitution.* New York: Little, Brown.

Cases

Abrams v. United States. 1919. 250 U.S. 616.

Chaplinsky v. New Hampshire. 1942. 315 U.S. 599.

Citizens United v. Federal Election Commission. 2010. 558 U.S. 310.

Cohen v. California. 1971. 403 U.S. 15.

Miller v. California. 1973. 413 U.S. 15.

Morse v. Frederick. 2007. 551 U.S. 393.

R.A. V. v. City of St. Paul. 1992. 505 U.S. 377.

Schenk v. United States. 1919. 249 U.S. 47.

Texas v. Johnson. 1989. 491 U.S. 397.

Tinker v. Des Moines Independent Community School District. 1969. 393 U.S. 503.

United States v. O'Brien. 1968. 391 U.S. 367.

Whitney v. California. 1927. 274 U.S. 357.

CAMPAIGN FINANCE

Campaign finance laws regulate how individuals, political parties, and organized groups raise and spend money during federal and state campaigns and elections. Often they are created in response to political scandals or for maintaining the integrity and fairness of elections. As a result, the governmental interest in preventing corruption or the appearance of corruption traditionally has oriented the analysis of Supreme Court cases that interpret the First Amendment's meaning in relation to campaign finance laws. In campaign finance cases, federal and state courts attempt to strike a proper balance between the legislative goal of trying to control corruption and countervailing constitutional requirements that encourage free speech under the First Amendment during political elections. In deciding cases, state or federal courts must reconcile these interests in light of what individuals, political parties, and organized groups try to do in using money to advance their political agendas through election activity. Beginning with *Buckley v. Valeo* (1976), the Supreme Court has used its authority to superintend the political process more closely in campaign finance cases. In doing so, the Court has increasingly placed fewer limits on how money is raised and spent during election cycles, and that trend has continued in the Roberts Court (2005 to present). Two controversial cases, *Citizens United v. FEC* (2010) and *McCutcheon v. FEC* (2014), demonstrate that there are virtually no First Amendment regulatory limits that can prevent outside interests from raising money and spending it on campaigns and elections.

Campaign Financing Laws

Democrat Jesse Unruh, a powerful Californian politician who wielded national influence as a legislator and state treasurer in the 1960s and 1970s, once quipped that "money is the mother's milk of politics" (Uhlig 1987). A well-funded political campaign is the type of nourishment that an office seeker needs to be electorally successful, in part because the cost of political campaigning is only spiraling upward. According to the Center for Responsive Politics, in the 2014 election cycle, each of the 832 Republican and Democratic candidates that ran for a seat in the U.S. House of Representatives raised and spent roughly an average of $1 million in their political campaigns. For Senate races, every one of the 102 candidates raised and spent on average between $6 and $8 million (Center for Responsive Politics 2016). In the run-up to the 2016 presidential and congressional campaigns in Ohio, a battleground state, affluent individuals and businesses have spent at least $28 million on the presidential race, nearly $40 million on the U.S. Senate contests, and $18 million on Ohio's remaining 16 congressional races (Troy 2016). Political money, which comes from a complex array of individuals, political parties, political action committees (PACs), corporations, labor unions, and organized interests, is raised and spent to advance partisan interests and to gain political influence. Campaign finance laws thus attempt to minimize the effect that money has by putting a cap on contributions, restricting expenditures, or creating public disclosure requirements of campaign finances.

Early campaign finance laws were enacted to prevent deep-pocketed individuals or groups from having disproportionate political influence. Bribing or extorting politicians affects the political system's legitimacy at its core. The growth of machine politics and receiving jobs through patronage appointments in the 1820s exposed the impact corruption has on politics. On the state level, in 1829, New York passed a law called "An Act to Preserve the Purity of Elections," which sought to prohibit anyone from making political contributions in elections. Mindful of the Credit Mobilier transcontinental railroad scandal in the early 1870s, in 1907, Congress forbade corporations and national banks from making campaign contributions in federal elections. With the Publicity Act of 1910, Congress imposed disclosure requirements that publicly recorded the contributions and expenditures of national party committees in congressional elections. A year later, the law was amended by creating monetary limits on House and Senate races. Campaign finance reform accelerated into the early 20th century when Congress passed the Tillman Act (1907), a measure that banned corporate expenditures in federal elections. A similar enactment, the Taft-Hartley Act (1947), prohibited labor unions from using its money to influence federal elections. Identical legislation was an integral part of state law as well. Whether prompted by political chicanery or not, the general thrust of these laws was to try to diminish the influence of corruption, or its appearance, on political elections in order to enhance their integrity and fairness (Banks 2001, 23–24).

Campaign Finance Reform and *Buckley v. Valeo*

In 1971, Congress enacted sweeping campaign finance legislation that later became the focus of *Buckley v. Valeo* (1976), a landmark ruling that set the parameters of subsequent Supreme Court jurisprudence in campaign and election law. In *Buckley*, the Court reviewed the 1971 Federal Election Campaign Act (FECA) and subsequent amendments that attempted to curb the abuse of fundraising linked to the Watergate scandal and the 1972 presidential campaign. In addition to requiring that candidates, party committees, and PACs publicly disclose the money that they raised and spent in federal campaigns, the FECA established contribution and expenditure restrictions that regulated donations and spending during elections. An independent agency, the Federal Election Commission (FEC), was created to enforce FECA provisions. A third element of FECA established public (voluntary taxpayer) funding for presidential campaigns: if a candidate agrees to spending limits, then the campaign can receive matching funds in primaries and even more public funding in general elections (Banks 2001).

In *Buckley*, the Supreme Court upheld the contribution restrictions but struck down the spending limits under the First Amendment. In balancing the interests at stake, the Court reasoned that the contribution limits reasonably prevented quid pro quos (exchanging money for political favors). However, independent expenditure limits (which are not directly coordinated with a candidate's campaign or from the candidate's personal funds) directly impairs "the quantity of expression by restricting the numbers of issues discussed, the depth of their exploration, and the size of the audience reached." Notably, the Court rejected the government's interest in trying to equalize the speaking power of individuals and groups that could not spend as much as those who were more affluent. The Court also upheld the public funding provision for presidential campaigns while striking down the parts of FECA that improperly appointed members of FEC.

After *Buckley*, soft money contributions (funds given to political parties instead of candidates to support campaign activities) and monies spent on certain types of political advertising referred to as issue advocacy, which do not specifically advocate the election or defeat of a specific candidate, became problematic because these activities did not fall under FECA requirements. Thus, Congress passed the Bipartisan Campaign Reform Act of 2002 (BCRA), or the McCain-Feingold Act, as a reform measure. Among other things, the BCRA banned soft money and issue advocacy practices. In terms of issue advocacy, corporations and labor unions were prohibited from using their general treasury funds to pay for advertisement expenses that clearly referred to a candidate's election or defeat within 30 days before a primary and 60 days before a general election.

Upon challenge, in *McConnell v. FEC* (2003), a badly divided Supreme Court under the leadership of Chief Justice William Rehnquist upheld both of the soft money and issue advocacy provisions. After 2005, however, John Roberts replaced Rehnquist as Chief Justice, and Justice Samuel Alito filled the vacancy created by Justice Sandra Day O'Connor's retirement. The changes in the Court's composition led the Roberts Court to begin reviewing not only *Buckley* as a precedent but also others that were set thereafter, including *McConnell*. In contrast to the Rehnquist Court, the Roberts Court began to reshape campaign finance law by imposing fewer First Amendment restrictions on election activities, especially by wealthy individuals and outside groups.

The Roberts Court's Campaign Financing Decisions

In a series of rulings, the Roberts Court (from 2005) signaled early on that it was less tolerant of campaign financing regulations that undermined the values of encouraging First Amendment free speech and political debate during elections (Norden et al. 2016). In *Randall v. Sorrell* (2006), the Supreme Court invalidated a Vermont law that placed spending and contribution limits in statewide races; the ruling is significant for observing that the contribution restrictions of $200 were set far below the $1,000 limit upheld in *Buckley*. Thereafter, in *FEC v. Wisconsin Right to Life, Inc.* (2007) the Supreme Court revisited, but did not expressly overturn, *McConnell* by invalidating the BCRA's issue advocacy requirements as applied to campaign ads generated by Wisconsin Right to Life and other groups. In *Davis v. FEC* (2008), the Court struck down the BCRA's "Millionaires' Amendment," a provision that tried to equalize the campaign finances of opposing candidates in federal elections by increasing the contribution limits for less affluent candidates when they were pitted against wealthier self-financed opponents.

With *Citizens United v. FEC* (2010), in a 5–4 ruling, the Roberts Court held that the First Amendment protected the right of corporations and labor unions to use their general treasury funds to pay for expenses that express their political support or opposition to candidates, a practice that was outlawed by federal law and earlier Supreme Court precedents. Shortly thereafter, *McCutcheon v. FEC* (2014) invalidated the aggregate contribution limits established by the FECA and its amendments, declaring that they did nothing to prevent quid pro quos, or actual corruption, a First Amendment principle that was also reinforced by the *Citizens United* ruling. *Citizens United* and *McCutcheon*—along with *Speech-Now.org v. FEC* (2010), which is a D.C. Circuit federal appeals court decision that nullified under the First Amendment federal restrictions that limited contributions to nonprofit, I.R.S. §527 groups that make only independent expenditures—have revolutionized campaign finance law by exponentially increasing the amount of unregulated and undisclosed political monies that can be contributed and spent in federal and state political elections by individuals and outside groups (Weiner 2015).

The changes in Supreme Court campaign finance law have corresponded to other transformations in the political system. In the past, political monies often flowed through political parties and PACs using segregated accounts that were under public regulation and scrutiny. In today's politics, parties have become less important, so the focus of election activity is more candidate-centered. Rapid technological revolutions have encouraged candidates to use the Internet, social media, and TV advertising as the preferred choices for attracting political support and in conveying partisan messages. In light of these changes, some argue that the Supreme Court's rulings are defensible because the unlimited spending expands the range and diversity of contemporary political debate under the First Amendment. Yet critics counter that decisions such as *Citizens United* diminish democratic participation and political equality by allowing a narrow set of wealthy individuals, or a large range of super-PACs (entities that can raise unlimited money from corporations, unions, political committees, and individuals to pay for independent expenditures that advocate the election or defeat of candidates if they are not made in coordination with a candidate's campaign) to gain a disproportionate influence in campaigns and elections. In a 2014 interview with legal scholar Jeffrey Rosen, Justice Ruth Bader Ginsburg (who dissented in *Citizens United*) declared that, "If there was one decision I would overrule, it would be *Citizens United* [because the] notion that we have all the democracy that money can buy strays so far from what our democracy is supposed to be" (Rosen 2014). For other critics, the Court's jurisprudence has also facilitated the rise of "dark money," or funds that are given to nonprofit §501(c) tax-exempt groups that are not under any legal obligation to disclose their donors. By one estimate, after *Citizens United*, about $618 million of nearly $2 billion in outside spending represent dark funds (Weiner 2015, 7). While direct impact of the Roberts Court's campaign financing cases remains controversial and subject to conflicting interpretations, clearly in their aftermath, there has been an infusion of billions of dollars of unregulated money into the American political system that is often not subject to public disclosure (Weiner 2015).

Christopher P. Banks

See also: Constitutional Interpretation; Judicial Campaigns and the First Amendment; Partisan Judicial Elections and Political Money

Further Reading

Banks, Christopher P. 2001. "The Supreme Court's Response to American Political Corruption: The Failure of Constitutional Law or the Success of Republican Liberty?" *Superintending Democracy: The Courts and the Political Process*, edited by Christopher P. Banks and John C. Green. Akron, OH: University of Akron Press.

Center for Responsive Politics. 2016. "Election Overview (2014 Election Cycle)." https://www.opensecrets.org/overview/index.php?cycle=2014&type=G&display=A.

Hasen, Richard L. 2016. *Plutocrats United: Campaign Money, the Supreme Court, and the Distortion of American Elections*. New Haven, CT: Yale University Press.

Norden, Lawrence, Brent Ferguson, and Douglas Keith. 2016. *Five to Four*. New York: Brennan Center for Justice.

O'Brien, David M. 2014. *Constitutional Law and Politics: Struggles for Power and Governmental Accountability*. 9th ed., vol. 1. New York: W. W. Norton.

Rosen, Jeffrey. 2014. "Ruth Bader Ginsburg Is an American Hero." *New Republic*, September 28. http://www.newrepublic.com/article/119578/ruth-bader-ginsburg-interview-retirement-feminists-jazzercise.

Troy, Tom. 2016. "How Money Talks: With Millions to Spend and Few Limits, Mysterious Groups Dominate Campaigns." *Toledo Blade*, May 15. http://www.toledoblade.com/Politics/2016/05/15/How-money-talks.html.

Uhlig, Mark A. 1987. "Jesse Unruh, A California Political Power, Dies." *New York Times*, August 6. http://www.nytimes.com/1987/08/06/obituaries/jesse-unruh-a-california-political-power-dies.html.

Weiner, Daniel I. 2015. *Citizens United Five Years Later*. New York: Brennan Center for Justice.

Cases

Buckley v. Valeo. 1976. 424 U.S. 1.
Citizens United v. FEC. 2010. 558 U.S. 310.

Davis v. FEC. 2008. 554 U.S. 724.

FEC v. Wisconsin Right to Life, Inc. 2007. 551 U.S. 449.

McConnell v. FEC. 2003. 540 U.S. 93.

McCutcheon v. FEC. 2014. 134 S.Ct. 1434.

Randall v. Sorrell. 2006. 548 U.S. 230.

SpeechNow.org v. FEC. 2010. 599 F.3d 686.

RELIGIOUS FREEDOM

Religious freedom is a prominent part of the constitutional and political development of the United States. It is grounded in the First Amendment to the U.S. Constitution and was ratified in 1791. It reads, "Congress shall make no law respecting an establishment of religion, or prohibiting the free exercise thereof." The establishment and free exercise clauses are different and guard distinct rights from government interference. The free speech clause, which is also in the First Amendment, has propelled the U.S. Supreme Court into the main policymaking institution that interprets the religious liberty clauses and places limits on government power.

The First Amendment religious liberty clauses were debated and passed 150 years after the end of religious warfare in Europe that arose out of the Protestant Reformation. The history of religious conflict, together with the growth of many religious traditions in the American colonies, such as the Puritans, Anglicans, Catholics, Quakers, and Jews, underscore the comprehensive protections for religious freedom that the First Amendment represents. One of the primary architects of religious freedom in American constitutionalism is James Madison who, along with Thomas Jefferson, articulated the basic principles of religious liberty in the First Amendment. Madison drafted the First Amendment in 1789, and its principles are in line with his earlier writings on religion, such as his *Memorial and Remonstrance against Religious Assessments* (1785) and his *Federalist Papers*, No. 10 (1787). Madison envisioned expansive protections for religious liberty that allowed for many different religious groups to grow and flourish. Although Madison viewed religious faith as a pillar of good citizenship, he also argued religion is one of the most fertile sources of conflict in a democracy. For Madison, religious belief and conduct must be allowed to flourish, yet there must be appropriate constitutional restraints to keep religious groups from oppressing each other.

Religious freedom in the United States has deep roots in Puritan political thought as well. The experiences of Roger Williams, who founded the Rhode Island colony, John Locke's *A Letter Concerning Toleration* from the 1600s, and even Adam Smith's *Wealth of Nations* from the mid-1700s, are testaments to those influences. Prior to the First Amendment, the colonists experimented with institutions and practices designed to protect and encourage freedom of religious belief and conscience and created a principle of equal liberty of conscience among all religions (Nussbaum 2008, 356).

The Establishment and Free Exercise Clauses

Constitutional law scholar Henry J. Abraham defines three constitutional facts that form the foundation for the Constitution's stringent protections of religious liberty. First, Article VI of the Constitution prohibits religious tests as a condition of public service. Government service cannot be based on whether an official has certain religious beliefs. Second, the First Amendment applies to all levels of government—federal, state, and local—and that principle is based on a series of cases in which the Supreme Court "nationalized" the clauses and made them applicable to all levels of government. Third, two separate clauses—establishment and free exercise—each protect different aspects of religious liberty, although they are related (Abraham 2004, 221–224).

Religious liberty principles are found in the establishment and free exercise clauses, but they are far from clear. Although the establishment clause is "commanding in tone and clear in syntax, it is utterly unclear in its intention" (Abraham 2004, 262). Likewise, the free exercise clause "brackets freedom of religious belief and religious action" while the freedom to believe is absolute; thus, the freedom act upon those religious beliefs is something the government can regulate. Yet the clause offers little guidance as to when government regulation of religious conduct is constitutionally permissible (Abraham 2004, 234).

Since the mid-20th century, the Supreme Court has been the primary political institution to decide constitutional controversies over religious freedom. Across several decades and hundreds of cases, the Court has interpreted the establishment and free exercise clauses to define the basic constitutional doctrines that give meaning of the clauses and establish limits on government power over religion. Supreme Court justices have not always been in agreement over the interpretation of the religious liberty clauses, which only makes it more difficult to find a common understanding.

Some constitutional law scholars and political scientists disagree with the Supreme Court–centric view of religious liberty. Constitutional law expert Louis Fisher argues that Congress, the presidency, and even state legislatures have actively protected religious liberty since the Constitution was adopted, thus any understanding of the religious liberty clauses must take account of other political institutions (Fisher 2002). For Fisher, religious groups have developed very successful lobbying tactics that, when coupled with increasing amounts of federal and state monies available to religious schools, hospital, and other charities, gives religious groups an active presence in the lawmaking process. When federal and state (and even local) legislators pass policies that affect religious groups and religious interests, they necessarily invoke First Amendment freedoms that interpret and apply the religious liberty clauses through the policymaking process (Fisher 2002). Other scholars have recognized the importance of the high court in resolving constitutional conflicts over religious liberty, but they observe that debates over religion and public affairs involve the mobilization and counter-mobilization of religious groups who use the political process to press their concerns on policymakers to protect their own interests (Jelen 2000). Therefore, the role of other political institutions and groups in resolving conflicts over the establishment and free exercise clauses should not be overlooked. In the end, the Supreme Court is the final arbiter of the interpretation of the religious liberty clauses.

The Free Exercise Clause

Reynolds v. United States (1878) is a significant case that interprets whether the free exercise clause protects the Mormon practice of polygamy in the Utah territory. Congress required the Utah territory to ban polygamy as a prerequisite for statehood, and the Court upheld the ban even though it interfered with a basic doctrine of Mormon theology at that time. Until the mid-20th century, the high court did not decide many free exercise disputes; but thereafter, they handled a wide range of issues, including whether imposing a state sales tax on the sale of religious items violated free exercise, whether religious groups have to comply with state minimum labor laws, whether the free exercise of religion protects the right of a Jewish Air Force office to wear a yarmulke even though it violated military regulations on appropriate head coverings while on active duty, and whether the clause exempts religious groups and churches from local zoning ordinances. Notably, the Court has never viewed the free exercise of religion as an absolute right; that is, it can be limited by the government, and the Court's jurisprudence helps define when the government can interfere with that right.

In general, the Court has required the government to show a compelling interest whenever a policy interferes with religiously motivated conduct. For instance, in *Sherbert v. Verner* (1963), the Court ruled that when state government's unemployment policy forced a Seventh Day Adventist to work on her Sabbath Day (Saturday), the government had to show that its policy was absolutely necessary and compelling even though it interfered with religious liberty. The compelling interest test is a very high burden for the government to show, thus in most cases, the individual right to free exercise will be protected. Yet, in *Employment Division, Department of Human Resources of Oregon v. Smith* (1990), the Supreme Court reversed course and held that if a law, such as a criminal law, is generally applicable to all people, then the compelling interest test does not apply even if the law regulates religious conduct. In *Smith*, the Court decided that states cannot be exempt from criminal drug laws that prohibit the use of peyote, a hallucinogenic drug, for Native American spiritualists who used the drug as part of their worship. Whereas *Sherbert* supplied a more liberal reading of the free exercise clause, *Smith* was more restrictive in that it prioritized criminal law over the protection of a religiously motivated act.

After *Smith*, Congress passed the Religious Freedom Restoration Act (RFRA) (1993) that required the compelling interest test be used for all federal and state policies that interfered with the free exercise of religion. Many states passed their own versions of RFRA. RFRA and other policies had been lobbied for by many different religious groups because they considered the *Smith* decision could easily be applied to any religious group and take away their religious freedoms, and not just those of Native American spiritualists. Religious groups perceived *Smith* increased the capacity of federal, state, and local governments to regulate them more, so they turned to another branch of government—Congress—to press for reform and to change policy.

The Establishment Clause

Whereas the free exercise clause protects individual religious belief and conduct, the establishment clause is a direct limit on the government's power to establish a religion. An understanding of the clause's meaning is contingent on diverse historical, philosophical, legal, and political arguments (Levy 1986; Witte Jr. and Nichols 2011). As with the free exercise clause, the Supreme Court is the final constitutional arbiter of what it means for a federal, state, or local government to "establish" religion. The Court has adjudicated many establishment clause disputes since the mid-20th century. Those disputes concern government-mandated prayer or Bible-reading in public schools, government use of taxpayer monies to support private religious schools, the display of religious items (e.g., the Ten Commandments on public property or in government buildings), prayers at public high school sporting events, and the usage of public school facilities by religious groups to hold worship services or prayer meetings for students. While by no means an exclusive list, the types of establishment clause disputes adjudicated by the Court over time have addressed a wide and diverse range of politically controversial issues.

For some scholars, the Court's establishment clause decisions tend to be either separationist or accommodating in orientation. A separationist decision views the clause as creating a "wall of separation" between church and state; thus, there can be very little government support for religion. The wall of separation doctrine is grounded in the "wall" metaphor that is traced back to Thomas Jefferson's views. For separationists, the establishment clause envisions little government support for religion. Key separationist decisions, such as *Engel v. Vitale* (1962), have established that a New York State law mandating that every public school classroom recite a Christian prayer is unconstitutional. In *Lemon v. Kurtzman* (1971), the Court struck down Pennsylvania and Rhode Island laws that allowed state monies to be used to purchase educational materials or to supplement teacher salaries in private religious schools. In *Lemon*, the Court concluded that intermingling state taxpayer money with private religious schools created "excessive entanglement between church and state" and therefore violated the establishment clause.

Yet not all government support for religion violates the clause. In some cases, the Court has allowed government to accommodate religion. In *Everson v. Board of Education of Ewing Township, New Jersey* (1947), the Court upheld a New Jersey state law that reimbursed parents who sent children to private religious schools for their transportation costs, such as bus fares. In *Marsh v. Chambers* (1983), the Court ruled that having a religious figure, such as a Christian minister, priest, or rabbi open a legislative session with prayer, does not violate the establishment of religion, so long as the legislature does not show favoritism to one religion over all others. Finally, *Zelman v. Simmons-Harris* (2002) declared that state governments do not violate the establishment of religion if taxpayer monies subsidize the costs of private religious education through "voucher" programs through which parents receive vouchers from the state to send their children to private schools, many of which will be religious schools.

At times, the Supreme Court has used the endorsement test, a judicial standard that prohibits government from endorsing a specific religion. Another approach is government neutrality, or a judicial standard mandating that government must remain neutral toward religion and can neither favor nor disfavor religious groups or institutions in its policymaking. Yet another judicial approach is the coercion doctrine, which allows government to show support for religion as long as it does not coerce individuals into participating in a religious event, program, or exercise (Witte Jr. and Nichols 2011, 177–186).

Conclusion

Many of the Court's decisions on the free exercise and establishment clauses might seem contradictory. Yet, explaining the inconsistencies of the Court's decision-making may relate to the fact that the Court remains the main political institution charged with protecting the individual right to religious liberty; thus, using its discretion, the Court delineates the conditions under which government may interfere with that right. Regardless, while the Court has been very protective of religious belief and conduct, it has erected barriers to government support. It has sought to protect religious minorities who have less of a voice in the political process from overbearing regulation, yet it has also allowed majority religious preferences to affect the policy process. Overall, the Court protects religious liberty, while it also recognizes the historical importance of religion to American political and constitutional development in its political and judicial interpretation of religious freedom.

John C. Blakeman

See also: Constitutional Interpretation; Incorporation Doctrine; Judicial Review

Further Reading

Abraham, Henry J., with Barbara Perry. 2004. *Freedom and the Court: Civil Rights and Civil Liberties in the United States.* 6th ed. New York: Oxford University Press.

Fisher, Louis. 2002. *Religious Liberty in America: Political Safeguards.* Lawrence: Kansas University Press.

Jelen, Ted G. 2000. *To Serve God and Mammon: Church-State Relations in American Politics.* Boulder, CO: Westview Press.

Levy, Leonard M. 1986. *The Establishment Clause.* New York: Macmillan.

Madison, James. (1785) 2010. "Memorial and Remonstrance Against Religious Assessments." *The Papers of James Madison Digital Edition*, edited by J. C. A. Stagg. Charlottesville: University of Virginia Press, Rotunda.

Madison, James. (1787–88) 1961. "Federalist Paper 10." *The Federalist Papers*, edited by Jacob E. Cooke. Middletown, CT: Wesleyan University Press.

Nussbaum, Martha C. 2008. *Liberty of Conscience: In Defense of America's Tradition of Religious Liberty.* New York: Basic Books.

Witte, John Jr., and Joel A. Nichols. 2011. *Religion and the American Constitutional Experiment.* 3rd ed. Boulder, CO: Westview Press.

Cases

Church of the Lukumi Babalu Aye v. Hileah. 1993. 508 U.S. 520.

Employment Division, Department of Human Resources of Oregon v. Smith. 1990. 494 U.S. 872.

Engel v. Vitale. 1962. 370 U.S. 421.

Everson v. Board of Education of Ewing Township, New Jersey. 1947. 330 U.S. 1.

Goldman v. Weinberger. 1986. 475 U.S. 503.

Lemon v. Kurtzman. 1971. 403 U.S. 602.

Marsh v. Chambers. 1983. 463 U.S. 783.

Reynold v. United States. 1878. 98 U.S. 145.

Sherbert v. Verner. 1963. 374 U.S. 398.

Zelman v. Simmons-Harris. 2002. 536 U.S. 639.

GUN OWNERSHIP RIGHTS AND RESTRICTIONS

In the United States, gun ownership and laws restricting the possession and use of firearms is a long-standing part of American history and legal culture. From the time of the American Revolution to the 21st century, the nature and scope of gun regulation has fluctuated in accordance with prevailing circumstances, political assassinations, national and state politics, interest group pressure, crime rates, mass shootings, and public opinion. Whereas the federal regulation of guns has been infrequent over the past century, the states have been more active in creating laws affecting gun ownership and use. In general, federal and state gun laws create relatively few restrictions on the ownership and use of firearms. The liberalization of gun rights and policy is reinforced by Supreme Court precedent interpreting federalism principles and the Second Amendment's meaning. Two rulings, *District of Columbia v. Heller* (2008) and *McDonald v. City of Chicago* (2010), are landmark decisions in constitutional law that expanded gun rights first in the District of Columbia and then across the nation. These cases set the parameters for the development of national and state policies affecting gun control and personal rights well into the future.

Gun Regulation in the United States

Early gun regulation in the United States centered on state laws governing militia requirements. During the Revolutionary War era, state governments used citizen militias and private arms to maintain the common defense. States imposed a variety of requirements for militia service that were a form of gun regulation, including the practice of "mustering," which recorded firearms on the public rolls after their inspection (Cook and Goss 2014, 163). Thereafter, various laws were passed by states and localities that controlled how gunpowder was stored or imposed legal restrictions that barred the discharge of weapons in towns and cities. Some state laws tied gun ownership to citizenship duties, and others prevented certain groups of people from having guns. Under Pennsylvania's Test Acts, citizens who did not swear an oath of loyalty were banned from public office and juries, and were banned from owning firearms. The same state also disarmed groups that were seen as a threat to public safety, such as Native Americans, slaves, freed blacks, or certain races of mixed ancestry (Cornell 2008, 27–29). Moreover, throughout this early history, militia officials and other local authorities regularly conducted gun censuses that let government keep track of how many (and what type) of weapons each household had in its possession (Spitzer 2015b, 38).

In the antebellum period, states and localities used their police powers (designed to protect health, safety, and welfare of citizens) to enact time, place, and manner restrictions and other laws that criminalized certain types of gun ownership. These laws went beyond the typical practice of restricting the use of firearms in public places or regulating hunting activities. Concealed weapons, which became a growing problem up until the Civil War, as citizens increasingly armed themselves for the purpose of self-defense, were outlawed in many states. In addition, several states placed criminal prohibitions on certain types of weapons that were deemed a public nuisance, such as bowie knives, pistols, dirks, or sword canes (Cornell 2008, 142).

In the post–Civil War period and into the early 20th century, states passed thousands of gun control laws that regulated a wide range of firearms-related activities, including categorical bans on the ownership, sale, or transfer of certain weapons or accessories (e.g., pistols, long guns, automatic and semi-automatic weapons, silencers, ammunition); brandishing laws (penalizing the use of weapons in a threatening fashion); open and concealed gun carry restriction laws; licensing requirements or taxes on the manufacture, purchase, or sale of firearms; and preventing felons, foreigners, minors, and mentally ill persons from having access to guns (Spitzer 2015b, 39–61).

On the federal level, Congress has enacted gun laws sporadically and with far less regularity than the states. During the Prohibition era and in response to gangster violence, in 1927 a national firearm control statute was enacted when Congress banned the shipment of handguns to individuals. In 1934, the National Firearms Act required the registration of machine guns and sawed-off shotguns, along with levying taxes on their transfer. Shortly thereafter, in 1938, the Federal Firearms Act put licensing, registration, and record-keeping requirements in place for the distribution of handguns, shotguns, and rifles in interstate commerce by gun dealers, manufactures, and importers. Congress did not enact any other gun control laws until 1968. Prompted by an increase in social unrest, a growing rate of urban violence, and the assassinations of Martin Luther King Jr. and Robert Kennedy, the Gun Control Act of 1968 (GCA) imposed significant restrictions on the interstate shipment and the commercial use of firearms. Thereafter, in 1986, the Firearms Owners Protection Act, which eased federal gun laws, was passed largely in response to conservative and interest group pressure exerted by the National Rifle Association (NRA). In 1993, President Bill Clinton signed the Brady Handgun Violence Prevention Act into law, which was a measure that required background checks and a waiting period on handgun purchases in the wake of the attempted assassination of President Ronald Reagan and the near-fatal wounding of his presidential spokesman, James Brady. Although Congress created a ban on assault weapons in 1993, the law was allowed to expire in 2004. As a result, with few revisions to national gun policy, the 1968 GCA remains the legal foundation for federal gun regulation today (Cook and Goss 2014, 98–103; Vizzard 2015, 881–883).

The Debate over the Meaning of the Second Amendment in the Courts

National and state gun control regulations must comply with constitutional requirements. The Second Amendment of the U.S. Constitution states, "A well regulated Militia, being necessary to the security of a free State, the right of the people to keep and bear Arms, shall not be infringed." The precise meaning of these words is subject to historical and contemporary academic, legal, and political debate. In terms of constitutional law, the debate primarily centers on the meaning of the amendment's prefatory clause ("A well regulated Militia, being necessary to the security of a free State . . .") in relation to, or independently construed from, the amendment's operative clause ("the right of the people to keep and bear Arms shall not be infringed."). For gun control advocates, the prefatory clause prevents Congress from disarming state militias and thereafter creating a national standing army that threatens the states and individual rights. For gun rights' activists, the operative clause vests citizens with an individual right to bear arms without significant (or any) governmental interference. In addition, the debate over the Second Amendment implicates issues of federalism and what role the federal government plays in controlling or limiting state sovereignty or states' rights in maintaining militias or enacting gun control laws.

The controversy over constitutional meaning and the interpretation of corresponding principles of federalism can be traced back to the nation's founding where the colonists had a long-standing aversion to British professional military forces, or standing armies. In 1776, Virginia's Declaration of Rights declared that, "standing armies, in times of peace, should be avoided, as dangerous to liberty." After the American Revolution, the Articles of Confederation (1777–1789) gave the states most of the authority to protect national security through their militias; also, Congress's exercise of military powers was made contingent upon a majority vote of 9 of 13 states. During the political controversy over whether the Constitution should replace the Articles, the Anti-Federalists, who opposed the Constitution's ratification, feared that the federal government would create standing armies and therefore abuse its constitutional powers at the expense of the states and their citizens (Spitzer 2015a, 22–29).

While the fear of a national standing army unequivocally influenced the founding debate, the history of the Second Amendment's creation and ultimate ratification is subject to conflicting interpretations about the amendment's original meaning and, therefore, whether the *collective rights* theory (linked to gun control advocacy) or the *individual rights* theory (associated with gun rights' advocacy) is correct (Legal Information Institute 2016; Cornell 2008, 199). These contrasting views are manifested in related historical interpretations of the Second Amendment's intent or meaning: whereas the *militia* theory posits that states enjoy the right to maintain an armed citizenry, or a militia, for the collective defense, the *individual rights* perspective holds that citizens have the right to own firearms regardless of their militia service. Moreover, a third *hybrid* theory asserts that individuals have a civic right and responsibility to own weapons for the collective defense (Cook and Goss 2014, 92).

These viewpoints and their federalism implications have shaped the Second Amendment's judicial interpretation in federal and state courts. Two Supreme

Court rulings, *United States v. Lopez* (1995) and *Printz v. United States* (1997), determined that Congress exceeded its authority in creating laws limiting gun rights. In *Lopez*, a closely divided Court invalidated the federal Gun-Free School Zones Act of 1990, a measure that banned guns within 1,000 feet of school property. Chief Justice William Rehnquist's opinion of the Court held that Congress could not regulate local gun possession under its Article I, Section 8 commerce clause powers because the law did not affect an activity that had a substantial relationship to interstate commerce. With *Printz*, a bare majority of the Court ruled that the Tenth Amendment and overriding principles of federalism were violated when Congress tried to "command" the states and local law enforcement officers to perform background checks on handgun buyers through the federal Brady Handgun Prevention Act.

Until 2008, a different line of cases interpreted the scope and meaning of the Second Amendment in a fashion that mostly reinforced the collective rights' interpretation that vested in states the authority to use militias for the collective defense. The Supreme Court's decisions in *Presser v. Illinois* (1886) and *United States v. Miller* (1939), plus an array of nearly 50 other lower federal court rulings from the 1940s until the early part of the 21st century, confirmed this militia-based view. In fact, no federal court had struck down a gun law as a violation of the Second Amendment until the Court's landmark *District of Columbia v. Heller* (2008) decision (Spitzer 2015b, 71). In *Heller*, in a 5–4 opinion written by Justice Antonin Scalia, the Court nullified the District of Columbia's stringent ban on handgun possession by declaring that the Second Amendment protected an individual's right to own handguns for self-protection in the home. While Justice Scalia's originalist construction of the Second Amendment endorsed the individual rights theory, it also gave the states the flexibility to create gun control laws that banned or restricted the ownership and use of firearms by felons or the mentally ill. In addition, it authorized legislation that prohibited guns from being carried into government buildings or on school grounds, as well as laws imposing restrictions on the commercial sale of firearms. Shortly thereafter, in *McDonald v. City of Chicago* (2010), the Supreme Court held that gun ownership was a fundamental right. As a result, the Second Amendment was incorporated under the Fourteenth Amendment's due process clause, thereby extending it to all of the states.

The horrific spate of mass shootings, including the massacre of innocent children in a Sandy Hook elementary school in Newtown, Connecticut; the attempted assassination of Arizona congressional representative Gabrielle Giffords; and police or citizen vigilante-inspired gun violence against African Americans in the Tamir Rice (Cleveland), Trayvon Martin (Florida), and Michael Brown (Ferguson, Missouri) cases, has not prompted any significant federal reforms of gun laws. As a result, the states will continue to be the primary emphases of gun control legislation. With an estimated 300 million firearms in the country, state legislatures will face the ongoing challenge of enacting gun regulations that withstand post-*Heller* and *McDonald* constitutional scrutiny. By one approximation, presently there are more than 400 meaningful state and local laws on the books. The content of these laws range from vesting citizens with a constitutional right to bear arms in state constitutions to others that regulate ownership or impose licensing, registration, and gun carry restrictions, or, less frequently, to create assault weapon or high capacity ammunition bans. The scope and application of these laws will be subject to the vagaries of court rulings, interest group politics, the crime narrative, high-profile mass shootings, and public opinion. Accordingly, given the lack of federal reform and the expansive nature of gun rights under the post-*Heller* and *McDonald* individual rights' theory court rulings, the most likely success for implementing gun control laws will be directed at a narrow set of policy initiatives that lessen the possession and use of guns by high-risk individuals or prohibited persons—mentally ill or felons (Vizzard 2015, 894; Cook and Goss 2014, 104–114).

Christopher P. Banks

See also: Constitutional Interpretation; Incorporation Doctrine; Judicial Federalism; Judicial Review

Further Reading

Cook, Philip J., and Kristen A. Goss. 2014. *The Gun Debate: What Everyone Needs to Know.* New York: Oxford University Press.

Cornell, Saul. 2008. *A Well-Regulated Militia: The Founding Fathers and the Origins of Gun Control in America.* New York: Oxford University Press.

Goss, Kristin A. 2006. *Disarmed: The Missing Movement for Gun Control in America.* Princeton, NJ: Princeton University Press.

Kozuskanich, Nathan, and Saul Cornell, eds. 2013. *The Second Amendment on Trial: Critical Essays on District of Columbia v. Heller.* Amherst: University of Massachusetts Press.

Legal Information Institute (of Cornell Law School). 2016. "The Second Amendment." https://www.law.cornell.edu/wex/second_amendment.

Spitzer, Robert J. 2015a. *The Politics of Gun Control.* 6th ed. Boulder, CO: Paradigm.

Spitzer, Robert J. 2015b. *Guns across America: Reconciling Gun Rules and Rights.* New York: Oxford University Press.

Vizzard, William J. 2015. "The Current and Future State of Gun Policy in the United States." *Journal of Criminal Law and Criminology* 104: 879–904.

Cases

District of Columbia v. Heller. 2008. 554 U.S. 570.

McDonald v. City of Chicago. 2010. 561 U.S. 3025.

Presser v. Illinois. 1886. 116 U.S. 252.

Printz v. United States. 1997. 521 U.S. 898.

United States v. Lopez. 1995. 514 U.S. 549.
United States v. Miller. 1939. 307 U.S. 174.

PROPERTY RIGHTS

The right to own property, and the government's power to regulate it, leads to some of the most politically contentious cases in state and federal courts. Property rights are a vital part of the constitutional and political traditions in the United States. State and federal laws and constitutions provide extensive protections for the right to own property, and state and federal political processes are likewise diligent about protecting private property. Yet, the right to acquire and use property is not absolute, and it is often up to state and federal courts to determine when it is lawful for government to interfere with property rights.

Most property disputes, which are diverse in nature, are adjudicated in state and local courts. Judges determine questions of property ownership and resolve disputes between private individuals over how property is used. Judges also decide when new property is acquired or created, and they define the circumstances under which government can exercise its power of eminent domain to take private property for public use or exercise its zoning powers to regulate the usage of property. While federal courts deal with fewer types of property disputes, they will have more influence over federal laws concerning trademarks and patents (both of which protect property rights), and their interpretation of the Fifth Amendment in the U.S. Constitution often determines the limits of the government's power to take property.

State and federal courts must follow the Fifth Amendment, and its interpretation by the Supreme Court is key to setting the conditions under which federal or state governments can take private property for the public's benefit. Eminent domain is a centuries old doctrine which holds that all private property is held subject to taking by the government for public benefit. The Fifth Amendment reflects the concept of eminent domain in the Constitution because it recognizes that government can take property, albeit for public purposes only and with compensation to the property owner.

What Is Property?

Property consists of the thing being owned and used by an individual or business along with the owner's expectation to use that thing in certain ways. Two conceptions of property have held sway over American law over the course of at least 200 years. The first view, which is found in the English common law as inherited by the American colonists, holds that the right to own property is based on the ability to exclude others from using it. This idea is best summed up by William Blackstone, the 18th century common law scholar who wrote that the right of property is "that sole and despotic dominion which one man claims and exercises over external things of the world, in total exclusion of the right of any other individual" (1979, 2).

Subsequent to Blackstone, a more contemporary definition of property emerged after the Civil War. It did not view property as the ability to exclude others from using something; rather, property was perceived more as a bundle of rights—a collection of rights to buy, sell, use, develop, exploit, and so forth. If one's right within the "bundle" is removed, the overall right to property remains intact. Significantly, this more progressive definition of property facilitated more government regulation of property in the public interest.

Importantly, conceptions of property rights have changed throughout American legal and constitutional history. Under Blackstone's exclusionary definition of property in the mid-1700s, property rights were virtually absolute and relatively immune from government regulation. Yet, as economic development took hold in the new American republic in the early 1800s, and as governments responded to the need to build infrastructure, such as canals, roads, drainage ditches, ports, and bridges in order to further development, legal understandings about property rights began to evolve into the "bundle of rights" perspective that exists today.

Property and American Constitutionalism

Although private property is not explicitly mentioned in the Constitution as a protected right, several clauses in the document protect the right to own property from government interference. For example, in Article I, Congress is vested with the legislative power to set policy for trademarks and patents, thus protecting the rights of those who create or market property. Under Article I, Section 10, the Constitution also prohibits state governments from interfering with the right to contract. As a result, this provision determines how property owners use and dispose of their property. After the Fifth Amendment was ratified as part of the Bill of Rights in 1791, property rights were placed on firmer ground with its takings clause, a prohibition that prevents government from taking private property except for public use and with just compensation paid to the owner.

The lack of clear directives on property rights reflects the founders' perception that the right to own and amass private property is one of the most deeply ingrained rights in American constitutionalism. As such, it is infused into American political culture, law, and the Constitution. It is fair to say that most if not all of the political thinkers and prominent citizens of the American colonies and early United States considered the right to property to be one of the most fundamental liberties that the colonists had because that liberty is vital to the proper functioning of republican government.

Of the many thinkers of the era who devoted attention to the political and legal connotations of property, such as John Adams, Alexander Hamilton, Thomas Jefferson, and George Mason, James Madison's thoughts on property are perhaps the most prescient. Madison clearly articulated the importance property had to sustaining republican government, especially in regards to the danger that unequal distributions of property could cause. Madison also understood that the new Constitution in 1787 would play a vital role in protecting property rights. In *Federalist Papers*, No. 10, Madison (1787) argued that the federal government would be best suited to controlling the factions, or divisions, among people that tend to destabilize democratic governments. One of the most destabilizing divisions was the unequal distribution of property. Madison's solution did not depend on government policies that equally distributed property among the people. His solution, instead, was based on designing government institutions so that property conflicts could be managed peacefully. For Madison, the right to own property is embedded in American political culture; yet that right can lead to political excess and turmoil because property will always be distributed unequally. Thus, an important goal of the Constitution and the national political system is to preserve property rights and dampen the negative effects that they cause.

State Courts and Property Rights

State courts resolve most property conflicts in the United States. A primary function of state judiciaries is to offer a neutral set of institutions in which property rights and disputes may be adjudicated and peacefully resolved. As a result, state courts have played a prominent role in developing property rights throughout American history, and they have been at the forefront of establishing the legal parameters of the government's power to regulate property on behalf of the public.

In the 1800s, state courts began to develop legal doctrines to facilitate the government's power of eminent domain over private property. Many state courts expanded the conditions under which government could take property for public use, and they imposed legal restrictions on the owner's ability to sue the government for redress. The property rights litigation in state courts resulted when state or local governments took property to develop infrastructure—such as canals, toll roads, or ports—that were vital to economic development and growth. By the mid-1800s, state courts facilitated the process by which private corporations could take advantage of the historic doctrine of eminent domain. Thus, private railroad companies that built railroads for public use could use eminent domain to take property that was used for constructing new railroads, and corporations built dams on waterways and flooded private property in order to create mill ponds to power gristmills that would grind grain for the public's use (Scheiber 1988). In this way, state courts caused a dramatic transformation about how the law affects property rights. Accordingly, it became much easier for government to take property for public purposes that were necessary to create economic growth and development that benefited the public good. By the Civil War, state courts had decided that "the American conception of property was harnessed to the paramount goal of economic development" (Horwitz 1988, 150).

Courts in western states further expanded the property doctrine by likewise linking the eminent domain power to the needs of private corporations and economic development. Irrigation companies were given authority to dig irritation canals over wide swaths of private lands in order to benefit agriculture. Similarly, mining companies in western states were given broad authority to build infrastructure, such as roads across private property in order to facilitate the extraction and transportation of minerals.

Federal Courts, Property, and the Constitution

Federal courts deal with far fewer property disputes than state courts. However, the U.S. Supreme Court has interpreted the Constitution to decide some of the most important, and contentious, cases concerning property rights in American constitutional history. A discussion of a few key historical cases illustrates that trend.

One case early in the new republic dealt with a vital and controversial question concerning property ownership in North America. *Johnson v. Macintosh* (1823) concerned a property dispute between two individuals who claimed ownership over the same piece of property. Johnson asserted that he had bought the land from a group of white settlers on the Illinois frontier who had previously acquired the property from Native Americans. Macintosh claimed title to the land from a grant to him by the U.S. government. In deciding in favor of Macintosh, the Court determined that he had superior title because it stemmed from the national government and could be traced back to the North American territory that was discovered by European explorers. In addition, Native Americans had a right to occupy the land, but the national government had the sole power to extinguish that right through treaties.

Macintosh established the principle of discovery in American property law, which meant that Native American tribes did not own land, and only occupied it, and therefore could not sell it to private owners. *Macintosh* also helped to formulate a positive principle by which clear title to land can be established in courts. This resulted in a more stable and predictable process for buying, selling, and transferring land during a time in which the population was growing and seeking new land to settle. The deplorable, negative impact of the Court's decision was to remove the right of ownership over that land from Indians who possessed much of the land long before European settlers arrived.

In 1837, *Charles River Bridge v. Warren Bridge* addressed whether the Commonwealth of Massachusetts could authorize the building of a free public bridge over the Charles River and thereby destroy the economic interests and property rights of an adjacent toll bridge. The Supreme Court ruled in favor of Massachusetts. In his opinion of the Court, Chief Justice Taney declared that "while the rights of private property are sacredly guarded, we must not forget that the community also has rights, and that the happiness and well-being of every citizen depends on their faithful preservation." *Charles River Bridge* thus indicated that the Court was willing early on to interpret the Constitution to balance the sacred right of private property with the government's and public's interest in building infrastructure, such as a bridge, to facilitate economic development.

Among the many property rights cases the Supreme Court has decided over the course of American history, a trilogy remains especially significant. Two of the three, *Pennsylvania Coal Co. v. Mahon* (1922) and *Penn Central Transportation Co. v. New York City* (1978), each concerned the extent to which state governments could regulate property without physically taking possession of it. As Justice Oliver Wendell Holmes noted in *Mahon*, "while property may be regulated to a certain extent, if a regulation goes too far it will be recognized as a taking." Thus, if the government regulates property to such an extent as to affect its value, it might be considered a taking of that property under the Fifth Amendment, thus forcing the government to pay compensation. In the *Penn Central* case, the Court similarly ruled that while a regulation affecting the use of property could be considered a government taking of property, a historical preservation policy by New York City that prohibited certain types of development of historical buildings was not extensive enough to be a taking of property. For the Court, even though the preservation policy placed restrictions on the ability of owners to modify their historical properties, the regulations did not interfere with property rights enough to be considered a taking or seizure of property.

In the third of the trilogy of cases and perhaps one of the Supreme Court's most contentious property cases—*Kelo v. City of New London* (2005)—the justices addressed the issue of whether a local government could use its power of eminent domain to take private property and then transfer the land to a private developer that would redevelop the land in order to revitalize the local area's economy. Generally, governments take property for public purposes such as public roads, ports, utilities, and the like. Here, though, the Court was confronted with a taking of property for private purposes that ostensibly would have a public benefit. In a 5–4 ruling, the Court deemed there was a taking for constitutional purposes, although it noted that takings of property for purely private purposes are generally prohibited by the Constitution. In response, many states passed statutes prohibiting local governments from pursuing similar policies, so the Court's decision has had a minimal impact. Yet, it illustrates how the Court has generally been deferential to governments that take property, and it has usually ruled such policies are constitutional.

John C. Blakeman

See also: Constitutional Interpretation; Judicial Federalism; Incorporation Doctrine

Further Reading

Abraham, Henry J. 1998. *The Judicial Process: An Introductory Analysis of the Courts of the United States, England, and France.* 7th ed. Oxford: Oxford University Press.

Blackstone, Sir William. 1979. *Commentaries on the Laws of England: A Facsimile of the First Edition of 1765–1769, Volume 2.* Chicago: University of Chicago Press.

Hall, Kermit L. 1989. *The Magic Mirror: Law in American History.* Oxford: Oxford University Press.

Hamilton, Alexander, John Jay, and James Madison. (1787–88) 1937. *The Federalist Papers.* New York: The Modern Library edition.

Horwitz, Morton J. 1988. "The Transformation in the Conception of Property in American Law, 1780–1860." In *American Law and the Constitutional Order*, edited by Lawrence M. Friedman and Harry N. Scheiber. Cambridge, MA: Harvard University Press.

Horwitz, Morton J. 1992. *The Transformation of American Law, 1870–1960.* Oxford: Oxford University Press.

Madison, James. (1787–88) 1961. "Federalist Paper 10." *The Federalist Papers*, edited by Jacob E. Cooke. Middletown, CT: Wesleyan University Press.

Merrill, Thomas W., and Henry E. Smith. 2010. *Oxford Introductions to U.S. Law: Property.* Oxford: Oxford University Press.

Sheiber, Harry N. 1988. "Property Law, Expropriation, and Resource Allocation by Government, 1789–1910." In *American Law and the Constitutional Order*, edited by Lawrence Friedman. Cambridge, MA: Harvard University Press.

Cases

Charles River Bridge v. Warren River Bridge. 1837. 36 U.S. 420.

Johnson v. Macintosh. 1823. 21 U.S. 543.

Kelo v. City of New London. 2005. 545 U.S. 469.

Penn Central Transportation Co. v. New York City. 1978. 438 U.S. 104.

Pennsylvania Coal Co v. Mahon. 1922. 260 U.S. 393.

DEFENDANTS' RIGHTS

In the United States, citizens accused of breaking the law are given substantive and procedural rights as defendants in criminal prosecutions. Defendants' rights under federal and state law originate from constitutional protections that safe-guard the accused from arbitrary government action that threatens to take away their basic rights to living free in society. The scope and application of defen-dants' rights in criminal prosecutions are determined by the judiciary in rulings interpreting federal and state constitutions and specific bill of rights' free-doms. In safeguarding defendants' rights, the operation of the crime control and due process models of criminal justice in the adversarial system is significant. These models intensify the tensions that are built in to the adversarial criminal justice system because the prosecution and defense must work against each other to uncover the facts that will resolve the accused's guilt or innocence in a trial. In the adversary system, the judiciary uses its discretion to grant defen-dants' rights by determining the political meaning of crime control and due process in accordance with the Fourth, Fifth, and Sixth Amendments to the U.S. Constitution.

The Crime Control and Due Process Models in the Adversarial Criminal Justice System

Criminal prosecutions involve public prosecutors and public defenders or private defense counsel that try cases in court under general principles of due process and justice, such as the presumption of innocence in criminal trials. Under this presumption, citizens accused of crimes are considered innocent until the government meets its burden of evidentiary proof that the defendant is guilty beyond a reasonable doubt. The contest between the prosecution and the defense is necessarily adversarial in nature where each side is pitted against the other in an effort to convince a neutral fact finder, which is the jury or judge (if a bench trial), that the defendant is guilty or innocent. Under the adversarial system, lawyers have considerable discretion to present only the facts that they consider to be most important in securing a conviction or an acquittal. For this reason, the criminal trial process is unpredictable and highly contentious because each side is determined to win their case, even if the truth of what happened is lost in the process (Frank 1949).

Resolving combative criminal cases in the adversarial system of justice reg-isters a basic conflict between safeguarding defendants' rights and guarantee-ing the public's right to remain safe through the swift prosecution of those who are guilty. Criminal sociologists have described this tension in terms of two competing models of criminal justice. Under the *crime control model*, police and prosecutors protect public safety by presuming that the defendants in criminal prosecutions are guilty; thus, they must be swiftly prosecuted in the criminal justice system. Under this view, criminal prosecutions are equated to assembly-line justice because convictions are secured through agreements between the prosecution and defense (plea bargains) instead of time-consuming trials that are really unnecessary because most defendants are, in fact, guilty. In contrast, the due process model is characterized as a type of obstacle course justice because the defense uses principles of due process and procedural objections to slow down criminal prosecutions that inherently are fraught with mistaken evidence and police misconduct. Under this perspective, defendants interpose formal evidentiary rules and principles of justice, such as the exclusionary rule, which excludes evidence in a trial if the police secured it unlawfully, to slow down the criminal justice system. This, in turn, limits abusive government authority and preserves the presumption of innocence (Packer 1968).

The differences between the crime control and due process models underscore rival views of adversarial justice that are registered in judicial decisions that are political in scope. While not always the case, liberal justices and courts are prone to expanding the rights of criminal defendants whereas conservatives are more likely to restrict them in favor of supporting police and prosecutorial actions. Under the U.S. Constitution, the scope of freedom afforded criminal suspects is tied to Supreme Court interpretations of the due process guarantees that are absorbed in the Fourteenth Amendment and made applicable to the states through the incorporation doctrine. Courts routinely address the constitutional issues that are raised during police searches and seizures, the interrogation of suspects while in police custody, and whether the accused has been given the right to appointed legal counsel.

The Fourth Amendment's Prohibition against Unreasonable Searches and Seizures

The Fourth Amendment states:

> The right of the people to be secure in their persons, houses, papers, and effects, against unreasonable searches and seizures, shall not be violated, and no warrants shall issue, but upon probable cause, supported by oath or affirmation, and particularly describing the place to be searched, and the persons or things to be seized.

This language captures the need to restrain government officials from conducting searches and taking the property of citizens with impunity. The framers were mindful of the need to limit government powers as a result of their experiences in the Revolutionary War when British authorities would conduct general searches of colonial homes and persons without any reason or evidence to support them. As a result, the Supreme Court has developed its Fourth Amendment jurisprudence from the principle that police searches and seizures cannot be unreasonable; that is, they must be supported by a warrant that is based on probable cause (showing that there are objective facts that a crime has been committed) and a specification of the area to be searched and the items to be seized. As an additional protection, warrants must be issued by judicial officers who can evaluate the basis for the warrant from a neutral and unbiased standpoint. In addition, *Weeks v. United States* (1914) and *Mapp v. Ohio* (1961) give federal and state courts the authority to monitor police misconduct through the exclusionary rule, a judge-made doctrine that prevents illegally obtained evidence from being used at trial.

The scope of permissible government action often turns on the question of whether the police conducted a "search" for Fourth Amendment purposes. In *Olmstead v. United States* (1928), the Supreme Court required that the search must be accompanied by a physical intrusion into constitutionally protected areas, such as entering a person's home or in taking personal effects. In recognizing the impact that evolving technologies have on the Fourth Amendment, the Court in *Katz v. United States* (1967) overturned a bookie's gambling conviction because placing a listening device on a telephone booth during the police investigation violated the defendant's reasonable expectation of privacy. As the Court declared, the Fourth Amendment "protects people, not places." The physical intrusion, or trespass theory, and the reasonable expectation of privacy standards do not seem to be mutually exclusive. In *United States v. Jones* (2012), several justices applied elements of *Olmstead's* trespass theory and *Katz's* reasonably expectation of privacy standard as grounds to hold that the police overstepped its authority in using a global positioning system device to secure evidence of illegal drug trafficking activity because putting the device on the defendant's car constituted a Fourth Amendment search.

The Fifth Amendment's Privilege against Self-Incrimination

One of the most important rights of the Fifth Amendment is the privilege against self-incrimination. A relevant part of the Fifth Amendment declares, "No person . . . shall be compelled in any criminal case to be a witness against himself." Several interests, among them respecting privacy and protecting against arbitrary punishments that violate general rules of due process and fair play, explain why government cannot force defendants to testify against themselves in criminal trials (O'Brien 2014, 1085–1087). These values are applied in *Miranda v. Arizona* (1966), a landmark ruling establishing that police have the constitutional duty to advise suspects of their rights during custodial interrogation. *Miranda* requires that the police follow procedural safeguards during interrogations which ensure that a suspect's incriminating statements are made on a voluntary basis and without government compulsion.

The procedural safeguards, or *Miranda* warnings, include admonishments informing suspects of the right to remain silent, of the right to request an attorney, and that statements of guilt will be used as evidence against them in criminal trials if they are made. Although *Miranda* was especially controversial for its time, and Congress has tried to repeal it with legislation, the Supreme Court has not yet overruled it. Instead, it has carved out exceptions that allow incriminating evidence to be introduced during trials on a case-by-case basis—a pattern of judicial behavior that has the effect of returning to a pre-*Miranda* approach that lets courts consider if the "totality of the circumstances" surrounding the prosecution show that the defendant was forced to give incriminating statements. The case-by-case approach gives the police more flexibility in interrogating suspects, thereby limiting *Miranda's* scope and application in many Fifth Amendment cases (O'Brien 2014, 1094–1100).

The Sixth Amendment's Right to Appointed Legal Counsel

In addition to guaranteeing defendants the rights to confront their accusers, be informed of the charges against them, and have a speedy trial, the Sixth Amendment also requires, "In all criminal prosecutions, the accused shall . . . have the assistance of counsel for his defense." While its text unambiguously safeguards the right to counsel in criminal prosecutions, courts have been reluctant to extend it to civil cases. The importance of legal representation was recognized early on in colonial laws that let defendants retain their own lawyers and afforded counsel to suspects accused of capital crimes. Still, as a general rule, there is little historical evidence to show that government had to pay for counsel for defendants that were poor. Until the mid-20th century, only a few states required the appointment of legal counsel in felony cases. While the Supreme Court held that due process principles and the right to counsel was denied to several black defendants that were accused of raping two white girls on a train in Alabama in the famous "Scottsboro Boys" *Powell v. Alabama* (1932) ruling, it only required appointed counsel in special circumstances, such as when the defendants suffered from "ignorance, feeble-mindedness, illiteracy, or the like."

The issue of when governments must provide legal aid was not fully addressed by the Supreme Court until the landmark ruling of *Gideon v. Wainwright* (1963). In *Gideon*, the Supreme Court overturned the defendant's state felony conviction for breaking and entering into a pool hall to steal money and other items. Although he requested it on the grounds of indigence, Gideon was denied appointed counsel. In reversing the lower court's decision, Justice Black indicated that Gideon's rights to an attorney and a fair trial were intrinsically linked together because "any person haled into court, who is too poor to hire a lawyer, cannot be assured a fair trial unless counsel is provided for him." In declaring that lawyers in criminal prosecutions are "necessities, not luxuries," Justice Black underscored an equality-of-arms principle that requires opponents that are clashing in court have an equal right to have comparable resources to make their case, including the help of an attorney.

In later cases, the Supreme Court expanded the reach of the *Gideon's* ruling to other contexts that may oblige state governments to subsidize the right to appointed counsel, such as all cases where incarceration is a possibility (*Argersinger v. Hamlin*, 1972), or during the first appeal of a conviction (*Douglas v. California*, 1963), and to cases involving the prosecutions of minor defendants (*In re Gault*, 1967) or mentally ill suspects who seek to represent themselves (*Indiana v. Edwards*, 2008). State governments that are financially challenged with budget shortfalls are increasingly pressed to implement the *Gideon* mandate, however. Many public defenders' offices with high caseloads and limited staff struggle to deliver legal services to those who need it on the grounds of indigence, leading some commentators to lament that the promise of giving access to justice and appointed counsel through *Gideon* is more of an illusion than reality without significant reforms being put in place (Giovanni and Patel 2013).

Christopher P. Banks

See also: Capital Punishment; Constitutional Interpretation; Incorporation Doctrine; Mandatory Sentencing; Privacy Rights

Further Reading

Bibas, Stephanos. 2012. *The Machinery of Criminal Justice*. New York: Oxford University Press.

Frank, Jerome. 1949. *Courts on Trial: Myth and Reality in American Justice*. Princeton, NJ: Princeton University Press.

Giovanni, Thomas, and Roopal Patel. 2013. "Gideon at 50: Three Reforms to Revive the Right to Counsel," April 9. http://www.brennancenter.org/sites/default/files/publications/Gideon_Report_040913.pdf.

Kanovitz, Jacqueline R. 2015. *Constitutional Law for Criminal Justice*. New York: Routledge.

Langbein, John H. 2003. *The Origins of Adversary Criminal Trial*. New York: Oxford University Press.

O'Brien, David M. 2014. *Constitutional Law and Politics: Civil Rights and Civil Liberties*. 9th ed., vol. 2. New York: W. W. Norton.

Packer, Herbert L. 1968. *The Limits of the Criminal Sanction*. Stanford, CA: Stanford University Press.

Cases

Argersinger v. Hamlin. 1972. 407 U.S. 25.
Douglas v. California. 1963. 372 U.S. 353.
Gideon v. Wainwright. 1963. 372 U.S. 355.
Indiana v. Edwards. 2008. 554 U.S. 162.
In re Gault. 1967. 387 U.S. 1.
Katz v. United States. 1967. 389 U.S. 347.

Mapp v. Ohio. 1961. 367 U.S. 643.
Miranda v. Arizona. 1966. 284 U.S. 436.
Olmstead v. United States. 1928. 277 U.S. 438.
Powell v. Alabama. 1932. 287 U.S. 45.
United States v. Jones. 2012.132 S.Ct. 945.
Weeks v. United States. 1914. 232 U.S. 383.

MANDATORY SENTENCING

Mandatory sentencing laws punish offenders in accordance with a legislative tough-on-crime attitude. Emerging in the mid-1980s, the laws arose under the political umbrella of doling out just punishment under determinate sentencing schemes that limit judges to giving offenders "fixed" or specific punishments for violating criminal law. Mandatory sentences are determinate sentences because they eliminate the ambiguity of not knowing precisely how long an offender will remain in prison after sentencing. They are labeled three-strikes-and-you're-out, habitual offender, mandatory sentences, mandatory minimum, truth-in-sentencing, and life without parole laws—and all aim to reduce judicial discretion to impose lenient sentences while insuring that offenders serve all of the time they deserve for deciding to break the law. The unintended consequences of mandatory sentencing laws include the imposition of longer prison sentences, or mass incarceration, which costs taxpayers more money to subsidize an expanding correctional infrastructure across the nation. They also impose a social cost on offenders and communities that struggle to assimilate offenders back into society when they are released from prison after doing their time, a significant challenge in tight budgetary times. There is increasing evidence that mandatory sentencing polices are inherently problematic because they are counterproductive, economically inefficient, and punish the wrong types of offenders with unduly harsh prison sentences. As a result, the Supreme Court and politicians from both sides of the aisle are revisiting the constitutionality and policy wisdom of determinate sentencing practices—a trend that is building momentum for reform in the future.

The Growth of Mandatory Sentencing Laws

The growth of mandatory sentencing laws can be traced back to the late 1970s and early 1980s. Aligned with a crime control theory of public safety, these laws sought to inflict severe punishments on offenders by playing on the public fear that it is necessary for criminals to "do the crime, do the time," and also "lock 'em up and throw away the key" (Kelly 2015, 2). In this light, the enactment of harsh sentencing laws is a political response to indeterminate sentencing laws that permit judges to consider a broad range of minimum and maximum punishments to punish offenders in the hope of rehabilitating them. With indeterminate sentencing, judges and parole boards retain the authority to reintroduce an offender back into the community or to revoke the terms of parole, if certain conditions for release are met. A key assumption is that treating the offender's underlying mental health or substance abuse difficulties helps solve the problems that led to illicit behavior and prevent repeat offending behavior. Contrary to popular impressions, though, offenders under this model of sentencing policy do not simply spend their days in idle group therapy or rehabilitation classes. Instead, correctional rehabilitation techniques proactively try to adjust miscreant behavior through a balanced program of "treatment, intervention, rehabilitation, and punishment while, at the same time, providing risk management through correctional control" (Kelly 2015, 23).

Although rehabilitation was the cornerstone of penal policy for much of the 20th century, it fell into political disfavor by the mid-1970s and increasingly thereafter. For crime control advocates, indeterminate sentencing laws are problematic for at least three reasons: (1) they give judges too much discretion to use extralegal factors, such as life, work, or personal circumstances of the offender, to levy sentences that are predictable and uniformly applied to offenders and crimes, a problem that creates sentencing disparities and discrimination among similarly situated offenders; (2) the existence of sentencing disparities suggests that judges are using their personal biases to sentence offenders more leniently than is appropriate; and (3) it is unfair not to have "truth" in sentencing because the sentences given to offenders do not honestly match the time they actually serve. As a result, determinate sentencing laws began to replace rehabilitative sentencing practices in the late 1970s and early 1980s, often with bipartisan support (Kelly 2015, 38–39, 337).

By 1984, the federal government adopted the Sentencing Reform Act, a measure that implemented sentencing guidelines with the administrative support of a newly created U.S. Sentencing Commission. Through the Commission, mandatory guidelines were generated to enhance the severity of punishment generally and to specify that certain malefactors, such as violent, repeat, or drug offenders, were treated especially harshly. Using a harm-based quantitative sentencing matrix, judges assign a sanction that is determined by the score an offender receives by committing the crime. The score takes into account the offense's severity and past criminal history and then uses those as controlling factors to quantify the amount of harm an offender inflicts during the crime. During sentencing, judges evaluate the facts of the case, such as whether there is physical harm, economic loss, a large quantity of drugs, or the defendant's role in the committing the crime, among other factors, to calculate a penalty that falls within a fixed range of punishment categories that sanction offenders for the harm they cause by committing crimes in light of their past criminal history. Notably, the guidelines discourage judges from weighing the types of aggravating or mitigating circumstances that were traditionally considered in the past, such as the defendant's poverty, drug or alcohol addictions, or mental illness. Judges are restrained and sometimes prohibited from "departing" from the guidelines if they choose to assign greater or lesser punishment in individual cases; and when they do, their decisions are subject to further review by an appeals court. Of the 258 cells in the federal sentencing guidelines' matrix, 92 percent of them require a prison sentence. As well, the Commission eliminated parole in the federal system, and the possibility of early release is also severely limited. All told, the Commission's work and the sentencing guidelines created harsher punishments by substantially reducing judicial discretion, ending parole, restricting probation, and increasing the length of time served in prison (Kelly 2015, 40; Stith and Cabranes 1998, 82–85).

Soon the federal guidelines became the template for state sentencing policies. However, there was far less uniformity and greater disparity in sentencing practices as the states revised their legislation. Whereas some states used presumptive sentences or guidelines (that require certain punishments to be imposed), others enacted *mandatory minimum sentences* for certain crimes or offenders (e.g., drug or weapons offenses or violent or habitual offenders), or *truth in sentencing laws* (that increased prison time for certain types of offenders). Still other states imposed *life-without-possibility-of-parole* or *three-strikes (and you're out)* laws that called for 25 years to life imprisonment penalties for certain crimes and repetitive criminal history. These laws had the single overriding purpose to keep offenders locked up in prisons after conviction (Banks and O'Brien 2015, 217–222).

While the federal guidelines could be faulted for being too draconian, state sentencing law and policy under a mandatory sentencing framework is also subject to the criticism of being too convoluted and unjust because the laws are unevenly applied across the 50 states and have pernicious policy effects. Critics argue that determinate sentencing laws wrongly keep less violent and low-level offenders in jail for unjustifiably long periods of time, a trend that originated from the political fight against the War on Drugs that began in the 1970s. Moreover, harsh punishment schemes have contributed to the United States having the highest rate of incarceration in the world with almost 7 million persons under correctional supervision, a phenomenon that comes at a high financial cost to governments and society in general. The expenses that are required to maintain the carceral state have climbed to a total of $1 trillion since 1980, and they remain virtually unsustainable for tight recessionary prone economies that cannot pay for a gargantuan prison state (Porter 2016, 3; Tonry 2016, 4; Kelly 2015, 1, 323).

Determinate Sentencing Laws in the U.S. Supreme Court

The ill effects of harsh sentencing policies also have constitutional implications. Starting with *Apprendi v. New Jersey* (2000), the Supreme Court ruled that all of the facts that increase sentences for offenders under the guidelines had to be established by juries instead of by judges in order to comply with the Sixth Amendment right to have a fair jury trial. The *Apprendi* principle led to subsequent rulings that question the constitutionality of not only federal but also state guidelines' sentencing law. In *Blakely v. Washington* (2004), the Supreme Court used the same Sixth Amendment logic to invalidate Washington's Sentencing Reform Act because it wrongfully let trial judges increase a defendant's sentence on the basis of facts that are not admitted by the defendant or determined by a jury. Notably, after *Blakely*, the states have not used binding legal sentencing guidelines. Rather, they have chosen to allow judges to apply them voluntarily as a form of sentencing advice about how to punish offenders (Frase 2013, xiii). Likewise, on the federal level, *United States v. Booker* (2005) nullified part of the U.S. Sentencing Guidelines and, in the process, ruled that they were only advisory in effect, which meant that federal judges also had the voluntary choice to consult the sentencing guidelines to make recommendations about how to punish defendants. In the aftermath of *Booker*, the U.S. Sentencing Commission has instructed judges to sentence defendants by first calculating the applicable sentencing range and then consider if there is any reasonable basis to depart from or vary the prescribed punishment established by the guidelines (U.S. Sentencing Commission 2015, 11–12).

Especially in light of the growth of mass incarceration, nonpartisan organizations, academic studies, and increasingly bipartisan political coalitions insist that mandatory sentencing laws are flawed policy initiatives because they are unjust, costly, and harm local communities (Porter 2016; Tonry 2016, 201; Kelly 2015, 322–340). As a result, there has been a growing movement to reform them by implementing new sentencing and crime containment strategies. The Sentencing Project's 2016 report finds that several states have enacted new sentencing laws that are directed at curbing the problem of rising prison population growth. As examples, Connecticut eased penalties for drug offenses, while Nebraska abolished the death penalty. Other states, such as Maryland, Oklahoma, and North Dakota, adjusted their mandatory sentencing laws to make it easier for judges to make departures from mandatory minimums. Several other states, among them Texas and Montana, revised probation and parole procedures so that offenders may avoid returning to prison for minor technical violations that relate to the conditions of their release (Porter 2016, 3). According to the National Conference on State Legislatures, state sentencing and correctional polices are returning to past practices, with 33 states now operating primarily indeterminate sentencing regimes, and only 17 states, plus the District of Columbia, using strictly determinate sentencing systems (Lawrence 2015, 4). At the federal level, similar initiatives, such as the Smart on Crime program adopted by the Obama administration, are using federal monies and resources to ensure fairer punishments for nonviolent, low-level offenders while easing legal restrictions that prevent prisoners who have served their sentences from having an easier time assimilating back into the community through reentry programs (U.S. Department of Justice 2015).

Christopher P. Banks

See also: Capital Punishment; Constitutional Interpretation; Defendants' Rights

Further Reading

Banks, Christopher P., and David M. O'Brien. 2015. *The Judicial Process: Law, Courts, and Judicial Politics.* Thousand Oaks, CA: CQ Press.

Clear, Todd R., and Natasha A. Frost. 2014. *The Punishment Imperative: The Rise and Failure of Mass Incarceration in America.* New York: New York University Press.

Frase, Richard S. 2007. "The Apprendi-Blakely Cases: Sentencing Reform Counter-Revolution?" *Criminology and Public Policy* 6: 403–431.

Frase, Richard S. 2013. *Just Sentencing: Principles and Procedures for a Workable System.* New York: Oxford University Press.

Haerens, Margaret, ed. 2010. *Mandatory Minimum Sentencing.* Farmington Hills, MI: Greenhaven Press.

Kelly, William R. 2015. *Criminal Justice at the Crossroads: Transforming Crime and Punishment.* New York: Columbia University Press.

Lawrence, Alison. 2015. "Making Sense of Sentencing: State Systems and Policies." http://www.ncsl.org/documents/cj/sentencing.pdf.

Porter, Nicole D. 2016. "The State of Sentencing 2015: Developments in Policy and Practice." http://sentencingproject.org/wp-content/uploads/2016/02/State-of-Sentencing-2015.pdf.

Stith, Kate, and Jose A. Cabranes. 1998. *Fear of Judging: Sentencing Guidelines in the Federal Courts.* Chicago: University of Chicago Press.

Tonry, Michael. 2013. "Sentencing in America, 1975–2025." *Crime and Justice* 42: 141–198.

Tonry, Michael. 2016. *Sentencing Fragments: Penal Reform in America, 1975–2025.* New York: Oxford University Press.

U.S. Department of Justice. 2015. "The Attorney General's Smart on Crime Initiative." https://www.justice.gov/ag/attorney-generals-smart-crime-initiative.

U.S. Sentencing Commission. 2012. *Report on the Continuing Impact of United States v. Booker on Federal Sentencing.* Washington, D.C.: Government Printing Office.

U.S. Sentencing Commission. 2015. *Federal Sentencing: The Basics.* Washington, D.C.: Government Printing Office.

Cases and Statutes

Apprendi v. New Jersey. 2000. 530 U.S. 466.

Blakely v. Washington. 2004. 542 U.S. 296.

The Sentencing Reform Act of 1984. 18 U.S.C. §§3551 et seq.
United States v. Booker. 2005. 543 U.S. 220.

CAPITAL PUNISHMENT

The death penalty, or capital punishment, has been a long-standing part of American law and human history. Its origins have ancient roots that go back to early civilizations around the world. While the penalty has sparked intense moral debate, the arguments for and against it also raise enduring constitutional and political questions that range from debating its permissibility to how and to whom it is applied by governments and juries in specific types of capital cases. Federal and state courts reviewing the issue look to their respective constitutions to determine if capital punishment violates the due process principle that government-sponsored executions must not be disproportionate to the offense or, as expressed in the U.S. Constitution's Eighth Amendment, cruel and unusual. While the Supreme Court and public opinion has shown support for the death penalty, recent case law and new advances in medical and criminal forensic technologies have reignited the concerns shared by capital punishment opponents that the penalty is not only immoral but also arbitrarily applied, as a result of convictions produced from inherently flawed police and trial procedures. The specter of wrongful convictions is juxtaposed against other criticisms that capital punishment is out of step with international human rights law and norms.

The Origins and Evolution of the Death Penalty

Putting people to death for breaking the law has always been a part of human history. In the ancient civilizations of Rome, Greece, Assyria, and China, capital punishment was used for a variety of purposes and with no shortage of means. In ancient China, for example, beheadings by the sword were common, whereas in Rome and Greece the deed was done by axe. The history of other early societies records that executions were performed by crucifixion, burning at the stake, boiling in oil, disembowelment, drawing and quartering, and breaking on the wheel (Streib 2013, 2–3). Between 1400 and 1700, governments in Europe used capital punishment to dispense justice and solidify the state's power over threats to public order and safety in the interest of protecting entrenched social orders. In this respect, executions often served a symbolic and political purpose. For this reason, death sentences were carried out in public spaces, and the most gruesome were used against political enemies—not just common murderers or ordinary criminals. As one criminal sociologist explains, "Traitors were hung, drawn and quartered, their heads placed on spikes, their body parts displayed around the kingdom" (Garland 2010, 76–77, 78). The popular fictional account of Scottish rebel William Wallace's horrific death in the movie *Braveheart* (1995) is emblematic of how political traitors were treated in this era.

The death penalty's adoption in Western cultures is neither surprising nor unusual given its prevalence throughout time. Although it has evolved in fits and starts in the United States after being transplanted from England, it was widely used in colonial America for a number of crimes. In addition to death sentences, colonial codes authorized many harsh punishments, among them mutilation, hanging, banishment, whipping, branding, forced labor, and public shaming. However, by the time of the 1787 Constitutional Convention and the ratification of the Bill of Rights in 1791, the Eighth Amendment prohibition against "cruel and unusual" punishments was generally understood to bar only extreme forms of execution, such as crucifixion or burning at the stake (Whitman 2003, 166).

In the decades that followed and for most of the 19th century, American states largely reserved the death penalty for murderers, but there were some notable exceptions. Western and southern states were known to inflict it on horse thieves, cattle rustlers, and rapists. In the Civil War period, the South used it as a tool of political and social repression against blacks. Although the federal government limited the death penalty to only a few specified offenses, the laws in many states extended it to a multitude of offenses well into the 20th century. The types of nonhomicidal offenses that triggered capital punishment included kidnapping, treason, carnal knowledge, armed robbery, train robbery, arson, espionage, and perjury in a capital case, among others (Bedau 1996, 3–7). For some scholars, the prevalence of harsh punishments is infused in an American culture that is not prone to mercy and, significantly, is only one of six political systems in the world that has shown a willingness to execute minors (Whitman 2003, 46).

According to the Death Penalty Information Center (2016), as of July 2016, the federal government and 31 states still retain the death penalty. Nineteen states, plus the District of Columbia, have abolished it. Since 1976, nearly 1,500 persons have been put to death, and most executions were concentrated in the southern states and Texas. In recent years, however, the rate of executions has been declining. Of the states that use it, the primary method of execution is by lethal injection, followed by electrocution, gas chamber, hanging, and firing squad. As of January 2016, close to 3,000 inmates languish on death row. Notably, the United States is one of the 58 countries around the world that retain the death penalty for ordinary crimes. Some of the others include Afghanistan, China, Cuba, Iran, Japan, Pakistan, Saudi Arabia, Thailand, and Vietnam.

The Death Penalty's Constitutionality in Federal and State Courts

Like the federal government, state courts are obliged to adhere to the provisions of their governing founding documents in reviewing the legality of capital punishment. For states with the death penalty, all have language that mirror the federal Constitution's guarantee of due process and the ban against inflicting cruel or unusual punishments. Those constitutional principles, along with the guarantee of equality under the law, have been incorporated and applied to the actions of state governments through the Supreme Court's incorporation doctrine. Furthermore, although the U.S. Constitution's Eighth Amendment also proscribes excessive bails and excessive fines, the Supreme Court has not yet made those provisions fully applicable to the states under the incorporation doctrine.

Key cases that establish parameters of permissible capital punishment laws include *Trop v. Dulles* (1958), *Furman v. Georgia* (1972), and *Gregg v. Georgia* (1976). While *Trop* is not a death penalty case, it required that punishments must comport with the "evolving standards of decency," a legal standard that allows courts to construe the Eighth Amendment as a living document that fits the tenor of the times. In *Trop*, the Warren Court (1953–1969) held that a native-born American who deserted his country during wartime could not be punished by the loss of his citizenship because it contradicted the "principle of civilized treatment guaranteed by the Eighth Amendment." As a result, denationalization violates "evolving standards of decency that mark the progress of a maturing society." *Trop*'s constitutional significance is twofold. Not only did it tap into ongoing abolitionists' claims that the death penalty violated civilized norms and practices, it also became the controversial basis for subsequent Supreme Court decisions that debated the scope and meaning of the Eighth Amendment's application to capital crimes in the modern era (Garland 2010, 216).

Trop's reasoning found its way into *Furman v. Georgia* (1972) when the country was beginning to abandon the death penalty. After 1967, most states put a moratorium on executions because there was growing concern from abolitionist reformers and interest groups that the penalty was applied arbitrarily. In *Furman*, in a per curiam (unsigned) opinion, but in a case also featuring nine separate opinions by each justice, a sharply divided Supreme Court invalidated the death penalty as a violation of the Eighth Amendment. Among the concurring opinions, Justice White concluded it was arbitrary. Justice Douglas agreed but added that it was discriminatorily applied against politically marginalized groups. Justice Stewart characterized it as a "unique penalty . . . [that is] so wantonly and so freakishly imposed." For Justices Brennan and Marshall, the death penalty is a violation of human dignity. Three dissenting justices, Blackmun, Powell, and Rehnquist, countered that the Court must show deference to legislative policy choices; and Chief Justice Burger thought that the punishment is neither cruel nor unusual. Significantly, though, he stated that the states ought to provide more guidance for how the penalty is to be applied by judges and juries by creating clear legal standards in their death sentencing laws.

In the aftermath of *Furman,* a majority of states rewrote their laws to reinstitute the death penalty. Many states opted to spell out the aggravating and mitigating factors that juries could take into account when determining if the defendant should live or die at the hands of the state. Others, such as North Carolina and Oklahoma, imposed mandatory death sentences for certain crimes, a penalty that takes away from juries the discretion to choose life or death during sentencing. As these laws went into effect, the death row population began to rise, prompting the Court to revisit the issue in *Gregg v. Georgia* (1976). In *Gregg,* with only Justices Brennan and Marshall dissenting, the Court reversed course and upheld Georgia's death penalty statute. Notably, how Georgia revised its law to meet constitutional standards is significant because it became a template for other legislation that specified aggravating and mitigating circumstances and also required separate trials to determine guilt and the ensuing sentence (Streib 2013, 44).

The Supreme Court continues to wrestle with the death penalty. Even so, it has not overruled *Gregg.* However, it has declared that mandatory death sentences are unconstitutional in *Woodson v. North Carolina* (1976) and, with *Coker v. Georgia* (1977), held that capital punishment cannot be applied to rapists of adult women. In subsequent cases, the Court decided that offenders suffering under a mental disability (*Atkins v. Virginia,* 2002) and that minors under the age of 16 could not be executed (*Roper v. Simmons,* 2005). The Roberts Court (from 2005) has weighed in on capital punishment by invalidating it for crimes of child rape (*Kennedy v. Louisiana,* 2008) but also authorizing the use of a three-drug lethal injection protocol (*Baze v. Rees,* 2008) and a specific type of drug, midazolam (a sedative), as the first drug used in the three-drug lethal injection protocol (*Glossip v. Gross,* 2015). In *Glossip,* a 5–4 decision, the justices acutely disagreed with each other along ideological lines, a signal that the issue will return to the Court—especially if a liberal president vested with the power of judicial appointment enters the White House after the 2016 presidential election. Each of the liberal justices dissented, and two of them, Sotomayor and Breyer, read parts of their opinions from the bench during the Court's announcement of judgment, a rare two-justice public display of judicial contempt. In her dissent, Justice Kagan went so far as to say that the Court in *Glossip* is letting prisoners be "exposed to what may well be the chemical equivalent of being burned at the stake" (Howe 2015).

The Future of the Death Penalty in the United States

The imposition of the death penalty remains politically controversial as a matter of domestic social policy and international human rights law. Human rights lawyers are quick to observe that most other civilized countries throughout the world have banned state-sanctioned execution under international law and human rights treaties. As a domestic and global issue, decisions by pharmaceutical companies to restrict the availability of the drugs used for lethal injections in the United States present ongoing challenges for states seeking to enforce its death penalty laws. The practical concern of whether lethal injection will remain viable as a death penalty option sits alongside basic moral and legal questions about whether executions can be administered fairly and without arbitrary, flawed, or cost-prohibitive procedures. While defenders of capital punishment insist that it is justified as a deterrent to homicidal behavior, abolitionists have pointed to a series of "botched" executions (where the inmate does not die right away and allegedly suffers inhumanely) to make their case. Furthermore, academic studies and organized interest group advocates observe that convictions are prone to human error in the trial process (e.g., admitting evidence of culpability when subsequent DNA evidence proves otherwise), which leads to wrongful convictions and the possibility that death row inmates could be executed for crimes they did not commit. Other lingering constitutional questions, such as whether budget-strapped public defenders' offices can supply effective appointed legal counsel to capital defendants or whether prosecutors overstep their authority by applying the death penalty in a racially discriminatory manner, ensure that federal and state courts will continue to examine the legal and policy wisdom of retaining capital punishment as a method of crime control and constitutional justice.

Christopher P. Banks

See also: Constitutional Interpretation; Defendants' Rights; Judicial Federalism; Mandatory Sentencing

Further Reading

Bedau, Hugo Adam, ed. 1996. *The Death Penalty in America: Current Controversies*. New York: Oxford University Press.

Death Penalty Information Center. 2016. "Fact Sheet." http://www.deathpenaltyinfo.org.

Garland, David. 2010. *Peculiar Institution: America's Death Penalty in an Age of Abolition*. Cambridge, MA: Belknap Press of Harvard University Press.

Howe, Amy. 2015. "Justices Again Spurn Lethal Injection Challenge: In Plain English." *SCOTUSblog*, June 29. http://www.scotusblog.com/2015/06/justices-again-spurn-lethal-injection-challenge-in-plain-english/.

Sarat, Austin, and Järgen Martschukat, eds. 2011. *Is the Death Penalty Dying?: European and American Perspectives*. New York: Cambridge University Press.

Streib, Victor. 2013. *Death Penalty in a Nutshell*. 4th ed. Saint Paul, MN: West Publishing.

Whitman, James Q. 2003. *Harsh Justice: Criminal Punishment and the Widening Divide Between America and Europe*. New York: Oxford University Press.

Zimring, Franklin E. 2003. *The Contradictions of American Capital Punishment*. New York: Oxford University Press.

Cases

Atkins v. Virginia. 2002. 536 U.S. 304.
Baze v. Rees. 2008. 533 U.S. 35.
Coker v. Georgia. 1977. 433 U.S. 584.
Furman v. Georgia. 1972. 408 U.S. 238.
Glossip v. Gross. 2015. 135 S. Ct. 2726.
Gregg v. Georgia. 1976. 428 U.S. 153.
Kennedy v. Louisiana. 2008. 554 U.S. 407.
Roper v. Simmons. 2005. 543 U.S. 551.
Trop v. Dulles. 1958. 356 U.S. 86.
Weems v. United States. 1910. 217 U.S. 349.
Woodson v. North Carolina. 1976. 428 U.S. 280.

PRIVACY RIGHTS

Privacy rights are personal freedoms that protect against unwanted or unjustifiable government interference. Broadly construed, the recognition of privacy rights encompasses personal autonomy and informational privacy interests. The right to privacy protects personal decision-making relating to issues of childrearing, marriage, reproductive freedom, human sexuality, gender identity, and death. In addition, the right to privacy insures that the information government gathers, stores, or communicates about individuals is subject to legal constraints. While the U.S. Supreme Court has determined that certain federal Bill of Rights include privacy interests that deserve judicial protection, the Court has also expanded the meaning of the right to privacy through its interpretation of the Fourteenth Amendment. In contrast, state courts have derived privacy rights from state constitutions as well as from federal law established by Supreme Court precedents. However, some state courts have enlarged the scope of privacy rights by going beyond the meaning given to them by Supreme Court precedents and federal law. Judicial decision-making in the area of privacy law will continue to assume greater legal and political significance in an increasingly globalized society that is being rapidly transformed by digital and scientific technologies and the challenges posed to national security in the post-9/11 era.

The Evolution of the Right to Privacy

As early as 1890, Samuel Warren and Louis Brandeis (who later became a Supreme Court justice) argued that the common law ought to recognize a right to privacy or, in their words, "the right to be let alone" (Warren and Brandeis

1890). Such judicial recognition was needed because the right to privacy is not explicitly mentioned in the U.S. Constitution. Certain provisions of the federal Bill of Rights imply one, however. Under the First Amendment, citizens have the freedom to make personal choices about their political expression, whom to associate with, or what religion to believe in. The Third Amendment protects the liberty to prevent military troops from occupying personal residences during peacetime. The Fourth Amendment safeguards citizens from unreasonable searches and searches from government officials. The Fifth Amendment protects individuals from incriminating themselves during police interrogations when they are in custodial interrogation. Many of these privacy components were etched into constitutional law by Justice William O. Douglas in *Griswold v. Connecticut* (1965), a landmark Supreme decision that implied a right to privacy from the Fourteenth Amendment's due process clause and other specific provisions in the federal Bill of Rights. Although some state courts recognized privacy rights that pertained to the nondisclosure of personal matters, self-autonomy, or natural rights in the early 20th century (Shaman 2006, 988–989), *Griswold* is the first Supreme Court case to declare that there is a fundamental right to privacy under the U.S. Constitution. As a result, *Griswold* is often the point of departure for understanding subsequent rulings by federal and state courts that address the scope and application of privacy rights (Soma et al. 2014, 61).

In *Griswold*, in a 7–2 decision, the Supreme Court invalidated an antiquated Connecticut law that prohibited the use or distribution of contraceptives because it violated a married couples' right to make intimate personal choices. After acknowledging that the case raises many questions about the meaning of the Fourteenth Amendment's due process clause, Justice Douglas reasoned that a right to privacy is implied by the First, Third, Fourth, and Fifth Amendments to the U.S. Constitution. In citing several cases interpreting those provisions, Justice Douglas concluded that the "specific guarantees in the Bill of Rights have penumbras, formed by emanations from those guarantees that help give them life and substance" which, therefore, "create zones of privacy." He added that the Ninth Amendment, which states that, "The enumeration in the Constitution, of certain rights, shall not be construed to deny or disparage others retained by the people," lent further support for articulating a fundamental right to privacy. In separate concurrences and dissents, several of the justices questioned whether the right to privacy, or whether any other rights that are expressed in the first eight amendments or implied elsewhere, can be incorporated and applied against the actions of state governments under the broad umbrella of judicially enforceable Fourteenth Amendment due process rights. In this respect, *Griswold* remains important in the judicial debate about not only the constitutional meaning of privacy rights but also in understanding the nuances of rival judicial theories about the scope and application of the Fourteenth Amendment's incorporation doctrine and the nationalization of civil rights and liberties.

Federal Courts and the Right to Privacy

Although *Griswold v. Connecticut* (1965) safeguarded the informational privacy interests of married couples, it also is the touchstone for conceptualizing the liberty that is attached to personal autonomy. In *Lawrence v. Texas* (2003), the Supreme Court struck down a state law banning homosexual sodomy because it violated a same-sex couple's Fourteenth Amendment due process right to make intimate and private choices about their consensual sexual practices. Similar privacy-based rationales have recognized the autonomy to possess obscene material in the home (*Stanley v. Georgia*, 1969); to have an abortion (*Roe v. Wade*, 1973); to let extended families live together in the same residence (*Moore v. City of East Cleveland*, 1977); to allow parents to control how they wish to raise their child, even though it means denying grandparents rights to visitation (*Troxel v. Granville*, 2000); and to permit persons of different races (*Loving v. Virginia*, 1967) or persons of the same biological sex (*Obergefell v. Hodges*, 2015) to wed. Notably, on occasion, the Supreme Court has chosen to limit personal autonomy rights. In *Washington v. Glucksberg* (1997), a state law banning physician-assisted suicide was upheld because the Court ruled that there is no due process right for terminally ill adults to choose to end their life because facilitating suicide offends traditional notions of ordered liberty and justice.

Apart from personal autonomy, the Supreme Court has extended privacy rights to cases implicating the government's use of personal information, a key issue that is often raised in exploring the constitutional limits of government action in criminal prosecutions. In *Katz v. United States* (1967), the high court reviewed a defendant's argument that a wiretap that was physically placed on a phone booth to gather evidence about illegal gambling activities violated the Fourth Amendment's prohibition against unreasonable searches and seizures. In ruling that the government overstepped its authority to gather incriminating evidence through an electronic device, the Court overruled prior case law establishing that the Fourth Amendment only safeguards citizens against physical intrusions, or "searches," of constitutionally protected areas. In doing so, the *Katz* Court held that the "Fourth Amendment protects people, not places," which meant in practice that citizens have a "reasonable expectation of privacy" that society is prepared to recognize as constitutionally valid, an argument that Justice John Marshall Harlan II made in his famous and influential concurring opinion.

In subsequent cases, the Supreme Court has looked to *Katz* and even more traditional property-based conceptions of privacy to rule that the Fourth Amendment prohibits warrantless searches of private residences through thermal imaging devices in drug investigations (*Kyllo v. United States*, 2001) and in reasoning that the police must comply with the Fourth Amendment's warrant requirement before attaching a global positioning system device to a suspect's car in a drug trafficking case (*United States v. Jones*, 2012). In *Riley v. California*

(2014), the Court held that the information stored on a defendant's cell phone could not be retrieved without a warrant in a gang-related shooting and attempted murder investigation, ostensibly because the criminal suspect's privacy interests in the digital age of the 21st century outweighed the government's need to secure evidence during an arrest in a criminal prosecution. In many respects, *Riley* is a harbinger of a federal court's decision that ordered Apple to assist the FBI to unlock an iPhone that was used by ISIS-inspired terrorism suspects who murdered several people in a San Bernardino, California, mass shooting in 2016 (Isaac 2016). To be sure, the Court's privacy cases will continue to regulate the parameters of official and private activities in the future that address the constitutional implications of anti-terrorism electronic and biometric surveillance, aerial drone use, mass data-mining operations, bulk data retention, online social media activities, new reproductive technologies, the collection of DNA evidence, LGBT rights, the theft of personal consumer or medical information by computer hackers, and so forth (Soma et al. 2014; Sarat 2015; Bernal 2014; Moore 2010).

State Courts and the Right to Privacy

Although influenced by the federal model of privacy rights protection, state courts have used their authority to ascertain but sometimes expand privacy law. Under principles of judicial federalism, state courts are obliged to respect, but not necessarily follow, Supreme Court precedents establishing privacy rights as long as their decision-making does not contradict federal law (Shaman 2006, 987). In this respect, state courts have more flexibility than federal courts to interpret the scope and meaning of privacy rights as originating from explicit or implied right to privacy provisions in state constitutions. To date, and unlike the U.S. Constitution, at least 10 state constitutions have explicit right to privacy clauses that spell out the limits to governmental action. The specific wording of the clauses is variable but often patterned after the language of natural rights found in the Declaration of Independence and early Supreme Court precedents or, in other instances, that are drawn from Fourth Amendment's unreasonable search and seizure principles. Whereas Article I, Section 1, of the California constitution states that, "All people . . . have inalienable rights [including] enjoying and defending life and liberty, acquiring, possessing, and protecting property, and pursuing and obtaining safety, happiness, and privacy," Article I, Section 10, of the South Carolina constitution declares that, "The right of the people to be secure in their persons, houses, papers and effects against unreasonable searches and seizures and unreasonable invasions of privacy shall not be violated." Other state constitutions, such as Alaska's, which proclaims that, "The right of the people to privacy is recognized and shall not be infringed," are more open-ended and therefore vest state courts will ample discretion to fill in the details (Soma et al. 2014, 186–193).

State courts have relied on the explicit right to privacy clauses or used their powers to imply a right to privacy to enlarge the personal autonomy or informational privacy freedoms of citizens. As early as 1922, in *Davis v. Davis*, the Supreme Court of Tennessee looked to its state constitution to announce that a divorced father could prevent his estranged spouse from donating her frozen embryos to a childless couple on the grounds that he had a right to "procreational autonomy" that protected his parental childbearing rights. More recently, a California court in *Burrows v. Superior Court* (1974) required police to obtain a warrant before seizing a customer's bank records, a ruling that went beyond a U.S. Supreme Court case which held that bank patrons do not have a reasonable expectation of privacy in keeping their records private. As these rulings suggest, state courts are sometimes ahead of the declarations (or at least take a different approach) that the U.S. Supreme Court makes in defining privacy rights in contemporary settings. While many states today are legalizing the medicinal or recreational use of marijuana, in 1975, in *Ravin v. State*, the Alaska Supreme Court determined that privacy rights protect citizens in possessing marijuana for their personal use in the home. Similarly, pathbreaking state supreme court decisions in Massachusetts in 2003 (*Goodridge v. Department of Public Health*) and elsewhere across the nation afforded same-sex couples the right to marry as a vindication of their privacy rights several years before the nation's highest court did so with its landmark decision in *Obergefell v. Hodges* (2015).

Christopher P. Banks

See also: Abortion Restrictions; Defendant's Rights; Freedom of Speech; Incorporation Doctrine: Judicial Federalism; Property Rights; Religious Freedom; Same-Sex Marriage

Further Reading

Bernal, Paul. 2014. *Internet Privacy Rights: Rights to Protect Autonomy.* New York: Cambridge University Press.

Isaac, Mike. 2016. "Explaining Apple's Fight with the F.B.I." *New York Times*, February 17. http://www.nytimes.com/2016/02/18/technology/explaining-apples-fight-with-the-fbi.html?_r=0.

Moore, Adam D. 2010. *Privacy Rights: Moral and Legal Foundations.* University Park: Pennsylvania State University Press.

Rotenberg, Marc, Julia Horwitz, and Jeramie Scott, eds. 2015. *Privacy in the Modern Age: The Search for Solutions.* New York: New Press.

Sarat, Austin, ed. 2015. *A World Without Privacy: What Law Can and Should Do?* New York: Cambridge University Press.

Shaman, Jeffrey M. 2006. "The Right of Privacy in State Constitutional Law." *Rutgers Law Journal* 37: 971–1085.

Soma, John T., Stephen D. Rynerson, and Erica Kitaev. 2014. *Privacy Law in a Nutshell.* 2nd ed. Saint Paul, MN: West Academic.

Warren, Samuel D., and Louis D. Brandeis. 1890. "The Right of Privacy." *Harvard Law Review* 4: 193–220.

Cases

Burrows v. Superior Court. 1974. 118 Cal. Rptr. 166.
Davis v. Davis. 1922. 842 S.W.2d 588.
Goodridge v. Department of Public Health. 2003. 798 N.E.2d 941.
Griswold v. Connecticut. 1965. 381 U.S. 479.
Katz v. United States. 1967. 389 U.S. 347.
Kyllo v. United States. 2001. 533 U.S. 27.
Lawrence v. Texas. 2003. 539 U.S. 558.
Loving v. Virginia. 1967. 388 U.S. 1.
Moore v. City of East Cleveland. 1977. 431 U.S. 494.
Obergefell v. Hodges. 2015. 135 S.Ct. U.S. 1039.
Ravin v. State. 1975. 537 P.2d 494.
Riley v. California. 2014. 134 S.Ct. 2473.
Roe v. Wade. 1973. 410 U.S. 113,
Stanley v. Georgia. 1969. 394 U.S. 557.
Troxel v. Granville. 2000. 530 U.S. 57.
United States v. Jones. 2012. 132 S. Ct. 945.
Washington v. Glucksberg. 1997. 521 U.S. 702.

ABORTION RESTRICTIONS

Although federal and state courts have long acknowledged privacy rights, the constitutional recognition of reproductive freedoms did not fully manifest itself until the mid-to-late 20th century. The right to have an abortion and the limitations placed on the government's constitutional authority to regulate a woman's personal autonomy in respect to abortions was first established in the landmark *Roe v. Wade* (1973) ruling. Thereafter, in light of mounting political pressures and judicial appointments from conservative presidents that have sought to restrict severely, or to eliminate entirely, the right of abortion, the Supreme Court altered the constitutional principles that govern the regulation of a woman's right to choose to abort an unborn fetus. Although *Roe* still remains intact as a precedent, in 1992, a sharply divided Court revised and weakened the judicial standard of review that determines the constitutionality of abortion restrictions in *Planned Parenthood of Southeastern Pennsylvania v. Casey*. *Casey's* declaration that abortion restrictions are permissible so long as they do not place a substantial obstacle in the path of women seeking to abort unborn fetuses has encouraged the states to enact regulations that increasingly constrict access to abortion providers throughout the United States. The legality of anti-abortion regulations has been the subject of ongoing political and judicial controversy, culminating in *Whole Woman's Health v. Hellerstedt* (2016), the Roberts Court's (2005 to present) most significant judicial declaration about the constitutional scope and application of *Casey's* undue burden test to date.

The Origin of Privacy Rights and Reproductive Freedoms

Although earlier cases such as *Boyd v. United States* (1886) recognized privacy rights in the Fourth and Fifth Amendments in the area of criminal procedure, the judicial development of privacy law in relation to personal intimate choices and private relationships originates in the 1920s. With *Meyer v. Nebraska* (1923), the Supreme Court overturned a state law that prohibited public and private schools from giving instruction on German and non-English modern languages. The legislation was enacted in the aftermath of World War I and a heightened antipathy to Germany and peace negotiations. In doing so, the Court recognized that the Fourteenth Amendment's due process clause meant that individuals have the right "to marry, establish a home and bring up children," among other freedoms. Similarly, *Pierce v. Society of Sisters* (1925) acknowledged that parents enjoyed the liberty to make basic educational and upbringing decisions about their children in striking down a state law requiring attendance in public, as opposed to private, schools. Apart from the marriage and child-rearing context, the Court subsequently addressed the area of reproductive freedom by at first sustaining a Virginia law providing for the compulsory sterilization of mentally challenged individuals who were confined to state institutions (*Buck v. Bell*, 1927), but then invalidating a state law that required the sterilization of habitual criminal on equal protection grounds (*Skinner v. Oklahoma*, 1942).

The first major cases creating a constitutional right to privacy that later was applied to the abortion context were decided in the 1960s and 1970s. In *Griswold v. Connecticut* (1965), the Supreme Court used the Fourteenth Amendment's due process clause to strike down a state law that interfered with the private choices of married couples' right to use contraceptives. In writing for the Court, Justice William Douglas held that there are "specific guarantees in the Bill of Rights [that] have penumbras, formed by emanations from those guarantees that help give them life and substance," which thus "create zones of privacy." In articulating a fundamental right to privacy, *Griswold* laid the basis for *Eisenstadt v. Baird* (1972), a subsequent decision that interpreted the Fourteenth Amendment's equal protection clause to protect the privacy rights of unmarried persons who were allowed to make the same type of personal choices that married people were legally permitted to make about using contraceptives in their relationships. Together, *Griswold* and *Eisenstadt* are the foundation for the Court's seminal abortion ruling in *Roe v. Wade* (1973) and, later, *Planned Parenthood of Southeastern Pennsylvania v. Casey* (1992).

Roe v. Wade to Planned Parenthood of Southeastern Pennsylvania v. Casey

In a 7–2 ruling, in *Roe v. Wade* (1973), the Supreme Court extended the right to privacy to strike down Texas's law that made performing abortions a crime except where they are necessary to save the mother's life. Justice Harry Blackmun's opinion of the Court reasoned that the Fourteenth Amendment's due process clause encompassed a right to privacy that also afforded to the mother the fundamental freedom to choose an abortion. Because the mother's right to choose is a fundamental right, any attempt by the government to regulate it is subject to the judicial standard of *strict scrutiny*. To meet strict scrutiny, the government must prove that it has a compelling interest to regulate the abortion procedure with a law that is narrowly tailored to accomplish its objective.

In applying strict scrutiny, Blackmun explained that the government's interest in protecting the mother's health and the potentiality of human life in the fetus becomes more compelling as the pregnancy continues to full term. Under the so-called trimester analysis, the Court must balance the privacy and health interests of women against those of the government in protecting the unborn. Thus, in the first trimester (three months) of pregnancy, the mother and her physician retain full control over the abortion decision. In the second trimester (three to six months), the government can regulate the abortion procedure up to the point of viability (the "compelling" point of time when the fetus has the capacity to sustain meaningful life outside of the mother's womb, usually between 24 to 28 weeks), so long as the restrictions are reasonably related to preserving the mother's health. After viability, or in the last trimester (six to nine months), the government has a compelling interest to regulate and perhaps prohibit abortions to safeguard the potentiality of fetal life, except when necessary to preserve the mother's health. In separate dissents, Justices William Rehnquist and Byron White argued that the Texas anti-abortion law was a reasonable regulation and that the Court overstepped its authority in striking it down.

Roe's controversial decision forced the states to revisit and sometimes rewrite their existing abortion laws. Whereas some jurisdictions put new restrictions on public funding for abortions, others banned abortions in public hospitals, and still others imposed spousal or parental (for a minor) informed consent requirements before having abortions. Other states mandated fetal lung and maturity tests, erected mandatory waiting periods, and outlawed advertisements for abortion clinics. *Roe* also became a rallying cry for anti-abortion opponents on the religious conservative right, and like-minded politicians intensified their resistance to it during the 1980s and Reagan presidency. Replacing Justice Lewis Powell on the Supreme Court after his retirement turned into a political battleground in 1987. In fact, the issue of abortion was pivotal in the Senate's decision to reject President Reagan's choice of Robert Bork to fill the vacancy, ostensibly because he was a conservative jurist that was labeled "out of the main-stream," in part because he was outspoken critic that refused to recognize an unenumerated (unwritten) right to privacy or abortion rights.

Amid the political turmoil, the Supreme Court reaffirmed *Roe* first in *Akron v. Akron Center for Reproductive Health, Inc.* (1983) and then in *Thornburgh v. American College of Obstetricians and Gynecologists* (1986). Justice Sandra Day O'Connor's dissent in *Akron* is especially noteworthy, for it laid the basis for the justices to alter the operative constitutional standards regulating abortion restrictions about a decade later. There, in an opinion joined by Justices Rehnquist and White, O'Connor argued that *Roe's* understanding about the precise point of fetal viability was based on outdated medical evidence and that its trimester approach was misguided and should be replaced by a new test that evaluates the constitutionality of anti-abortion laws by determining if they posed an undue burden on women seeking to have them. Subsequently, the undue burden test became the focus of the Court's unusual joint opinion by justices O'Connor, David Souter, and Anthony Kennedy in *Planned Parenthood of Southeastern Pennsylvania v. Casey* (1992) that affirmed the "essence of *Roe*" but weakened it considerably.

As the Court's composition shifted its jurisprudence to the right in the late 1980s, many court watchers suspected that *Roe* was destined to be placed in the constitutional dustbin of history in light of the growing judicial skepticism about its underlying constitutional logic. Even *Roe's* author, Justice Blackmun, was quoted in the national media as fearing the worst. Before a class of first-year law students at the University of Arkansas, he said, "Will *Roe v. Wade* go down the drain? I think there's a very distinct possibility that it will, this term. You can count the votes" (Associated Press 1988). So, in 1989, while a badly split Court in *Webster v. Reproductive Health Services* upheld many of Missouri's anti-abortion restrictions (including requirements banning public facilities from performing abortions and the performance of fetal viability tests), anti-*Roe* proponents were disappointed that the justices could not muster enough votes to jettison *Roe*, an outcome that was replicated in the Court's next landmark ruling in *Casey*. Still, *Webster* signaled to state legislatures that the Court was willing to tolerate even more restrictive abortion regulations in state law (Shimabukuro 2015, 3).

In *Planned Parenthood of Southeastern Pennsylvania v. Casey* (1992), several abortion clinics challenged a Pennsylvania abortion law that required women (1) to be informed by doctors about fetal development; (2) to get their spouse's consent to an abortion, and, if they were a minor, to get their parent's consent; and, (3) to wait 24 hours to have an abortion after they gave their informed consent. Pennsylvania's law also imposed reporting and public disclosure requirements on doctors performing abortions. In delivering the ruling, which upheld all of the provisions except the one requiring spousal notification, Justices O'Connor, Kennedy, and Souter announced the judgment of the Court, joined in part by Justices Harry Blackmun and John Paul Stevens. In doing so, the Court refused to overturn *Roe* because the doctrine of stare decisis (let the prior decision stand) compelled that the Court retain a precedent that the people have come to rely on to set their legal expectations; thus, overruling *Roe* would lead to a loss in the Court's public legitimacy as a judicial institution as well as undermine the national commitment to the rule of law. The most important *Roe* principle that was kept intact is the woman's right to end her pregnancy before fetal viability. Still, *Casey* had the effect of significantly weakening *Roe* by eliminating the trimester analysis and replacing it with a new test; that is, a law regulating abortions is unconstitutional if it puts an undue burden on a woman's ability to make the choice to end her pregnancy. In other words, the law must not have "the purpose or effect of placing a substantial obstacle in the path of a woman seeking an abortion of a nonviable fetus."

The Partial Birth Abortion Rulings and *Whole Woman's Heath v. Hellerstedt*

Although *Casey* did not reverse the basic right to choose an abortion, the Court has reviewed the politically controversial issue of "late-term" or "partial-birth" abortion bans. In *Stenberg v. Carhart* (2000), a closely divided Supreme Court invalidated a state ban on partial-birth abortions on the grounds that the law omitted a medical exception for permitting abortions if the mother's health was in jeopardy. In response, Congress enacted the Partial-Birth Abortion Ban Act, or legislation that banned late-term abortions under federal law. Thereafter, in *Gonzales v. Carhart* (2007), the Roberts Court sustained the federal ban even though it suffered from the same constitutional defect that caused the state law to be overturned in *Stenberg v. Carhart*. As a result, the constitutionality of states' partial-birth abortion bans remains an open question until the Court elects to return to the issue.

Moreover, in an important ruling interpreting the parameters of the undue burden test, the Roberts Court struck down a Texas law that severely limited access to abortions in *Whole Woman's Health v. Hellerstedt* (2016). The Texas law was challenged because it required that abortions could only be performed by physicians with admitting privileges in a hospital within 30 miles of the abortion facility, and it forced abortion clinics to meet the higher standards of medical care that are set for ambulatory surgical centers. Both provisions, the Court ruled in a 6–3 decision, were unconstitutional because they placed an undue burden on the woman's right to choose, and to have access to, abortions. In writing for the Court's majority, Justice Stephen Breyer rejected Texas's argument that each provision was designed to improve abortion safety and patient health. In dismissing these claims, Breyer reiterated that *Casey* required that the judiciary must evaluate "the burdens a law imposes on abortion access together with the benefits those laws confer." In weighing the record evidence of the facts in the case, the Court concluded that the Texas law had little or no medical benefits and, moreover, that it had the adverse effect of greatly limiting the availability of, and access to, abortions because many clinics were forced to close with the restrictions in place. The dissenting justices collectively made two basic points. In writing for himself, Justice Clarence Thomas complained that the Court was showing a preference for sustaining abortion rights in comparison to other freedoms. Justice Samuel Alito's dissent, joined by Chief Justice Roberts and Justice Thomas, argued that the Court should not have reviewed the case at all because it should have been dismissed on procedural grounds (Denniston 2016).

While the long-term impact of *Hellerstedt* remains unclear, its short-term effect is that it refines the precedent set in *Casey* and provides additional guidance to courts and litigants that are certain to need it as the fight over abortion restrictions will surely consume the judiciary's time in future litigation. In addition, there is little doubt that the Supreme Court will be asked to revisit the abortion controversy in light of *Hellerstedt* and its application to health care reform and the legal implications of Obamacare, or the Patient Protection and Affordable Care Act.

Christopher P. Banks

See also: The Affordable Care Act; Constitutional Interpretation; Privacy Rights; Same-Sex Marriage

Further Reading

Associated Press. 1988. "Justice Fears for Roe Ruling." *New York Times*, September 14. http://www.nytimes.com/1988/09/14/us/justice-fears-for-roe-ruling.html.

Denniston, Lyle. 2016. "Opinion Analysis: Abortion Rights Reemerge Strongly." *SCOTUSblog*, June 27. http://www.scotusblog.com/2016/06/opinion-analysis-abortion -rights-reemerge-strongly/.

O'Brien, David M. 2014. *Constitutional Law and Politics: Struggles for Power and Government Accountability*. 9th ed., vol. 2. New York: W. W. Norton.

Shimabukuro, Jon O. 2015. "Abortion: Judicial History and Legislative Response." *Congressional Research Service* (RL 33467, September 16). Washington, D.C.: Government Printing Service.

Cases

Akron v. Akron Center for Reproductive Health, Inc. 1983. 462 U.S. 416.
Boyd v. United States. 1886. 116 U.S. 616.
Buck v. Bell. 1927. 274 U.S. 200.
Eisenstadt v. Baird. 1972. 405 U.S. 438.
Gonzales v. Carhart. 2007. 550 U.S. 124.

Griswold v. Connecticut. 1965. 381 U.S. 479.

Meyer v. Nebraska. 1923. 262 U.S. 390.

Pierce v. Society of Sisters. 1925. 268 U.S. 510.

Planned Parenthood of Southeastern Pennsylvania v. Casey. 1992. 505 U.S. 833.

Roe v. Wade. 1973. 410 U.S. 113.

Skinner v. Oklahoma. 1942. 316 U.S. 535.

Stenberg v. Carhart. 2000. 530 U.S. 914.

Thornburgh v. American College of Obstetricians and Gynecologists. 1986. 476 U.S. 747.

Webster v. Reproductive Health Services. 1989. 492 U.S. 490.

Whole Woman's Health v. Hellerstedt. 2016. 136 S.Ct. 2292

RACIAL DISCRIMINATION

From the founding to today, racial conflict has been an enduring issue in American politics and for U.S. courts. While the Declaration of Independence enshrined the principle that "all men are created equal" in American society, achieving full equality for persons of color has been more of an aspirational goal than reality for much of American history. The political compromises that led to the U.S. Constitution's ratification meant that the founding document silently embraced the institution of slavery, an issue that was not resolved until the Civil War. With the enactment of the Thirteenth, Fourteenth, and Fifteenth Amendments, slaves were freed from bondage and given political rights. However, during Reconstruction and afterward, the Supreme Court did not always protect those freedoms, and the South continued to take them away with the passage of discriminatory Jim Crow laws. It was not until the mid-20th century that the Supreme Court began to interpret the Fourteenth Amendment in a way that limited the impact of racial inequality in society, a process that coincided with the civil rights movement and the passage of landmark civil rights and voting rights legislation in the 1960s. Since then, the Supreme Court has been at the forefront of deciding issues of racial discrimination that arise in school desegregation, interracial marriage, criminal procedure, executive powers, and affirmative action cases, among others.

The Constitution, Slavery, and the Civil War

During the colonial era, slaves represented a significant portion of the population in the South. Even though a draft of the Declaration of Independence had a section that condemned the international slave trade, it was removed from the final version. Although slavery was losing its grip on the North by the time of the 1787 Constitutional Convention, the South retained it as a way to grow its economy and build individual wealth by expanding property rights. The differences between the North and the South over the issue of slavery could not be resolved completely in the founding document, so a compromise was reached to ensure the Constitution's ratification. While the words "slave" and "slavery" are absent in the original Constitution, it nonetheless preserved the institution of slavery with Article I, Section 2, Clause 3 (the three-fifths clause, counting each slave as 3/5th of a free person for taxation and representation purposes); Article I, Section 9, Clause 1 (the slave trade clause, barring Congress from restricting the slave trade for 20 years); Article IV, Section 2, Clause 3 (the fugitive slave clause, providing for the return of fugitive slaves); and Article V (preventing constitutional amendments involving the slave trade before 1808) (Davis and Graham 1995, 1–2). Abolitionist William Lloyd Garrison referred to these compromises and the Constitution as a "covenant with death" and "an agreement with Hell." Historian William M. Wiecek similarly analogized the founding debate over slavery to a fairy tale, the "Witch at the Christening," because those discussions were haunted by an evil uninvited guest that put a curse on the new American nation (Finkelman 2014, 3, 163).

In the decades leading up to the Civil War, the federal courts wrestled with defining the legal parameters of the slave trade and the return of slaves. However, as the abolitionist movement and sectional conflict grew, the most contentious and politically controversial issues involved how to deal with slavery in the territories and the admission of new states. With assorted legislation, including the 1820 Missouri Compromise (admitting Missouri as a slave state while admitting Maine as a free state and banning slavery north of Missouri's southern border), Congress could not settle the issue. Neither could the Supreme Court, as its infamous *Dred Scott v. Sandford* (1857) decision attests. In *Dred Scott*, in a 7–2 decision, the Supreme Court invalidated the 1820 Missouri Compromise and declared that a slave had no rights as a U.S. citizen to sue for his freedom after his owner took him from Missouri, a slave state, to Illinois and other territories that banned slavery, and then back to Missouri. As Chief Justice Roger Taney declared, slaves "had no rights which the white man was bound to respect, and that the negro might justly and lawfully be reduced to slavery for his benefit" (Davis and Graham 1995, 8).

Plessy v. Ferguson and the "Separate but Equal" Doctrine

The racial and sectional differences over the issue of slavery were settled by the Civil War, President Lincoln's Emancipation Proclamation, and Congress's enactment of the Civil War amendments that banned slavery (Thirteenth); gave freed slaves citizenship, due process, and equality rights (Fourteenth); and voting rights (Fifteenth). Still, the emergence of Southern black codes and Jim Crow laws after Reconstruction kept blacks from enjoying their freedom by barring them from jury service and erecting barriers to voting with literacy tests and poll taxes, among other things.

When challenged, the Supreme Court provided some relief but not consistently. To illustrate, *Strauder v. West Virginia* (1880) invalidated a state law banning blacks from juries, but the *Civil Rights Cases* (1883) struck down a federal civil rights law that prevented blacks from being discriminated against in public places, such as inns, theaters, and transportation. Significantly, the *Civil Rights Cases* are crucial for helping to reinforce the "state action" doctrine, which holds that Congress can only enforce Fourteenth Amendment rights against laws enacted by state governments, not private entities or individuals.

By the 1890s, blacks were also discriminated against by railroad segregation laws in the South. In *Plessy v. Ferguson* (1896), the Supreme Court upheld a Louisiana law requiring the segregation of blacks and whites on a railway car by declaring it was valid so long at the public accommodations are "separate but equal." In spite of Justice John Harlan's lone dissent in *Plessy* which argued that the "Constitution is color-blind, and neither knows nor tolerates classes among citizens," *Plessy* remained good law until the middle of the 20th century.

Brown v. Board of Education and the Civil Rights Movement

The Supreme Court led by Chief Justice Earl Warren revolutionized due process, criminal, procedural, and egalitarian rights from 1953 to 1969. One of its most important decisions is *Brown v. Board of Education* (1954), a ruling that civil rights activists and lawyers brought before the high court in the aftermath of earlier decisions such as *Missouri ex rel. v. Gaines* (1938) that held that equal protection was denied to blacks seeking admission to law schools when the state did not establish one as a separate facility. In a unanimous opinion, *Brown* declared that the Fourteenth Amendment's equal protection clause is violated because schoolchildren are psychologically harmed by having to attend separate public schools because they are placed into an inferior status to white children. Chief Justice Warren relied on the Fourteenth Amendment to reach this conclusion, but he also used social science studies as evidence to show that separate facilities make black schoolchildren feel inferior. Doing so created an ongoing controversy about the legitimacy of using extralegal sources to write a constitutional principle of equality into law that effectively overturned the separate but equal doctrine. In *Bolling v. Sharpe* (1954), the Court also used the Fifth Amendment's due process clause to invalidate racial segregation in the District of Columbia's public schools, which is under the federal government's control, an outcome that meant equal protection principles applied not only against state governments but also to federal actions.

The *Brown* desegregation mandate generated massive resistance in local communities, especially in the South, and many school boards refused to comply with it. The Supreme Court had little capacity to enforce its decree, a problem that was illustrated by *Brown v. Board of Education* (1955), a ruling that held states and local school authorities were only obliged to desegregate "with all deliberate speed." With no judicial guidance or enforcement mechanisms, opposition to the desegregation mandate remained firm and did not ease up until the federal government took action and threatened to sue or defund school districts that refused to integrate their schools in the early to mid-1960s. In addition, the movement to implement desegregation was helped by Congress's enactment of the Civil Rights Act of 1964, a measure that outlawed segregation in public accommodations and in employment (O'Brien 2014, 1472; Klarman 2004, 362–363).

Brown's Meaning and Other Supreme Court Rulings on Racial Discrimination

The difficulties of implementing *Brown's* desegregation decree intensified as the country and membership of the Supreme Court grew more conservative in the 1980s and thereafter. Two rulings, *Board of Education of Oklahoma City Public Schools v. Dowell* (1991) and *Freeman v. Pitts* (1992), held that federal court supervision of segregated school districts could stop if the courts were convinced that school boards reasonably acted to put into place their desegregation plans. Later, in *Parents Involved in the Community Schools v. Seattle School District No. 1* (2007), the Roberts Court (2005 to present) added that racial factors could not be taken into account in desegregation plans that were voluntarily adopted by school boards in assigning students to high schools that were racially isolated due to housing patterns. In a 5–4 ruling, the justices sharply disagreed on *Brown's* meaning in evaluating the school board's efforts to achieve integration and racial balance. For Chief Justice Roberts, his plurality opinion concluded that, "The way to stop discrimination on the basis of race is to stop discriminating on the basis of race." The dissenters, led by Justice John Paul Stevens, countered that the Supreme Court's interpretation of *Brown* represents a "cruel irony" that "rewrites the history of one of this Court's most important decisions."

Apart from educational discrimination cases, the Supreme Court has helped to break down racial barriers by refusing to sanction restrictive covenants, or deed restrictions that prevent blacks from being able to buy a house in a private real estate transaction in *Shelley v. Kraemer* (1948) and, in *Loving v. Virginia* (1967), striking down bans on interracial marriages. In the area of criminal procedure, with *Batson v. Kentucky* (1986), important limitations were placed on the exercise of prosecutorial discretion when the Court held that the Fourteenth Amendment's equal protection clause prevents prosecutors from using peremptory challenges (that are based on any reason) to exclude purposefully selecting black persons from serving on juries. The *Batson* rule was applied to *Foster v. Chapman* (2016), a Roberts Court decision that overturned a black defendant's death sentence when a Georgia prosecutor could not justify on race-neutral grounds his use of peremptory challenges to strike four black jurors during the capital sentencing proceeding. As Chief Justice Roberts explained, "The contents of the prosecution's file . . . plainly belie the State's claim that it exercised its strikes in a 'color-blind' manner."

Still, in other cases, the Supreme Court has adopted a more restrictive approach that arguably cuts back on the full range of rights that persons of color might otherwise be entitled to receive if race were in fact taken into account. In *Korematsu v. United States* (1944), the Supreme Court authorized the president to detain Japanese Americans into military detention camps in the interest of national security during World War II, a decision that the dissenters criticized as racist. In affirmative action cases, while the Supreme Court has upheld such programs to increase educational diversity in higher education (*Regents of the University of California v. Bakke,* 1978), in later precedents, the justices have struggled with the implications of using a color-blind or race-neutral approach in upholding the University of Michigan's College of Literature, Science and the Arts' affirmative action program in *Gratz v. Bollinger* (2003) while striking down the same University's law school affirmative action plan in *Grutter v. Bollinger* (2003). A recurring issue in these cases is the wisdom of permitting minorities to gain what critics label as "preferential treatment" through affirmative action programs, or, instead, requiring that all persons be treated equally on the basis of their individual merits, an argument that is also criticized as unjust by affirmative action proponents who argue that race should be taken into account to ensure full equality. Issues of race also factor into voting rights and redistricting decisions, and those cases will only become more significant as the Court and country wrestles with the new questions of racism that have increasingly become part of the national discourse through the "Black Lives Matter" social movement that emerged in the aftermath of police shootings of unarmed black men in Ferguson, Missouri, and other cities across the United States.

Christopher P. Banks

See also: Affirmative Action; Constitutional Interpretation; Incorporation Doctrine; Voting Rights

Further Reading

Browne-Marshall, Gloria J. 2007. *Race, Law, and American Society: 1607 to Present.* New York: Routledge.

Davis, Abraham L., and Barbara Luck Graham. 1995. *The Supreme Court, Race, and Civil Rights.* Thousand Oaks, CA: Sage Publications.

Finkelman, Paul. 2014. *Slavery and the Founders: Race and Liberty in the Age of Jefferson.* 3rd ed. Armonk, NY: M. E. Sharpe.

Klarman, Michael J. 2004. *From Jim Crow to Civil Rights Laws: The Supreme Court and the Struggle for Racial Equality.* New York: Oxford University Press.

O'Brien, David M. 2014. *Constitutional Law and Politics: Civil Rights and Civil Liberties.* 9th ed., vol. 2. New York: W. W. Norton.

Cases

Batson v. Kentucky. 1986. 476 U.S. 79.
Board of Education of Oklahoma City Public Schools v. Dowell. 1991. 498 U.S. 237.
Bolling v. Sharpe. 1954. 347 U.S. 497.
Brown v. Board of Education. 1954. 347 U.S. 483.
Brown v. Board of Education. 1955. 349 U.S. 294.
Civil Rights Cases. 1883. 109 U.S. 3.
Foster v. Chapman. 2016. 136 S.Ct. 1737.
Freeman v. Pitts. 1992. 503 U.S. 467.
Gratz v. Bollinger. 2003. 539 U.S. 244.
Grutter v. Bollinger. 2003. 539 U.S. 306.
Korematsu v. United States. 1944. 323 U.S. 214.
Loving v. Virginia. 1967. 388 U.S. 1.
Missouri ex rel. v. Gaines. 1938. 305 U.S. 337.
Parents Involved in the Community Schools v. Seattle School District No. 1. 2007. 551. U.S. 701.
Plessy v. Ferguson. 1896. 163 U.S. 537.
Regents of the University of California v. Bakke. 1978. 438 U.S. 265.
Shelley v. Kraemer. 1948. 334 U.S. 1.
Strauder v. West Virginia. 1880. 100 U.S. 303.

AFFIRMATIVE ACTION

The Fourteenth Amendment's equal protection clause guarantees that all persons are to be treated equally under the laws of the U.S. Constitution. Although the Fourteenth Amendment is one of the Civil War amendments (Thirteenth, Fourteenth, and Fifteenth Amendments) that were enacted in the post–Civil War Reconstruction era in an effort to preserve the civil rights and liberties of newly emancipated slaves, in subsequent years, its principle of equality has been applied by the Supreme Court to contemporary issues of racial discrimination, including affirmative action. Affirmative action is a shorthand description for a governmental policy that gives a preference to individuals who have membership in groups that have been historically discriminated against over others that compete for jobs, contracts, educational admission, or other scarce resources (Kennedy 2013, 20). Affirmative action programs are controversial because they allow race, ethnicity, or gender to be taken into account in hiring, contracting, or admission decisions, which, in turn, has the effect of denying those benefits to meritorious applicants who are not in the designated group. Since their inception in the 1960s, the legality of affirmative action programs has been subject to ongoing constitutional challenge in the U.S. Supreme Court with mixed results. While affirmative action remains constitutional as a matter of equal protection jurisprudence, the Court has narrowed its application to specific types of cases through its interpretation of a judicial standard of review that is called strict scrutiny. As a result, as one legal scholar put it, "For now, affirmative action is like an injured bear: too strong to succumb to its wounds but too hurt to attain full vitality" (Kennedy 2013, 15).

The Origin and Debate over Affirmative Action Programs

As an official governmental policy, affirmative action is widely acknowledged to originate in the early 1960s with President John F. Kennedy's (JFK) Executive Order 10925, which mandated that federally funded government contractors must "take affirmative action to ensure that applicants are employed, and that employees are treated during employment, without regard to their race, creed, color, or national origin." JFK's order was then followed by President Lyndon B. Johnson's (LBJ) Executive Order 11246, an edict requiring federal contractors to "take affirmative action" in employing and treating applicants "without regard to their race, color, religion, sex, or national origin." LBJ's order, as amended, specifies that large employers (with 50 or more employees and federal contracts over $50,000) file written affirmative action plans with the federal government that include minority and women hiring goals along with deadlines in order to facilitate good-faith compliance. For its part, Congress helped solidify the basis for affirmative action programs by enacting the Civil Rights Act of 1964 (banning racial discrimination in the private sector) and the Voting Rights Act of 1965 (outlawing racial discrimination in voting). Notably, the inroads establishing race-conscious policies were achieved in the civil rights era and in the aftermath of the Supreme Court's landmark ruling in *Brown v. Board of Education* (1954), a decision that forbade racial segregation in public schools. Subsequent rulings over the next 20 years imposed an affirmative action duty on local school boards to integrate their educational systems (Feder 2015, 1–2).

Banning racial discrimination through the use of affirmative action programs is typically accomplished in government, the private sector, and in higher education with set-asides, quotas, and preferences that are applied to a variety of workplace, hiring, promotion, contracting, and educational admission decision settings. Still, the debate over affirmative action has persisted in the national discourse since the 1960s. For supporters, affirmative action programs are legitimate because they provide equal opportunities for politically disadvantaged minorities who have been historically discriminated against in society. In addition, they facilitate diversity and racial integration, which, in turn, helps to eradicate deep-seated norms and practices of racial bigotry. In contrast, critics counter that affirmative action policies are unjust because they unnecessarily cast minorities into a role of playing a victim and, in practice, only benefit the most privileged of minorities who can take advantage of them. In addition, using racial preferences discriminates against nonminorities, including qualified whites who also deserve an equal chance to compete on merits for favored scarce resources. An underlying theme that works through all of the objections to affirmative action programs is the idea that the U.S. Constitution is "color-blind," an argument that Justice John Marshall Harlan first made in dissenting from the Supreme Court's endorsement of the "separate-but-equal" doctrine in *Plessy v. Ferguson* (1896). A modern restatement of the color-blind theory comes from Chief Justice John Roberts who declared in *Parents Involved in the Community Schools v. Seattle School District No. 1* (2007) that, "The way to stop discrimination on the basis of race is to stop discriminating on the basis of race" (Kennedy 2013, 78, 148–149).

Affirmative Action in Higher Education

A key battleground for establishing the legality of affirmative action programs relates to making admission decisions in higher education. At first, the Supreme Court was reluctant to address the issue, as evidenced by the Burger Court's (1969–1986) to dismiss a white applicant's challenge to an affirmative action program at the University of Washington law school by invoking the mootness doctrine in *Defunis v. Odegaard* (1974). Notably, though, liberal Justice William O. Douglas dissented and argued that, "Whatever [DeFunis's] race, he had a constitutional right to have his application considered on its individual merits in a racially neutral manner." Justice Douglas's endorsement of racial neutrality became a harbinger for modern-day arguments asserting that affirmative action programs are inherently unequal because race-conscious admission decisions unfairly penalize persons from reaping the benefits of their individual merits.

In *Regents of the University of California v. Bakke* (1978), a fragmented Supreme Court held that it was constitutional under the Fourteenth Amendment's equal protection clause to use racial preferences in an affirmative action program but only if racial quotas were not employed in a plan that was trying to advance the goal of achieving diversity in the student population. With the election of Ronald Reagan to the presidency in 1980, conservative special interest groups began to accelerate their attack on affirmative action through litigation in the federal courts, especially as the appointments from Presidents Richard Nixon, Reagan, and George H. W. Bush increasingly shifted the Supreme Court's composition to the right. While the Rehnquist Court (1986–2005) did not reverse *Bakke*, the justices showed that they were growing skeptical of race-conscious affirmative action programs. In *Gratz v. Bollinger* (2003), the Rehnquist Court invalidated the University of Michigan's undergraduate admissions program because it used racial considerations in a point system to grant or deny admissions to applicants. Still, the Court went in an opposite direction in deciding *Grutter v. Bollinger* (2003), a 5–4 ruling that endorsed the University of Michigan's law school's affirmative action program. In her opinion of the Court, Justice Sandra Day O'Connor favorably evaluated the affirmative action plan by using the *strict scrutiny* judicial standard of review. In doing so, she reiterated that the *Bakke* principle of achieving educational diversity in the study body is a compelling governmental interest, and, because the admission program used a holistic approach that took into account a variety of admissions' criteria in order to generate a critical mass of minority students, the affirmative action plan was narrowly tailored to achieve the goal of educational diversity. For the dissenters, which included Chief Justice William Rehnquist and Justices Antonin Scalia, Clarence Thomas, and Anthony Kennedy, the Court missed the mark in applying the strict scrutiny test and argued instead that the plan operated more like an impermissible quota system.

In a series of rulings, the Roberts Court (2005 to present) has grappled with the issue of affirmative action and its public policy implications in at least two different contexts. In the late 1990s and throughout the first decade in the new millennium, the voters in several states—among them Arizona, California, Michigan, Nebraska, Oklahoma, and Washington—evaluated the merits of affirmative action programs through the state ballot and initiative process (National Conference of State Legislatures 2014). By 2014, at least seven states banned affirmative action policies. In 2006, Michigan voters amended the state constitution to prohibit the use of race-based preferences as part of the admission process for public universities, a decision that was challenged on appeal to the Supreme Court as a violation of equal protection. In a 6–2 ruling, the Court in *Schuette v. Coalition to Defend Affirmative Action, Integration and Immigrant Rights and Fight for Equality By Any Means Necessary* (2014) rejected that argument by reasoning that Michigan voters had properly exercised their prerogative to amend the state's constitution as part of the democratic process. While Justice Kennedy's opinion of the Court asserted that the case "is not about the constitutionality, or the merits, of race-conscious admissions policies in higher education," but rather about "who may resolve" the "debate about racial preferences," the ruling clearly signaled that the judiciary will not stand in the way of the electorate's judgment to enact laws that diminish raced-based policies in public higher education. In this light, dissenting Justice Sonia Sotomayor argued that allowing Michigan voters to change the political process in a discriminatory fashion only makes it extremely difficult for politically disadvantaged minorities to defend the legitimacy of affirmative action programs in the future (Denniston 2014).

Still, in *Fisher v. University of Texas at Austin* (2016) (*Fisher II*), the justices addressed the underlying merits of affirmative action directly and upheld the

University of Texas at Austin's (UT-A) admissions policy. Notably, the 2016 ruling emerged only after the Court sent the case back to the Fifth Circuit in *Fisher v. University of Texas at Austin* (2013) (*Fisher I*) on the grounds that it did not apply the strict scrutiny test correctly; thereafter, the Fifth Circuit reaffirmed its earlier ruling that upheld the plan, which, in turn, was reviewed by the Court in *Fisher II* for a second time.

At issue in the *Fisher* litigation was the constitutionality of UT-A's so-called Top Ten Percent rule, which automatically admitted applicants if they were in the top 10 percent of their graduating high school class; however, the plan, using a holistic approach, then used race and a host of other factors, including leadership skills, community service, awards, honors, and other special talents or circumstances, to admit the rest to achieve a critical mass of minority students. Abigail Fisher, a white applicant that was denied admission, challenged the affirmative action plan on the basis that it violated her rights under the Fourteenth Amendment's equal protection clause. In rejecting that argument, in *Fisher II*, Justice Kennedy's opinion of the Court ruled in a 4–3 decision that UT-A's admission program served the compelling interest of increasing diversity in the student body, and the use of race and ethnicity to make admission decisions was narrowly tailored to achieve that interest, thus satisfying the strict scrutiny standard of review. The principal dissent, written by Justice Samuel Alito and joined by Chief Justice Roberts and Justice Thomas, countered that there was insufficient evidence to show that the affirmative action plan served a compelling interest or that it used race-based considerations in a way that was narrowly tailored to promote educational diversity. Because the plan fails to meet strict scrutiny, Justice Alito stated that the conclusion the Court reached in validating the affirmative action plan is "remarkable—and remarkably wrong."

In spite of *Fisher II's* endorsement of UT-A's affirmative action plan, it is unlikely that the Court's pronouncement is the last word or the final resolution of the affirmative action debate. Additional lawsuits have been filed in federal district courts that challenge the affirmative action plans and admission policies of Harvard University and of the University of North Carolina at Chapel Hill. In addition, 130 Asian American organizations have asked the Justice Department and the Department of Education to investigate the admission practices of Yale University, Brown University, and Dartmouth College for alleged discrimination against Asian American applicants. If any of the ongoing cases or investigations succeed in reaching the Supreme Court, then the constitutionality of affirmative action in the future may very well rest on the outcome of the 2016 presidential election and whether President Barack Obama's successor will be able to appoint a liberal or conservative to the Supreme Court (Slattery 2016).

Christopher P. Banks

See also: Constitutional Interpretation; Racial Discrimination; State Ballot Initiatives and Referendums

Further Reading

Denniston, Lyle. 2014. "Opinion Analysis: Affirmative Action—Up to the Voters." *SCOTUSblog*, April 22. http://www.scotusblog.com/2014/04/opinion-analysis-affirmative-action-up-to-the-voters/.

Deslippe, Dennis. 2012. *Protesting Affirmative Action: The Struggle over Equality after the Civil Rights Revolution.* Baltimore: John Hopkins University.

Feder, Jody. 2015. "Federal Affirmative Action Law: A Brief History." *Congressional Research Service (RS22256) (October 19, 2015).* Washington, D.C.: Congressional Research Service.

Hasan, Zoya, and Martha C. Nussbaum, eds. 2012. *Equalizing Access: Affirmative Action in Higher Education in India, United States, and South Africa.* Oxford: Oxford University Press.

Kennedy, Randall. 2013. *For Discrimination: Race, Affirmative Action, and the Law.* New York: Pantheon Books.

National Conference of State Legislatures. 2014. "Affirmative Action: State Action: April 2014." http://www.ncsl.org/research/education/affirmative-action-state-action.aspx.

Slattery, Elizabeth. 2016. "Symposium: A Disappointing Decision, but More Lawsuits are on the Way." *SCOTUSblog*, June 24. http://www.scotusblog.com/2016/06/symposium-a-disappointing-decision-but-more-lawsuits-are-on-the-way/.

Cases

Brown v. Board of Education. 1954. 347 U.S. 483.

Defunis v. Odegaard. 1974. 416 U.S. 312.

Fisher v. University of Texas at Austin. 2013. 133 S.Ct. 2411.

Fisher v. University of Texas at Austin. 2016. 136 S.Ct. 2198.

Gratz v. Bollinger. 2003. 539 U.S. 234.

Grutter v. Bollinger. 2003. 539 U.S. 306.

Parents Involved in the Community Schools v. Seattle School District No. 1. 2007. 551. U.S. 701.

Regents of the University of California v. Bakke. 1978. 438 U.S. 265.

Schuette v. Coalition to Defend Affirmative Action, Integration and Immigrant Rights and Fight for Equality By Any Means Necessary. 2014. 134 S.Ct. 1623.

GERRYMANDERING

Gerrymandering takes its name from the redistricting process used by the 1812 Massachusetts legislature to draw the geographical lines of legislative districts that are part of campaigns and elections. How the geographic lines are drawn is important because the elected officials within districts are representing the will of the citizens who put them in office. As governor of Massachusetts, Elbridge Gerry worked with the legislature to develop a redistricting plan that favored his political party and interests. His critics quickly described the plan, which looked like an odd-shaped salamander, as a "gerrymander." Gerrymandering, then, is drawing legislative district lines to preserve the influence of a party that has control of the political process and lawmaking in general. The role courts play in supervising campaigns and elections in reviewing challenges to redistricting plans is controversial because, before the 1960s, courts opted to remain out of the political thicket by invoking the political question doctrine. With *Baker v. Carr* (1962), the Supreme Court reassessed its positon and decided that hearing redistricting cases is a justiciable controversy that is not always barred by the political question doctrine. The decision to review redistricting cases lets the judiciary supervise the electoral process more closely. As a result, the Supreme Court has used its authority to establish the constitutional parameters of whether redistricting plans violate the Fourteenth Amendment's equal protection clause in different types of redistricting and gerrymandering cases. While the Supreme Court remains at the forefront of deciding political representation questions, it nonetheless struggles to identify and apply clear constitutional standards to redistricting and gerrymandering cases that are inherently political in scope.

Redistricting and Gerrymandering

State legislatures perform congressional and state redistricting in most states, although some states legally authorize independent commissions to accomplish the task in order to make the redistricting process less political. Under the U.S. Constitution, state legislatures have the authority to draw the lines for U.S. House of Representative and state legislative districts, and the redistricting process occurs at the 10-year mark after the national census is taken in order to take into account population shifts within the state. The redistricting process is inherently political, and the lines that are drawn to configure election districts go a long way in determining which party and candidates control the political agenda and lawmaking decisions that are made in state and national assemblies. In 2015, more than 150 redistricting bills were introduced in 34 states and Puerto Rico. In general, the redistricting legislation addresses the administrative logistics of redrawing the electoral lines and districts through redistricting commissions, public input, and establishing the criteria for redistricting decisions (National Conference of State Legislatures 2015).

Scholars have identified three types of gerrymandering. *Political* or *partisan gerrymandering* occurs when redistricting plans are created to secure an electoral advantage for one political party over another. *Incumbent* or *bipartisan* (or sometimes, *sweetheart*) *gerrymandering* is redistricting designed to safeguard the electoral fortunes of incumbents from both parties. *Racial gerrymandering* consists of redistricting plans that work to the benefit of a certain race or ethnicity, which then has the effect of excluding groups of voters that fall into either category. Gerrymandering is typically accomplished by "packing" or "cracking" the districts. With packing, voters identified with the opposing party are packed or concentrated into a few districts to reduce their voting influence. In contrast, cracking occurs when voters from the other party are divided or spread out among many districts in order to dilute their voting power (Tokaji 2013, 77078).

Citizens or groups that are unhappy with redistricting decisions bring their challenges to court for resolution. In general, the lawsuits involve claims that the redistricting process results in plans that violate constitutional standards of equality and political representation because they are driven by partisan interests or seek to gain a political advantage by excluding or diluting the vote of citizens or groups of voters on the basis of political factors or race. Before the 1960s, the judiciary was very reluctant to review redistricting cases on the grounds that legislatures, and not courts, are the proper venue for hearing political questions. In *Colegrove v. Green* (1946), Justice Felix Frankfurter invoked the political question doctrine to avoid hearing a constitutional challenge to how Illinois configured its election districts. In doing so, he declared that "courts ought not to enter this political thicket." However, with *Baker v. Carr* (1962), the U.S. Supreme Court reversed course and ruled that evaluating the constitutionality of redistricting plans is a justiciable issue and is not necessarily barred by the political question doctrine.

Chief Justice Earl Warren said in his *Memoirs* that *Baker* is the most important case the Warren Court ever decided because it offered the promise of allowing the judiciary to pave the way for the political system to allow for equal and effective political representation among all citizens (Cottrill and Peretti 2013, 262). *Baker* has been the catalyst for subsequent Supreme Court rulings that evaluate the constitutionality of district line-drawing resulting in unequal, or "malapportioned," legislatures (that do not represent the voters on the basis of equal population), and related political and racial gerrymandering cases.

The "One Person, One Vote" Principle

A series of cases during the Warren Court's (1953–1969) "egalitarian revolution" helped expand voting rights by establishing the "one person, one vote" principle of constitutional law. Georgia's county unit system, a voting procedure that let candidates in statewide primary elections receive all of the county's unit votes if they had the highest number of votes in a county, was deemed to be a violation of the Fourteenth Amendment's equal protection clause in *Gray v. Saunders* (1963). Justice William O. Douglas's opinion of the Court agreed with the petitioner's claim that his vote meant less because he was an urban voter, and the unit system had the effect of overrepresenting the votes coming from rural counties even though they consisted of about one-third of the state's population. For Douglas, "The conception of political equality from the Declaration of Independence, to Lincoln's Gettysburg Address, to the Fifteenth, Seventeenth, and Nineteenth Amendments can mean only one thing—one person, one vote." The one person, one vote rule was later applied to strike down the malapportionment of congressional districts in *Wesberry v. Sanders* (1964) and then to state legislatures in *Reynolds v. Sims* (1964).

The Roberts Court (2005–present) revisited the implications of the one person, one vote principle in *Evenwel v. Abbott* (2016). In *Evenwel*, a group of voters argued that Texas's redistricting of State Senate districts must be based on the number of eligible voters instead of the state's total population. The voters reasoned that drawing legislative districts on the basis of total population creates unequal districts that dilute their votes when compared to using the voter-eligible population. In rejecting that claim, Justice Ruth Bader Ginsburg's opinion of the unanimous Court observed that configuring districts off of a voter-eligible baseline is contrary to the framing history of the U.S. Constitution and the Fourteenth Amendment. In addition, using voting population is against the practice that all the states use in their redistricting processes that equalize districts by the total population numbers derived from the decennial census. Notably, adopting the total population standard has a political impact that favors the Democratic Party because its voter base is typically concentrated in urban areas that include ineligible voters, such as children, prison inmates, ex-convicts, and immigrants. In contrast, the Republican Party is disadvantaged by the total population standard because its voting base is often found in rural areas that have more eligible voters (Denniston 2016).

In another unanimous opinion the Court in *Harris v. Arizona Independent Redistricting Commission* (2016) rebuffed a challenge by a group of Arizona voters which argued that a redistricting map created by Arizona's independent redistricting commission was an unconstitutional partisan gerrymander because it had districts that were unequal in population and worked only to the advantage of the Democratic Party. In rejecting the claim, Justice Stephen Breyer's opinion of the Court held that the Fourteenth Amendment's equal protection clause is satisfied by the good faith and practical efforts of state legislatures to construct districts that are nearly equal in population. As he wrote, "The Constitution . . . does not demand mathematical perfection." Breyer applied that standard by reasoning that Texas's redistricting plan met the one person, one vote principle because it had a maximum population deviation (between the largest and smallest districts) of 10 percent or less, and the voters could not prove that the plan was created for an illegitimate purpose. With *Harris*, the Court reiterated that state legislatures have the flexibility to deviate from perfect population equality in drawing their state and local districts so long as they try in good faith to take into account other goals and criteria that are an ordinary part of the redistricting process, such as respecting existing political boundaries and not drawing irregular-shaped district lines that destroy geographic compactness, among others (Howe 2016).

Political and Racial Gerrymandering

The goal of achieving fair and effective political representation is undermined by political gerrymanders that favor the re-election of incumbents by drawing district lines that favor only one party and diminish electoral competition in political elections. In confronting the issue, in *Davis v. Bandemer* (1986), the Supreme Court was united in deciding that political gerrymandering cares are justiciable; however, the justices could not agree on what standards to use in evaluating the constitutionality of an Indiana restricting plan that favored the Republican Party under the Fourteenth Amendment's equal protection clause. After *Davis*, most lower courts used a standard that emerged from a four-justice bloc that asked if the plan had a discriminatory intent and effect; that is, redistricting plans are unconstitutional if legislatures intended to draw the lines with certain political consequences in mind, and the plan itself had the effect of "consistently degrad[ing] a voter's or a group of voters' influence on the political process as a whole" (Tokaji 2013, 84).

Even so, how to apply the *Davis* standard remained unclear, and subsequent decisions were equally ambiguous. Thus, in a challenge to a partisan gerrymander of Pennsylvania's congressional districts by Republicans in *Vieth v. Jubeliver* (2004), the Supreme Court could not agree on either of the justiciability or standards' issues. A third case, *League of United Latin American Citizens v. Perry* (2006), upheld the state Republican-controlled legislature's decision to redraw Texas's congressional districts at mid-decade in order to give the Republicans an electoral advantage. However, as in the prior cases, there was no agreement by a majority of the justices as to how political gerrymanders should be constitutionally evaluated. In the aftermath of these cases, one scholar concluded that, "Partisan gerrymandering is still justiciable, but no manageable standard exists upon which the Court can provide relief" (Schultz 2014, 156). The next decennial census in 2020 may provide more guidance as the Supreme Court is surely to confront the issue again in challenges to partisan gerrymanders after that date.

An important and recurring question in redistricting cases is whether race can be used as a factor in drawing election district lines, an issue that grew in significance after the Voting Rights Act of 1965 (VRA) was enacted. Before then, *Gomillion v. Lightfoot* (1960) established that reconfiguring the lines into odd shapes for the purpose of protecting white voting interests and disenfranchising African American voters in Tuskegee, Alabama, is a violation of the Fifteenth Amendment. After the VRA was passed, legislatures began to create "majority-minority" districts that enhanced African American and Hispanic political representation. With *United Jewish Organizations v. Carey* (1977), the Supreme Court upheld a New York redistricting plan that Hasidic Jews challenged because it divided their representation into different communities in the interest of creating two nonwhite voting districts that met VRA requirements. In rejecting the Hasidic Jews' claims of voter dilution, the Court indicated that the deliberate use of racial quotas for the purpose of increasing minority representation and complying with the VRA did not violate the Fourteenth or Fifteenth Amendments.

Yet after the Court's composition changed and became more conservative, the justices adopted a more rigorous standard of strict scrutiny that disfavored the use of race in redistricting decisions. The Rehnquist Court (1986–2005) in *Shaw v. Reno* (1993) upheld a challenge from voters objecting to a redistricting plan that created two majority-minority districts that increased the political representation of African American and Hispanic voters in North Carolina. Justice Sandra Day O'Connor's opinion of the Court reasoned that the bizarre shapes of the districts "bears an uncomfortable resemblance to political apartheid" and thus shows that race was used to segregate the voters along racial lines without a compelling reason and at the exclusion of considering other traditional redistricting factors. After *Shaw*, the constitutional validity of majority-minority restricting plans may be evaluated under strict scrutiny, an approach which means that they can only be constitutionally defended under the VRA if there is a compelling interest to use race as a factor in conjunction with other redistricting criteria. Still, in light of *Easley v. Cromartie* (2001), which upheld a North Carolina redistricting plan that was revised in light of the *Shaw* litigation, the Supreme Court has signaled that legislatures can avoid incurring a *Shaw* equal protection violation if they can show that nonracial political factors were responsible for drawing the lines of election districts in a particular way (Tokaji 2013, 146).

Christopher P. Banks

See also: Affirmative Action; Jurisdictional Doctrines and Procedures; Racial Discrimination; Voting Rights

Further Reading

Cottrill, James B., and Terri J. Peretti. 2013. "Gerrymandering from the Bench?: The Electoral Consequences of Judicial Redistricting." *Election Law Journal* 12:261–276.

Denniston, Lyle. 2016. "Opinion Analysis: Leaving a Constitutional Ideal Still Undefined." *SCOTUSblog*, April 4. http://www.scotusblog.com/2016/04/opinion-analysis-leaving-a-constitutional-ideal-still-undefined/.

Howe, Amy. 2016. "Opinion Analysis: A Narrow, but Unanimous Ruling on Texas Redistricting." *SCOTUSblog*, April 20. http://www.scotusblog.com/2016/04/opinion-analysis-a-narrow-but-unanimous-ruling-on-arizona-redistricting/.

National Conference for State Legislatures. 2015. "2015 Redistricting Legislation." http://www.ncsl.org/research/redistricting/2015-redistricting-legislation.aspx.

O'Brien, David M. 2014. *Constitutional Law and Politics: Struggles for Power and Governmental Accountability.* 9th ed., vol. 2. New York: W. W. Norton.

Schultz, David. 2014. *Election Law and Democratic Theory.* Burlington, VT: Ashgate Publishing Company.

Tokaji, Daniel P. 2013. *Election Law in a Nutshell.* St. Paul, MN: West Academic Publishing.

Cases

Baker v. Carr. 1962. 369 U.S. 186.

Colegrove v. Green. 1946. U.S.

Davis v. Bandemer. 1986. 478 U.S. 106.

Easley v. Cromartie. 2001. 532 U.S. 234.

Evenwel v. Abbott. 2016. 136 S.Ct. 1120.

Gomillion v. Lightfoot. 1960. 364 U.S. 339.

Gray v. Saunders. 1963. 372 U.S. 368.

Harris v. Arizona Independent Redistricting Commission. 2016. 136 S.Ct. 1301.

League of United Latin American Citizens v. Perry. 2006. 548 U.S. 399.

Reynolds v. Sims. 1964. 377 U.S. 533.

Shaw v. Reno. 1993. 590 U.S. 630.

United Jewish Organizations v. Carey. 1977. 430 U.S. 144.

Vieth v. Jubeliver. 2004. 541 U.S. 267.

Wesberry v. Sanders. 1964. 376 U.S. 1.

VOTING RIGHTS

Voting rights is a key part of the original U.S. Constitution, but the states have wide latitude to determine voting qualifications. While the states ultimately extended the franchise to white nonproperty owners, other groups of people, including women, African Americans, and young adults, did not have the right to vote until the Constitution was amended. After the Civil War and in spite of the ratification of the Fourteenth and Fifteenth Amendment, the states began to disenfranchise African Americans through the operation of discriminatory laws such as grandfather clauses, literacy tests, and poll taxes. In the 20th century, the Nineteenth, Twenty-Fourth, and Twenty-Sixth Amendments established greater electoral protections for those who did not enjoy full voting rights. During the civil rights movement in the 1960s, Congress passed the Voting Rights Act (VRA) of 1965, a key law that helped protect African Americans against state voting discrimination laws. While the Supreme Court has upheld Congress's authority to enact voting rights legislation, decisions in 2015 undercut congressional authority and encouraged states to enact restrictive voter identification laws.

The U.S. Constitution and Voting Rights

During colonial times, the states adopted a model of voting rights that they inherited from Great Britain. Under the British model, the colonies only allowed "freeholders," or white men owning property that were 21 years or older, to vote. After the American Revolution, the Articles of Confederation did not put any restrictions on the states to determine voting eligibility requirements, and generally the same approach was taken in defining the parameters of political representation and voting rights in the U.S. Constitution (O'Brien 2014, 852). While the U.S. Constitution does not specify that there is a general right to vote, Article 1, Section 2, stipulates that electors voting in elections for House of Representative members must have the same qualifications that are imposed by state legislatures. Article I, Section 4, the elections clause, grants the power to states to regulate the "Times, Places, and Manner" of holding congressional elections while also giving Congress the authority to alter those restrictions. For Senate elections, whereas the original constitution gave state legislatures the power to choose their senators, the Seventeenth Amendment (1913) removed that provision by allowing for the popular and direct vote of senators.

The wide latitude given to the states under the U.S. Constitution to determine voting qualifications allowed them to deny the franchise to nonpropertied whites in the 18th century. Still, the growth of political parties led to reforms that expanded voting rights and the electorate. During President Andrew Jackson's administration (1829–1837), many states changed their laws to either end or replace the property requirement with taxpayer qualifications. The disenfranchisement of nonproperty owners increasingly became unpopular because many military veterans were denied voting rights. Thus, by the mid-19th century, all states had removed the condition of owning property as a voting qualification. Even so, other groups that represented a large part of the nation's population, such as women and African Americans, were not extended the franchise or given voting rights' protections until subsequent constitutional amendments were put in place (Tokaji 2013, 15, 33; O'Brien 2014, 853).

The Civil War Amendments and Voter Disenfranchisement Laws

After the Civil War, two of the so-called Civil War amendments (the Thirteenth, Fourteenth, and Fifteenth Amendments) theoretically expanded voting rights. Section 2 of the Fourteenth Amendment (1868) stipulates that Congress has the power to reduce the political representation of any state that denies voting rights Likewise, the Fifteenth Amendment (1870) protects African American voting rights by preventing their abridgement "by the United States or by any State on account of race, color, or previous condition of servitude." In spite of these measures, many southern states used a variety of laws to disenfranchise persons of color in the aftermath of the Civil War. To illustrate, in 1903, Alabama's constitution specified that persons who had registered to vote before January 1, 1903, were registered for life unless they were ineligible for committing certain crimes. The provision had the effect of "grandfathering" in, or guaranteeing the right to be registered and vote, to mostly white persons. In addition, the constitution also imposed burdensome registration requirements (literacy tests, good character tests, poll taxes, etc.) for persons seeking to vote after January 1, 1903, and many African Americans that had not registered before that time also could not meet the voter qualifications. In a class action suit challenging the voter registration system, in *Giles v. Harris* (1903), the Supreme Court ruled that it lacked the jurisdiction to hear the case by invoking the political question doctrine—the principle holding that the political branches, and not the federal courts, are the proper venue for resolving disputes that are inherently political in nature. As Davis and Graham observe, *Giles* "legitimated the widespread disfranchisement of Southern blacks during this era" (1995, 26).

Although the Supreme Court invalidated the use of grandfather clauses in later rulings (*Guinn v. United States*, 1915), southern states prevented African Americans from voting with literacy tests and poll taxes. Literacy tests, which required persons to read or comprehend certain texts as a prerequisite to voting, persisted until they were outlawed by the federal VRA in the mid-1960s. Before then, in *Lassiter v. Northampton County Board of Elections* (1959), the Supreme Court upheld Louisiana's requirement that all persons of any race must be able to read or write any section of the state's constitution. Justice William O. Douglas's opinion of the Court determined that a literacy test that is fairly administered to all persons in a race-neutral manner does not violate the Fifteenth Amendment. In contrast, in *Louisiana v. United States* (1965), the Court struck down a similar state constitution "interpretation" requirement because it vested in state voting officials too much discretion to deny persons the right to vote on the basis of racial considerations.

Along with literacy tests, poll taxes were an effective deterrent that helped to disenfranchise African American voters. In *Breedlove v. Suttles* (1937), the Supreme Court sustained the use of a Georgia poll tax that had been imposed on men but not women or minors. In doing so, the justices ruled that neither the Fourteenth Amendment's equal protection or privileges or immunities clause, nor the Nineteenth Amendment (which bans deprivations of voting rights on the basis of sex), is violated because poll taxes and the exemptions created by the state law are reasonable, long-standing electoral and taxation practices. Even so, poll taxes increasingly became controversial by the time of the civil rights movement, and all states but four eliminated them by 1960. In addition, in *Harper v. Virginia State Board of Elections* (1966), the Court declared that Virginia's poll tax violated the Fourteenth Amendment's equal protection clause; the decision ended the use of poll tax in state elections. Shortly before

Harper, the Twenty-Fourth Amendment's ratification in 1964 had already outlawed them in federal elections.

The Voting Rights Act of 1965 and *Shelby County v. Holder*

Two constitutional amendments in the 20th century extended the franchise to women and younger citizens. The Nineteenth Amendment (1920) highlighted the women's suffrage movement that began in earnest in Elizabeth Cady Stanton's 1848 Declaration of Sentiments (a manifesto for equal voting and legal rights for women) at the Seneca Falls Convention in New York. By its terms, the Nineteenth Amendment declared that, "The right of citizens of the United States to vote shall not be denied or abridged by the United States or by any state on account of sex." Some 50 years later, the Twenty-Sixth Amendment (1971) was ratified, which prohibited the denial of voting rights to citizens that were 18 years or older.

Congress enacted civil rights laws in 1957, 1960, and 1964 that tried, but failed, to expand the voting rights of blacks due to white resistance and noncompliance. By the mid-1960s and amid growing social unrest and increasing political demonstrations, Congress enacted the VRA of 1965 as legislation that safeguarded African American voting rights. The VRA was passed in response to the disenfranchisement of black citizens in many southern states. In Section 2, the VRA adopted a general prohibition of state laws that denied voting rights on the basis of race or color, a principle that originated from the Fifteenth Amendment, and backed it up with judicial enforcement mechanisms (Laney 2008, 12). Shortly after its enactment, the Supreme Court upheld the VRA's constitutionality in *South Carolina v. Katzenbach* (1966).

The VRA and its subsequent amendments and reauthorizations used other legislative strategies to enlarge voting rights. It banned literacy tests. It enlisted the help of the federal government to supervise election procedures in states that historically discriminated against African Americans. Sections 4(b) and 5 of the VRA adopted the use of a coverage formula and preclearance mechanism that compelled certain jurisdictions, such as Alabama, Georgia, Louisiana, Mississippi, and other southern states, that historically discriminated against African Americans to get the federal government's approval before they were permitted to make changes to their election laws. Federal preclearance was required whenever a covered state contemplated making changes to not only specific laws that affect voting registration procedures but also to laws that structurally provided the basis for holding elections, such as switching from having an election by single-member districts to one with at-large elections, which dilutes voting power of minorities, or by altering the boundaries of single-member electoral districts through redistricting plans (Laney 2008, 8–11).

In 2006, the VRA was reauthorized for another 25 years, but, afterwards, the preclearance mechanism's constitutionality was attacked in litigation in federal courts. A main line of criticism and the legal basis for the lawsuits opposing the preclearance provision is that the formula that determined which states had to comply with preclearance was antiquated and did not appropriately take into account improvements that were made in election practices that lessened discriminatory impacts (Tokaji 2013, 109). In *Northwestern Austin Municipal Utility District No. One v. Holder* (2009), the Roberts Court (2005–present) signaled that it might be receptive to those legal arguments (Denniston 2013).

Thereafter, in a case that was split along ideological lines in a 5–4 decision, the Court in *Shelby County v. Holder* (2013) invalidated the VRA's Section 4(b) coverage formula and, in the process, immobilized Section 5 preclearance and effectively rendered it meaningless without subsequent congressional action to fix the law's defects. In writing the opinion of the Court, Chief Justice John Roberts Jr., joined by Justices Antonin Scalia, Anthony Kennedy, Clarence Thomas, and Samuel Alito, first reasoned that the VRA preclearance provision is inconsistent with federalism principles requiring that all states retain equal sovereignty without undue federal interference. Next, in striking Section 4(b) down, it determined that the coverage formula was based on outdated election data that did not correctly reflect that voting practices had changed for the better in the states affected by the preclearance requirement.

In a dissent that was joined by liberal Justices Stephen Breyer, Sonia Sotomayor, and Elena Kagan, Justice Ruth Bader Ginsburg countered in *Shelby County* that the Court should defer to Congress's decision to reauthorize the VRA in 2006 because there is ample evidence to show that the law is an effective remedy to fixing past and present issues of racially inspired voting discrimination. As she lamented, "The sad irony of today's decision lies in its utter failure to grasp why the VRA has proven effective." In this light, critics of *Shelby County* have observed that in the aftermath of the Court's ruling, at least 10 of the 15 states that were subject to federal preclearance have begun to introduce new laws that create barriers to voting, including voter identification laws that require photo IDs and others that reduce early voting opportunities and eliminate same-day voter registration (Lopez 2014, 5).

Christopher P. Banks

See also: Affirmative Action; Constitutional Interpretation; Gerrymandering; Jurisdictional Doctrines and Procedures; Racial Discrimination

Further Reading

Davis, Abraham L., and Barbara Luck Graham. 1995. *The Supreme Court, Race, and Civil Rights*. Thousand Oaks, CA: Sage Publications.

Denniston, Lyle. 2013. "Opinion Recap: Voting Law in Deep Peril." *SCOTUSblog*, June 25. http://www.scotusblog.com/2013/06/opinion-recap-voting-law-in-deep-peril/.

Laney, Garrine P. 2008. "The Voting Rights Act of 1965, As Amended: Its History and Current Issues." *CRS Report for Congress (Updated June 12, 2008)*. Report 95–896. Washington, D.C.: Congressional Research Service.

Lopez, Tomas. 2014. "Shelby County: One Year Later." Brennan Center for Justice, June 24. http://www.brennancenter.org/sites/default/files/analysis/Shelby_County_One_Year_Later.pdf.

Lowenstein, Daniel Hays, Richard L. Hasen, and Daniel P. Tokaji. 2012. *Election Law: Cases and Materials*. Durham, NC: Carolina Academic Press.

O'Brien, David M. 2014. *Constitutional Law and Politics: Civil Rights and Civil Liberties*. 9th ed., vol. 2. New York: W. W. Norton.

Tokaji, Daniel P. 2013. *Election Law in a Nutshell*. St. Paul, MN: West Academic Publishing.

Cases

Breedlove v. Suttles. 1937. 302 U.S. 277.

Giles v. Harris. 1903. 189 U.S. 475.

Guinn v. United States. 1915. 238 U.S. 347.

Harper v. Virginia State Board of Elections. 1966. 383 U.S. 663.

Lassiter v. Northampton County Board of Elections. 1959. 360 U.S. 45.

Louisiana v. United States. 1965. 380 U.S. 145.

Northwestern Austin Municipal Utility District No. One v. Holder. 2009. 557 U.S. 193.

Shelby County v. Holder. 2013. 570 U.S. 2.

South Carolina v. Katzenbach. 1966. 383 U.S. 301.

Glossary of Concepts, Laws, and People

Acquittal: A finding that the defendant is not guilty of the charges brought by the government. This finding may be reached by the trial judge either in a case tried before the judge or on a motion for judgment of acquittal made by a defendant or the judge in a jury trial. The jury may make such a finding in a case tried before it.

Action: A legal dispute brought to court for trial and settlement (can also be described as a case or as a lawsuit).

Active judge: A judge in the full-time service of the court.

Adjudication: Giving or pronouncing a judgment or decree; also, the judgment given. The courts provide this service, that is, the settling of disputes and the application of laws and rules.

Administrative Office of the U.S. Courts (AO): The federal agency responsible for collecting court statistics, administering the federal courts' budget, processing the federal courts' payroll, and performing other administrative functions under the direction and supervision of the Judicial Conference of the United States.

Admissible: A term used to describe evidence that may be heard by a jury and considered by a judge or a jury in federal civil and criminal cases.

Adversary system: The system of trial practice in the United States in which each of the opposing or adversarial parties has full opportunity to present and establish its contentions before the court. Through the adversary process, each side in a dispute has the right to present its case as persuasively as possible, subject to the rules of evidence, and an independent fact finder, either judge or jury, decides in favor of one side or the other.

Advisory opinion: A nonbinding opinion of a court that suggests how the court might react if the constitutionality of a particular law was challenged. Although federal courts do not issue advisory opinions, some state courts are required to provide legislatures or governors with such input on request.

Affidavit: A statement made both voluntarily and under oath.

Amicus brief: A document filed by an amicus curiae in support of a party in a lawsuit.

Amicus curiae: A Latin term meaning "friend of the court." An amicus curiae is a person or organization that is not a party in the case on appeal yet has a strong interest in the outcome of the case and thus files a brief with the court of appeals called an "amicus brief." This brief may call important legal or factual matters to the court's attention and thus help the court reach a proper decision in the case.

Answer: A pleading by which a defendant resists or otherwise responds to the plaintiff's allegation of facts (presented in a complaint).

Appeal: After a trial, a request by a party that has lost on one or more issues for a higher court (appellate court) to review the trial court's decision to determine if it was correct. To make such a request is "to appeal" or "to take an appeal." One who appeals is called the "appellant"; the other party is the "appellee." Appeals are only heard on matters of law (rules of procedure and substantive rules applied to decide the outcome of the trial below) and not of fact (what happened, when, and to whom).

Appearance: The formal proceeding by which a defendant submits himself or herself to the jurisdiction of the court.

Appellant: The party appealing a decision or judgment to a higher court.

Appellate court: A court having jurisdiction to review the judgments of a "trial court."

Appellate jurisdiction: The authority of a higher court to review the decisions of a lower court.

Appellee: The party against whom an appeal is filed.

Arraignment: The stage in the criminal process during which a judge formally informs the defendant of the charges against him or her. The defendant enters a plea during this hearing.

Article I: The first section of the U.S. Constitution. Article I outlines the powers and authority of Congress.

Article I courts: Federal courts organized under the authority of Congress as set out in Article I of the U.S. Constitution. Article I courts include immigration courts, Social Security courts, and military courts. The judges who serve in these courts serve for set terms (usually 14 years), not for life.

Article III: The section of the U.S. Constitution that places "the judicial Power of the United States" in the federal courts.

Article III courts: Federal courts organized under the authority of Article III of the U.S. Constitution. Article III courts include the U.S. Supreme Court, the circuit courts of appeals, and the district courts. Judges of these courts serve for life.

Article III judges: Judges who exercise "the judicial Power of the United States" under Article III of the U.S. Constitution. They are appointed by the president, subject to the approval of the Senate. Supreme Court justices, courts of appeals judges, district court judges, and Court of International Trade judges are Article III judges; bankruptcy and magistrate judges are not.

Assistant U.S. attorney (AUSA): A federal prosecutor who assists the U.S. attorney in the judicial district by prosecuting criminal cases for the federal government and representing the government in civil actions. It is important to distinguish a U.S. attorney from a district attorney (DA), who prosecutes criminal cases for a state, county, or city.

Attorney general: The executive branch official appointed by the president to head the Justice Department—the nation's lawyer.

Bail: The money, bonds, or other valuable deposit put forward as security to allow a defendant to be released from jail during the trial process.

Bench trial: Trial without a jury where a judge decides which party prevails.

Brief: (a) A written summary of a specific court decision. This type of brief reports the name, year, and citation of the case; circumstances of the case; the disputed legal question; a summary of arguments; the vote of the court's members and the court's rationale; any novel legal principles announced or applied; and dissenting opinions. (b) A legal argument, written to inform and persuade a court. These briefs follow format guidelines required by the court.

Calendar: The clerk of the court's list of cases with dates and times set for hearings, trials, or arguments.

Case file: A complete collection of every document in a case.

Case law: The law as reflected in the written decisions of the courts; the law in cases that have been decided. Case law is different from statutory law in that statutes are written by Congress, and case law is shaped by the rulings of the federal courts.

Case management: Techniques used to process cases from one stage of the proceeding to another, such as setting deadlines for discovery or scheduling a series of pretrial conferences. Case management calls for different approaches from one case to the next and is the primary responsibility of judges, assisted by lawyers and clerks' office personnel.

Cause: A lawsuit, litigation, or legal action.

Cause of action: Facts giving rise to a lawsuit.

Certiorari, writ of: Literally, an order to "make us informed." The order issued by an appellate court to a lower court calling for transcripts and documents relating to a case. The grant of a writ of certiorari means the higher court has voluntarily agreed to review a case.

Chambers: The offices of a judge.

Change of venue: Moving a trial to a new location, generally because pretrial publicity has made it difficult to select an impartial jury.

Chief judge: The judge who has primary responsibility for the administration of a court but also decides cases. Chief appellate and chief district judges take office under rules that account for age and seniority; chief bankruptcy judges are appointed by the district judges of the court.

Chief justice: The "first among equals" on the U.S. Supreme Court, who has numerous responsibilities for the administration of the federal judicial system as well as for hearing cases. The president appoints the chief justice, with approval of the Senate, when a vacancy occurs in the office.

Circuit: The regional unit of federal judicial appeals. Congress has divided the federal judicial system into 12 regional circuits (the 11 numbered circuits and the District of Columbia circuit). In each circuit is a court of appeals to hear appeals from district courts in the circuit and a circuit judicial council to oversee the administration of the courts of the circuit. A specialized circuit court also sits in Washington, D.C. and is known as the Circuit Court for the Federal Circuit.

Circuit court: see U.S. Court of Appeals.

Circuit Judicial Council: A governing body in each federal circuit created by Congress to ensure the effective and expeditious administration of justice in that circuit. Each council has an equal number of circuit and district court judges; the chief judge of the circuit is the presiding officer.

Citation: A reference to a source of legal authority.

Civil actions: Noncriminal cases in which one private individual or business sues another to protect, enforce, or redress private or civil rights.

Civil law: Law governing private rights of individuals and relationships between individuals, as opposed to criminal law.

Clerk of court: An officer appointed by the judges of the court to assist in managing the flow of cases through the court, maintain court records, handle financial matters, and provide other administrative support to the court.

Common law: The legal system that originated in England and is now in use in the United States that relies on the articulation of legal principles in a historical succession of judicial decisions. Common law principles can be changed by legislation.

Common law action: A case in which the issues are determined by common law legal principles established by courts and tradition, as opposed to statutes.

Complaint: A written statement filed by the plaintiff that initiates a civil case stating the wrongs allegedly committed by the defendant and requesting relief from the court.

Concurring opinion: Where an appellate judge agrees with the majority's ruling (outcome or judgment in a case) but has different reasons for this approval.

Constitutional courts: Article III courts.

Contempt of court: The deliberate disobedience of a court order, or the disruption of a court proceeding.

Court costs: The expenses in addition to legal fees of prosecuting or defending a lawsuit.

Court of last resort (COLR): The final court that decides a case on appeal (e.g., the Supreme Court of the United States or the supreme court of any state).

Court reporter: A person who records, transcribes, or stenographically takes down testimony, motions, orders, and other proceedings during trials, hearings, and other court proceedings.

Courts of record: Courts whose proceedings are permanently recorded and have the power to fine or imprison for contempt.

Criminal law: Law concerned with the relationship between the community and the individual.

Damages: Monetary compensation that may be recovered in the courts by any person who has suffered loss, detriment, or injury to his or her person, property, or rights through the unlawful act or negligence of another.

Decision: The judgment reached or given by a court of law.

Declaratory judgment: A judgment that declares the rights of the parties or expresses the opinion of the court on a question of law, without ordering anything to be done.

Decree: A decision or order of the court. A final decree is one that finally disposes of the litigation; an interlocutory decree is a provisional or preliminary decree that is not final.

Defendant: A person charged with a crime in a criminal case, or the party responding to a civil complaint.

Deposition: Testimony taken under oath but outside of court.

Directed verdict: The determination of a judge that a jury should provide a certain decision; the decision by a judge made prior to the conclusion of trial testimony that the prosecution's case is too weak to sustain charges against a defendant.

Discovery: The pretrial period where lawyers for opposing sides provide each other with the information, names of witnesses, and the evidence that will be used at trial.

Dismissal: A court order terminating a case. May be voluntary (at the request of the parties) or involuntary.

Dissenting opinion: The written rationale explaining the vote of the justices on an appellate court who disagrees with the majority's decision.

District courts: see **U.S. district court.**

Diversity jurisdiction: The federal district courts' authority to hear and decide civil cases involving plaintiffs and defendants who are citizens of different states (or U.S. citizens and foreign nationals) and who meet certain statutory requirements.

Docket: A log containing the complete history of each case in the form of brief chronological entries summarizing the court proceedings.

Due process: U.S. law in its regular course of administration through the courts. The constitutional guarantee of due process requires that everyone receive such constitutional protections as a fair trial; assistance of counsel; and the rights to remain silent, to a speedy and public trial, to an impartial jury, and to confront and secure witnesses.

En banc: "In the bench" or "as a full bench." Refers to court sessions with the entire membership of a court participating rather than the usual number. U.S. circuit courts of appeals usually sit in panels of three judges, but all the judges in the court may decide certain matters together. They are then said to be sitting en banc (occasionally spelled in banc).

Enjoin: To require a person, through the issuance of an injunction, to perform or to abstain from some specific act.

Equal protection of the law: Guarantee of the Fourteenth Amendment of the U.S. Constitution that all persons receive equal treatment under the law.

Equitable action: An action that may be brought for the purpose of restraining the threatened infliction of wrongs or injuries and to prevent threatened illegal action. An action seeking an injunction is an equitable action.

Equity law: Legal principles based on ideals of fairness, rather than written laws.

***Erie Railroad Co. v. Tompkins* (1938):** The Judiciary Act of 1789 allowed for diversity jurisdiction in the federal courts. It further held in Section 34 that "the rules of the several states . . . shall be regarded as rules of decision in trials at common law in the federal courts." This rule required the federal courts to follow state laws when deciding diversity law cases. Left undefined, however, was just which laws the courts had to follow: statutory and common law (i.e., written laws and judicial precedents) or just statutory (written laws). After the *Swift v. Tyson* ruling in 1842, the answer was just statutory law. Federal judges were free to develop their own interpretations of these laws—even where the interpretations were at odds with existing state court interpretations. The federal courts took great advantage of this power following the Civil War. *Erie* changed this pattern. In it, Justice Louis Brandeis declared that, "there is no federal general common law." *Swift* was not only a bad decision, it was unconstitutional as a violation of the Tenth Amendment, which reserved all ungranted powers to the states or the people.

Exclusionary rule: The legal principle, under the Fifth and Fourteenth Amendments, that judges may forbid prosecutors from presenting improperly acquired evidence at a criminal trial.

Executive order: The commandments, rules, or regulations issued by the authority of the highest administrative officer of some unit of government, such as mayor, governor, or president. Executive orders often provide details on how an administration will implement a statute or court order.

Ex parte: By or for one party; done for, on behalf of, or on the application of one party only.

Federal courts: Courts established under the U.S. Constitution. The term usually refers to courts of the federal judicial branch, which include the Supreme Court of the United States, the U.S. courts of appeals, the U.S. district courts (including U.S. bankruptcy courts), and the U.S. Court of International Trade. Congress has established other federal courts in the executive branch, such as immigration courts.

Federalism: A principle of the U.S. Constitution that gives some functions to the U.S. government and leaves the other functions to the states. The functions of the U.S. (or federal) government involve the nation as a whole and include regulating commerce that affects people in more than one state, providing for the national defense, and taking care of federal lands. State and local governments perform such functions as running the schools, managing the police departments, and paving the streets.

Federal-question jurisdiction: Jurisdiction given to federal courts in cases involving the interpretation and application of the U.S. Constitution, acts of Congress, and treaties.

Federal rules: Bodies of rules developed by the federal judiciary that spell out procedural requirements. The federal rules are the Federal Rules of Civil Procedure, the Federal Rules of Criminal Procedure, the Federal Rules of Appellate Procedure, the Federal Rules of Evidence, and the Federal Rules of Bankruptcy Procedure. Rules can take effect only after they are forwarded to Congress for review, and Congress declines to change them.

Felony: The most serious type of criminal offenses, eligible for punishments of more than 365 days in prison.

Final decision: A court's decision that resolves the claims of the parties and leaves nothing further for the court to do but ensure that the decision is carried out. The U.S. courts of appeals have jurisdiction over appeals from final decisions of U.S. district courts.

Finding: A formal conclusion by a trial judge or jury regarding the facts of a case.

Grand jury: A group of laypersons who review and hear police evidence to decide if there is enough evidence to press charges. This group usually has 23 people, and it may review many cases.

Habeas corpus: Literally, "you have the body." A writ of habeas corpus is used by courts to determine whether the government is properly, or improperly, detaining someone.

Hearing: Any form of judicial, quasi-judicial, or legislative proceeding at which issues are heard or testimony is taken.

Hearing on the merits: A hearing before a court on the legal questions at issue, as opposed to procedural questions.

Holding: The legal conclusion or principle that provides the basis for a court's judgment.

Hung jury: A jury unable to reach a verdict.

Inadmissible: Evidence that cannot be admitted in court under the rules of evidence.

In camera: Literally, "in chambers," or in private. Judicial proceedings between the judge and opposing lawyers, outside of public view.

Indictment: The formal charge issued by a grand jury stating there is enough evidence that the defendant committed the crime to justify having a trial; it is used primarily for felonies. See also "information."

In forma pauperis: An expression meaning "in the manner of a pauper." Permission given by the court to a person to file a case without payment of the required court fees because the person cannot pay them.

Information: A formal accusation by a government attorney that the defendant committed a misdemeanor. See also "indictment."

Injunction: An order of the court prohibiting (or compelling) the performance of a specific act to prevent irreparable damage or injury.

Instructions: A judge's explanation to the jury before it begins deliberations of the questions it must answer. Judge's instructions include information about law governing the case.

Interlocutory appeal: A proceeding brought to an appellate court before a trial is finished. These decisions affect temporary disposition of money, children, or progress on something until the trial verdict can be rendered.

Issue: The disputed point in a disagreement between parties in a lawsuit.

Jay, John: First chief justice of the U.S. Supreme Court (1789–1795).

Judge: An official of the judicial branch with authority to decide lawsuits brought before courts. Used generically, the term judge may also refer to all judicial officers, including Supreme Court justices.

Judgment: The official decision of a court finally resolving the dispute between the parties to the lawsuit.

Judicial activism: A philosophical approach that says courts are duty-bound to correct perceived injustices, even when there is no grant of authority in statute or established legal principle for the court to do so.

Judicial restraint: (a) The philosophical approach that says courts are duty-bound to adhere to established legal principles and remain within the boundaries of their authority when making decisions, even when doing so allows a perceived injustice to occur. (b) The belief that judges should not express personal views or emotions in court.

Judicial review: The authority of a court to review the official actions of other branches of government. Also, the authority to declare unconstitutional the actions of other branches.

Judiciary Act of 1789: The act of Congress that organized the federal court system. It set up a three-tiered court system with the Supreme Court at the top. At the bottom were the district courts (trial courts), each of which covered an entire state. In the middle were the circuit courts. These courts, which heard appeals from the district courts and had original jurisdiction on the more significant criminal and civil law matters, were manned by a mix of district judges and Supreme Court justices riding circuit. There were originally three circuits: Northern, Middle, and Southern.

Judiciary Act of 1801: A revision of the Judiciary Act of 1789. This act of Congress was passed for partisan reasons, as the outgoing Federalist Party sought to create a preserve within the federal courts for federalist judges to "watch out for" the incoming Republican Congress and presidency. (The appointments under this act were known as the "midnight appointments.") Though the act's reforms—the creation of permanent circuit courts with appointed judges and the end of circuit riding for the Supreme Court justices—were needed, the act was repealed in 1802.

Jurisdiction: (1) the legal authority of a court to hear and decide a case; (2) the geographic area over which the court has authority to decide cases.

Jurisprudence: The study of law and the structure of the legal system.

Justice Department: The agency of the federal executive branch with responsibilities in a wide range of areas bearing on the administration of justice and enforcement of laws passed by Congress. The Justice Department is responsible for investigating alleged criminal conduct, deciding which cases merit prosecution in the federal courts, and prosecuting those cases. It also represents the U.S. government in many civil actions.

Justiciable claim: A claim that is capable of being resolved in the courts.

Lawsuit: A legal action started by a plaintiff against a defendant based on a complaint that the defendant's failure to perform a legal duty resulted in harm to the plaintiff.

Legislative courts: Courts organized under Article I, which explicitly deals with the powers of Congress, of the U.S. Constitution. These courts are situated in the executive agencies and oversee administrative hearings. Article I courts include immigration courts, Social Security courts, and military courts. The judges who serve in these courts do not serve for life but rather serve for set terms (usually 14 years).

Litigant: The individual bringing a lawsuit. Participants (plaintiffs and defendants) in lawsuits are also called litigants.

Litigation: A case, controversy, or lawsuit. Participants (plaintiffs and defendants) in lawsuits are called litigants.

Litigator: A lawyer representing a litigant in court.

Magistrate judge: A judicial officer of a district court who conducts initial proceedings in criminal cases, decides criminal misdemeanor cases, handles many pretrial civil and criminal matters on behalf of district judges, and decides civil cases with the consent of the parties.

Majority opinion: The ruling in an appellate court where a majority of the judges hearing the case agree as to the outcome of the case—that is, their ruling or judgment. This majority opinion is also known as the "opinion of the court" and can create a precedent that lower federal courts must follow.

Mandamus: Literally, "we command." The court order that compels a governmental official to carry out some action.

Mandate: A judicial command directing the proper officer to enforce a judgment, sentence, or decree.

Mandatory jurisdiction: The requirement of a court to decide a case.

Marbury v. Madison **(1803):** At the end of his term, Federalist president John Adams appointed William Marbury as justice of the peace for the District of Columbia.

The secretary of state, John Marshall, failed to deliver the commission to Marbury and left that task to the new secretary of state, James Madison. Upon his inauguration, the new president, Thomas Jefferson, told Madison not to deliver the commissions. Marbury filed suit and asked the Supreme Court to issue a writ of mandamus to require Madison to deliver the commission. In his opinion, Chief Justice Marshall said that while Marbury was entitled to the commission, the Supreme Court did not have the power to issue the writ of mandamus because the Judiciary Act of 1789, the act written by Congress that authorized the Supreme Court to issue such writs, was unconstitutional. Thus, the Court gave up the power to issue writs but affirmed its power of judicial review, saying that if a law written by the legislature conflicts with the Constitution, the law is "null and void."

Marshall, John: Fourth chief justice of the United States (1801–1835). Marshall served longer than any other chief justice. He is credited with leading the Court into its first "golden age." Marshall is best known for his ruling in *Marbury v. Madison* (1803), wherein he described the power of judicial review.

Misdemeanor: A minor criminal offense, usually punishable by fewer than 365 days in jail or fines less than $5,000.

Mistrial: An invalid trial, caused by fundamental error. When a mistrial is declared, the trial must start again with the selection of a new jury.

Motion: A litigant's request for a judicial decision on an issue relating to the case.

Motion to dismiss: A formal request for the court to dismiss a complaint because of insufficiency of evidence or because the law does not recognize the injury or harm claimed.

Natural law: Those obligations that are placed on all persons, or rights recognized for all people, because of human nature.

Opinion: A judge's written explanation of the decision of the court. Because a case may be heard by three or more judges in the court of appeals, the opinion in appellate decisions can take several forms. If all the judges completely agree on the result, one judge will write the opinion for all. If all the judges do not agree, the formal decision will be based on the view of the majority, and one member of the majority will write the opinion. The judges who did not agree with the majority may write separately in dissenting or concurring opinions to present their views. A dissenting opinion disagrees with the majority opinion due to the reasoning or the principles of law the majority used to decide the case, or both. A concurring opinion agrees with the decision of the majority opinion but offers further comment or clarification or even an entirely different reason for reaching the same result. Only the majority opinion can serve as binding precedent in future cases. See also "precedent."

Oral argument: An opportunity for lawyers to summarize their position before the court and also to answer the judges' questions.

Order: A command from the court directing or forbidding an action.

Ordinance: The rules and regulations enacted by a city or county legislature.

Original jurisdiction: The authority to hear the initial proceedings in a case. A court of origin is the court in which a case originates. Appellate courts do not have original jurisdiction, except in exceptional cases.

Panel: (1) In appellate cases, a group of judges (usually three) assigned to decide the case; (2) in the jury selection process, the group of potential jurors; or (3) the list of attorneys who are both available and qualified to serve as court-appointed counsel for criminal defendants who cannot afford their own counsel.

Party: One of the litigants. At the trial level, the parties are typically referred to as the plaintiff and defendant. On appeal, they are known as the appellant and appellee, or in some cases involving administrative agencies, as the petitioner and respondent.

Per curiam: Literally, "for the court." An unsigned decision of an appeals court; usually a unanimous decision.

Petition for rehearing: A document filed by a party who lost a case in the U.S. Court of Appeals to ask the panel to reconsider its decision. If the panel grants the petition, it may ask the parties to file additional briefs and reargue the case.

Petit jury: A trial jury, usually with between 6 and 12 individuals, authorized to hear a trial and decide the facts of a case.

Plaintiff: The person who files the complaint in a civil lawsuit. A person who brings an action; the party who complains or sues in a personal action and is so named on the record.

Plea bargain: A negotiated settlement in a criminal case. Usually a prosecutor agrees to reduce a charge or seek a reduced sentence, and the defendant agrees to plead guilty.

Pleadings: Written statements filed with the court that describe a party's legal or factual assertions about the case.

Police power: The authority of government to protect the health, safety, well-being, and morals of a community.

Positive law: Rights and obligations created by governments, as opposed to those thought to be inherent in human nature.

Precedent: A court decision in an earlier case with facts and legal issues similar to a dispute currently before a court. Judges will generally "follow precedent"—meaning that they use the principles established in earlier cases to decide new cases that have similar facts and raise similar legal issues. A judge will disregard precedent if a party can show that the earlier case was wrongly decided or that it differed in some significant way from the current case.

Pretrial conference: (1) In a civil case, a meeting of the judge and lawyers conducted pursuant to Federal Rule of Civil Procedure 16(d) to decide which matters are in dispute and should be presented to the jury, to review evidence and witnesses to be presented, to set a timetable for the case, and sometimes to discuss settlement of the case; (2) in a criminal case, a meeting that the court may conduct, pursuant to Federal Rule of Criminal Procedure 17.1, upon motion of any party or on its own motion, "to consider such matters as will promote a fair and expeditious trial."

Procedure: The rules for conducting a lawsuit; there are rules of civil procedure, criminal procedure, evidence, bankruptcy, and appellate procedure.

Pro se: A Latin term meaning "on one's own behalf"; in courts, it refers to persons who present their own cases without lawyers.

Prosecute: To charge someone with a crime. A prosecutor tries a criminal case on behalf of the government.

Record: A written account of the proceedings in a case, including all pleadings, evidence, and exhibits submitted in the course of the case.

Record on appeal: The record of a case made as proceedings unfold in the U.S. district court, and assembled by clerks in the district court clerk's office and transmitted to the U.S. Court of Appeals. It consists of the pleadings and exhibits filed in the case, the written orders entered by the trial judge, a certified copy of the docket entries, and a transcript of the relevant court proceedings. Courts of appeals judges review parts of the record, along with briefs presented by the parties, when considering appeals of lower courts' decisions.

Recuse: To withdraw or disqualify oneself as a judge in a case because of personal prejudice, conflict of interest, or some other good reason why the judge should not sit in the interest of fairness.

Remand: The act of an appellate court sending a case to a lower court for further proceedings.

Reverse: The act of an appellate court setting aside the decision of a trial court. A reversal is often accompanied by a remand to the lower court for further proceedings.

Rule of court: An order made by a court having jurisdiction. Rules of court are either general or special: the former are the regulations by which the practice of the court is governed; the latter are special orders made in particular cases.

Rule to show cause: A court order obtained on motion by either party to demonstrate why the particular relief sought should not be granted. This order is generally used in connection with contempt proceedings.

Senior judge: A judge who has retired from active duty but continues to perform some judicial duties, usually maintaining a reduced caseload. Compare with "active judge."

Settlement: An agreement between the parties to a lawsuit to resolve their differences among themselves without having a trial or before the judge or jury renders a verdict in a trial.

Standing: The legal prerogative of an individual or organization to sue or be sued in a particular situation. To have standing, a party must have a direct stake in the outcome of a case.

Stare decisis: The doctrine that, when a court has once laid down a principle of law as applicable to a certain set of facts, it will adhere to that principle and apply it to future cases where the facts are substantially the same.

Statute: Law enacted by legislatures or executive officers, such as codes.

Stay: The postponement or halting of a judicial proceeding or judgment. A motion for a stay pending appeal seeks to delay the effect of a district court order or agency order until a U.S. Court of Appeals decides whether that order is valid.

Strict construction: The narrow interpretation of statute, precedence, or a constitutional provision.

Subpoena: A court order to provide testimony or evidence.

Substantive law: Law dealing with rights, duties, and liabilities, as distinguished from law that regulates procedure.

Swift v. Tyson (1842): The Judiciary Act of 1789 allowed for diversity jurisdiction in the federal courts. It further held in Section 34 that, "the rules of the several states . . . shall be regarded as rules of decision in trials at common law in the federal courts." This rule required the federal courts to follow state laws when deciding diversity law cases. Left undefined, however, was just which laws the courts had to follow:

statutory and common law (i.e., written laws and judicial precedents) or just statutory (written laws). *Swift* answered this question by noting that it was just statutory. Federal judges were free to develop their own interpretations of these laws—even where these interpretations were at odds with existing state court interpretations.

Taney, Roger B.: Fifth chief justice of the United States (1836–1864). Taney led the Supreme Court during the turbulent period leading up to the Civil War. He was appointed by President Andrew Jackson. Taney is best known for his rulings in the *Charles River Bridge Case* (1837; an economic development case in which he discussed the doctrine of "creative destruction") and *Dred Scott v. Sandford* (1857; slavery in the territories).

Temporary restraining order: A decision compelling someone to discontinue some action, usually until judicial proceedings have been exhausted in a case.

Term: The time during which the U.S. Supreme Court sits for the transaction of business, also referred to as a session. Each year's term begins on the first Monday in October and ends when the Court has announced its decisions in all the cases it has heard during the term, usually in late June or early July.

Transcript: A written, word-for-word record of what was said, either in a proceeding such as a trial, or during some other formal conversation, such as a hearing or oral deposition.

Trial: The proceeding at which parties in a civil case, or the government and the defense in a criminal case, produce evidence for consideration by a fact finder in court. The fact finder, who may be a judge or a jury, applies the law to the facts as it finds them and decides whether the defendant is guilty in a criminal case or which party should win in a civil case.

Uphold: The appellate court agrees with the lower court decision and allows it to stand.

U.S. attorney: A lawyer appointed by the president in each judicial district to prosecute and defend cases for the federal government. The U.S. attorney employs a staff of assistant U.S. attorneys who appear as the government's attorneys in individual cases.

U.S. Bankruptcy Court: A federal court that hears and administers matters that arise under the Bankruptcy Code. Although it is a unit of the district court and technically hears cases referred to it by the district court, it functions as a separate administrative unit for most practical purposes.

U.S. Court of Appeals: A federal court that reviews decisions of the district court when a party in a case asks it to. Some use the term *circuit court* to refer to the court of appeals, although technically *circuit court* refers to a federal trial court that functioned from 1789 to the early 20th century.

U.S. Court of Appeals for the Federal Circuit: A federal court of appeals located in Washington, D.C., whose jurisdiction is defined by subject matter rather than geography. It hears appeals only in certain types of cases, including those involving patent laws and those decided by the U.S. Court of International Trade and the U.S. Court of Federal Claims. The judges on these courts are among the group often referred to as Article III judges because their power to hear and decide cases stems from Article III of the U.S. Constitution, and they thus have tenure during good behavior and irreducible salaries.

U.S. Court of Appeals judge: A judge of one of the 13 U.S. courts of appeals. When a party appeals a district court decision in a case, appeals judges review what happened in the district court to see if the district judge made any mistakes that would require them to change or modify the decision or to order that the case be retried. Court of appeals judges are among the group often referred to as Article III judges because their power to hear and decide cases stems from Article III of the U.S. Constitution, and they thus have tenure during good behavior and irreducible salaries.

U.S. Court of Federal Claims: A special trial court with nationwide jurisdiction that hears cases involving money damages in excess of $10,000 against the United States, including disputes over federal contracts, federal takings of private property for public use, and rights of military personnel. The president appoints, with the approval of the Senate, U.S. Court of Federal Claims judges for 15-year terms.

U.S. district court: A federal court with general trial jurisdiction. It is the court in which the parties in a lawsuit file motions, petitions, and other documents and take part in pretrial and other types of status conferences. If there is a trial, it takes place in the district court. It is also referred to as a trial court. Every state has at least one district court. Larger states can have as many as four districts.

U.S. district judge: A judge of the federal district courts, appointed by the president, subject to the approval of the Senate. District judges are among the group often referred to as Article III judges because their power to hear and decide cases stems from Article III of the U.S. Constitution, and they thus have tenure during good behavior and irreducible salaries.

U.S. Marshals Service: An agency of the Justice Department charged with providing courtroom security in federal district courts, apprehending federal fugitives, transporting federal prisoners, and supervising the Justice Department's Federal Witness Protection Program.

Venire: Literally, "to appear at court." The panel of citizens from which a petit jury will be selected.

Venue: The geographical location in which a case is tried.

Verdict: The decision of a trial jury or a judge that determines the guilt or innocence of a criminal defendant, or that determines the final outcome of a civil case.

Voir dire: The process by which judges and lawyers select a trial jury from among those eligible to serve by questioning them to make certain that they would fairly decide the case. Voir dire is a phrase meaning "to speak the truth."

Warrant: A written court order permitting police to arrest a specific individual, or authority to search for and seize evidence from a particular place.

Warren, Earl: Chief justice during the turbulent era of the civil rights movement (1953–1969). Warren is best known for his ruling in *Brown v. Board of Education* (1954). His name is also associated with a noticeable shift on the Court toward protecting civil liberties and civil rights.

Writ: A formal written command or order, issued by the court, requiring the performance of a specific act.

Writ of certiorari: An order issued by the U.S. Supreme Court directing the lower court to transmit records for a case that it will hear on appeal. This is the primary method by which the Supreme Court hears cases.

Writ of execution: A means of enforcing a judgment in which, at the plaintiff's request, the clerk directs the U.S. marshal to seize the defendant's property, sell it, and deliver to the plaintiff the amount of money necessary to satisfy the judgment.

Writ of garnishment: A means of enforcing a judgment in which the defendant's property (e.g., a bank account, wages, or any debt owed to the defendant by someone else) is to be seized and then held in the hands of a third person.

Writ of habeas corpus: A document filed as a means of testing the legality of a restraint on a person's liberty, usually imprisonment. The writ commands the officials who have custody of a prisoner to bring the prisoner before the court, so that the court may determine whether the prisoner is being detained lawfully.

Annotated Bibliography

Abraham, Henry J. 1998. *The Judicial Process: An Introductory Analysis of the Courts of the United States, England, and France*. 7th ed. New York: Oxford University Press.

A well-written and well-presented textbook on the workings of the U.S. judicial system, with comparisons drawn to the English and French legal systems. This book is a good place to start for an introduction into the legal process as practiced in the courts, especially for those wanting a comparative format.

Advisory Council to the United States Court of Appeals for the Federal Circuit. 2004. *United States Court of Appeals for the Federal Circuit: A History: 1990–2002*. Washington, D.C.: U.S. Court of Appeals for the Federal Circuit.

A series of essays exploring the history of the federal circuit court sitting in Washington, D.C.

Alexander, Roberta Sue. 2005. *A Place of Recourse: A History of the U.S. District Court for the Southern District of Ohio, 1803–2003*. Athens: Ohio University Press.

A well-written and insightful history of the Southern District Court of Ohio. This book emphasizes both the major cases argued and the court's personnel. In addition, Alexander seeks to place this court's actions into a wider historical context.

Anderson, Terry L., and Peter J. Hill. 2004. *The Not So Wild, Wild West: Property Rights on the Frontier*. Stanford, CA: Stanford University Press.

The not-so-violent story of how the West was won. Rather than being a legacy of the spoils of gunslingers, the authors see the settlement of the West as a triumph of entrepreneurship and the protection of property rights in frontier court systems. Cooperation and the rule of law overcame violence among free people acting in their economic rights.

Banks, Christopher P., and David M. O'Brien. 2015. *The Judicial Process: Law, Courts, and Judicial Politics*. Thousand Oaks, CA: CQ Press.

A concise and comprehensive core text that introduces students to the significance and nature of the judicial process in the United States and around the world. The authors offer an uncomplicated and unique insight into very complicated, highly relevant, and cutting-edge issues that surround the judicial process.

Banks, Christopher P., and John C. Blakeman. 2012. *The U.S. Supreme Court and New Federalism: From the Rehnquist to the Roberts Court*. Lanham, MD: Rowman & Littlefield.

Two constitutional scholars investigate how the U.S. Supreme Court rulings have formed the political principle of federalism.

Barrow, Deborah J., and Thomas G. Walker. 1988. *A Court Divided: The Fifth Circuit Court of Appeals and the Politics of Judicial Reform*. New Haven, CT: Yale University Press.
Details the decision to split the old Fifth Circuit Court of Appeals (covering Georgia, Florida, Alabama, Louisiana, Mississippi, and Texas) into two circuits—the Fifth (Louisiana, Mississippi, and Texas) and the Eleventh (Georgia, Florida, and Alabama). This book provides a very good description of the politics behind the running of the federal courts.

Barrow, Deborah J., Gerard S. Gryski, and Gary Zuk. 1996. *The Federal Judiciary and Institutional Change*. Ann Arbor: University of Michigan Press.
Discusses the staffing of the federal district and appellate courts from 1869 to 1992. The primary focus of this book is to show the importance of government control (unified versus divided) to institutional change.

Baum, Lawrence. 2012. *American Courts: Process and Policy*. Boston: Houghton Mifflin.
An excellent series of essays examining the work of state and federal courts, with insights into the history and workings of U.S. courts. Baum's offering is primarily descriptive and explanatory in nature, with the focus largely on processes. Generally avoiding normative discussions and details about outcomes, Baum instead provides careful and succinct discussion of the various theories of judicial behavior.

Cahan, Richard. 2002. *A Court That Shaped America: Chicago's Federal District Court from Abe Lincoln to Abbie Hoffman*. Evanston, IL: Northwestern University Press.
Relates the history of the Northern District Court of Illinois. The book emphasizes both the major cases argued and the court's personnel. In addition, Cahan seeks to place this court's actions into a wider historical context.

Carp, Robert A., and C. K. Rowland. 1983. *Policymaking and Politics in the Federal District Courts*. Knoxville: University of Tennessee Press.
Discusses the ways that federal trial courts—the district courts—can affect and even make policy by their actions as they seek to "enforce" federal laws. This is an important work in the ongoing discussion of the roles and functions of the federal courts.

Carp, Robert A., Ronald Stidham, and Kenneth L. Manning. 2011. *The Federal Courts*. 5th ed. Washington, D.C.: CQ Press.
The best single-volume study of the structure and workings of the federal court system. Covering topics from workloads to jurisdictions and personnel, this is the best place to go to seek additional and more detailed analysis of the workings of the federal court system.

Champagne, Anthony, Cynthia Harrison, and Adam Land. 1992. *A Directory of Oral History Interviews Related to the Federal Courts*. Washington, D.C.: Federal Judicial History Office, Federal Judicial Center.
Lists manuscript collections that hold interviews by and about federal judges. Published by the History Project, this is an invaluable resource for anyone seeking to research the history of the federal judicial system.

Clark, Mary L. 2004. "One Man's Token Is Another Woman's Breakthrough? The Appointment of the First Women Federal Judges." *Villanova Law Review* 49: 487–550.
Explores the politics behind the appointment of the first women federal judges.

Ellis, Richard. 1971. *The Jeffersonian Crisis: Courts and Politics in the Young Republic.* New York: W. W. Norton.
Explores the politics of judicial activism and reform in the early 19th century. Ellis lays out the struggles to determine the proper function of the federal courts in this early period. He also shows how these courts were as political an institution as the executive and legislative branches.

Fish, Peter Graham. 1973. *The Politics of Federal Judicial Administration.* Princeton, NJ: Princeton University Press.
An examination of the way the federal courts are administered as a component of the federal government. This book focuses on the politics of this administrative effort, emphasizing interactions between the courts and the other branches of government.

Fish, Peter Graham. 2002. *Federal Justice in the Mid-Atlantic South: United States Courts from Maryland to the Carolinas, 1789–1835.* Washington, D.C.: Administrative Office of the United States Courts.
Another history of the early formation of the federal courts, in this case in the mid-Atlantic states of Maryland, Virginia, and the Carolinas. This work emphasizes the judges who served during this period, from both biographical and doctrinal perspectives, in addition to the major cases argued before them. In addition, Fish seeks to place the actions of these courts into a wider historical context.

Frankfurter, Felix, and James Landis. 1927. *The Business of the Supreme Court: A Study in the Federal Judicial System.* New York: Macmillan.
A detailed summary and analysis of the legislation that shaped the work of the federal courts from their creation in 1789 through 1925. This work is especially interesting in that one of the authors would later serve as an associate justice of the U.S. Supreme Court.

Frase, Richard S. 2013. *Just Sentencing: Principles and Procedures for a Workable System.* New York: Oxford University Press.
Advocates for an expanded version of the theory of limiting retributivism and other limits on sentence severity, while at the same time accommodating crime control and other nonretributive punishment purposes.

Goldman, Sheldon. 1999. *Picking Federal Judges: Lower Court Selection from Roosevelt through Reagan.* New Haven, CT: Yale University Press.
One of the most widely cited and complete descriptions of the appointment process for federal judges in the 20th century. This book provides some of the best currently available statistical data on federal judges in this century.

Hall, Kermit L., ed. 2005. *The Oxford Companion to the Supreme Court of the United States.* New York: Oxford University Press.
Useful summaries of aspects of the history and structure of the Supreme Court. This is the best single source for information on the U.S. Supreme Court and

includes new entries on key cases such as abortion, voting rights, freedom of speech, and freedom of religion.

Hall, Kermit L., and Peter Karsten. 2008. *The Magic Mirror: Law in American History.* New York: Oxford University Press.
Ideal reading material for anyone interested in the history of law in the United States. It recounts the role that law has played in the United States, from how the first settlers worked with each other, as well as indigenous peoples, up through contemporary law and society in 2007.

Holt, Wythe. 1989. "To Establish Justice: Politics, the Judiciary Act of 1789, and the Invention of the Federal Courts." *Duke Law Journal* 38: 1421–1531. http://scholarship .law.duke.edu/cgi/viewcontent.cgi?article=3097&context=dlj.
One of the best accounts of the beginning of the judicial system.

Howard, J. Woodford, Jr. 1981. *Courts of Appeals in the Federal Judicial System: A Study of the Second, Fifth, and District of Columbia Circuits.* Princeton, NJ: Princeton University Press.
A path-breaking and seminal look at the impact of regional variation on the work and doctrines of three federal circuit courts of appeals. Howard finds not only that these different circuits faced different types of cases, but that these differences shaped the doctrinal stance of the courts.

Judicial Research Initiative. 2016. U.S. Appeals Courts Database. http://artsandsciences .sc.edu/poli/juri/appct.htm.
An extensive database, designed by Donald R. Songer, that encourages studies done over time for the courts.

Kritzer, Herbert M. 2015. *Lawyers at Work.* New Orleans, LA: Quid Pro Books.
A collection of essays and articles by the author that draw on his extensive research—both qualitative and quantitative—on the legal practice of lawyers over the past 35 years, including his work on the Civil Litigation Research Project, which was a massive undertaking funded by the Carter administration. This is for anyone interested in understanding the work of lawyers in day-to-day litigation-like settings, as well as those seeking more knowledge about the nature of legal practice and the structure of the legal profession.

Lyles, Kevin L. 1997. *The Gatekeepers: Federal District Courts in the Political Process.* Santa Barbara, CA: Praeger.
Explores the workings of the federal district courts. This book emphasizes how these courts shape which issues are heard within the system and, conversely, how they can keep issues out of the system. This is best read in conjunction with Carp and Rowland's *Policymaking and Politics in the Federal District Courts.*

Marcus, Maeva, ed. 1992. *Origins of the Federal Judiciary: Essays on the Judiciary Act of 1789.* New York: Oxford University Press.
A series of well-written and informative essays on the formation of the lower federal courts in 1789. This book is perhaps the best single work on the history of the Judiciary Act of 1789 and is best read in combination with Wythe Holt's article on the same topic.

McCarthy, Cathy A., and Tara Treacy. 2000. *The History of the Administrative Office of the United States: Sixty Years of Service to the Federal Judiciary*. Washington, D.C.: Administrative Office of the United States Courts.

A government pamphlet that describes the origins, development, and functions of the Administrative Office of the United States Courts—the primary agency for running the federal court system. Among other duties, this agency keeps track of federal caseload trends.

Nagel, Robert F., ed. 1995. *Intellect and Craft: The Contributions of Justice Hans Linde to American Constitutionalism*. Boulder, CO: Westview Press.

Collection of Justice Hans Linde's writing. Linde is one of the most significant figures in modern judicial theory in the United States. A scholar, diplomat, and jurist, Linde may be most remembered for advancing the idea of new judicial federalism by finding within the Oregon Constitution libertarian principles not to be found in parallel language of the U.S. Constitution. Linde's work remains current in its consideration of models of interpretation for judges and the bounds that federalism places on the federal government in interfering in the prerogatives of the states. Readers with a firm footing in legal theory will appreciate this collection.

National Center for State Courts. 2016. http://www.ncsc.org/.

Website for the National Center for State Courts (NCSC). The NCSC oversees the Court Statistics Project (CSP, http://www.courtstatistics.org), which collects an enormous amount of data on the workload of state courts. The CSP monitors what type of cases are filed, which types of courts do the most work, and changes in this data over time. The center also provides detailed diagrams highlighting the structure and jurisdictional makeup of every state court system.

Peltason, J. W. 1961. *58 Lonely Men: Federal Judges and School Desegregation*. Urbana: University of Illinois Press.

A powerful description of the role played by southern federal judges in the early days of the civil rights revolution following the Supreme Court's ruling in *Brown v. Board of Education*. Peltason argues that the Supreme Court placed these judges out on a limb as they attempted to enforce civil rights in a region that did not want to desegregate.

Posner, Richard A. 1999. *The Federal Courts: Challenge and Reform*. Cambridge, MA: Harvard University Press.

Updated version of Posner's influential 1985 book that offers a comprehensive evaluation of the federal judiciary and judicial reform. It examines the caseload of judges, how they are still able to maintain quality when administering justice, and the challenges inherent in that administration.

Posner, Richard A., Lee Epstein, and William M. Landes. 2013. *The Behavior of Federal Judges: A Theoretical and Empirical Study of Rational Choice*. Cambridge, MA: Harvard University Press.

An attempt to explain the secretive behavior of judges. A judge, a political scientist, and an economist join forces to construct a unified theory on judicial decision-making.

Purcell, Edward A. 2000. *Brandeis and the Progressive Constitution: Erie, the Judicial Power, and the Politics of the Federal Courts in Twentieth-Century America*. New Haven, CT: Yale University Press.

Explores the shift in emphasis within the federal courts of its roles and functions from diversity-based private suits to federal-question–based public lawsuits. Purcell argues that the Supreme Court's ruling in *Erie* was an attempt by the Progressive justice Louis Brandeis to rein in the power of the federal courts.

Purcell, Edward A. 2014. *Originalism, Federalism, and the American Constitutional Enterprise: A Historical Inquiry*. New Haven, CT: Yale University Press.

Traces federalism through the centuries in a lively recounting that leads scholars in the field to refute the widely accepted notion that the founding fathers successfully created a constitutional balance of power between the federal and state governments.

Rehnquist, William H. 2001. *The Supreme Court*. New York: Knopf.

A solid, if unimaginative, history of the U.S. Supreme Court. This book is most interesting for having been written by the then-sitting chief justice.

Resnik, Judith. 2009. *Federal Courts Stories*. Campbell, CA: Foundation Press.

Political insiders look at the personalities and stories behind major court cases.

Rosen, Jeffrey. 2007. *The Supreme Court: The Personalities and Rivalries That Defined America*. New York: Times Books.

A recent history of the workings of the Supreme Court with emphasis on the various conflicts between justices. This book serves as a companion to the PBS video series (see entry under Other Media later in this list).

Rowland, C. K., and Robert A. Carp. 1996. *Politics and Judgment in Federal District Courts*. Lawrence: University Press of Kansas.

A useful study on how federal district judges decide cases.

Scalia, Antonin. 1997. *A Matter of Interpretation: Federal Courts and the Law*. Princeton, NJ: Princeton University Press.

A frank discussion by a sitting Supreme Court justice on his views of the powers and jurisdictions of the federal courts.

State Supreme Court Data Project. 2016. Project Overview. http://www.ruf.rice.edu/~pbrace/statecourt/.

Web page describing a collaborative project between Rice University and Michigan State University and sponsored by the National Science Foundation. The State Supreme Court Data Project provides this database with information on state supreme court decisions in all 50 states.

Stith, Kate, and José A. Cabranes. 1998. *Fear of Judging: Sentencing Guidelines in the Federal Courts*. Chicago: University of Chicago Press.

Explores the uses and abuses of the federal criminal sentencing guidelines. The authors argue that the guidelines are inappropriate.

Supreme Court Database. 2016. http://supremecourtdatabase.org/.

Contains a wealth of information about each case decided by the Court from 1791 to 2014, with more current cases continually being added. Information includes how the justices voted, the parties to the suit, the legal provisions considered in the case, and so on.

Tarr, G. Alan. 2012. *Without Fear or Favor: Judicial Independence and Judicial Accountability in the States*. Palo Alto, CA: Stanford University Press.
Review of broad legal and political arguments in regard to how politics and methods of judicial selection relate to democratic accountability in the state court systems.

Whittington, Keith E., R. Daniel Kelemen, and Gregory A. Caldeira. 2010. *The Oxford Handbook of Law and Politics*. New York: Oxford University Press.
A contemporary compilation of traditional subjects in the fields of politics and law, including comparative federalism and the role of the judiciary, international law, constitutionalism, feminist theory and the law, the legal profession, jurisprudence, and filling the bench, among other topics.

Wilson, Steven Harmon. 2002. *The Rise of Judicial Management in the U.S. District Court, Southern District of Texas, 1955–2000*. Athens: University of Georgia Press.
An excellent history of the Southern District of Texas, exploring the cases and issues before the court in the past four decades of the 20th century. Wilson shows how the job of a district court changed over time as private law cases declined and public law cases grew, which required a shift in the function of district judges toward a more administrative and even managerial role in pushing cases through the system.

GOVERNMENT REPORTS AND CASE REPORTS

Annual Report of the Attorney General of the United States (1870–1939)
Annual Report of the Director of the Administrative Office of the United States Courts (1940–present)
Provide basic statistical information on the workings of the federal courts. In particular, these reports show the evolving caseload of the federal courts, as well as discuss significant administrative changes (e.g., the addition of a new court or the appointment of additional judges).

Annual Report of the Proceedings of the Judicial Conference of the United States (1945–present)
Summarizes both the current conditions in the courts and the policies adopted. The Judicial Conference is the governing body of the federal courts and is made up of the chief justice of the United States, the chief judges of the circuit courts of appeals, and selected other judges. The Conference sets broad policy for the running of the federal courts.

Federal Reports (Circuit Court of Appeals Cases)
Federal Supplement (District Court Cases)
U.S. Reports (Supreme Court Cases)
Provides the opinions of the federal courts. These reports are available in all law libraries and many public and university libraries. By providing easy access to the federal judiciary's output, they are an invaluable resource for reading and understanding the workings of the federal court system.

U.S. Statutes at Large
Published source of all federal legislation. This includes the legislation organizing the federal courts reprinted in this volume.

OTHER MEDIA

The Supreme Court. PBS Video, Ambrose Video Publishing. Release date January 2007. A recent documentary on the history of the U.S. Supreme Court. This documentary includes interviews with many major constitutional law scholars and with Chief Justice John Roberts.

About the Editor and Contributors

Christopher P. Banks is a professor at Kent State University. In 1980, he earned his BA in political science and, in 1984, graduated with his law degree. Before receiving his doctorate in American politics from the University of Virginia in 1995, he practiced law in civil and criminal litigation in Connecticut and was active in local and state politics. In Connecticut, he ran for state representative in 1988. Thereafter, he received a gubernatorial appointment to serve as an administrative hearing officer for the Connecticut Commission on Human Rights and Opportunities. At Kent State University, he teaches undergraduate and graduate courses in the judicial process, constitutional law, civil rights and liberties, terrorism and human rights, American political thought, racial inequality and judicial policymaking, and American politics. He is the author of *Judicial Politics in the D.C. Circuit Court* (John Hopkins University Press, 1999); the coauthor of *The U.S. Supreme Court and New Federalism: From the Rehnquist to Roberts Court* (Roman & Littlefield, 2012), *The Judicial Process: Law, Courts, and Judicial Politics* (Sage/CQ Press, 2015), and *Courts and Judicial Policymaking* (Prentice Hall, 2008); and the co-editor of *The Final Arbiter: The Consequences of Bush v. Gore for Law and Politics* (State University of New York Press, 2005) and *Superintending Democracy: The Courts and the Political Process* (University of Akron Press, 2001). He has published numerous book chapters, book reviews, and journal articles on judicial behavior, law and politics, federalism, terrorism, and human rights in *PS: Political Science and Politics*, *Justice System Journal*, *Publius: The Journal of Federalism*, *Judicature*, *International Journal of Human Rights*, *Public Integrity: The Journal for the American Society of Public Administration*, *Social Science Quarterly*, *Southeastern Political Review*, and *The Journal of Law & Politics*, among others.

Roberta Sue Alexander is distinguished service professor of history and professor emeritus at the University of Dayton in Ohio. A specialist in U.S. political and legal history, she is the author of *North Carolina Faces the Freedmen: Race Relations During Presidential Reconstruction, 1865–1867* (Duke University Press, 1985) and *A Place of Recourse: A History of the U.S. District Court for the Southern District of Ohio, 1803–2003* (Ohio University Press, 2005).

John C. Blakeman is professor and chair of the Political Science Department at the University of Wisconsin-Stevens Point. His main teaching and research interests focus on constitutional law, religion and politics, sports and politics, and federalism. In addition to authoring several articles and book chapters, he is the author of *The Bible in the Park: Religious Expression, Public Forums, and Federal District Courts* (University of Akron Press, 2005) and the coauthor of *The American Constitutional Experience*, 3rd ed. (Kendall Hunt Publishing, 2012), and *The U.S. Supreme Court and the New Federalism: From the Rehnquist to the Roberts Court* (Roman & Littlefield, 2012).

Timothy Dixon is assistant professor of history at Nova Southeastern University in Fort Lauderdale, Florida. He is the coauthor of *Democracy and Judicial Independence: A History of the Federal Courts of Alabama, 1820–1994* (New York: Carlson Press, 1996) with Tony Freyer.

Lisa Hager is an assistant professor of Political Science at South Dakota State University in the Department of History, Political Science, Philosophy, and Religion. She received her PhD in political science from Kent State University in 2016, and she holds a master of arts in political science from Kent State University (2013) and a bachelor of arts in political science from Wartburg College (2009). During the 2015–2016 academic year, Hager was an American Political Science Association (APSA) Congressional Fellow in the office of Representative Daniel Lipinski (IL-3).

Sean O. Hogan is a survey research director for the Research Triangle Institute (RTI International). His research interests include opinion and behaviors of decision makers, such as medical professionals, elected officials, lawyers, and judges. He has conducted survey research on behalf of state and federal agencies and for groups concerned with state judicial selection reform and tort innovation. His research on the decision making of state Supreme Court justices, Chicago aldermen, and voters has appeared in peer-reviewed publications. His book contributions include chapters on state judicial systems and the field of survey research and survey methods. Hogan earned his PhD in public policy analysis from the University of Illinois at Chicago.

Ginny Hollinger received her degree, with honors, in political science with a minor in international studies from Texas State University. Her next goal is working toward earning her PhD. In her spare time, Ginny volunteers with HeadCount Voter Registration and assists with food drives, community carnivals, and animal rescue services.

Charles F. Jacobs is an associate professor of judicial process and American politics at St. Norbert College in De Pere, Wisconsin. He also serves as the pre-law advisor. He has conducted research on the judicial philosophy of Stephen

Breyer in the area of criminal law and procedure and is currently exploring the role of retired justices on the politics of the U.S. Supreme Court.

Lester Lindley is professor emeritus at Nova Southeastern University in Fort Lauderdale, Florida, where he taught constitutional and legal history. He is the author of *Contract, Economic Change, and the Search for Order in Industrializing America* (Routledge, 1993) and *The Impact of the Telegraph on Contract Law* (Taylor and Frances, 1991).

Thomas Mackey is professor of history and adjunct professor of law at the University of Louisville in Kentucky, where he teaches constitutional and legal history. He is the author of three books on U.S. legal history.

Mathew Manweller is an assistant professor of political science at Central Washington University in Ellensburg, Washington. Direct democracy, tort reform, and constitutional law are among his research interests, and his work has been published in *American Research Politics, American Review of Politics, Business and Politics,* the *Independent Review,* and the *Journal of Socio-Economics.* His book, *The People Versus The Courts: Initiative Elites, Judicial Review and Direct Democracy in the American Legal System,* was published in 2004. He sits on the research advisory board for the Seattle-based Washington Policy Center. Manweller earned his PhD in political science from the University of Oregon.

Steven C. Tauber is an associate professor and director of the School of Interdisciplinary Global Studies (formerly the Department of Government & International Affairs) at the University of South Florida. His research areas focus on American politics and law and society, with a special emphasis on the animal advocacy movement. He recently published *Navigating the Jungle: Law, Politics, and the Animal Advocacy Movement* (Routledge, 2015).

James L. Walker earned a bachelor's degree from Santa Clara University and a PhD from the University of California at Berkeley. For 33 years, he was professor in the department of political science at Wright State University in Dayton, Ohio, before retiring in 2002. He is coauthor with Michael Solimine of *Respecting State Courts: The Inevitability of Judicial Federalism.* He is also author or coauthor of several articles on the state and federal judiciaries.

Ruth Ann Watry holds a PhD in political science from the University of Delaware. She is an associate professor of political science and public administration at Northern Michigan University. Watry is the author of *Administrative Statutory Interpretation: The Aftermath of Chevron v. Natural Resources Defense Council* (2002). Her research and teaching interests include state courts, state and federal level administrative law, women and politics, and constitutional law.

Charles L. Zelden is a professor of history at Nova Southeastern University in Fort Lauderdale, Florida. A specialist in U.S. political and legal history, he has published numerous articles and books on the subject, including *The Battle for the Black Ballot: Smith v. Allwright and the Defeat of the Texas All-White Primary* (University Press of Kansas, 2004); *Voting Rights on Trial: A Handbook with Case, Laws, and Documents* (ABC-CLIO, 2002); *Justice Lies in the District: The U.S. District Court, Southern District of Texas, 1902–1960* (Texas A&M University Press, 1993); and also worked on a history of the case of *Bush v. Gore* and the 2000 presidential postelection published by the University Press of Kansas in 2008 and a book for CQ Press on the Supreme Court and election law published in late 2008.

OTHER CONTRIBUTORS

Kwame Badu Antwi-Boasiako
Stephen F. Austin State University

Sara Buck
University of Southern Mississippi

Doug Goodman
Mississippi State University

Vicki Lindsay
University of Southern Mississippi

Lana McDowell
University of Southern Mississippi

Elizabeth Corzine McMullan
University of Southern Mississippi

James A. Newman
Idaho State University

Lisa S. Nored
University of Southern Mississippi

Barbara Patrick
Mississippi State University

John David Rausch Jr.
West Texas A&M University

La Shonda Stewart
Mississippi State University

R. Alan Thompson
Old Dominion University

Index